THE HANDBOOK OF STUDENT AFFAIRS ADMINISTRATION

THE HANDBOOK OF STUDENT AFFAIRS ADMINISTRATION

SECOND EDITION

Margaret J. Barr, Mary K. Desler,
and Associates

Jossey-Bass Publishers
San Francisco

Published by Jossey-Bass
A Wiley Imprint
989 Market Street, San Francisco, CA 94103-1741   www.josseybass.com

Jossey-Bass books and products are available through most bookstores. To contact Jossey-Bass directly call our Customer Care Department within the U.S. at 800-956-7739, outside the U.S. at 317-572-3986 or fax 317-572-4002.

Jossey-Bass also publishes its books in a variety of electronic formats. Some content that appears in print may not be available in electronic books.

Library of Congress Cataloging-in-Publication Data

Barr, Margaret J.
  The handbook of student affairs administration / Margaret J. Barr, Mary K. Desler, and associates.— 2nd ed.
      p. cm. — (The Jossey-Bass higher and adult education series)
      Includes bibliographical references and index.
      ISBN 0-7879-4720-2
      1. Student affairs services—United States. 2. Student activities—United States—Management. 3. Student affairs administration. I. Desler, Mary K. II. Title. III. Series. LB2342.92 .B37 2000
      378.1'94'0973—dc21   99—098002

FIRST EDITION
HB Printing   10 9 8 7 6 5 4 3

THE JOSSEY-BASS HIGHER AND ADULT
EDUCATION SERIES

CONTENTS

10 The Political Dimensions of Decision Making   178

Paul L. Moore

11 Planning, Managing, and Financing Facilities and Services   197

George S. McClellan and Margaret J. Barr

PART THREE: ESSENTIAL SKILLS AND COMPETENCIES FOR STUDENT AFFAIRS MANAGERS 229

NATIONAL ASSOCIATION OF STUDENT PERSONNEL ADMINISTRATORS

The National Association of Student Personnel Administrators (NASPA) is the leading voice for student affairs administration, policy, and practice. It addresses critical issues in student affairs and seeks to enrich the educational experience for all college and university students. As a national association, NASPA promotes leadership in higher education, advocates for students, and provides cutting edge tools and programs to higher education practitioners. Since 1918, student affairs administrators have turned to NASPA as the premier resource for high quality programs and information on current issues affecting campus policies and students' needs.

NASPA's mission is to serve student affairs administrators, faculty, students, and other professionals who are actively involved in facilitating student learning in higher education. NASPA fulfills this mission by

- Providing professional development to higher education professionals through the dissemination of high-quality information and exemplary models of practice.
- Providing strong leadership in higher education through policy development and advocacy for students on the most important national issues.
- Promoting pluralism, diversity, and internationalism in NASPA and the profession.
- Providing leadership for promoting, assessing, and supporting student learning and successful educational outcomes.

- Maintaining, evaluating, and developing a high-quality association infrastructure to meet current needs and to anticipate future trends.

With 8,000 members from more than 1,500 U.S. and international higher education institutions, NASPA is one of the leading nonprofit higher education associations for student affairs administrators, faculty, and students. Its members are shaping the profession with innovative programs and resources that will provide leadership and guidance for the many challenges ahead.

For additional information on NASPA or its membership, publications, professional development programs, or other information, visit the NASPA website at http://www.naspa.org or contact the national office at:

NASPA
1875 Connecticut Avenue, NW
Suite 418
Washington, D.C. 20009–5728
Phone: 202–265–7500
Fax: 202–797–1157
E-mail: office@naspa.org

PREFACE

Many challenges face higher education and student affairs as we move into the new century. Our success will depend on how well we cope with the changing environment both within and without the higher education enterprise. Our success also depends on how well we prepare for the challenges and opportunities that will face us in the future. As we know, higher education, and thus student affairs, is not insulated from the challenges facing the greater society. Every indication is that those challenges will grow even greater in the future. Under such conditions student affairs professionals must confront a number of questions including: What are the skills, knowledge base and competencies I need to effectively confront the challenges of the future? What opportunities are available to me to continue to grow and develop as a student affairs professional? What are the issues facing higher education and student affairs?

Purpose

This book has been written to help the student affairs professional answer those questions. It is a second edition adding new materials to aid practitioners with our ever-evolving set of challenges and opportunities. The volume contains specific, practical advice from respected practitioners as well as broad approaches to problem solving and solutions. While we cannot hope to answer all questions, our hope is that this second edition of *The Handbook of Student Affairs Administration* will become a basic reference for student affairs professionals at all levels of administration and management. In addition to updating materials provided in the first edition, a number of new topics have been added to this volume. These include: a discussion of our historic and philosophic roots, a focus on planning for and financing facilities, understanding assessment, translating theory and assessment results to practice, creating partnerships with academic affairs, fundraising and a discussion of the principles of good practice. We believe these additions will provide current and helpful materials to our readers.

The second edition of the handbook is a result of the collaboration of a number of people. It is again being sponsored by the National Association of Student Personnel Administrators (NASPA). This new edition was undertaken because there was a need to bring material contained in the volume up to date and to continue to provide a resource book written by practitioners *for* practitioners. We hope this new edition meets that goal.

Audience

The volume is designed to be particularly helpful to those assuming middle management or senior management positions in student affairs for the first time. It will also be useful to those individuals who come to student affairs from another area of the academy. In addition, it is designed to be of assistance to senior student affairs officers interested in professional renewal and development. Finally, the book can be used as a basic text in doctoral preparation programs.

Overview of the Contents

The Handbook of Student Affairs Administration is organized in five parts, which can be read in any order. Within these parts, the chapters are designed to be read independently although references are made to other chapters in the volume regarding specific points and issues.

Part One focuses on the administrative environment for student affairs. Understanding the history and philosophy of student affairs (Chapter One) is an important first step in managing the environment. Obviously student affairs does not stand alone; instead it is part of a complex web of missions (Chapter Two), governance (Chapter Three), campus environments (Chapter Four), finances (Chapter Five) and constituency group relationships (Chapter Six).

In Part Two, the focus shifts to the practical organizational and management issues associated with the field. Administrative relationships, the role of middle management and staff issues are discussed in detail in Chapters Seven, Eight and Nine, respectively. Other chapters emphasize the political dimensions of our administrative role (Chapter Ten), facility management (Chapter Eleven), and the technological issues influencing administration (Chapter Twelve). Each of these issues contributed to the effectiveness of student affairs within the educational institution.

Part Three focuses on the essential skills and competencies for successful management in student affairs. The emphasis in this section is on practical advice to practitioners. How do we: identify and use relevant theories and models? (Chapter Thirteen), identify the key elements of assessment? (Chapter Fourteen), measure student satisfaction and needs? (Chapter Fifteen), translate assessment results and theory to practice? (Chapter Sixteen), develop effective programs? (Chapter Seventeen), manage fiscal resources? (Chapter Eighteen), confront legal constraints? (Chapter Nineteen), develop effective relationships? (Chapter Twenty), manage conflict? (Chapter Twenty-One), maintain ethical standards? (Chapter Twenty-Two), partner with academic affairs (Chapter Twenty-Three), and deal with campus crises? (Chapter Twenty-Four) Each chapter attempts to provide guidance to professionals struggling with these issues on their own campus.

In Part Four the emphasis changes to the methods and means to acquire and develop essential administrative skills, competencies and knowledge. The authors in Chapters Twenty-Five through Twenty-Eight explore staff development programs, the role of professional associations, doctoral education and alternative methods for professional development.

Part Five becomes future oriented focusing on: characteristics of new students (Chapter Twenty-Nine), diversity issues (Chapter Thirty), fund raising and development (Chapter Thirty), applying professional standards and principles of good practice (Chapter Thirty-Two), and the leadership challenges for the future (Chapter Thirty-Three).

ACKNOWLEDGEMENTS

We would be remiss if we did not thank the contributors to this volume. Our colleagues from across the country took time out of very busy and demanding schedules to contribute to this endeavor. Specific thanks goes to NASPA for sponsoring this volume a second time as a contribution to the profession. Jossey-Bass staff members made important contributions to the volume by providing critical conceptual and editorial feedback. Vádal Redmond, from Northwestern University, deserves special recognition for her long hours in final manuscript preparation. Our colleagues at Northwestern deserve special thanks for their forbearance during this project—their patience has been outstanding. Family and friends do make a difference. We are grateful to our parents for their continued love and support through our professional struggles and growth. Peggy would like to extend special thanks to her colleagues in the National Vice Presidents Group and her dear friend, Sharon Justice, for support and help. Mary would like to thank the following individuals who have served as mentors or allies at various points in her career: Rose Knudsen, Ruth Bamford, Marie Johnson, Ernest Pascarella, and most of all, Margaret Barr.

January, 2000   Margaret J. Barr
Northwestern University   Mary K. Desler

THE AUTHORS

Margaret J. Barr currently serves as vice president for student affairs at Northwestern University. She received her B.S. degree (1961) in elementary education from Buffalo State College, her M.S. degree (1964) in college student personnel from Southern Illinois University, Carbondale, and her Ph.D. degree (1980) in higher education administration from the University of Texas, Austin. Author of more than thirty books, book chapters, and monographs, Barr received the Outstanding Contribution to Literature and Research Award from the National Association of Student Personnel Administrators (NASPA) in 1986 and the Professional Service Award from the American College Personnel Association (ACPA) in that same year. In 1990, she received the Contribution to Knowledge Award from ACPA.

Long active in professional associations, she served as president of ACPA in 1985 and, before that, as vice president for commissions, chair of Commission II and a Senior Scholar of that association. She served as program chair for the ACPA national convention in Cincinnati in 1980. Barr was also a member of the committee that authored *A Perspective on Student Affairs* published by NASPA in 1987. She was director of the Richard F. Stevens Institute in 1989 and 1990 and served on the NASPA Foundation Board for two terms.

Among her publications are the first edition of *The Handbook of Student Affairs Administration* (with Associates, 1993); *New Futures for Student Affairs: Building a Vision for Professional Leadership and Practice* (1990, with M. Lee Upcraft and Associates);

Student Affairs and The Law (ed. 1988), and *Developing Effective Student Services Programs: Systematical Approaches for Practitioners* (1985, with L. A. Keating and Associates). She served for twelve years as editor of the New Directions for Student Services series published by Jossey-Bass.

Barr previously served as vice chancellor for student affairs at Texas Christian University, vice president for student affairs at Northern Illinois University, assistant vice president for student affairs at Northern Illinois University, associate dean of students at the University of Texas, Austin, and assistant dean of students at that same institution. She also has served in various administrative positions at Trenton State College and the State University of New York at Binghamton.

Mary K. Desler is the assistant vice president for student affairs at Northwestern University. She received her B.Ed. (1968) degree in elementary education from the University of Wisconsin, Whitewater, an M.A. degree (1974) in communications from Wheaton College in Illinois, and her Ph.D. (1985) in higher education administration from Michigan State University.

She has been active in NASPA IV-East serving as a faculty member in the New Professionals Institute (1996, 1997), program co-chair of the regional conferences (1991, 1992) and co-chair of the local arrangements committee for the 1990 regional conference. Desler is also the recipient of the 1987 NASPA Dissertation of the Year Award. Desler is co-author of five journal articles.

Desler previously served as vice president for enrollment management and student affairs at North Central College, assistant vice chancellor for academic affairs at the University of Illinois, Chicago, associate dean of students at the University of Illinois, Chicago, director of residence living at Central Washington University and as a residence hall director at Michigan State University and Wheaton College.

David A. Ambler, vice chancellor for student affairs at the University of Kansas, received his B.S. degree (1959) in business administration, his M.P.A. degree (1961) in political science, and his Ed.D. degree (1966) in educational administration, all from Indiana University. He was chair of the NASPA Foundation for two terms, chair of the ACPA/NASPA Task Force on Professional Preparation and Practice from 1987 to 1989 and has served on both the ACPA and NASPA journal editorial boards.

Gregory S. Blimling is vice chancellor for student affairs and professor of human development and psychological counseling at Appalachian State University in North Carolina. He is the current editor of the *Journal of College Student Development.* Blimling has been named a senior scholar for ACPA and received the Greenleaf Distinguished Alumni Award from Indiana University.

Kelly A. Carter is an assistant director for residential life at Northwestern University. Previously, she was a coordinator of residence life at Pennsylvania State University where she received her M.Ed in counselor education. She received her

B.A. from Virginia Polytechnic Institute and State University. Carter is the 1998 recipient of the American College Personnel Association, Standing Committee for Lesbian, Gay, Bisexual, and Transgender Awareness, New Professional Award.

Joan Claar is vice president and dean of students at Cornell College. She received her B.A. degree (1961) in English and her M.S. (1963) in college student personnel from Southern Illinois University, Carbondale, and her Ph.D. (1971) in higher education from the State University of New York, Buffalo. A former president of NASPA, she has also served as vice president for Region IV-E, national conference chair and member of the journal board. She is currently vice president of the NASPA Foundation and is an adjunct faculty member in the student development program at the University of Iowa.

Jann M. Contento is completing his Ph.D. in education leadership and policy studies at Arizona State University. He previously served as a policy analyst at the Arizona Board of Regents and held various positions in student affairs administration.

Michael J. Cuyjet is an associate professor and coordinator of the College Student Personnel Program in the Department of Educational and Counseling Psychology at the University of Louisville. He earned his B.S.(1969) in speech communications from Bradley University, his M.S.Ed. (1973) in counseling from Northern Illinois University and his Ed.D. (1983) in counselor education from that same institution. A former student affairs practitioner, he served in various capacities at Northern Illinois University and the University of Maryland-College Park. He has been an active participant in NASPA, ACPA and the National Association of Campus Activities for over twenty-five years.

Marsha A. Duncan currently serves as vice president for student affairs at Florida Technological Institute. She received both her B.S. degree (1969) in government and her M.S. degree in college student personnel from Southern Illinois University, Carbondale. Active in professional associations, she has served both on the judicial affairs directorate of ACPA and the board of directors of NASPA. She is a former president of NASPA.

Cathy McHugh Engstrom is an assistant professor of higher education at Syracuse University. She earned her B.A. in biology at Holy Cross, her M.Ed. in student personnel services in higher education at the University of Vermont, and her Ph.D. in counseling and personnel services at the University of Maryland, College Park. She previously served in a variety of student affairs positions at the University of California, Davis, University of Maryland, College Park and Virginia Tech. She co-edited *Using Technology to Enhance Student Services and Promote Student Learning.*

Robert H. Fenske is professor of higher education at Arizona State University. He is a frequent contributor to the literature on college students. His research interests include student financial aid, and policy analysis on access, retention, and program completion.

Jane M. Fried is an associate professor at Central Connecticut State University. She earned her B.A. degree(1966) in American and world literature from Harper College (now the State University of New York, Binghamton). Her M.A. degree is from Syracuse University in student personnel (1968) and her doctoral degree (1977) from the Union of Experimenting College and Universities, Cincinnati, Ohio. She received the Esther Lloyd Jones Award for Professional Service from ACPA and chaired the ethics committee, the standing committee on women and the affirmative action committee of ACPA. Author of several chapters and monographs, she currently serves on the NASPA Research Advisory Group.

Donald D. Gehring is a professor of higher education at Bowling Green State University. He received his B.S. degree (1960) in industrial management from Georgia Institute of Technology, his M.Ed degree (1966) in math education from Emory University, and his Ed.D. degree (1971) from the University of Georgia. Gehring was the recipient of the NASPA Contribution to Literature and Research Award in 1985, and the Robert Schaefer Award for Excellence as a Graduate Faculty Member in 1990, and the American College and University Housing Officers-International (ACUHO-I) Distinguished Service Award in 1989.

Harold Goldsmith is the vice president for student affairs at Indiana University of Pennsylvania. He earned his A.B. degree (1968) in government from Indiana University, Bloomington, his M.Ed degree (1972) in student personnel from The American University, and his Ed.D. degree (1975) in higher education administration from Indiana University, Bloomington. He has served as president of the Virginia Association of Student Personnel Administrators, on the directorate of ACPA Commission I and on the executive board of the Pennsylvania Association of Student Personnel Administrators. He is the chair of the Technology Network for NASPA Region II.

Michael L. Jackson is vice president for student affairs at the University of Southern California. He earned his B.A. degree (1972) in anthropology at Stanford University and both his M.Ed (1974) and Ed.D. (1976) at the University of Massachusetts, Amherst. Prior to USC, he served as dean of students and assistant to the provost at Stanford University. He has served on the board of directors of NASPA and as vice-president for Region VI of that association.

Susan R. Komives is associate professor of counseling and personnel services and the College Student Personnel (CSP) program director at the University of Maryland, College Park. She also serves as a faculty associate in the division of student affairs. She earned both her B.S. degree (1968) in mathematics and chemistry and her M.S. degree (1969) in higher education and student personnel administration from Florida State University, and her Ed.D. degree (1973) in educational administration and supervision from the University of Tennessee. A former president and senior scholar of ACPA, she was a member of the ACPA/NASPA Task Force on Professional Preparation and Practice.

Kevin Kruger is the associate executive director of NASPA. He earned his M.A. (1981) and Ph.D. (1991) in counseling and student personnel services from the University of Maryland, College Park. Before joining NASPA, he worked at both the University of Maryland, College Park and the University of Maryland Baltimore County in a variety of student affairs roles. He was co-editor of *Using Technology To Promote Student Learning: Opportunities for Today and Tomorrow.*

George D. Kuh, professor of higher education at Indiana University in the Center for Postsecondary Research and Planning, received his B.A. degree (1968) in English and history from Luther College, his M.S. degree (1971) from Saint Cloud State University and his Ph.D. degree (1975) in counselor education and higher education. Kuh received the Contribution to Knowledge Award (1986) from ACPA and was named a Senior Scholar in that group. NASPA awarded him the Contribution to Literature and Research Award in 1987. He was a member of the committee that collaborated on *A Perspective on Student Affairs.* He has authored or co-authored over 125 publications including *Involving Colleges: Successful Approaches to Fostering Student Learning and Development Outside the Classroom* (with J. H. Schuh, E. J. Whitt and Associates).

George S. McClellan is the director of graduate and off-campus housing at Northwestern University. He received his B.A. degree (1982) in English and American literature and his M.S.Ed (1999) in higher education administration from Northwestern University. McClellan has served as NASPA Region IV-East technology coordinator, chair of the Graduate and Professional Student Services Network in NASPA and host of the GRDSTUSV.

Thomas E. Miller is the vice president for student affairs and dean of students at Eckerd College. He received his B.S. degree (1970) in natural science from Muhlenberg College and both his M.S. degree (1972) in education and his Ed.D. degree (1979) in higher education from Indiana University. He previously served as vice president for student affairs and dean of students at Canisius College. He has served as a board member or officer of several professional associations including NASPA, the Fulbright Association, the National Consortium for Academics and Sports, and the Eastern Association of Deans.

Donald B. Mills is vice chancellor for student affairs at Texas Christian University. He earned his B.A. degree (1968) in government from Harvard University, his M.Div. degree (1972) in Christian ethics from Texas Christian University (TCU) and his Ed.D. degree (1985) in higher education administration from the University of North Texas. Prior to assuming his current role, he held various administrative positions in student affairs at TCU. He received the Distinguished

Service Award from the Texas Association of College and University Personnel Administrators in 1988. He is highly involved in local community activities.

Keith M. Miser is vice president for student affairs and associate professor in the school of education at Colorado State University. He has served as a chief student affairs officer for 28 years including service as dean of students and associate vice president for administration at the University of Vermont. Active in professional associations, he has served on the editorial board for the *Journal of College Student Personnel* and as editor of the *NASPA Journal*. He earned his B.S. degree in biology, the M.S. degree in counseling and guidance and the Ed.D. degree in higher education administration all from Indiana University.

Leila V. Moore is vice president for student affairs at the University of New Hampshire. She has a B.S. degree (1961) in English literature from Carnegie Institute of Technology (now Carnegie-Mellon University), and M.A. degree (1983) in student personnel from Syracuse University, and an Ed.D. (1975) in counseling and personnel services from the State University of New York at Albany. She is past president of ACPA and the recipient of professional service awards from both the Pennsylvania and New York State Divisions of ACPA. She is the author of four books and monographs, eleven book chapters and thirteen articles in refereed journals.

Paul L. Moore is vice president for university advancement and student affairs at California State University, Chico. He received his B.A. degree (1965) from the University of Oregon, his M.A. degree (1966) in counseling from the University of Oregon and his Ph.D. degree (1977) in sociology of education from the University of Southern California. Active in NASPA, he has served as vice president of Region VI and as a member of the editorial board of the *NASPA Journal*. Moore's recent publications include *Managing the Political Dimension of Student Affairs*.

Elizabeth M. Nuss is vice president and dean of students at Goucher College. She served as executive director of NASPA for eight years. She received her B.A. degree (1967) in Spanish and secondary education from the State University of New York, Albany, her M.Ed. degree (1969) in higher education and student personnel administration from The Pennsylvania State University, and her Ph.D. degree (1981) in education policy, planning and administration from the University of Maryland, College Park. She is the author or co-author of numerous publications and was the recipient of the NASPA Dissertation of the Year Award (1982) and the Free Turner Award for Outstanding Service to NASPA (1996).

James J. Rhatigan was appointed senior vice president at Wichita State University in 1997 after a long career as vice president for student affairs and dean of students. He was NASPA president in 1975–76 and has served as NASPA historian since 1978. He served on the committee that wrote *A Perspective on Student Affairs*.

James A. Rund is an affiliate professor in educational leadership and social policy studies and associate vice president for student affairs at Arizona State University. He previously served as dean of students at the University of South Dakota.

C. Arthur Sandeen is a profesor at the University of Florida. He previously served as vice president for student affairs at the University of Florida. Sandeen earned his B.A. degree (1960) in religion and psychology from Miami University Ohio, his M.A. degree (1962) in college student personnel from Michigan State University, and his Ph.D. degree (1965) in higher education administration from Michigan State University. He served as president of NASPA and received both the Fred Turner Award (1983) and the Scott Goodnight Award (1990) from that association. He chaired the committee that collaborated on *A Perspective on Student Affairs* (1987). A respected author, his most recent work is *The Chief Student Affairs Officer: Leader, Manager, Mediator and Educator* (1991).

John H. Schuh is professor and executive officer of the Department of Educational Leadership and Policy Studies at Iowa State University. He earned his B.A. (1969) degree in history from the University of Wisconsin, Oshkosh and both his M.C. (1972) degree and Ph.D. (1974) degree from Arizona State University. He received the Contribution to Knowledge Award 1990), the Presidential Service Award (1991) and has been designated as a Senior Scholar Diplomate by ACPA. Schuh also received the Contribution to Literature and Research Award from NASPA in 1992. He has served as a member of the ACUHO-I executive board, the ACPA Media Editor, and as member-at-large of the NASPA Executive Board. He is the author, co-author or editor of 13 books or monographs, 30 book chapters and 65 articles including *Involving Colleges: Successful Approaches to Fostering Student Learning and Development Outside the Classroom* (with G. D. Kuh, E. J. Whitt and Associates) and *Assessment in Student Affairs* (with M. Lee Upcraft). He is editor of the *New Directories for Student Services*, monograph series.

James E. Scott is the vice president for student services at Georgia State University. Scott received his B.S. (1969) degree in history and his M.A. (1971) degree in counseling from Eastern Michigan University and his Ph.D. degree (1978) in higher education administration from the University of Michigan. Active in professional organizations, he chaired the 1992 NASPA national conference committee and served as NASPA president in 1994–95. In 1997, he received the NASPA Region III Service Award and in 1988, he received the Fred Turner Award for Outstanding Service to NASPA.

Deborah J. Taub is assistant professor of educational studies and coordinator of the graduate program in college student affairs at Purdue University. She earned her B.A. degree (1978) in English from Oberlin College and both her M.A. degree in college student personnel (1989) and her Ph.D. degree (1993) in college student personnel administration from the University of Maryland, College Park. She received ACPA's Annuit Coeptis Award for emerging professionals in 1994 and serves as a member of the directorate for Commission XII of that association.

Saundra L. Taylor is vice president for campus life at the University of Arizona. Previously, she served as vice president for student affairs and interim vice president for student affairs at Western Washington University. She received her B.A. degree in psychology (1963) from DePauw University, an M.A. in clinical psychology from Bowling Green State University (1965) and a Ph.D. in clinical psychology from Ohio University (1969). She is active in NASPA having served on the national board, the *NASPA Journal Board* and currently is national coordinator of the Minority Student Fellowship Program.

Vincent Tinto is a Distinguished University Professor at Syracuse University and department chair of the higher education department. He received his Ph.D. (1971) in education and sociology from the University of Chicago. He has written extensively on student attainment in higher education and on issues of higher education reform. His publications include *Leaving College: Rethinking the Causes and Cures of Student Attrition* (1987, 1993).

M. Lee Upcraft is a research associate in the Center for the Study of Higher Education, assistant vice president for student affairs emeritus, and an affiliate professor of higher education at The Pennsylvania State University. He received both his B.A. degree (1960) in social studies and his M.A. degree (1961) in guidance and counseling from the State University of New York, Albany. He received his Ph.D. degree (1967) from Michigan State University. An active scholar, his most recent book is *Assessment in Student Affairs* (with J. H. Schuh).

Mark von Destinon, dean of students at Cohise College, has a B.A. degree (1978) in political science, a M.A. degree (1985) in higher education and a Ph.D. degree (1989) in higher education, all from the University of Arizona. He has been actively involved in NASPA serving on the Gay, Lesbian, and Bisexual Concerns Network and as member at-large for the Research and Program Division of NASPA.

Elizabeth J. Whitt is associate professor and coordinator of graduate programs in student development in postsecondary education at the University of Iowa. She serves on the editorial board of *The Journal of College Student Development* and is associate editor of the *New Directions for Student Services* monograph series. She is a past member of the board of directors of NASPA and the executive council of division J of the American Educational Research Association. She received her B.A. degree (1973) in history from Drake University, her M.A. (1977) in college student personnel administration from Michigan State University, and her Ph.D. (1988) in higher education administration and sociology from Indiana University.

Christine Kajikawa Wilkinson serves as vice president for student affairs at the University of Arizona and has previously served as director of admissions at the same institution. She has also served as acting athletic director and has been actively involved in the Phoenix community. She received her B.A. degree (1966) in education and her M.A. degree (1967) in counseling psychology from the University of California at Berkeley, and a Ph.D. (1976) in higher education administration from Arizona State University.

Dudley B. Woodard Jr. is professor of higher education at the Center for the Study of Higher Education, University of Arizona where he previously served as vice president for student affairs. Woodard earned his B.A. degree (1962) in psychology from McMurray College, and both his M.A. degree (1965) in human relations and his Ph.D. degree (1969) from Ohio University. He is a past president of NASPA and chaired the NASPA Foundation Board. Woodard is co-editor (with S. R. Komives) of *Student Services: A Handbook for the Profession, Third Edition.*

PART ONE

THE ADMINISTRATIVE ENVIRONMENT OF STUDENT AFFAIRS

Institutions of higher education are complex and oftentimes confusing organizations. Whether the institution is large or small, commuter residential, or four- or two-year, it is essential for the effective student affairs professional to develop a sound understanding of the administrative environment. Part One discusses the framework in which we must practice our profession. Higher education is part of the larger society and is shaped by forces beyond the control of the institution. In addition, campus governance structures and constituent relationships within the institution also influence the role of student affairs. The chapters included in this section discuss the broader issues involved in determining the climate in which we function.

Our history and what we believe in—our philosophy—are at the core of understanding the work of student affairs. In Chapter One, James Rhatigan, who is known widely as the student affairs historian, takes us back to our roots, reminds us of the influence of those that went before us, and traces the development of the values and beliefs on which the profession of student affairs is founded.

The history and philosophy of student affairs are the same, regardless of the institution. Even so, institutions can also be very different from one another. A number of factors affect the place of student affairs within institutions of higher education. None is more important than that of the institutional mission. Each of us must appreciate and use that mission to guide our work with students. In Chapter Two, Margaret Barr discusses the importance of the mission of the institution in developing student affairs programs, activities, and services.

Internal and external governance structures also influence the work of administration in student affairs. Questions of complexity, bureaucracy, union, councils, and committees plague all of us from time to time. In Chapter Three, Thomas Miller provides guidance for understanding such organizational structures and the specific parts they play in the effective administration of student affairs.

Campus climate, tradition, community, and other phrases have become part of the lexicon of student affairs. What do they really mean, and how can you as a practitioner begin to assess your campus environment. George Kuh provides helpful assistance in answering these difficult questions in Chapter Four and introduces us to the complexity of that process.

Money—the lack of it, the loss of it, or the prudent use of it—presents a number of challenges for successful practice in student affairs. In recent years, rapid growth of higher education has ended, and fiscal support for the academy has diminished. In Chapter Five, John Schuh provides an overview of the fiscal constraints facing higher education and draws salient conclusions for each of us on our campuses.

Many have called administration an art rather than a science. Good administration is dependent on developing strong working relationships with others both on and off the campus. In chapter Six, Dudley Woodard provides framework to assist student affairs professionals in identifying key constituency groups.

Part One sets the stage for understanding the complicated administration of student affairs programs and services within institutions of education.

CHAPTER ONE

THE HISTORY AND PHILOSOPHY OF STUDENT AFFAIRS

James J. Rhatigan

This chapter will provide an overview of the history and philosophy of student affairs administration in higher education. A primary focus will be on our professional beginnings, the role of the dean and the personnel worker, and the specific contribution of the early deans of women. The value of understanding and appreciating a historical perspective on our work will be discussed. A review of the influence of the *Student Personnel Point of View* and subsequent documents will be presented. Post-World War II changes in focus and the work of student affairs will be covered. The chapter will conclude with a view of our professional future as it is shaped by these historical perspectives.

It is commonly believed that student affairs administrators are not interested in history. This belief is a misleading, indeed, expensive miscalculation. Thoughtful people are concerned about how the present came to be. They understand that both purpose and expectations are rooted in history. Unfortunately, we do not see the true nature of our work reflected in the dusty accountings of an earlier day. This issue must be corrected.

Much of our written history lacks passion and excitement, neglects true context, and fails to convey the spirit of our work. How could student affairs, with its array of responsibilities in a dynamic century, fail to tell a more compelling story? The answer simply is that those best equipped to tell the story have not been inclined to do so.

Professional writings about "student personnel administration" frequently center on secondary sources even when primary documents are available. When primary sources are cited, writers have not always interpreted those documents contextually. This is how "accepted" history has been created and how stereotypes are maintained.

Two prominent examples of our history that merit better telling are the dean as disciplinarian and the dean serving *in loco parentis*. The roles played by deans in those two areas typically are seen as harmful, negative behaviors that detract from the professional reputation we desire. Actually the opposite case could be made. These stories are greatly misunderstood, void of the fuller explanations that they deserve (Rhatigan, 1978a; Fley, 1963).

A review of *in loco parentis*, for example, centers on its outdated legal status and its intent to validate the control of student behavior; as such, the concept is not relevant to the preponderant number of students on campus today. But a historical analysis indicates an institutional commitment to caring, respect, and a concern for a student's growth and development. Souls were at stake. Here is found the roots of the idea of the "wholeness" of the individual, the philosophical underpinning of modern student personnel work. Here is a commitment consistent with the notion of "seamless learning" discussed currently. Here we pay homage to the centuries-old idea of *alma mater*, a nurturing mother, portraying the institution as a living thing, a place where relationships are deep and abiding. These views are a strong antidote to some contemporary views about higher education's relationship to students.

Our field grew from the campus up, not from theory down. Our history must be developed in the same way. It should include an examination of men and women from individual campuses, their encounters with the profound dramas of individual lives in their time, the joys and sorrows they experienced, their political and ethical encounters, and the lessons they learned and conveyed. The intent of student affairs has always been to connect people who need with people who care (Chambers, 1987). The many ways this happens provide the story of student affairs. To tell it, a comprehensive insight is needed, one that recognizes the vital relationships between us and all who came before us, between us and all who will follow. Professional identity is rooted in the past. This is a quiet truth but a powerful one.

There are reasons to be encouraged. A handful of dissertations in recent years have uncovered primary documents on individual campuses (Tuttle, 1996; Bashaw, 1992; Gilroy, 1987). Sheeley (1991) found sufficient archival material to profile all of the past presidents of ACPA. Murphy (1988) demonstrated that a writer without formal training in history can present material effectively as he summarized the first hundred years of student affairs history at Oklahoma State University. More of these resources undoubtedly exist and a comprehensive effort to find them should be organized. A number of professional associations are now depositing their papers on a regular basis in the archives at Bowling Green State University. History articles offering new perspectives are appearing more frequently in our professional journals (Cross, 1998; Roberts, 1998; Blimling and Alschuler, 1996; Caple, 1996; Ruekel and Harris, 1986; Coomes, Whitt, and Kuh, 1987). Indications are that one day sufficient sources will be developed to enable one among us to write the definitive history our predecessors deserve.

Beginnings

Some writers have pointed to antecedents of student affairs in Athenian education (Bathurst, 1938), others to universities in the Middle Ages (Cowley, 1940; Haskins, 1940; Kibre, 1948; Rait, 1912; Rashdall, 1895). However, student affairs is largely an American higher education invention. It had a small but important beginning in the nineteenth century, but for the most part is a twentieth century phenomenon.

Some original scholarship of high quality has been produced. Cowley's two-part piece on the history of college residence halls is an excellent example (1934a, 1934b). So is Leonard's work (1956), which traces student affairs to its origins in the Colonial period. Hers is the most extensive treatment and contains an excellent bibliography for those wishing to explore further these early efforts.

The steady growth and resilience of student affairs administration are sources of amazement and its development vex many. Some writers have suggested that the field was born merely because the president needed help in regulating student behavior. Arguments abound as to whether it is a profession. Some of its own practitioners show a lack of understanding about it; its future is frequently seen as tenuous. Some energetic group or prophet is nearly always working at the task of reorganizing, reevaluating, reshaping, reforming, or renaming it. A more thoughtful understanding requires an appreciation of its historical roots.

In retrospect, it is evident that several factors influenced the development of this new field of work, including the development of land-grant institutions and the rise of public colleges and universities; expanding enrollments and the accompanying increase in the heterogeneity of student populations; social, political, and intellectual ferment in the United States; the rise of coeducation and the increase in numbers of women entering educational institutions; the introduction of the elective system in higher education; and an emphasis on vocationalism as a competitor to the traditional liberal arts. In addition, the impact of science and the scientific method; the struggle between empiricism and humanism; impersonalism on the part of faculty educated in German institutions; expanding industrialization and urbanization and the closing of the American "frontier"; the view of higher education as a social status phenomenon, with less student motivation for "academic" subjects; the establishment of a true "university" system; massive European immigration; and the changing roles of students in higher education influeced the development of student affairs. Undeniably other factors exist, but certainly all of those above are related to the changes that occurred.

For an understanding of the dramatic features of these changes, one must return to an earlier setting. The early American college was heavily value-oriented, with the president serving as the chief moral font. As Rudolph (1976) has observed, "moral purpose, values, and the reality of heaven," (p. 32) were dominant characteristics of those institutions and their primary administrators. College embodied the totality of student life but emphasized spiritual needs. Few public institutions existed, and the central religious emphasis did not erode until secular institutions gained a permanent foothold.

Public institutions developed in substantially different ways. Some of the early public schools, particularly those stemming from the Morrill Act of 1862, were established to serve pragmatic needs (e.g. agriculture, technological subjects, and home economics). The establishment of Johns Hopkins as the first true American "university" had a dramatic and opposite effect. Institutions responded by searching for scholars interested in research. A growing number went to Germany for their education and returned with a rigid model of education that ignored student issues outside the classroom. As the number of elective courses grew, so did the fragmentation of higher education. The resulting fractionalization of formal learning continues today in most institutions.

During this period, the moral force of the president was diminished greatly. The president's efforts were diverted to the problems of finance, capital construction, faculty recruitment, the establishment of new programs, and the politics of growth. The problem of accommodating increasing numbers of students worsened because many were not well prepared for higher education. Rudolph (1976) notes that the senior course in moral philosophy, often taught by the president of the old-time college, was its "most effective and its most transparent repository of values . . . . Once that died, as in time it did, there would really be no way to prevent the formation of the National Association of Student Personnel Administrators" (p. 33).

Contending philosophies in the United States were vigorously at work during the period 1870–1929, and students were as tied to them as were other Americans. In reviewing educational philosophies that had an impact on student personnel work, Lloyd-Jones and Smith (1954) list more than a dozen influences. "There has been a regrouping of the ideas exemplified in French, German, and English education, with additional fresh emphases and new ideas that are indigenous to American education . . ." (pp. 8–9). The authors focused on rationalism, neo-humanism, and instrumentalism and came to the view that the latter philosophy, instrumentalism, provides the best hope for "student personnel work as deeper teaching."

The concerns of the early deans of men and deans of women were not always incidental to higher education as suggested earlier, but they were incidental in the last decades of the nineteenth century, extending into World War I. The deans in this period were humanists in a field increasingly dominated by empiricists. It is probably useful to consider that if faculty at the turn of the century had viewed what the deans did as important, the field would have taken a different organizational form.

The early efforts to restore the concern for students were principal conditions leading to the birth and growth of the field of student affairs. No one knew for sure what needed to be accomplished, or how, but only that needs were present. The field began by serving needs that had been pushed to the periphery, and it has been argued that the field has remained there ever since (Fenske, 1980). How to become, or whether to become, a part of the mainstream is a continuing dilemma, replete with contradictions, contumely, and irony. Whether this is the glory or the failure of student affairs remains a favorite subject of interest, particularly at professional meetings.

One thing is clear. A rapidly growing and heterogeneous population of students entered higher education needing substantial assistance in other than curricular matters at approximately the same time that much of higher education was jettisoning that responsibility. If student affairs is a constant reminder to the faculty of their failure, or unwillingness, to cope with the lives of students, it could well be a continuing irritation. This is a legacy that can be overcome, if indeed it is true.

The Dean and the Personnel Worker

Factors contributing to the emergence of the field surfaced in different ways in different places. Three separate sources were involved: the dean of women, the dean of men, and the personnel worker. Their vestiges are still apparent in the existence of three major professional organizations (National Association of Student Personnel Administrators, American College Personnel Association, National Association of Women in Education), as well as several organizations with specific focuses. Anyone doubting the influence of history should examine the several failed efforts to merge or combine the three principal organizations. The lack of success may be attributed to a variety of circumstances, but a dominant reason is related to the history of each group.

A review of the *Proceedings* of the early deans of men and deans of women reveals a collection of diverse people with high ideals, warmth, optimism, and genuineness. Students writing later about these deans emphasized their affection, compassion, and concern for students. The deans also evidenced strong qualities of leadership, and many of them were deeply religious. Most of them came from teaching roles in the liberal arts. The profession's kinship with liberal arts is a facet of our history that warrants further attention (Kuh, Shedd, and Whitt, 1997).

Cowley (1937) identified the first of student personnel deans as LeBaron Russell Briggs of Harvard, who assumed his position in 1890. Thomas Arkle Clark of Illinois claimed to be the first administrator to carry the title "Dean of Men," beginning in 1909, although he assumed the responsibilities earlier. Blackburn (1969) reports the existence of women deans by a variety of names, but believes the title was first used at the University of Chicago in 1892, with Alice Freeman Palmer and Marion Talbot as central figures. Tuttle (1996) believes that Adelia Johnston was first, serving from 1869 at Oberlin as lady principal, and designated as dean of women in 1894.

The roles and activities of the early deans emerged as they worked. Dean Stanley Coulter of Purdue observed, "When the Board of Trustees elected me Dean of Men, I wrote them very respectfully and asked them to give me the duties of the Dean of Men. They wrote back that they did not know but when I found out to let them know." Thomas Arkle Clark noted, "I had no specific duties, no specific authority, no precedents either to guide me or to handicap me. It was an untried sea upon which I was about to set sail. My only chart was the action of the Board of Trustees when they said I was to interest myself in the individual student" (Secretarial Notes, 1924, p.9). With this kind of indefinite status, why were positions needed? One can infer that, in the minds of trustees, something was missing on the individual campus, perhaps the connection to those with needs to those who care.

Fley (1977), writing on the life of Dean Briggs, offers an explanation from Briggs's biographer, Rollo Brown: "Of President Eliot I saw very little . . . .But about Dean Briggs there could be no doubt. He was human: he was intimate, personal, vastly gentle and kind. To me and to my brethren he meant Harvard, and Harvard meant nothing less than Dean Briggs" (p. 24).

These men and women moved without the benefit of prior history or professional preparation as we know it today. They lacked both budget and clearly outlined duties. There was little communication across campuses, no agreed-upon agendas, and no tools of any kind save their own education, values, personal skills, and leadership ability. Nevertheless, they began the process of preparing a foundation upon which a field of work could later be built. This was reflected in a growing campus influence that was not always appreciated but earned grudging recognition. From the beginning, our predecessors talked about the wholeness of persons and the need to deal with issues in that framework. From the beginning, other voices felt this point of view was unrealistic, unnecessary, and unattainable.

Slowly definitions began to take shape. A typical definition of the dean of men was "that officer in the administration who undertakes to assist the men students [to] achieve the utmost of which they are individually capable, through personal effort on their behalf, and through mobilizing in their behalf all the forces within the University which can be made to serve this end" (Secretarial Notes, 1928, p. 37). President Cloyd Heck Marvin of George Washington observed, "The Dean of Men is most free to interpret his position in terms of modern university life because he is handling problems dealing with the adaptation of student life to the constantly changing social surroundings . . . . You are dealing in men, helping the student to get hold of life, to find the right environment in which he can develop himself to his fullest capacity" (Secretarial Notes, 1929, p. 23).

When the "student development" movement emerged in the late 1960s, writers differentiated the "service" function attributed to the early deans with their own conceptions about students (Brown, 1972; Crookston, 1972). These later writers took the view that service was an insufficient basis upon which the profession could develop a future. Regardless of the merit of their position, it is regrettable that they used a superficial definition of service and applied it to the work of the early deans. A more accurate picture is provided by Cowley, in 1983: "Personnel work constitutes all activities undertaken or sponsored by an educational institution, aside from curricular instruction, in which the student's personal development is the primary concern" (p. 65).

Issues facing the early deans of women overlapped with those of their male counterparts but had understandably unique features. Many educators were unenthusiastic about the increasing enrollment of women students, feeling they were physically and emotionally ill-equipped to cope with the rigors of higher education. As early as the mid–1800s, Horace Mann commented on women's enrollment to the Regents of the University of Michigan, who were considering coeducation. "The advantages of a joint education are great. The dangers of it are terrible" (Fley, 1966, p. 108). He argued that either the moral dangers facing women had to be dealt with or he would prefer that the "young women of that age" not have the advantages of an education. Deans of women were expected to deal with these issues. While the deans may have privately despaired of their situation, they embraced the opportunity to participate. Many of them reported to the president and were given campus-wide visibility and opportunities to serve in policy-making settings. Being in these circles did not exempt them from the skepticism, but it was a matter of importance. The success of coeducation, ironically, eventually would destroy the position of dean of women (Tuttle, 1996).

Most of the early deans of women were nonconformists. They were a first-of-a-kind in institutions that were first-of-a-kind (coeducational). The frustrations they encountered were enormous, a function of working in an alien environment dominated by men. Nonetheless, the inroads they made were permanent. Their ambitions for women were not always respected, but through nuance, poise, and skill they worked to expand opportunities for women students.

In 1903, Martha Foote Crow, the dean of women at Northwestern, and her colleague, Marion Talbot, at the University of Chicago, founded a group that later would become the American Association of University Women (AAUW). This was a vigorous voice for women in the years that followed, yet the historical role of deans of women in AAUW is not well remembered (Truex, 1971).

Student discipline was thrust upon them. Many faculty saw this as a central role for the deans of women, whose annoyance was circumspect and often translated into language and behavior that could serve women. Matthews (1915) set the pattern for women writers who acknowledged the obligations they had to endure, but who then set out to broaden perspectives, inspire, and subtly advocate change. She identified academic, administrative, and social roles for the deans and argued that the dean of women was to be a specialist in women's education. One could imagine this kind of language had special meaning to her informed colleagues. The seriousness she gave to her position is recorded in her assertion that the dean of women had a primary and unique responsibility for an entire generation of young women. This sense of destiny was a shield against the daily resistance they encountered, and not just from their male counterparts. Matthews believed that any woman considering being a dean must be prepared to experience a wide gamut of joy and sorrow. This admonition seems appropriate for student affairs even now.

As was the case with their male counterparts, the position of dean of women varied greatly from campus to campus. In an early history, Holmes (1939) observed that the position was not standardized and, given the uniqueness of each campus, probably should not be. Hopkins (1926) and Cowley (1937) would make the same observations about deans of men. Holmes identified diverse obstacles, opportunities, and quality programs in her study of various campuses. She belied the stereotype of these women as gray-haired ladies looking after routine chores, reporting that sixty percent had faculty rank and taught regularly. The early deans saw this recognition not only as earned, but as essential to their credibility as deans. Fley (1963) has observed of these women that a remarkable breadth of interest, keen insight, and scholarship were evident from the beginning.

Why are we left with only a stilted caricature of deans of women? Except for their own professional journals, little credit has been paid to them. Fley believes many are remembered as "snoopy battle-axes" (1963). We have forgotten their essential courage in the face of formidable circumstances; their dedication in attempting to open new fields of study to women; their persistence even in failure; the stereotype they rose above; the ethical standards evidenced in their work and writing; and the example they set for all who followed. That these women have been diminished, when they should stand as inspirational models, is a matter of ignorance rather than malice, but the result is very nearly the same. Are we interested in correcting this injustice?

The third group comprising the field was the "personnel" worker. None of the early deans of men or deans of women thought of themselves as personnel workers and one seldom finds the word "personnel" used by them.

In 1911, Walter Dill Scott, a psychologist at Northwestern University, published the first book known to apply principles of psychology to employees in industry. As World War I approached, Scott was asked to offer assistance to the U.S. Army to develop a classification system for the Army. In 1917, a Committee on Classification of Personnel was formed that, in retrospect, included a "Who's Who" in the emerging field of psychology, measurement, and educational psychology. Among them were E. K. Strong Jr., E. L. Thorndike, W. V. Bingham, John B. Watson, Louis M. Terman, Robert M. Yerkes, and J. K. Angell.

When Scott accepted the presidency of Northwestern in 1919, he did so with the understanding that he could develop a personnel program for the institution. In a meeting with the Northwestern Board of Trustees, Scott described his concept of personnel work: "It is my belief that the emphasis would be on the individuality of the student and his present needs and interests. The student should be looked upon as more than a candidate for a degree, he is an individuality that must be developed and must be trained for a life of service . . . . Inadequate attention has been given to the fundamental problem of personnel. The great problem in our nation today is the problem of people" (Blackburn, 1969).

The focus Scott chose was to guide students intelligently into the proper field of work. Vocational guidance was to be performed by the personnel administrator. The work was a natural extension of Parsons' pioneering effort, offering psychological measurement as an indispensable tool in vocational guidance. Both the number of personnel workers and the variety of services they offered multiplied rapidly, but the emphasis on vocational guidance became such a dominant theme that, in time, for many the terms "guidance" and "student personnel" were seen as nearly synonymous (Cowley, 1934).

Psychological measurement gained considerable momentum both from the Army classification test and from seminal work in the field of intelligence. Although Cattell has been credited with instituting the first American testing and data collection (at Columbia University), the work of Alfred Binet was of major influence. His tests were translated into English and produced in several versions, the most important of which was the Stanford-Binet, first produced by Lewis Terman in 1916. Thorndike and Strong, among others, turned their creative attention to the educational implications of "aptitude" and "interest" testing. The enthusiasm generated from developments in measurement was pronounced, but the field has been unable to achieve the ambitious goals of its founders. A reading of student affairs journals reveals a fascination with measurement, but many view its claims as overreaching. There are thousands of instruments in the test archives of the ERIC Clearinghouse on Assessment and Evaluation. Few of these are known to practitioners in student affairs or practitioners anywhere. Schon's observation is pertinent: professional knowledge often is mismatched to the realities of practice (Cross, 1998).

The work Scott envisioned for the field entailed efforts already underway by deans of men and deans of women. On some campuses they coalesced immediately, but on others turf battles ensued and instances of hostility resulted.

A number of other events coincided with the work of Scott, involving the scholars engaged in the activities of the Army Classification System. A discussion of these issues would require an outline of the history of psychology in the United States. This discussion is available elsewhere (Hunt, 1993), but the impact of these influences on the field of student personnel administration must be acknowledged.

The status of psychology in the United States was altered by John B. Watson. The introspective psychology that Wundt had formulated proved frustrating because it was found lacking in objectivity. Predictability was difficult and replication was nearly impossible. Lowe (1969) argues that disillusionment with introspection led to behaviorism—the application of the objective methods of animal psychologists to human beings. This opened a field of study that has remained popular since. It is clear that the field of student personnel owes a debt to behaviorism, but as is characteristic of much of our dilemma, the weighting of that debt could be enhanced by historical analysis.

A final "personnel" element emerged from the field of mental health. "It came to be recognized that mental health really depended on the way people got along with each other on the college campus. Increasingly, it was seen that it was closely tied up with the morale of the college, with the presence or absence of conflicts in the environment or within personality" (Brubacher and Rudy, 1976, p. 342). (An examination of the college environment would develop later.) The American public had a growing interest in mental health, stimulated by Clifford Beers' *A Mind That Found Itself,* published in 1909. Mental health came to be considered as one aspect of the "whole" student. Its roots are found in the medical profession, but Blackburn (1969) believes the "medical model" and its focus on "adjustment" has been a mixed blessing for student affairs.

Other issues in the rapidly changing United States affected the development of student affairs, and certainly those touched upon above were complex and interacted in ways that we do not fully understand. But they do explain the separate emergence of the "personnel" professional. From the beginning, these persons sought to use the tools of science and humanistic learning to the extent those tools were available, adapting them to the needs of the student. Conflicts would surface later as to whether claims made in the personnel literature were supportable.

These overlapping constituencies would be resolved by the creation of a dean of students. The new position had an immediate impact. After losing the battle to the broader-based personnel workers, the dean of men frequently won the campus war by moving to the position of dean of students. The expanded enterprise was "his" to command because an additional casualty was the dean of women. Further, the new dean was no longer (necessarily) an inspirational figure, but purportedly was selected for administrative abilities. The idea of a campus "environment" resulted in organizational planning and programs that were more comprehensive than the personal agendas of the deans of men and deans of women.

Within two decades, yet another new position surfaced: the vice president for student affairs. The change resulted from a growing acceptance of student affairs as a major division of the institution. The title proliferated during the period of student unrest in the 1960s. For a period of time, the title "vice president for student affairs and dean of students" reflected both a reluctance of senior student affairs officers to move further from the lives of students and the beckoning of the executive role many would find more useful in their campus efforts.

The long history of women in student affairs resurfaced in the 1980s with the vice president's position. On most campuses, no women were employed at a vice presidential level in the university administration. Student affairs became a natural area of entry. Today a substantial number of vice presidents of student affairs are women, perhaps a final vindication of the dean of women. Minority professionals have also found student affairs to be an avenue for participation in central administrative roles. The full impact in higher education of these new opportunities will be seen more clearly in the decades ahead.

Values in Historical Perspective

The early deans were deeply concerned about values although they may be remembered more as "moralizers" than as "moral." The question of what is of value in human life remains one of life's most central issues, but there is little appreciation or understanding of its historical influence on the student affairs profession.

In every age, thoughtful men and women have pondered values. Cowley (1960) defines a value as "a subjective attitude of a human individual or group at a given point in time and space about the worth of any objective, projective, or subjective entity." Normally we develop a set of values over time. It is through this set that we transcend momentary pain and pleasure and are enabled to coordinate a virtually unlimited number of experiences encompassing the whole of life.

One area of formal philosophical inquiry is devoted entirely to values. It is evident in many enduring pieces of literature about human dilemmas. Our field was formed and has developed as a response to values existing beyond higher education. These values influenced, and continue to influence, our work because they pervade the culture in which we live. They guide the way we make choices, shaped how our predecessors made choices, and identify how such choices were allowed to be made in the face of forces at work in the world.

Our interest is not merely with the content of values or the way they are acquired, but with their relevance to self-appraisal and ultimate behavior. Values imply choices made or not made, deeds done or not done, satisfactions experienced or not experienced.

We do not live alone. The way any segment of society behaves is a product of values. Culture can be seen as a system of consensually validated social expectations derived from the personal values of diverse individuals. This is how the "good" and "bad" connotations become the morals in our time.

Humanism contains a set of values that profoundly affected the work of the early deans. Originating in the Renaissance and gaining its full stature during the European Age of Reason, humanism's principal characteristics include a belief in human rationality; confidence in the possibility of human perfectibility; and recognition of the importance of self-awareness.

Reason, it was averred, should result in action, and reason and achievement became joined in ways unique to the American nation. Its existence coincided with rapid industrial growth, and for a time the two continued side by side. As the American frontier closed and people were thrown into close contact in burgeoning cities, the unfettered enthusiasm for the right to achieve was not as attractive. The exploitation of immigrant workers, women, and children began to cast doubt on the virtue of unbridled individualism, and humanists are still confronting these issues. Higher education encountered them toward the end of the nineteenth century.

The second humanist tenet points directly to the actualization of one's inner potential. As Lowe (1969) puts it, "Humanists continue to emphasize individual initiative and to believe in progress and in man's ability to perfect his world." It is in this second humanist value that the notion of achievement sets its deepest roots. As a matter of fact, it yokes the idea of rationality with the concept of self and self-awareness.

Attention to the third tenet of humanism, that of self-awareness, characterizes our field. The notion of a self-concept has broadened to the point that it has many variations in psychological usage. Maslow offered the concept of self-actualization, which humanists see as the highest good (Hunt, 1993). Carl Rogers made this point in the 1950s. A positive regard for oneself is so important, in Rogers' view, that he wrote an entire book about it (1951). *Client-Centered Therapy* is a well-known idea among those in the profession with counseling backgrounds. His views reflect classical humanism. Failing in self-awareness, in a concept of self, individuals encounter singular difficulties that are obstacles to a productive life. The goal of therapy is to expand self-awareness. Rogers saw the effort as a process, a direction, but it was a crucial process.

Perhaps the most enduring American humanist is Fromm. While arguing for the self in *Escape from Freedom* (1941), Fromm notes that the price of individual freedom may be too high for many, resulting in loneliness and isolation. He was deeply concerned with the persuasive reasons that could be developed for conforming to more dominant voices. This view was expanded six years later in *Man for Himself* (1947), in which Fromm introduces the idea of a "marketing orientation" as a fearful trend in American life. Here the self must conform and please in order to get along, a function of living in an industrial nation. This assertion remains a concern. A fear of group rejection is a paramount fear, a pervasive anxiety for many. In *The Sane Society* (1955), he expands the notion by observing the tendency in American life to redefine long-held values. His concern is evident. Even simple distinctions like "right" and "wrong" are vulnerable to redefinition.

It is impossible here to offer more than a sketch of humanistic values. But their centrality to the purpose and direction of student affairs must be understood.

The Student Personnel Point of View

It can be argued that the foundation document for our work is *The Student Personnel Point of View*, 1937 (National Association of Student Personnel Administrators [NASPA], 1989). In 1937, the American Council on Education (ACE) called together an influential group of educators interested in examining the status of growing out-of-class programs and activities loosely called personnel services. Hardee (1987) provides useful information on the background of these participants. From the discussions held by the group, two members took the responsibility for preparing a summary document. They were W. H. Cowley, professor and director of the personnel bureau at Ohio State University, and Esther Lloyd-Jones, chair of guidance and student personnel, Teachers College, Columbia University. The document was entitled *The Student Personnel Point of View* which was accepted largely unchallenged for thirty years, and has not been superseded even now. The core philosophy is contained within two concise paragraphs that reflect a humanist perspective.

One of the basic purposes of higher education is the preservation, transmission, and enrichment of the important elements of culture: the product of scholarship, research, creative imagination, and human experience. It is the task of colleges and universities to utilize this and other educational purposes as to assist the student in developing to the limits of his potential and in making his contribution to the betterment of society.

This philosophy imposes upon educational institutions the obligation to consider the student as a whole—his intellectual capacity and achievement, his emotional make-up, his physical condition, his social relationships, his vocational aptitudes and skills, his moral and religious values, his economic resources, and his aesthetic appreciation. It puts emphasis, in brief, upon the development of the student as a person rather than upon his intellectual training alone [NASPA, 1989].

When Walter Dill Scott established the "Personnel Office," as he had promised the trustees at Northwestern, he selected L. B. Hopkins to direct the office. Esther Lloyd-Jones was an outstanding undergraduate student who worked with Hopkins but felt his program was geared mostly for men. She conducted a study of women undergraduates and their needs that so impressed Scott that he sponsored her master's program at Teachers College, Columbia and established an associate director of personnel position for her when she returned. She returned to Teachers College in 1926, beginning a forty-year career there. She would become one of the most influential figures in our professional history.

As Lloyd-Jones began her career at Teachers College, only a few blocks away, John Dewey was concluding his long tenure at Columbia University. The humanist influence in the United States was reformulated in Dewey's work that would be referred to varyingly as experimentalism, instrumentalism, or pragmatism.

Dewey believed in the humanist propositions of human growth and development and gave to the schools an important role in encouraging these outcomes. Central to his work was an analysis of the psychology of learning, his belief in the wholeness of students, and his advocacy for student-centered learning. He did not abandon the centrality of intellectual development but argued that it would prosper if it was accompanied by experience. He saw both the successes and the abuses of the industrial revolution and believed the tools of science could be used in service to the nation (Dewey, [1916] 1952).

At the time of the ACE meeting, Cowley had developed an interest in the growing field of student personnel. He wrote during that period about the variety of functions performed and argued for closer cooperation among the various campus programs and national organizations, a point of view that found its way into the statement.

The Student Personnel Point of View contained strengths and flaws that might be expected from a document developed over just a few days. Its strength is found in the men and women who created it. They were among the most outstanding people of their day, drawn from a variety of backgrounds, possessing an ability to articulate their views and a keen understanding of potential of the field they were asked to describe. They correctly predicted that "student personnel" would join business affairs and academic affairs as a major division of college and university life. The criticism today is that by outlining so many separate services, they failed to see how this would affect relationships with other divisions and how specialization would undercut the idea of wholeness central to the espoused philosophy. The group did call for cooperation between and within institutions, believing that good practice would be a matter of discovery over time.

The document was redrafted by ACE in 1949 to reflect the major changes in American life and on the campus following World War II. Only Cowley and Lloyd-Jones were left from the original committee. E. G. Williamson (University of Minnesota) chaired the new effort and three new goals were offered:

- Education for a fuller realization of democracy in every phase of living.
- Education directly and explicitly for understanding and cooperation.
- Education for the application of creative imagination and trained intelligence to the solution of social problems and to the administration of public affairs (NASPA, 1989).

The "preservation, transmission, and enrichment of the culture" changed from *one* of higher education basic purposes (1937) to *the* basic purpose (1949). This may reflect Williamson's concern that student personnel administration was seen as soft intellectually. This caused him to comment on one occasion that the field needed to consider the whole student, "intellect and all" (1961, p. 429).

In a thoughtful passage in *Student Personnel Work as Deeper Teaching* (Lloyd-Jones and Smith, 1954), Lloyd-Jones reminded her readers of the common beliefs held by those "who profess themselves as student personnel workers."

1. "A belief in the worth of the individual; that human values are of the greatest importance; that the common good can be promoted best by helping each individual to develop to the utmost in accordance with his abilities. There is growing agreement that the mores, the way in which groups subtly and unconsciously assign roles to persons, and the social expectancies to which individuals respond are powerfully controlling in stimulating or inhibiting an individual in the development of his abilities.

2. The belief in the equal dignity of thinking and feeling and working; that these aspects are inseparable. Personnel work is interested in the *whole* person and

not merely in his mind or his economic productivity or some other one of his aspects.

3. The belief that the world has a place for everybody: a place in the social world, a place in the civic world, a place in family life, and a place in the vocational world; that it is education's task to offer youth not only an invitation, but also positive stimulation carefully adapted to his needs to help him to grow to full stature in all of these roles. A stimulating and rich environment provides for the exploration of resources (relationships: who and what he is); and for the accomplishment of developmental tasks appropriate for his age level which will carry the young person into effective adult life, and on further into a rich later life.

4. The belief that what an individual gathers from his experiences continues on in time; it is not what is imposed, but what is absorbed that persists. Personnel workers see the person—at whatever age—not as a single moment independent of the past and the future, but as a transition point in a stream of experience that goes back to infancy and will continue on into the future; they believe that each person can move progressively from dependence toward independence, from interest to responsibility, from casual concern to good work habits, from superficial to logical associations, from egocentric to social behavior" (p. 5).

The Postwar Years

In one sense, the end of World War II transformed student personnel administration. The enterprise grew phenomenally, both in the introduction of new programs and services and the expansion of old ones. Philosophical issues in student affairs were secondary to the requirements of time and energy needed to serve the returning veteran. The role of women in the war effort, whether in the military or in industry, led them to college in greater numbers. Racial minorities, while small as a percentage, grew substantially in absolute numbers from the prewar years.

Blaesser (1945) and his colleagues were concerned about a number of these issues. Rules and regulations, they correctly predicted, "are probably in for a bad time." They believed that mental health would be an issue, particularly for veterans with combat experience. What would racial attitudes be like? they pondered. Would religious counseling need to be expanded?

Of course, most worrisome of all, what would be the needs of a postwar American, and how should a college education be altered to meet those needs? The introduction of the Serviceman's Readjustment Act, familiarly known as the G. I. Bill of Rights, introduced students to the campus who were the first in their family to attend college. Hundreds of thousands of students would flock to newly developed public two-year colleges across the United States. Married students would be coming to campus in huge numbers. Where would they live? What would be their requirements?

Some immediate realities dampened the postwar period. The Soviet Union kept its war machine in place and began to exert its will throughout Europe. The "Cold War" began under President Truman and remained as a serious issue until the Berlin Wall was torn down in 1989. The brief alignment of the Russians with mainland China was worrisome, and efforts to "contain" the spread of Communism emerged as foreign policy. These events were made more urgent by Soviet achievements in space technology.

At home, the federal government used its power to condemn Communism, as it was perceived as an internal threat. Senator Joseph McCarthy of Wisconsin emerged as the leader of a political right wing and was joined by the Committee on Un-American Activities in the House of Representatives.

Racial tension also surfaced in the 1950s and would affect the country's equilibrium. Segregation was under attack everywhere and military force occasionally was used to contain passions. Groundwork was laid for the "women's movement." These events would presage the more disruptive decade of the sixties.

A number of issues coalesced in the 1960s to make the decade violent on and off the campus. The assassination of three national leaders, John F. Kennedy, Robert F. Kennedy, and Martin Luther King, Jr., demonstrated the fragile nature of human progress. The undeclared war in Vietnam hardened hearts and minds, dividing the nation. A counterculture emerged with drugs as a sacrament. Efforts to increase rights along racial lines intensified. A revolution in communication and information introduced messages into one's living room nearly simultaneous to their occurrence across the globe.

College students were not isolated from these events. In fact, in some instances they led the dissent. Many were disturbed by the collaboration between war industries and higher education institutions. Eisenhower had warned the country of the military-industrial complex and his admonition was taken seriously on the campus. College students' ideals led them to politics, but what they found there was not appealing. Campus dissent became violent in a number of instances and occasionally was met by repressive responses that worsened matters.

Revel (1971) points to the 1960s as a series of interrelated events in the United States that were revolutionary in nature. He argues that no other nation in the world could have survived this many-faceted attack on itself.

Serious as these issues were, the decade of the 1960s produced successful legislation that would transform civil rights. The Civil Rights Act of 1965 contained a number of separate titles that over the years would be pervasive influences. The Higher Education Acts of 1965 (amended in 1972) improved the life of students in a number of ways, not the least of which was financial support unparalleled in the nation's history.

This brief history ends at 1970, because perspective becomes more difficult when one is personally engaged in events. The late 1960s in student affairs produced a fundamental review of current practices and called for "student development" as a means of describing the profession. Brown (1972), Miller and Prince (1976) led the early discussions, and the efficacy of their ideas is still being pondered. Clearly the field has been energized by those discussions.

Looking Forward to a New Century

History unfolding need not be a spectator sport. We will all need to think, write, and participate in *our* time about matters of importance if we hope to influence the future. Writing about current issues in student affairs and beyond should be considered a matter of stewardship. We owe our present circumstances to the earlier deans who made it possible. We repay this debt not to them, but to those who follow us. This responsibility cannot be accomplished solely through segmented, restrictive articles in research journals. Broad issues will command attention:

1. What will it mean to be educated through a "higher education"? In answering, we will be concerned about the fields of knowledge and principal skills to which students must be introduced and how they are acquired. Will ignorance be our major foe? If so, we can claim to be at the *center* of the academy. There we will enjoy common purpose with others while professing and demonstrating unique ideas and contributions of our own.

2. If there are human values identified as good, worthy, and important to us all, will they find a way into the purposes of a higher education? Will professional colleagues in the future argue that effective citizenship can be taught, that bigotry cannot be tolerated, that personal integrity is more vital than material success or personal power, that the ideal of human worth and dignity is central to all that we call good? Will there be an effort to "preserve, transmit, and enrich" values or will they be viewed as a byproduct of education? Will student affairs invoke this debate or eschew it?

3. We have lived in a century of hierarchical power, in politics and in work. The college campus, collegial in many ways, has been hierarchical at the core. Wheatley (1992) believes that substantial change is now evident. She talks about the quantum world. In the quantum world, she says, charts and hierarchies are going to surrender entirely to the power of relationships. Relationships will not merely be interesting to examine, they will be all there is to organizational reality. She stresses the need to see things *in their wholeness* rather than in ever-

narrowing parts if one seeks to understand and influence future organizations. The disruption of hierarchy would be a promising development for student affairs. Growing numbers of faculty and staff would look for ways to make a higher education useful for students, be less concerned about formal status, and be more interested in people with imagination, skill, and energy wherever they are found on the campus.

4. What will be the future relationship between a student and a higher education? As students of all ages, different races and creeds, full- and part-time status, of differing backgrounds, orientations, and circumstances, come to higher education, will there be a common underpinning? What will be the relative influence of student interests, corporate America, and professional educators and scholars on the content, purposes, and methods of higher education? There has been a growing acceptance of the notion of students as consumers, students as customers. What do these metaphors mean? Is the historical university worth defending? What will student affairs professionals have to say on such matters?

5. The use of technology today in higher education is accelerating, but will be seen as primitive by future standards. Discussions by the most knowledgeable among us today need to give direction to a technology that serves rather than dominates. Student affairs can use the tools of technology to advance broader goals. For example, it should be possible, figuratively, to disassemble entire student populations, rebuilding them student by student as learning communities, involving persons with common needs (Rhatigan, 1986). Students should be able to join in several learning communities at any one time or across time to meet the temporary or enduring issues that are important to them. Will technology require a new student affairs philosophy or will it merely encourage the realization of long-held aspirations?

In an effort to encourage active participation in the large events that await us, the ordinary, pressing issues of the day cannot be neglected. This is a problem for dedicated student affairs professionals who must choose how to spend their energy. Reading and writing may not be their first choice (Rhatigan and Crawford, 1978b). We do not need to write *for publication* to be effective. In campus committees, memoranda, classes, newspapers, seminars, presentations, and conversations, we can use the tools of history to achieve goals seen as important.

Campus practitioners will need to find a way to retreat from their labors to be active learners. A major limitation in work is lacking the ability to see possibilities, failing to employ imagination, wasting time on undeserving tasks, or doing things *others* have identified as important. Yet, the professional literature must take practitioners into account in far more effective ways than seem to exist at the time of this writing.

Practitioners do not enjoy the luxury of certainty. It is profoundly true that student affairs administrators must often proceed without knowing exactly what they are doing. We either act or step aside. This requires judgment and faith, the willingness to be vulnerable and to take risks. There is much to celebrate in these ordinary days of our lives, part of the fellowship we share with those who came before. We must work hard to allow colleagues years from now to glimpse this evidence of goodness.

References

Bashaw, C. T. "We Who Live off on the Edges: Deans of Women at Southern Coeducational Institutions and Access to the Community of Higher Education," 1907–1960. Unpublished doctoral dissertation, University of Georgia, 1992.

Bathurst, J. E. "What Is Student Personnel Work?" *Educational Record*, 1938, 19, 502–515.

Blackburn, J. L. "Perceived Purposes of Student Personnel Programs by Chief Student Personnel Officers as a Function of Academic Preparation and Experience." Unpublished doctoral dissertation, Florida State University, 1969.

Blaesser, W. W. and others. *Student Personnel Work in the Postwar College*. Washington, D.C.: American Council on Education, 1945.

Blimling, G. S., and Alschuler, A. S. "Creating a Home for the Spirit of Learning: Contributions of Student Development Directors." *Journal of College Student Development* 1996, 37, (2), 203–223.

Brown, R. D. *Student Development in Tomorrow's Higher Education: A Return to the Academy*. Monograph 16, ACPA, 1972.

Brubacher, J., and Rudy, W. R. *Higher Education in Transition* (3rd ed.) New York: Harper Collins, 1976.

Caple, R. B. "The Learning Debate: A Historical Perspective," *Journal of College Student Development*, 1996, 37(2), 203–213.

Chambers, J. Untitled Remarks, Opening Session, ACPA/NASPA Joint Conference, Chicago, March 15, 1987. Audiotape.

Coomes, M. D., Whitt, E. J., and Kuh, G. D. "Woman for a Changing World," *Journal of Counseling and Development*, 1987, 65, 407–414.

Cowley, W. H. "The History of Student Residential Housing," *School and Society*, 1934a, 40 (1040), 705–712.

Cowley, W. H. "The History of Student Residential Housing, II," *School and Society*, 1934b, 40 (1041), 758–764.

Cowley, W. H. "The Disappearing Dean of Men," *Proceedings of the Nineteenth Annual Conference of Deans and Advisors to Men*, Austin, TX: University of Texas, (mimeograph), 1937, 85–99.

Cowley, W. H. "The History and Philosophy of Student Personnel Work," *Journal of the National Association of Deans of Women*, 1940, 3, 153–162.

Cowley, W. H. "A Holistic Overview of American Colleges and Universities," (mimeograph), 1960, 69–86.

Cowley, W. H. "The Nature of Student Personnel Work," In G. L. Saddlemire and A. L. Rentz (eds.), *Student Affairs—A Profession's Heritage*, Carbondale, IL: Southern Illinois Press, 1983, 47–73.

Crookston, B. B. "An Organizational Model for Student Development," *Journal of the National Association of Student Personnel Administrators*, 1972, 10(1), 3–13.

Cross, K. P. "Why Learning Communities? Why Now?" *About Campus*, 1998, 3(3), 4–11.

Dewey, J. *Democracy and Education*. New York: Macmillan Company, 1952. (Originally published 1916.)

Fenske, R. H. "Historical Foundations." In U. Delworth and G. R. Hanson (eds.), *Student Services: A Handbook for the Profession*, San Francisco: Jossey-Bass, 1980.

Fley, J. "Discipline in Student Personnel Work: The Changing Views of Deans and Personnel Workers." Unpublished doctoral dissertation, University of Illinois, 1963.

Fley, J. "An Honorable Tradition," *Journal of the National Association of Women Deans and Counselors*, 1966, 29(3), 106–110.

Fley, J. "LeBaron Russell Briggs: He Meant Harvard." *Journal of the National Association of Women Deans, Advisors and Counselors*, 1977, 40 (Fall), 21–24.

Fromm, E. *Escape from Freedom*. New York: Farrar and Rinehart, Inc., 1941.

Fromm, E. *Man for Himself*. Greenwich, Connecticut: Fawcett Publications, 1947.

Fromm, E. *The Sane Society*. New York: Rinehart, 1955.

Gilroy, M. "The Contributions of Selected Teachers College Women to the Field of Student Personnel." Unpublished doctoral dissertation, Teachers College, Columbia University, 1987.

Hardee, M. D. Untitled Keynote Address, ACPA/NASPA Joint Conference, Chicago, March 15, 1987.

Haskins, C. H. *The Rise of Universities*. New York: Peter Smith, 1940.

Holmes, L. *A History of the Position of Dean of Women in a Selected Group of Co-educational Colleges and Universities in the United States*. New York: Teachers College, Columbia, University, 1939.

Hopkins, L. B. "Personnel Procedure in Education," *The Educational Record*, 1926, 3, 3–96.

Hunt, M. *The Story of Psychology*. New York: Doubleday, 1993.

Kibre, P. *The Nations in the Medieval Universities*. Cambridge: Medieval Academy of America, 1948.

Kuh, G. D., Shedd, J. D., and Whitt, E. J., "Student Affairs and Liberal Education: Unrecognized (and Unappreciated) Common Law Partners." In E. J. Whitt (ed.) *College Student Affairs Administration*. ASHE Reader Series. Needham Heights, MA: Simon & Schuster, 1997, 60–69.

Leonard, E. A. *Origins of Personnel Services in American Higher Education*. Minneapolis: University of Minnesota Press, 1956.

Lloyd-Jones, E., and Smith, M. R., *Student Personnel Work as Deeper Teaching*. New York: Harper and Bras, 1954.

Lowe, C. M. *Value Orientations in Counseling and Psychotherapy*. San Francisco: Chandler Company, 1969.

Matthews, L. K. *The Dean of Women*. Boston: Houghton Mifflin, Co., 1915.

Miller, T., and Prince, J. *The Future of Student Affairs*. San Francisco, Jossey-Bass, 1976.

Murphy, P. M. *Student Life and Services*. Stillwater: Oklahoma State University Centennial Series, 1988.

National Association of Student Personnel Administrators [NASPA], *Points of View*. Washington, D.C.: NASPA, 1989.

Rait, R. S. *Life in the Medieval University*. Cambridge, MA: Harvard University Press, 1912.

Rashdall, H. *The Universities of Europe in the Middle Ages*. 3 vols. New York: Oxford University Press, 1895.

Revel, J. *Without Marx or Jesus*. Garden City, New York: Doubleday and Co., 1971.

Rhatigan, J. J. "History as a Potential Ally," *Journal of the National Association of Student Personnel Administrators*, 1974, 11(3), 11–15.

Rhatigan, J. J. "Student Services Versus Student Development: Is There a Difference?" *Journal of the National Association for Women Deans, Administrators, and Counselors*. 1975, 38(2), 51–58.

Rhatigan, J. J. "A Corrective Look Back." In J. R. Appleton, C. M. Briggs, and J. J. Rhatigan, *Pieces of Eight*. Portland: NIRAD, 1978a, 9–43.

Rhatigan, J. J. "Developing a Campus Profile of Commuter Students," *Journal of the National Association of Student Personnel Administrators*, 1986, 24(1), 4–10.

Rhatigan, J. J., and Crawford, A. E, III, "Professional Development Preferences of Student Affairs Administrators," *Journal of the National Association of Student Personnel Administrators*, 1978b, 15(3), 45–52.

Roberts, D. C. "Student Learning Was Always Supposed To Be the Core of Our Work," *About Campus*, 1998, 3(3), 18–22.

Rogers, C. R. *Client-Centered Therapy, Its Current Practice, Implications and Theory*. Boston: Houghton Mifflin, 1951.

Rudolph, F. "The American College Student: From Theologian to Technocrat in 300 Years." *Journal of the National Association of Student Personnel Administrators*, 1976, 14(1), 31–39.

Ruekel, P., and Harris, A. R. (eds.) "NAWDAC Celebrates Seventy Years," *Journal of the National Association for Women Deans, Administrators and Counselors*. 1986, 49(2).

Secretarial Notes on Sixth Annual Conference of Deans and Advisers of Men held at University of Michigan, April 24–26, 1924, p. 9.

Secretarial Notes on Tenth Annual Conference of Deans and Advisers of Men held at University of Colorado, May 10–12, 1928, p. 37.

Secretarial Notes on Eleventh Annual Conference of Deans and Advisers of Men held at Washington, D.C., April 11–13, 1929, p. 23.

Sheeley, V. L. *Fulfilling Visions: Emerging Leaders of ACPA*. ACPA, 1991.

Truex, D. "Education of Women, the Student Personnel Profession, and the New Feminism," *Journal of the National Association of Women Deans and Counselors*, 1971, 34, 13–20.

Tuttle, K. N. "What Became of the Dean of Women? Changing Roles for Women Administrators in American Higher Education, 1940–1980." Unpublished doctoral dissertation, University of Kansas, 1996.

Wheatley, M. *Leadership and the New Science*. San Francisco: Berret-Koehler, Inc., 1992.

Williamson, E. G. *Student Personnel Services in Colleges and Universities*. New York: McGraw Hill, 1961.

CHAPTER TWO

THE IMPORTANCE OF THE INSTITUTIONAL MISSION

Margaret J. Barr

When discussions focus on the mission of an institution, often the rhetoric is grand and the generalizations are sweeping. But the mission of an institution influences all aspects of the day-by-day institutional life and the future growth and development of the college or university. Failure to understand, appreciate, and translate the mission of the institution into programs and services can rank among the biggest mistakes a student affairs administrator can make. The complexity and diversity of higher education in the United States makes appreciation and understanding of the mission more difficult and challenging, for what is supported at one institution may be a foreign concept at another college or university.

"American higher education has never been forced to conform to any one uniform pattern of organization, administration or support" (Brubacher and Rudy, 1976, p. 59). Instead, a rich tapestry characterizes higher education in the United States. Institutions can be found that are large or small, public or independent, church-related or church-controlled, four year or two year, post-baccalaureate or community colleges, selective or open in admissions, and rural or urban. These characteristics, as well as others, do not develop by accident. Institutional characteristics, including how the institution conducts itself in large and small ways, flow from the mission of the institution.

Other chapters in this volume will explore the characteristics of students, the roles and purposes of various functions in student affairs, the intricacies of financial and facility management, and the ways individuals and organizations in higher education can assess progress toward goal accomplishment. This chapter will focus instead on why the mission of the institution is important and on the role of the mission in shaping the tone and direction of the educational enterprise and professional practice in student affairs. Examples of how the mission of the institution influences daily practices within specific educational settings will be provided. Finally, the chapter will provide suggestions for how student affairs professionals can increase their effectiveness in translating the mission of the institution to students, their parents, and others.

Why is a Mission Statement Important?

The distinctive character of an institution is usually imbedded in its mission statement. A mission statement helps those who work at, teach at, contemplate attending and support an institution understand what the institution is attempting to accomplish.

A mission statement should provide guidance to the day-by-day practices within the institution. William Bryan Martin states: "A statement of institutional mission, at its best, formally represents assumptions and purposes that will guide the planning as well as the activities of a college or university. Despite flights of rhetoric, sweeping generalizations and other evidence that the reach exceeds the grasp, a good mission statement helps members of the community decide when to say no and when to say yes. It is a statement of intention that affects practice. It is informed by tradition and experience yet transcends both" (Martin, 1982, p. 85). The purposes of an institutional mission as outlined by Martin are powerful and essential to setting the tone and direction of the institution.

According to Welzenback (1982), the mission statement should also provide a statement of the broad long-term purpose of the institution. Simply stated, the mission statement articulates why the institution was created and defines the constituencies the institution will serve.

In addition, an institutional mission statement should guide the academic leadership of the institution in determining what educational programs are appropriate within the context of the institution (Carnegie Council on Policy Studies in Higher Education, 1980). In part, the mission of the institution determines what contributions a specific institution should make to the broader higher education enterprise. In an era of restricted resources, an analysis of the institutional mission statement may prevent inappropriate ventures from being launched. If the new program is not consistent with the mission it will inevitably fail.

The mission statement also provides specific guidance to student affairs professionals in developing policies and implementing new program initiatives. To illustrate, if an institution is church-controlled and committed to strongly held views regarding the behavior of students, development of policies that run contrary to the mission of the institution will not be supported. Thus social activities, health education programs, and residence hall rules and regulations must all be congruent with the mission of the institution. Or, if an institution is founded to serve the community, policies and practices that restrict access of community members to the institution will not be tolerated. One reality of a community-based institution is a focus on providing educational opportunities at low cost to those in the community. Efforts to drastically raise tuition or charge extra fees to support programs in such institutions will be viewed as inconsistent with the institutional mission.

Finally, a mission statement may provide guidance to students by providing information regarding the expectations of the institution for students. For example, if the institution believes that an honor code is important, students should be able to understand that expectation by reading the mission statement. Or, if dancing is prohibited on campus, a prospective student should be able to understand this prohibition from reading the institutional mission statement.

Kuh, Schuh, and Whitt (1991) indicate that an institutional mission "can be based on religious, ideological, or philosophical beliefs about human potential, teaching and learning" (p. 41). Whatever the basis for the institutional statement, in order for it to be a useful guide for the student affairs practitioner, it must be understood. A number of factors contribute to the understanding of the mission of the institution and attention to those factors can help the practitioner develop programs and services that are congruent with the institutional mission. These factors may be referred to as the living mission of the institution (Lyons, 1993).

Factors Influencing the Mission

Affiliation

The mission of church-controlled or church-related institutions influences the daily life of students, faculty, and staff. As Lyons (1993) points out, Earlham, Haverford, and Guilford colleges are distinctive institutions because they all were founded by Quakers (Society of Friends). To this day, according to Lyons, "the Quaker tradition continues to play an significant role in determining how things get done, how members of the campus community relate to each other, and how policy is conceived and implemented" (p. 8).

Notre Dame, Georgetown, DePaul, Loyola of Chicago, and Loyola of New Orleans, as examples, are shaped by their religious affiliation with the Catholic Church. That affiliation influences the life of the campus related to governance structures, control, behavioral expectations for students, and the recognition of student organizations. The situation at Georgetown University illustrates the conflicting issues facing student affairs administrators at some religiously affiliated institutions. Two gay student organizations were refused recognition from the institution based on church doctrine condemning homosexuality. If the student groups were not recognized, they could not use the facilities of the institution, use institutional mail, or request funds in support of programs and activities. Georgetown University is also subject to the antidiscrimination law of the District of Columbia prohibiting, among other things, discrimination on the basis of sexual orientation. The student groups sued under the statute. The court, according to Kaplin and Lee (1997), "reached a collective result of not requiring the university to recognize the groups but requiring it to give them access to facilities, services and funding" (p. 401). Kaplin and Lee go on to say that "the District of Columbia's compelling interest in eradicating discrimination based on sexual preference outweighed any burden on the university's freedom of religion that providing equal access would imply" (p. 401). Although the United States Congress later amended the law governing the District of Columbia to permit religious institutions to discriminate on the basis of sexual orientation, the case is illustrative of the confusing and difficult paths sometimes trod by administrators at some institutions.

There are also many examples in higher education where private institutions have been transformed into public colleges and universities. In almost all cases, vestiges of that former affiliation can be found in the life of the campus through traditions, the names of buildings, and the mission statement.

Characteristics

Another way to understand the mission of the institution is to carefully look at the characteristics of the institution and the students attending the college or university. Is it residential or commuter? The design of student affairs programs and delivery systems will differ substantially between the two types of institutions. For example, residential campuses rely on floor meetings, resident assistants, and residence hall staff to assure that students receive information in a timely and useful fashion. On a commuter campus, more emphasis is placed on the campus newspaper, signs, direct mailings, and e-mail to assure that students can access information that is important to their academic experience.

What degrees are offered? Is it a limited curriculum or a more expansive one? Are graduate and professional students served? Is the enrollment part-time or full-time? The answers to all of these questions will also shape the role and scope of student affairs programs. Institutions with substantial graduate programs often must examine family housing opportunities, support services for international students, and access to medical care for student dependents. Those issues are far less relevant at institutions with a primarily undergraduate population of traditional age. The issue of full- or part-time status of the student body also shapes the range of student services provided by the institution. Part-time learners often get medical insurance, for example, through family or work rather than through the institution.

What does it cost to attend? What financial aid is available for students? The answers to these questions will shape the socioeconomic status of the student body. That will influence the types of student activities provided and programs initiated in the institution. Financial aid policies may, but not necessarily, also influence the ethnic make-up of the student body. The racial and ethnic composition of the student body influences all that we do and try to accomplish in student affairs.

The answers to these questions also help bring form and substance to the mission of the institution. In order to understand an institution, one must fundamentally understand who is served and in what manner. That understanding then brings helpful guidance to administrators planning programs and activities.

One of the important characteristics is institutional size. This characteristic, perhaps more than any other, influences the role of student affairs. Smaller, more intimate, institutions allow student affairs staff members to know students and interact with them on a daily basis. For example, at Cornell College in Iowa, the dean of students has an opportunity to know a greater proportion of students on a more informal level than can be achieved by the vice president for student affairs at the University of Michigan.

These and other characteristics of the institution are evidence of the institutional mission in the everyday life of the campus. Many small liberal arts colleges struggling with enrollment made a decision to engage in the development of educational programs for adult students. If that decision was made without regard to the mission of the institution, the programs were sure to fail because all parts of the institution had not embraced the new program emphasis. In instances where the decision to expand whom the institution serves was made with broad community input and even adjustment of the written mission of the institution, such programs succeeded. In those instances, the new efforts and the institutional mission were brought into congruence.

History

Many factors influence the specific mission of an institution. The first is the intention of the founders—whether the institution is a creation of the state legislature or the collective will of a private group of individuals. One of the key questions to ask is, what did those who created the institution intend to accomplish through establishment of the college or university? Sometimes that intention is easy to discern from the original statutes, reference to an institution in the state constitution or the articles of incorporation. Sometimes understanding the intention of those who created the institution is more complex. For example, one private institutional mission statement indicates it should be " . . . a university of the highest order of excellence, complete in all of its parts . . . " (Northwestern University, 1852). Clearly much more needed to be done (and has been done) to define just what the highest order of excellence means for the students, faculty, staff, and alumni of the institution.

In addition, institutions that were church-related or church-controlled have evolved into secular enterprises. Under such circumstances, it is very likely that the institutional mission statement and the daily life of the campus will still reflect some of the values of the earlier affiliation. For example, baccalaureate services and university creeds may still be a part of campus life although the institution is independent and has no religious affiliation.

As Lyons (1993) indicates, "the heritage of the institution can be one of the building blocks of its mission" (p. 41). Lyons cautions, however, that although history is important, it is only one of many ways to understand the mission of the institution (p. 41).

Focus

Some institutions have focused missions with regard to whom they serve and how they serve them. Community colleges, for example, serve a bounded geographic community and develop programs and activities to uniquely meet the needs of the communities where they are located. For example, as residency patterns change, it is often the community college that offers the first organized programs in English as a second language. Or, as the needs of business and industry change from manufacturing to technology and service, the community college usually offers both credit- and noncredit-bearing opportunities for citizens of the surrounding community to gain new skills and competencies. In such circumstances, student affairs units may, for instance, provide more support to first-time learners than in other kinds of institutional settings.

Lyons (1993) also cites Berea College as an institution with a focused mission "to educate the able but poor children in Appalachia" (p. 13). That mission has translated into specific campus programs requiring that the student body be limited to those who can pay little or no tuition, and that all students work for the institution to offset the cost of their education. Thus, in this institution, student services pay a great deal of time and attention to supervising work programs.

Historically black colleges and universities and tribal colleges were founded to serve those unserved or underserved by established institutions of higher education. Historically black institutions have a unique history and heritage of fighting for survival against almost insurmountable odds. Many such institutions were and are religiously affiliated, and in both the private and public sector, the struggle for resources to support these institutions is constant. The unique mission of the historically black colleges has been challenged by the integration of public and private institutions of higher education after passage of the Civil Rights Act. Some historically black institutions have developed a unique presence in American higher education and have served as the educational foundation for many African American leaders in our country. In recent years, there has been an increased interest from African American students in attending such institutions.

The development of true tribal colleges has occurred since the beginning of the twentieth century. Prior to that time, higher educational institutions for Native Americans were developed as "non-reservation boarding schools" focused on technical training (Brubacher and Rudy, 1976, p. 83). Currently, there are almost thirty tribal colleges, each supported by an Indian nation with assistance from the Bureau of Indian Affairs. It is interesting to note that only two of those colleges are inter-tribal. The issue of education for Native Americans is one that is not yet fully resolved.

Governance

The independent or public nature of the institution is shaped by an important part of the institutional mission. The very nature of the institution is influenced by the statutory, constitutional, or charter provisions governing the formation of the institution. A valuable discussion regarding the differences in governance between independent and public institutions can be found in the chapter by Miller in this volume. Without discussing those issues in detail, it is important to note that the corporate governance structure of the institution influences much of the day-by-day work of the institution. Even the terms *public* or *private* have great meaning in terms of the expectations of students, parents, and major donors. The governance structure of the institution is one of the major components in understanding the mission of the institution and defining who will be served.

Higher Education System

Several institutions of higher education may be connected through the development of a public university system. When such systems are present, the individual campuses have less autonomy and many policies and procedures are administered on a system-wide basis. Although there may be uniformity of some aspects of institutional life, it would be a mistake to assume that all campuses within a system are the same and function in the same way. In the University of California system, for example, the University of California at Davis, with a rich heritage based on the environment and agriculture, is substantially different from the campus at the University of California at Berkeley. Although linked in important ways, the campuses retain a distinctive character that influences the actual ways through which systems policies are enacted and enforced.

The State University of New York is also a system with some degree of centralized control on issues of policy, program development, and facility construction. However, each campus in that large and complex system varies considerably from each other in focus, history, and the traditions of the institution. The State University of New York at Stony Brook differs remarkably from the State University of New York at Albany, Binghamton, or Buffalo. The State University College at Fredonia and the State University College at Oswego also have distinctive characters influencing the day-to-day lives of students, faculty and staff. In all of these cases, much more than the governance through a system shapes the ways in which the institution grows, prospers, and serves students, faculty, staff, and the larger community.

Geographic Location

The physical location of the institution also influences the mission of the institution. Those who created the institution located it in a particular place to meet a particular need. The history of higher education is replete with examples of such institutions. Population sometimes dictates geographic location as is demonstrated by the number of historically black institutions located in the south rather than the north. Native American tribes created their own institutions to meet both their own educational and cultural needs.

Therefore, it should not be surprising that academic programs at the various campuses of the University of Alaska focus on the unique aspects of the culture, climate, and economy of Alaska. Or that institutions in urban settings are less likely than those located in agrarian areas to have academic programs related to veterinarian medicine.

Geographic location also influences the role and scope of student affairs work on campus. For example, an isolated campus in a rural area is much more likely than an urban campus to have a campus infirmary where students can check in for overnight stays. The urban campus has many hospital options located in the immediate vicinity, whereas those resources may not be available on the rural campus.

There usually is a reason for the location of a specific institution. The growth of "normal schools" in the early twentieth century responded to the need for educated persons to serve as teachers in communities across the country. The conversion of these institutions to other purposes also was done to meet a specific need, although part of that need may have been political.

All of these factors and others contribute to a richer understanding of the institutional mission and the influence that mission will have on the role and function of student affairs.

Links Between Institutions

There may be other links between and among institutions both public and independent that are not dependent on governance. Such links might include joint programs, the ability to share library and other facilities, discounts for students to attend certain events, faculty training grants, and joint grant proposals. Each of these relationships and linkages between institutions helps shape the scope and purpose of the institution and, thus, of student affairs. Policies will be influenced by such arrangements. For example, should a student from another institution attending classes through a consortia arrangement have access to the host institution's psychological or health services? Whenever such arrangements are developed, they must be consistent with the mission of the institution and serve the constituencies that institution was designed to serve.

Predetermination

The institutional mission can also proscribe how student services will be organized and how students will access services. For example, the adherence to the English model of undergraduate colleges (with residence units and faculty involvement) has influenced the organization of student services at institutions such as Harvard,

Princeton, and Yale. Although some services (such as health care, placement, and psychological services) are provided centrally, most are decentralized into the collegiate sub-units under the control of a faculty master. For example, food service may or may not be offered through a central dining unit. Students take greater responsibility than in some other settings over the quality of their out-of-class experience.

The faculty members in such units assume responsibility for academic advising, support for individual students, and a reflective adult presence in the college. Structures similar to residential colleges are not unique to the Ivy League, but instead can be found in diverse institutions such as the University of the Redlands, Western Washington University, Northwestern University, and the University of California at Santa Cruz.

Other institutions, because of their mission, require certain staff skills and competencies. At Gallaudet University and Rochester Institute of Technology, for example, a foolish inconsistency would exist if staff members were hired who were not able to communicate with the hearing impaired. In one case, the campus was created to serve the hearing-impaired; in the other a large group of students have hearing difficulties. Given these populations, units to serve them are essential on both campuses, and the majority of those hired must be able to communicate with these students, parents, and alumni.

A decision to grow and nurture a specific academic program can also influence the array and function of student services on a campus. For example, the growth of rehabilitation counseling programs at several campuses in Illinois has shaped the response of those campuses to providing services for the mobility impaired. On those campuses, special attention has been paid to the physical access of mobility-impaired students to campus buildings and programs. The academic program has helped influence a campus response.

Suggestions for Professionals

Understanding the institutional mission is not always easy. While the words may be written in plain prose, the meaning shapes the character of the institution. Some practical steps to enhance understanding of the institutional mission include the following:

1. Read the history of the institution if it is available. Most institutions either have a written history or an archival collection that can shed light on the mission of the institution as developed by the founders.

2. Follow the institutional mission over time as it is reflected in catalogs and other documents. Determine if it has altered. Usually the mission statement evolves over time, reflecting changing needs and priorities of the institution. Question why and when those changes occurred and position them in your mind against the larger events happening in the world at that time.

3. Talk to persons who have been a part of the institution for some time. Retired professors and staff members can help you understand the past so you can better understand the present.

4. Test new program ideas against the mission statement. Identify some trusted confidants who can help you understand what is acceptable in this institution at this time.

5. Read the mission statement carefully and uncover the core values that drive the institution and its supporters.

6. Review old yearbooks and memorabilia. Both will help you understand the roots of the college or university.

7. Ask for help. If you are unsure whether what you are doing is consistent with the mission of the institution, inquire. In the process, you may gain an ally for a new and innovative program idea.

8. An essential part of any job search process should focus on understanding the institutional mission of a potential employing institution. Only when you understand that mission will you understand if you fit the environment in question.

Summary

Full understanding of the institutional mission statement is essential to the development of sound and effective student affairs programs and services. Failure to understand the institutional mission statement can result in program failure and inappropriate services for students. Each campus is unique. Understanding the written mission statement is important, but it is also essential that student affairs professional understand the living mission of the institution. The living mission is demonstrated through language, history, location, purpose, academic programs, and campus governance processes. When the written and living institutional mission is understood, the nuances involved in institutional culture can be woven into the creation of effective and useful programs for students. The overarching goal for higher education should not be forgotten when we try to understand a specific institution. Peter Flawn, former president of the University of Texas at Austin, said it best: "The central mission of the university is human development and that is a very good thing in which to be involved" (1990, p. 16).

References

Board of Trustees, Northwestern University. *Resolution of the Board of Trustees*. Northwestern University: University Archives, September 22, 1852.

Brubacher, J., and Rudy, W. *Higher Education in Transition*. (3rd ed.) New York: Harper Collins, 1976.

Carnegie Council on Policy Studies in Higher Education. *A Summary of Reports and Recommendations*. San Francisco: Jossey-Bass, 1980.

Flawn, P. *A Primer for University Presidents*. Austin, TX: University of Texas Press, 1990.

Kaplin, W. A., and Lee, B. A. *A Legal Guide for Student Affairs Professionals*, San Francisco: Jossey-Bass, 1997.

Kuh, G., Schuh, J., and Whitt, E. *Involving Colleges*. San Francisco, 1991.

Lyons, J. W. "The Importance of Institutional Mission," In M. J. Barr (ed.), *The Handbook of Student Affairs Administration*. San Francisco: Jossey-Bass, 1993.

Martin, W. B. *A College of Character*. San Francisco: Jossey-Bass, 1982.

Welzenback, F. F. (ed.), *College and University Business Administration*. Washington, D.C.: National Association of College and University Business Officers, 1982.

CHAPTER THREE

INSTITUTIONAL GOVERNANCE AND THE ROLE OF STUDENT AFFAIRS

Thomas E. Miller

Understanding how the governance structures in colleges and universities work is essential to the success of student affairs. This chapter is designed to help the practitioner understand the role student affairs can and should play within the educational enterprise. The contextual background associated with college and university governance in the United States will be described. The important role of governing boards will be discussed within the current context of higher education.

Higher education institutions have great diversity in structure and organizational arrangements. Focus will be placed on a description of how those differences affect governance structures and issues. Distinctions between public and private institutions will be discussed, as will the impact of size on governance structures and procedures.

Next, the chapter will describe how student affairs administrators work with trustees to present strategies for developing effective working relationships with members of the governing board to advance the interests of the institution. Faculty also have important roles in governance. Those roles will be described as well as the principles student affairs administrators should employ to work with faculty in the governance process. The roles of students and of staff personnel in governance matters will also be discussed, including ways for student affairs professionals to engage and enable those roles.

Contextual Parameters

Colleges and universities are communities of learners and scholars. Those communities exist in the context of corporate charters granted by states in accordance with each state's laws. The charters, based in corporate law, make the community a single legal entity, a corporation. The charters assign to the trustees of the institutions the obligations associated with directing the activities of the corporation and assuming the fiduciary responsibility for its programs and the welfare of its members.

The corporate structure of higher education is a uniquely American development. It has been modeled in other settings, but it was developed and refined in the United States. From the time of the formation of the colonial colleges, the states have been given the responsibility of establishing and overseeing educational programs. The responsibility for executing educational law and overseeing institutional policy and management has been assigned by the states to trustees in a corporate model of governance.

Providing roles for faculty in institutional governance is not an original American development; the concepts are borrowed from the European model of university governance. It is founded in common law, granting to faculty a role in setting the direction for institutional curriculum development and the responsibility and freedom to teach without prescriptive intervention regarding content.

Students have less defined roles in higher educational institutional governance, with wide variance by type and nature of institution. However, as the higher educational market has become more competitive and restricted, students have been given an increased voice as consumers and partners in the teaching and learning process. Student affairs administrators serve as guides for students, and helping students to be effective participants in the governance process is an important role for them to fulfill.

Institutional Distinctions

Observers of higher education know well the differences between public institutions and private ones. Size distinctions also affect the manner in which institutions operate. The ways in which those differences can influence the governance process are powerful.

Public Institutions. Student affairs staff at public institutions need to be alert to the concerns of the legislature that governs their status. For state-controlled or state-supported colleges and universities, this means paying attention to affairs and developments at the state capitol and being familiar with individual legislators and the concerns they have for higher education, particularly in student life areas. For many community colleges, it also means attending to matters and personnel in local legislation, often at the county level.

Lawmakers are an additional constituency for these administrators because they are accountable to them and must keep them informed about ways in which the law, or at least proposed legislation, could affect student life. A campus visit by a member of the legislature must be treated as an opportunity to represent the institution and its concerns in a favorable light.

Many public institutions in statewide systems employ persons in the state capitol to keep the campuses informed about legislative and funding developments. These persons are additional contacts to be cultivated for the understanding of student life issues.

For multicampus systems, there is usually a central office, often near the capitol, staffed by administrators working to coordinate the efforts on the campuses. In some states, a specific administrator is assigned the task of working with student affairs professionals on all campuses, helping them serve students while conforming to norms established at the central level. This person represents another important relationship for the chief student affairs administrator.

Most governing boards in the public sector of higher education tend to be smaller, some with as few as six or seven members. Large, multiple-campus systems such as those found in California and New York will have larger boards appointed by the governor with the advice and consent of the state senate. In some states these appointments are apolitical, but in others they are divided through a strict political party distribution system. On a small number of campuses, the voters in the state elect regents or trustees for the state university system.

No matter what the means of appointment, governing boards at public institutions focus on overall institutional governance within the context of needs of the state. Often, public board issues and debates are associated with cost and access more so than their private sector counterparts. For multicampus systems the boards tend to delegate much of the authority for management to the centralized office for the institution. Such system-wide boards serve as the governing authority for the system, working to preserve individual campus integrity and independence while insuring system-wide uniformity in matters such as financial affairs and personnel policies.

Among the challenges for systemwide or other public sector boards of trustees is the fact that they often do not set the terms for fiscal policy. Many times it is the legislature that determines fees and tuition students will pay as well as compensation levels for staff and faculty. The challenge of the board in those circumstances is to strive for equity and support institutional advancement as much as possible within the fiscal framework established.

The interests and concerns for chief student affairs officers in these circumstances relate to knowing who the players are and where the influence is located. They must keep communication lines open and be prepared to give guidance and collect information on a widely varying set of topics. In addition, they need to support the president and the interests of the institution however possible and be alert to changes in conditions that could affect student or institutional welfare.

Student affairs staff should also keep students informed about legislative or regulatory initiatives that could affect their lives. Students can be very interested and energetic participants in the legislative or governmental process and can be very effective spokespersons for their own welfare. Student affairs staff can help inform the process by routinely preparing students to represent themselves and informing them about issues that affect them.

Independent or Private Institutions. Working with boards and with government is far different for student affairs staff at independent, private institutions. A key factor is the greater control that the board has over fiscal matters. Boards of trustees at private institutions set fees for students, control compensation levels for faculty and staff, and decide the general parameters for budget decisions. If trustees want to provide greater compensation to faculty and staff, they can simply make it affordable by increasing charges to students. This is a far cry from a public institution board waiting for legislative direction regarding fiscal matters. In this circumstance, the student affairs administrator can help the board understand student issues associated with fee and tuition increases and other charges.

Another factor is that governing boards in the private sector tend to be much larger. There are private institutions with boards of trustees numbering more than fifty members. This can create quite a different working dynamic for the chief student affairs officer. With larger boards, individual and small groups of trustees at private institutions might be more able to take special interest in aspects of the institution, such as student life. As described earlier, the energy that trustees can bring to such special interest can be challenging to the administrator affected.

Trustees are usually benefactors, often expected to take the lead in fund raising efforts of the institution. These dual roles, trustee and benefactor, should be factored in when the board member is engaged by an administrator. The chief student affairs officer also needs to be alert to other benefactors because some of them are prospective trustees. Nurturing and attending to these relationships is the work of all of the senior staff of the institution, including those from student affairs.

Although the burdens of attending to legislative developments are far greater in the public sector, it is worth noting that senior student affairs offices at private institutions are well served by paying attention to proposed legislation and regulatory initiatives. A number of state laws have been passed recently that have had an onerous effect on student affairs and student life, and that is made more likely when student affairs staff in both the public and private sectors do not pay attention to legislative proposals and developments.

Size Distinctions. Governance issues vary among institutions according to their size. This certainly influences the role of the chief student affairs officer. Larger institutions need representative groups for faculty, staff, and students to be effectively involved in governance. In those settings, the student affairs staff should know the membership of the groups and interact with them from an informed perspective. At larger institutions, members of the institutional community feel more distance from the decision-making process and, sometimes as a result, do not feel confidence or trust in the decision-making process. Such circumstances can present an additional challenge to the chief student affairs officer, who may need to assume the role of information-giver and representative of the decision-making process.

Smaller institutions do not necessarily need those same representative structures because the groups that would need representation are often small enough to represent themselves. At smaller institutions, there is often widespread familiarity with those making decisions and those representing constituencies. Size, in this instance, gives members of the community a sense of confidence in and contact with the process of governance and the people involved. That is the case, though, only when there are good systems of communication and coordination of the governance process. The familiarity of smaller institutions can present an additional problem associated with information that is confidential or should be closely held. The ease with which rumors can spread on a smaller campus has taught many a lesson about the need to keep confidences and to know who can be trusted with sensitive information. This concern must be monitored and managed by all involved, and certainly by every responsible administrator.

Governing Boards

The legal responsibility for boards of trustees is, in effect, to serve as the final authority for all institutional decision-making. Trustees delegate much of the management of colleges and universities to administrators and to faculty. However, unless that delegation is explicit, the board has the duty to direct every aspect of the institution's management. Boards almost always reserve for themselves final authority regarding fiscal matters because they often consider their ultimate duty is the development of sound fiscal practices and the financial health of the institution. Other responsibilities associated with institutional management are often assigned to the administration, with the board reserving for itself final authority regarding major policy changes or developments. As far as their duties to students, trustees have the general responsibility to insure that student rights are protected and that their interests and welfare are at the highest priority level for the conducting of institutional business. In many circumstances when there are questions regarding what is best for students, trustees will seek the counsel and advice of the chief student affairs officer. In all cases, the chief student affairs officer should be sure to report interactions with trustees to the president so that he is not left out of the communications loop. Independent, noncoordinated interactions with trustees can create problems regarding trust, power, and authority.

Selection and Preparation. Board members are selected for service in different ways, depending on institutional type and upon procedures and standards detailed in the institutional charter. At public institutions, some trustees are appointed through a process managed by the state government or are elected. Both public and private institutions may have trustees elected by alumni. Private institutions, though, typically have boards of trustees that are self-selecting and self-perpetuating. Those institutions with religious affiliation control or histories may have some of their trustees nominated through a process managed by a church or another religious organization or order.

Many board members come to higher education from professional experiences in business, law, medicine, philanthropy, or other areas. As a result, quite a few of them have little knowledge about higher education and its culture and must be informed of institutional characteristics. Special programs to orient the board or new members usually involve the chief student affairs officer. When involved in such programs, student affairs professionals should reflect carefully on those aspects of their work that are of most interest and importance to trustees and, together with the president, plan to provide information that is most helpful and related to the duties of trustees.

Activities and Operations. A key function of the board is to select and supervise the president of the institution, who often serves as a nonvoting member of the board of trustees. The president is often the only member of the administration serving on the board, but there are instances when other administrators serve as members of the board. The chief financial officer may serve the institution as treasurer and an officer of the board, or the chief development officer may function as secretary to the board. Each institution or system has a unique governance structure and it should be understood by student affairs professionals.

The legal authority of the governing board is only as a corporate body. Individual trustees, unless assigned by the board, have no inherent authority associated with their membership on the board. The board acts as a collective entity, not as a collection of individuals. However, individual trustees may take great interest in certain aspects of the institution. This is one way in which a student affairs administrator might engage the governance process, but it can be a hazardous practice. Working with individual trustees can be easily interpreted as attempting to exert unwarranted or unwelcome influence.

Board members may take a particular interest in students or in a special student issue or concern. A board member might make contact with a chief student affairs officer to discuss such a matter. The prudent administrator would respond very carefully. It is not good practice to use individual relationships with board members to further specific issues associated with student affairs. The board has to view the institution from a broad perspective. When departmental or specific constituent interests are in conflict, trustees make the best decisions when they have a balanced, unbiased view of the issues. When they are individually persuaded to take particular positions, the situation can be a risk to their objectivity. In any event, the careful administrator ensures that the president is informed about all contacts with individual board members, at least when they are outside of the norms associated with the business of the institution.

Many boards of trustees engage in special board development activities such as retreats, special strategic planning days, and goal-setting exercises. There are times when a student affairs administrator who is knowledgeable about organizational development can be helpful to the board development process. Helping the president or leaders of the trustees to plan a developmental experience is often the very kind of work that student affairs staff members perform for their own staffs or for student organizations. This expertise can be shared and can be quite helpful to the board, while creating excellent relationships between the board and the responsible administrator.

Student Life Committee. Boards of trustees usually conduct much of their work through committees. Committees examine issues in some detail and then recommend action to the full board as part of their reporting duties. Those committees, which may meet in relation to full board meetings or independently of them, are often designed to match the administrative organizational structure of the institution. Clearly, under such a framework the key committee for the student affairs professional is the student life or student affairs committee, if one exists.

The chief student affairs administrator is usually assigned the responsibility of staffing the student life committee. That often involves making suggestions about agenda topics, meeting with the committee chair and the president to discuss the agenda, and gathering the necessary information and materials to make for effective and productive meetings.

Students may be invited to be a part of student life committee discussions or they may be asked to make presentations to the committee about specific issues. It is usually the duty of the chief student affairs officer to coordinate such involvement and to manage the presentation to the committee. There may also be a systematic means of communicating with student life committee members, such as routine mailing of the student newspaper, and these will often be the duty of the chief student affairs officer.

The student life committee is usually commissioned with the responsibility of representing student interests in the policymaking activities of the board. The chief student affairs officer as well as individual student representatives to the committee have the duty to see that board members have the necessary information to perform this task effectively. The committee may also have a duty to see that student services and programs have appropriate resources. The chief student affairs officer can inform this function, but only with delicate care and great prudence to avoid the appearance of using trustees in a manipulative way. The student life committee needs to be informed about students and any changes in the nature of the student body, and the chief student affairs administrator should be a prime conduit of information to the committee on these matters.

Other Board Committees. There are other committees that the chief student affairs officers might engage. Most boards have a buildings and grounds committee charged with the duty of overseeing policy and development of the physical plant of the institution. Many campus buildings are central to the purposes of the student life operation, and some are under the direct supervision of the student affairs staff. Residence halls, student union buildings, and athletic or recreational facilities are good examples of such buildings. When new construction or remodeling of these buildings is being evaluated and implemented by a buildings and grounds committee, the chief student affairs officer becomes an important advocate of student interests and needs and a central member of the design team. Many student affairs officers have found themselves working with architects or construction managers in coordination with trustees serving on a buildings and grounds committee and have discovered that they are the least informed about building design, construction, and funding. The learning curve can be a steep one, but trustees will at least expect the student affairs staff to know about student needs and how a building can be best designed to meet those needs.

Still other committees may on occasion call on a chief student affairs officer. Some boards of trustees have established committees on enrollment management for which student affairs staff might be important consultants, particularly on matters associated with student retention. Boards with finance committees routinely use the senior officers of the institution as consultants, and development committees might seek counsel from student affairs staff on development issues or on public relations concerns. In all of these instances, the chief student affairs officer needs to have done the homework about the particular interests of the committee and know what the expectations are in order to be of the greatest service.

In work with all board committees, the chief student affairs officer should attempt to seek ways to engage students with board members. Trustees of colleges and universities understand their obligations to students and are generally very interested in first-hand expressions about the institution by students. Some view students as customers, some see them as a product, but all of them have obligations to students and interest in them. It is the student affairs staff who often serve as the connection between students and trustees and help trustees understand students and their concerns. When appropriate, student affairs administrators need to stimulate and manage circumstances for student interaction with trustees. Student affairs staff should design programs and activities for students to interact with trustees and describe their observations and experiences. Those activities can be social in nature or they can be part of business meetings, but they should be encouraged and stimulated.

Faculty Governance

Faculty, like trustees, have long-standing and traditional roles associated with institutional governance. Engaging those roles can be challenging for a student affairs staff member, but it also can be quite rewarding and helpful.

Roles and Functions. Few constituencies in the higher education community have positions as complex as do faculty. They are expected to lead scholarly development in their fields, provide service to their institutions and communities, and be expert in imparting knowledge. Few faculty members accomplish everything to which they once aspired. The life of a faculty member is demanding, exacting, and often not as rewarding as was anticipated. In addition to their roles as scholars and teachers, faculty are expected to participate in the governance of the institution and of their own affairs as a constituent group on the campus.

Faculty members generally direct the processes of selection of their peers, and they also direct the decision-making process for promotion and tenure status for each member of the faculty. At many institutions, faculty control the development of the curriculum, the design and delivery of new courses, and the process of changing major offerings. In short, at many institutions, faculty govern their own affairs.

The typical student affairs staff member has little role in these matters. Some student affairs personnel have faculty status; some came from faculty posts and are tenured, but those are exceptions. This may have less to do with faculty or institutional perspectives about student affairs than how administrators as a group are perceived by faculty. Higher education has a system of almost parallel decision-making structures and processes. One is for faculty and academic matters, and the other is for more broad institutional matters. Student affairs staff participate little in the former, but they are usually prominent in the latter.

Institutions have varying ways in which faculty participate in general institutional governance. Even how faculty are represented differs greatly across institutional types. Larger institutions have faculty councils or senates, representative of the faculty and their interests. Through such bodies, the faculty exercise their influence on institutional affairs. Few such representative bodies have positions reserved for student affairs staff, so those staff members have little influence on the decision-making of such groups. Smaller institutions often engage the faculty as a whole in governance and decision-making, and student affairs staff are commonly party to that process.

Building Relationships. The wise administrator spends a good amount of time and energy engaging the faculty and informing them of the issues and concerns involved in serving students and directing student life. Even when student affairs staff do not participate directly in faculty decision-making, a great, but indirect, impact can be made when faculty opinion-makers and leaders are aware of and sensitive to student life issues. This is far from official participation in faculty decision making, but it can be as powerful and important.

Some student affairs staff have had success building such relationships by establishing faculty consulting or advisory groups in association with functional areas in student affairs. A career services advisory council, made up of faculty, or a residence halls advisory council, similarly configured, can generate faculty advocates for student affairs and protect or even enhance the quality of student affairs work.

The advent of collective bargaining has made student affairs involvement in faculty roles in governance more complicated. Faculty collective bargaining agreements are contractual in nature and generally spell out carefully the roles and functions of faculty representatives and administrators in decision making. Even the casual influence of faculty opinion can be difficult because the ways in which faculty members use their time is often a matter of contract.

Student Roles

Somewhat like the faculty, students have some control, or at least influence, on those matters that most directly affect them. Student government is often a vehicle for student programming and student representation in decision-making. Students often direct their own budget decisions related to student organization funding. Student fees often fund student publications and activities, and student responsibility in these areas is often independent of institutional control.

Students do not have the same representative influence on institutional matters. They often have a voice, but because the student community and student leadership turn over so frequently, student representatives to faculty groups or to trustees are often uninformed and not grounded in an understanding of the norms for decision-making in those groups.

At many institutions, students have a representative who attends trustee meetings, in most cases without voting privileges. Those students become observers or consultants to the board and, when called upon, give the student perspective on an issue or problem being discussed. Many times, a chief student affairs officer can provide useful background or perspective to a student who is representing her peers to governing or decision-making bodies. It is good practice, when students are first engaging a group such as a faculty committee, the institutional budget committee, or trustees, for the chief student affairs officer to offer to meet with the student. At that meeting the student can be briefed on the purpose and configuration of the group and generally guided on what to expect. In this way, student affairs staff can help make student representation most effective and useful to students and to the decision-making process.

Students can benefit from other guidance about their representation in the governance process. Knowing how to determine what is confidential, for example, is an important consideration for students. Those who are representing their peers often want to report to them about matters being discussed by trustees, administrators, or faculty. The student affairs staff can help them fulfill their duties to inform their peers without compromising the integrity or confidentiality of the decision-making process.

Student affairs staff can also serve the process of governance by guiding students on strategies for involvement and ways to engage the process. For example, students often present problems and complaints about how the institution works to those who work most closely with them. These moments are opportunities for describing to students ways in which they can get involved in institutional improvement and, to an extent, governance. Other good opportunities to stimulate student interest in governance occur frequently and should be taken.

Staff Roles

At many institutions, staff have roles in the governance process, at least when aspects of the process or decisions affect their welfare. Many institutions have staff committees or staff councils that represent concerns of staff. Some institutions use staff representatives as observers and commentators at trustee meetings.

When trustees are considering staff benefit programs, for example, staff may well be appropriately involved in those decisions. The modification of various benefit plans, such as health care, dental care, or retirement plans, often involve representatives of those affected. As part of their responsibility for fiscal control, trustees might be involved in decision-making that has the effect of eliminating or altering staff positions. Consultation with staff may be an essential part of that process.

The student affairs administrator has no special role in this function, except to support it and help communicate information about matters that can affect staff. The most effective student affairs operations are those where staff feel valued and respected and efforts are made to sustain their morale and recognize their hard work. In that context, supporting staff roles in participation in governance is natural and easy.

Summary

Student affairs staff engage the governance process in many ways. The nature and form of governance structures affect the extent and quality of that engagement, but it is something to which all student affairs administrators should be sensitive.

Working with trustees is a very important aspect of the duties of the chief student affairs officer. Recognizing the difference between the authority and influence of individuals who serve on a board of trustees and the trustees as a corporate or organizational entity is essential to good working relationships with trustees. Keeping the chief executive informed about work with trustees is extremely important. Consulting with and supporting trustee committees and, as called upon, the full board is the official way in which the chief student affairs officer engages the governance process associated with the board.

Working with faculty and their roles in governance is usually a consultative role for the student affairs professional. Fostering strong, affirming relationships with faculty is an important part of that work. Helping students be effective participants in governance is an instructional role that student affairs staff can perform.

There are substantial differences between the governance structures in public higher education and in the private sector. Further, institutional size makes a big difference in how governance structures function and in how the student affairs professional becomes involved.

The savvy student affairs staff member looks at involvement in the governance process as an opportunity to help the institution set direction in a way that actively considers student interests. Knowing how the structure works is essential to being effective within it, and that knowledge informs the quality of the impact that is possible. The following publications will be useful to readers wanting to learn more about this subject.

Recommended Reading

Armacost, P. "Student Personnel Administration Policies." In A. Knowles (ed.), *Handbook of College and University Administration*. New York: McGraw-Hill, 1970.

Barr, M. J. "Legal Organization and Control of Higher Education." In M. J. Barr (ed.), *Student Services and the Law*. San Francisco: Jossey-Bass, 1988.

Chait, R., Holland, T., and Taylor, B. *Improving the Performance of Governing Boards*. Phoenix, AZ: Oryx Press, 1996.

Correnti, R. "How Public and Private Institutions Differ Under the Law." In M. J. Barr (ed.), *Student Services and the Law*. San Francisco: Jossey-Bass, 1988.

Goodale, T. G. *Student Affairs Committee*. Washington, D.C.: Association of Governing Boards of Universities and Colleges, 1984.

Ingram, R. T. and Associates. *Handbook of College and University Trusteeship*. San Francisco: Jossey-Bass, 1980.

Kreiser, R. (ed). *Policy Documents and Reports*. Washington, D.C.: American Association of University Professors, 1990.

Pembroke, W. J. "Institutional Governance and the Role of Student Affairs." In M. J. Barr (ed.) *The Handbook of Student Affairs Administration*. San Francisco: Jossey-Bass, 1993.

Sandeen, C. A. *The Chief Student Affairs Officer*. San Francisco: Jossey-Bass, 1991.

CHAPTER FOUR

UNDERSTANDING CAMPUS ENVIRONMENTS

George D. Kuh

Colleges and universities have many things in common. Most institutions offer a variety of major fields. Academic years, usually divided into semesters or quarters, run from fall to spring. Classrooms, laboratories, and studios provide structured settings for regular interactions between teachers and students. Through out-of-class learning experiences, students acquire practical competence in such areas as making decisions and working with people who are different from themselves. Although asynchronous learning opportunities will become more numerous, patterns and rhythms will continue to characterize the undergraduate experience.

At the same time, institutions of higher education differ in many respects, such as size, control (public or private), curricular emphasis (e.g., liberal arts, science and technology), and the amount and type of external funding. These and other variables frequently are considered by prospective students applying for admission and by scholars studying faculty productivity and satisfaction. Contrary to popular belief, however, such variables as institutional size, prestige, and affluence are unrelated to student learning and personal development (Braxton, Smart, and Thieke 1991; Pascarella and Terenzini, 1991).

All things considered, what and how much a student learns is more a function of what the student *does* in college than any other factor. And, as Pascarella and Terenzini (1991) pointed out, the contextual conditions of an institution are more important in encouraging student engagement in learning opportunities than involvement in any organizational or programmatic variables. Equally important, the amount of effort students devote to learning is, in part, a function of the degree to which their institution provides opportunities for, supports, and rewards student learning.

This chapter provides an overview of some of the more important "contextual conditions" that foster student learning and personal development and how these conditions can be assessed. Key concepts with which student affairs professionals must be familiar in order to understand and shape learning environments are considered. First, the relationship between the institutional context and student learning is briefly summarized. Then, a framework is presented for identifying and understanding how contextual conditions work together to influence student learning. Finally, issues are discussed that warrant attention when assessing the contextual conditions of a given campus.

The Importance of the Institutional Context on Student Learning and Personal Development

From their review of more than 2,600 studies of the impact of college on students, Pascarella and Terenzini (1991) drew the following four conclusions about the role of an institution's contextual conditions on student learning. First, students benefit more from their college experience when their "total level of campus engagement (academic, interpersonal, extracurricular) is mutually supporting and relevant to a particular educational outcome" (Pascarella and Terenzini, 1991, p. 626). That is, students get more from college when they engage in a variety of educationally purposeful activities.

Second, involvement in the academic and social life of the institution enhances student learning (Pascarella and Terenzini, 1991). Students have considerable latitude in choosing how to allocate their time and effort. Two institutional characteristics are particularly important in engendering student involvement in educationally purposeful activities. The first is a clear, coherent (preferably distinctive) mission that focuses faculty and student behavior and gives direction to student learning. In large institutions, the major field environment, including the influence of one's peers, often substitutes for the larger campus mission in focusing student effort. The second institutional characteristic is sufficient opportunities for meaningful participation in the life of the institution, such as leadership roles in academic and social organizations, recreation, campus jobs, and off-campus work or internships.

Third, integrated and complementary academic and social programs, policies, and practices enhance student learning (Pascarella and Terenzini, 1991). No single experience, policy, or program is likely to have a dramatic influence on the attitudes and behaviors of most students. Curricular and cocurricular policies and practices (such as links between the living environment and one's studies; for example, academic theme housing or between one's studies and community service) are more likely to have positive effects on student learning when they support students' learning goals and are consistent with the institution's educational purposes and values.

Finally, students who feel they belong and are valued as individuals are more likely to take advantage of the resources the institution provides for their learning (Pascarella and Terenzini, 1991). When ethics of membership and care characterize a college or university, students perceive that they cannot be anonymous, that the institution is concerned about their welfare and committed to their success, and that the psychological size of the institution is appropriate, comfortable, and manageable (Kuh and others, 1991).

Taken together, these four conclusions suggest that an institution's contextual conditions are more important to student learning and personal development than faculty productivity, library holdings, organizational structures, or particular academic or student life programs. Therefore, student affairs professionals must know how the various aspects of their campus environments influence student behavior (American College Personnel Association, 1994; National Association of Student Personnel Administrators, 1987). To acquire this knowledge, student affairs staff have to discover how various institutional properties (location, physical, social, and psychological environments) and faculty and student cultures work together to promote or inhibit students' engagement with learning and personal development opportunities.

A Framework for Assessing the Influence of Contextual Conditions on Student Learning

Many institutional properties interact in complex ways to create an institution's context for learning. Student affairs professionals must be familiar with these properties in order to analyze how their college's environment influences students and to address those contextual conditions that can be intentionally modified to have a stronger, more positive effect on how students spend their time and what they gain from attending college. Toward these ends, two frameworks are needed to identify and examine an institution's contextual conditions. The first, the substantive frame, takes into account the physical and psychological properties that influence learning, such as the size and shape of built structures, the campus use of green space, and students' perceptions of what the institution emphasizes and quality of relations among different groups (faculty, students, administrators). These aspects of an institutional environment typically can be measured or assessed to identify the primary points of contact between students and the institution, such as interactions with peers and faculty members in various venues inside or outside the classroom and the effects of these interactions on student effort and learning. The second framework is needed to interpret how the various substantive elements of the environment work together to affect student behavior. This interpretive frame serves as a filter or lens through which to analyze and understand how students' interactions with the institution's contextual conditions influence their behavior. As with any theoretical lens, what one sees or attends to is in large part a function of the perspective taken on the phenomenon. For example, just as some student development theories account for certain aspects of growth and behavior but not others, so it is with interpretive views of the effects of interactions between students and their college environments.

Substantive Frames

In this section, three sets of institutional properties are discussed that can substantially influence student learning: the institution's mission and philosophy; opportunities for learning as well as support and rewards for student effort; and faculty and student cultures.

Institutional Mission and Philosophy. As Barr indicated in Chapter Two, no institutional factor is more influential in directing student and faculty behavior than the institution's mission and philosophy (Kuh and others, 1991). For this reason, creating institutional conditions that encourage students to take advantage of learning and personal development opportunities must begin with clarifying institutional aims and translating these aims into appropriate expectations for student behavior.

Clarifying the mission seems to be a fairly straightforward task. But although every college has a mission, it may or may not be congruent with how the college describes itself regarding the statement of educational purposes in the catalog or other documents. In addition, institutional missions may change, intentionally or in response to changes in the external environment, as many single-sex colleges did in response to student preference for coeducational learning experiences. For these reasons, a necessary step in understanding the influence of an institution's contextual conditions on student learning and personal development is to discover the institution's enacted mission by talking with students, faculty, administrators, graduates, and others in order to learn what the college is at present and what it aspires to be.

When members of various groups consistently use similar terms to describe what their college is trying to do with its resources, the institution's mission can be said to be clear and coherent. In some instances, particularly small colleges and universities, the institutional mission may be salient, meaning that even people who are not "insiders" (people who live and work in close proximity to the institution and call it their own), or are not members of one of the college's major constituent groups, have a fairly clear understanding of what the institution stands for and is trying to accomplish. Too often, however, institutions are unclear about what they are trying to accomplish or communicate their aims in confused or convoluted ways. As a result, they send mixed messages about their purposes and values. When institutional leaders assert that both research and teaching are important, but tenure decisions depend primarily on research contributions, faculty can become confused or jaded about what their institution values.

Just as every college has a mission, each has a philosophy, although it is rare that it is stated in writing (Kuh and others, 1991). However, an institution's philosophy can be discerned from its acts which represent the institution's values and beliefs as they are enacted by institutional agents or policies, practices, and standard operating procedures (Kuh, 1993).

One aspect of an institution's philosophy is the degree to which faculty and student affairs staff trust students. For example, at some institutions student codes of conduct include many stipulations. Other institutions rely on academic and social honor codes to foster student responsibility. Student learning can be promoted using either type of philosophy, provided that the philosophy is clearly and coherently expressed throughout all aspects of institutional life and the philosophy is compatible with the ability of students to behave in ways that are consistent with the philosophy; that is, students have the capacity for responsible, independent judgment, and good decision-making.

As colleges have grown larger, their philosophies and core values have sometimes become incoherent and, worse, inconsistent with their educational aims. When students are told at orientation that the institution has high expectations for their learning, but faculty rely on multiple choice tests and provide little or no feedback on written work other than a grade, students understandably may become confused. The same situation will occur if students are told they are expected to manage their own affairs independently and yet are constantly monitored by the student affairs staff. Such circumstances make it difficult, if not impossible, for institutional agents to articulate a moral basis for challenging student behavior that is inconsistent with the institution's aspirations.

Opportunities, Support, and Rewards. According to Blocher (1974, 1978), an optimal learning environment has three subsystems operating simultaneously:

opportunity, support, and reward. These subsystems warrant attention because they can help explain how an institution's contextual conditions promote or discourage engagement and, ultimately, student learning and personal development.

Most colleges and universities have social programming bodies, governance structures, performing arts venues, intercollegiate and intramural athletic teams, recreational sports venues, and so on. When the availability, frequency, and the intensity of these opportunities is great, an adequate infrastructure of opportunities exists and "people tend to be busier, more vigorous, more versatile, and more involved" (Walsh, 1978, p. 7). Iowa State University, for example, has more than 400 formally recognized clubs. Students at the University of North Carolina at Charlotte offer a comprehensive series of training programs to help students develop leadership skills (Kuh and Schuh, 1991). At Indiana University, peer instructors for freshman interest groups (FIGs) assist students in adjusting to the university and making connections between the three courses in which they are co-enrolled that make up the FIG. The peer instructors themselves also benefit in that their own learning and personal development is enriched through their interactions with members of their FIG.

The opportunity subsystem of a college should encourage spontaneous interaction among students and between students and institutional agents consistent with the institution's educational purposes. Stanford University has four ethnic theme houses and four ethnic community centers that encourage students from historically underrepresented groups to become involved in campus life. Grinnell College and Wichita State University make it very easy for student groups to organize themselves and receive funding (Kuh and others, 199). When the physical dimensions of a campus are "human scale," students enjoy a sense of being in control; small residences (no more than 300 students) permit students to more easily identify with and take ownership for their living unit.

High expectations for the performance of all students is a characteristic of powerful learning environments (Kuh, forthcoming). Such settings provide structure and support that enable students to successfully deal with ambiguous, complex, and novel situations that require responses beyond the students' repertoire. Support may take the form of an ethic of care, a belief system that permeates the institution that encourages faculty, staff and students to reach out to those in need (Kuh and others, 1999). Safety nets made up of faculty and staff (paraprofessional as well as professional) are available to intervene with students encountering difficulty. The optimal amount of structure students need depends on their ability to exercise responsibility, their academic preparation and background, and their religious background. For example, Berea, Xavier of New Orleans (both Roman Catholic affiliated institutions), and Iowa State provide more rules than Earlham, Grinnell, Mount Holyoke, and Stanford.

Students learn best when they receive frequent feedback about their performance relative to institutional expectations (American College Personnel Association/ National Association of Student Personnel Administrators, 1997; Chickering and Gamson, 1987) and are encouraged to integrate their in-class and out-of-class experiences through senior seminars or experiential learning activities such as service learning or internships. Many colleges recognize student achievement through convocations and honors society memberships, athletic banquets, deans' lists, announcements of scholarship and fellowship recipients, and selection of high-performing students to serve as tutors, laboratory assistants, and peer advisors (Kuh, Vesper, Connolly, and Pace, 1997). At Xavier University of New Orleans, photographs of those admitted to graduate and professional schools are featured on the walls of academic buildings.

When the three subsystems (opportunity, support, reward) are operating at a satisfactory level, are mutually supporting, and complement the institution's educational purposes, they create powerful conditions for learning.

Faculty and Student Subcultures. Student learning is in large part a function of academic effort and the frequency and quality of interactions between students and important agents of socialization: faculty, student affairs professionals, and peers. Therefore, it is important to determine whether faculty and student cultures foster or discourage student engagement in the activities that matter to their learning and personal development (Kuh, 1994).

The amount of time faculty devote to students is influenced by the type of institution in which they work and the expectations that institutional leaders and others have for faculty and student performance. Teachers at many institutions spend less time with undergraduates outside the classroom than their counterparts of a several decades ago. Of course, there are always exceptions: institutions where the quality of interaction between students and faculty are unusually rich and rewarding (Kuh and others, 1991). Moreover, there is perceptible shift in the role of the faculty member from dispensing information to arranging activities that promote student learning (Barr and Tagg, 1995) and in the amount of attention being given to undergraduate education, even at research universities (Diamond and Adam, 1997).

However, this shift toward a student- or learner-centered philosophy is a long way from being fully realized in most colleges and universities. For example, in state-assisted colleges, where the heavy emphasis on undergraduate instruction is often coupled with institutional aspirations to move up in the pecking order, teaching loads remain heavy even as expectations for publications increase. In addition, many faculty members often feel conflicted between research (to which many were socialized in graduate school to value over teaching) and the daily demands of teaching and student advising.

At the same time, record numbers of students are matriculating at colleges or universities with B+ or better high school grades even though they studied fewer than eight hours a week on average (Astin, 1997). While they have high expectations for their performance in college (the majority expect to earn B+ or better grades as they did in high school), they are devoting less effort to their studies than previous cohorts (Kuh, 1999). That is, students still have lots of discretionary time (even though a larger fraction are employed), but many do not use it to take advantage of institutional resources for learning and personal development, such as the library and laboratories. Students appear to spend as much time watching television on a weekly basis as they do studying (Marchese, 1998). Something is amiss when students can get good grades by devoting so little time to their studies.

The combination of demands on faculty to improve their instructional approaches, incorporate technology in their work, and engage in scholarly inquiry, and the high-grades-for-low-effort student cohort matriculating in the 1990s appears to have given rise to a tacit agreement between students and faculty that essentially says, "You leave me alone and I will leave you alone." That is, I (the faculty member) won't require you to work too hard, if you won't make many demands on my time such as making appointments to talk or challenge a grade. In return, the student expects a reasonably good grade, at least a B. So far, this disengagement compact seems to be working as undergraduate grades are at an all-time high even though student academic effort is down slightly (Kuh, 1999).

Taken together, student cultures and one's peers exert a nontrivial influence on student learning because they determine the kinds of people with whom one spends time and, therefore, the values and attitudes to which one is exposed (Weidman, 1989). No matter what institutional agents say or do, within four to six weeks following the start of an academic term, new students are exposed to the prevailing student culture that tells them which classes and instructors are to be taken seriously, and where, how much, and what to study (Holland and Eisenhart, 1990; Moffatt, 1989).

Complicating attempts to understand the influence of the institution's cultures on student behavior is that different student affinity groups develop and perpetuate their own distinctive interaction patterns and norms that influence how their members behave and are to relate to others. These groups include, but are not limited to, Greek organizations, students who live together on or off campus, honors students, athletes, and members of minority racial and ethnic groups, including international students. Recognizing how these groups shape student behavior is important because they have established expectations, attitudes, and values that are incongruent with those of the faculty. While faculty are primarily interested in teaching and research, students are more concerned with other matters such as grades, making friends, taking care of themselves, and managing their time. For example, such student groups as fraternities organize around social themes, whereas athletes are focused on competition; both value orientations may conflict with those of the faculty.

Even so, many colleges and universities condone and even support the activities in which some student subcultures engage because those groups do things that no other organization in the institution can achieve. For example, "collegiates" (Clark and Trow, 1966), such as fraternity and sorority members, tend to be satisfied with college life and are loyal to their college. They help their college attract new students and typically support the institution financially after graduation (Nelson, 1984).

One unfortunate irony of college life is that most colleges and universities ignore what student subcultures teach their student members. Only by becoming more knowledgeable about the various student cultures on campuses will we have a good chance of effecting positive change with those groups that are antithetical to the institution's educational aims (Kuh, 1994). There is always more to learn about the influence of student cultures on student learning as the characteristics, aspirations, and attitudes of students change from one cohort to the next. Of course, in order to do this task well, some resources must be committed to it.

Interpretive Frames

In this section, three perspectives are discussed that can be used to understand how a college's contextual conditions influence student learning: ecology; climates; and cultures. The terms *ecology*, *climate*, and *culture* often are used interchangeably, but they emphasize different aspects of an institution's environment that need to be clarified and understood for student affairs staff to discover how the contextual conditions of their campus influence student learning and personal development. Ecology is the broadest of these concepts, encompassing both climate and culture. The plural form of climate and culture suggests that the contextual conditions of a college are not monolithic. Many sub-environments exist on a campus and can be approximated by examining climates and cultures at different levels, such as the institution, academic department or major field, living unit, and affinity group(s). Institutional environments also have variable influences on student behavior. This explains why campus climates and cultures have competing, sometimes contradictory effects on the behavior of students, faculty, and student affairs professionals.

Ecology. Student learning and personal development are products of the reciprocal interactions between individuals or groups of students, faculty and administrators, and the physical, perceived, and enacted environments of the college. That is, behavior is a function of students interacting with the college environment broadly defined to include physical spaces, policies, people, and other physical, biological, chemical, and cultural stimuli. This relationship between students and their college has been described as transactional (Aulepp and Delworth, 1976) or mutually shaping—that is, students shape their environment and are shaped by it.

Because collegiate environments affect the behavior of students, students tend to behave in similar ways despite their individual differences (Barker, 1968; Huebner, 1979, 1989). Some environments are more congruent with certain students' needs than others. For example, "If a student reported a high need for achievement and the campus environment was consensually identified as exerting a press for achievement, a congruent situation would exist, leading to satisfaction and good functioning" (Huebner, 1989, p. 169). Similarly, if a student is surrounded by people with compatible personality characteristics, the environmental setting can be said to be congruent (Holland, 1973). When the mismatch is great between environmental demands and student needs, dissonance results and the student becomes dissatisfied, academic performance suffers, and premature departure occurs (Tinto, 1993).

The ecology frame (the institution's size, location, facilities, open spaces, and other permanent attributes) can also be used to interpret the influence of physical properties of the campus on behavior. The amount, locations, and arrangement of physical spaces shape behavior, for instance, in that they facilitate or inhibit social interaction and the development of group cohesiveness (Myrick and Marx, 1968). In general, the less crowded and more organized and neat the physical environment, the lower the level of stress (Ahrentzen and others, 1982). In densely populated areas, such as high-rise residences, indicators of social pathology (deviant behavior, frustration) tend to be higher (Moos, 1979). The proximity of academic buildings to permeable socially catalytic spaces can promote or discourage interaction between students from different majors. For example, when the engineering building is in a far corner of the campus some distance from the student union, the amount of interaction engineering students will have with students in other fields will likely be low. Locating enrollment-related offices such as registrar, financial aid, admissions, and bursar in different parts of the campus affects student satisfaction. The physical design of counseling centers (Iwai, Churchill, and Cummings 1983), the dean of students office (Hurst and Ragle, 1979), college unions (Banning and Cunard, 1986), and commencement programs (Banning, 1983) and campus markings (Banning, 1992; Banning and Luna, 1992) can also affect student perceptions and performance.

Territoriality is an example of an ecological property that may warrant attention. When arriving in a new environment, it is not uncommon for people from similar backgrounds or who knew each other prior to coming to the university to congregate in a specific public area at certain times of the day. At one urban university, African American students perceive that there are a limited number of places on campus where they feel comfortable in freely socializing with their friends. One of these is around a red couch in the middle of the ground floor of the student union. Whether this and other similar actions expand or place limits on their network of social relations is not known. However, when student affinity groups are highly segmented by ethnic background, academic interest, or other characteristics, learning and personal development may be unnecessarily blunted. This is especially problematic if students perceive that intermingling with students from other groups is discouraged at the university.

The ecology of a campus affects students' behavior in complicated ways. Although it is difficult to discover and describe the ecology of a given campus, this interpretive frame has great potential for helping student affairs staff understand how their institution influences student learning because it emphasizes the interrelatedness of a large number of institutional factors and conditions (Banning, 1989).

Climates. Climate refers to how students, faculty, student affairs staff, and other institutional agents *perceive and experience* their institution (Baird, 1988; Peterson and Spencer, 1990). For example, institutions differ in the degree to which students believe faculty and administrators are supportive of their learning and personal development goals (Kuh and others, 1997). If students view the campus as "chilly" or "inhospitable," it can negatively affect their academic performance as well as appraisal of themselves and others (Lyons, 1990). Indeed, students' perceptions of their institution always have a nontrivial influence and directly and indirectly affect learning and personal development. Most climate measures focus on perceptions of organizational functioning, such as goal setting, decision making, and resource allocation; and affective responses to experiences with the institution, such as feelings of loyalty and commitment, morale and satisfaction, and a general sense of belonging (Baird, 1988).

Such instruments as the *College and University Environment Scales (CUES)* (Pace, 1969) assess institutional attributes that encourage students to behave in certain ways, such as a high need for achievement or the quality of relations between faculty and students (Astin and Holland, 1961). *The College Student Experiences Questionnaire (CSEQ)* (Pace and Kuh, 1998) is designed primarily to estimate student effort devoted to various learning activities, but also includes ten scales that represent students' perceptions of aspects of the institution that are related to student engagement, learning, and personal development. Seven of the scales depict the degree to which students feel that their college emphasizes scholarship, estheticism, critical thinking, diversity, information literacy, vocational competence, and the practical relevance of courses. The remaining three *CSEQ* environment scales refer to the quality of relations between students, faculty, and administrators.

The University Residence Environments Scale (URES) (Moos, 1979), provides information about the climates of residential sub-environments. The *URES* provides information about whether groups of residents are more interested in social activities or academic pursuits, and whether these same students view their living environments as, for example, highly structured and competitive, or interpersonally supportive and achievement-oriented. Student affairs professionals can use these data to intentionally modify, through indirect or direct means, the climate of residences by grouping students with certain characteristics in order to create the desired climate (Schroeder, 1976, 1981).

Results from the *CUES, CSEQ, URES* and similar instruments (*College Student Questionnaire*, Peterson, 1968; *Institutional Functioning Inventory*, Peterson and others, 1970; see Baird, 1988 for additional information about these instruments) can be interpreted according to student's sex, year in school, major field, and race and ethnicity to compare the perceptions of different groups of students. As a result, campus climate measures can reflect the multiple realities that exist among various groups (Kuh, Whitt, and Shedd, 1987). By administering climate measures periodically, student affairs staff can monitor progress toward making living unit environments, attitudes of subgroups of students (e.g., fraternities), and the general campus climate more congruent with the institution's educational purposes.

Cultures. Whereas measures of climate reflect individual or group perceptions of certain aspects of the institution, campus culture encompasses both the espoused and enacted character of an institution (Kuh, 1993). Institutional culture is the collective, mutually shaping pattern of institutional history, mission, physical settings, norms, traditions, values, practices, beliefs, and assumptions that guide the behavior of individuals and groups in college or university (Kuh and Whitt, 1988). The espoused character of an institution's culture is that which people on and off the campus wish the institution to be, its best public image congruent with its announced educational values and programs. The enacted character of the institution's culture is the myriad elements and interactions that make up institutional life on a daily basis and may or may not be consistent with espoused values and commitments. For example, at some colleges, the dominant student culture values activities that complement the institution's educational purposes, while at other institutions, students routinely engage in activities that are antithetical to their college's mission (Kuh, 1990). Viewing institutional life through a cultural lens provides a frame of reference with which to interpret the meaning of events and actions on and off campus (Kuh and Whitt, 1988).

Specifying a college's culture is a challenging task. This is because collegiate cultures are made up of holistic, complex webs of physical and verbal artifacts, enduring behavioral patterns, embedded values and beliefs, and ideologies and assumptions that represent learned products of group experience (Kuh and Whitt, 1988). Cultural values and beliefs are perpetuated through traditions (e.g., graduation ceremonies, induction experiences for new students and faculty), major campus events, heroic individuals, and language (Eaton and Manning, 1993; Kuh, 1998; Ott, 1989). The meanings that various members of the campus community attach to these cultural elements, however, are not always easy to deduce, nor can they be easily derived by people unfamiliar with the institution.

Institutional cultures tend to be relatively stable, but they are not stagnant. Cultures change over time through a dynamic interplay between the institution's structural and cultural elements, forces in the external environment (shifting demographics), cataclysmic events (destruction of facilities or accidents that take the lives of senior administrators or athletic teams) (Peterson and others, 1986), and the presence of people, such as women and members of historically underrepresented ethnic and racial groups, whose beliefs and assumptions differ somewhat from those held by the majority.

Cultures also change as a result of the mutual shaping of cultural properties. That is, such properties as the physical attributes of a campus, established practices, celebratory events, symbols and symbolic actions, and subcultures influence each other while simultaneously shaping the behavior of students, faculty, and staff. Similarly, the presence of newcomers whose backgrounds are different than those of previous cohorts of students and faculty members also has an influence on cultural properties. In this sense, culture is both product and process (Peterson and others, 1986), influencing such behavioral outcomes as student performance and satisfaction, as well as being influenced by the characteristics, attitudes, and behavior of faculty, staff, students, and the external environment.

Earlier an example was given of African American students congregating around a red couch in the student union where they enjoyed their only meaningful social interaction on campus. The cultural lens is useful here because the red couch is not only an important gathering place for African American students; it is to them their most visible symbol of a black presence on campus.

Key Issues in Assessing Environmental Influences on Learning

To discover how the contextual conditions of a campus influence student learning and personal development, a comprehensive, in-depth study of an institution's culture and its policies and practices is needed. This section discusses some key issues related to conducting an audit of how a college's contextual conditions influence student learning. Although this section assumes a comprehensive campus-wide audit, the same issues pertain if the focus of the project is circumscribed, such as assessing the impact of the residence halls or the campus union on student performance.

Institutional audits are labor-intensive. However, they provide high quality, policy-relevant information that cannot be obtained any other way. The following suggestions are distilled from Austin (1990), Austin, Rice, and Splete (1991), Crowson (1987), Fetterman (1990), Kuh (1993), Kuh and others, (1991), Schein (1985), Whitt (1993), and Whitt and Kuh (1991).

Determine the Institution's Commitment to the Project. Some colleges request a study of their learning environment, but are not clear about what they wish to accomplish with the project. They lack the institutional will to learn from the process and implement recommendations that follow either those suggested by the study team or those that emerge from campus discussions from the findings. Clarifying the purpose of the study is critical. One or some combination of a wide range of issues call attention to the need for such a study—from the self-study required by regional accreditation agencies to the factors that contribute to student abuse of alcohol to promoting collaboration between academic and student affairs to assessing the learning climate for diversity. No matter what the study team has been asked to focus on, support from the highest administrative levels, including the governing board, is essential for a successful campus audit. Publicity about the project, including what it is intended to accomplish and institutional responses to the emerging findings are also essential. A variety of venues should be used including the student newspaper, faculty newsletters, alumni publications, e-mail, and local, as well as campus, radio, and television.

Assemble a Credible, Qualified Study Team. Assuming that campus policymakers have agreed that an audit is needed, the first step is to create a partnership of people familiar with the institution (insiders) and consultants (outsiders) knowledgeable about conditions that foster student learning. Outsiders are needed to help insiders "make the familiar strange" (Whitt, 1993). That is, most faculty, student affairs staff, and students are so familiar with the institution that they are unable to note how such taken-for-granted aspects of campus life as traditions and ritualistic practices positively and negatively influence student learning of various groups (women, minorities, older students). The team must be perceived as credible, fair, tactful, discrete, truthful, and trustworthy by the various stakeholders likely to be affected by the findings or charged with implementing recommendations from the study. Sensitivity to and appreciation for the mission and purposes of the type of institution being examined are essential. While many student affairs professionals embody these characteristics, it also will be important that faculty members and academic administrators be represented on the study team. Faculty members are more likely to talk freely with another faculty member or with a respected outsider; therefore, a study team that includes several faculty members will likely obtain higher quality data. The team should also reflect an appropriate gender, racial, and ethnic balance.

Conduct the Audit with Integrity, Goodwill, and an Open Mind. Respect the unique qualities of the institution and the worth of all individuals, groups, and points of view. This advice is obvious, but is difficult to adhere to because in the process of the audit, team members will encounter some people with whom they have more in common and tend to be more accepting of interpretations that are consistent with their own cognitive maps. Keep to a minimum evaluative judgments about the relative merits of perceptions of individuals and groups, policies, practices, symbols, and other cultural artifacts. Emphasize institutional strengths as well as limitations so an appropriate tone for improving the quality of campus life can be created. Most important, determine what the data mean in the context of the college and clearly explicate how they influence student learning.

For example, on commuter campuses, the classroom is the primary, and often the only significant, point of contact between the majority of students and the institution. No matter how much effort student affairs and academic support staff devote to trying to make campus life meaningful to more students, certain circumstances are unalterable, such as the responsibilities of many students that make traditional campus-based functions and programs unattractive, impossible to attend, or irrelevant to their needs and concerns. The national norms of the College Student Experiences Questionnaire research program (Kuh and others, 1997) show that the majority of students at urban universities never use campus outdoor recreational facilities (67%), play on an intramural team (84%), attend a meeting of a campus club (54%), work on a student organization (75%) or committee (81%), or attend social events in the campus union (63%). And typically no more than 10–15% engage in any of these activities more than occasionally. Clearly, for understandable reasons, many students at urban universities do not engage in the activities typically associated with building a sense of community. The implication of this is that when studying the learning environments of such institutions, the classroom must receive a disproportionately large share of attention because it is the primary locus of social relations as well as the primary (but not exclusive) source of intellectual stimulation and discipline-based information.

Obtain As Much Relevant Information as Possible from Different Sources. It is essential to obtain high quality information from a variety of sources (faculty, current, former and prospective students, graduates, student affairs staff, others) using multiple data collection methods (interviews, observations, survey data, document analysis) in order to create a complex, accurate understanding of campus life. To yield the most useful results, audits should incorporate some combination of interviews, observations, and self-report pencil and paper instruments completed by students and perhaps others such as faculty and student affairs professionals (Austin, 1990; Kuh, 1990). Data produced by multiple methods of data collection almost always are mutually reinforcing and add legitimacy to the findings because those who prefer either the qualitative or quantitative paradigm will be able to locate information that they can "believe."

One approach is to use open-ended interviews with students, faculty, and others to identify critical issues which deserve immediate attention. Based on this information, an appropriate instrument, such as the *CSEQ*, may be used to collect additional information from a larger number of students. In certain instances, the best approach may be to construct a survey designed to obtain the needed information. Following the collection of survey data, additional interviews with individual and groups of students, faculty members, and student affairs staff will provide more detailed insights into how the institutional context affects student learning and personal development.

To determine if the espoused values and aspirations of the institution are congruent with the enacted policies and practices that shape daily interactions, the audit team must examine the written and oral statements of institutional leaders and important institutional documents, such as the mission statement, past and current catalogs, and statements of student rights, responsibilities, and ethics. These tacit assumptions and other enacted patterns of behavior and understanding often go unchallenged and unrecognized, which makes their influence on student learning difficult to ascertain and address.

The nature of the project will dictate whether both process indicators and outcomes measures are needed. Process indicators are measures of how students and faculty spend their time and are highly correlated with desired outcomes of college, such as critical thinking, knowledge acquisition, and moral and ethical reasoning. Among the more familiar process indicators are good practices in undergraduate education (Chickering and Gamson, 1987) and student affairs (Blimling and Whitt, 1999). These include such things as high expectations, active learning, peer cooperation, and interaction with faculty. To estimate the relative quality of the undergraduate experience of various groups (women and men, students of color, students majoring in different fields), measures of both the amount of effort students invest in their education (process indicators) and what they get out of it (outcomes) should be made.

Seek Different Points of View. Obtain as much diverse information as possible by seeking out contradictions and differences of opinion. Avoid simplifying complicated issues and prematurely drawing conclusions. Particular attention should be given to what the institution *espouses* (says about itself in publications and public statements, but may or may not actually do) with regard to the philosophy, values, policies and practices and what seems to be *enacted* (what people put into practice). Espoused values may take the form of institutional aspirations, such as an announced commitment to health-enhancing behavior or to increasing the number of students and faculty from historically underrepresented groups. If these goals are not realized, however, the gap between espoused and enacted values can create considerable confusion in students and others.

Test Impressions Early and Often. Feedback from insiders about emerging interpretations is critical to obtaining high quality data. That is, as mentioned above, the audit team must have their emerging understandings and impressions validated and corrected by those whose experiences are being described (Lincoln and Guba, 1985). Treat emerging interpretations as speculations to be confirmed and reconfirmed by subsequent data. Feedback should be given to participants throughout the process. Participating in the study should be educative; that is, through the data collection and reporting processes, the team and various groups should learn a good deal about themselves and student learning before any "final report" is circulated. Indeed, perhaps the most important outcome of the audit process is getting people together to talk about or discover matters of mutual interest and importance to institutional vitality and student learning.

Whitt's (1993) caution warrants emphasis here: obtain the permission of participants; be clear about your purposes and the ways information obtained from participants will be used; do not report preliminary findings except to check your evolving impressions, explanations, and interpretations; be explicit about how the results of the campus audit can and cannot be used.

Treat Every Participant and Every Piece of Information as Important. Many inextricably intertwined institutional properties influence student learning. Therefore, the audit team must assume that every aspect of institutional life may have an influence—positive or negative—on student learning. Attention must be given to the routine as well as the more unusual, celebratory aspects of campus life. By focusing on events that are the most obvious or most colorful, such as new student orientation, induction ceremonies, honors programs, scholarship banquets, and commencement, one may overlook the mundane routines by which institutional values are expressed and reinforced for most students and that shape faculty and student aspirations and behavior on an ongoing basis (Kuh, 1997).

Significant Improvements Take Time. As mentioned earlier, it is important that key institutional leaders be ready and willing to accept feedback about the quality of contextual conditions for learning (Schein, 1985). Audits often shed light on the "shadow side of campus culture," aspects of faculty and student cultures about which just enough is known so people know they are not to discuss such matters (Kuh, 1993). Therefore, it probably will be useful to have people from different groups of faculty, students and administrators participate in some aspects of the investigation. Expect the audit results to confirm as well as challenge one or more taken-for-granted assumptions about student life. Several studies have shown, for instance, that attendance at large lecture classes on a typical day may draw only about 60% of the students taking the course (Marchese, 1998). A study at one large university found that more than 50% of undergraduates skip three or more class sessions per course per semester (Wolf, Schmitz, and Ellis, 1991). Although the reasons for missing class vary (some use the time to study for exams in other classes, some to sleep), that so many students miss what amounts to a week or more of instruction surprised and disappointed many faculty and academic administrators.

Certain physical attributes of a campus are not always viewed as welcoming or hospitable by people who have been historically underrepresented and may belie espoused institutional aspirations to be open to members of these groups. For example, artwork and portraits featured in public places often reflect the institution's history and preferences of administrators. As a result, artifacts manifest mostly white, mostly male views. While it seems a simple matter to add artifacts that reflect the experiences of different groups of people, a college simply cannot exchange one set of paintings for another. Some will object to what appears to be revisionist history or "politically correct" behavior. Moreover, a college must pay attention to whether its values are consistent with its educational purposes.

No institution is perfect, so it is easy to criticize the current state of affairs anywhere. At the same time, the most important goal of an audit is to help faculty, student affairs professionals, and students become aware of the rich harvest of learning opportunities inherent in collegiate environments and how their institution can encourage more students to take greater advantage of these opportunities. This means that, among other things, faculty and staff must have current relevant information about the characteristics of their students in order to understand and interpret the findings from a campus audit and use the information to improve the learning climate.

Summary

An institution of higher education is more than a collection of students and faculty, buildings, and green spaces. Greater than the sum of its many parts, a college or university is at once a behavior setting that regulates the behavior of its members; a theater-in-the-round where the scripts of the past get played out in the process of seeking solutions to contemporary ills; a highly leveraged subsidiary that annually consumes an increasing amount of its parent company's resources; a social club with numerous cliques of faculty, students, and administrators; a cultural and recreational oasis where the number and variety of events and activities outstrip any one individual's capacity to partake of them all; a game of chance in which members of various groups are assigned to physical spaces not always compatible with their personal or academic preferences and aspirations; and an intellectual theme park where the only limits to what one can discover are imposed by the learner.

All of the actions and events described above, and more, occur simultaneously. At some colleges, this maelstrom of activity is more coherent and consistent with the institution's educational purposes than at others. This is because the various properties of a college work together in complicated, almost mysterious ways to promote or discourage student learning. While the way these properties work together may seem mysterious, the properties themselves are not.

In the final analysis, a college or university is what its faculty, administrators, students, graduates, trustees, and others believe it to be (Wilkins, 1989). Knowledge about graduation rates and library holdings is not enough to create and sustain an educationally purposeful learning community. Students, faculty, administrators must *believe* in something. To paraphrase (Murchland, 1991, p. 15), a high quality learning environment "is a bit like religion . . . We have to believe in it to make it work." Student affairs staff can use the substantive and interpretive frames described in this chapter to identify and better understand the influence of their institution on the learning and personal development of students. Such knowledge coupled with a firm belief in the importance of their work and what their college stands for will enable student affairs professionals to make even more valuable contributions to their institutions and students.

References

Ahrentzen, S., Jue, B. M., Skorpanish, M. A., and Evans, G. W. "School Environment and Stress." In G. Evans (ed.), *Environmental Stress*. Cambridge, MA: MIT Press, 1982.

American College Personnel Association. *The Student Learning Imperative*. Washington, D.C.: American College Personnel Association, 1994.

American College Personnel Association/National Association of Student Personnel Administrators. *Principles of Good Practice for Student Affairs*. Washington, D.C.: American College Personnel Association/National Association of Student Personnel Administrator, 1997.

Astin, A. W. "The Changing American College Student: Thirty Year Trends, 1966–1996." *The Review of Higher Education*, 1997, 21, 115–135.

Astin A. W., and Holland, J. L. "The Environmental Assessment Technique: A Way to Measure College Environments." *Journal of Educational Psychology*, 1961, 52, 308–316.

Aulepp, L., and Delworth, U. *Training Manual for An Ecosystem Model*. Boulder, CO: Western Interstate Commission for Higher Education, 1976.

Austin, A. E. "Faculty Cultures, Faculty Values." In W. G. Tierney (ed.), *Assessing Academic Climates and Cultures*. New Directions for Institutional Research, no. 68. San Francisco: Jossey-Bass, 1990.

Austin, A. E., Rice, R. E., and Splete, A. P. *The Academic Workplace Audit*. Washington, D.C.: Council for Independent Colleges, 1991.

Baird, L. L. "The College Environment Revisited: A Review of Research and Theory." In J. C. Smart (ed.), *Higher Education: Handbook of Theory and Research*, Vol. IV. New York: Agathon, 1988.

Banning, J. H. "The Built Environment: Do Ivy Walls Have Memories?" *Campus Ecologist*, 1983, 1(2), 1–3.

Banning, J. H. "Creating a Climate for Successful Student Development: The Campus Ecology Manager Role." In U. Delworth and G. Hanson (eds.), *Student Services: A Handbook for the Profession*. San Francisco: Jossey-Bass, 1989.

Banning, J. H. "Visual Anthropology: Viewing the Campus Ecology for Messages of Sexism." *The Campus Ecologist*, 1992, 10(1), 1–4.

Banning, J. H., and Cunard, M. "Environment Supports Student Development." *ACU-I Bulletin*, 1986, 54(1), 8–10.

Banning, J. H., and Luna, F. C. "Viewing the Campus Ecology For Messages About Hispanic/Latino Culture." *The Campus Ecologist*, 1992, 10(4), 1–4.

Barker, R. G. *Ecological Psychology: Concepts and Methods for Studying the Environment of Human Behavior*. Stanford, CA: Stanford University Press, 1968.

Barr, R. B., and Tagg, J. "From Teaching to Learning—A New Paradigm for Undergraduate Education." *Change*, 1995 (November/December), 13–25.

Blimling, G. and Whitt E. (eds.), *Good Practices in Student Affairs*. San Francisco: Jossey-Bass, 1999.

Blocher, D. H. "Toward an Ecology of Student Development." *Personnel and Guidance Journal*, 1974, 52, 360–365.

Blocher, D. H. "Campus Learning Environments and the Ecology of Student Development." In J. Banning (ed.), *Campus Ecology: A perspective for Student Affairs*. Cincinnati, OH: National Association of Student Personnel Administrators, 1978.

Braxton, J. M., Smart, J. C., and Thieke, W. S. "Peer Groups of Colleges and Universities Based on Student Outcomes." *Journal of College Student Development*, 1991, 32, 302–309.

Chickering, A. W., and Gamson, Z. F. "Seven Principles for Good Practice in Undergraduate Education." *AAHE Bulletin*, 1987, *39*(7), 3–7.

Clark, R., and Trow, M. "The Organizational Context." In T. M. Newcomb and E. K. Wilson (eds.), *College Peer Groups: Problems and Prospects for Research*. Chicago: Aldine, 1966.

Crowson, R. L. "Qualitative Research Methods in Higher Education." In J. C. Smart (ed.), *Higher Education: Handbook of Theory and Research*, Vol. III. New York: Agathon Press, 1987.

Diamond, R. M., and Adam, B. E. *Changing Priorities At Research Universities: 1991–1996.* Syracuse, NY: Syracuse University Center for Instructional Development, 1997.

Eaton, S., and Manning, K. "Loosening the Ties That Bind: Shaping Student Culture." In G. D. Kuh (ed.), *Using Cultural Perspectives in Student Affairs Work.* Alexandria, VA: ACPA Media, 1993.

Fetterman, D. "Ethnographic Auditing: A New Approach to Evaluating Management." In W. G. Tierney (ed.), *Assessing Academic Climates and Cultures.* New Directions for Institutional Research, no. 68. San Francisco: Jossey-Bass, 1990.

Holland, D. C., and Eisenhart, M. A. *Educated in Romance: Women, Achievement, and College Culture.* Chicago: The University of Chicago Press, 1990.

Holland, J. L. *Making Vocational Choices: A Theory of Careers.* Englewood Cliffs, NJ: Prentice-Hall, 1973.

Huebner, L. A. (ed.). *Redesigning Campus Environments. New Directions for Student Services*, no. 6. San Francisco: Jossey-Bass, 1979.

Huebner, L. A. "Interaction of Student and Campus." In U. Delworth and G. Hanson (eds.), *Student Services: A Handbook for the Profession* (rev. ed.). San Francisco: Jossey-Bass, 1989.

Hurst, J. C., and Ragle, J. D. "Application of the Ecosystem Perspective to a Dean of Students' Office." In L. Huebner (ed.), *Redesigning Campus Environments.* New Directions for Student Services, no. 8. San Francisco: Jossey-Bass, 1979.

Iwai, S., Churchill, W., and Cummings, L. "The Physical Characteristics of College and University Counseling Services." *Journal of College Student Personnel*, 1983, 24, 55–60.

Kuh, G. D. "Assessing Student Culture." In W. G. Tierney (ed.), *Assessing Academic Climates and Cultures.* New Directions for Institutional Research, no. 68. San Francisco: Jossey-Bass, 1990.

Kuh, G. D. "Appraising the Character of a College." *Journal of Counseling and Development*, 1993, 71, 661–668.

Kuh, G. D. "Creating Campus Climates That Foster Learning." In C. C. Schroeder, P. Mable, and Associates, *Realizing the Educational Potential of Residence Halls* (pp. 109–132). San Francisco: Jossey-Bass, 1994.

Kuh, G. D. "Strengthening the Ties that Bind": Cultural Events, Rituals, and Traditions." In J. N. Gardner, G. Van der Veer, and Associates, *The Senior Year Experience: Facilitating Integration, Reflection, Closure, and Transition* (pp. 152–170). San Francisco: Jossey-Bass, 1997.

Kuh, G. D. "How Are We Doing? Tracking the Quality of the Undergraduate Experience from the 1960s to the Present." *The Review of Higher Education*, 1999, 22, 99–119.

Kuh, G. D. "Setting the Bar High to Promote Seamless Learning." In G. Blimling and E. Whitt (eds.), *Good Practices in Student Affairs.* San Francisco: Jossey-Bass, 1999.

Kuh, G. D. and Schuh, J. H. "The Ecology of Involving Colleges." *Campus Ecologist*, 1991, 9(4), 1–3.

Kuh, G. D., Vesper, N., Connolly, M. R., and Pace, C. R. *College Student Experiences Questionnaire: Revised Norms for the Third Edition.* Bloomington: Indiana University Center for Postsecondary Research and Planning, 1997.

Kuh, G. D., and Whitt, E. J. *The Invisible Tapestry: Culture in American Colleges and Universities.* AAHE-ERIC/Higher Education Research Report, no. 1. Washington, D.C.: American Association for Higher Education, 1988.

Kuh, G. D., Whitt, E. J., and Shedd, J. D. *Student Affairs, 2001: A Paradigmatic Odyssey.* ACPA Media Publication, no. 42. Alexandria, VA: American College Personnel Association, 1987.

Kuh, G. D., and others. *Involving Colleges: Successful Approaches to Fostering Student Learning and Development Outside the Classroom.* San Francisco: Jossey-Bass, 1991.

Lincoln, Y., and Guba, E. G. *Naturalistic Inquiry.* San Francisco: Jossey-Bass, 1985.

Lyons, J. W. "Examining the Validity of Basic Assumptions and Beliefs." In M. J. Barr, M. L. Upcraft, and Associates, *New Futures for Student Affairs.* San Francisco: Jossey-Bass, 1990.

Marchese, T. "Disengaged Students." *Change,* 1998, 30(2), 4.

Moffatt, M. *Coming of Age in New Jersey: College and American Culture.* New Brunswick, N.J.: Rutgers University Press, 1989.

Moos, R. *Evaluating Educational Environments.* San Francisco: Jossey-Bass, 1979.

Murchland, B. "Knowledge, Action, and Belief." *Public Leadership Education,* 1991, 4, 13–15.

Myrick, R., and Marx, B. S. *An Exploratory Study of the Relationship Between High School Building Design and Student Learning.* Washington, D.C.: Bureau of Research, Office of Education, U.S. Department of Health, Education and Welfare, 1968.

National Association of Student Personnel Administrators. *A Perspective on Student Affairs.* Iowa City, IA: American College Testing Program, 1987.

Nelson, T. *A Comparison of Selected Undergraduate Experiences of Alumni Who Financially Support Their Alma Mater.* Unpublished doctoral dissertation, Indiana University, Bloomington, 1984.

Ott, J. S. *The Organizational Culture Perspective.* Chicago: Dorsey, 1989.

Pace, C. R. *College and University Environment Scales: Technical Manual* (2nd ed). Princeton, N.J.: Educational Testing Service, 1969.

Pace, C. R., and Kuh, G. D. *College Student Experiences Questionnaire* (4th ed). Bloomington: Indiana University Center for Postsecondary Research and Planning, 1998.

Pascarella, E. T., and Terenzini, P. T. *How College Affects Students: Findings and Insights from Twenty Years of Research.* San Francisco: Jossey-Bass, 1991.

Peterson, M. W., and others. *The Organizational Context for Teaching and Learning: A Review of the Research Literature.* Ann Arbor, MI: National Center for Research to Improve Postsecondary Teaching and Learning, 1986.

Peterson, M. W., and Spencer, M. G. "Understanding Academic Climate and Culture." In W. G. Tierney (ed.), *Assessing Academic Climates and Cultures.* New Directions for Institutional Research, no. 68. San Francisco: Jossey-Bass, 1990.

Peterson, R. E. *College Student Questionnaire: Technical Manual.* Princeton, N.J.: Educational Testing Service, 1968.

Peterson, R. E. and others. *Institutional Functioning Inventory: Preliminary Technical Manual.* Princeton, N.J.: Educational Testing Service, 1970.

Schein, E. H. *Organizational Culture and Leadership.* San Francisco: Jossey-Bass, 1985.

Schroeder, C. S. "New Strategies for Structuring Residential Environments." *Journal of College Student Personnel,* 1976, 17, 386–390.

Schroeder, C. S. "Student Development Through Environmental Management." In G. Blimling and J. Schuh (eds.), *Increasing the Educational Role of Residence Halls. New Directions for Student Services,* no. 13. San Francisco: Jossey-Bass, 1981.

Tinto, V. *Leaving College.* Chicago: University of Chicago Press, 1993.

Walsh, W. B. "Person-Environment Interaction." In J. Banning (ed.), *Campus Ecology: A Perspective for Student Affairs.* Cincinnati, OH: National Association for Student Personnel Administrators, 1978.

Weidman, J. "Undergraduate Socialization: A Conceptual Approach." In J. Smart (ed.), *Higher Education: Handbook of Theory and Research* (vol. V). New York: Agathon, 1989.

Whitt, E. J. "Making the Familiar Strange: Discovering Culture." In G. D. Kuh (ed.), *Using Cultural Perspectives in Student Affairs Work*. Alexandria, VA: ACPA Media, 1993.

Whitt, E. J., and Kuh, G. D. "Qualitative Methods in Higher Education Research: A Team Approach to Multiple Site Investigation." *Review of Higher Education*, 1991, 14, 317–337.

Wilkins, A. L. *Developing Corporate Character: How To Successfully Change an Organization Without Destroying It*. San Francisco: Jossey-Bass, 1989.

Wolf, B., Schmitz, T., and Ellis, M. "How Students Study: Views from Bloomington Campus Undergraduates." Bloomington: Indiana University Office for Academic Affairs and Dean of Faculties, 1991.

CHAPTER FIVE

FISCAL PRESSURES ON HIGHER EDUCATION AND STUDENT AFFAIRS

John H. Schuh

This is not an easy time to be a budget officer or financial manager in an institution of higher education. As this chapter will describe, students are coming to our institutions underprepared, in some cases, to do adequate academic work; the federal government is requiring institutions of higher education to comply with legislation without providing the resources to do so; and the overall costs of obtaining a higher education continue to escalate far beyond the cost of living. In addition, institutions of higher education face increased costs for services, and deteriorating physical plants (nationally deferred maintenance is estimated to be $26 billion according to one study [National Commission on the Cost of Higher Education, 1998]) place further financial burdens on both public and private institutions. Perhaps most importantly, as Balderston (1995, p. xi) asserts, "In the past these institutions were capable of growing in many directions without having to assess mission or scope and without being specifically accountable, financially or otherwise, to funding agencies, the taxpaying public, faculty or students. That period is over, and universities are now asked to justify themselves."

Fiscal policy, constraints, and conditions have a profound effect on programs, services, learning opportunities, and activities developed by and offered in the student affairs division. This chapter will examine a variety of factors that influence the fiscal environment in which the student affairs division operates. First, the economic implications of demographic and social trends will be examined. Second, several federal initiatives will be presented in the context of their economic impact on institutions of higher education. Third, a quick look will be taken at state financing of higher education and the compliance requirements states are placing on colleges and universities. Finally, issues related to the cost of attending institutions of higher education and financial aid will be discussed. Brief implications for student affairs will be presented in each section. The fiscal environment for higher education is difficult. As Woodard (1995, p. 1) points out, "The fiscal roller coaster of the 1970s and 1980s prompted many institutions of higher education to tighten their budgets by reducing, consolidation, and merging programs, which reduced human resources and operating costs. The 'fiscal woes' lament by the higher education community has not led to any broad-based support but rather has heightened the public debate over the efficiency and effectiveness of human education." Let us examine some of the factors that have contributed to this environment.

Demographic and Social Trends

Demographic influences on student affairs will be addressed in detail elsewhere in this book. This section will discuss selected demographic and social trends in the context of their financial implications for higher education.

Kuh (1990) observes that student affairs officers will have to deal with social issues that will affect the practice of student affairs in the future. In fact, the future is just around the corner. For reasons that we will examine later, many college students of the future may be at risk and may need additional support to be successful. This will take the form of tutorial help, counseling, financial aid, and other assistance specific to individual campuses. Consider the following information about the students who will be coming to college at the start of the twenty-first century.

The Family

The percentage of two-parent households has declined in the United States over the past twenty-five years from 84.3 percent in 1972 to 71.2 percent in 1997, the percentage of whereas families with the mother as head of household has grown substantially. These families have grown from 13.7 percent of all families in 1972 to 23.8 percent in 1997 (U.S. Department of Education, 1998e, p. 136). The United States heads a list of ten developed countries in divorce rates. In 1993, for example, there were 20.5 divorces for every one thousand women in the United States, compared with 14.9 in 1970, 9.2 in 1960, and 10.3 in 1950 (U.S. Department of Education, 1996b, p. 20). Many traditional-age college students will continue to come from homes where divorce has occurred. As a result, many of these students may need help from their institution of higher education in forms as support groups, individual counseling, or other assistance in order to cope with a changed family structure. Expansion of or introduction of such services very well may result in additional fiscal pressures on student affairs divisions.

In addition to the effect of divorce rates, the increasing proportion of single-parent families also influences young people. The U.S. Department of Education (U.S. Department of Education, 1996b, p. 34) reports that the percentage of children living in single-parent families nearly doubled from 11.3 percent in 1970 to 24.9 percent in 1994. More than half (59.5 percent) of all African American children lived in single-parent households in 1994, compared with 29.1 percent of Hispanic children and 18.7 percent of white children according to the U.S. Department of Education (1996b, p. 34). These statistics lead to the second demographic trend that will affect students of the future: economic deprivation.

Poverty

Absence of a parent often means limited financial support, lack of nurturing, and negative psychological and social effects on children (Bianchi, 1990). The economic consequences of growing up in single-parent households are particularly dramatic and disturbing. O'Hare, Pollard, Mann, and Kent (1991) estimate that the median family income for two-parent families was $31,757, compared with $9,590 for families with only the female parent present.

Another interesting dimension is that the average number of children in households with children has an inverse relationship to family income. Typically, families with larger incomes have fewer children according to the U.S. Department of Education (1996b, p. 46). Perhaps the most telling statistic is offered by Hodgkinson (1985), who writes that every day in America forty unwed teenage girls give birth to their third child. One wonders what opportunities will be available to the children who grow up in these families.

In fact, the U.S. Department of Education (1996b, p. 54) determined that 52.9 percent of all children in female-headed households lived in poverty in 1994. About 43 percent of all African American children, 41 percent of Hispanic children, and 16.3 percent of white children lived in poverty in 1994. Moreover, the increase of poor children coming from female-headed households has grown dramatically since 1960, from under 24 percent to 57 percent for all children in 1994. Children of the unmarried are also more likely to live in poverty as adults (Griffith, Frase, and Ralph, 1989).

Many traditional-age students of the future will come from one-parent families where the only provider was the mother. As we have seen, the data reveal that the income of these families is often below the poverty line. Students from these families will probably need substantial amounts of financial aid in order to enroll in college. Additionally, the students may require special efforts on the part of colleges and universities to attract them to college in the first place because many of them may come from families where the remaining parent has not graduated from college or even thought about attending an institution of higher education. This situation, in turn, will make it more costly to recruit these students. It may be incumbent on institutions to provide more programming for parents that describes the benefits of college attendance because individuals unfamiliar with institutions of higher education may find the language, traditions, and culture of colleges complex and difficult to understand (Kuh and Whitt, 1988).

School Enrollment

The percentage of young people of color enrolled in elementary and secondary schools has grown dramatically over the past two decades and should be an indication of the next century's college population. Unfortunately, young people from underrepresented minority groups are not present in college and university student bodies to the extent that they attend elementary and secondary schools, according to the U.S. Department of Education (1997). For example, whites comprised 70.4 percent of the enrollment in elementary and secondary schools in 1986, and 64.8 percent in 1995 (U.S. Department of Education, 1998a, p. 14); however, they accounted for 78.1 percent of the students enrolled in institutions of higher education in 1986, and 74.5 percent in 1995 (U.S. Department of Education, 1997, p. 221). African Americans have increased their numbers from 16.1 percent of children attending elementary and secondary schools in 1986 to 16.8 percent of those enrolled in 1995 (U.S. Department of Education, 1998a, p. 14). But they constituted only 10.6 percent of all students attending college in 1986 and 11.7 percent in 1995 (U.S. Department of Education, 1997, p. 221), although that percentage had increased from 4.8 percent in 1965 (U.S. Department of Education, 1997, p. 221).

Similarly, the representation of Hispanic youth has increased in elementary and secondary schools, but they are not enrolled proportionately in institutions of postsecondary education. The percentage of Hispanic children enrolled in elementary and secondary schools grew from 9.9 percent of all those enrolled in 1986 to 13.5 percent in 1995 (U.S. Department of Education, 1998a, p. 14). Hispanics, however, made up only 6.4 percent of college students in 1986 and 8.4 percent in 1995 (U.S. Department of Education, 1997, p. 221).

It is clear that student bodies of the future will contain more students of color. Campuses are already struggling to provide appropriate support to historically underrepresented students. As the number of students of color increases on college campuses, additional financial investments may be required to provide staff time, perhaps staff members, and targeted programs as Cuyjet and his colleagues (1998) have recommended. Ramirez (1993, p. 437) asserts that "Programmatic development in an institution characterized by changing student populations ultimately comes down to choosing from an array of activities that will require fiscal and staff support."

Federal Higher Education Initiatives

The federal government continues to be interested in opening access for historically underserved populations. Clearly, that will be an ongoing focus of federal involvement in higher education. This section is dedicated to reviewing selected federal legislative and regulatory developments of recent years with specific attention on the fiscal implications of these initiatives.

Access for Those with Disabilities

One category of federal regulation of higher education stems from legislation adopted in 1973. "Section 504 of the Rehabilitation Act of 1973 was enacted by the United States Congress to provide protection for handicapped persons against various forms of societal discrimination" (Bills and Hall, 1994, p. 58). Section 504 mandates that programs offered by campuses receiving federal funds be accessible to persons with disabilities. Certainly, no one could argue with the premise that everyone ought to be able to pursue a college education; indeed, there are tremendous benefits to making higher education available so that disabled people can more easily become independent, productive citizens. However, this legislation (like many other federal laws) mandates certain institutional responses without providing funding for implementation.

With the passage of the Americans with Disabilities Act (1990) and an increasing emphasis on including individuals who heretofore had not participated in campus life, additional costs will be incurred by colleges and universities. Students with learning disabilities who previously may not have been welcomed by institutions of higher education are now enrolling and require special services. As more children with disabilities participate in mainstream educational experiences in elementary and secondary schools, one can be sure that such students will want to enroll in postsecondary institutions. The percentage of students who were served by federally supported programs for students with disabilities increased from 8.3 percent of all public K − 12 enrollment in 1977 to 12.4 percent in 1996 (U.S. Department of Education, 1998e, p. 138).

An area of continuing growth will be accommodations for students with learning disabilities. Students with learning disabilities comprised the largest percentage of all students with some form of disability being served by federally supported programs, 46.3 percent, according to the U.S. Department of Education (1998e, p. 138). El-Khawas (1996) advises college administrators to work closely with high schools to stay aware of changes in serving students with disabilities and to become better aware of the numbers and patterns of students with disabilities.

Among the implications of this legislation for student affairs officers are that housing reserves may be tapped for residence hall modifications; staff must be identified and programs developed to assist those with disabilities; documents, brochures, and other printed material may have to be provided in Braille; interpreters will be needed for public events; assistive technology will need to be provided; and that those with disabilities will expect student affairs officers to serve as their advocates, even though the potential costs associated with the changes they desire may be substantial.

Regulatory Compliance

Another category of federal initiatives deals with regulatory compliance as exemplified by draft registration and illegal immigration. The burdens of some of these regulations are relatively light because all that is required is a certain degree of documentation. In other cases, the costs can be massive. Stanford University is cited as paying $20 million per year in costs related to complying with a variety of regulations (National Commission on the Cost of Higher Education, 1998). Nevertheless, the regulations point to the philosophical direction in which the federal government appears to be heading: Institutions will have to keep more records and assist the federal government in achieving its objectives. In the case of draft registration, for example, the goal is that all 18-year-olds eligible for draft registration will comply with the law. In the case of immigration legislation, the objective is that all persons hired by institutions of higher education will conform with federal law concerning eligibility for employment. In each situation, the institution is asked to help enforce federal laws by providing certain assurances that specific individuals are in compliance with certain statutes or regulations. In all cases, there is no funding to assist institutions with this task.

Consumer Protection

A third category of the federal agenda, which might be termed consumer protection legislation, has placed additional financial burdens on colleges and universities for the foreseeable future. Recent laws have stipulated that institutions of higher education notify faculty and students on a regular basis about the institution's substance-abuse policy, laws related to the use of alcohol and other drugs, and programs available to provide assistance to those who seek help (Drug-Free Schools and Communities Act Amendments of 1989, Public Law 101–226). Starting with the 1992–93 academic year, institutions were required to provide a variety of individuals (including current and prospective students) with information related to graduation rates, campus safety, and criminal activity (Student Right-to-Know and Campus Security Act, Public Law 101–542). In each case (substance abuse and criminal activity), failure to comply with Department of Education regulations could result in the forfeiture of financial aid dollars. As Fenske and Johnson (1990, p. 120) assert, "The federal government is now willing to use the threat of withdrawal of student aid as a club to enforce desired student behaviors unrelated to and beyond the direct control of the colleges and universities."

The implications of consumer legislation include costs related to preparation and distribution of materials. For example, the law requires that every student receive certain information about campus crime each year. At a college where each student has a campus mailbox this has minimal implications, but the costs associated with a commuter student body may be considerably greater. As crimes are detected and members of the campus advised of the criminal activity, additional personnel costs will be incurred in the notification process.

Although one can only speculate about what may be next on the agenda of the federal government, it is clear that recent activities will have an impact on the financial resources of colleges and universities for several reasons. Failure to comply with the regulations may result in the termination or withholding of federal financial assistance (Gehring, 1994).

Issues Related to State Finance

Before reviewing specific factors and trends influencing the financing of higher education, it is useful to take a moment to describe some of the financial issues faced by the states. Although public institutions rely on state support to a much greater degree than private institutions, virtually every college or university in the country is affected to some degree by the amount of financing that the states can provide, whether through direct support to institutions or financial aid programs to students. State governments have had to contend with a fundamental shift in their relationship with the federal government that has had dramatic implications for their budgets. Consider several issues listed here in cursory form that have both short- and long-term implications for higher education.

Transfer of Fiscal Responsibility to the States

During the 1980s, the federal government transferred partial or full responsibility for many domestic programs to the states (McGuire, 1991). General revenue sharing (GRS) ended in 1987 (Steel, Lorrich, and Soden, 1989). As GRS accounted for five percent of cities' general funds and three percent of all operating revenues (Marando, 1990), cities and counties have turned to state governments for increased aid (Gold and Erickson, 1989). Local governments have become competitors with higher education for state funds.

A number of the programs that have been transferred to the states have become competitors with higher education for state funding. Included in this group are hazardous waste control, transportation, and welfare. Added to this are the costs of operating prisons for an ever-growing population, health care and housing, and a continuous pressure to reduce taxes. With these factors in mind, one can paint a fairly dismal scenario for higher education support. Indeed, when one examines sources of current fund revenue for public institutions of higher education, state appropriations have declined from 1980–81 to 1994–95. In 1980–81, state appropriations comprised 45.6 percent of all current fund revenue. In 1994–95, this funding had declined to 35.9 percent (U.S. Department of Education, 1997, p. 341). Much of the decline has been made up by tuition increases. Over this same period of time, tuition income as a percentage of income increased from 12.9 percent to 18.4 percent.

Institutions should not look to their states for relief from regulation. State governmental regulation has also placed additional burdens on colleges and universities. State involvement has taken on many forms (budgeting, program assessment, and political intrusion) and exists for many purposes (improving academic quality, economic competitiveness, access, and degree attainment [Fenske and Johnson, 1990]). "Public colleges and universities, and to a lesser but still significant extent, private institutions, are just beginning to sense the dimensions and long-term impact of state governors, legislatures, and statewide higher education agencies" (Fenske and Johnson, 1990, p. 124).

The pressures on state budgets appear to be getting worse rather than better and make clear that most institutions of higher education will not be able to turn to their legislatures for substantial increases in funding. In the best scenario, public institutions may be able to receive adjustments in their budgets that correspond to the cost of inflation. But it is unlikely that a majority of public colleges and universities will be successful in their attempts to receive much more support from their state governments.

Private institutions face similar economic pressures due to the current and projected economic climate in the country. At private institutions, tuition income as percentage of general fund revenues has increased from 36.6 percent in 1980–81 to 42.4 percent in 1994–95 (U.S. Department of Education, 1997, p. 342). Private support cannot meet all the perceived needs of these institutions. Indeed, as a percentage of general fund revenue, private gifts and contracts have remained stable from 1980–81 (9.3 percent) to 1994–95 (8.8 percent) at private institutions (U.S. Department of Education, 1997, p. 342).

As institutions of higher education are adversely affected by state budget problems, student affairs units will be fortunate to maintain the status quo that has existed over the past two decades. Student affairs expenditures at all public universities were 3.7 percent of all educational and general expenditures in 1976–77 and remained 3.7 percent in 1994–95 (U.S. Department of Education, 1997, p. 358). Those student affairs units funded by general revenues (state support and tuition) will be in fierce competition with academic units for resources. Those funded by user fees and fees for service (such as student housing or student unions) can expect to contribute more money into their institutions through overhead charges for such items as accounting and purchasing services, security, and the like. Regardless of the funding source, student affairs units will be forced to struggle to maintain an adequate funding base for the foreseeable future.

The Public-Private Dilemma

An especially difficult issue confronting state financing of higher education is the extent to which government ought to support private institutions. Though private colleges and universities constitute over half of the country's institutions of higher education ("Almanac," 1998, p. 18), their total enrollment is only approximately twenty percent of all individuals attending institutions of higher education ("Almanac," 1998, p. 19). The average in-state resident cost of attending a four-year residential public institution in 1996—97 was just $7,331, whereas similar costs at a residential four-year private institution averaged $18,476 (U.S. Department of Education, 1997, p. 326). As a result of a variety of factors, a spirited debate over just how much state support should go to private institutions continues. Among the questions in this debate, according to Floyd (1982), are the following:

1. What is the desirability of government aid to private institutions?
2. What is the appropriate differential between tuition for public and private institutions?
3. If the private sector in a particular state is especially large, should the government choose between having to subsidize it or absorb increased public sector enrollments?

4. If states provide money to private institutions, most commonly through financial aid programs to students, should these institutions participate in statewide planning efforts?

5. If states provide support to private institutions, how will the institutions maintain their traditional role of independence?

The answers to these questions and others do not come easily. Nonetheless, there is no doubt that the competition between public and private institutions for state dollars—often revolving around whether states ought to provide direct support to students (through financial aid programs, thereby favoring private colleges) or direct support to institutions (thereby favoring public colleges)—has the potential to become more heated. Regardless of the direction of the debate, Lennington (1996, p. ix) asserts, "Many state governments, in response to their own fiscal and deficit problems, have reduced subsidies for state institutions of higher education and scholarship programs for private institutions."

Factors Affecting State Finance of Higher Education

When one examines the relationship of higher education to the states, it is important to remember that the United States does not have a national system of higher education. As Levy (1986, p. 255) points out, "Discussions about U.S. higher education finance should really be pursued on a state-by-state basis. The fifty state systems, not to mention more local networks, put intranation comparative analysis at a premium. Variation is enormous." There are, however, some factors influencing state financing of higher education. Munitz and Lawless (1986) identify several issues related to resource allocation that are germane to the current fiscal environment.

Review of Expenditures. Increasingly, expenditures of higher education institutions are being scrutinized by governing boards, legislatures, coordinating councils, students, parents, and virtually anyone else who has a perceived interest in this area. As mentioned earlier, state funding is being squeezed, and the result is that careful attention is being paid to how financial resources are being spent.

Munitz and Lawless (1986) posit that a fundamental shift has occurred in the framework being used to determine if higher education institutions are spending funds wisely. Their position is that through the 1970s, higher education was viewed in a broader context, and such ideas as encouraging lifelong learning and viewing vocational achievements over a lifetime were considered important. Munitz and Lawless (1986) assert that a philosophical change occurred in the 1980s: higher education has come to be regarded as an experience that provides immediate socioeconomic mobility and strengthened earning potential. The result of this shift is that resources have had to be reallocated and curricula and other learning experiences have had to be revised. Higher education may also be seen as having direct economic benefit to individuals, rather than to society as a whole. Those holding this position believe that the recipients of higher education ought to pay more since they gain directly from the experience (for example, Kassebaum, 1991).

Student affairs officers can expect that expenditures will receive careful scrutiny for the balance of this century and beyond. This is not to suggest that care has not been exercised in the past. It has. But as resources become increasingly restricted, institutions will examine their funding for student affairs and other units with a heightened degree of care and perhaps with an eye to finding resources that could be diverted to other institutional purposes.

Disenchanted Taxpayers. As witnessed by the tax revolt in California (Proposition 13), taxpayers across the country are demanding and winning cuts in property taxes (Yinger, 1990). "Many state governments, in response to their own fiscal and deficit problems, have reduced subsidies for state institutions of higher education and scholarship programs for private institutions" (Lennington, 1996, p. ix). In one state, a combination of economic issues, voter-initiated efforts to reduce property taxes, and concerns for public safety and corrections resulted in reduction for higher education in succeeding biennia of two percent, twelve percent, twenty percent, and thirteen percent (Trow, 1995). The relative priority of higher education compared to other governmentally funded activities has been questioned. As noted previously, higher education has become a competitor with other activities for state funds: "Citizen movements like California's Proposition 13 can have an impact on higher education, as a decline in local tax revenues places greater burdens on the state to provide services previously assumed by the localities" (Hauptman, 1990, p. 16).

Academic Productivity. As part of the call for increased accountability, institutions have been asked to develop measures of productivity. Munitz and Lawless (1986, p. 69) argue, "In higher education there are no indices as quantifiably specific as widgets produced per hour of labor." Faculty and academic administrators represent the largest concentration of expenditures in higher education (Lennington, 1996, p. 116) and will be called upon to demonstrate greater levels of productivity because they represent the largest proportions of institutional expenditures. Similar demonstrations will be required of student affairs practitioners. For example, Kuh and Nuss (1990), citing Scott, Wards, and Yeomen (1978), point out that student affairs expenditures usually receive even greater scrutiny than those of academic units because student affairs expenditures have been justified more on the basis of idealistic or humanistic grounds than on tangible evidence or results. Upcraft and Schuh (1996) assert that student affairs needs to respond to global pressures of accountability as well as to internal pressure to justify the allocation of resources to programs and services that appear to be nonacademic and, therefore, less essential.

Student affairs units are seen by some as adding to the cost of higher education (for example, Lennington, 1996). One approach to student affairs is described by Balderston (1995), who reports that (student) service units should be self-financing and "charge each user a price that will ostensibly at least, cover the cost" (pp. 128–129). Charging user fees, however, is merely a means of shifting the costs from tuition charges to other sources and has little or no effect on the student, who pays for the service either as part of the tuition bill or the fee bill. Still another option is to charge specific users for services. More detailed information about student fees is provided by Levy (1995).

Increased productivity will be sought throughout institutions of higher education. Student affairs will be no exception. Staff can expect to work more efficiently, harder, and perhaps longer, and technology probably will not make jobs easier or help staff be more productive. "There is no evidence to date that the use of technology in higher education has resulted in widespread savings to colleges and universities" (National Commission of the Cost of Higher Education, 1998). "Introduction of new technology rarely, for example, reduces personnel requirements or saves money" (Mills, 1990, p. 139). Indeed, technology often results in additional costs for students. "Some campuses have instituted mandatory computer/instructional technology fees" ranging from $55 per student in community colleges to $140 in public universities (National Commission on the Cost of Higher Education, 1998).

One approach to limiting costs related to academic personnel has been an increasing reliance on part-time and adjunct faculty. According to one report, the percentage of part-time faculty and staff has grown from thirty-three percent in 1987 to forty-two percent in 1992, whereas the percentage of tenured faculty and staff has declined from fifty-eight to fifty-four percent (National Commission on the Cost of Higher Education, 1998). The substitution of part-time and adjunct faculty, who are paid by the course or the credit hour taught, can represent a significant cost saving for an institution. On the other hand, adjunct and part-time faculty may be less available to meet with students before or after class, serve as members of institutional committees, or help shape curriculum, which can be interpreted as lowering the quality of the student experience. Nonetheless, the cost saving of using adjunct or part-time faculty members can be dramatic, given that the average salary of a faculty member for all ranks was $50,837 in 1996–1997 (U.S. Department of Education, 1998d).

Selected Factors Influencing the Financial Health of Institutions

Revenues

Revenues have a dramatic and important effect on the financial status of colleges and universities. Among the revenue sources for institutions of higher education are students, government, private and foundation donors, corporations, and investments. Students pay tuition, fees, and room-and-board expenses and buy books and supplies. State governments, as mentioned earlier, provide direct aid to public institutions and financial aid to students who attend private institutions. The federal government sponsors financial aid programs and supports research and creative activities. Individuals, foundations, and corporations furnish gifts and grants to colleges and universities; and financial markets provide income for these institutions through revenue generated from investments of endowments and operating funds.

In general, the mix of revenues changed from 1980–81 to 1994–95. Income from tuition and fees, private gifts and contracts, and sales and services grew over this period of time, whereas federal support and state appropriations declined as revenue sources (U.S. Department of Education, 1997, p. 341).

Tuition. Tuition is the most important source of income for private institutions of higher education. In 1980–81, tuition represented 36.6 percent of general fund revenue, whereas by 1994–95, this percentage had increased to 42.4 percent (U.S. Department of Education, 1997, p. 342). Taylor and Massy (1996) concluded as a result of a study of nearly 1,000 institutions that almost all private institutions are tuition-driven, and tuition and fee income is also significant for public institutions.

Fund Raising. Private colleges depend more on private, foundation, and corporate contributions than public institutions, but the latter have also begun to rely more on donations—a situation that puts them squarely in competition for these funds with the private sector. During the 1996–97 fiscal year, 12 of the 20 institutions receiving the most money in voluntary (gift-donor) support were private ("Almanac," 1998, p. 35). Revenues from investments reflect the fruits of gifts and donations. In recent years, the return on endowment investments has been substantially greater than the rate of inflation. For example, the consumer price index has increased at an annual rate of 3.5 percent from June 30, 1987 through June 30, 1997; however, the return on all investment pools for institutions of higher education was 18.2 percent in fiscal 1998 (Lively, 1998). Thus, the real return on these funds (the rate of return minus the rate of inflation) has been substantial, although it may not be sustainable in the future.

Student Costs

The cost of attending college continues to rise, often at a rate much higher than the commonly accepted measure of inflation, the Consumer Price Index. Since 1973–74, consumer prices have tripled, but the cost of attendance at public two-year colleges has increased four times, at public universities five times, and at private universities nearly six times (Oblinger and Verville, 1998). To illustrate the growth in student costs, the average in-state cost of attending a four-year public institution in 1964–65 was $950 for room, board (seven-day meal plan), and tuition. By 1996–1997, the cost had risen to $6,534. Similarly, the cost of private higher education had risen dramatically. In 1964–65, the average cost of room, board, and tuition at a private institution was $1,907. By 1996–97, the cost of a year at a private college had grown to $18,071 according to the U.S. Department of Education (1997, pp. 326–327). None of these costs were adjusted for increases in inflation. One report summarizes the situation this way:

> Between 1987 and 1996, median family income rose 37 percent and disposable per-capita income rose 52 percent. During the same period, both measures of net prices rose considerably faster. Specifically, the price of attendance minus grants rose 114 percent at public four-year institutions, 81 percent at private four-year institutions, and 159 percent at public two-year institutions. Total price minus all financial aid (grants, loans, and work study) demonstrates a similar pattern: this measure of net price increased 95 percent at four-year institutions, 64 percent at private four-year institutions, and 169 percent at public two-year institutions (sic) (National Commission on the Cost of Higher Education, 1998, p. 7).

The cost of attendance varies widely from state to state; however, the national average was $7,331 for room, board, and tuition for an in-state student attending a public college or university and $18,476 at a private institution (U.S. Department of Education, 1997, p. 327). For example, in such states as Vermont, New York, Massachusetts, Rhode Island, Connecticut, Pennsylvania, and Maryland, the cost of attendance was more than $9,000 for room, board, and in-state tuition in 1996–97 at public institutions. This compares with less than $6,000 for in-state tuition, room, and board at public institutions in Kansas, Arkansas, North Carolina, Texas, and North Dakota.

Costs to attend private institutions also reflect a wide range in average costs for room, board and tuition using 1996–1997 as an illustration. The average was more than $20,000 for private institutions in Vermont, Rhode Island, Pennsylvania, New York, New Jersey, and New Hampshire, whereas it was less than $12,000 in Arkansas, Mississippi, Montana, North Dakota, Utah, and Oklahoma according to the U.S. Department of Education (1997, p. 328). To be sure, no claims are made to equate cost with quality. But the point is this: the cost of education varies widely from state to state and averages can be a bit misleading. Put another way, a student attending a private institution in one state very well could pay less than a student attending a public four-year institution in another.

Although always a low-cost option for students, the cost of attending a two-year public institution has increased as well. Tuition was $99 per year for an in-state student at a public community college in 1964–65 and it had risen to $1,283 in 1996–97 (U.S. Department of Education, 1997, pp. 326–327). Again, the cost of attendance varied widely from state to state. Whereas the average tuition for an in-state student was $1,283 in 1996–1997, such states as California, Texas, Arizona, and North Carolina charged less than $800 for a year's tuition, and such states as Vermont, Maine, South Dakota, and New York charged more than $2,500 per year. The point of all this should be clear: National averages related to the cost of attendance can be misleading because such a wide variance exists from state to state.

Financial Aid Trends

Clearly, one of the responses to the growth in the cost of attendance has been the widespread development of financial aid programs. Over two-thirds (68.4 percent) of all full-time undergraduate students who attended college in 1995–1996 received some form of financial aid. The most common source of this aid was federal programs (55.6 percent) followed by institutional aid programs (27.7 percent), state programs (19.8 percent) and then other programs (10.9 percent) (U.S. Department of Education, 1997, p. 332). Students attending private institutions were more likely to participate in financial aid programs (80.3 percent) than those attending public institutions (62.8 percent). This difference, in part, can be attributed to participation in institutional aid programs. More than half of the students who attended private colleges and universities (56.3 percent) participated in institutional aid programs, compared with 18.8 percent of students who attended public institutions. These data reflect full-time enrollment (U.S. Department of Education, 1997, p. 332).

During the past decade, the pattern of financial aid has evolved so that the majority of federal dollars is now devoted to loans rather than grants. Of the approximately $38 billion allocated to financial aid programs by the federal government in 1996–1997, more than half of the aid was earmarked for loan programs ("Almanac," 1998, p. 17). Hartle and Galloway (1997, p. 35) explain the change this way, " . . . the shift in emphasis from grants to loans has undermined the social compact that assumed that the adult generation would pay for the next generation's college education." The typical financial aid package in the late 1970s consisted of approximately 80 percent grants, 17 percent loans, and 3 percent student employment; in the late 1980s, the mix was 50 percent loans, 46 percent grants, and 4 percent student employment (Margolin, 1989). Only 16 percent of freshmen received Pell grants in 1988, fewer than half the number of students who received Pells in 1980 (Cutler, 1989). To make matters worse, the purchasing power of Pell grants has eroded over the past two decades. In 1976–1977, the average Pell grant covered 19 percent of the average price of attendance at private institutions and 39 percent of the average price of attendance at public institutions. By 1996–1997, the percentages had dropped to 9 percent of the cost of attendance at private institutions and 22 percent at public institutions (The Education Resources Institute, 1998, p. vi).

Loan Programs. One federal report observes, "Since 1970, borrowing, working, and part-time attendance have all increased, in some cases dramatically. For example, loans have made up about 39 percent of federal financial aid programs (grants, loans, and work-study), whereas in 1970–71, they made up 65 percent of federal aid in 1990–91" (U.S. Department of Education, 1998b, p. 2).

This trend has continued into the 1990s. For example, in 1992, 33.6 percent of all full-time students participated in some form of loan program. By 1995–1996, this figure had increased to 43.7 percent of all students. The increase is about equal in terms of growth whether the student attended a public or private four-year institution. The growth was from 26.9 percent in 1992–93 to 37.2 percent participation in loan programs at public institutions in 1995–1996, and from 46.5 percent to 56.9 percent at private colleges and universities. Students who attended two-year public colleges borrowed less than their counterparts who enrolled at four-year institutions. Here the increase was from 12.7 percent to 21.8 percent (U.S. Department of Education, 1997, p. 333).

Students attending graduate or professional school have to deal with even greater financial challenges. McWade (1995, p. 53) observes, "Managing the debt they (graduate students) carry in a graduate program can be a major concern for students, especially if it is complicated by the debt they incur while there." The data suggest that a substantial majority of students seeking a first professional degree borrow. According to the U.S. Department of Education (1997, p. 336), 74.4 percent of first professional students received loans, compared with 25.2 percent of doctor's degree students and 43.1 percent of master's degree students. The difference between these cohorts of students lies in the greater availability of graduate assistantships for master's and doctoral students. Such support typically is not available for professional students.

Stafford loans have emerged as the most common form of federal aid. More than half (55.6 percent) of all full-time undergraduates received federal aid in 1995–96. A total of 42.2 percent of all undergraduates received Stafford loans, followed by Pell grants (30.1 percent), SEOG grants (9.1 percent), college work-study (9.0 percent), Perkins loans (7.6 percent and 5.0 percent) (U.S. Department of Education, 1997, p. 334). Stafford loans were especially popular among students at four-year private colleges and universities, where 55.1 percent of all undergraduates participated in the program.

Tuition Discounting. Another strategy is the development of tuition discounting, which is an increasingly common strategy at private institutions. Tuition discounting, in effect, is providing a student a lower cost of attendance than the "sticker price," meaning the published cost of tuition and fees. This form of financial aid is designed to attract students to attend the institution and persist to graduation. Willcox (1991) asserts that this form of financial aid can enhance initial and continued enrollment. Tuition discounting, however, has financial implications for the institution engaging in this practice. Dickmeyer (1997, pp. 139–140) concludes that "the result has been a skyrocketing of tuition prices, much slower growth of net tuition (tuition less institutionally-funded grant aid), and a burgeoning fraction of the total expense budget dedicated to institutionally-funded student aid."

Work Study. Not only has there been a shift from grants to loans (which moves some of the financial aid responsibility from the federal government to the student), there has also been a change in the funding composition of the college work-study program. In 1964, this program consisted of 80 percent federal and 20 percent institutional funding (Organization for Economic Cooperation and Development, 1990), whereas in 1998, federal funding accounted for 70 percent, with the balance coming from institutions.

Recall that students of the twenty-first century increasingly will come from single-parent families or families with modest financial resources. To pay for the costs of attending college, these students will be forced to assume larger debts than those of preceding generations. As a result, when they graduate from college and enter the work force, they may have to defer any additional debt because of their student loan obligations. Moreover, those interested in attending private institutions must contemplate even more substantial debt if their resources are insufficient to finance their education. For private institutions, the potential burden of student debt is a real problem if they would like to attract a diverse student body because some economic classes will simply be excluded from attendance and some are very adverse to additional debt accumulation. In addition, private institutions must balance increased tuition rates against the dollars required for financial aid.

As an economic policy issue, the matter of students increasingly turning to loans to finance their college education does not augur well for the future financial health of the United States, where consumer spending represents approximately two-thirds of all economic activity. Students who are strapped with heavy college loan debts will be less able to buy appliances, cars, homes, or other items that require long-term financing.

College Attendance and Low Income

One of the objectives of federal policy, almost regardless of administration, has been to provide greater access to postsecondary education for students from modest economic backgrounds. The demographic trends in the first section of this chapter indicate that an increasing proportion of college students will be from low-income backgrounds, so this objective is consistent with the population trends of the country. Using a definition of low income as " . . . 125 percent of the federally established poverty threshold for their family size" (U.S. Department of Education, 1996a, p. 3), more than one student in five (20.2 percent) was from a low-income family (U.S. Department of Education, 1996a, p. 5). Typically, these students were more likely to be female, of color, and attending a two-year college than their counterparts who were not low-income status.

A substantial proportion of low-income students participated in financial aid programs. More than 84 percent received some form of aid, whereas 76 percent received a Pell grant. Nearly half (49.2 percent) also participated in federal loan programs (U.S. Department of Education, 1996a, p. 39). More than half (52 percent) received institutional aid while attending private four-year institutions. Institutional assistance is an important source of aid for these students, although institutional aid was seen as being less important at public institutions. According to one study, "Public institutions usually have relatively little need-based aid to distribute. In many states, most need-based aid at public institutions is awarded directly to students through state grant programs rather than through the institutions" (U.S. Department of Education, 1996a, p. 47).

Work as a Financing Option

One other option for students who attend institutions of higher education is to work while they are enrolled. This is an option that a large proportion of undergraduates use to finance college attendance. For example, in 1995–1996, 79 percent of undergraduates reported working, most commonly 21 to 34 hours (17 percent), or 35 or more hours (37 percent) per week (U.S. Department of Education, 1998c, p. 5). In another study, half reported that the primary reason they worked was to help pay for their education (U.S. Department of Education, 1998e, p. 122). Among the students who work, students who worked fewer hours were likely to be employed on campus, while those who worked more hours tended to work off campus (U.S. Department of Education, 1998c, p. 13). Just fifteen percent of all students worked on campus, whereas the balance worked off campus, presumably for employers who were less sensitive to the academic calendar, including mid-terms and final examinations.

Students who worked more hours reported that work had a negative effect on their academic performance. For example, 17.1 percent of students who worked one to fifteen hours per week reported that work was a negative effect on their academic performance, whereas 22.3 percent reported that it had a positive effect. Students who indicated they worked sixteen to twenty hours indicated that work was more negative than positive (34.3 percent compared with 13.8 percent), whereas 46 percent of those working twenty-one to thirty-four hours reported a negative effect. Lastly, 55.4 percent of those working thirty-five or more hours reported work as having a negative effect, whereas 9.7 percent indicated that work had a positive effect on their academic performance (U.S. Department of Education, 1998c, pp. 14–15). According to another study, "Among students who worked to pay school expenses, the more hours they worked, the more likely they were to report that their work schedule limited their class schedule, reduced the number of classes they could take and reduced their class choices" (U.S. Department of Education, 1998e, p. 122).

Students who worked more hours, however, were less likely to participate in loan programs. Those who worked one to fifteen hours per week participated in loan program at a 46.3 percent rate, compared with 25.7 percent of those who worked 35 or more hours per week. Similarly, the amount of loan aid had a relationship with the number of hours worked. Those who worked fewer hours (one to fifteen per week) borrowed an average of $4,344 compared with $3,810 for those who worked thirty-five or more hours per week (U.S. Department of Education, 1998c, p. 16).

One other aspect of work is worth noting: its influence on persistence. "For both first-year and continuing students, those working one–fifteen hours per week were less likely to interrupt their enrollment than students working sixteen–thirty-four hours per week" (U.S. Department of Education, 1998c, p. 18). Working a few hours a week actually had a positive effect on persistence. "Students who did not work while enrolled were less likely to attend for a full academic year than those working one–fifteen hours. This result held for both first-year (15 percent versus 6 percent) and continuing students (6 percent versus 2 percent)" U.S. Department of Education, 1998c, p. 19).

Still, not all students who work will suffer from the experience. Pascarella and others (1998) found in a study of 3,840 students enrolled at twenty-three institutions that " . . . for the most part, work during college that does not exceed 15–20 hours per week does not seriously inhibit students' intellectual growth." It would appear that when students work longer hours, that is, more than 20 hours per week, this activity inhibits their education.

It is difficult to predict the future of higher education, but the financial aid trends identified may have a serious impact on higher education delivery systems of the future. The Education Resources Institute (1998) identifies the following potential implications for higher education from the current financial aid situation:

- Increasing proportions of students are working full- or part-time to finance their education;
- The increasing popularity of distance education may be a result of students needing alternatives to traditional campus-based courses;
- Disadvantaged students may limit their postsecondary education to public two-year institutions, or as an alternative will take half of their bachelor's degree at a two-year college as a cost-saving measure.

Summary

This chapter has examined four wide-ranging issues that influence the fiscal environment of higher education and student affairs. Demographic trends assure that our future students will more commonly be people of color, less likely be affluent, and more often be from single-parent families. It is likely that many of these will be first-generation college students. These trends have direct implications related to the cost of higher education in terms of requiring increased staff time, programming, and direct support.

Federal initiatives of the last decade have resulted in a variety of initiatives that have increased the cost of delivering higher education to students. Access to higher education opportunities has been broadened for people with disabilities and students with learning disabilities, are enrolling in increasingly greater numbers. The cost of providing educational experiences to these students can require substantial financial resources. Typically, such services require expensive assistive technology or are delivered on an individual or small group basis by highly skilled individuals including signers/interpreters, psychometrists, or others who are specialists in individualized learning. Legislation has been passed that requires institutions to initiate what could be classified broadly as consumer information activities, but funding has not been forthcoming to help institutions comply. As a consequence, institutions incur greater costs by being required to provide a wide variety of information to all students, whether they seek the information or not.

Pressures have mounted on states even in this time of relative affluence. The shift of the responsibility for many programs from the federal government to the states has created substantially increased obligations for state governments; accordingly, higher education has to compete vigorously for state support against other state agencies and programs for financial support. A growing population of prison inmates drains funds from state treasuries as well. Other factors that are putting pressures on states as sources of support are programs to cut taxes and initiatives seeking greater accountability and productivity from institutions. In the case of the former, revenue streams are becoming more limited; in the case of the latter, institutions have to spend more time justifying what they do and how they do it. Finally, we find a philosophical shift in thinking about state support of higher education, whether this be directly to students who attend private colleges through financial aid programs or to institutions operated in the public sector. The argument goes something like this: As the benefits of college are seen to accrue primarily to those who graduate (typically demonstrated in the form of higher income) rather than to society as a whole, it becomes more philosophically palatable in the minds of some to argue that students and their families should bear more of the burden of paying for these benefits than the citizens of the taxing unit.

The financial health of institutions, the fourth general area of discussion of this chapter, also has been affected in a variety of ways. Institutions continue to rely more on tuition, fee charges, and fund-raising as sources of income. Increased costs continue to be passed along to students. In turn, students look to financial aid as the means by which they can satisfy their financial obligations. The problem with this pattern is that the most common form of financial aid has become loans (nearly half of all students enrolled in college will be receiving loans to pay for at least a portion of the cost of attendance in the near future).

This scenario has been developed in relatively good economic times. What might occur as a consequence of an economic downturn? No one knows for sure, but it certainly would appear that the economic waters upon which our institutions of higher education will sail in the future will be choppy at best.

References

"Almanac." *Chronicle of Higher Education.* Aug. 28, 1998, pp. 3–42.

Balderston, F. E. *Managing Today's University* (2nd ed.) San Francisco: Jossey-Bass, 1995.

Bianchi, S. M. "America's Children: Mixed Results." *Population Bulletin*, 1990, 45 (4), 3–41.

Bills, T. A., and Hall, P. J. "Antidiscrimination Laws and Student Affairs." In M. D. Coomes and D. D. Gehring (eds.), *Student Services in a Changing Federal Climate.* New Directions for Student Services Sourcebook, no. 68. San Francisco: Jossey-Bass, 1994.

Cutler, B. "Up the Down Staircase." *American Demographics,* 1989, 11 (4), 3226, 41.

Cuyjet, M. J. (ed.) *Helping African American Men Succeed in College.* New Directions for Student Services Sourcebook no. 80. San Francisco: Jossey-Bass 1998.

Dickmeyer, N. "Enrollment Goals, Tuition Pricing and Institutional Aid Commitments." In J. S. Davis (ed.), *Student Aid Research: A Manual for Financial Aid Administrators.* Washington, DC: NASFAA, 1997.

El-Khawas, E. "Student Diversity on Today's Campuses." In S. R. Komives, D. B. Woodard Jr., and Associates, *Student Services: A Handbook for the Profession* (3rd ed.) San Francisco: Jossey-Bass, 1996.

Fenske, R. H., and Johnson, E. A. "Changing Regulatory and Legal Environments." In M. J. Barr, M. L. Upcraft, and Associates, *New Futures for Student Affairs: Building a Vision for Professional Leadership and Practice.* San Francisco: Jossey-Bass, 1990.

Floyd, C. E. *State Planning, Budgeting, and Accountability: Approaches for Higher Education.* AAHE-ERIC Higher Education Research Report, no. 6. Washington, D.C.: American Association for Higher Education, 1982.

Gehring, D. D. "Protective Policy Laws." In M. D. Coomes and D. D. Gehring (eds.), *Student Services in a Changing Federal Climate.* New Directions for Student Services Sourcebook, no. 68. San Francisco: Jossey-Bass, 1994.

Gold, S. D., and Erickson, B. M. "State Aid to Local Governments in the 1980s." *State and Local Government Review,* 1989, 21 (1), 11–22.

Griffith, J. E., Frase, M. J., and Ralph, J. H. "American Education: The Challenge of Change." *Population Bulletin,* 1989, 44 (4), 3–37.

Hartle, T. W., and Galloway, F. J. "Federal Guidance for a Changing National Agenda." In M. W. Peterson, D. D. Dill, L. A. Mets, and Associates (eds.), *Planning and Management for a Changing Environment.* San Francisco: Jossey-Bass, 1997.

Hauptman, A. M. "Helping Colleges Survive Bad Times." *State Government News,* 1990, 33 (9), 16–17.

Hodgkinson, H. L. *All One System: Demographics of Education, Kindergarten Through Graduate School.* Washington, D.C.: Institute for Educational Leadership, 1985.

Kassebaum, N. L. "Perspectives from Washington." Speech presented at the Kansas Conference on Postsecondary Education, Topeka, Oct. 1991.

Kuh, G. D. "The Demographic Juggernaut." In M. J. Barr, M. L. Upcraft, and Associates, *New Futures for Student Affairs: Building a Vision for Professional Leadership and Practice.* San Francisco: Jossey-Bass, 1990.

Kuh, G. D., and Nuss, E. M. "Evaluating Financial Management in Student Affairs." In J. H. Schuh (ed.), *Financial Management for Student Affairs Administrators.* Washington, D.C.: American College Personnel Association, 1990.

Kuh, G. D., and Whitt, E. J. *The Invisible Tapestry: Culture in American Colleges and Universities,* ASHE-ERIC Higher Education Report, no. 1. Washington, D.C.: Association for the Study of Higher Education, 1988.

Lennington, R. L. *Managing Higher Education as a Business.* Phoenix, AZ: Oryx, 1996.

Levy, D. C. "Policy Controversies in Higher Education Finance: Comparative Perspectives on the U.S. Private-Public Debate." In S. K. Gove and T. M. Stauffer (eds.), *Policy Controversies in Higher Education.* Westport, CT.: Greenwood Press, 1986.

Levy, S. R. "Sources of Current and Future Funding." In D. B. Woodard, Jr. (ed.), *Budgeting as a Tool for Policy in Student Affairs.* New Directions for Student Services Sourcebook, no. 70. San Francisco: Jossey-Bass, 1995.

Lively, K. "College Endowments Earned 18.2% Return in Fiscal 1998." *The Chronicle of Higher Education,* November 27, 1998, p. A33.

Marando, V. L. "General Revenue Sharing: Termination and City Response." *State and Local Government Review,* 1990, 22 (3), 98–107.

McGuire, T. J. "State and Local Tax Reform for the 1990s: Implications from Arizona." *Journal of Policy Analysis and Management,* 1991, 10 (1), 64–77.

Margolin, J. B. "Financing a College Education." New York: Plenum Press, 1989.

McWade, P. "Financial Aid for Graduate Study." In A. S. Pruitt-Logan and P. D. Isaac (eds.), *Student Services for the Changing Graduate Student Population.* New Directions for Student Services Sourcebook, no. 72. San Francisco: Jossey-Bass, 1995.

Mills, D. B. "The Technological Transformation of Student Affairs." In M. J. Barr, M. L. Upcraft, and Associates, *New Futures for Student Affairs: Building a Vision for Professional Leadership and Practice.* San Francisco: Jossey-Bass, 1990.

Munitz, B., and Lawless, R. "Resource Allocation Policies for the Eighties." In S. K. Gove and T. M. Stauffer (eds.), *Policy Controversies in Higher Education.* Westport, CT: Greenwood Press, 1986.

National Commission on the Cost of Higher Education (1998). *Straight Talk About College Costs and Prices.* Washington, D.C.: American Council on Education, 1998.

Oblinger, D. G., and Verville, A-L. *What Business Wants from Higher Education.* Phoenix, AZ: Oryx, 1998.

O'Hare, W. P., Pollard, K. M., Mann, T. L., and Kent, M. M. "African Americans in the 1990s." *Population Bulletin,* 1991, 46 (1), 1–40.

Organization for Economic Cooperation and Development. *Financing Higher Education: Current Patterns.* Paris: Organization for Economic Cooperation and Development, 1990.

Pascarella, E. T., and others. "Does Work Inhibit Cognitive Development During College?" *Educational Research and Policy Analysis,* 1998, 20, 75–93.

Ramirez, B. C. "Adapting to New Student Needs and Characteristics." In M. J. Barr and Associates, *The Handbook of Student Affairs Administration.* San Francisco: Jossey-Bass, 1993.

Steel, B. S., Lorrich, N. P., and Soden, D. L. "A Comparison of Municipal Responses to the Elimination of Federal General Revenue Sharing in Florida, Michigan, and Washington." *State and Local Government Review,* 1989, 21 (3), 106–115.

Taylor, B. E., and Massy, W. F. *Strategic Indicators for Higher Education.* Princeton, NJ: Peterson's, 1996.

The Education Resources Institute. *Do Grants Matter?* Boston: Author, 1998.

Trow, J. A. "Budgeting Climate." In D. B. Woodard, Jr., (ed.), *Budgeting as a Tool for Policy in Student Affairs.* New Directions for Student Services Sourcebook, no. 70. San Francisco: Jossey-Bass, 1995.

Upcraft, M.L., and Shuh, J.H. *Assessment in Student Affairs.* San Francisco: Jossey-Bass 1996.

U.S. Department of Education. "Drug-Free Schools and Campuses: Final Regulations." *Federal Register*, Aug. 16, 1990, 34 CFR Part 86.

U.S. Department of Education, National Center for Education Statistics. *How Low Income Undergraduates Financed Postsecondary Education: 1992–93.* Washington, D.C.: U.S. Department of Education, National Center for Education Statistics, 1996a.

U.S. Department of Education, National Center for Education Statistics. *Youth Indicators, 1996.* Washington, DC: Author, 1996b.

U.S. Department of Education, National Center for Education Statistics. *Digest of Education Statistics 1997.* Washington, D.C.: U.S. Department of Education, National Center for Education Statistics, 1997.

U.S. Department of Education, National Center for Education Statistics. *Mini-Digest of Education Statistics 1997.* Washington, D.C.: U.S. Department of Education, National Center for Education Statistics, 1998a.

U.S. Department of Education, National Center for Education Statistics. *Postsecondary Financing Strategies: How Undergraduates Combine Work, Borrowing, and Attendance.* Washington, D.C.: U.S. Department of Education, National Center for Education Statistics, 1998b.

U.S. Department of Education, National Center for *Education Profile of Undergraduates in U.S. Postsecondary Institutions with an Essary on Undergraduates Who Work.* Washington, D.C.: U.S. Department of Education, National Center for Education Statistics, 1998c.

U.S. Department of Education, National Center for Education Statistics. *Salaries, Tenure, and Fringe Benefits 1996–97.* Washington, DC: U.S. Department of Education, National Center for Education Statistics, 1998d.

U.S. Department of Education, National Center for Education Statistics. *The Condition of Education 1998.* Washington, D.C.: U.S. Department of Education, National Center for Education Statistics, 1998e.

Willcox, L. "Evaluating the Impact of Financial Aid on Student Recruitment and Retention." In D. Hossler (ed.), *Evaluating Student Recruitment and Retention Programs.* New Directions for Institutional Research Sourcebook, no. 70. San Francisco: Jossey-Bass, 1991.

Woodard, D. B. Jr. "Editor's Notes." In D. B. Woodard, Jr. (ed.), *Budgeting as a Tool for Policy in Student Affairs.* New Directions for Student Services Sourcebook, no. 70. San Francisco: Jossey-Bass, 1995.

Yinger, J. "States to the Rescue? Aid to Central Cities Under the New Federalism." *Public Budgeting and Finance*, 1990, 10 (2), 27–44.

CHAPTER SIX

IDENTIFYING AND WORKING WITH KEY CONSTITUENTS

Dudley B. Woodard, Jr. and Mark von Destinon

Higher education is undergoing a slow but profound and fundamental trans-formation. It is deep, pervasive, and intentional (Eckel, Hill, and Green, 1998). The conditions that have set this process into motion are well known, but the outcome is uncertain. What will our institutions look like in another decade? Who will they serve and how will they be funded? How will institutional missions change to respond to new clientele, a rapidly changing marketplace, ac-countability demands, privatization and commercialization, technological ad-vances, and a global economy? (Altbach, Berdahl, and Gumport, 1998) Campus leaders have turned to strategic planning and successful corporate models to help them understand how to restructure their institutions to be competitive and suc-cessful in this new reality. Because our institutions are tradition-bound and labor-intensive, often they find it difficult to use new technologies and methodologies to achieve savings, increase productivity, and exploit new market opportunities. And, because we are a labor-intensive organization, it is clear that our future suc-cess is predicated on how we use our human capital in the restructuring of our institutions.

How well we work with different on- and off-campus constituencies is one of the core conditions for the successful restructuring of our institutions. This chap-ter focuses on working with the constituency groups that influence and affect the collegiate institution. Sociological, leadership, and organizational theories are presented to describe and assist in the understanding of the interaction of institutional culture and group behaviors. Theory is used as a bridge to understanding the beliefs, behaviors, and power sources of various constituent groups followed by a discussion of interpreting the meaning of their actions in the context of different theoretical lenses. Institutions should set into motion an ongoing program of educating constituents about the critical issues faced by the institution and the choices to be made in order to gain constituent support and prepare them for change (Haenicke, 1991). Environmental scanning is offered as one way to keep abreast of constituent attitudes, lifestyles, tastes, and opinions in order to cultivate meaningful relationships between the institution and members of the constituent groups. The final section of the chapter offers some advice in working with different constituent groups.

Theoretical Frameworks

This section provides the theoretical framework to help understand the behavior, motivation, and actions of constituent groups. The theories we use determine what we see and what we do. Many organizational problems occur because managers use theoretical frames that are too simple or too narrow (Bolman and Deal, 1984, p. 25). Sociology is a proper unit for analysis because it is the study of social interaction and culture. Culture, the way of life, especially the general customs and beliefs of a particular group of people at a particular time, is a useful lens to study the behaviors of constituent groups in higher education. The cultural view holds that to understand and appreciate behavior, assumptions and beliefs shared by a group of people must be considered. In the higher education context, culture is the "collective, mutually shaping patterns of norms, values, practices, beliefs, and assumptions which guide the behavior of individuals and groups and provide a frame of reference within which to interpret the meaning of events and actions on and off the campus (Kuh, 1993, p. 2)." The functionalist, conflict, and symbolic interaction paradigms are offered as broad methods to understand and interpret group behaviors (Bolman and Deal, 1991).

Leadership theory is useful in understanding the roles, perspectives, assumptions, and styles of decision-makers and how leaders exhibit different behaviors and decision-making processes depending on conditions and challenges. New leadership paradigms have emerged that challenge traditional beliefs and assumptions about leadership and shift from focusing on the behaviors of the leader to the process of leadership with an emphasis on the followers and group members themselves. A reconstruction of the leadership view is seen as "not something a leader possesses so much as a process involving followership . . . a relational process of

people together attempting to accomplish change or make a difference to benefit the common good" (Komives, Lucas, and McMahon, 1998, p. 11).

Organizational theory helps us to understand processes such as reallocation
of resources, personnel management, decision-making, policy development and
implementation, planning, and restructuring activities. There has been a shift from
viewing organizations as closed and hierarchical systems to complex open systems,
influenced by external events and changing conditions. Organizational theory usually focuses on structure and processes, whereas organizational behavior focuses
on the interactions among the actors and subsequent influence on organizational
processes and outcomes. Examining the interactions among institutional actors
deepens our understanding about an organization's beliefs, assumptions, and work
processes (Kuh, 1996).

Functional, Conflict, Symbolic Perspectives

Functionalists focus on issues of order and stability in society. They define society
as a system of interrelated, interdependent parts. The parts are connected so
closely that each one affects all the others as well as the system as a whole. Functionalists consider a function to be the contribution of a part to the larger system and its effects on other parts of the system (Ferrante, 1998, p. 32). A
functionalist would suggest that the roles of the different constituent groups each
serve a purpose within the institution and influence the decision-making process.
The input from different groups serves a balancing function to ensure that decisions are not made without input.

The conflict perspective focuses on conflict as an inevitable fact of social life
and as the most important agent for social change. Conflict can take many forms
besides outright physical confrontation, including subtle manipulation, disagreement, dominance, tension, hostility, and direct competition. Conflict theorists emphasize the role of competition in producing conflict. Dominant and subordinate
groups in society compete for scarce and valued resources (access to material
wealth, education, health care, well paying jobs, etc.). Those who gain control of
these resources strive to protect their own interests against the resistance of others. Conflict theorists draw their inspirations from Karl Marx, who focused on
class conflict (Ferrante, 1998, p. 42). However, everything cannot be explained by
the Marxist variables of race, class, and gender.

The symbolic interaction perspective is concerned with how people define reality, how people make sense of the world, how they experience and define what
they are doing, and how they influence and are influenced by one another. George
Herbert Mead focused on how the self develops, how people attach meanings to
their own and other people's actions, how people learn these meaning and how

meanings evolve. He focused on people and their relationships with one another. He maintained that people learn meanings from others, that we organize our lives around these meanings, and that meanings of symbols change as conditions change (Ferrante, 1998; Mead, 1934).

According to symbolic interactionists, symbols play a central role in social interaction. A symbol is any kind of physical phenomenon—a word, object, color, sound, feeling, odor, movement, taste—to which people assign a meaning or value (White, 1949). The meaning is not evident from the physical phenomena alone. People must share a symbol system if they are to communicate; problems arise when involved parties place different interpretations on the same event. They also show that during interaction, the parties involved do not respond directly to the surroundings and to each other's actions, words, and gestures. Instead they interpret first and then respond on the basis of those interpretations (Blumer, 1969). The interpretation-response process is taken for granted. Usually we are not conscious that the meanings we assign to objects, people, and settings make our world understandable and shape our reactions.

Organizational Frames

The three broad frameworks discussed above are useful to the campus manager who is attempting to understand campus organizational culture. Bolman and Deal (1991) narrow and combine these frameworks to suggest four frames with which organizational culture can be examined: the structural frame, the human resource frame, the political frame, and the symbolic frame.

The structural frame examines the context in which individuals relate and work together. This emphasizes the importance of formal roles and relationships and the organizational structures as well as policies and procedures created to manage them. Problems arise when the structure does not fit the situation and then reorganization occurs to address the problem. The admissions and registration functions are considered to be closely linked at most institutions, but at some institutions a demand for increased enrollments and enrollment management have resulted in separation of the functions. Admissions is reorganized under an institutional advancement unit and registration functions are assigned to academic or student affairs. This structural change is made to provide better service to both new students and continuing registrants. Organizationally, it may make sense for the institution, but the uncoupling of these functions can cause coordination and transition problems.

The human resource frame focuses on the fit between the individual and the organization. Bolman and Deal (1984) state that this results because "organizations are inhabited by people with needs, feelings and prejudices" and they have "both skills and limitations (p. 5)." This relates closely to the concept of environmental pressure and personal needs theorized by Stern (1970) and expanded upon by Walsh (1973) and Huebner (1980; 1989). The fit, or congruence, between a person and their environment or organization is seen as the key to effectiveness and emphasizes the need to tailor organizations to people. For example, the development of summer bridge programs focusing on students of low socioeconomic status and minority students to help them in the transition to an institution is rooted in this frame.

The political frame sees power and politics as central to organizations. This concept "views organizations as arenas of scarce resources where 'power' and 'influence' are constantly affecting the allocation of resources" (Bolman and Deal, p. 5). Conflict is expected because of differences in needs, perspectives, and lifestyles. "Coalitions form around specific interests and change as issues come and go. Problems arise because power is unevenly distributed" (Bolman and Deal, 1984, p. 5). For example, a university decides to build a research facility rather than upgrade classrooms and spaces for students and faculty. This illustrates power playing to market forces for reputational enhancement rather than enhancing the learning environment.

The symbolic frame emphasizes the complexity and ambiguity of organizational phenomena and the extent to which symbols mediate the meaning of organizational events (Bolman and Deal, 1984). "Organizations are viewed as held together more by shared values and culture than by goals and policies" (p. 6). This theoretical construct was offered by Woodard and von Destinon (1993) to help interpret "how constituents perceive a decision" and to "shed light on their subsequent actions" (p. 71). For example, students may protest and occupy the campus library when faced with budget cuts that will reduce library hours. Instead of prohibiting the action, student affairs professionals could work with the protesters and student government to accomplish a protest without incident. The shared values within the culture and the supportive management by student services permits the symbolic action of the students without violating university policy regarding assembly and protest.

Organizational Culture. To further reduce the analysis of culture we look to Schein (1985) who divides culture into three levels: artifacts, values, and basic assumptions and beliefs. Artifacts include both material and non-material culture. Material culture consists of physical objects to which people have attached status or meaning. Non-material culture consists of intangible creations like beliefs, values, and norms. Both offer appropriate concepts to examine institutional behaviors. Kuh and Whitt (1991) suggest three categories of artifacts—rituals, language, and stories—as descriptive of collegiate culture.

Rituals in higher education are social constructions to serve different purposes: communicating important values, (athletic events); welcoming and socializing new colleagues, (orientation) (Gardner, 1986); and celebrating accomplishments, (graduation). Such activities are important because they structure social interaction and provide insight into the quality of life within the community (Kuh and Whitt, 1988; Kuh and Whitt, 1991, p. 55).

Language, both spoken and written, transmits values, thoughts, perceptions, and feelings (Langer, 1953). Every institution has developed a language to communicate with its constituents. The language may be common among institutions, like the "drop/add" process or, although it may be understood by different institutions, it may refer to something or some place different, like "Old Main." And last, the institutional language may be only institution-specific and not understood by anyone outside of the campus culture, like "A Day" at the University of Arizona when the freshmen repaint the large cement "A" on a mountainside overlooking the campus announcing their presence and membership in the university community. Policy statements, operating procedures, and written statements regarding the institutional mission and purpose also communicate important messages to faculty, students, and others. Because colleges are rich in symbolism and ceremony, sensitivity to the nuances of language across groups is important for accurately interpreting events and actions (Kuh and Whitt, 1991, p. 56).

Stories also provide information about student affairs and the institution. As stories are passed on from one student generation to another, they become part of the institutional culture. One example is the story that driving across the state or county line in order to phone in your registration magically grants access and a priority to your call. Such stories are often influential in determining institutional priorities (Kuh and Whitt, 1991, p. 56), although often nothing can be done to dissipate the campus myth.

Schein's (1985) second conceptualization of culture includes values, defined as beliefs about the importance of goals, activities, relationships, and feelings. Many values espoused by student affairs professionals are expressed as themes or guiding principles such as every student is unique (American Council on Education, 1937) and students are ultimately responsible for their own behavior (National Association of Student Personnel Administrators, 1987). Cultural values are likely to be tightly linked to, or at least congruent with, basic beliefs and assumptions (Kuh and Whitt, 1991, p. 56–57).

The third level consists of assumptions and beliefs about the culture. Schein (1985) asserts these are learned responses to threats to institutional survival and exert a powerful influence over what people think about and what they do. Indeed, assumptions and beliefs determine the way in which reality is perceived and unconsciously guide behavior (Kuh and Whitt, 1991, p. 57). This is obvious in the funding appropriations of state legislators who may favor one state institution over another due to their beliefs about campus and community populations and priorities.

Leadership

Boundary management (Morgan, 1986) is a way for leaders to build power. It is the act of "monitoring and controlling boundary transactions" (p. 181). By monitoring, one can identify critical knowledge that places an individual in a position to exercise power as a function of that knowledge. By controlling an individual, one can block or facilitate cross-functional activities. Boundary management is an example of a traditional notion about leadership. As Rogers (1996) points out, a paradigmatic shift has occurred and the view of leadership is changing from a positional authority and power perspective to a relational and cooperative perspective. Power is not used in the sense of controlling over, but rather, power is the collective will and interests of the people working together.

There are many views on leadership. What is important in working with constituent groups is to understand the culture of the group(s) and the context of the issue or problem; different conditions may call for different styles of leadership and different leaders; leaders are not born, but rather leadership qualities can be developed; and leadership is getting people to work together to bring about real change (Komives, Lucas, and McMahon, 1998). Kouzes and Posner (1990) capture the changing paradigm on leadership in describing the five practices common to successful leaders. Leadership is challenging the process; inspiring a shared vision; enabling others to act; modeling the way; and encouraging the heart (p. 8–13). When working with constituent groups, understandings and practices are key to bringing about a resolution to a problem or facilitating real change growing out of shared visions and mutual interests.

Constituent Groups

This section discusses how to develop an understanding of institutional constituent groups through examination of characteristics such as historical or social construction, identity, and informal or external types. "Moreover, it is important to examine both characteristics and types using the various lenses of smaller institutions, private institutions, institutions serving students who were historically denied access to mainstream institutions (Cross, 1996, p.4), and community colleges as well as public colleges and universities."

Characteristics

The work of Pat Cross (1971) represents a sociological view of student differences. Cross argued that the new student coming into the academy in the 1970s had unique characteristics that institutions of higher education were not prepared to address. She defined new students as those who score in the lowest one third among national samples of high school students taking traditional academic ability tests; have had difficulty performing traditional academic tasks; and do not find existing forms of education appropriate. The continuing pressure for institutions to increase enrollment and to reach a wider range in society has resulted in recruitment from this population. Conversely, these students are coming to college as a result of society's emphasis on college degrees as a path to a better life (Cross, 1971; Widdick, Knefelkamp, and Parker, 1980).

The changing mosaic pattern of enrollments is both encouraging and enriching and will continue to expand. Thus, even as educators respond to greater student diversity than in the past, future generations of educators will need to respond to student populations that are even more diverse.

Through a political dynamic lasting several decades, certain groups of students have become recognized as worthy of specific attention. Trow (1973) points out that greater student diversity is accompanied by an evolving social and political consciousness in which groups that have distinctive needs and experiences increase in number and then gain a collective identity that enables them to articulate their concerns and call for appropriate responses. Colleges and universities have taken action to develop special programs appropriate for these students. The process has been a gradual one. A certain number of these students must be present at an institution before they find their voice and seek group-conscious forms of assistance. Typically, adequate institutional response has developed slowly and unevenly with some responding more quickly than others.

Thus far, demographic or personal background factors have gained the most attention. Other characteristics relevant to learning and academic accomplishments have not readily entered into discussion. To spur broader thinking and to help anticipate the future, El-Khawas (1996) suggests characteristics that include two separate dimensions relevant to understanding students and their needs: diversity of background and situational differences.

The first dimension, diversity of background, includes race, ethnicity, class, gender, sexual orientation, students with disabilities, international students, and older and younger students. The second dimension, situational differences, includes the full- or part-time differences by degree objective, intermittent students, transfer students, and differences by type of institution (El-Khawas, 1996). Situational factors also include systematic differences arising from the degree sought (associate's or bachelor's) and the type of institution attended (community college, four-year liberal arts, or university).

These are analytical categories constructed to meet practical objectives, but nevertheless limited and necessarily narrow: an individual's circumstances are affected by multiple, overlapping characteristics, and some characteristics are more meaningful than others for different students at different times. The task for the educator is to make use of distinctive categories as a first step in understanding students; it is also important to develop the ability to integrate information related to several dimensions when approaching any particular situation.

Each of the characteristics that help define today's students will certainly remain important in the future. It is likely that new categories will emerge as well, possibly in response to demographic and economic changes, but also because of the growing awareness that no set of categories can adequately reflect the full array of students. Further sub-groupings will emerge, both in regard to student background and situational differences. Use them all, taking advantage of the strengths of each for suitable purposes or occasions. The theories that you take with you as a manager will influence what you see, what you understand, what you do, and, ultimately, how effective you are as a manager (Bolman and Deal, 1984, p. 25).

Types of Constituent Groups

Faculty. All institutions have some level of faculty governance. Whether existing for their own political or self-serving interests, groups such as the faculty senate, undergraduate and graduate councils, college and departmental councils or advisory groups, and groups like the American Association of University Professors (or self-appointed "watchdog" groups) all attempt to exert their formal or informal influence on institutional governance. The following guidelines are offered to position student affairs professionals as knowledgeable individuals regarding the role of faculty in institutional governance.

First learn which groups have campus-wide support and have been effective. Second, identify the splinter groups and learn about their issues and power base. Third, do not underestimate the influence and role of different factions and temporal groups. Fourth, know the leadership and gain an understanding of which issues drive the group; for example, personnel, budget, curriculum, or quality of the educational experience. Finally, make use of the different governance/advisory groups according to function through information sharing, consultation, and, where appropriate, presentation of agenda items for debate and resolution.

Staff. Federal law separates employees into two categories: exempt and nonexempt. Generally, these groups are identified as classified staff; for example, clerical, secretarial, or physical plant employees and professional and administrative staff. The classified staff council or advisory group is generally organized for the purpose of representing employees on the conditions of employment (salary raises, merit distribution, paid holidays, child care, or tuition reimbursement for family members) as well as representing a voice on major non-academic policy issues. On some campuses, these groups are unionized and the activity is limited to conditions of employment. The professional/administrative council is usually organized for the purpose of handling issues/concerns with respect to the functions and operations of the institution. Some councils, however, handle conditions of employment either as a recognized function by the institution or on a case-by-case basis when requested by the administration. In some cases, the professional/administrative staff may also be unionized.

Staff and professional organizations serve a useful function but, unless unionized, their role may often be ignored or downplayed. If the action and presence of these groups are not recognized, it may lead to alienation and cynicism on the part of the staff within the organization. To help recognize these groups and affirm their contribution, student affairs professionals should be sure to understand the functions of these groups and their decision-making powers. In addition, know the leaders, ask to receive their mailings, newsletters, or other materials, and occasionally meet with the groups. Demonstrate support for the groups when possible by sponsoring some of their programs and advocating some of their causes. Finally, be cautious not to go beyond the group's institutional role or unintentionally grant authority the group does not or should not have.

Students. Most institutions recognize some form of student governance. The most common form is an elected executive branch, senate or assembly, and judicial branch. Depending on the size and complexity of the institution, there may be separate undergraduate and graduate governance functions as well as governance functions within professional schools/colleges and residence halls. By nature, the interests, characteristics, temperament, and composition of these groups are transient; therefore, the student affairs professional must always guard against stereotyping and becoming insensitive to the changing interests and characteristics of student governance groups. These cardinal rules may help to smooth the annual transition with student governments:

1. Don't be judgmental.
2. Students are knowledgeable and have experiences and perspectives that should be valued.

3. Remember that student government is a learning experience for the students.
4. Maintain an accepting attitude in order to help shape student experience, actions, and future.
5. Above all, stay out of student politics. Commit yourself to work with the elected and appointed officers, whomever they may be.
6. Be an advocate, advisor, information giver, challenger, and arrange opportunities for a fair hearing of student issues regardless of your position or the perceived position of the institution.

Other Student Organizations. There are many constituent groups, but the most important groups to the student affairs professional are the formal or informal student organizations. Working with student organizations is the mainstay of the practitioner's work. Student organizations reflect the size, type, and complexity of an institution and, like student governing associations, are dynamic, changing, and transient in nature.

Formal groups usually are recognized by or registered through student government or some institutional process; organized for a social, service, educational, or honorary purpose; and function according to an approved constitution or statement of purpose. Formal organization and recognition by the institution provides certain privileges to the group, such as funding assistance, and use of facilities and services.

Informal groups tend to be temporal and issue- or interest-specific. For example, concern swept the nation over the murder of Matthew Shepard, a gay student at the University of Wyoming. In response, many vigils, services, and even protests were held on campuses across the nation, yet participants often were not recognized groups, rather they represented communities of concerned constituents. In other cases, these coalitions varied and vanished as concern waned, but in some cases new, recognized organizations were formed. Informal groups also tend to be campus barometers, therefore, the issue/interest they represent should be taken seriously. However, it is important to take other soundings to validate their issue or claim. It is equally important not to invalidate legitimate interests of other recognized campus groups. Again, the sad death of Matthew Shepard provides an example when we remember the controversy of the conflict between the constituents concerned over human rights contrasted against the anti-gay rights advocates and the religious doctrine of some institutions.

Local and State Community. Another major constituency is the local and state community. Groups representing interests in these arenas are just as varied as the campus groups and represent a wide range of governance, professional or business, and special interest groups, as well as friends and alumni.

Governance groups include elected or appointed trustees, regents, and boards, as well as city or county councils, state legislatures and other officials.

Professional and business groups include higher educational institutions, businesses that rely on graduates, and other stakeholders in the local economy.

Special interest groups include groups organized to lobby for specific interests of groups such as minority groups, neighborhood associations, donors, sports fans, or parents. Constituents in this category are not directly connected to the institution through employment or enrollment. Their interest is based on an experience, cause, conflict, or program related to the institution and rooted in their own perceptions of issues. And, their expressions of interest are not always supportive of institutional actions.

National Groups. National groups are less likely to have a physical presence on the campus. Their interests may be strong; however, they are less apt to be physically involved in a debate over campus issues. Instead their presence and pressure is more often exerted in subtle ways. National constituents include Congress, educational associations (like the American Council on Education or the American Association of Community and Junior Colleges), and professional organizations (like the American Association for Counseling and Development or the National Association of Student Personnel Administrators).

Local chapters of a national group may arouse provincial sentiment and exert strong influence on campus. This is usually a factor of strong and committed student leadership or national circumstances that focus attention on the cause. In either case, the presence of the interest group cannot be denied; however, the pressure they exert is often sporadic following a change in leadership and shifting attention on issues.

Interpretation

Tea leaf reading is an apt metaphor to describe the daily analysis of life and culture at an institution. Watching the campus environment is often like watching a pot of tea set to boil. Tea must then steep "so that exactly the right color and strength result" (Leek, 1969, p. 14). Campus managers must assess when to put the lid on an activity and when to add or remove the tea (or catalyst) from the brew. And campus managers, like tea leaf readers, know that, "The quantity of tea leaves is not synonymous to a bigger or better fortune reading" (Leek, 1969, p. 14). Reading the patterns and interpreting the symbols that one sees is the important part. "Many readers have developed their own free interpretation of the symbols formed by the tea cup patterns" (Leek, 1969, p. 16).

The analytical framework best utilized to read tea leaves and to study constituent actions is derived from "symbolic interaction" theory, which draws upon the sociology of everyday life as an organizing framework (Blumer, 1969; Woodard and von Destinon, 1993). The relationship between the individual and society is critical. Symbolic interaction emphasizes the role of interpretation in the mediation of human experiences (Blumer, 1969). Objects, people, situations, and events are intrinsically without meaning and acquire meaning only when it is conferred by humans. According to Bogdan and Biklen (1982, p. 33), the meaning people give their experience, including the process of interpretation, is "essential and constitutive, not accidental or secondary to what the experience is." Human behavior, then, is understandable to the extent that definitions and the process by which they are manufactured are understood (Bogdan and Biklen, 1982). The process of interpreting is not an autonomous act, nor is it determined by any particular force, human or otherwise; individuals interpret with the help of others, but others do not do it for them. Through interaction, the individual constructs meaning. People in a given situation—for example, students in a specific major or student organization—often develop common perspectives because they share common experiences, problems, and backgrounds.

An individual student's actions may be viewed as a product of prior interactions with society and culture and present interactions with the social and cultural characteristics of the institution (von Destinon, 1989). Symbolic interaction theory provides a direction for interpreting these student interactions. The symbolic interactionist, like the campus administrator, will often enter a setting and inquire, "What's going on here?" (Freeman, 1980).

It is important to keep in mind Craven's (1951) criticism that researchers of student behaviors "do not seem to attempt insight into the frame of reference of the student himself" (p. 13). There is no consistency in the variables that have been used at different institutions to assist in understanding the students' point of view and even if there were, it would probably be difficult to measure them quantitatively or to test their relationships statistically. However, there should be an attempt to test their validity through non-statistical methods.

One method of cross-validation, triangulation, supports a finding by showing that other information agrees with it, or at least, does not contradict it (Miles and Huberman, 1984). Webb and others (1965) first used the term triangulation, borrowing it from the field of surveying, to identify the procedure of checking findings against other data to provide convergent evidence. The resources used to attempt triangulation of data are cross validation, if more than one individual reports the same occurrence or perception thereof; responses to questionnaires like the Cooperative Institutional Research Program (CIRP), College Student Experiences Questionnaire (CSEQ), or other institutionally designed instruments; campus police reports; participation and enrollment patterns; etc.

Because the purpose is to learn of constituencies' perceptions and how they influence behavior, it is necessary to consider an analytic method that compares student and group behavior and experiences. Cross-validation is a type of content analysis that aims at a classification of material in terms of a system of categories devised to yield data relevant to specific hypotheses (Berelson, 1954). Miles and Huberman (1984) referred to this as the "modus operandi approach" or "analytic induction" where the finding emerges by seeing or hearing multiple instances of it from different sources (p. 234). Glaser and Strauss (1967, p. 114) also suggest that an "inductive method" of data analysis is required.

Data analysis may be said to be subjective, based on the sensitivity of the campus manager to the nature of the information received. The symbolic view is that the actions of individuals are based on what experiences mean, or symbolize, to them. Like the tea leaf reader, success of analysis depends upon the administration correctly interpreting the campus climate. Decisions on the importance of data, a type of weighting, are dependent on the nature of the data. Certain data may be considered stronger or weaker than others. Miles and Huberman (1984) stated "[s]tronger data can be given more weight in the conclusion. Conversely, a conclusion based on weak or suspect data can be, at the least, held lightly, and optimally, discarded if there is an alternate conclusion with stronger data back of it" (p. 235). Miles and Huberman (1984) also listed markers an analyst can use in deciding to give more weight to some data than to others: data from some informants are "better" because of the informant's knowledge and circumstances; the circumstances of the data collection may have strengthened or weakened the quality of the data; the quality of the data may be stronger because of validation efforts (p. 235–236).

Awareness of these preconceived notions attempts to control the biases of the interpretive campus manager. Certain methodologies are designed to remove subjective elements from the analysis and most view values as separate from facts. Lincoln and Guba (1985) raise four objections to the idea of value-free methodologies: it seems sounder to adopt the axiom of multiple, constructed realities than that of a single, tangible reality; theories are value-determined and facts are theory-laden, therefore, facts are value-determined; values determine the decisions about what to study, how to study it, and what interpretations to make; values influence inquiry (p. 162). Bogdan and Biklen (1982) concur that a value-free methodology is a utopian concept and state, " . . . most opinions and prejudices are rather superficial. The data that are collected provides a much more detailed rendering of events than even the most creatively prejudiced mind might have imagined prior to the study" (p. 42).

The major analytical biases identified by researchers are related to the issues of "representativeness," "availability," and "weighting" (Miles and Huberman, 1984). The archetypal analytical biases include holistic fallacy (interpreting events as more congruent than they really are); elite bias (over-weighting data from articulate, well informed, high-status informants and underrepresenting data from intractable, less articulate, lower status ones); and going native (losing one's perspective and being co-opted into the perceptions and explanations of local informants) (Wax, 1971; Miles and Huberman, 1984, p. 230).

To mitigate the effects of bias, both in the analysis and in the data collection, Nesbitt and Ross (1980) list twelve tactics for confirming conclusions: check for representativeness; check for researcher effects; triangulation; weight the evidence; look at differences (contrast/comparisons); check the meaning of outliers; use extreme cases; rule out spurious relations; replicate a finding; check out rival explanations; look for negative evidence; get feedback from informants (Nesbitt and Ross, 1980; Miles and Huberman, 1984, p. 231).

In order to "attempt insight into the frame of reference of the student himself" (Craven, 1951, p. 13), the theoretical foundation of symbolic interaction analysis can be used to examine the separate findings and to search for important patterns—that is, to yield the "insider's view,"—for example, the meanings students attach to the events of their college lives. This analytical approach to interpretation emphasizes the reciprocal influence of society and culture upon the individual. Symbolic interaction analysis emphasizes the ways individuals' interpretations mediate their experiences.

Constituent groups are able to provide some excuse or justification for their activities by constructing a meaning filtered through their interpreted experiences for any incident or set of circumstances (Rose, 1962). This interpretation of meaning has two facets. First is a psychological meaning—the meaning to the individual, which is highly subjective and personal, and second is the social meaning—the meaning to the collective. Because interpretations of meaning occur through symbols with a learned meaning and value (Rose, 1962), the experiences of students can be said to have meaning only through the values they have attached to symbols they learned through social interactions. Thus, people with similar backgrounds will interpret symbols in a similar manner. This is an unconscious process: the symbols are said to "bubble up" from the individual and collective unconscious carrying shared meanings (Jung, 1964; Rose, 1962). The response of the institution should emerge from those shared meanings, but the interpretation of what the experiences symbolize to the constituents is less concrete.

Working Guidelines and Advice

After issues, leaders, and options have been identified, there are some practical guidelines to follow in working with constituent groups. Constituent groups expect to be treated with respect and taken seriously. Action on the part of the institution that suggests otherwise will antagonize and create unnecessary barriers, and perhaps doom discussions before they begin. Taking the time to understand the characteristics, purposes, and power sources of the constituent group will facilitate discussions and coalesce relationships.

Know Constituents

It is important to identify both the formal and informal leaders and to become acquainted with some of the constituents. Find something in common to talk about. Learn something in advance about the members, their jobs, families, community service, and children. Work on establishing personal relationships and make certain to attend some functions sponsored by the group, this should be an ongoing commitment. Reframing El-Khawas' (1996) advice about students applies to all groups: be open to changing definitions and conditions; use encompassing language; recognize distinctive subgroups while paying attention to broadly felt student needs; and take risks by considering ways in which changing student interests and experiences help identify institutional practices that are outmoded or narrowly conceived (p. 65).

Define and Define Again

This technique provides a hedge against complacency, a call for continuous exploration of exactly what makes students tick, what their concerns are, and how they define issues. The danger is that a certain view of students can become a blinder, obscuring new meanings given by students to what otherwise appear to be the same attitudes. Educators must be aware that in many aspects of communication with students, time-honored approaches may have lost their meaning (El-Khawas, 1996).

Recognize Legitimacy

Groups often feel or believe that the institution does not recognize their legitimacy. For established groups, the institution can recognize the group in many ways, such as attendance at group-sponsored functions and honoring the group or its leaders during a campus ceremony. Be careful not to give a group authority and power beyond their role through exuberance and kindness! Less well known or temporal groups may be recognized by acknowledging their mission or through public statements that support or acknowledge their efforts or actions.

Seek Advice

If you have an upcoming decision that will interest or effect one or more constituencies, seek their advice and include these groups in an advising session. You may have to mediate disputes, but it sometimes helps to defuse the situation by allowing the groups to have input, or feel that they have input, before the decision is made. After the decision has been made, it is difficult to backtrack and try to include the opinions and interests of the differing constituencies. As El-Khawas (1996) points out, the reality of student diversity is too complex for any one person to comprehend it. A pooling of experience and insights by campus professionals will yield better insights and decisions.

Environmental Scanning

Campus managers should continually scan their surroundings for clues to important changes and try to anticipate events. Listen to the stories of students and faculty. Seek out information from external constituents. Keeping an open mind and listening is a powerful way to become alerted to trends and indicators that signal fundamental, long-term change.

Symbolism

Experiences are made powerful by the meanings and values people attach to them. A university seeking to meet student/constituent needs, for example, must recognize that the commonplace policies and procedures of mundane university operations symbolize barriers to be overcome. Effective interventions to empower student/constituents can then be planned.

Scheduling of Meetings

Make certain people have agreed on time, place, and agenda for the meeting. A letter of confirmation should be sent to participants and, when possible, the meeting place should rotate between the institution and a preferred site of the constituent group.

Briefings

After an issue arises, constituents should be kept informed and involved in its development. Serve constituents by presenting a positive attitude toward the issue and not permitting it to wane or ignite. Provide constituents with data they need to assist them in their decision-making process and to educate them on the scope of the issues. Do not withhold information unless it is confidential or cannot be released based on legal grounds or personnel policies. Trust is built on openness and a group will quickly distrust the institution if it believes the institution is withholding information. Remember the symbolic interaction theory—any action on your part will be interpreted by the group, so try to give a clear message.

Secure Feedback

This strategy helps to keep a high level of interest in the issue and permits all groups an opportunity to have input into the decision-making process. This involves both quantitative and qualitative data collection. Not only will important information be collected, but also the constituents will have been provided a documented opportunity to participate.

Recognize Differences

Constituent groups may come from diverse cultural backgrounds or have values that are different from those advocated by an assumed community norm. Through words and actions the institution can influence how the issues are addressed and how divergent values are accepted. Modeling acceptance behaviors may have as strong an effect on the outcome as any other factor in the negotiations. A little sensitive foresight may facilitate the decision process. Remember the legendary wisdom of King Arthur who planned a round table so that no one would assume a higher status from their seating position.

Accept Responsibility

This also means that at times you may have to accept the responsibility for enforcing unpopular decisions made by others. In such a case, do not express your disagreement with the decision, but assert that you are upholding the decision and remind the constituency group that you are responding to their social obligation to recognize the decision even if they do not agree with it.

Do Not Procrastinate

Answer each constituency question as soon as possible. Delays will be inevitable, but dragging your heels over an issue that you know will provoke dissent may only increase the magnitude of that dissent.

No Secrets

Be open about the decision-making process, clear on whose responsibility it is to make the decision, and how and when the decision will be made. Being secretive about the decision-making process will only serve to increase curiosity and foster distrust.

Approve Releases and Agreements

Most accords reached by an institution and a constituent group run the risk of disintegration if there is not a written document signed by both parties and approved press releases. It is also appropriate to designate spokespeople for both groups. Letting others speak usually runs the risk of unintentionally giving misinformation or false impressions.

Summary

In summary, working with constituent groups is based on a sound working knowledge of the beliefs, behavior, and power source of the group; an understanding of how decisions are influenced and made; an identification of the leadership, issues, and options through environmental scanning; and following some simple tips for success on working with constituent groups. Institutions should set into motion an ongoing program of educating constituents about the critical issues faced by the institution and the choices to be made in order to gain constituent support and prepare them for change (Haenicke, 1991). And, the more institutions know about constituent attitudes, life-styles, tastes, and opinions, the easier it is to cultivate a meaningful relationship between the institution and members of the constituent group.

Perhaps the best way to describe and assess the conditions which characterize successful and quality constituent relationships is to reframe the Carnegie principles based on the report, *Campus Life: In Search of Community* (Carnegie Foundation, 1990). These principles are a necessary condition to establishing successful, quality constituent relationships. Constituent relations should be based on

A clear and agreed upon purpose and direction. An institution is an educationally purposeful community where faculty, staff, and students share academic goals and work together for teaching and learning. This is a foundation concept in building strong constituent relationships.

Openness, freedom of expression, and civility. The Carnegie Foundation affirms that freedom of expression and civility on campus should be recognized and protected. This is an important principle to remember, especially, in light of the vigorous campus debates on fighting words, hate speech, and First Amendment rights.

A sense of fair play and respect for each individual. A campus is a just community where individual rights, differences, and diversity are valued and balanced.

Expressing sensitivity to and caring for others. A campus should be a caring community incorporating not just compassion, but empathy and outreach. The well being of each member of the community is of concern and service to others is respected.

Concern for the common good. Members of the campus community must recognize and accept their obligation to the group and agree to procedures intended to guide behavior for the common good.

Respect for the heritage, traditions, and rituals of other groups. Members of different groups must recognize and celebrate, learn from, and understand the diversity of historical and cultural traditions present on campus. Whether these are the customs and traditions of the campus, an ethnic or religious group, or of the locality, understanding and celebrating heritage is an important learning experience.

Each of the Carnegie principles is essential to establishing strong and functional constituent relationships. The University, as a microcosm of society, has a responsibility to educate students to the fundamental values of human rights. If we as practitioners and educators can transmit that premise to students and instill in them an awareness of and respect for the beliefs and actions of others, we help to fulfill our responsibility for shaping society. Teaching civic responsibility should be a central role of our institutions and successfully working with diverse and profoundly different constituent groups is an excellent way to teach and model civic responsibility.

References

American Council on Education. The Student Personnel Point of View. *American Council on Education Studies* (series 1, vol. 1, no. 3). Washington, D.C.: American Council on Education, 1937.

Altbach, P. G., Berdahl, R. O., and Gumport, P. J. *American Higher Education in the Twenty-First Century*. Baltimore: John Hopkins University Press, 1998.

Berelson, B. "Content Analysis." In G. Lindzey (ed.), *Handbook of Social Psychology*. Reading, MA: Addison-Wesley, 1954.

Blumer, H. *Symbolic Interactionism: Perspective and Method*. Englewood Cliffs, NJ: Prentice Hall, 1969.

Bogdan, R. C., and Biklen, S. K. *Qualitative Research for Education: An Introduction to Theory and Methods*. Boston: Allyn and Bacon, 1982.

Bolman, L. G., and Deal, T. E. *Modern Approaches to Understanding and Managing Organizations*. San Francisco: Jossey-Bass, 1984.

Bolman, L. G., and Deal, T. E. *Reframing Organizations: Artistry, Choice, and Leadership*. San Francisco: Jossey-Bass, 1991.

Carnegie Foundation for the Advancement of Teaching. *Campus Life: In Search of Community.* Princeton, NJ: Carnegie Foundation for the Advancement of Teaching, 1990.

Craven, C. J. *Why We Withdrew: An Investigation into the Reasons Male Students Left Syracuse University During the Year 1948, and into Their Attitudes Toward Their College Experience.* Unpublished dissertation, Syracuse University, 1951.

Cross, K. P. *Beyond the Open Door: New Students to Higher Education.* San Francisco: Jossey-Bass, 1971.

Cross, K.P. *New Lenses on Learning.* About Campus, 1996, 1(1) p.4–9

Eckel, P., Hill, B., and Green, M. "On Change: En Route to Transformation." *American Council on Education,* 1998.

El-Khawas, E. "Student Diversity on Today's Campuses." In S. R. Komives and D. B. Woodard, Jr. (eds.) *Student Services: A Handbook for the Profession.* San Francisco: Jossey-Bass, 1996.

Ferrante, J. *Sociology: A Global Perspective,* 3rd ed., Belmont, CA: Wadsworth Publishing Company, 1998.

Freeman, C. R. "Phenomenological Sociology and Ethnomethodology." In J. D. Douglas (ed.), *Introduction to the Sociologies of Everyday Life.* Boston: Allyn and Bacon, 1980.

Gardner, J. W. *The Heart of the Matter: Leader-Constituent Interaction.* Leadership Papers, no. 3. Washington, D.C.: Independent Sector, 1986.

Glaser, B. G., and Strauss, A. L. *The Discovery of Grounded Theory.* Chicago: Aldine Publishing Company, 1967.

Haenicke, D. "Presidential Perspective." *Currents,* 1991, 17 (1), 18–21.

Huebner, L. "Interaction of Student and Campus." In U. Delworth and G. Hansen (eds.), *Student Services: A Handbook for the Profession.* San Francisco: Jossey-Bass, 1980.

Huebner, L. "Interaction of Student and Campus." In U. Delworth and G. Hansen, *Student Services: A Handbook for the Profession,* 2nd ed., San Francisco: Jossey-Bass, 1989.

Jung, C. G. *Man and His Symbols.* New York: Dell Publishing, 1964.

Komives, S. R., Lucas, N., and McMahon, T. R. *Exploring Leadership: For College Students Who Want to Make a Difference.* San Francisco: Jossey-Bass, 1998.

Kouzes, M. J., and Posner, B. Z. *The Leadership Challenge: How to Get Extraordinary Things Done in Organizations.* San Francisco: Jossey-Bass, 1990.

Kuh, G. D. *Cultural Perspectives in Student Affairs Work.* American College Personnel Association: University Press of America, 1993.

Kuh, G. D. "Organizational Theory" in S. R. Komives and D. B. Woodard, Jr. (eds.) *Student Services: A Handbook for the Profession.* San Francisco: Jossey-Bass, 1996.

Kuh, G. D., and Whitt, E. J. *The Invisible Tapestry: Culture in American Colleges and Universities.* ASHE-ERIC Higher Education report, no. 1, Washington, D.C.: Association for the Study of Higher Education, 1988.

Kuh, G. D., and Whitt, E. "Organizational Theory: A Primer." In T. K. Miller and R. B. Winston (eds.), *Administration and Leadership in Student Affairs,* 2nd ed., Muncie, IN: Accelerated Development Inc., 1991.

Langer, S. K. *Feeling and Form.* New York: Scribner and Sons, 1953.

Leek, S. *The Sybil Leek Book of Fortune Telling.* Toronto: Macmillan Company, 1969.

Lincoln, Y. S., and Guba, E. G. *Naturalistic Inquiry.* Beverly Hills: Sage Pub., 1985.

Mead, G. H. *Mind, Self and Society.* Chicago: University of Chicago Press, 1934.

Miles, M. B. and Huberman, A. M. *Qualitative Data Analysis.* Beverly Hills, CA: Sage Publications, 1984.

Morgan, G. *Images of Organization*. Beverly Hills, CA: Sage Publications, 1986.

National Association of Student Personnel Administrators. *A Perspective on Student Affairs*. Iowa City, IA: National Association of Student Personnel Administrators, 1987.

Nesbitt, R. E., and Ross, L. *Human Inference: Strategies and Shortcomings of Social Judgment*. Englewood Cliffs, NJ: Prentice Hall, 1980.

Rogers, J. L. "Leadership." In S. R. Komives and D. B. Woodard, Jr. (ed.), *Student Services: A Handbook for the Profession*. San Francisco: Jossey-Bass, 1996.

Rose, A. M. "A Systematic Summary of Symbolic Interaction Theory." In A. M. Rose (ed.), *Human Behavior and Social Processes*. London: Routledge, 1962.

Schein, E. H. *Organizational Culture and Leadership*. San Francisco: Jossey-Bass, 1985.

Stern, G. G. *People in Context: Measuring Person-Environment Congruence in Education and Industry*. New York: Wiley, 1970.

Trow, M. *Problems in the Transition from Elite to Mass Higher Education*. San Francisco: Carnegie Commission, 1973.

von Destinon, M. A. *The Integration, Involvement, and Persistence of Chicano Students*. Unpublished dissertation, University of Arizona, 1989.

Walsh, W. B. *Theories of Person-Environment Interaction: Implications for the College Student*. The American College Testing Program, 1973.

Wax, R. *Doing Fieldwork: Warnings and Advice*. Chicago: University of Chicago Press, 1971.

Webb, E. J., Campbell, D. T., Schwartz, R. D., and Sechrist, L. *Unobtrusive Measures*. Chicago: Rand McNally, 1965.

White, L. A. *The Science of Culture: A Study of Man and Civilization*. New York: Farrar, Strauss, 1949.

Widdick, C., Knefelkamp, L., and Parker, C. "Student Development." In U. Delworth and G. Hansen (eds.), *Student Services: A Handbook for the Profession*. San Francisco: Jossey-Bass, 1980.

Woodard, D. B., Jr., and von Destinon, M. A. "Identifying and Working with Key Constituent Groups." In M. J. Barr (ed.), *The Handbook of Student Affairs Administration*. San Francisco: Jossey-Bass, 1993.

PART TWO

ORGANIZATIONAL AND MANAGEMENT ISSUES

There is not a perfect and correct model for organizing the services and functions associated with student affairs. Higher education is much too diverse for that and institutions have unique organizational structures. A number of organizational and management issues exist, however, that influence the direction, character and effectiveness of the student affairs enterprise on the college or university campus. Part Two focuses on those issues directly related to the organizational structure and the role of student affairs administrators in higher education.

Chapter Seven focuses on models of administrative oversight for student affairs along with methods to organize the internal functions of student affairs. The strengths and weaknesses of such organizational structures are also presented.

The chapter provides valuable advice when dealing with organizational issues on our individual campuses.

Most student affairs professionals serve as middle managers within their divisions. Department heads, deans and others in the field will profit from the analysis provided by Donald Mills in Chapter Eight.

Staff members are our most important resource as we attempt to meet the challenges of today and tomorrow. Saundra Taylor and Mark von Destinon provide valuable insight and advice on the tasks of selecting, training, supervising and evaluating professional and support staff members in Chapter Nine.

As much as we would like to believe otherwise, higher education is an extremely political environment. In Chapter Eleven, Paul Moore provides cogent advice on negotiating this difficult area of administration.

Planning for, managing and financing facilities has become a central task for many student affairs administrators. In Chapter Twelve, George McClellan and Margaret Barr provide information and advice to those who take on these complex tasks.

Technology has had an enormous impact on student affairs administration.

In Chapter Thirteen, Lee Upcraft and Harold Goldsmith offer new perspectives on a growing field for consideration in student affairs.

Understanding of these management issues is essential to the success of a student affairs administrator. Part Two offers opportunities and options for administrators dealing with complex issues within their institutional environments.

CHAPTER SEVEN

ORGANIZATIONAL AND ADMINISTRATIVE MODELS

David A. Ambler

As we enter the twenty-first century, it is important for the student affairs profession to reflect on its incredible development during the first century of its organized existence. We trace our beginning to 1890 with the appointment of LeBaron Russell Briggs as the first personnel dean at Harvard. As Sandeen notes, Briggs was " . . . a one person student affairs staff!" He had " . . . no job description, no organizational chart, and no set of professional standards to guide him . . ." (Sandeen, 1996, p. 435).

A century later, we find the profession as a highly organized and well established major element of American higher education with a growing presence in countries throughout the world. Student affairs programs are found in every type of postsecondary institution; services are comprehensive and complete and are accepted as essential to the success of every institution's educational mission.

The paradox, however, is that the personnel movements that hatched this unique American educational profession did not necessarily envision the role of student affairs as a part of the higher education establishment. Rhatigan suggests that the profession " . . . was predicated upon being out of the mainstream; how to become (or whether to become) a part of the mainstream is our continuing dilemma . . . ." (Appleton, Briggs, and Rhatigan, 1978, p. 12). Knock, however, believes that "while the student personnel point of view calls for an institutional response to the education of the whole student, the most visible organizational development at most colleges and universities during the 1950s, 1960s, and 1970s was the creation of a separate student personnel services structure (student affairs division)." (Knock, 1985, p. 36).

Intentional or circumstantial, the student personnel movement did in fact become a legitimate part of the higher education bureaucracy. It is the assumption of this chapter, therefore, that the establishment of student affairs as a major administrative element of higher education is the primary reason for its success; this corporate model has served the profession well in the past and will be the source of our success in the new century. But we cannot afford to be complacent; if this profession is to remain a vital element of the American higher education establishment, student affairs must become more sophisticated with regard to delivery of services and partnerships with faculty support of institutional goals.

This chapter will examine several organizational models for higher education and review approaches for administrative oversight in student affairs. The focus then turns to the unique organizational issues within student affairs administrative units. Finally, the strengths and weaknesses of each organizational model will be identified.

Organizational Models in Higher Education

It is important to note that "no universal reporting structure exists that will assure the effectiveness of the student affairs organization. These structures only acquire meaning by demonstrating their worth within a specific institution" (Barr, 1993, p. 96). However, understanding the organizational models that influence the general higher education enterprise is of great value. Kuh (1989) identifies four conventional models by which one can examine different institutional organizational systems. Those models are the rational, the bureaucratic, the collegial and the political models. They are useful tools for understanding the diversity of organizational approaches found in American colleges and universities.

The Rational Model

An appealing model for academicians, the rational model is based on such academic values as rules of logic, order, purposeful direction, and rational and predictable behavior. Such a model requires minimal structure and demonstrates less reliance on formalized regulations and personnel supervision. The model assumes a consensus and common mission for all members and units of the institution. While such a model is more evident in small, private, or religious-oriented colleges, it fails to explain the structures found in large, multipurpose institutions where many of the members have diverse and often competing agendas.

The Bureaucratic Model

Max Weber (1947) developed this model which gives priority to hierarchical power, limits on authority, division of labor, specialization, technical competence, standard operating procedures, rules of work and differential rewards (Hage, 1980). The bureaucratic model is perhaps the most visible model in American colleges and universities; yet its rigidity often renders it inefficient in the creative environment of the academic enterprise. In the student affairs organization, this model frequently restricts or conflicts with the ability of staff members to respond to the unique or special needs of students or the unconventional opportunities for student development.

The Collegial Model

Frequently considered the ideal way to organize an academic community, the collegial model has as its central value the participation of all members of the enterprise in the decision-making process of establishing institutional mission and goals. It assumes a common commitment to the scholarly life. Kuh (1989) identifies the major advantages of the collegial model as consistency with academic traditions, responsiveness to persuasive arguments, roots in democratic traditions, and guarantee of representation in the decision-making structure. However, Kuh indicates that this model is inefficient, insensitive to power differentials, resource availability, and the realities of policy implementation. With respect to student affairs functions, Millett (1978) observes that the collegial model requires reluctant faculty involvement with such issues as student conduct.

The Political Model

This model places emphasis on the importance of power, influence, and conflict resolution. Further, the model encourages the involvement of disparate groups in decision-making and gives priority to policy development as the means of resolving complex problems and issues (Kuh, 1989). Power is most often derived from the ability to control resources and to influence the development of institutional policy. Although this model is often the antithesis of the nature of student affairs work, it does help to explain the sometimes limited ability of student affairs organizations to influence academic policy or secure significant amounts of institutional resources.

While no institution is a pure reflection of any one of these models, elements of each are usually found at every college or university. An understanding of the various elements of organizational models can provide perspective on the different structures for supplying oversight to student affairs and can promote an understanding of the varied internal management structures found in student affairs today.

Models for Administrative Oversight of Student Affairs

Many factors influence the position of the student affairs program in the structure of the college or university. Chief among them are the people and traditions of the institution. Institutions in general and higher education in specific are slow to change. More than most organizations, higher education values tradition. The mission of the institution impacts organizational structure. Private undergraduate colleges frequently extol student development and, consequently, elevate student affairs in the organizational structure. Comprehensive research institutions, on the other hand, may subjugate student affairs to the institutional academic leadership. Finally, the will of the chief executive officer, the president or chancellor, plays a major role in determining the reporting status of the chief student affairs officer.

Whatever the model or the factors that dictate an institution's organizational structure, there are four major models of administrative oversight of student affairs that have emerged over the latter half of the twentieth century: reporting to the chief executive officer, reporting through another institutional officer, the dual reporting structure, and a decentralization model.

Reporting to the Chief Executive Officer

In 1992, this author surveyed one hundred and thirteen institutions from 47 states regarding various aspects of their student affairs organizational structure such as services offered, internal organizational structures, nomenclature and titles, span of control, and location in the university or college hierarchy. At that time, the elevation of the chief student affairs officer to the executive management level of the institution was virtually universal. Most reported to the president or chancellor. This major change in the reporting level of the chief student affairs officer generally occurred in the 1960s and 1970s as student protest regarding civil rights, student rights, and the Vietnam war forced a change in the legal, social, and educational relationships of students with their universities. For the student affairs leader, it created new opportunities to influence institutional, educational, social, and financial policy. While there are always extra risks and liabilities at the top of the organization, this change in the reporting relationship of student affairs is perhaps the most significant factor in the increased importance of the profession today.

Reporting through Another Institutional Officer

The 1992 survey, however, reported that a growing number of institutional vice presidents, including student affairs, were reporting to a campus chief administrative officer such as an executive vice president or provost. A recent survey of a random sample of these same institutions indicates that this trend has continued over the past seven years. The revival and popularity of the "provost model" seems to account for this change in reporting status.

Although some are alarmed by this trend, it appears to be more related to the changing role of the chief executive officer than a diminishing role for the institution's vice presidents. Others, however, viewed the provost as an academic officer with less commitment to student affairs than the president. The important aspect of this model, however, is the locus for decision-making regarding institutional educational policy and financial support: direct access to the provost and the level of participation in the decision-making process seem to determine the degree of satisfaction of student affairs practitioners with this reporting model.

The Dual Reporting Responsibility

In spite of the inherent problems of "serving two masters," the dual-line reporting model remains common in many institutions. It has its "up and down sides" and has several variations. A dual reporting model can bridge the problems of reporting to the president or reporting to another campus officer. It may allow the student affairs officer to participate in policymaking with the president, and at the same time facilitate more frequent support for student affairs operational problems from an executive vice president or provost.

In some institutions where the chief student affairs officer has responsibilities for the financial aspects of certain auxiliary services, a dual-line reporting responsibility may exist with the president and the chief financial officer. For example, a chief student affairs officer may be responsible for all aspects of student housing, but may find that she reports to the president with respect to residential life policies while being accountable to the financial vice president for bond indebtedness, food service, housekeeping, etc. Of the officers surveyed, those who experienced this type of dual-line reporting generally were dissatisfied with this arrangement.

Student affairs officers who report to both the president and the chief academic officer or provost also have mixed feelings about the desirability of this model. Some prefer the consistency of working with the president, whereas others value the close relationship with the provost, academic deans, and the involvement with educational policy development that this type of dual-line reporting permits.

The Decentralized Organizational Structure

Under this model, many student services that might otherwise be part of a central division of student affairs are distributed to academic units or are selectively related to certain academic or non-student affairs administrative units. For example, some academic schools or colleges might be responsible for a variety of services such as orientation, advising and counseling, financial aid, placement, etc. for the students enrolled in their unit. In some colleges and universities, certain services might be provided by academic units specializing in that service. Intramural and recreational services, for example, might be provided by the department of physical education; services for students with disabilities could be assigned to the special education department.

While this model rarely exists in the extreme form, some elements of this model can be found in many institutions. Some would argue for it on the basis of dealing with the whole student; others would advocate it as a way of reducing central administration size and cost. But a decentralized organizational structure usually results in less efficient services, inconsistency of policy, and the treatment of students and, finally, higher costs.

Guiding Principles for Student Affairs Organization and Management

The student affairs profession has seen an evolution in its organizational structure and management style in the several decades since the "personnel deans" were the principal, if not the only, administrators of the program.

"The deans of men and deans of women had relied heavily on the force of their personalities and their reputations as effective teachers in their work as deans. They had no special corner on administrative skills . . . The dean of students position was established to bring some order out of the substantial overlapping which resulted on some campuses. Persons with administrative skills were hired to direct the various staff and offices involved in working with students outside of the classroom . . . The leader was no longer (necessarily) an inspirational figure, but was more likely selected for his/her ability to develop or manage a variety of programs and services in behalf of students" (Appleton, Briggs, and Rhatigan, 1978, p. 20). Only recently has much attention been devoted to understanding and developing effective management styles and structures to address new organizational assignments and political realities. In many ways, the profession has found it difficult and uncomfortable adapting to these new roles and assignments. Our recent history is replete with an unfortunate debate on whether we are educators or administrators. Chief student affairs officers frequently express guilt or remorse at their inability to attend equally to the needs of students as well as those of the organization. The "many hats" that student affairs officials wear in being officers of the institution on the one hand and advocates or student concerns on the other is frequently presented as an unreconcilable paradox. The failure of student affairs to resolve this dilemma stalled our development of effective internal management structures appropriate to our various campuses. We have been slow to provide the would-be chief student affairs officer with the necessary administrative mind-set, the organizational skills, and the management techniques to be successful in our ever-increasing complex and technical institutional structures.

The rationale supporting the administrative or corporate model for student affairs' internal management is based on five assumptions:

1. First, the effective development and delivery of services and programs are the historical and legitimate basis of the profession and its only viable means of accomplishing its educational goals.
2. There is no inherent conflict or dichotomy between the profession's administrative orientation and its educational and developmental goals.
3. In order to effect desired educational outcomes, student services must be effectively managed and coordinated with academic programs and services.
4. Identification with the administrative structure permits student services to influence policy formulation and resource allocation to effect its educational goals.
5. The administrative model provides the student services profession with the greatest flexibility for responding to student and institutional needs with the ability to reach large segments of the student population (Ambler, 1989, pp. 250–251).

With an appreciation for the rationale of the administrative model in student affairs, some guiding principles can be identified that are useful in the development of effective internal management systems. These principles have evolved as much from the observations and practice of the profession as they have from any systematic study of administrative theory.

Origins of Organizational Structures

As noted earlier, organizational structures are more the result of history and personalities than any particular management theory. As Sandeen (1989) suggests, few, if any, executives are given a clean slate when developing their organization. The history of the institution, its mission, the personalities and competencies of its people, the ambiance of its environment, and other such non-objective factors have all played an important role in developing the unique character of an institution. A wise administrator takes cognizance of such factors in planning and implementing any organizational structure.

Role of the Chief Student Affairs Officer

The ascribed role of the chief student affairs officer (CSAO) is the single most important factor in shaping the design and structure of the division of student affairs. If the institution desires that the CSAO function as a member of the executive management team, the internal administrative structure of the division must be developed to permit that role to be effectively met. Conversely, if the CSAO is limited to directing the student services program, a different management structure will be in order.

Organizational Symmetry

The concept of symmetry is important to the efficient operation of a student affairs division. Organizational symmetry suggests that officers of an organization holding positions of similar importance or value should be located in the same administrative stratum. Horizontal communications are of equal importance as the traditional communications "up and down" the organizational ladder. Symmetry permits effective interaction and integration of various units within student affairs and with their counterparts in other sectors of the colleges or university. Middle managers in student affairs must perceive themselves as equals if voluntary coordination of services and programs is to be achieved. "Personnel deans" must feel some equality with their academic counterparts if genuine coordination of student services with academic instruction is to be achieved.

Stability

Although change is often defined as a permanent organizational fixture, there are important advantages to maintaining some stability over time with regard to the structure, titles and administrative responsibilities of the various student affairs programs. Faddish and elaborate titles frequently do not have the same identification and respect of their more traditional predecessors. When a unit has developed a history and reputation for good service, student affairs officers should be cautious about initiating precipitous or superficial organizational changes.

Autonomy

Organizational autonomy should be balanced with program integration. The value of permitting individual administrative units to achieve a high degree of autonomy is constantly debated. Admittedly, such ownership usually promotes responsibility and creativity, yet the danger of isolation from the needs of students and other services is always possible. Functional interdependence of units within the division of student affairs must be balanced with the virtues of individual unit integrity.

Staff Involvement

Individual staff members must be allowed a role in designing the organizational structures in which they will be expected to operate. The corporate model frequently is described as a "top-down" structure with little latitude for individual participation. Yet a wise administrator clearly understands the need to make allowances for individual differences and participation. In designing organizational structures, a responsive CSAO will draw broad parameters and allow subordinates to fill in most of the missing details. Encouraging participation in organizational design releases creativity; giving ownership to the administrative structure insures responsibility.

Titles

Titles are important both to individuals and institutions. Assigning titles that are descriptive and simple, yet reflective of the value of the position and the function, should be a goal of every CSAO. Developing some consensus regarding student affairs nomenclature should be a goal of our national professional organizations.

Titles should also reflect the culture of the campus and have meaning within the institution. Others, within the campus community, should be able to understand the scope of authority of an individual with a specific title. For example, the title dean of students has meaning on most college campuses, whereas the title of dean of human development might send a confusing message regarding the role and scope of the position.

Organizational Communications

Student affairs organizational structure should be viewed as efficient communications systems with a primary goal of minimizing violations of the organization's integrity. Effective communications across the division as well as "up and down" the structure should be a major factor in organizational design. A clear sign of a defective organization is when the classic "end run" becomes a necessary or accepted behavior. The CSAO must have a system and a style that permits communications to flow in various directions without violating the integrity of individuals or the organization. It is possible for the chief executive in student affairs to listen to people on the lower rungs of the organization. If the CSAO has such an "open door" policy, clear and honest communication must occur on a regular basis between the CSAO and the mid-managers within the organization. Failure to do so will contribute to feelings of inadequacy or lack of inclusion by the middle manager.

Models of Internal Management Structures for Student Affairs

In the 1992 survey of more than one hundred student affairs divisions by this author, a wide variety of unique and different organizational structures were evident. In the more recent sample survey of these same student affairs programs, many had experienced institutional changes that affected the division's structure. Common institutional changes that have impacted student affairs structures include the adoption of the provost model, establishment of an institutional executive officer for enrollment management, use of technology, and privatization of services. While these factors have frequently added to or subtracted from the responsibilities of the division of student affairs, the four basic models of management structures for student affairs remain evident in these institutions.

The Revenue Source Model

This model is most common in public universities, where a more complete separation of revenue sources is frequently mandated by state statute. Private institutions may utilize this model as well, but they frequently are less concerned about the differentiation of revenue sources as "commingling" of funds is possible and sometimes desirable.

This model is relatively new in student affairs for it has only been in recent years that many CSAOs have been given responsibility for the financial management of auxiliary services. Such services funded by their own revenue streams or fee-generated income might include housing, student unions, health services, food services, and bookstores. Frequently, the management of these funds will represent as much as eighty percent or more of the chief student affairs officer's fiscal responsibility.

How services are organized in this model will depend on the number of auxiliary units involved, the financial restrictions and requirements of each service, the amount of funds involved, and the extent of other student service functions funded by the general or state appropriated budget of the institution. Frequently, the size of the budget of the auxiliary services will dictate that these units report directly to the CSAO along with other units funded by the institution's budget. A more simplified version of this model has two associates reporting to the chief, each responsible for the functions funded by the two different revenue streams.

This model has the primary advantage of direct accountability for these important financial functions. Because programmatic responsibility is also included, the CSAO can insure that the services operate with a unified philosophy balancing student needs and financial requirements. The primary disadvantage to such a model is the disproportionate amount of time that the chief spends on financial matters, sometimes at the neglect of other student life concerns.

The "Affinity of Services" Model

In those large student affairs divisions where the services and programs offered are quite numerous and diverse, the "Affinity Model" is most attractive. Services are clustered by the nature or commonality of their purpose, usually along the lines of some standard taxonomy of services. A typical set of classifications for this model would include enrollment services (admissions, records, financial aids, registration, and orientation), student life (student activities, discipline, residential life, Greek organizational advising, etc.), student services (counseling, placement, foreign student services, remedial services, etc.), and auxiliary services (student housing, student unions, health services, bookstore, etc.).

Usually this organizational model will have specialists responsible for each cluster of services who report in turn to the CSAO. Each supervisor becomes an expert on the services in that area or cluster and maintains a certain degree of autonomy in fulfilling the responsibilities of the position. The model permits the

CSAO to exercise executive control over all the functions and ensure proper coordination and integration. Specialization remains the primary feature and chief virtue of this model.

There are several potential problems with this model, the most obvious being the highly elongated and bureaucratic structure it entails. The CSAO is at some distance from the various services and runs the danger of becoming isolated from staff and student concerns. Communications become a constant concern and decisions affecting a variety of activities are slowed because of the difficulty in cross-unit consultation. Specialization frequently creates problems of territorial boundaries. In spite of these inherent difficulties, it remains the most common model among large public and private universities.

The "Staff Associates" Model

Between the highly elongated "Affinity of Services" model and the "flat" structure associated with direct supervision, the "Staff Associates" model permits the chief student affairs officer to provide general leadership to the various units in the division while controlling the technical and bureaucratic aspects of administration through a cadre of staff associates. Such associates operate in staff capacities and exercise little or no line authority. They may function with such titles as assistant, associate, coordinator, staff specialist, etc. They usually specialize in such functional areas as budgeting, personnel, program development, research, or systems development and create an infrastructure of services that support the division as well as the chief student affairs officer.

This model has the primary advantage of permitting the CSAO to maintain close contact with each unit and provide leadership through program development and integration. It provides the technical and specialized assistance that unit leaders need without encumbering the time and energies of the CSAO. Specialization is possible without creating artificial territorial boundaries between units. The CSAO can function with ease as part of the executive management of the institution.

Disadvantages of this approach must also be noted. Staff associates can become "power brokers" by using the authority and autonomy they amass in providing their specialized services. There is a constant danger that staff associates can become autonomous authorities unto themselves. The units of the division tend to receive fragmented assistance because no one staff associate can deal with all of a unit's problems. Because of the high degree of specialization and loyalty of the associates to the CSAO, it is sometimes difficult for a unit head to successfully appeal an action to that level.

The Direct Supervision Model

This model is usually found in small colleges or in student affairs units with a limited number of programs and services. In the expanding realm and complexity of student services, this model is a disappearing operational plan, but it does have its strong advocates. Others long or argue for its return. In this model, all student service units report directly to the chief. Assistant vice presidents or assistant deans fulfill staff functions only and regular contact between the CSAO and the unit directors is the norm. The chief becomes both a generalist and a specialist in the areas that comprise the division. Communications are usually complete and decision-making channels are clearly defined and understood. The CSAO is well known to staff, other colleagues, and students.

The primary disadvantage of this model is that there are few institutional settings today where it can be effectively implemented. Few CSAOs are afforded the luxury of operating in such a simplistic fashion. If one or two institutional management functions are added to the responsibilities of the chief, the need for a different organizational model may be triggered.

Summary

The growth and achievement of student affairs programs and organizational structures are among the most unique and remarkable developments in American higher education in the twentieth century. From faculty members serving as "student deans," the student affairs profession has developed into a large and complex major administrative unit in every type of post-secondary higher education.

As we enter the new century, the student affairs units of our colleges and universities are well respected and influential components of the higher education establishment. The profession may be justly proud of its progress in becoming efficient and effective organizational entities, providing sophisticated and well managed programs and services.

Yet the student affairs profession must be mindful of its roots and that its obligations and responsibilities to students must never be lost in its location among the educational power elite. Sandeen astutely warns: "It is very important for student affairs staff to understand that to accomplish their goals they must work in collaboration with their colleagues in academic affairs, business, and development. The relationship of the student affairs organization to the institutional organization as a whole is very important, but it is not as critical to the success of student affairs as the relationships, coalitions, and cooperative programs that can be developed. Student affairs does not become effective on a campus as a result of the power arrangements described on an organizational chart; it earns its role by successfully accomplishing tasks deemed important to the institution" (Sandeen, 1996, p. 436).

References

Ambler, D. "The Administrator Role." In U. Delworth, G. R. Hanson, and Associates, (eds.) *Student Services A Handbook for the Profession.* (2nd. ed.) San Francisco: Jossey-Bass, 1989.

Appleton, J., Briggs, C., and Rhatigan, J. *Pieces of Eight.* Portland, OR: National Association of Student Personnel Administrators Institute of Research and Development, 1978.

Barr, M. J. "Organizational and Administrative Models," in M. J. Barr and Associates, (eds.) *Student Affairs: The Handbook for the Profession.* San Francisco: Jossey-Bass, 1993.

Hage, J. *Theories of Organization: Form, Process, and Transformation.* New York: Wiley, 1980.

Knock, G. H. "Development of Student Services in Higher Education." In M. J. Barr, L. A. Keating, and Associates, (eds.) *Developing Effective Student Service Programs: Systematic Approaches for Practitioners.* San Francisco: Jossey-Bass, 1985.

Kuh, G. D. "Organizational Concepts and Influences," In U. Delworth, G. R. Hanson, and Associates, (eds.) *Student Services: A Handbook for the Profession.* (2nd ed.) San Francisco: Jossey-Bass, 1989.

Millett, J. D. *New Structures of Campus Power: Success and Failures of Emerging Forms of Institutional Governance.* San Francisco: Jossey-Bass, 1978.

Sandeen, A. "Issues Influencing Organization." In U. Delworth, G. R. Hanson, and Associates, (eds.) *Student Services a Handbook for the Profession.* (2nd ed.) San Francisco: Jossey-Bass, 1989.

Sandeen, A. "Organizations, Functions, and Standards of Practice." In S. R. Komives, D. B. Woodard, Jr., and Associates, (eds.) *Student Services: A Handbook for the Profession.* (3rd ed.) San Francisco: Jossey-Bass, 1996.

Weber, M. *The Theory of Social and Economic Organization.* London: Oxford University Press, 1947.

CHAPTER EIGHT

THE ROLE OF THE MIDDLE MANAGER

Donald B. Mills

To paraphrase Charles Dickens, middle management is the best of jobs; it is the worst of jobs. Middle managers frequently have significant responsibilities, but may not have final authority. They implement policy, but may not always feel an integral part of the decision-making process. Often middle managers supervise other staff, but final decisions about staffing levels and compensation may be made by others. They are expected to empower students, but may feel powerless themselves. But even with these limitations, the middle manager plays a vital role in the student affairs function on the campuses of institutions of higher education.

This chapter will discuss the parameters of the middle management role in student affairs and the responsibilities and issues associated with it. The importance of developing positive relationships with subordinates and supervisors will be examined. Career and mobility questions will be presented. The chapter concludes with recommendations for effective practice as a middle manager.

Defining Middle Management in Student Affairs

A precise definition of what constitutes a middle manager proves to be as elusive as developing an exact definition of middle age. Clearly, there are differences between entry-level staff managers and executive-level administrators. But where do the middle managers fit in the structure, and what do they do?

135

The simple answer is that middle managers manage people, money, information, and programs. But perhaps the best starting place is to examine an organizational chart. White, Webb, and Young indicate that middle managers provide support services and other administrative duties linking vertical and horizontal levels of an organizational hierarchy (1990). Allison and Allison declare that a middle manager position is the first rung on a career, rather than just a job (1984). A middle manager always provides supervision of programs (White, Webb, and Young, 1990). Depending on institutional size, middle managers may also supervise staff. Thus, the work is fundamentally different from that of a junior staff member. The trend to teams in management, however, means middle managers may be asked to supervise projects in addition to people.

Because of their position in the organizational hierarchy, middle managers implement and interpret policy, but do not create it. Policy decisions are generally the prerogative of executive-level administrators. Middle managers most often have influence, however, in those decisions directly related to their area of expertise and responsibility. In contrast to lower-level management staff, the middle manager may not be in direct contact with students, but may have a primary relationship with staff. Positions in student affairs that would be classified as middle management include directors and associate directors of functional departments, facilities, and programs such as admissions, residence life, counseling center, student center, alcohol education, and recreation.

Managing Information

Drucker has indicated that industry's definition of a middle manager as someone who is responsible for the production of goods and services is no longer a complete one. Whereas the traditional middle manager was in charge of carrying out production routines, management responsibilities have evolved so that now the middle manager has the added role of knowledge professional (Drucker, 1974). This concept is transferred easily to student affairs and higher education and has become important to the understanding of management in higher education.

Like organizations everywhere, the importance of information in student affairs cannot be underestimated. As institutions of higher education have grown increasingly complex, and the competition for students and resources more intense, gathering and interpreting information has become more important. Successful institutions adapt to changing environmental conditions. Such conditions can be determined only by accurate information. Therefore, the middle manager can assure the success of programs and services only by receiving information and making decisions based on an appropriate interpretation of that information. The implication is that managing information is as integral to the middle manager's job as supervising and as providing programs for students, faculty, and staff.

The middle manager must be familiar with the effects and benefits of technology. Not only must the successful middle manager be computer-literate, but she or he should also be knowledgeable about various methods of using technology to provide better information. Technology is a tool that has the potential to provide more information in support of effective decision-making. From budgeting to research, from analysis to reports, proper use of available technology is a valuable tool for the middle manager.

Types of essential information include demographic data for admissions, retention, housing, and financial aid. In addition, changes in student lifestyles affect virtually all student affairs departments, and economic conditions of the society influence programs like food and health services and the student employment or placement center. Successful managing of data and data collection will maximize the ability of the middle manager to serve students well. But the amount of information can be overwhelming. What are the critical factors? What makes a difference at this institution? What is the important information needed for good decisions at all levels of the organization? The effective middle manager, in consultation with executive level officers, will answer these questions prior to commencing data collection.

Managing Funds

Perhaps the most obvious use of information is involved in managing funds. As funds either become more scarce or have more stringent accountability requirements, the middle manager must not only understand changing conditions but must also develop alternative means of supporting programs.

The budget is the basic document the middle manager uses to implement plans and to develop strategies to achieve objectives. The process of creating an annual budget requires setting programmatic priorities, evaluating staffing needs, and determining levels of material support necessary to accomplish objectives. These priorities, staffing levels, and necessary support are determined in conjunction with the executive-level supervisor and must be consistent with institutional priorities and strategic plans. After budgets have been approved, it is the middle manager's responsibility to execute departmental objectives within those constraints. Funds must be spent for the purpose for which they were budgeted. Changing priorities within a fiscal year should occur only in unusual circumstances and with approval of executive-level officers. Failure to maintain budget integrity has a significant impact on the entire division of student affairs and the institution.

Regardless of the most careful budgeting, situations arise when funds available differ from estimates used in budgeting. The effective middle manager will have well-developed contingency plans. If priorities have been established during the budget process, the programs and services to be deferred during a shortage of funds should easily be determined. In the instance of surplus funds (admittedly more rare), the middle manager should have programs and services identified that could usefully be expanded or added to those existing efforts.

Managing funds, however, also means maintaining an accurate record of expenditures (and income, if appropriate) throughout the fiscal year. Financial reviews should occur on a regular and relatively frequent basis. Midyear corrections due to unexpected expenditures should be initiated by the middle manager. If the middle manager does not make a regular, careful review of financial status, corrections will be imposed by higher management. Although the focus for the middle manager will be the annual budget, long-term financial trends and costs must be considered as well. Costs may escalate and must be predicted well in advance to assure proper budget management.

While the focus for the middle manager will be the annual budget, long-term financial trends (costs and revenues) should be considered as well. Escalating costs or declining revenues (or the reverse) must be predicted as far in advance as possible to assure proper financial and programmatic management.

Influencing the Culture

The middle manager in student affairs has a unique opportunity to understand and change the culture of an institution. By their nature, academic programs are composed of focused knowledge and fields; by contrast, administrative functions are more specific to the institution. Additionally, frequent interaction with students places the profession's middle managers in a unique position to hear institutional myths and traditions and to gain access to institutional information. All these are items that play a part in defining the institutional culture. A skilled middle manager in student affairs processes and shares such information in order to assist in solving problems. Kuh and Whitt (1988) provide valuable insight in understanding the complexity of the culture of institutions of higher education, and middle managers will profit from reading their work (See Chapter 4 of this volume, "Understanding Campus Environments.").

The culture of an organization is composed of its mission and value system. The mission keeps a focus within the organization on doing the right thing. Values define the culture of the organization. The manager understands both and is comfortable in the particular institutional setting. The question is not only what does a person know, but are their values, decision-making styles, and methods of adapting to changing conditions compatible with the institution (Hanaka and Hawkins, 1997)?

At the center of the culture of higher education is the academic enterprise. Faculty sometime maintain that the functions performed by middle managers in student affairs take funds from necessary academic programs and are contrary to the essential institutional culture. The astute middle manager develops positive and fruitful relationships with the faculty. Even though the institutional culture may have an academic core, middle managers in student affairs are in a unique position to understand that culture and to impart it to students and other staff.

Managing a Career

Executive-level positions will usually be filled from the ranks of the middle manager. Because of this potential for advancement, middle managers must be conscious of the career aspects of a position, not just the job requirements (Allison and Allison, 1984). Of course, not all of these managers want to be promoted to an executive level. Whatever their ultimate career decision—movement up the organization or the equally important role of increasing skills and competency at the current job level—a path and goals must be established.

Benke and Disque (1990) describe the difficulty of promotion for the middle manager in higher education. Typically, the higher education hierarchy is organized as a pyramid with many jobs at the base and fewer positions at the summit. Although this situation is true of other organizations as well, in higher education the concept of a career ladder is not well-defined and the number of midrange positions compared to entry-level positions is limited. Further, the means of promotion in institutions is often ill-defined (White, Webb, and Young, 1990). It is, therefore, incumbent upon a middle manager to make deliberate decisions about career aspirations. Individuals should establish career and personal objectives, determine the additional training or information necessary to advance, and develop an individual career plan (Allison and Allison, 1984). Advancement to executive levels in student affairs also requires another important decision on the part of the middle manager. The chief student affairs officer has a general control over a broad range of functional areas. The typical middle manager has specific responsibilities. In preparing for advancement, the middle manager must determine whether a career path should include experience in several areas or a concentration in just one (Allison and Allison, 1984).

Several issues must be considered when planning a career. Factors include individual choice (individual desires, goals, and lifestyles), institutional promotion practices and criteria, and economic conditions (supply and demand). Recognition that promotions can be achieved both by staying within an organization and by moving to another institution is important in determining a career path (White, Webb, and Young, 1990).

Role Issues for Middle Management

The middle manager must resolve many issues to function effectively within the organization, including scope of authority, supervision responsibilities, planning, and the importance of staff development.

Authority

Questions of power and authority are inherent for the middle manager. What can the middle manager decide, and what must receive approval from a higher authority? Should decisions be approved before implementation, or is notification of them appropriate? These questions are especially difficult to resolve when the middle manager has recently been appointed to the position.

Role ambiguity occurs when there is a conflict between expectations and the actual issues that confront the middle manager. Drucker (1974) indicates that an efficient organization demands clear decision-making authority. The participants in the process must agree on what determinations can be made and at what level. Unless authority for decisions is precisely articulated, confusion will result. The responsibility for clarifying any questions rests with both the middle manager and the supervisor. However, experience indicates that the clarification should be initiated by the middle manager, as the results are more critical to his or her performance.

The authority issue is complicated by the development of teams. One management implication of the team approach is that individuals must learn to work at the same time in different organizational structures. For one task they may work in a team, whereas in another they will work in a traditional hierarchical structure. "The executive of the future will require a toolbox full of organizational structures. He will have to select the right tool for each specific task" (Drucker, p. 26, 1998). The middle manager must learn to work in an environment of ambiguity that team approaches and project management creates.

The question of power is also fraught with ambiguity. Although power has its roots in authority, it has many other dimensions of importance to the middle manager. The organizational chart and clarification of authority will create guidelines, but the middle manager must also recognize the power that comes from a variety of sources. In addition to those that are structural elements of a student affairs division (position, budget, size of staff), other sources of power include knowledge, skills, longevity at the institution, and strength of personality. Additionally, some individuals are able to stop projects (passive power) even though their position in the institution is outside student affairs. Recognition of those who have influence greater than their position would indicate will assist the middle manager in determining how to make decisions within the power structure (Allison and Allison, 1984).

Supervision of Staff

Managing staff is a critical element of the middle manager's responsibility. Although it is never an easy task, it is frequently the most rewarding. Entry-level staff members work primarily with students, but the middle manager probably works most closely with staff. The ability to manage staff successfully is generally the determinant of success for the middle manager.

When acting as a supervisor, the middle manager must be more than a manipulator; he or she must be a leader. The middle manager must develop the skills of motivation, delegation, performance appraisal, and staff selection.

Any manager accomplishes goals by working through others. Therefore, inspiring staff to accomplish goals is the essential task of management. Carr (1989) suggests that managers cannot do their other jobs and be constantly "motivating." Only staff members can motivate themselves, so the manager's job is to create an environment in which excellent work by staff is rewarded. Congruence must exist between the achievement of student affairs division objectives and how staff members are rewarded. Staff should be commended for good work and highly rewarded for great work that leads to goal achievement. Mediocre work does not deserve special acknowledgment. Further, the manager has the responsibility to assure that a person's skills and interests are appropriate for the task to be accomplished.

Salary is one form of reward, but not the only one. Other forms include praise, more challenging work assignments, autonomy, and a pleasant work environment. The good manager understands what is important to each staff person. A necessary and effective reward is to involve staff in setting objectives and priorities. Failure to take critical motivating factors into account can lead to diminished work quality (Carr, 1989).

The middle manager has the responsibility to assure that staff groups have the ability to accomplish what is expected. One technique that has gained currency is the supervisor as coach rather than commander. In this approach, the manager adopts a style of guiding rather than dictating. The manager is able to supervise more staff, creates a more flexible work force by providing employees the tools to be self-reliant, and enhances employee job satisfaction by encouraging greater individual responsibility (Gendron, 1998b).

Careful delegation frees the manager to do the job of managing and allows staff the role of accomplishing specific tasks. Three principles are central. First, both responsibility and authority for work should be delegated, and certain boundaries must be clearly understood. Second, middle managers must delegate only what a staff person is ready to handle. Third, they must keep abreast of the items that have been delegated (Carr, 1989).

Performance appraisals are one of the middle manager's most useful tools. Brown (1988) recommends that performance appraisal be approached the way a coach views working with a player or a mentor with a student. It is designed to improve performance and to enhance an individual's skills. Appraisal should be conducted consistently as part of the developmental process for staff. Lack of a formal approach to performance appraisal leads to a system that does not improve morale, appears biased, and may be considered ineffective. A successful program provides the manager with information that can be used to improve performance, determine goals, and evaluate progress (Brown, 1988).

The process of staff selection is obviously key to good staff performance. A well developed position description is the first condition for hiring competent staff. As Gendron (1998b) notes, leading-edge organizations develop clear descriptions of each job that needs to be filled, how the job may evolve in the future, and the type of person needed to fill the position.

Planning

As the twentieth century comes to a close, strategic planning becomes more important to all organizations. Forces external to organizations demand increased effectiveness if they are to thrive in an environment of increased competition and public accountability. To combat the negative possibilities of these forces, organizations have turned to various planning approaches. Traditionally upper management creates plans for implementation by middle management. But any organization that is essentially a knowledge organization recognizes that information flows up as well as down. Successful executives will seek and accept information wherever it is available. And the information available at all levels has the potential to be critical in establishing a successful strategic plan.

Gendron (1998a) states that middle managers can play important roles in the strategic planning process. The middle manager acts as a strategy ambassador bringing information about corporate strategy to front-line workers and brings front-line knowledge back to executives. The cascade of information in this paradigm flows both downward and upward. When the middle manager is involved in the planning process, several important benefits accrue to both the middle manager and the organization. The middle manager assumes a sense of ownership and is motivated by the challenge to provide critical information that will be used by the organization in its future plans. The organization benefits because of the improved quality of information.

The form planning takes will vary depending on the culture of the particular institution. In some cases, a very formal planning structure exists which develops detailed plans complete with benchmarks to measure the level of plan achievement. In these instances, the middle manager may primarily be a provider of information. Mintzberg (1987), however, maintains that strategic plans can take forms other than a deliberate, structured plan. Plans can also emerge. In emergent planning environments, the learning that occurs as the plan is implemented is recirculated into the plan. So the plan is constantly being reworked and rewritten. The middle manager is key in this environment.

If the middle manager works in an environment that does not include them in the formal institutional planning process, the middle manager is not necessarily precluded from involvement in the planning process. The organizational chart should not limit managers. Middle managers may be the first to recognize when existing strategies or processes no longer are effective. For example, an admissions director or residential life director may first recognize changes in student culture that would necessitate changes in institutional plans. Or a financial aid director recognizes changes in governmental policy that will influence institutional plans. When the middle manager recognizes that changes have occurred in the operating environment and there is not a mechanism to provide this information to the executive level, it is appropriate, perhaps vitally important, that middle managers develop a response to the challenges.

The ability to develop a logical argument and present it in a logical way is an extremely powerful tool available to the manager. All organizations will attend to a good idea (Gendron, 1998a). Most institutions value ownership of institutional culture by all levels of the organization and will support the strategic plans developed below the executive level or outside the mindset of the distinct planning function in the organization.

Staff Development

Staff development is a necessary aspect of the middle manager's work. Programs should be designed that not only improve skills, but also challenge individuals intellectually and philosophically. Staff members must be made to feel that they are not stagnating, but are continuing to grow. Staff development can occur through formal programs, individual mentoring, performance appraisals, and self-directed learning (Bryan and Mullendore, 1990). (Part Four of this volume discusses in detail a range of staff development options.)

The middle manager should consider encouraging staff to continue formal education. The development of communication and critical-thinking skills is always an addition to the group. Further, involvement in research and exposure to a breadth of knowledge will provide valuable support to the middle manager (Young, 1997). The value placed on scholarship within the academy will translate into an improved image of the division of student affairs as the educational levels of staff members increase.

Finally, a commitment to a comprehensive staff development plan for staff members in a unit is the manager's best interest. Drucker indicates that one criterion for promotion of a middle manager is whether or not staff members in the unit are prepared to fill the mid-management role, at least on a temporary basis (Drucker, 1974).

Ethics and Credibility

"First, do no harm." The famous admonition from Hippocrates forms the basis of all ethical systems. For the middle manager, generating a solid value system and behaving in an ethical manner is critical to achieving success. The responsibilities of the middle manager create ethical challenges. There are obvious legal issues where the proper courses of action are prescribed by law. And generally there are institutional policies and ethical codes of conduct that define appropriate behavior. But all ethical issues can never be fully codified. Each person is left to develop an ethical system that provides a guide to his own behavior. Young (1997) suggests that building an identity based on values is an essential part of adult development. For Young, essential ingredients of a value-based identity for those in higher education include truth, an understanding of the possibilities and limitations of freedom, equality of opportunity, an environment of justice, community, and spirituality. These same values provide an appropriate foundation for an individual's ethical system.

Essentially the middle manager manages through a variety of techniques, but at root is the sense that a person is honest, fair, credible and can be trusted. In their book *Credibility*, Kouzes and Posner (1993) maintain that leadership is a relationship, "a reciprocal relationship between those who choose to lead and those who decide to follow" (Kouzes and Posner, 1993, p. 1). The essential ingredient in this relationship is credibility. Credibility has a significantly positive experience on the performance of the individual and the organization. Service to the institution and the people of the institution, values consistent with the values of the institution, competency, honesty, and fairness are qualities found in the successful manager. Those who report to and those who supervise the middle manager expect both ethical conduct and credibility from her.

Relationships with the Supervisor

Just as the relationship with those being supervised is crucial to the success of the middle manager, so too is the relationship with the supervisor—most generally the chief or associate chief student affairs officer. The quality of that connection is dependent on a number of factors. A clear authority structure is critical to the middle manager and the whole functional unit. Even though a middle manager may serve as part of a team, there still remains a definite reporting structure. In addition, the person who will make decisions in an emergency situation when the chief student affairs officer may not be present must be clearly designated. Although emergencies cannot be predicted in advance, the responsibility to respond to them can be preassigned (Drucker, 1974).

Responsibility

Although there is a close link between authority and responsibility, there are distinct differences as well. Middle managers may have both responsibility and authority in some areas, but they are also charged with implementing decisions from a higher level. The unpopular message as well as the popular one is often delivered by the middle manager. The middle manager may have to bear the brunt of such a decision, but it is inappropriate to transfer the responsibility for management decisions to the supervisory level. Developing an ability to handle unpopular decisions assists the manager in confronting the inevitable difficulties that are part of management.

Communication

It is especially useful for the middle manager to provide information about issues not directly related to student affairs. An effective student affairs division will interact with units across campus, and keeping the chief student affairs officer informed about these relationships is most important. There must be constant communication between the middle manager and the chief student affairs officer. The supervisor should never be surprised by events on campus. Even though unforeseen problems will develop, middle managers must try to keep the supervisor up to date. It is equally true that the chief student affairs officer should work to keep middle managers well informed about issues being discussed at the executive level.

The communication system should encompass both formal and informal routes. Regularly scheduled, frequent meetings are important, but informal communication is important as well. The middle manager should use all forms of communication, including the phone, e-mail, written reports, and memorandums. Communication should cover both the status of present conditions and also future issues, goals, and plans. These will form a basis for new programs and activities with ongoing guidance from and approval of the supervisor. Any concerns will be resolved before extensive work has been completed. Work will progress in a more orderly and efficient fashion when communication is open and frequent.

Accountability

The middle manager must be accountable to a variety of constituencies—a difficult balancing act because there are competing needs associated with each. Among these constituencies are students, staff, the chief student affairs officer, colleagues, and the institution itself. These competing groups and individuals require differing levels of accountability and especially require that the mid-manager set priorities. It may not be possible to please all constituencies, but acting responsibly toward the institution and chief student affairs officer will almost always assure that other constituencies are properly treated.

A relationship also exists between accountability and authority. To be accountable for performance, middle managers must have the authority to control the functions for which they are answerable. This requirement does not diminish the function of the chief student affairs officer; rather, it is a positive statement of the necessity to clarify lines of control and authority (Drucker, 1974). The need for control reinforces the importance of regular communication with the chief student affairs officer.

Reengineering

At a time when resources are in short supply and therefore ever more precious, and at a time when accountability from external sources is increasing, institutions may take a fresh look at operations to determine if the organization should be structured in a way that better uses available resources. The institution may choose to outsource certain functions or redefine the expectations of institutional units, including student affairs. The middle manager is frequently caught in the center of the process. Although there is no assurance that the middle manager will remain with the institution after reengineering, the effective middle manager will do everything possible to make the process effective. The success of reengineering are openness of decision-making, involvement of employees throughout the organization, an enlargement of job responsibilities, and the redesign of organizational units (Balderston, 1995). The middle manager is best served by making the process work smoothly and successfully.

Middle Manager as Politician

The middle manager by definition serves between other institutional managers. The nature of the position thus requires that political skills be honed and employed as part of the work routine. It should be noted that the word *politician*, as used in this context, carries neither positive nor negative connotations. It is merely a statement of a specific type of necessary skill. (See Chapter 10 in this volume, "The Political Dimensions of Decision Making.".) Coalition building, mediation, negotiating, and bargaining skills are important tools for the manager.

Decision-Making

Every middle manager must develop a style for making decisions. Obviously, all these are made within an environmental context. Hersey and Blanchard (1972) state that the style of decision-making is dependent on the qualities present in those who make up the organization. The middle manager must make judgments about what style best suits the situation. The goal is to choose the style that produces the most effective results. It becomes an important task to assess staff members accurately to determine their readiness to participate in decisions.

Some would maintain that a democratic approach is the most fair way to make decisions, but that is impossible in a bureaucratic organization. The majority does not rule. However, the more a middle manager can share responsibility for decision-making, the more staff members are willing to support decisions and are motivated to achieve common objectives. Involvement is dependent on factors such as experience, staff attitudes, executive staff attitudes, the guidelines for the decision, the amount of time available, and preferred style (Allison and Allison, 1984). Of course, one should not confuse involvement with authority; decisions must still rest with appropriate levels of the organization. Still, effective middle managers will seek ways to share responsibility with staff members and with their senior student affairs officers.

Competition

The middle manager may choose to seek advancement within the student affairs division or within the institution. Although it is generally true that decisions for advancement are based on ability, political issues are also present. Most student affairs organizations are not blatantly political, but they too have their "insider" struggles.

Advancement within the existing structure can occur in three ways. First, a vacancy occurs at a position above the present level, and the middle manager is promoted. Second, the middle manager has assumed more responsibility and has demonstrated worth to the organization beyond what was expected. A position may then be created to promote the middle manager. Third, the middle manager may move to other responsibilities that bring new opportunities and challenges within the organization. In any case, the middle manager must have a career track in mind, a plan to achieve career goals (including additional education, if necessary), and a commitment to the performance levels necessary for advancement (Allison and Allison, 1984).

For advancement to occur, one must also become known to the administrative decision-makers. The best means of increasing visibility is to perform at a high level. Volunteering for institution-wide responsibilities provides that opportunity. Institutional culture and traditions will also determine to a great extent how middle managers interact with those at the top.

Middle managers may find themselves in competition with colleagues for advancement to senior-level positions. This competition should not be allowed to degenerate into an open political fight for the appointment. Neither the individuals nor the institution would benefit. White, Webb, and Young (1990) state that a significant amount of intrinsic support in a student affairs middle management position comes from colleagues. Support from within the institution is much more important to job satisfaction than that from colleagues outside the institution. Therefore, competition for a position can be a source of organizational and personal disruption. The professional attitude of all interested parties should deter the negative aspects of competition for advancement.

The middle manager must also serve as a mediator at times to control competition that may occur between members of the departmental staff. The successful middle manager must recognize and assist those seeking to elevate themselves, but their desire for advancement can never be allowed to come at the expense of another staff member.

Political skills are needed not just for personal success and advancement, however. Student unrest, unhappy parents, angry staff, or disappointed alumni may all come to the attention of the middle manager. Failure to effectively communicate and to defuse a situation may cause serious adverse effects for the institution and for student affairs. The full range of political skills, including coalition-building, persuasion, mediation, and negotiation, as well as clearly stated policies, are often necessary to resolve these issues.

Mobility

For many middle managers, respect from their superiors is a highly significant aspect of their positions. However, almost equally significant is a career commitment and a desire to move to more responsible positions. White, Webb, and Young

(1990) state that most middle managers expect to relocate to achieve advancement. Movement to another institution seems to be required for many student affairs middle managers with fewer than ten years of experience who wish to advance. For those with more than sixteen years experience, institutional loyalty has increased significantly, and advancement is often achieved by accruing more and varied responsibilities within the organization.

Benke and Disque (1990) report that the tenure of chief student affairs officers in their positions is increasing. Moreover, some institutions appoint faculty members to executive-level positions, a situation creating limited opportunities for advancement from mid-management positions. Mobility then must be considered both within the institution and externally.

Though lateral moves may be seen as negative, there is evidence that the path to the chief student affairs office is smoothed by obtaining experience beyond a specific functional unit (White, Webb, and Young, 1990). The middle manager interested in mobility would do well to investigate lateral moves as providing necessary experience for later opportunities.

Professional Development

The middle manager must seek means to develop new skills and competencies. Although these are key to advancement, Drucker argues that they are important for performance as well. Drucker maintains, "We need . . . manager development precisely because tomorrow's jobs and tomorrow's organization can be assumed, with high probability, to be different from today's job and today's organization" (1974, p. 424). The effective middle manager will make new skills a priority.

This kind of development can come from a variety of sources, but a crucial aspect of the undertaking is the evaluation of which skills are to be developed. Both the National Association of Student Personnel Administrators (NASPA) and the American College Personnel Association (ACPA) have provided survey results indicating those skills and competencies that college presidents and chief student affairs officers consider important (White, Webb, and Young, 1990). These include the ability to communicate with a variety of constituencies, analyze needs and create programs, establish policies, understand students, and select and train staff. Obviously, there are others unique to particular institutions, but those listed demonstrate the chief student affairs officer operates from a much more general point of view than the functional unit manager.

Professional associations can be critical for the mobility of middle managers. Not only do they provide opportunities to increase knowledge, develop new abilities, and learn of professional developments, but they can also be used to build networks with colleagues across the country or within a region. It is rare that the middle manager will face a challenge that has not been faced by someone, somewhere. A network can identify those who have faced a similar problem and provide the "voice of experience" to the manager seeking a solution. A network proves exceedingly useful to a person interested in moving to another institution as well as to someone attempting to understand the opportunities available for advancement. The placement centers operated by professional associations are of limited value; however, the informal network can be most helpful. Middle managers should be active in professional associations for several professional reasons, but forging links with colleagues is a major one. (See Chapter 26 in this volume, "The Role of Professional Associations." for more information.)

Opportunities for formal education should not be dismissed by the middle manager. The doctorate is essential for advancement in many institutions. Further, it fosters improved communication and critical thinking skills, improves the ability to conduct research, and exposes the middle manager to a breadth of knowledge necessary for advancement (White, Webb, and Young, 1990). For those who have completed their formal education, many associations and institutions of higher education offer seminars and training sessions designed to respond to critical issues in the field. These have both immediate and long-term benefits for the middle manager.

Some Career Issues

The midlife crisis has become a point of discussion in much of the popular literature of recent years. The scientific literature has also examined the transitions that coincide with middle age. During this time, adults examine careers and career aspirations, take a closer look at family and those relationships, and search for a sense of meaning to life (Schlossberg, Lynch, and Chickering, 1989). These issues are particularly relevant to the middle manager, especially one who has been in a position for several years. The middle manager is "likely to find himself in a spiritual crisis in his early or mid-forties. By that time the great majority will have reached, inevitably, their terminal positions . . . .Suddenly their work will not satisfy them anymore" (Drucker, 1974, p. 420). The successful middle manager will seek ways to ensure a meaningful career.

Middle managers examine their relationship to employing institutions as they might ties to family. The motivation to continue in student affairs and to excel is frequently based on this relationship. The meaning of a position, and ultimately a career, has its roots in the fundamental relationship between the manager and the institution. Failure to find a satisfactory answer to the quest for meaning in the relationship often causes persons to seek career opportunities outside student affairs (White, Webb, and Young, 1990).

Those elements that create the most satisfaction throughout a career have been investigated by White, Webb, and Young (1990). They report that extrinsic sources are support from a supervisor, ability to develop or influence policy, the degree of authority in the position, salary, staff development opportunities, and support from colleagues outside the institution. Intrinsic sources of satisfaction are opportunities to influence students' development, flexibility and freedom to establish daily routine, variety of job responsibilities, freedom to control or change job responsibilities, respect from superiors, and respect from colleagues. An environment that makes possible these elements enhances job satisfaction for the middle manager and minimizes the likelihood of a career midlife crisis.

Summary

The role of middle manager in student affairs, as of those in other organizations, is difficult to define. The nature of the position virtually assures ambiguity about the exact nature of responsibilities. However, middle managers can adopt several approaches to aid in achieving success.

- First, they should define clearly for themselves the position, its authority, and its accountability. The middle manager and the supervisor should agree on this definition.
- Second, middle managers should commit themselves to provide the best supervision of staff possible and to meet institutional goals and objectives.
- Third, they must adopt a management style that helps staff members while enabling the manager to meet performance expectations.
- Fourth, the relationship with the chief student affairs officer or other supervisor should be open and designed to enhance the middle manager's role in the institution.
- Fifth, middle managers must take responsibility for personal development of new skills and competencies.
- Sixth, they should be involved in professional associations to create a network of colleagues for assistance and support.
- Seventh, they should establish a personal career path, with contingencies, to keep professional decisions in focus.
- Eighth, middle managers should analyze which factors that provide job satisfaction and create situations where those factors can be exploited to the maximum extent.

The middle manager has a unique function in a student affairs program. Mid-level managers must select, train, and develop staff. They must implement policy and programs. They must furnish communication both up and down the organizational ladder. They may provide direction to a specific functional program and yet are expected to have an institutional view on issues. Middle-managers may be asked to provide direct assistance in institutional planning and organization reengineering. Finally, middle managers may have designs on a chief student affairs position, but a direct path to that position in one organization is unlikely.

Even with the ambiguities and seeming contradictions inherent in their positions, middle managers provide the leadership of functional areas that form the basis of student affairs programs. They are the knowledge professionals of student affairs programs and have an important influence on each student's development and that of staff members who will be the professional leaders of the next generation. Sandeen (1991) offers insight to the aspiring CEO: know yourself, have a philosophy, pay your dues, be willing to move, select your institution, and love the students. These insights are good advice for the middle manager as well.

References

Allison, M. A., and Allison, E. *Managing Up, Managing Down.* New York: Simon & Schuster, 1984.

Balderston, F. E. *Managing Today's University.* San Francisco: Jossey-Bass, 1995.

Benke, M., and Disque, C. S. "Moving In, Out, Up, or Nowhere? The Mobility of Mid-Managers." In R. B. Young (ed.), *The Invisible Leaders: Student Affairs Mid-Managers.* Washington, D.C.: National Association of Student Personnel Administrators, 1990.

Brown, R. D. "The Need for the Purpose of a Performance Appraisals System." In R. D. Brown (ed.), *Performance Appraisal as a Tool for Staff Development.* New Directions for Student Services, no. 43. San Francisco: Jossey-Bass, 1988.

Bryan, W. A., and Mullendore, R. H. "Professional Development Strategies." In R. B. Young (ed.), *The Invisible Leaders: Student Affairs Mid-Mangers.* Washington, D.C.: National Association of Student Personnel Administrators, 1990.

Carr, C. *The New Manager's Survival Manual.* New York: Wiley, 1989.

Drucker, P. F. *Management: Task, Responsibilities, Practices.* New York: Harper Collins, 1974.

Drucker, P. F. "Management's New Paradigms." *Forbes,* October 5, 1998.

Gendron, M. "Strategic Planning—Why It's Not Just for Senior Managers Anymore." *Harvard Management Update,* vol. 3, #5, May 1998a.

Gendron, M. "Keys to Retaining Your Best Managers in a Tight Job Market." *Harvard Management Update,* vol. 3, #6, June 1998b.

Hanaka, M. E., and Hawkins, B. "Organizing for Endless Winning." In F. Hesselbein, M. Goldsmith, and R. Beckhard (eds.), *The Organization of the Future.* San Francisco: Jossey-Bass, 1997.

Hersey, P., and Blanchard, K. H. *Management of Organizational Behavior: Utilizing Human Resources.* Englewood Cliffs, NJ: Prentice-Hall, 1972.

Kouzes, J. M. and Posner, B. Z. *Credibility.* San Francisco: Jossey-Bass, 1993.

Kuh, G. D., and Whitt, E. J. *The Invisible Tapestry: Culture in American Colleges and Universities.* ASHE-ERIC Higher Education Report, no. 1. Washington, D.C.: Association for the Study of Higher Education, 1988.

Mintzberg, H. "Crafting Strategy." *Harvard Business Review,* Jul.-Aug., 1987.

Sandeen, C.A. *The Chief Student Affairs Officer.* San Francisco: Jossey-Bass, 1991.

Schlossberg, N. K., Lynch, A. Q., and Chickering, A. W. *Improving Higher Education Environments for Adults: Responsive Programs and Services from Entry to Departure.* San Francisco: Jossey-Bass, 1989.

White, J., Webb, L., and Young, R. B. "Press and Stress: A Comparative Study of Institutional Factors Affecting the Work of Mid-Managers." In R. B. Young (ed.), *The Invisible Leaders: Student Affairs Mid-Managers.* Washington, D.C.: National Association of Student Personnel Administrators, 1990.

Young, R. B. *No Neutral Ground.* San Francisco: Jossey-Bass, 1997.

CHAPTER NINE

SELECTING, TRAINING, SUPERVISING, AND EVALUATING STAFF

Saundra L. Taylor and Mark von Destinon

The selection, development, and retention of staff has become more difficult and critical in the second half of this century due to increases in the mobility of our population and the complexity of positions. The pace of change has
resulted in increases in education, social mobility, and a global economy (Ferrante,
1998). As we move into the third millennium the pace of change is accelerating.
In the Agricultural Age it took centuries to implement change, the Industrial Age
reduced the centuries to decades, and now the rate of change has been compressed into years, if not months, thanks to the advent of the Information Age
(Breivik, 1998; Dolence and Norris, 1995; Emmi, 1998; Ferrante, 1998; Toeffler,
1970). Colleges and universities are essential to producing the "knowledge workers" to fill the new positions and changing position requirements demanded
(Emmi, 1998, p. 3). Institutions of higher education must serve as not only academic training fields to provide curriculum and instruction, but also as supple-
mentary training fields to provide both life skills and work experience.

The divisions of student affairs and human resources serve to operationalize
life skills and experiential training. Combining these entities allows us to integrate
the services provided by these areas consciously and holistically. These campus
divisions are labor-intensive human services providers who work to meet the needs
and goals of both the providers and recipients of those services. Some of these mutual needs include a safe and healthy environment, a learning environment, com-

petitive salaries and benefits, diversity in the work place, a just and honorable community, mutual respect and recognition, and work-life connections (Hadley, 1997). How well they do this is measured in each area by student and employee success, commitment, and retention. The linkage between these areas looks at students as present or future employees and at employees, as continuing students in an era of information literacy and resource-based learning (Breivik, 1998; Hadley, 1997).

This chapter offers an examination of the blending of the cultures of student affairs and human resources within higher education. To provide a context for the examination of this cultural shift, we draw on a sociological paradigm that looks at the philosophy, mission, operation, and experience of the student affairs and human resources areas. As an explanatory thread for the blending and interaction of these cultures, we draw upon proverbs of the mid-nineteenth century African American culture as it transitioned from bondage to freedom (Mieder, 1989; Prahlad, 1996). The proverbs grew out of the forced blending of many African cultures with the European cultural roots of the masters and they express common values related to work ethics. Their relationship to the blending of the higher education cultures lies not in the concept of forced cultural clash, but in the spirit of a work ethic towards accomplishing similar goals.

This chapter focuses on the role of organizational culture in staff selection and development and how they affect human behavior within organizations. It is rooted in the experience of the University of Cincinnati and the University of Arizona where the student affairs and human resources units have been combined under one administrative umbrella because of their commonalities of mission and purpose. The importance of multicultural awareness and person-environment interaction as they apply to campus culture and climate are examined. The impact of technology and institutional size on the hierarchy within staff lines and employee turnover are reviewed. The employee evaluation process, its legal requirements, and implications are discussed. The chapter ends with a review of the guidelines and advice offered to the student affairs practitioner.

Organizational Climate and Culture

"You've got eyes to see and wisdom not to see."

In the mid–19th century African American culture, ignoring or pretending not to know about something could keep a person out of trouble. This emphasizes the values of prudence and caution and relates to the concept we know today as environmental scanning. Woodard and von Destinon (1993) describe environmental scanning as looking "for any trend or event that may have an impact on the institution" (p. 73). Scanning our institutional environments reveals pressing demands for technologically competent knowledge workers and issues include an organizational culture change that reflects an emphasis on not only the productivity, but also the selection, training, development, and retraining of knowledge workers. Kuh and Whitt (1991) laid the groundwork to explain this cultural shift in student services in their review of human relations management. They suggest that the answer lies in the study of productivity in the workplace at the Hawthorne, Illinois electric plant (Filley, House, and Kerr, 1976) which found that human factors such as worker involvement, motivation, morale, and group dynamics were significant determinants of productivity (Hersey and Blanchard, 1982; Owens, 1981). Human relations management is the area which shares a common body of theory with the area of student development.

The study of human relations management focuses on the people in organizations by studying their emotional and social nature, as well as their experiences and interactions within diversified organizations (Kuh and Whitt, 1991). Human relations management theory provides operational paradigms for understanding the functions of human resources units (Hersey and Blanchard, 1982) and student development theory provides similar underpinnings to the field of student affairs. Both disciplines operate within the context of organizational culture which Richardson and Skinner (1991) defines as the assumptions and beliefs shared by members. They examined how institutions change to achieve a better balance between the emphasis given to student retention and the focus on changing the environment to promote higher levels of student achievement. This examination of student services functions and their relation to student success and achievement provides a conceptual parallel to the mission and goals of the human resources unit. The answer to institutional change suggested by Richardson and Skinner (1991) involves the management of organizational culture.

Human Behavior within Organizations

"The old sheep wonder where the yarn socks come from."

This African American proverb suggests that everything is not as it appears, and draws attention to cause and effect relationships. When examining human behavior within organizations, it is natural to consider motivations, cause, and effect for that behavior. Clark (1985) describes organizational behavior theory as "neo-orthodox" theory, a concept that acknowledges that the psychological and social environments that make up organizations also shape human behavior. Organizational performance is also affected by their social, economic, political, and technological contexts (Clark, 1985; Kuh and Whitt, 1991).

Schneider (1990) offers a behavioral perspective on organizational culture that suggests there are many cultures in an organization. This provides a rationale to identify the functions of student affairs and human resources as independent subcultures. A dominant culture evolves when behavioral influences emerge. Each influence must be reviewed from the perspective of its contribution to an understanding of the culture from a behavioral viewpoint and in terms of its implications for cultural formation, maintenance, and change. Management has a definite stake in the development of a culture that will be compatible with institutional goals. Various aspects of both a student's and an employee's environment, whether they are perceived separately or collectively, can affect culture formation and can be managed. The development of a culture combining student affairs and human resources can be influenced over time with consistent application of behavioral principles (Thompson and Luthans, 1990).

Organizational Culture and Leadership

"Tomorrow might be the carriage-driver's day for plowing."

This expression emphasizes the distinction of roles within a culture and speaks not only to an acceptance of a cultural hierarchy, but also to shifting paradigms. In the higher education context, culture is the collective patterns of norms, values, practices, and beliefs which guide behavior and provides a framework toward interpreting events and actions (Kuh and Whitt, 1988). This view contends that to understand and appreciate behavior, the assumptions and beliefs shared within the culture must be considered. To analyze behavior, Schein (1985) divides culture into three levels: artifacts, values, and beliefs. Kuh and Whitt (1991) used three categories of artifacts to illustrate Schein's concept: rituals, language, and stories.

Rituals. Colleges, as cultures, are rich in traditions, symbolism, and ceremony. In college and university settings, rituals are social constructs that communicate values, socialize new colleagues, and celebrate accomplishments. Examples of rituals include orientation, convocation, registration, commencement, and social activities like student functions, annual staff holiday gatherings, and end of the year celebrations. These activities are important because they provide structure for social interaction and give insight into the quality of life within the community. Rituals also serve as standards through which members of the culture assess, define, and refine their behavior (Kuh and Whitt, 1988, Kuh and Whitt, 1991) and become part of the context for performance evaluations of staff.

Language. Language, both spoken and written, is the vehicle through which values, thoughts, perceptions, and feelings are transmitted (Langer, 1953). Both student affairs and human resources professionals have developed a language which revolves around people to communicate within their respective cultures. Yet now they need to develop a common language to communicate with each other. Concepts such as "student development" or "faculty and staff development" have different meanings inside the organization, with individuals interpreting them in their own way and for their own purposes. Policy statements, operating procedures, and written statements of philosophy and mission, also communicate important messages to faculty, staff, and students about institutional values, but translating these into practice differs from one campus subculture to another. The concept of student development must evolve from the notion of intellectual, physical, and personal development to include skills training. At the same time, the concept of faculty and staff development needs to be more holistic and give thought to the personal development of employees beyond the skills that contribute to their jobs. Having a common language, and being sensitive to the nuances of that language, recognizes the importance of interpreting events and actions in order to make progress towards institutional goals (Kuh, Whitt, and Shedd, 1987; Kuh and Whitt, 1991; Masland, 1985).

Stories. Stories are narratives, anecdotes, or urban legends that provide information about student affairs, human resources, and the institution. As stories are passed on from one student or employee generation to the next, they may become legends that are tightly woven into the institutional culture. Examples of such myths are the academic legends that students must wait fifteen minutes for an instructor who is late for class or the belief that institutions never hire doctorates earned at their own institution. Such stories often have a profound impact upon the decisions relating to institutional priorities and actions (Kuh and Whitt, 1988; Kuh and Whitt, 1991).

Values. Schein's (1985) second level of culture is made up of values, which he defines as widely held beliefs about the importance of certain goals, activities, relationships, and feelings. Many values embraced by student affairs are shared by human resources. This can be seen in the beliefs and assumptions inherent in the report *Campus Life: In Search of Community* (Carnegie Foundation, 1990), which can be reframed to illustrate the functions of both student affairs and human resources:

- Purposeful Community: where faculty staff and students share goals and work together for teaching and learning.
- Open Community: where freedom of expression and civility on campus are recognized and protected.
- Just Community: where individual rights, differences, and diversity are valued and balanced.
- Caring Community: where the well-being of each member of the community is of concern, and service to others is respected.
- Disciplined Community: where members of the campus community recognize and accept their obligation to the common good.
- Celebrative Community: where there is respect for the heritage, traditions, and rituals of others (Carnegie Foundation, 1990).

Cultural values are likely to be congruent with these basic assumptions. Institutional statements about the drug-free workplace serve to communicate the institution's values under certain circumstances (Gehring, 1996). For example, when statements are repeated often and are accompanied by behaviors, like programming, it suggests a depth of institutional attention to and commitment on the issue. Of course, some values are merely espoused (Argyris and Schon, 1978) and although they "should" predict what people say in certain situations, they may not "be" represented in their actions. Espoused values are more like aspirations or rationalizations (Schein, 1985). Examples of espoused values abound in student affairs and human resources divisions. There are public statements about the need to increase minority representation among students and staff while few people of color are admitted or hired. There is the assertion that individuals are responsible for their actions while each year additional rules are added to the student code of conduct. And last, there are policies that underscore the institution's commitment to holistic development of students and staff while practice shows a disproportionate amount of time spent on grievance and discipline (Kuh and Whitt, 1991).

Beliefs. The third level focuses on beliefs identified by Schein (1985) to be the core of culture. These consist of basic, yet often unstated, assumptions that underlie artifacts and values. Schein contends that these beliefs are responses to threats and exert a powerful influence over how students and employees think and act. An example of an unstated assumption includes the notion of social mobility (that an individual can achieve a desired level of education, income, and standard of living through hard work) (Ferrante, 1998). Assumptions and beliefs determine the way in which reality is perceived and unconsciously guide behavior (Kuh and Whitt, 1991; Schein, 1985).

Multicultrual Awareness

"Sometimes the runt pig beats the whole litter growing."

This observation developed from a perception of livestock and its use in the vernacular and here draws an almost offensive parallel between ownership of livestock and the status of people. It refers to people who may, at first, seem at a disadvantage in some way, yet often end up amounting to more than their peers, and reinforces the notion that appearances can be deceiving. The blending of ethnic and social cultures, within the construct of an institution of higher learning, gives emphasis to the need for multicultural awareness as we combine attention to student affairs and human resources. This proverb also emphasizes the need for institutions to bear in mind that students and employees have needs, rights, and emotions that must be acknowledged.

According to Pusch and Hoopes (as cited in Pusch, 1979) "multiculturalism is a state of being in which an individual feels comfortable and communicates effectively with people from any culture, in any situation, because she or he has developed the necessary knowledge and skills to do so." Talbot (1996) also points out, "Multiculturalism is not an inherent characteristic of an individual, no matter his or her race, ethnicity, or gender; rather, it is based on an individual's ability and openness to learn" (p. 381). Comfort within the workplace and educational setting results not only from physical amenities, like heating, cooling, and parking, but also to the psychological assurances of respect, acceptance, justice, appreciation, and belonging within the campus community.

"A multicultural organization is one that is genuinely committed to diverse representation of its membership; is sensitive to maintaining an open, supportive and responsive environment; is working toward and purposefully including elements of diverse cultures in its ongoing operation; and . . . is authentic in its response to issues confronting it" (Barr and Strong, 1988, p. 85). The goal of achieving a multicultural workplace and learning environment is essential to shaping the selection of staff and students, the kind of training afforded to staff and students, and the evaluation of individuals and the institution making progress toward a diverse community.

Employee Selection

"A new broom sweeps clean, but an old broom knows the corners."

This adage is relevant to the issues of employee selection. Do you choose an experienced employee or one fresh out of college with training in the latest technology? One answer to this human resources dilemma can be found in student affairs theory in the models of person-environment interaction. This model provides a paradigm that transfers easily to the selection of personnel.

The models of person-environment interaction (Huebner, 1989) provide a framework within which institutions can redesign human resources policies to improve employee selection procedures as well as their rewards and employee recruitment techniques. Lessons can be learned from the food service industry, a service-oriented profession, which has already realized the importance of a paradigm shift that suggests human development opportunities will make people want to come to work for the organization (recruitment), be more satisfied on the job (productivity), and more satisfied with their opportunity for longevity and promotion (retention) (Martin, 1998). Human resources can benefit from the lessons in effective recruiting, screening of candidates, and the most effective techniques to do so that have been learned by student services through theory and practice. Conversely, student services can learn from human resources theory to manage organizational culture through strategic planning, by coordinating and controlling the implementation of plans, by selecting new staff who embody the values and behaviors desired, and by providing incentives and support to existing staff to encourage them to change in desired directions (Richardson and Skinner, 1991).

Too often the culture of higher education is organized along "silo" lines, and that has a strong impact on employee selection, training, supervision, and evaluation. A silo is a contained unit used for storage and separate from other structures around it. The many divisions of an institution cannot stand alone like silos. The challenge is for the profession to transform itself (Komives and Woodard, 1996) and many have called for a shift away from the conventional concepts about teaching and learning and how educational systems have been organized (Breivik, 1998; Komives and Woodard, 1996; Kuh, 1996; Rogers, 1996). The activities of employee selection, training, supervision, and evaluation of staff cannot be left to a "hit or miss" approach or seen as the province of human resources with no sense of partnership across units or divisions. Often conflicts exist between human resources and other divisions within the institution resulting from perceptions of immediate need versus fair hiring practices or appropriate procedures. The challenge and ultimate goal is that the student learning environment and the quality of student, faculty, and staff life on campus "are as good as circumstances permit" (Brown, 1988, p. 4).

Often the selection to fill a staff vacancy presents a dilemma for managers and the ensuing selection process becomes a "no win" situation. When defining mission and purpose, it is advantageous to spend time establishing ground rules for employee recruitment and selection. Educating the staff through discussion, understanding the selection, establishing selection criteria and process for all staff levels, and holding them consistent helps to reduce interoffice conflict over position vacancies and contributes to the perception of a fair system.

The debate rages over whether internal candidates have an advantage in the hiring process. It can be argued that internal candidates' knowledge of and experience with institutional processes will insure a smooth transition and many believe it is better to hire a known, rather than an unknown, quantity. Yet critics argue that it permits a degree of social control by the administration, promotes "inbreeding" and maintains the status quo. Opponents of internal selection will argue that often "familiarity breeds contempt." While preselection is against the law, favoritism in the selection process is not, although many consider it unethical.

Human Relations and Technology

"Rails split before breakfast will season the dinner."

This adage from the pre-industrial background of sharecropping and intense manual labor draws attention to the work ethic and seasonal nature of agricultural labor in the fields. The notion that hard work now will make other tasks easier in the future turns attention to the continued need for training in both human relations and technology, as well as increased productivity offered by technology. Training must be firmly focused on continuous learning. The pace of change in the world is so great that managers and their staff need to constantly update their skills (Breivik, 1998; Toffler, 1970) and institutions should allow time and opportunities for people to do so. Organizations that fail to promote skill development are likely to suffer as their employees struggle to keep pace with changes in technical areas (Hastings, 1998). Technological advancements are here and traditional staff and student support services now need to catch up. Specifically, students and all levels of staff "must learn to anticipate the directions and rate of change. All of this will require broad, imaginative innovations in our educational system" (Toffler, 1970, p. 25).

Breivik (1998) contends that both the explosion of and access to information are reshaping both learning and teaching and offers the concepts of information literacy and resource-based learning as a new educational paradigm. The definition of information literacy is summarized as the "abilities to locate, organize, evaluate, and communicate information" (Breivik, 1998, p. 6). Students, as well as faculty and staff, have to be schooled not only in how to find the information but how to interpret and understand it. Resource-based learning shifts the focus from teaching to learning by making students responsible for selecting their own learning materials from the information resources available (Breivik, 1998). This recognizes the impact of the Internet and other technological advancements that have placed information at our fingertips, and the impact of technology on instructional methods. In addition, it provides a mechanism to address differences in students' educational styles and needs.

Resource-based learning brings the Montessori (1984) method of education, focusing on the development of a child's own initiative, into lifelong learning. The work and learning opportunities presented in higher education through cooperative education programs, internships, and practicums bring the role of a student/worker's initiative into job preparation. Peterson (1983) suggests "andragogy" to describe the instructional process for adults as differentiated from pedagogy, the instructional process for children. The traditional pedagogical view is that knowledge is transmitted from the teacher to the student, but that view is no longer appropriate because knowledge changes so rapidly. Andragogy emphasizes the development of learning skills and the continuing practice of those skills throughout the lifetime (Knowles, 1980; Peterson, 1983). This is true of on-the-job training and employee retraining. Now, perhaps more than at any time previous, we expect students and employees to be lifelong learners and not only to know how, but to have the desire, to access information.

It can be argued that information literacy and resource-based learning operate on the student or employee's need to know where to find information for a specific interest or task and not on the general mastery of a particular content area. Under this model, instruction becomes facilitation as motivated students and employees are guided to establish the contextual relationships between the simple acquisition of data and knowledge as well as between theory and practice. The development of career programs and technological innovations in the community colleges led to increasingly close relationships with business and industry, and provided those institutions many opportunities to attract already employed students, a clientele that needed no changing to benefit from the work-related programs their employers helped to establish (Richardson, 1991). Thus, the foundation for on-the-job training and employee skill development has already been laid. The challenge to institutions now is to utilize the programs already developed to implement technology to benefit employees within their own organizations.

Staff Hierarchy

"Raindrops can't tell broadcloth from jeans."

This expression recognizes differences in skills and preparation as well as in experience and ability, yet, at the same time, notes the commonalities of purpose and mission. In the antebellum culture of the old South, there were small farmers and large plantations each with specific needs, just as we have institutions of higher education today that vary by size and type. Just as the reentry and older-than-average students are blurring the meaning of college class standing, so too have the distinctions between students and staff and on-the-job responsibilities been blurred based on preparation, experience, and employment.

How we select and train our students, faculty, and staff has become of critical importance. Just as student development has focused on the holistic development of the student, so too must human resources recognize the untapped potential within faculty and staff and work to develop it. The diligent, motivated individual who may start out as a resident assistant and educates herself throughout the institution could one day be your senior student affairs officer (Singer and Kamin, 1998). Imagine the response from our staff if we fostered their development in the same way in which we try to provide student development programming in the residence halls!

The Operations Staff. Operations refer to the front-line staff, and this area represents the focal point for identifying threats and opportunities to the routine processes, especially because these departments (i.e., admissions, financial aid, registration, etc.) usually see the students or the paperwork first. The front-line staff also includes paraprofessionals such as orientation leaders, peer counselors, resident assistants, student aides, and others who work in order to complement their academic curricula, but whose primary reason for being on campus is to graduate (Schuh and Carlisle, 1991, p. 500).

Operational education means teaching each employee on the front line how to handle functional responsibilities and to show how each position interacts with others in forming both an early detection system for problems as well as a cultural work ethic. A comprehensive understanding of the significance of each person's role in the organization results in better job performance in general, and more reliable information to enable the supervisor to make educated, fact-based decisions. Unreliable or wrong information can lead to incorrect conclusions, bad decisions, and ultimately the loss of resources (students, tuition, faculty, staff, service providers, etc.). The importance of educating the front-line staff has become even more essential given the high turnover in these positions. The front-line staff members are often the first contact with the institution and are likely to identify fluctuations in the daily routine and avert student, faculty, and staff problems before they start (Singer and Kamin, 1998).

Specific skills required in front-line operations positions in student affairs vary greatly and depend on the service area, yet admonitions about the impact of technology (Breivik, 1998; Emmi, 1998; and Toffler, 1970) cannot be denied. Computers, including laptop, desktop, and mainframe, as well as fax machines, e-mail, and "smart" cards, have revolutionized the service delivery areas and require special attention in order for staff to stay abreast of their uses and possibilities. Continuing education allows student affairs staff to broaden their perspective and opens them to additional opportunities and assignments, "When you invest in people, they recognize that fact" (Barbrick in Martin, 1998, p.3). Continuing education shows employees that the institution is interested in their growth within the organization, both personally and professionally (Martin, 1998).

Middle Management. The middle manager is the institution's guiding light (see Chapter 8 "The Role of the Middle Manager" in this volume). Many issues and problems that could otherwise remain undetected by managers/supervisors and the higher level administration can be detected by the middle manager, permitting appropriate action to be taken (Singer and Kamin, 1998). Using the experience of your middle managers and having those individuals interact and interface regularly with your front-line operations staff is critical. Less experienced middle managers need to undergo rigorous assessment so that an action plan can be prepared to guide each of them through their subsequent training to fill in knowledge or skills deficits.

"While few student affairs staff enter the profession to become managers, almost every advancement in leadership requires greater skills in human resources management" (Dalton, 1996, p. 494). All operations staff need training in strategic leadership and accountability. Training, along with on-the-job performance, permits a functional assessment of the employee's capabilities and develops a pool of middle-management candidates. If more positions in student services were viewed as of professional stature, with career opportunities as well as commensurate responsibilities and higher earning potential, institutions would find themselves on firmer footing in the new millennium. There lies the challenge for higher education (Martin, 1998).

Managerial/Administrative Staff. Student affairs administrators should already have successful experience and expertise in leadership and management, either in institutions of higher education or elsewhere, combined with relevant professional knowledge and understanding. Historically student affairs leaders were drawn from faculty ranks and often the excellent instructor was not well-suited to the demanding task of managing large staff and budgets (Tester, 1998). Dalton (1996) summarized this best by noting that, "to be successful as a leader in the profession, one must understand the nature of student affairs organizations as well as how to effectively manage their staff and resources" (p. 494).

Candidate recruitment for administrative/managerial positions within our institutions of higher learning needs to focus on a demonstrated potential to manage complex organizations. Institutions also must look for candidates who can develop a strategic educational vision committed to raising achievement, and then show that they can turn that vision into practice. Candidates must be able to monitor, evaluate, and review an institution's effectiveness and be accountable to legislators, faculty, staff, students, parents, donors, and the cultural community (Tester, 1998; Woodard and von Destinon, 1993).

These administrative competencies result from a combination of experience and training, and specific programs (like an MBA or an administrative endorsement on a teaching credential) are assumed as selection characteristics to ensure a good match. Human resources traditionally screens for selection criteria as requested, but the humanistic qualities long respected and identified in student affairs offer less quantitative, yet equally needed criteria in staff selection. Administrative positions may also need to pursue further training on issues such as managing and motivating, effective communication, developing professional capabilities, and deploying staff and resources in an effective and efficient manner (Tester, 1998).

The immediate impact of the introduction of management training for administrators may not be all that noticeable to the casual observer, but the move is one of the best ways to respond to the challenge of raising standards (Tester, 1998). Student affairs has moved towards identifying training and competencies required for administrative/managerial positions through the development of comprehensive professional standards in higher education (Council for the Advancement of Standards for Student/Development Programs, 1986; Miller, 1997). Boyett and Conn (1992) forecast a future where technology, global competition, and consumer demands will increasingly require more flexible, creative, and team-oriented workplaces. These changes are already underway in American business and industry, and they are becoming increasingly common in American colleges and universities. Employees of the future will make greater use of technology to manage services, be more directly involved in a wider array of problem solving, and give greater priority to continual improvement in the quality of programs and services for both employees and students. These changes will require operational staff, middle-management and administrative/managerial staff who are flexible, innovative, and good communicators who can work effectively in teams and who are committed to continual growth and learning (Dalton, 1996).

Employee Turnover

"Don't fatten frogs for snakes."

This proverb is an admonition not to allow others to reap what you have sown and suggests that you must look out for your own best interests. In today's mobile society, employers often do not value their employees and overlook the costs associated with the loss of experience, and the training and selection when an employee must be replaced. The defense of this management position is always that there are other, possibly better educated, candidates willing to join the workforce for less money than the longer term employees. As this proverb suggests, our forbearers knew better and recognized the investment of human experience and potential. The managerial concept to replace rather than retrain also disproportionately emphasizes the cost of continuing education and retraining without realizing that it is cost-beneficial because it boosts employee morale and reduces turnover (Martin, 1998).

Career Advancement

"The one that drops the crutch the best gets the most biscuits."

The moral of this proverb is that the person who asks for attention gets it. It emphasizes positive rewards for behavior. One way to get attention on the job is to have a goal and to work hard on the job towards your goal. Career advancement in education used to be a relatively simple matter. An ability to teach well could draw attention to your performance and thereby "qualify" you to be an administrator. Today the situation is very different. The layers of bureaucracy are deeper and advancement may take several steps, sometimes upward, sometimes lateral, and sometimes in different areas, while one learns the multiple roles of the profession.

Major reforms in education over the last twenty years have effectively given institutions more ability to control their own organizational structures and affairs. However, greater freedom has been accompanied by far greater responsibility. Today's department head is burdened with wide-ranging managerial duties covering almost every aspect of a school's operation: outreach, recruitment, admission, advising, registration, financial aid, activities, tutoring, special services, graduation, and placement. Education experts expect a rapid increase in administrative support staff to do the routine tasks, such as paperwork, that teachers indicate prevent them from actually teaching (Tester, 1998).

Networking. Mutual support networks like professional associations exist because staff realize the importance of networking and learning through sharing common problems and solutions. In student affairs, the two major national organization are the American College Personnel Association (ACPA) and the National Association of Student Personnel Administrators (NASPA). In addition, there are numerous other organizations that address the interests of specific functions within the profession. Human resources has similar organizations such as the Society for Human Resource Management (SHRM), the College and University Personnel Association (CUPA), and the American Compensation Association (ACA). Such associations provide a vehicle and foundation for staff training and development as well as opportunities for career advancement by increasing your visibility in the profession. Administrators should encourage and celebrate the participation of their staff in professional associations for the training, development, and networking they provide that benefits not only the employees, but also the institution. Being a supervisor at any level can often be a lonely job, so we must create a strong ethos of professional support that staff can draw on throughout their careers.

On-campus programs can encourage networking among their employees as an aspect of training and development. Networking can be fostered through formal employee activities (such as a staff advisory council or classified staff association) or through informal volunteer activities (a canned food drive or organizing the staff Christmas party). Mentoring programs have become popular both on campus and at professional organization conferences. On campus, experienced staff may be drafted to act as mentors to their new colleagues. Moore and Salimbene (1981) define a mentor as "a more experienced and powerful individual who guides, advises and assists in any number of ways the career of a less experienced, often younger, upwardly mobile protégé in the context of a close professionally-centered relationship usually lasting one year or more" A less formal type of mentoring program occurs when established staff have the opportunity to be counseled by and work with senior-level executives during training programs that deal with staff appraisal, resource allocation, and time management. (Schuh and Carlisle, 1991, p. 503). Institutions need to foster and promote these programs for all levels of staff.

Performance Appraisal

"What you don't have in your head you've got to have in your feet."

This proverb refers to an evaluation of a person's skills and abilities. Of course, the determination of which is the preferred skill or ability is dependent upon the requirements of the job at hand and the judgement of the evaluator. The Professional Standards for Higher Education state that, "All functional areas must have a regular system of staff selection and evaluation, and must provide continuing professional development opportunities for staff . . ." (Council for the Advancement of Standards for Student Services/Development Programs, 1986, p. 6). This section reviews the area of staff evaluation.

Job Descriptions. On paper, the job descriptions, relationships among personnel, and procedures for performing work-related tasks are well defined and predictable. However, the actual work of organizations is not as predictable because the people involved with organization vary in the extent to which they adhere to rules and regulations. Three factors that influence how people act are the informal relationships they form with others, the way they are trained to do their jobs, and the way their performances are evaluated (Ferrante, 1998, p. 205). So far we have examined organizational culture and job training: this section will review strategies for performance evaluation.

Mission and Purpose. To lay a foundation for performance evaluation, we must first establish a defining mission statement (see Chapter 2 "The Importance of Institutional Mission"). The institution, including the student affairs and human resources divisions should have well-defined mission statements that can be translated into policy statements, major objectives, and division goals. The more the staff understands the why and what of their jobs as well as the when, where, and how much, the more likely they are to be satisfied and contributing members (Brown, 1988, p. 14). We can define a college or university mission as that of education and as a tool for teaching students of any age how to think, how to learn, how to create, and how to transfer expertise in the context of highly complex symbolic information (Furman, 1998). Those, in turn, are the skills on which their performance may be judged. After a mission statement has been established, it is then necessary to define a specific strategy for its accomplishment. Clear, concise and specific mission statements should influence budget decisions, allocation of staff time, and what staff do daily (Brown, 1988, p. 15). The establishment of a strategy requires institutional leaders to reassess the skills and abilities of the supporting staff.

After defining specific strategies for the accomplishment of a mission, the next step is to educate employees as to how the institution accomplishes its mission, and then to delegate strategies or programs to the appropriate member of the "team." Continued education and reinforcement for the members of an organization is no less essential than the continued education and reinforcement of the public. Employees, students, and the public must understand where the institution is going and how it intends to get there; in other words, they must understand both the mission and strategy to accomplish it (Furman, 1998).

Behavioral Evaluation

"You can hide the fire, but what are you going to do with the smoke?"

This saying refers to the consequences of actions. Although your deeds may be hidden, the consequences of those deeds will be noticeable. The ethic of prudence and caution is inherent in this saying because it is true that a person is judged by his or her actions. This is the theory behind employee performance appraisal. The term performance appraisal is used because "it connotes both assessing and making judgements about worth" (Brown, 1988, p. 5). Staff and administrators think of appraisal primarily as an event rather than a process, but it should be viewed as a system. Appraisal is not an event that occurs once a year, nor is it a form to be filled out (Brown, 1988). The goal of an appraisal system is not to have highly sophisticated assessment tools or an intricate interview process, but to have an appraisal process that is fair, effective, and that improves morale and staff performance.

Behavioral Measures. Brown (1988) recommends evaluating employees on the behaviors rather than by ranking or goal setting. Behaviorally anchored rating scales ask respondents to rate descriptions of behaviors that are consistent with job descriptions. The raters respond to questions that ask them to evaluate the staff member based on behaviors they have observed over a specified period of time. Two variations have evolved: behavioral observation scales (BOS), for observed behaviors, and behavioral expectation scales (BES) that are used when direct observation of the behavior is not always possible (Brown, 1988).

Statistical Measures. The evaluation process can provide the supervisor with knowledge about areas of weakness that can be strengthened through a career development plan (Schuh and Carlisle, 1991, p. 502). The decisions made in performance appraisal include providing feedback for professional development, assessing individual and group training needs, determining promotions, making salary decisions, and selection of staff (Brown, 1988). In large organizations, supervisors often compile statistics on absenteeism, customer satisfaction, and goal attainment as a way to measure individual, departmental, and overall organizational performance. Such measures can be convenient and useful management tools because they are considered to be objective and because they permit systematic comparison of individuals across time and departments.

One problem with statistical measures of performance is that a chosen measure may not be a valid indicator of what it is intended to measure, or it may measure performance by too narrow a criteria. For example, occupational safety is often measured by the number of accidents that occur on the job. On the basis of this indicator, the chemical industry has one of the lowest accident rates of all industries. This indicator, however, has been criticized as too narrow and lacking validity: Chemical workers may be less likely to suffer physical injury on the job than to suffer illnesses whose symptoms go unrecognized as related to chemical exposures. Furthermore, exposure-related illnesses may take years to develop (Ferrante, 1998).

A second problem with statistical measures of performance is that they encourage employees to concentrate on achieving a good score and to ignore other problems and issues. In other words, people tend to pay attention only to those areas that are being measured and to overlook those for which no measures exist.

Many potential problems are associated with statistical measures of performance. To ensure that important conditions such as occupational safety are monitored, it is advisable to develop thoughtful and accurate indicators to measure them, assign responsibility to a definite position, and tie the measures to the evaluation of performance by persons occupying that position. When no such system is in place, responsibility for accident prevention never rests squarely with specific people. This diffusion of responsibility also can occur when decision-makers rely on experts for advice or when the power to make decisions is concentrated in the hands of a few people at the top.

Legal Issues

"Don't say more with your mouth than your back can stand."

This is another admonition for cautionary behavior, but also suggests responsibility for your actions. Used here, it serves to introduce the legal areas of civil rights and management responsibilities that are products of federal statutes and programs like Affirmative Action and the Americans with Disabilities Act. Student affairs administrators frequently are called upon to make decisions relating to staff employment and civil rights liability. In order to make appropriate decisions in employment circumstances, administrators need to understand the legal parameters within which these decisions can and must be made. (See "Legal Constraints on Professional Practices" in this volume.)

Administrators often are expected to deal with employment-related practices such as determining position descriptions and qualifications; recruiting candidates; or making decisions regarding appointments, promotions, tenure, continuation, non-renewal, or dismissal. Institutions appreciate administrators who can spot warning signs and raise questions of legality and liability before any action is taken (Gehring, 1991).

The following discussion is not intended as legal advice; instead, it is intended as a cautionary admonition to administrators to broadly scan the environment for threats and opportunities in the legal arena. Legal counsel should be consulted concerning issues and concerns of legal requirements when making employment and evaluation decisions. There are six federal statutes that have significant impact on hiring decisions in higher education: Title VI and Title VII of the Civil Rights Act of 1964; Title IX of the Educational Amendments of 1972; Section 504 of the Rehabilitation Act of 1973, the Family Education Rights and Privacy Act of 1974, and the Americans with Disabilities Act of 1990 (Bills and Hall, 1994,

p. 47). It is imperative that student affairs professionals have a sound understanding of the rights that students and employees derive from these statutes.

Employment issues concerning staff evaluation and due process procedures for termination as well as handling the consequences of financial cutbacks also require sound legal advice. Employment issues will normally relate to designing job descriptions and deciding qualifications, position advertising, candidate interviews, hiring, salary determination, position evaluation, promotion, termination, and layoffs (Hollander and Young, 1991). A number of legal considerations are inherent in the evaluation process and should be recognized by everyone concerned.

The principles involved in Affirmative Action came into vogue in the 1970s. The guiding principle behind Affirmative Action plans is to provide equal opportunities for members of minority groups and women who in the past have been deprived of equal opportunity. Much controversy and debate has arisen from implementation of Affirmative Action plans, with opponents claiming that Affirmative Action is often synonymous with reverse discrimination. The legality of Affirmative Action has been challenged often (Hollander and Young, 1991).

Educational institutions that qualify as federal contractors or subcontractors are subject to Executive Order 11246 and the institution's attorney should be consulted on whether the college must follow it. If so, the essential purpose of this mandate is to prohibit discrimination in employment on the basis of race, color, religion, sex, and national origin in hiring, upgrading, salaries, fringe benefits, training, and other conditions of employment (Hollander and Young, 1991).

Guidelines

"Stand further is better than beg pardon."

We end with another cautionary proverb, one that suggests it is better to stay out of trouble than to beg forgiveness or pardon for getting into it. However, organizations are run by humans and, thus, mistakes do occur. When that happens the best advice is to beg pardon, or for administrators to apologize for the error and get back on track. This does not mean to forget that the error occurred, but to attempt to identify the cause and affect relationship so that a similar problem does not occur in the future. This section provides some guidelines and advice identified in the process of this discussion.

One of the most important pieces of advice for the blending of the cultures of student affairs and human resources within an institution is for the two units to develop a common language in order to communicate with each other. Effective communication and the understanding of it are critical to the success of any enterprise. To help in communication and understanding, we look to the two institutions where human resources is under the umbrella of student affairs, the University of Arizona and the University of Cincinnati.

The vice president for student affairs at the University of Cincinnati and his staff, (Livingston, Hadley, and Michaud, 1997) presented at the joint ACPA/NASPA conference on student affairs and human resources as "Partners in the New Learning University." Their recommendations for combining these units were to realign, redesign, redefine, and reengineer processes, roles, and responsibilities within the new organization.

- Realign refers to the institution and its changing environment that is evolving from a faculty-oriented culture with rigid, predetermined processes to a self-correcting, self-informing, learner-oriented culture.
- Redesign the structure of the institution to be a more flexible and responsive organization that is learner-focused, technology-supported, and strives to eliminate structural barriers.
- Redefine individual roles and responsibilities at planning and program levels so employees are empowered to improve services, enhance the learning environment, and strengthen alliances across the campus.
- Reengineer processes to emphasize quality methodologies, new technologies, information systems, and working alliances (Livingston, Hadley, and Michaud, 1997).

Following in this context, the University of Arizona has focused on rethinking the organizational paradigm and reeducating the faculty, staff, and students through structure of a new organizational unit identified as Campus Life. This new unit combines the traditional areas of student affairs with human resources and emphasizes the units of health and wellness, student life, cultural arts, along with human resources to promote the concept of a learning community (Taylor, 1997).

Environmental scanning teaches us to be on the watch for threats and opportunities on the horizon (Woodard and von Destinon, 1993). The area of employee performance appraisal is one that presents, in any organization, both threats and opportunities. The recommendations offered by Brown (1988) are repeated and summarized here.

Use the term "performance appraisal" because it refers to the process of assessment and making value judgements.

Promote the concept of appraisal primarily as a system or process rather than an event.

Use behavioral evaluations consistent with the position descriptions and based on behaviors observed over a specified period of time (Brown, 1988).

Administrators, when called upon to make decisions relating to employment, must have an understanding of the legal scope of the issues. Hollander and Young (1991) suggest four guidelines to keep in mind.

1. Familiarize yourself with the employment process and what employment-related constitutional and statutory mandates apply at both the federal and state levels.
2. Read and understand official documents of the institution, which includes governing board policies; faculty, staff, and student handbooks; and college catalogs. In addition, review the institution's past practices and customs regarding employment.
3. Know the terms and conditions of your own contract. This understanding should be in writing. Be clear about all employment responsibilities and rights.
4. Be aware of institutional policies regarding risk management, insurance coverage, and the mechanisms that exist for handling liability claims, court costs and awards. (Hollander and Young, 1991, p. 441–442).

In addition, we advise you to seek legal guidance when necessary under the old philosophy that it is "better to be safe than sorry." This suggests that you develop a working relationship with your institution's legal counsel.

Summary

This chapter offered an examination of the blending of two cultures within higher education, those of student affairs and human resources. It suggests a sociological paradigm that looks at the philosophies, missions, operations, and experiences of the student affairs and human resources cultures. It also draws upon the experience of the African American culture of the mid-nineteenth century, which faced cataclysmic social changes and challenges in its transition from bondage to independence and self-sufficiency. That culture provides us with common sense metaphors to enlighten the shifting cultural paradigms facing our profession as we approach the new millennium.

This chapter does not advocate the combination of student affairs and human resources within the institution, but it does offer a theoretical paradigm to allow for such a change and discusses not only the parallels between units, but also how they complement each other. Working to combine these two functional units can be done to streamline the provision of services and to foster understanding and communication across organizational lines. It has the added benefit of providing much-needed staff training and development as well as promoting the reality and perception of career advancement within the organization and reducing staff turnover. Regardless of the willingness or ability of an institution to combine these functions, student affairs units should set into motion an ongoing program for staff training and development. If practitioners and educators can establish training and development programs for our operations, we middle management and managerial/administrative staff will help to fulfill our responsibility for preparing our institutions as well as our profession for the twenty-first century.

References

Argyris, C. and Schon, D. *Organizational Learning: A Theory of Action Perspective Reading*, MA, Addison-Wesley, 1978.

Barr, D. J., and Strong, L. J. "Embracing Multiculturalism: The Existing Contradictions." *NASPA Journal*, 1988, 26, 85–90.

Bills, T. A., and Hall, P. J. "Antidiscrimination Laws and Student Affairs." In D. D. Gehring (ed.), *Student Services in a Changing Federal Climate*. New Directions for Student Services, no. 68. San Francisco: Jossey-Bass, 1994.

Boyett, J. H., and Conn, H. P. *Workplace 2000: The Revolution Reshaping American Business*. New York: Penguin, 1992.

Breivik, P. S. *Student Learning in the Information Age*. Phoenix, AZ: Oryx Press, 1998.

Brown, R. D. *Performance Appraisal as a Tool for Staff Development*. New Directions for Student Services, no. 43, 1988.

Carnegie Foundation for the Advancement of Teaching. *Campus Life: In Search of Community*. Princeton, NJ: Carnegie Foundation for the Advancement of Teaching, 1990.

Clark, D. L. "Emerging Paradigms in Organizational Theory and Research." In Y. Lincoln (ed.), *Organizational Theory and Inquiry: The Paradigm Revolution*, 1985, pp. 43–78. Beverly Hills, CA: Sage Publications.

Council for the Advancement of Standards for Student Services/Development Programs. *CAS Standards and Guidelines for Student Services/Development Programs*. Washington, D.C.: Council for the Advancement of Standards for Student Services/Development Programs, 1986.

Dalton, J. C. "Managing Human Resources." In S. R. Komives, and D. B. Woodard, Jr. (eds.) *Student Services: A Handbook for the Profession*. (3rd ed.) San Francisco: Jossey-Bass, 1996.

Dolence, M. G., and Norris, D. N. *Transforming Higher Education: A Vision for Learning in the 21st Century*. 1995.

Emmi, M. J. *Workforce Development: Skilled Workers in Demand*. Keynote address, Corporate Higher Education Forum, Banff, Canada, Sep. 24, Malvern, PA: Systems and Computer Technology, 1998.

Ferrante, J. *Sociology: A Global Perspective*. (3rd ed.) Belmont, CA: Wadsworth Publishing Company, 1998.

Filley, A. C., House, R. J., and Kerr, S. *Managerial Process and Organizational Behavior*. (2nd ed.) Glenview, IL: Scott, Foresman, 1976.

Furman, M. E. "Creating Corporate Culture: Step Two-Defining Strategies and Educating Employees." *Incentive*, vol. 172, no. 6, Jun. 1998.

Gehring, D. D. "Legal Issues in the Administration of Student Affairs." In T. K. Miller and R. B. Winston (eds.) *Administration and Leadership in Student Affairs.* (2nd ed.) Muncie, IN: Accelerated Development, Inc., 1991.

Gehring, D. D. *Campus Crime, College Policy, and Federal Laws and Regulations.* New Directions for Higher Education, no. 95, San Francisco: Jossey-Bass, 1996.

Hadley, T. D. "Shared Benefits: Student Afffairs and Human Resources." Unpublished paper, University of Cinncinnati, 1997.

Hastings, P. "Lifelong Development for Supply-Chain Management." *Logistics Focus,* 1998, vol. 6, no. 6, Jul./Aug, 16–18.

Hersey, P., and Blanchard, K. H. *Management of Organizational Behavior: Utilizing Human Resources.* Englewood Cliffs, NJ: Prentice-Hall, Inc., 1982.

Hollander, P. A., and Young, D. P. "Legal Issues and Employent Practices in Student Affairs." In T. K. Miller and R. B. Winston (eds.), *Administration and Leadership in Student Affairs.* (2nd ed.) Muncie, IN: Accelerated Development, Inc., 1991.

Huebner, L. A. "Interaction of Student and Campus." In U. Delworth and G. Hansen (eds.), *Student Services: A Handbook for the Profession.* (2nd ed.) San Francisco: Jossey-Bass, 1989.

Knowles, M. S. *The Modern Practice of Adult Education.* Chicago: Association Press, 1980.

Komives, S. R., and Woodard, D. B., Jr. *Student Services: A Handbook for the Profession.* (3rd ed.) San Francisco: Jossey-Bass, 1996.

Kuh, G.D. "Organizational Theory." In S. R. Komives and D. B. Woodard, Jr. (eds.), *Student Services: A Handbook for the Profession.* (3rd ed.) San Francisco: Jossey-Bass, 1996.

Kuh, G. D., and Whitt, E. J. *The Invisible Tapestry: Culture in American Colleges and Universities.* ASHE-ERIC Higher Education report, no. 1, Washington, D.C.: Association for the Study of Higher Education, 1988.

Kuh, G., and Whitt, E. "Organizational Theory: A Primer." In T. K. Miller and R. B. Winston (eds.), *Administration and Leadership in Student Affairs.* (2nd ed.) Muncie, IN: Accelerated Development Inc., 1991.

Kuh, G. D., Whitt, E. J., and Shedd, J. D. *Student Affairs, 2001: A Pragmatic Odyssey.* Alexandria, VA: American College Personnel Association Media, 1987.

Langer, S. K. *Feeling and Form.* New York: Scribner and Sons, 1953.

Livingston, M. D., Hadley, T. D., and Michaud, P. J. "Redesigning Organizational Boundaries: Student Affairs and Human Resources—Partners in the New Learning University." Presentation at the ACPA/NASPA joint conference, Chicago: March, 1997.

Martin, R. "Operators: Retrain to Fight Labor Deficit." *Nation's Restaurant News,* 1998, vol. 32, no. 20, May 18, 3–8.

Masland, A. T. "Organizational Culture in the Study of Higher Education." *Review of Higher Education,* 1985, 8, 157–68.

Mieder, W. *American Proverbs: A Study of Texts and Contexts.* New York: Peter Lang Publishing, Inc., 1989.

Miller, T. K. *CAS: The Book of Professional Standards for Higher Education.* Washington, D.C.: Council for the Advancement of Standards in Higher Education, 1997.

Montessori, M. *The Absorbent Mind.* New York: Dell Publishing, 1984.

Moore, K. M., and Salimbene, A. M. "The Dynamics of the Mentor-Prote[as]ge[as] Relationship in Developing Women as Academic Leaders." *Journal for Educational Equity and Leadership,* Fall 1981, 2 (1), 51–64.

Owens, R. G. *Organizational Behavior in Education.* (2nd ed.) Englewood Cliffs, NJ: Prentice Hall, 1981.

Peterson, D. *Facilitating Education for Older Learners.* San Francisco: Jossey-Bass, 1983.

Prahlad, S. A. *African-American Proverbs in Context.* Jackson, MS: University Press, 1996.

Pusch, M. D. (ed.). *Multicultural Education: A Cross-Cultural Training Approach.* La Grange Park, IL: Intercultural Network, 1979.

Richardson, R. C., Jr., and Skinner, E. F. *Achieving Quality and Diversity: Universities in a Multicultural Society.* New York: American Council on Education and MacMillan, 1991.

Rogers, J. L. "Leadership." In S. R. Komives and D. B. Woodard, Jr. (eds.), *Student Services: A Handbook for the Profession.* (3rd ed.) San Francisco: Jossey-Bass, 1996.

Schein, E. H. *Organizational Culture and Leadership.* San Francisco: Jossey-Bass, 1985.

Schneider, B. (ed.). *Organizational Climate and Culture.* San Francisco: Jossey-Bass, 1990.

Schuh, J. H., and Carlisle, W. "Supervision and Evaluation: Selected Topics For Emerging Professionals." In T. K. Miller and R. B. Winston (eds.), *Administration and Leadership in Student Affairs.* (2nd ed.) Muncie, IN: Accelerated Development, Inc., 1991.

Singer, R. M., and Kamin, L. J. "The Need to Educate: From the Bottom Up." vol. 54, no. 1, Jan./Feb., 1998, National Commercial Finance Association, 34–40.

Talbot, D. "Multiculturalism." In S. R. Komives and D. B. Woodard, Jr. (eds.), *Student Services: A Handbook for the Profession.* (3rd ed.) San Francisco: Jossey-Bass, 1996.

Taylor, S. L. *Campus Life, a National Model: Redefining the University Community,* 1997.

Tester, N. "Mr. Chips Learns to Manage." *Management Today,* Jul. 1998, 50–53.

Thompson, K. R., and Luthans, F. "Organizational Culture: A Behavioral Perspective." In B. Schneider (ed.), *Organizational Climate and Culture.* San Francisco: Jossey-Bass, 1990.

Toffler, A. *Future Shock,* New York: Random House, 1970.

Woodard, D. B., Jr., and von Destinon, M. A. "Identifying and Working with Key Constituent Groups." In M. J. Barr (ed.), *The Handbook of Student Affairs Administration.* San Francisco: Jossey-Bass, 1993.

CHAPTER TEN

THE POLITICAL DIMENSIONS OF DECISION MAKING

Paul L. Moore

In organizational life, the term *politics* may be the most employed and least understood concept among the words we use to describe important aspects of our work. For many faculty members and administrators, it has negative connotations, suggesting trickery, manipulation, and self-interest; as a result, it causes some discomfort when used (Block, 1987; Pfeffer, 1981). It is a topic we would prefer to talk about privately or euphemistically. The training of student affairs professionals with its anchors in the helping professions and our focus on the personal development of students may create greater ambivalence for us than others when confronted with "politics." At the same time, however, we understand it to be a necessary and ubiquitous process through which important decisions are made in society and in our institutions. As Appleton (1991, p. 5) notes, "Political behavior is inevitable in every organizational setting, is found at every level in the hierarchy, and intensifies as the decision making possibilities are greater and more important."

Clearly, an understanding of institutional decision-making must be a priority for all those who hope to make and influence policies affecting their work and institutions. Whether an institution is large or small, secular or non-secular, whether it is a research university or community college, an important part of its management involves decision making about direction, strategy, and resource allocation. How these decisions are made is the essence of organizational politics.

One important caveat is that the political approach is not the only useful one in understanding organizations in general and higher education in particular. Bolman and Deal (1984) have identified four major theoretical frameworks for organizations: rational, human resource, political, and symbolic. Each has an interesting perspective that adds to our understanding of organizations. Rational theorists deal with the goals, roles, and technology of organizations. The human resource writers are concerned with the interaction of the needs and capabilities of people with the roles and relationships within organizations. Meaning within organizations is the interest of symbolic theorists. Power, conflict, and resource allocation are the concerns of political theorists. Each approach has its strengths and weaknesses; and although we have emphasized in this chapter the political perspective as being useful to student affairs professionals, it is helpful to acknowledge Pfeffer's (1981, p. 2) caution when speaking of politics and its essential ingredient, power: "While power is something, it is not everything."

The purposes of this chapter are to identify and define key concepts necessary to an understanding of organizational politics, highlight elements of institutions of higher education that distinguish them from other societal institutions and affect their political processes, and suggest political perspectives strategies and tactics for student affairs practitioners.

Basic Concepts

As used in this chapter, *politics* refers to the processes that influence the direction of and allocate resources for an organization. Political behaviors are those designed to shape or determine institutional direction and policy and are as rational or irrational and altruistic or self-serving as the people involved. As we are concerned here with the political processes and activities that occur within colleges and universities, Pfeffer's (1981, p. 7) definition of organizational politics is instructive: "Organizational politics involves those activities taken within organizations to acquire, develop, and use power and other resources to obtain one's preferred outcomes in a situation in which there is uncertainty or dissensus about choices."

Key aspects of this definition are power, preferences, and uncertainty. *Power* may be defined as "the ability to produce intended change in others, to influence them so that they will be more likely to act in accordance with one's own preferences" (Birnbaum, 1988, p. 13). *Preferences* suggest what an individual or group would like to see happen within the organization. And *uncertainty* implies that a decision is yet to be made or a direction chosen.

In his study of New York University as a political system, Baldridge (1971, p. 24) describes its major elements: "The broad outline of the political system looks like this: a complex social structure generates multiple pressures, many forms of power and pressure impinge on the decision makers, a legislative stage translates these pressures into policy, and a policy execution phase finally generates feedback in the form of new conflict." Important ideas in this description are differing interests, intergroup disagreement or conflict, use of power in pursuit of interests, efforts to influence decision-makers, and decision-making itself.

Important Conceptual Considerations

The purpose of this section is to introduce major elements that will help with the discussion of power and politics and perhaps encourage the reader to pursue an independent review of the literature. The intent is not to review in depth all the theoretical concepts that underpin a discussion of organizational politics; excellent discussions of these already exist (Baldridge, 1971; Pfeffer, 1981; Bacharach and Lawler, 1980; and Birnbaum, 1988).

The Political Model. This view of organizations assumes that they are not completely rational and harmonious entities, but are composed of constantly shifting coalitions that bargain for desired outcomes and use strategies and tactics designed to influence results. Organizational life is seen as a series of political transactions involving the use of power to obtain resources or achieve other ends (Bacharach and Lawler, 1980). Organizations are not typically homogeneous but rather pluralistic, being composed of all sorts of subgroups and subcultures. Conflicts arising from these differences are natural and are to be expected in political organizations (Baldridge, 1971). Power, differing preferences, conflict, influence, coalitions, negotiation, and compromise are key ingredients in a political system.

To suggest that a college or university is a political system that experiences the use of power, conflict, and mutual influence is not to argue that rational processes, bureaucratic incrementalism, and strong organizational cultural tendencies are not at work or nonexistent. Other methods of making decisions and controlling activity exist that assist with the ongoing activity of an organization. Careful accumulation of information and examination of alternatives frequently inform academic, student welfare, and fundraising decisions. Organizations will make some decisions based on closely held values, such as those that might be made in an institution with religious roots. And certainly incrementalism will determine many budget allocations.

Political activities tend to be accentuated when normal patterns or processes do not produce coherent direction, strategies, or accepted resource allocations. Active disagreement may be stimulated by external sources, such as an important institutional constituency, or by internal sources, such as the protest generated by the proposal of a new program having perceived negative financial implications for others in the organization. Pfeffer (1981) has identified several elements that produce political activity in organizations: interdependence of the interest groups or actors, goals that are inconsistent, resource scarcity, issues of importance, and decentralized decision-making.

The political model assumes that the power of the various participants will determine the outcome. Thus, understanding "who participates in decision making, what determines each player's stand on the issues, what determines each actor's relative power, and how the decision process arrives at a decision" is an important managerial and political consideration (Pfeffer, 1981, p. 28). All groups and individuals are not concerned with all issues. Even when interested, they will exhibit differing levels of intensity and ability to influence a particular decision. And as the results are primarily the consequence of negotiation and compromise, they are rarely the perfect expression of any specific individual or group preferences (Pfeffer, 1981).

Power. Earlier, power was defined as the ability to influence others in such a way that they will more likely do what we prefer. "Compared to influence, power is the potential for influence, and influence is the result of actualized power" (King, 1975, p. 7). Power describes relationships among people that are given particular meaning by the organizational context. Further, the person to be influenced assigns meaning to the behavior or communications that are designed to influence (King, 1975). All relations need not require or manifest the ingredient of power. The organizational setting and the roles of individuals significantly affect the nature and extent of power in the relationship.

French and Raven (1959) identify five bases of power relating to organizational context that describe what groups or individuals use to affect the behavior of others: coercive, reward, expertise, referent, and legitimate power. Some writers have added a sixth: information (Bacharach and Lawler, 1980).

Coercive power suggests the ability to punish, such as dismissal or demotion or, in a group situation, job action by a labor union.

Reward power involves giving something of value (a promotion or raise) if certain behavior is exhibited; in a group situation, it might mean representation on an important board of directors.

Expert power is specialized knowledge about issues or activities of interest to the organization. Examples are the special knowledge of lawyers, medical doctors, and accountants.

Referent power is based on identification with another person, such as the deference shown to charismatic leaders. An example is the credibility often accorded the assistant to a college president.

Legitimate power, sometimes called bureaucratic power, is "power based on rights of control and concomitant obligations to obey" (Bacharach and Lawler, 1980, p. 33). Legitimate power is essentially authority as ascribed to senior university officers, such as presidents, vice presidents, and deans. By virtue of their positions, they are empowered to make certain decisions and are expected to do so by others.

Legitimate power or authority is not the same as influence. Authority is the ability and right to make and enforce decisions; either one has the right to make decisions or not. Influence, by contrast, is the opportunity for almost anyone in an organization to seek to affect decisions arising from any of the bases of power rather than from organizational right (Bacharach and Lawler, 1980).

Information refers to the opportunity that social actors have to gain information about internal matters or the organization's relations to the environment.

Influence does not occur in a vacuum; it requires both that someone wishes to influence and that someone is willing to be influenced. Writing about social influence and communication, King (1975, p. 12) states: "For communication and social influence to occur, the receiver must be affected. The receiver assigns meaning to behavior." The bases of power noted above are conceived similarly; someone employs one or a combination of these sources to induce someone else to do something. These processes, therefore, cannot exist independently of context.

Needs, Motivation, and Expectations

How people behave in an organization reflects in part their motivations for being there, such as pay, prestige, or fellowship, and expectations about how the organization will treat them or respond to certain behaviors on their part (Appleton, 1991). What motivates them and what they expect from an organization are strongly related to their perceived needs. Personal needs may include safety and security, love and affiliation, social esteem and prestige, power and autonomy, self-esteem and competence, and achievement and creativity (Webber, 1979). Needs, motivations, and expectations are as varied as the people who work in an organization and will be influenced by personal values, beliefs, age, experience, gender, and ethnicity.

Political behavior, designed to influence organizational direction and policy through the use of power and other resources, is directly connected to individual motivations and personal or group expectations of the organization. How people respond to efforts to influence them requires that they give meaning to the actions taken, and that meaning is affected and filtered by needs, motivations, and expectations. The exercise of power does not guarantee that the person or group that is to be influenced will respond as hoped. It all depends on the context—

individual perceptions, immediate or long-term needs, personal values and beliefs, and the stakes to be won or lost.

Self-Serving Versus Productive Behavior

If behavior depends in part on the motivations and expectations of the individual, how can an organization elicit behavior that supports its goals? Is self-serving behavior necessarily negative, as some have contended? (Block, 1987) If a person is behaving politically, is that necessarily at odds with institutional goals and culture? How can one distinguish between political activities that support institutional goals and those that do not?

The answer lies, in part, in the extent to which the political actor's expectations and the results of specific actions are congruent with the goals of the organization. Figure 10.1 illustrates the notion of congruence.

We know, of course, that the motives of the involved actors and purposes behind particular actions are not always apparent. Organizational politics are consequently complex and ambiguous; things may not be as they appear. Although long-term results may provide definitive answers to questions of motivation and purpose, decisions will be made in the short-run based on perceptions of those purposes, whether clearly articulated or not.

Into those judgments are brought all the contextual elements of organizational life—the individual and organizational values, purposes, technologies, histories, and perspectives. Whether or not political behavior is fundamentally self-serving or in the interest of both the individual and organization is frequently a matter of opinion.

Leadership

Influence, and by implication the use of power, is basic to managerial leadership (Webber, 1979). What then is the role of leadership in a political organization? Appleton (1991, p. 13) argues, "The leader must be prepared to use power in an effective manner and to understand the extent to which individual differences and expectations and self-serving political interests will affect the functioning of an organization." Managing the political process and political conflict is at the heart of leadership (Yates, 1985).

Important Elements of Institutions of Higher Education

If power, influence, and politics exist, are based upon relationships and organizational structures, and are central to administrative life (Pfeffer, 1981; Yates, 1985),

FIGURE 10.1 GOAL: FUNCTIONAL BEHAVIOR

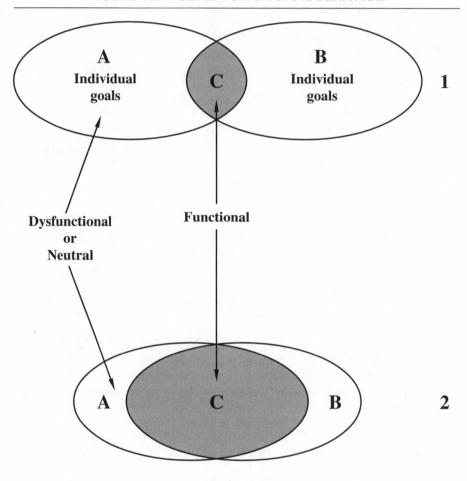

Source: Appleton, 1991, p. 12. Reprinted with permission.

it follows that the practitioner ought to understand the unique aspects of institutions of higher education that shape their political environments.

Goal Diffusion. Colleges and universities typically exhibit a lack of clarity and agreement on institutional goals (Birnbaum, 1988; Baldridge, 1973). Teaching, research, and service are the three most frequently stated goals, but they exist in differing combinations and degrees of emphasis on each campus; moreover, goals may even be assigned a different importance on a single campus. However, other goals may be widely embraced, such as intercollegiate athletics or a particular religion. The result is often a lack of agreed-upon, mutually consistent goals—that is, a number of conflicting or inconsistent goals are accepted. Almost inevitably, such an environment sets the stage for disagreement and competition over institutional direction and the allocation of resources.

Uncertainty of Means or Technologies. Not only are the goals of higher education diffuse, but the means that should be used to educate students are not always clear. Which classroom strategies (lectures, small discussion seminars, laboratory activity, or independent study) are most productive and when? Many techniques seem to work, but how they create change in students and which ones are best are not known (Birnbaum, 1988). Because our technologies are not clear, major choices about how to allocate resources are often not easily and decisively made. Again, the stage is set for disagreement and political activity.

Dual Control. Another feature of higher education that contributes to political activity is the dual nature of institutional control (Birnbaum, 1988). Responsibility for decision-making is vested in an administration, including a board of trustees, a president, and a generally elaborate structure. Simultaneously, responsibility is endowed upon faculty structures, schools, departments, senates, and committees that make a number of important curricular and personnel decisions. The authority in the former tends to be hierarchical and in the latter, professional. Moreover, the two structures are not necessarily clearly defined and integrated; thus, opportunity for dissent and conflict abounds.

Structural Uniqueness. Not only do colleges and universities have dual decision-making systems, they are filled with other distinctive features adding ambiguity and complexity to their functioning. As noted previously, there is both a management structure and an employee governance structure. In each, labor unions may organize employees in a context structured by complex state government regulations. Outside groups, particularly the federal government, alumni associations, supporters (such as athletic or arts fundraising groups), and accrediting associations, have their say. And staff and students may be effectively organized and represented in official governance bodies. Clearly, the variety of interests, institutional complexity, and the nature of the decision-making apparatus, whether direct or advisory, suggest the conditions necessary for a political organization.

Organizational Culture. Culture, according to Schein (1985, p. 9), is "a pattern of basic assumptions—invented, discovered, or developed by a given group as it learns to cope with its problems of external adaptation and internal integration—that has worked well enough to be considered valid and, therefore, to be taught to new members as the correct way to perceive, think, and feel in relation to those problems." Colleges and universities have cultures, as do the structures within them: schools, departments, senates, and groups. In addition, those affiliated with the institution, such as accrediting associations, alumni and support groups, and professional associations, exhibit cultural characteristics. The cultures of universities differ from those of other societal institutions as well as from each other. Culture, then, affects how a particular organization reacts to issues of organizational strategy, technology, conflict, communications, socialization, and productivity. Culture helps deal with issues of organizational survival and internal functioning (Schein, 1985).

Limits on Leadership. Birnbaum (1988) has analyzed the limitations on leadership in higher education brought about by the organizational, governance, and cultural uniqueness of colleges and universities. Dual decision-making systems, decentralization of academic decision-making, the influence of external authorities and interests, and the lack of agreement on institutional goals—all impose constraints on leadership. It is no wonder that although transformational leadership is almost always desired, it is much less frequently achieved.

Nonetheless, the importance of leadership remains. An understanding of the political dimension of universities is a critical element in providing effective leadership. Strategies and tactics that can be helpful in managing the political environment for the benefit of students and the institution are available to the student affairs leader.

Perspectives and Strategies

The assumption of this chapter is that most of us experience sufficient organizational politics in our daily administrative lives to warrant thinking about ways to improve our effectiveness in dealing with it. The following suggestions may provide some guidance.

The President and Senior Colleagues. Depending on professional level, the term *boss* may be substituted for *president;* the ideas are the same. Although we might wish it were not so, the most important relationship is with the boss. Without a strong or at least respectful relationship, a student affairs leader will struggle with many aspects of his or her responsibility. It is important to take whatever time and do whatever is necessary to secure this relationship, including informing, training, protecting, and supporting senior colleagues. There are, of course, personal and ethical limits that must be understood and acted on, even if it means resignation (Brown, 1991).

Senior colleagues, particularly at the vice-presidential level, require attention. Without good, constructive relationships, a sense of teamwork cannot be cultivated, and the normal turf, budget, and policy battles may take on a more partisan tone. Student affairs professionals must recognize their colleagues' biases, strengths, and weaknesses in order to strengthen their relationships, shape their approaches, and protect their interests.

Roles, Issues, and the Institution. To perform well in the political arena, it is critical for those in student affairs to understand thoroughly their role, whether as the chief student affairs officer (Sandeen, 1991) or as a middle manager (Young, 1990; Ellis and Moon, 1991). Being clear about the expectations of one's boss and key constituencies will translate into personal confidence when dealing with the managerial as well as the political dimensions of a position. For example, Brown (1991) sees key roles of the chief student affairs officer as being surrogate, shield, and defender for the president. Without an appreciation of these expectations, the student affairs vice president may be paralyzed by the conflicting expectations of the president, faculty, and students.

It is equally important to know the issues. Although it is not possible to be aware of all that goes on in a division or large department, it is nonetheless critical to have a good sense of the substance of everything within a job's area of responsibility, especially where criticism or territorial battles are likely.

Following and understanding institutional issues is necessary, whether or not they impinge directly on a practitioner's responsibilities. This practice will be helpful in establishing a reputation as an officer or professional with institution-wide interests and role. Such a perception by others may lead to greater involvement in and influence on the full range of institutional concerns. On the formal side, student affairs officers must keep abreast of relevant current issues through perusal of their professional journals and general publications such as the *Chronicle of Higher Education* and the *Journal of Higher Education*. It may be useful to have a working knowledge of the informational sources followed by other important administrators, such as the publications of the National Association of College and University Business Officers typically reviewed by business and administrative vice presidents.

The Importance of Competence. The power of personal competence cannot be overly emphasized. We normally think of competence in relation to student affairs "business" or management, but as a source of power it goes well beyond professional expertise. Professionals in the field must strive to be highly skilled in their work, but that is not sufficient if they are to play a broader institutional role. Political competence, the subject of this chapter, suggests an understanding of power and its uses, of the personal motivations of others in the organization, of the opportunities provided to influence decisions about institutional direction and resource allocation, and of the potential of staff work to shape alternatives.

Proper Positioning. One cannot influence decisions unless one is organizationally, professionally, and personally in a position to do so. Opportunities for influencing unit or institutional decisions do not necessarily occur because an individual knows a lot or is recognized as a strong professional by colleagues on other campuses; such opportunities usually occur because that person has taken steps to be known as competent, interested, and involved in the fortunes of his unit, division, or institution.

Visibility on the campus, and perhaps in the larger community in which the institution resides, is an important and not-always-understood notion. Being visible simply means attending meetings, socials, and programs of importance to various important constituencies within and without the college or university. Participation may be seen by others as much more beneficial to a program or idea than might be obvious. The positive aspects of visibility can, however, be squandered through overexposure or participation in unimportant activities. One must, therefore, monitor the importance and frequency of involvement.

Officers in student affairs must keep track of what they and their units accomplish. Acknowledgment of accomplishments serves both as a reinforcement of strong and innovative performance and a method of ensuring that organizational efforts are directed toward unit goals.

Accomplishments should also be shared with senior administration officials, colleagues, and faculty members. A performance will be judged with or without information; thus, it is important that others are informed of activities and achievements. Informing others also has the benefit of establishing competence, interest, and involvement in institutional issues and strengthening the ability to participate effectively in the institution's political environment.

Being informed about campus issues and individual responsibilities is, of course, required of those who would influence the course of institutional development. This requirement extends to a clear understanding of institutional history and culture.

Those in the field should also be thoughtful about their public presence—that is, their personal style, which relates to how they do things and how they are perceived by others: "Personal style is the professional demeanor by which each of us is known. It denotes how we behave in our work, as distinguished from what we do" (Appleton, Briggs, and Rhatigan, 1978, p. 139). Style, though rooted in personal characteristics and experiences, can be understood and shaped to enhance effectiveness in the educational and political environment. Do student affairs officers use jargon or language readily understood and accepted by their audiences? Do they and those on their staff show a level of professionalism appropriate for students, their parents, or trustees? Do they dress in a way that meets the expectations of important constituencies? Are they willing and accomplished public speakers readily available to campus and community groups? The point of these and other similar questions is to argue that one needs to act, look, and see oneself as a major player in institutional decision-making and leadership.

Relationships, or Getting to Know Others. Like close ties to the president, relationships with others are essential to effective participation in the political processes of colleges and universities. With the possible exception of legislative activities such as faculty senates, relationships are the best vehicle for building coalitions, resolving conflict, and creating consensus. With such a pivotal function, building and maintaining relationships must be an active concern for student affairs officers.

Brown (1991) refers to the "positive value of gossip," information that gives some hint of situations, motives, or fast-moving events. By working at knowing others, those in student affairs position themselves in key places in the informal communication network of their campus. The information gained can be enormously helpful in countering resistance or informing others of interests or proposals.

Moore (1991) describes a strategy for getting to know and routinely working with academic deans through regular visits or lunches. These periodic contacts need not require agendas other than simply checking in to see how faculty members and students are doing, what issues are developing, and what else might be done. The contact will be appreciated and may build a relationship that will prove mutually beneficial during extraordinary situations.

Time Requirements. It must be clear by now that managing the political dimension of a job can be, and frequently is, enormously time-consuming. The time requirement seems to increase as the organizational level of a position rises: the higher and more central the responsibilities, the greater the opportunities for political activity and the higher the demand on time. In an unpublished study of the political involvement of chief student affairs officers (Moore and Moore, 1991), seventy-four percent of the 243 responding chief student affairs officers reported that political activities consumed a significant amount of their work time.

Politics is not a function to be managed like budget or planning; it is a backdrop. It is not our work, but it affects our work. Its effect on our time must be accommodated and managed so that it does not overwhelm the requirements of our institutions and our students.

Perhaps politics should be thought of as a consideration—one that must be factored into our efforts at conflict resolution, pursuit of goals, and decision-making. In some sense, it is like the notion of student development, which guides and influences much of our work. As such, the time that it takes can be managed so as not to squeeze out other productive activities.

The importance of spending sufficient time on the political process is illustrated by Birnbaum (1988), who writes, "People who spend time on a decision will be disproportionately successful."

Accepting Conflict. Conflict will be more or less present, more or less visible, and more or less a factor in student affairs depending on institutional culture and history and the personalities and motivations of current players. Whatever its degree, however, university administrators must anticipate that conflict over priorities, turf, and resources will occur. It is not unusual or extraordinary.

Differences, and indeed conflict, are necessary ingredients to a political system. This observation implies that student affairs officers must be able to deal with conflict, understand the political system, and know how to operate in it. The marriage of the two, conflict and institutional politics, is a fact that must be considered in confronting problems both between individuals in student affairs and between student affairs personnel and representatives of other areas within the institution.

On a personal level, student affairs officers may not wish to deal with conflict, but must have a willingness and strategies to manage it. Individual styles will obviously reflect personal and contextual characteristics.

Fighting, or the Rules of Battle. Inevitably, all administrators will encounter disagreements over territory or resources that will require a struggle. Personal values and style will, of course, determine much of what they do. Nevertheless, there are some points to keep in mind.

Battles should not be fought if they cannot be won. There will be some matters of principle that require a fight even though winning is very unlikely; however, fighting hopeless battles will only dissipate energy and resources. Fighting uses resources, may damage relationships and future interactions, and, thus, should be engaged in only for important reasons. Personal ego is not such a reason.

It is essential to be well informed. Until preparation is complete, the battle should be postponed. A neutral ground for the conversation should be chosen and privacy ensured. Above all, student affairs officers must maintain their dignity. Fights have consequences, and nothing is worth the loss of one's self-respect and the regard of others.

Integrity. In the final analysis, consistent ethical behavior is the most important strategy. When the battles are over and the dust settles, people will follow leaders of high integrity even when the won-lost record is less than they would hope. To lose integrity is to lose claim to leadership and the support of the boss, staff, and students.

Other Tactics. There are a great number of tactics that might be identified as potentially useful in addition to those formally explored above. Several of these deserve brief mention.

1. The participation of the opposition should be encouraged (Birnbaum, 1988). Participation may help opponents appreciate the real constraints faced by the institution and the consequences inherent in any particular political situation. It may have a tempering effect.
2. Birnbaum (1988) describes another method for dealing with politically sensitive issues. The "garbage can" strategy is based on the notion that new proposals often attract all sorts of unrelated solutions and problems. By increasing the possible solutions, one may reduce the probability that a specific idea or strategy will survive the process. Committees often serve the function of developing so many ideas and solutions that none can get support or be implemented. In addition, sometimes it is strategically important to overload the decision-making system with proposals on various matters. When that occurs and time is limited, chances increase that some proposals will not get through the process of evaluation and decision making by committees and other governance groups.
3. Efforts should be focused on the relevant persons and situations related to an objective. "[The] persons who are there have the power" (Baldridge, 1971, p. 26).
4. Service on committees is crucial; they are where the work gets done (Baldridge, 1971). By being present, doing the work of the committee, and staying until the job is done, student affairs officers will influence what happens.
5. Persistence is vital (Birnbaum, 1988; Baldridge, 1971). Even though a policy is written, the issue may not be settled. Evolving interpretations should be constantly monitored.
6. Management should be unobtrusive (Birnbaum, 1988). Managing small changes without much fanfare may elicit less attention and resistance.

Staff Education

Although many will be reluctant to involve their staff in the normal political skirmishes, it is important that they understand institutional history and culture. For example, many business schools have faculty consultants in the area of organizational culture who can be quite helpful to student affairs staff. An informed staff will be more sensitive to issues and interactions that may have political overtones; the result is that the leadership's network is expanded and more consistent organizational responses to political situations can be made. It is also helpful to inform senior staff members of the details of situations that either may cause political disagreement or that invite collaboration with others.

Clear Purposes and Values. A clearly and consistently stated set of purposes and supporting values can help provide a context within which actions and initiatives related to responsibilities can be understood and interpreted. Explicitness is a virtue in itself in that it informs the opinions of others and helps reduce uninformed speculations and the suspicion of secret motivations and agendas. Speculation will always be present in organizations and should, therefore, be anticipated and countered by information. Actions rooted in core values are more understandable and less subject to misunderstanding.

Explicit and consistently stated values and purposes are important not only to external, but also to internal audiences, such as the staff or division. Staff members, fully cognizant of organizational values and direction, will act more reliably in pursuit of them and will likely make fewer mistakes that can be seized upon by other interest groups within the organization.

At the same time, it is important that student affairs leaders and staff work to attain and respond to an institutional perspective. Partisan politics is frequently rooted or finds its voice in narrow matters. Budget requests and program proposals that respond to general institutional goals will more likely gain supporters and ultimate approval and less likely attract opposition because of petty issues. Further, embracing institutional purposes and values signals membership on a team committed to institutional advancement.

Performance. Extremely competent people performing at high levels are more likely to be successful in pursuit of objectives and able to counter opposition to organizational activities and initiatives. A uniformly able staff is an invaluable political asset. Political competence can be encouraged through consistent investment in staff development activities.

Faculty

A widely understood and broadly applicable approach to faculty is an important institutional strategy. Faculty members will be supporters or opponents depending on what they know or how they are involved and supported in a given process by student affairs personnel. Importantly, such a strategy must reflect the typical commitments of the faculty, as well as the values and mission of the institution (Bloland, 1991). Managers should think often of faculty in their program planning and evaluation and follow through when faculty participation is secured or interest expressed.

Staff should also be encouraged to develop strong relations with academic units through teaching, writing, or consultation. Teaching is the most traditional approach, but consultation on such issues as the handling of difficult students or training on student diversity is increasingly possible. Staff members should be encouraged to respond to faculty concerns quickly and positively, regardless of how insignificant or uninformed the request or question might seem.

Faculties will influence institutional decisions through their senates, institutional standing committees, and school and department governance structures. Although many faculty members may be uninformed about student affairs issues and commitments, they will influence, perhaps negatively, decisions affecting student affairs.

Communication

The student affairs organization must actively communicate with those it would seek to influence. Communication must be consistent, frequent, and of high quality and should originate in all parts of the organization, not just from the top. Each office or function has a constituency with which communication is vital. The form of communication may be a newsletter, a computer bulletin board, or a personal visit, depending on institutional size and purposes. It may involve the sharing of ideas about common interests through the circulation of articles. Internal articles on student trends or interests can furnish useful information about reentry student characteristics or employment trends. Communication strategies must also contain active opportunities for listening and feedback through an open-door policy, letters to the editor, or a constituent survey.

Ethical Considerations

A number of good resources on ethics are available for the student affairs practitioner (Canon and Brown, 1985; Upcraft and Poole, 1991). It seems, however, that the issue of ethical behavior is more important when examining our political roles within the organizations in which we work—perhaps especially because institutions of higher education are committed to the pursuit of truth. The perceived importance of this behavior also stems from our understanding that when we confront institutional politics, we are not necessarily dealing with an idealized good, but with a world in which people do not always act nobly.

Yet groups and individuals disagree on institutional direction and resource allocation decisions, attempt to influence decisions that have an impact on themselves or their interests, and exercise power when they do so. Organizational politics are real and ubiquitous and are, thus, an important aspect of administrative decision-making and life. As such, organizational politics must be considered from an ethical perspective. After all, as Appleton (1991) states, it is "the acquisition and right use of power" (p. 6) that ought to be of great interest to the professional operating in the political dimension of administrative life.

Special Considerations

Although institutions and personal situations will provide an array of administrative and political challenges, some deserve special mention to encourage practitioners to think differently or more broadly about them; these include issues of gender, ethnicity, institutional size, and institutional affiliation or sponsorship.

Gender and Ethnicity. There are expected differences in administrative experiences related to gender and ethnicity, but these factors may present special challenges. In a study of female and African American chief student affairs officers (Mamarchev and Williamson, 1991), respondents reported a number of common issues that affected their ability to manage their political environments. There were perceived differences in the ways that they had been socialized, in the availability of mentors during the formative years of their careers, in familiarity with the territory of senior administration, in their inclusion in some informal social and information-sharing situations, and in others' understanding of their role and competence because of their gender or ethnic background. These situations caused the respondents to find ways to augment their training and experience and to develop strategies to help them cope with a political environment perhaps different from that normally associated with the position held.

Institutional Size. Institutional size clearly affects how one operates, administratively and politically. Size may limit access to decision-making, create administrative decentralization and specialization, lessen social interaction, and diminish the accuracy of communication (Smith, 1991). Each of these dimensions will require the tailoring of strategies and tactics designed to influence institutional decision-making. Birnbaum (1988) provides an excellent discussion of institutional function based partly on organizational size.

Mission. Institutional sponsorship and, therefore, mission can have an enormous impact on institutional goals. A Jesuit college, for example, may well have a different social agenda because of a commitment to service than a public, technical university. Private institutions may more vigorously defend their independent status than some other values that public institutions may deem more important, such as broad student access. These differences, as well as those in institutional culture, will also influence the approaches to political systems and situations that student affairs officers will adopt.

Summary

This chapter has argued that the political dimension of institutional life exists and is important and manageable. The student affairs practitioner will be affected by political struggles about institutional direction, plans for pursuing these purposes, and allocation of resources to implement the plans. It is, therefore, critical for student affairs administrators to know the history, culture, and people in their institutions and to take into account their colleagues who also wish to influence events. They should know their business, actively participate in institutional life, and be students of the inevitable political processes of their institutions, including the tactics, strategies, and possibilities that are available to them. Institutional politics should be understood, appreciated for its potential and limitations, and practiced as competently as possible.

Certainly, the practice of politics without values is bleak. Lacking a clear sense of fairness, high level of integrity, and commitment to the students, faculty, and institutions we serve, organizational politics can disintegrate to the distasteful, self-serving spectacle too often seen in our political institutions. There is another way—one that understands the processes necessary to create consensus about where we are going and how we will get there, but that demonstrates the best values of higher education.

References

Appleton, J. R. "The Context." In P. L. Moore (ed.), *Managing the Political Dimension of Student Affairs.* New Directions for Student Services, no. 55. San Francisco: Jossey-Bass, 1991.

Appleton, J. R., Briggs, C. M., and Rhatigan, J. J. *Pieces of Eight.* Portland, OR: National Association of Student Personnel Administrators Institute of Research and Development, 1978.

Bacharach, S. B., and Lawler, E. J. *Power and Politics in Organizations: The Social Psychology of Conflict, Coalitions, and Bargaining.* San Francisco: Jossey-Bass, 1980.

Baldridge, J. V. *Power and Conflict in the University.* New York: Wiley, 1971.

Baldridge, J. V. "Organizational Change Processes: A Political Systems Approach." In J. R. Appleton (ed.), *Selected Major Speeches and Excerpts from National Association of Student Personnel Administrator's 55th Annual Conference,* Monograph no. 4. Washington, D.C.: National Association of Student Personnel Administrators, Oct. 1973.

Birnbaum, R. *How Colleges Work. The Cybernetics of Academic Organization and Leadership.* San Francisco: Jossey-Bass, 1988.

Block, P. *The Empowered Manager: Positive Political Skills at Work*. San Francisco: Jossey-Bass, 1987.

Bloland, P. A. "Key Academic Values and Issues." In P. L. Moore (ed.), *Managing the Political Dimension of Student Affairs*. New Directions for Student Services, no. 55. San Francisco: Jossey-Bass, 1991.

Bolman, L. G., and Deal, T. E. *Modern Approaches to Understanding and Managing Organizations*. San Francisco: Jossey-Bass, 1984.

Brown, R. M. "Working with the President and Senior Administrators." In P. L. Moore (ed.), *Managing the Political Dimension of Student Affairs*. New Directions for Student Services, no. 55. San Francisco: Jossey-Bass, 1991.

Canon, H. J., and Brown, R. D. (eds.). *Applied Ethics in Student Services*. New Directions for Student Services, no. 30. San Francisco: Jossey-Bass, 1985.

Ellis, H., and Moon, J. "The Middle Manager: Truly in the Middle." In P. L. Moore (ed.), *Managing the Political Dimension of Student Affairs*. New Directions for Student Services, no. 55. San Francisco: Jossey-Bass, 1991.

French, J. R. P., and Raven, B. H. "The Bases of Social Power." In D. Cartwright (ed.), *Studies in Social Power*. Ann Arbor: University of Michigan Press, 1959.

King, S. W. *Communication and Social Influence*. Reading, MA: Addison Wesley, 1975.

Mamarchev, H. L., and Williamson, M. L. "Women and African Americans: Stories Told and Lessons Learned—A Case Study." In P. L. Moore (ed.), *Managing the Political Dimension of Student Affairs*. New Directions for Student Services, no. 55. San Francisco: Jossey-Bass, 1991.

Moore, P. L. "Ideas for the Chief." In P. L. Moore (ed.), *Managing the Political Dimension of Student Affairs*. New Directions for Student Services, no. 55. San Francisco: Jossey-Bass, 1991.

Moore, P. L., and Moore, S. C. "Survey of Political Involvement of Chief Student Affairs Officers." Unpublished data, 1991.

Pfeffer, J. *Power in Organizations*. Marshfield, MA: Pitman, 1981.

Sandeen, A. *The Chief Student Affairs Officer: Leader, Manager, Mediator, Educator*. San Francisco: Jossey-Bass, 1991.

Schein, E. H. *Organizational Culture and Leadership: A Dynamic View*. San Francisco: Jossey-Bass, 1985.

Smith, D. G. "Small Colleges and Religious Institutions: Special Issues." In P. L. Moore (ed.), *Managing the Political Dimension of Student Affairs*. New Directions for Student Services, no. 55. San Francisco: Jossey-Bass, 1991.

Upcraft, M. L., and Poole, T. G. "Ethical Issues and Administrative Politics." In P. L. Moore (ed.), *Managing the Political Dimension of Student Affairs*. New Directions for Student Services, no. 55. San Francisco: Jossey-Bass, 1991.

Webber, R. A. *Management: Basic Elements of Managing Organizations*. Homewood, IL: Irwin, 1979.

Yates, D., Jr. *The Politics of Management. Exploring the Inner Workings of Public and Private Organizations*. San Francisco: Jossey-Bass, 1985.

Young, R. B. (ed.). *The Invisible Leaders: Student Affairs Mid-Managers*. Washington, D.C.: National Association of Student Personnel Administrators, 1990.

CHAPTER ELEVEN

PLANNING, MANAGING, AND FINANCING FACILITIES AND SERVICES

George S. McClellan and Margaret J. Barr

Management in student affairs is "the process of organizing human and fiscal resources to meet institutional and program goals in an efficient, effective, ethical, and fiscally responsible manner." (Barr, 1988a, p. 9) One major management activity for student affairs staff involves planning for and operating facilities that serve the broad campus community. Whether the facility is a residence hall, a student union, or a recreation center, it is essential that student affairs professionals understand the strategic and operational considerations in facility management and construction.

At a college or university, facilities are more than just buildings. A student union, for example, becomes a location for student involvement and participation. A residence hall becomes a place for students to learn about and appreciate differences. Recreation centers become places for informal interaction between students, staff, and faculty. The programs, activities, and services within the building and the individuals and groups who use the facility all shape what the building means to a campus community. Thus, a campus facility, whether it is new, established, or in the process of being renovated, presents a unique set of problems and issues for the student affairs professional.

This chapter will discuss strategic and operational issues involved in managing facilities. Specific issues regarding renovation and construction of a facility will also be reviewed. Next, the challenges presented to managers of facilities as campus environments and populations change will be discussed. Methods to assess those changes and use the data for sound facility management will be addressed. Finally, the chapter will conclude with specific recommendations for practice.

Central Issues in Facility Management

Consideration of both strategic and operational issues is essential for effective management of facilities. "One shot" or static approaches may yield satisfactory short-term results, but the changing character of campus constituencies and campus environments make it highly unlikely these short-term successes will sustain user satisfaction. A well designed ongoing assessment program can serve as a valuable resource in both strategic and operational planning. The feedback gathered through assessment can provide insight into both perceptions of existing facilities and services and the changing characteristics of user groups.

Strategic Aspects of Facilities Management

A number of strategic questions influence the effective management of facilities.

What Is the Mission? The mission statement for a student affairs division should reflect the core values and purposes of that division within the broader context of the institutional mission. Similarly, the mission statement of a specific department in student affairs should reflect the core values and purposes of the department within the context of the student affairs division's mission statement.

Daily decision-making processes must include intentional efforts to test the ramifications of decisions for congruence with the mission statement of the department, division, and institution. Given the importance of the mission statement as a guiding management document, it cannot be allowed to reside in a binder on a shelf in an office. The mission statement should be shared with new staff members and new facility advisory board members as a part of their training program. Proposals for decisions regarding the facility and its services should demonstrate a connection to the values and purposes expressed in the facility mission statement. In addition, display of the facility mission statement in the building provides an opportunity for patrons to review it, comment on it, and evaluate whether or not the facility is meeting stated goals. Finally, the facility mission statement should be the subject of periodic review to assure congruence with the institutional mission statement and needs of those who use the facility.

Who Uses the Facility? Understanding who uses the facility and under what circumstances is an essential first step in facility management and planning. While simple counts of the number of individuals served provide useful information, such data is usually not enough. In addition, the astute manager learns who uses the facility under what circumstances and at what times. For example, a residence hall is used primarily by students and staff during the academic year. However, in the summer months conference groups or athletic camps are often in residence. Each of these client groups have unique needs, but those needs cannot be accommodated unless the differentiation among users is clearly understood by the facility manager. It usually is helpful to look at the types of activities that take place in the space (i.e., receptions, meetings, lounging, eating), the time of the event (morning, noon, afternoon, evenings, weekends), and whether the clientele is primarily students, staff, faculty, or members of the larger community. Specific data regarding the use of the facility helps plan for staffing needs as well as for any facility modifications that might be needed.

What Are the Needs? Understanding both the needs of those who use the facility and the institution is essential to facility development and management. Upcraft's and Schuh's chapter on needs assessment in this volume provides valuable guidance to managers attempting to gather useful data about the needs of those using a facility. Careful attention must be paid to the needs assessment process, and differentiation should be made between and among client groups. For example, students, staff, and faculty may have very different reasons and expectations for use of a campus recreation facility. Students may want more opportunities for interaction with others through organized classes or recreation programs. Staff and faculty may need facility access at times convenient to their work schedules to play racquetball or swim. Each set of needs is legitimate. They are, however, different, and those differences must be understood.

At times, student affairs staff members fall into the trap of creating and maintaining facilities and programs to meet their own needs rather than those of the broader community. A cardinal rule of facility management is to not assume that what works in one institution is completely transferable to another place or time. Systematic assessment of community member needs helps keep the focus of the manager on those who use the facility rather than on the needs of those who work in it.

Finally, it is important to understand the theoretical underpinnings of our shared profession for those theories inform practitioners about our clients. Developmental and other theories provide a useful lens through which a situation or question can be explored; however, they are not templates for decision-making. Potential needs identified through the application of theory should be locally tested through the professional experience of staff and the responses of the users of the facility.

Is Diversity Valued? One reason for caution in the use made of developmental theory is the limitations many theories have with respect to diversity. Students, staff, and faculty are all increasingly diverse. Diversity issues on our campuses include a range of persons reflecting differences in age, sexual orientation, marital status, ability, religion, and the full rainbow of ethnicity and race. Valuing diversity in facilities management is evidenced through affirmative recruitment and selection processes for staff; an inclusive management style; use of diverse decorations and artwork; and sensitivity to the varied needs of the user population. The increasing diversity of our campus communities is at once one of the greatest challenges and one of the greatest opportunities in higher education today.

Is Management Inclusive? There are benefits to be derived from the inclusive management of facilities beyond the obvious benefit derived from enjoying multiple insights into decision-making. Users who perceive their opinions have been given appropriate weight in the decision-making process are more likely to support the results of that process even when those results are not exactly what they might have wished. Staff members, many who work long hours for modest compensation, may perceive the opportunity to be involved in the process as a benefit both in terms of feeling valued and as a matter of professional development. Finally, others inside and outside the student affairs division are more able to understand and support the initiatives of a department when they have been involved in the formative discussion of those initiatives.

Who Are the Partner Departments? The effective and efficient operation of facilities and services on most campuses would not be possible without the active partnership of a wide array of partner departments. Depending on the campus organizational structure, these partner departments may report within or outside of the student affairs division. Physical plant, campus police, grounds keeping, legal affairs, purchasing, accounting, and budgeting are examples of typical partner departments. It is important for the director and key associates throughout the facility to know counterparts across campus and communicate effectively with other key players to facilitate operations.

Who Are Potential Political Partners? Just as productive relationships with partner departments are important to the effective management of facilities, political partnerships are important in achieving and maintaining support for funding both facilities and services. Fiscal resources are finite even at the most well funded institutions, and the debate on how best to employ those resources to meet the institution's goals often is reduced to a discussion regarding which good idea will receive funding support. Developing key faculty and staff partners who are willing to support funding requests for facilities helps assure the approval of those requests when the discussion narrows the choice between equally attractive project alternatives.

Political partnerships are also important in situations where there is disagreement on campus regarding an issue, initiative, or policy matter important to a facility and its services. As an example, many facilities managers have experienced the rancor that results from efforts to implement no-smoking policies in building commons. The likelihood of successful implementation of such a policy is enhanced if political allies in student, staff, and faculty governance groups publicly support the change in policy.

It is important to keep in mind political partnerships, like all partnerships, are reciprocal relationships. The persons or groups to whom facilities management staff turn for support have needs of their own, and the skillful facilities manager will be proactive in identifying and addressing their partners' needs. A more complete discussion of political partnerships can be found in Chapter Ten by Paul Moore, "The Political Dimensions of Decision-Making," in this volume.

Operational Aspects of Facilities Management

Budget, staff, and maintenance are essential issues that must be addressed in facility management.

Developing a Budget. Building a budget based solely on an incremental increase over the previous year's allocation is a poor management practice. Incremental approaches to budgeting enable the institutionalization of outdated facilities and services because periodic reviews are not required. Wasteful spending may result because funding is not tied to specific goals. Facilities managers who have relied on incremental funding as their primary tool of budget are likely to find departments having lesser success in the budgetary process as institutions adopt increasingly rigorous budgetary processes.

A more efficient and effective means available to obtain needed funding support is to assure that funding requests submitted reflect goals articulated in established planning documents. Boyle explains that "budgets flow naturally from good planning—good planning does not emanate from adequate budgets" (1995, p. 52). Explicitly articulating the link between a request for funding and the mission statement, strategic plan, or current capital campaign goals will help those making budget decisions understand the importance of the request both to the facility and to the broader campus community.

Building a budget based on established planning documents also helps assure the available funding will be used efficiently. Funding based on sound planning focuses resources on projects and programs that have been agreed to by the management team.

Budgeting for Utilities, Overhead, and Equipment Replacement. Budgets should be developed to reflect goals articulated in planning documents, but they must also account for the less glamorous realities of ongoing facilities operations. One such item is utilities. The facilities manager needs to know if the cost for utilities is included in the department's budget. If so, it is important for a facilities manager to account for rate increases in the budget planning process.

Institutional overhead costs also may be included in the operations budget if the facility is considered an auxiliary enterprise. Is the facility charged for its use of central services provided by the institution? Such central services may include payroll, purchasing, risk management, insurance, accounts receivable, or other business functions. Each institution develops a formula for such charges that must be understood by the facility budget manager.

A replacement schedule should be established for equipment and furnishings and a funding mechanism developed to support such purchases. On some campuses, reserve funds are established to support replacement needs and regular transfers are made to reserves from the operating budget. On other campuses, excess income over expenses are designated as equipment and furniture replacement funds. The important issue is to develop a realistic plan for replacement and fund it over a period of years.

New construction, as well as existing facilities, requires a well thought-out replacement plan that ideally should be funded from the day the building opens. Failure to plan for equipment and furnishing replacement creates problems for future facility managers.

Budget Implications of Deferred Maintenance. Planning for deferred maintenance is an integral part of facilities management. As buildings age, money is required to maintain infrastructure such as plumbing, electrical, roofs, elevators, interior and exterior walls, windows, and heating/ventilation/air conditioning. Costs for such repairs, maintenance, or facility improvements can easily be hundreds of thousands of dollars each year.

Several key questions need to be asked in addressing the issue of deferred maintenance. Is the facility responsible for funding its own deferred maintenance program? What insurance exists to cover expenses resulting from unforeseen emergencies such as flood, fire, tornado, and earthquake? Are there other sources of funds available to the facility to meet needs in the event of an unforeseen circumstance? Should a reserve account be established and routinely funded to cover such expenditures? A facilities manager should be aware of the answers to all of these important budget questions.

Establishing Maintenance Cycles. In addition to the issue of deferred maintenance, facilities management must address the issue of ongoing maintenance for the facility. Users may not observe the need for repair of a ceiling or pipes, but they do notice when a hallway carpet becomes frayed or the ballroom ceiling needs painted. The one-time purchase of paint, furniture, or carpet is not as expensive as replacing a roof, but over time these recurring annual maintenance expenses are a significant investment.

A practical approach to these important ongoing maintenance issues is to develop an annual maintenance cycle for the facility. A maintenance cycle involves establishing a list of items to be repaired or refurbished and then establishing a life cycle for each item. For example, carpet in residence hall rooms might be replaced every six years and walls in meeting rooms painted every three years. A maintenance cycle can be developed based on the identified life cycles, and the anticipated annual resources for maintenance projects can be included in budget preparation.

Staffing. The two largest areas of ongoing expense in the operating budgets of most facilities are facilities maintenance and facilities staff. The two elements are inexorably tied. Well built and maintained facilities and well planned and implemented programs come about as the result of the efforts of well chosen, well trained, and well motivated staffs.

Recruiting and selecting staff is one of the most important decision-making processes for any organization. The scope of the recruitment and selection process is determined by the level of position available, but the elements of an effective process are the same no matter what the staff level. An inclusive search and selection process focusing on providing both candidates and employer the opportunity to realistically assess the fit between person and position will help assure a successful selection. More on this subject can be found in the Chapter Nine, "Selecting, Training, Supervising, and Evaluating Staff," by Saundra Taylor and Mark von Destinon, elsewhere in this volume.

Facilities staff groups also frequently include a large number of student paraprofessionals working in a wide array of positions. These employment opportunities are important to students as a source of income, but also these work experiences can be important in the development of the students' sense of competency, autonomy, and leadership. Facility managers should be mindful of their responsibility in helping all staff members to develop. It is, however, particularly important for these managers to be intentional in their role as educators in dealing with student paraprofessionals.

Training Programs. Training programs for student paraprofessional staff usually should be conducted in groups to achieve operating efficiencies and to provide a sense of connection to a cohort of fellow student staff members. It may be possible to coordinate with other departments to provide training to a variety of student paraprofessional staff members on information that is important to all of them. Again, the benefits from such a coordinated approach would include economies of scale and a sense of connection by the paraprofessional staff to a larger cohort and a larger enterprise.

Training programs should exist for all positions, student and non-student. These programs should include a list of the information and skills that need to be obtained and who will help the new staff person obtain them. Staff members focused on facility management should receive specific training in service skills. Front-line staff members, student and non-student, are the first to learn of a user's frustration with a particular facility feature or service. Customer service and conflict resolution training for a staff member can mean the difference between the successful resolution of a difficult situation and the escalation of that difficult situation into an intractable dilemma.

An updated staff handbook for every position can be particularly useful in the training process. In addition to information specific to that position and contact information for persons or departments that are important to the position, the handbook should contain information about the facility and its services, the institutional context within which it operates, and mission statements for the department and its parent division. Training programs for all staff members should be ongoing. This will help the staff continue to develop, and the training discussions can help bring to light areas for possible improvement in the facilities and their services.

Professional Staff Issues. It is all too common to find friction in facility management between those staff members working in operations positions and those working in programming positions. Operations staff members' concerns about building issues are perceived by programmers as undercutting important programs, and programmers' plans to host demanding programs in the facility are seen by operations staff as being insensitive to important maintenance issues. Both sets of concerns are valid, and the existence of friction between the two groups is more a comment on the ways in which staff members are being involved in management rather than on the staff members themselves. Defining staff positions as either operations or programming, or allowing positions to be understood as such, denies the fundamental interconnectedness of the two functions. The facility manager should encourage blending of responsibilities. Operations staff members should be encouraged to advise a student group, and programmers should be invited to participate in facilities maintenance meetings.

Similar friction can develop between shifts of workers in facilities that operate for extended hours each day. Staff members become identified, either by title or by their own perception, as being day staff, evening staff or night staff. The distinction is an artificial one. Staff members should be encouraged to understand their role as being tied to particular functions, processes, services, and areas of responsibility. Further, staff members should also understand their roles in the broader context of the department. Neither the facility nor its services belongs exclusively to one staff group or another; and all staff groups should be involved in all of the decision-making processes for the department.

Contract Services. One consequence of the mounting pressure on institutional budgets has been an increased frequency of contracting with an external vendor for facilities management or services. Contractual arrangements with bookstores, food service vendors, laundry machine services, and coin-operated vending have been commonplace for decades in higher education. Recently, however, similar contractual arrangements have been made by institutions for health services, counseling services, residence halls, athletic facilities, and physical plant services among others. The use of contract services is likely to continue to be a matter of discussion and decision on campuses for years to come. Student affairs facility managers should become familiar with the issues involved in contracting and the positive and negative consequences of such decisions. Moving to contracted services is a major step and involves changes for employees as well as the institution. If the decision is made to go to contract services, careful consideration should be given to both the intended and unintended consequences of the decision for both employees and patrons.

The first step is the development of a request for proposals (RFP). The RFP should include background information regarding the institution requesting the proposal, the nature of facilities or services for which proposals are being sought, detailed information regarding the needs to be addressed in the proposal, financial information, and information regarding the proposal process. The latter information should include a mandatory information session for any vendors wishing to submit proposals, contact information for vendors having questions concerning the process, and a deadline and destination for submission of proposals. Requests for proposals should be developed and distributed in accordance with any applicable institutional regulation or state law, and they should always be developed in partnership with legal counsel.

The process for reviewing proposals may be conducted by an individual or a representative committee. In either case, the process should be an inclusive one designed to provide both the department and the vendors with an opportunity to realistically assess the potential for a contractual relationship. After a vendor is selected, the contracts should be developed in partnership with legal counsel.

Legal Issues. The increasingly litigious nature of our society presents unique challenges for facility managers. An injury due to a frayed or slick surface may result in a lawsuit far more costly, regardless of outcome, than the cost of replacing the carpet or replacing the non-skid stripping on the steps would have been. Although facilities managers should not allow the possibility of litigation to prevent them from achieving important goals, neither should managers pursue those goals without due consideration for the legal framework within which they operate.

One important legal framework for facilities managers is the Americans with Disabilities Act (ADA, [42 U.S.C. § 12101 et seq.]). The influence of this federal law on managing facilities and services is far-reaching. The ADA addresses issues of access and accommodation. Such issues can be as simple as the addition of Braille signs into a building or as complex as the need to provide signing services for hearing impaired patrons at a public program or conference.

The law also addresses employment issues for persons with disabilities. The matter can be as simple as providing additional lighting at a workstation for a person with a visual disability or as complex as responding to the needs of a staff member with an allergy to substances in the work environment. ADA establishes thresholds that must be met by facilities and employers over time. Facilities managers should seek legal advice regarding both the requirements of the ADA as written and the current legal interpretations of those requirements. It is also important, however, for facilities managers to understand and appreciate the difference between their facilities and services being accessible and being welcoming to persons with disabilities. The guiding ethical principles of care and inclusion should inform the work of facilities managers with respect to civil rights as much as any federal law in this area.

A specific legal issue for facility managers is the potential liability for unrelated business income tax (UBIT, [26 U.S.C. § 501(c)(7), § 501(c)(9), and § 501(c)(17)]) liability. Nonprofit educational enterprises enjoy tax-exempt status when conducting business in pursuit of their educational mission. When the business activities of those enterprises stray outside the boundaries of that mission, the income from those activities may be subject to taxation. The precise line between activities that do comport with the educational mission of the institution and those that do not is open to interpretation. Facilities managers seeking to expand revenue for their units should be particularly cautious when considering new ventures. Any activity triggering an UBIT audit is likely to invite a broader investigation of activities of the department as well. Again, consultation with legal counsel regarding the UBIT implications of any particular program or service is advised when there is any doubt as to the ability of that program or service to qualify as a part of the institution's mission.

Finally, the astute facility manager should be aware of applicable state and federal law with regard to employment including anti-discrimination statutes, occupational health and safety of employees, and, in the case of facilities renovation, removal of hazardous materials. The best approach to all legal questions facing a facility manager, however, is to consult competent legal advice early and often.

Audit. Facilities generate a large number of business transactions. Examples of typical transactions include room and board contracts, submission of payroll, receipts from cash sales, placement of purchase orders, and payment of accounts. Each one of these transactions presents the opportunity for the intentional or unintentional mishandling of institutional assets. It is the fiduciary responsibility of facilities managers to develop and assure the participation of the department in an ongoing program of periodic audit of the department's business procedures. Auditing services may be provided by the institution's own auditing department, or these services may be arranged through contract with an external vendor depending on institutional policies. Care should be exercised to assure all business practices conform to institutional policies and established accounting procedures.

Issues in Renovation and Construction of Facilities

Many of the issues involved in managing a recently renovated or newly constructed facility are the same as those involved in managing a facility that has existed for some time. The process of planning and implementing the renovation or construction of a facility, however, presents unique opportunities and challenges for the facilities management team.

Planning the Project

The planning process for renovation or construction of a campus facility should be inclusive. Representatives of important user groups should be invited to participate. This representation should be as broad as possible. This will help assure a more balanced view than might otherwise be developed by a group of facility managers. Care should also be taken in assembling the planning team to reflect the diversity of current and potential user populations. As the planning process progresses to a point where there are defined alternatives to be reviewed, these options should be presented in appropriate community forums as a means for gathering input from anyone interested in the project.

The first step in planning for the renovation or construction of a facility is development of a program statement. The goal of a program statement is to accurately and completely describe the programmatic needs for the facility without proscribing the means by which those needs should be met. The experts in defining the needs are the facilities management team and those who use the facility. The expert in identifying ways in which space might be used to meet identified needs is the architectural firm or consultant hired for the project. The program statement should reflect the identified user group needs that are consistent with the mission of the facility. The constraints of project funding might necessitate that some of these needs not be met as a part of the renovation being planned, but the articulation of those needs is a critical step in facility planning.

Although it is important to open up the planning process by thinking imaginatively, it is equally important not to raise false expectations or waste community resources on ostentatious or impractical planning. The focus of the planning process should be on the future, and not on fad or fashion. The planning group's definition of quality, a characteristic frequently mentioned in program statements, should include the concepts of durability and timelessness.

Financing the Project

Barr (1988b, p. 28) notes, "Construction of new facilities and renovation of existing facilities present some of the most complicated fiscal problems in higher education." Developing strategies to finance major repair, renovation, or new facility construction takes time, energy, and expertise. Several options are available to an institution, but the choice will be dictated by both the legal status of the institution and the philosophy of the institution regarding debt.

Self-Financing. If the institution is able, self-financing of major renovation or construction is the most desirable option. Usually, if that option is chosen, the financing plan for the facility must also account for interest payments to the institution for the use of the money during the period of the loan. Unfortunately, most institutions are not able to completely self-finance major facility renovation or construction.

Gift Support. In rare circumstances, gift support provides the entire cost for a new facility or renovation. The generosity of donors to American higher education is remarkable, and naming opportunities abound on most college and university campuses. Gift support does not occur by accident and often requires years of work with potential donors. The astute facility manager should always have institutionally approved plans for facility construction and renovation ready to present when donors request proposals. Most often, however, it is a combination of gift support and other financing options that make the construction or renovation possible.

Bonds. Bonds have become a popular form of financing at public and private institutions. Bonds are sold by the institution to finance projected facility debt and future revenues are used to finance the debt. In public institutions, bonds are often backed by a dedicated student fee that is used to pay back both bonds and interest. In both public and private institutions, revenues from room rentals, user fees, and facility rentals can be dedicated to bond repayment (Barr, 1988, p. 30). Ratings for bonds are provided through a bond rating service, and those ratings will determine the interest rates paid for the bonds. The interest rates in turn will determine whether or not issuance of the bonds is feasible.

There are restrictions on the amount of bonding authority for any institution. Those restrictions are determined by federal and state statute. Consultation with legal counsel and institutional finance officers is essential in order to determine if the opportunity to issue bonds is even an option.

Joint Enterprises. One emerging approach to facility development is that of establishing a joint venture with a private entrepreneur or local government. "Usually this approach occurs when both parties benefit and when the project meets a central educational need of the college or university" (Barr, 1988b, p. 30). In such ventures, the institution may provide the land, planning support, and pledge long-term operation of the facility. The private or governmental sector provides the initial capital for construction and start-up costs. Although such projects have the advantages of expediency, agreements should be carefully negotiated to assure ultimate control by the institution is consistent with the mission of the enterprise.

Renovation Concerns

After a program statement has been developed for a renovation project, the project design firm or consultant working on the project should be asked to develop design concepts and preliminary planning documents including estimated costs. Facilities managers need to monitor those cost estimates to assure that allowances for the hidden costs of renovation are included. It is not uncommon to experience a lack of accurate information about the infrastructure of older buildings. Older buildings also frequently contain asbestos in floors, walls, and ceilings, and removal of asbestos is costly. A contingency line sufficient for responding to hidden costs should be included as a part of the budget planning for the renovation. The renovation of a facility also may trigger elevated standards for compliance with fire, safety, and other codes (including the need for access for the handicapped and improved life safety systems), as well as local, state, and federal regulations.

After the renovation project is designed and funded, the next step is planning the actual work. Facilities managers are then often faced with the challenge of operating the facility and its services while renovation work is taking place. The technique of using a phased approach to construction can be very helpful in minimizing the disruptive impact of renovation. Phasing of a project involves taking one area out of service, completing renovation in that area, and then returning it to service before moving on to another area. Phasing usually means that the project will be more costly.

Even when a project can be phased to minimize disruption, it is unlikely that the phasing will eliminate inconvenience for users. There are a number of techniques that may help facilities managers to address the inconvenience. User group representatives who were included in the planning process can be asked to help convey to their constituencies the benefit that will be derived from the renovations when complete. A model or other visual representation of the facility as it will appear when renovated can be displayed so that users can have a sense of what improvements will be made. Advance notice and ongoing reports to users regarding the project can be distributed using newspaper articles, fliers, listserv announcements, and Web sites. Facilities staff should not seek to minimize or understate the inconvenience presented to users, but the staff should also encourage users not to overstate the matter either. Simply acknowledging the inconvenience and assisting in finding alternate solutions is the best approach to dealing with users unhappy as a result of the work being done. Finally, invite users to a celebration marking the completion of the renovation and the opening of the fully renovated facility.

Construction Issues

As is the case with renovation projects, there are hidden costs to be avoided in the planning of a new facility. Some relate to legal issues and local code compliance. Others involve the hidden costs of high-maintenance features. Something as simple as standardizing light fixtures can be the source of significant savings in the operating budget of the facility. Making sure that the types of finishes and equipment being used can be cleaned and maintained at a reasonable cost is another means of avoiding future high-maintenance problems. The time to think about the ongoing consequences of decisions is during planning. It will be too late or too costly to do anything about high-maintenance problems when the building is under construction or in operation.

Just as the facilities management team is excited by the construction of a new facility, the members of the campus community are also excited by such a project. Helping these community members to feel they are a part of the process is a responsibility of the facilities management team. The community should be kept informed about the project through newspaper articles, fliers, listserv announcements, building models, and Web sites. Finally, the completion of the project could be marked by celebrations involving those who planned, constructed, and funded the facility.

Prior to beginning service delivery in the new facility, the management team should conduct a "soft" opening—a test of the readiness of the facility and its services for operation. Selected members of the campus community should be invited to serve as volunteer users for the "soft" opening. This test might be linked to the celebrations for those involved in the planning, design, and construction of the facility. Following the resolution of any issues surfaced during the soft opening, the campus community should be invited to a grand opening ceremony as a means of marking the inauguration of service in the new facility.

Shared Fiscal and Operational Responsibility

Sometimes responsibility for facility management, planning, financing and construction is a shared responsibility between student affairs and another unit of the university. Most often that responsibility is shared with business affairs units. Under such arrangements, student affairs holds responsibility for the programmatic aspects of the facility such as advising groups, supervising resident assistants, and providing activities. Business affairs handles maintenance, cleaning services, financing issues, and the like. For such arrangements to be successful, student affairs staff involved in the facility must be both assertive and inclusive. Demonstrating assertive behavior involves the articulation of just what needs to be done to meet the needs of students. Demonstrating inclusive behavior means informing colleagues in business affairs of issues and concerns.

Conflict usually arises between units with shared responsibility if any of the following conditions exist:

- Lack of clear communication
- Take unilateral actions
- Failure to understand the fiscal implications of program initiatives or suggested physical renovations
- Failure to alert the other unit about problems that may come to them
- Lack of clear, easily understood policies and procedures

Most problems stem from poor communication. When faced with joint responsibility arrangements for facilities, it is important for student affairs staff to use their communication and problem-solving skills. Take the initiative to develop regular communication and joint planning mechanisms. Learn about fiscal issues and think about them when planning new initiatives. Finally, do not avoid the conflict but instead deal with it in a straight forward, respectful manner.

Change and Facilities Management

The strategic and operational issues in the management of facilities and its services are influenced by changes in campus environments. Frequently those changes on campuses are reflective of changes in the broader society. Among the societal changes having the greatest influences at colleges and universities are increasing diversity; rising expectations; the emerging use of technology; assessment; and the renewed emphasis on the value of community.

Students, staff, faculty, and other user groups come to campus facilities and services with an array of cultural and experiential backgrounds. They come with differing abilities, ages, genders, and faiths. They come as undergraduates, graduate students, and adult learners. They come alone, partnered or married, divorced, and with or without dependents. They all come, however, hoping to see some sign of themselves in their new place of study, work, or research. Campus facilities and its services play an important role in sending a welcoming message to these potential users. This message can be sent in a number of ways including the following:

- Making sure publications speak to the unique needs of diverse groups and depict a range of people as members of the community
- Displaying artwork created by an array of artists reflecting a rainbow of experience
- Presenting programs that provide the opportunity to celebrate holidays and other special occasions that are religiously or culturally significant and that help others to understand the origins and importance of these holidays
- Assuring that the decision-making process is inclusive and respectful of divergent points of view
- Assuring that within diverse groups all people are individuals and will be responded to accordingly

Diverse users also reach campus with very different expectations for personal security and safety. Reflecting the broader social concern with crime, users of facilities are demanding improved lighting, additional security phones, active monitoring of building entrances, and sophisticated systems for control of access.

Many also believe there is an increasing sense of consumerism on the part of users. The relationship between the facility and users is increasingly perceived and expressed as being that of merchant and customer. This increasing consumerism parallels the rising demand by the broader constituencies of higher education for accountability and improved performance.

The explosive growth in the use of computers and computer-assisted communications has altered facilities management. Providing routine services online has potential benefits for facilities management. Making routine functions (repair requests, meeting room reservations, scheduling appointments, submitting housing applications, and others) easily available online provides convenience of service for users. Although facilities managers should take advantage of the opportunity presented by technology to both facilitate user service and redirect staff resources, on-line service delivery is not a universal solution. Complex interactions are best served by personal interaction, and human development requires human contact. Finally, while access to computing is growing rapidly, it is not universal. Delivering services exclusively by computer, or preferentially by computer, may disenfranchise some community members from equal opportunity to make use of facilities and its services.

It is interesting that, at the same time many have withdrawn to their workstations as the center of their campus activity, interest in the notion of the campus as community is on the rise. The rhetoric of community can be found in some of the most active conversations on our campuses: diversity, civility, and service learning. Facilities and services can play an important role in the discussions of all these topics and in the movement toward an understanding of campuses as communities. Facilities staff can model behavior, present programs, host programs, and design spaces in ways that encourage a sense of community among users.

Budgetary constraints, rising consumerism, increased demands for accountability, and the forces of change (including diversity and technology) all mitigate to make effective assessment more important than ever for student affairs professionals. Upcraft and Schuh (1996, p. 315) state, "Assessment is a key to the survival of student affairs, as well as a tool for policy development, decision making, ensuring quality, accountability, and accessibility, strategic planning, and responding to political pressures." A comprehensive assessment program is an essential element of sound facility management. Upcraft and Schuh (1996) suggest that an assessment program should include a blend of quantitative and qualitative studies.

Recommendations for Practice

Whether managing an existing, newly renovated, or recently constructed facility, the management of facilities and their services is a complex and demanding role. The information in this chapter and the recommendations that follow are intended to help new practitioners in developing their facilities management skills and to assist more seasoned managers in enhancing their professional practice.

Facilities managers should constantly evaluate why things are being done the way they are in the facilities. It is almost certain that at least some of the users of the facility and its services are asking the same question. Exploring the answers will either reaffirm the purpose of the current practice, or it will prompt consideration of alternative approaches. Either result is a healthy one for the facility and its users.

Management of the budget of a facility and its services should always be a shared responsibility. The development of budget materials for a facility and its services should be an inclusive process involving advisory board members, staff members, and management team members. The budget should reflect the established goals and mission of the department based on existing planning documents. Ongoing compliance with the budget should be the joint responsibility of the entire management team, and review of the budget status should be included as a periodic activity of management meetings. Feedback regarding budget performance should be provided to staff members as a group, and formal feedback on budget management should be included in the performance evaluation of management team members.

Facilities managers must keep up to date regarding facilities management issues, best practices, changes in law, and the changing needs of those who use their facilities. Involvement in appropriate professional associations is an effective means of keeping current while providing other important professional development opportunities. Taking time to read the publications offered through these associations, and from other sources, is an essential investment of time for facilities managers. Engaging in reflection and dialogue with other professionals in the field is equally important.

Management theory, like developmental theory, can be a useful tool for facilities managers. The use of management theory, like the use of developmental theory, is not without limitations. It is not always easy or appropriate to use an artificial construct to resolve a real-life human issue. The most consistently useful management theory for facilities managers is MBWA—management by walking around. Remember, it is a nice facility. Get out of the office and see all of it on a regular basis.

Finally, facilities managers should be careful not to confuse the facility for its function. The facility and its furnishings are a vehicle for the delivery of services provided. Few would visit the facility were it not for the services, and the delivery of services would be impossible without the facility. Skillful management teams understand that the highest calling of their profession is to coordinate the facilities and services with the intention of meeting the basic and developmental needs of the users.

References

Barr, M. J. "Managing Money." In M. L. Upcraft and M. J. Barr (eds.), *Managing Student Affairs Effectively*. San Francisco, CA: Jossey-Bass, 1988a.

Barr, M. J. "Managing the Enterprise." In M. L. Upcraft and M. J. Barr (eds.), *Managing Student Affairs Effectively*. San Francisco, CA: Jossey-Bass, 1988b.

Boyle, T. P. "Good Questions for Sound Decision Making." In D. W. Woodard (ed.), *Budgeting as a Tool for Policy in Student Affairs*. San Francisco: Jossey-Bass, 1995.

Upcraft, M. L., and Schuh, J. H. "Making Assessment Work: Guiding Principles and Recommendations." In M. L. Upcraft and J. H. Schuh (eds.), *Assessment in Student Affairs: A Guide for Practitioners*. San Francisco: Jossey-Bass. 1996.

Statutory References

20 U.S.C. § 1092

20 U.S.C. § 1232g

26 U.S.C. § 501(c)(7), § 501(c)(9), and § 501(c)(17)

42 U.S.C. § 12101 et seq.

CHAPTER TWELVE ·

TECHNOLOGICAL CHANGES IN STUDENT AFFAIRS ADMINISTRATION

M. Lee Upcraft and Harold Goldsmith

Technological innovations and applications are rapidly transforming our society. This transformation has touched almost every aspect of our lives and its impact seems to be accelerating. Bill Gates has said technology is the revolution about which we have no choice (Gates, 1995). Higher education has lagged behind many other sectors of society in the adoption of technology as an administrative, learning, and communication tool. This, however, is changing as external forces and internal adaptations are compelling the adoption of new technological tools to compete successfully with both other higher education institutions and the corporate sector, as well as meet the challenges of an increasingly computer literate student body. There are many examples of these trends:

- At California State University's newest campus at Monterey Bay, one building is conspicuously absent from their blueprints: the library. The campus will instead rely on technology for information retrieval.
- The Western Governors' University, with its cyberspace campus and virtual classrooms, has taken steps toward full accreditation. Many other campuses, states, and regions are developing "virtual" campuses and enrolling students worldwide.
- At a leading research university, it is now possible to inquire about and apply for admission, get admitted, accept admission, receive advising, and enroll for

courses entirely through technological means without ever talking to another human being, either face to face or by telephone.

All of these trends, of course, directly and indirectly impact student affairs. The nature of our work, our investment in face-to-face relationships, and our reliance on students being physically present on our campuses has made our adoption of technological innovations somewhat cautious. As with most technological changes, early adopters have shown the way and advocated for its use. Student affairs administrators, however, have many questions. "Is the technological revolution a journey to higher levels of human experience or a gigantic leap into the abyss of total mechanization of the human race? Or will it be neither?" (Upcraft and Terenzini, 1999, p. 1) It is clear that student affairs professionals will need to become more knowledgeable about the uses and limitations of technology as well as the influence it will have on students and their learning and development if we are to fulfill our obligations to future student generations.

In this chapter, we will discuss the larger context of the technological revolution and the impact of technology on student learning and the delivery of student services and programs. The "downsides" of technology will also be discussed. Finally, the implications for student affairs policy and practice will be reviewed.

Technology, Society, and Higher Education

We are now in a time of unprecedented change. Naisbitt and Aburdene (1990) assert that "new technologies have changed the importance of scale and location and extended the power of individuals" (p. 301). They describe how technology empowers individuals by connecting them with the world electronically. Naisbitt and Aburdene also assert that the truly global cities of the 21st century will be the smartest and not the largest. These themes of individual empowerment and global networks are echoed by Louis Perleman (1992) who describes the technological transformation of the late 20th century and ends with the optimistic idea that "the same technology that is transforming work offers the new learning systems to solve the problems it creates" (p. 50).

The relationship between learning, technology, and work is the central theme of the work of Davis and Botkin (1994). Their thesis is that since learning is now the work of most businesses, learning is too important to be left to traditional higher education organizations. Business and industry should take over much of what is called traditional higher education in order for American business and industry to remain or get competitive in the global economy. Dollence and Norris

(1995) assert that the need for learning in the knowledge society is so great that not enough traditional institutions could be built to accommodate the need, but see a great opportunity for higher education to meet this need through the adoption of technology.

The debate outside and inside higher education has been intense. Few would argue that, on the whole, American higher education has been a success by most measures. That it is still one of America's most popular exports attests to its value. The question is the ability of higher education to respond to the opportunities and challenges presented by technology. Western Governor's University is one such response. Thirteen western states decided not to build additional campuses in the face of double-digit enrollment growth projections for the next ten years, but rather to create and offer entire degree programs to all students on-line. Daniel (1996) argues that this need for access to higher education is a worldwide problem and the only way to provide it is through alternative instructional models, including technology.

That this transformation of society and higher education will influence student affairs should be evident from the context provided. As the delivery systems and missions of higher education are influenced by technology, the profession and practice of student affairs will be greatly affected in many ways.

Comparing Traditional and Emerging Learning Models

In the traditional higher education and student affairs model, learning and campus are synonymous. The campus is essential because it is a place where the physical facilities—laboratories, libraries, classrooms, residences—are located; where faculty, students, and administrators reside. The dominant mode of delivery of education—the classroom and the lab—requires that groups of students and a faculty member be in the same place at the same time on a regularly scheduled basis over some period of time, usually a semester. In the new learning models (see Figure 12.1), the learner will have many more choices about the way in which learning occurs. The traditional classroom is now in competition with compressed video, the Internet, videotape, computer self-guided learning and simulations, interactive learning, and other technology-based learning environments. Because technology can mediate so many kinds of instruction, competency rather than in-class time is the measure of learning, the traditional academic calendar is obsolete, learning may be pursued on an individual basis, and the pace of learning is modified to meet learner needs.

Given these changes, the out-of-classroom environment also undergoes a radical transformation. The physical presence of groups of students in one place is no longer required and those students who do assemble on a campus will have

FIGURE 12.1 THE IMPACT OF TRADITIONAL AND EMERGING TECHNOLOGY ON STUDENT AFFAIRS (GOLDSMITH, 1992)

Feature	Traditional	Emerging
Campus	Phsyical Place	Information Node
Teaching	Face to Face	Multiple Options
Programs	Campus Based	Student Based
	Face to Face	Audio/Video
	Small Groups	Computer Assisted
Student Development	18–21 Age Focus	Resources
	Creation of:	Creation of:
	Environments	Interventions
	Experiences	Resources
	Interactions	Options
Student Services	Campus Focused	Student Focused

their lives outside the classroom greatly influenced by technology. The practice of student affairs, therefore, must shift from a campus-based model to a learner-based model, wherever that learner is. The implications for the delivery of student services and programs are enormous. The emphasis will shift from providing resources in a campus environment to linking the learner with those resources wherever the learner is located and whenever those resources are needed.

The Impact of Technology on Student Learning

Upcraft and Terenzini (1999) posit the increased reliance on technology in the classroom as one of the emerging trends. Even conventional courses are being impacted by available technology. Students are often required to search the Web in order to write papers or do class projects. Faculty members' expectations about the use of the most recent information are heightened by the availability of the Internet. In some cases, video conferencing is used to bring experts into class or to have discussions with students from other parts of the world. In some laboratory classes, advanced simulations are used to conduct chemical experiments, study anatomy, or practice world politics.

E-mail is used for students to communicate with instructors or with other classmates. Some faculty members are now establishing class "chat rooms" and class listservs that allow students to link to one another. Some faculty members are requiring students to use e-mail to submit papers and class assignments and giving students feedback in the same way.

Students are also taking courses by compressed video or satellite feeds. A faculty member may not even be in the same location as the students, but can see and hear students in remote locations. E-mail connections, the telephone, and often, an on-site supervisor complement this technology and assure that students remain connected to the instructor and others in the class.

At the high end of the technology scale are course offerings on the Internet. These courses are often self-paced, have tests built in to allow the student to assess learning, provide learning resources, and permit access to an adviser or tutor to answer questions or solve problems. The student's need to interact with other students or even the instructor is diminished because of the support provided by the technology of the course. Nowadays, students may not only take entire courses on the Web, but entire degree programs as well (Van Dusen, 1997). The permutations are endless and are limited only by the creativity of the faculty and the availability of learning technologies.

These changes in the use of technology require changes in the skills necessary to become a successful learner. The active listening, note-taking, test-taking, and questioning skills of the traditional classroom may be of limited use in a technologically mediated environment. The technological learning environment, time management, software savvy, computer "comfort," personal motivation, and synthesis may be as important as skills required in a traditional classroom.

Perhaps more importantly, the relationship between the learner and the faculty member is changed dramatically, and each must assume different roles. In the traditional classroom, learning is operationally defined as a faculty member in the physical presence of many students at the same time, in the same place, over some sustained period of time, with the instructor as "expert" and students as mostly passive learners. With technology, all of these assumptions are challenged. Learning becomes a continuum in which the learner may choose what, how, when, and where to learn, and the faculty member becomes the manager of the learning experience. The oft-repeated expression that a faculty member's role shifts from the "sage on the stage" to the "guide on the side" is very trite, but very true in technology-based learning.

The Impact of Technology on Student Services and Programs

Technology has also entered nearly every facet of student life. Network connections from residence halls, campus computer labs, and students' homes allow them to access the Internet and other campus networks, and to search remote databases and libraries. We offer just a few examples:

- In career placement centers, students can link to employer Web pages for information about companies and jobs, place resumes on the Web, and present their credentials to hundreds of employers. They can formulate cover letters or home pages, send them electronically to apply for jobs, and arrange for on-campus or on-site interviews. All this can be done from the friendly confines of their rooms or homes without any contact with campus placement services.

- As stated previously, at some institutions prospective students can access admissions information, apply for admission, accept admission, apply for financial aid, receive academic advising information, and schedule courses without ever talking to an institutional representative.

- In residence halls, students can create professional-looking posters using computer graphics, advertise programs on cable channels and Web sites, participate in chat rooms, access floor Web pages, and even hold virtual floor meetings.

- In the area of group educational programs, information that was formerly presented in person can now be offered through CD-ROM and other electronic media. Speakers can use advanced technology to demonstrate or visit remote places that bring even arcane topics to life.

- The use of integrated data bases allow student affairs administrators to provide access to students so they can review their tuition bill, examine financial aid data, find other students on campus, or search for a student organization of interest. We can create personalized letters inviting students to particular events based on an interest inventory and personal profile they provide at registration. This mass customization of contact with students permits more targeted creation and marketing of programs.

- In the personal development area, self-help sessions can be created on-line that help students prepare for tests, learn better study skills, manage stress, alleviate depression, or just plain relax.

- Cyberspace lounges and cafes are great new sources of entertainment and socializing which may expand students' social interactions. Compressed video technology or interactive chat rooms permit communication with persons who may be hundreds or thousands of miles away. For students away from home for the first time, communication with family and old friends can help ease the transition to college.

- In academic advising, students and administrators can keep track of academic progress through "degree audit" programs and create "what if" scenarios that allow students to test alternative majors or course sequences, freeing up advisers to focus on more personal issues.

- Students can access various forms of entertainment, from computer games to movies to television programs.

- Students with disabilities may access information and programs in the comfort of their rooms, rather than be challenged by campus physical barriers. However, accommodations must be made for those students whose disability may interfere with various learning technologies.

The list is almost endless, and because of the rapidly changing nature of technology, will be hopelessly out of date by the time this chapter is in print. The trend toward wireless computing expands these capabilities to anywhere the student happens to be. Research, communication, and entertainment are all available on demand (Upcraft and Terenzini, 1999).

Downsides of Technologies. With all these exciting, potentially positive capabilities, there are some downsides to the influence of technology that must be considered if we as student affairs professionals are to continue to act in the best interests of students' academic and psychosocial development and create communities that are, according to Boyer (1990), purposeful, just, open, disciplined, and caring. These downsides may include

- *Less face-to-face interactions*: Face-to-face interactions among students and formation of student groups may be diminished, and the development of common purposes and joint actions may be thwarted, thus inhibiting students' sense of community.
- *Less effective communication*: Instant communication does not necessarily mean better or more thoughtful communication. The impulse to write an e-mail message can give license to expression without reflection and could be damaging. Saying something abusive or unkind on e-mail may be easier than a face-to-face interaction. Anonymous e-mail messages may further accelerate the potentially harmful consequences of instant communication.
- *More academic dishonesty*: Technology may, in fact, make it easier for students to engage in plagiarism and other forms of academic dishonesty. For example, acquiring term papers on the Internet is relatively easy, and wireless communication can facilitate cheating on examinations. Further, it may be much harder to catch students engaged in electronic dishonesty, and to prove their guilt once charged.
- *A narrowed definition of an education*: Especially with technologically driven distance education, we run the risk of reducing education to knowledge transfer. A college education becomes a commodity and learning is purely instrumental, leading exclusively to vocational preparation. The idea that education develops the whole person (interpersonal development, civic responsibility, intrapersonal development, cognitive development, values development, and other traditional educational outcomes) can become diminished or totally lost in a cyber-education.
- *Endangered mental/physical health*: For some students, computers can become an addiction that takes over most of their life. Examples include checking e-mail every few minutes, playing video games incessantly, participating in multiple

chat rooms, and surfing the Internet excessively. Although establishing relationships based on e-mail conversations can sometimes lead to positive face-to-face relationships, reports of stalking, physical threats, and invasion of privacy are not uncommon.

- *Economic bifurcation of the campus community*: Technology creates the possibility of creating technological "haves" and "have-nots." Those who had access to computers prior to college and those who can afford their own computers will have an edge over those who have no experience with computers prior to college and who cannot afford them. Most often, this will result in putting poorer students at a distinct disadvantage, unless institutions focus on computer literacy programs and providing equal access to computers and computer technology to all students.

Implications for Student Affairs Policy and Practice

The following questions adapted from those posed by Upcraft and Terenzini (1999) must be addressed if we are to focus on the opportunities and challenges presented by the integration of technology into our higher education institutions.

How Will the Philosophy and Goals of Student Affairs Be Affected? From its inception, student affairs has been concerned with the development of the whole student—both their cognitive and affective dimensions. Indeed, a number of thinkers and writers in student affairs are calling for an end to the bifurcation of the student into "cognitive" and "affective" dimensions, arguing that student learning is an intricate web of experiences and consequences for learning that cannot be meaningfully disentangled. There are calls for blurring the boundaries between academic and student affairs, for collaborating across divisional lines and for integrating students' in-class and out-of-class experiences.

Computer technology, however, has the potential to bifurcate rather than integrate. In an "asynchronous learning environment" with "anywhere-anytime learning," not to mention "just in time learning," what is to be the role of student affairs? How is the full development—psychosocial and cognitive—to be promoted in a purposeful, integrated, mutually reinforcing environment or set of experiences? It seems clear that computer technology may pose a significant threat to the goals and educational effectiveness of what Kuh, Schuh, Whitt and Associates (1991) have termed involving colleges, unless they are conceived in ways that will accommodate a broader conception of student learning. This means that student affairs must develop new ways to promote educational goals and effectiveness that take into account the technological reality of today's campuses and student life. Will the goals traditionally espoused by student affairs (e.g. student development, the whole student, student learning) be judged no longer worthwhile or important elements of postsecondary education? Will these goals, if deemed appropriate, be achievable in a partial or completely virtual learning environment? If so, how?

How Can Student Affairs Use the Positive Aspects of Technology While Minimizing the Negative Aspects?

How Can Student Affairs Use the Positive Aspects of Technology While Minimizing the Negative Aspects? Evidence cited in this chapter should provide ample proof that technological innovation can improve service delivery, enhance communication, and facilitate student learning. The question then becomes how can student affairs professionals use technology to serve the best interests of students? First, we can make sure that all students have equal access to computer technology, particularly those who have been historically underserved by higher education: adult students, part-time students, commuting students, those students whose race/ethnicity is underrepresented, and economically disadvantaged students. Second, we can use technology to communicate with students, and "customize" our interactions with them without being restricted by time or place. Third, technology can enable us to make students more knowledgeable about the many resources available to them, and provide needed information when they encounter a problem. Fourth, we can use technology to make our services, programs, and facilities more efficient and user-friendly.

We must also minimize the downsides of technology. First, we must work harder at integrating technology into our effort to build student communities. Second, we must develop programs that make technology accessible to all and not just to those who are already computer literate and have computers. Third, we must revise our judicial policies to deal effectively with technologically based infractions such as illegal access, plagiarism, security breaches, use of institutional resources for private entrepreneurship, harassment, and other offenses. Fourth, we must not be left behind because we do not have adequate technological resources. We must have staff experts who monitor the latest technological developments, recommend computer hardware and software purchases, design local area networks (LANs), ensure accessibility to institutional computer networks, and provide other advice and consultation. Fifth, we must be knowledgeable about how different student learning styles are affected by different types of technologically mediated instruction. For example, some students may prefer the immediate feedback provided by a self-paced learning program, whereas others may need the interpersonal reinforcement that a traditional class provides. Finally, we must be advocates for the appropriate use of technology, ever vigilant to ways in which technology may not serve the best interests of students.

How Can We Insure that Technology Will Not Depersonalize the Campus and Reduce Student and Faculty Contact?

How Can We Insure that Technology Will Not Depersonalize the Campus and Reduce Student and Faculty Contact? A significant body of empirical evidence indicates that some of the most powerful forces in higher education are faculty members and other students (Pascarella and Terenzini, 1991). According to Upcraft and Terenzini (1999) research consistently points to students' interactions with faculty members (inside and outside the classroom) and with peers as powerful, positive influences on a wide array of educationally desirable outcomes. Technology has the potential of reducing this powerful, positive influence. For example, what is the impact on the community? While academic planners and distance education staffs are busy designing new ways to apply technology, student affairs administrators often commiserate about the loss of community and depersonalization of interpersonal relations. This opposition is not useful. A more constructive approach is to understand these new applications and consider the positive as well as negative consequences. For example, a campus network can provide valuable new ways to communicate with students and may have the potential to "personalize" the environment by facilitating communication among students, between faculty and students, and between students and student affairs staff members. After the positive aspects are acknowledged, questions can be raised about community and interpersonal relations. The question is no longer "if" technology will affect community and interpersonal relations, but how and under what conditions? These questions are particularly salient in institutions where some or all students are studying at a distance.

Student affairs administrators can also encourage the creation of on-campus discussion lists and communication mechanisms that can bring faculty, administrators, and students together in useful but previously underutilized ways. For example, student affairs staff might publish their e-mail addresses in the student newspaper and invite students to use e-mail to discuss issues, share concerns, or provide feedback. The use of technology to assess student services and programs through needs and satisfaction surveys is just beginning to be tapped as a means of systematic student feedback.

How Does Technology Affect Our Mission? What Responsibility, if any, Do We Have to Deliver Student Services and Programs to Students Learning at a Distance? How Will these Services and Programs Differ from Those Offered in a Traditional Campus Setting?

Increasingly, more and more students will spend part of their time engaged in field experiences away from campus or earn their entire degrees without ever setting foot on our campuses (Upcraft and Terenzini, 1999). How do we serve these students? Obviously, they will require different services and programs delivered in different ways. Unfortunately, in institutions whose mission is evolving to include distance education, students affairs has lagged behind in meeting these students' needs. If serving students at a distance is a major initiative, student affairs must determine how to provide student services and programs to those students. This means understanding the needs of these new learners and designing and assessing programs and services that meet those needs. As more customized academic programs are offered, student affairs must customize its programs and services. Even at institutions that choose to emphasize more traditional delivery of academic and student services and programs, there may be some instances where students are taking a combination of traditional courses and distance courses, and we must respond accordingly.

But this problem extends beyond revamping the delivery of student services and programs. It strikes to the heart of the way student affairs educates students. Traditionally, we have relied on intervening in students' out-of-class environment to affect development and learning, which assumes face-to-face interaction of students, faculty, and staff over some sustained period of time in a particular place. And there is substantial evidence (Pascarella and Terenzini, 1991), that most educational outcomes (e.g. psychosocial development and even cognitive development such as content mastery and critical thinking) are as much a result of what happens in this out-of-class environment as what happens in the classroom. The questions then become, what is the out-of-class environment for distance learners? How do student affairs professionals educate students whose out-of-class environment is more likely to be work and family rather than peer and faculty interaction? This is perhaps technology's greatest challenge of all for student affairs.

How Can We Ensure that Students with Less Accessibility to Computer Resources Will Not Be Disadvantaged? Louis Perleman (1992) argues that the term handicapped will be redefined by the development and use of new technology. The handicapped in the information society will be those who do not understand or use the new technology. The question of access is one of the most central to the discussion of the impact of technology on higher education. As discussed previously, technology has the potential to create "haves and have-nots," putting the economically disadvantaged behind the technology curve.

A role for student affairs administrators is to ensure equitable access. Some institutions have determined that all students must have computers and have built that cost into tuition. Others require computers and provide generous financing packages, training, and support for student users. For those institutions not requiring computers, student affairs staff will need to advocate adequate public access to computer laboratories. Wiring residence halls for computer access does not help students who do not have the resources to purchase a computer. Inferior public computer laboratories do not make for an equal playing field. In addition to access, training must be provided that will enable those students who have little prior experience with computers to overcome computer anxiety and learn computer skills.

How Does Student Affairs Keep Up with Technological Advances, and How Will They Be Funded? This is perhaps the most important question of all: Is technology worth it? Technology costs a lot of money. It also has the potential of saving a lot of

money, although there is scant evidence that technologically proficient campuses have saved anything. The rate of technological change is stunning. New software is introduced almost weekly; new advances in hardware render previously very adequate computers inadequate; and the capabilities of the Internet expand constantly. The current wisdom is that hardware and software will need to be replaced every three or four years. How can student affairs administrators make these decisions within already tight budgets? We suggest that such decisions be made within the hardware and software policies of the institution, thus opening up the possibility of some combination of internal unit resources and institutional support. Among a number of competing choices, what do we decide to support from institutional budgets, what services should students pay for, and what services, although desirable, are not affordable?

After initial decisions are made, we must anticipate the need for upgrades and establish a phased repair and replacement schedule. One hopeful development is the information and computing power being transferred to the Web and to campus-wide networks. As this trend continues, computers that permit access to these networks or the Web need less power and the software is stored on the network and Web. Thus, network administrators can do updates and investment in hardware is minimized.

Conclusion

The technological transformation sweeping organizations is also affecting higher education. As this transformation progresses, student affairs professionals need to acquire the skills and knowledge necessary to use emerging technologies to design and deliver programs, enhance communication, and facilitate learning. This changing technology will redefine the environment in which we work, impact the policies and practices that govern our work, and demand that we, as a profession, engage in continuous learning about technology that will serve the best interests of students.

Our work environment will shift from the campus-based learner to the learner who may be thousands of miles away. Meeting learner needs in these various physical and virtual settings becomes the challenge of the future for our profession. It becomes even more critical that we define our learning outcomes and design ways of assessing those outcomes so that our services can improve. Our programs and facilities must then be redesigned to achieve those outcomes, using a variety of technological and traditional interventions. This approach parallels an emerging technological trend in academic affairs that measures learning outcomes rather than in-class time.

Perhaps most importantly, our own learning must change. Through our staff professional development efforts and academic preparation programs, we must address the many issues identified in this chapter. How do we support students we never see, or see much less often? How can we build connection, awareness, and community in an institution that has multiple locations? How do we organize student affairs in these environments?

To date, there has been little discussion and even less research on the impact of technology on student learning and the implications for student affairs. We must align student services and programs with the missions of the institutions we serve. We must also advocate access to technology, identify for whom certain kinds of learning are most appropriate, and help find solutions to the administrative and learning challenges created by the increased use of technology in higher education.

References

Boyer, E. L. *Campus Life: In Search of Community.* Princeton, NJ: The Carnegie Foundation for the Advancement of Teaching, 1990.

Daniel, J. S. *Mega-Universities and Knowledge Media: Technology Strategies for Higher Education.* London: Kogan Page Limited, 1996.

Davis, S., and Botkin, J. *The Monster Under the Bed: How Business is Mastering the Opportunity of Knowledge for Profit.* New York: Simon Schuster, 1994.

Dollence, M. G., and Norris, D. M. *Transforming Higher Education: A Vision for Learning in the 21st Century.* Ann Arbor, MI: Society for College and University Planning, 1995.

Gates, W. *The Road Ahead,* New York: Viking Press, 1995.

Goldsmith, H. "The Future of Student Affairs: New Environments and New Technology." *The Journal of Student Affairs Administration,* 1992, vol. 1, (3).

Kuh, G. D., Schuh, J. H., Whitt, E. J., and Associates. *Involving Colleges: Successful Approaches to Fostering Student Learning and Personal Development Outside the Classroom.* San Francisco: Jossey-Bass, 1991.

Naisbitt, J., and Aburdene, P. *Megatrends 2000: Ten New Directions for the 1990s.* William Morrow and Company, 1990.

Pascarella, E. T., and Terenzini, P. T. *How College Affects Students.* San Francisco: Jossey Bass, 1991.

Perleman, L. J. *School's Out: Hyperlearning, the New Technology, and the End of Education.* New York: William Morrow and Company, 1992.

Upcraft, M. L., and Terenzini, P. T. "Technology," from Johnson, C. S. and Cheatham, H. E. (eds.), *Higher Education Trends in the Next Century: A Research Agenda for Student Success.* Washington, D.C.: American College Personnel Association, 1999.

Van Dusen, G. C. *The Virtual Campus: Technology and Reform in Higher Education,* ASHE-ERIC Higher Education Report, vol. 25, no. 5. Washington, D.C.: The George Washington University Press, 1997.

PART THREE

ESSENTIAL SKILLS AND COMPETENCIES FOR STUDENT AFFAIRS MANAGERS

In a world that is rapidly changing, it is essential that student affairs managers possess skills and competencies to aid them in dealing with new issues and new concerns. This section of the volume is written by practitioners for practitioners and focuses on our best thinking about the skills necessary for success in student affairs now and in the future.

An overview of the most relevant theories and models for student affairs practice is provided by George McClellan and Kelly Carter in Chapter Thirteen. Upcraft and Schuh then focus on the key elements in assessment and how they can be used in program development in Chapter Fourteen. Schuh and Upcraft focus on the critical importance of measuring student satisfaction and needs in Chapter Fifteen. The task of translating theory and assessment results to practice

is addressed by Mary Desler in Chapter Sixteen. Joan Claar and Michael Cuyjet provide practical advice to practitioners about program planning and implement in Chapter Seventeen.

Money is always an issue and Dudley Woodard focuses on key issues related to budget development and fiscal management in student affairs in Chapter Eighteen. Legal issues influence much of the work of student affairs and, in Chapter Nineteen, Donald Gehring provides valuable guidance to practitioners regarding the legal constraints on their practice. In Chapter Twenty, Art Sandeen draws on his years of experience to provide practical advice to practitioners regarding the development of effective campus and community relationships. As hard as we try, however, conflict is an inevitable condition in higher education and, in

Chapter Twenty-One, Leila Moore provides key insight into this important skill area.

It is critical that we always engage in our work in an ethical and responsible manner. In Chapter Twenty-Two, Jane Fried provides guidance to practitioners regarding ethical responses to vexing questions.

Any review of the literature in student affairs would find an intense interest in establishing effective relationships with academic affairs. In Chapter Twenty-Three, Cathy Engstrom and Vincent Tinto provide models and practical advice on how to establish strong and viable working relationships.

Lastly, student affairs professionals are often in the forefront of dealing with any campus crisis situation. Whether it is an issue with an individual student, a group of students or a natural disaster affecting the entire campus, dealing with crisis is an inevitable part of the career of a student affairs professional. In Chapter Twenty-Four, Marsha Duncan and Keith Miser provide practical advice on dealing with such difficult situations.

All student affairs professional have room to grow in one area or another of professional competence. This section of the book highlights important growth areas in order to meet the challenges of the future and of today.

CHAPTER THIRTEEN

AN OVERVIEW OF RELEVANT THEORIES AND MODELS FOR STUDENT AFFAIRS PRACTICE

Kelly A. Carter, and George S. McClellan

What use is theory, and how does it influence our practice as student affairs professionals? Kerlinger (1964) indicates that the purpose of theory is to explain and predict phenomena (p. 177). Hoy and Miskal (1978) agree with Kerlinger, but go further and indicate that the major function of theory is not only to describe, explain and predict behavior, but also to stimulate and guide further knowledge development (p.21). Theory helps us answer the questions of why some program, activity, policy, procedure, or intervention is or is not working (Rodgers, 1991, p. 205). Theory may even inform practitioners about what might work with a particular student, group of students, organization, or system.

Informal theories guide much of what we do as people and how we act as professionals (Argyris and Schon, 1978). We all develop theories and use them on a daily basis. Examples include what routes we take to and from work, what days are the best to bring a new idea to our supervisors, and our "knowledge" that something just will not work. We have a theory about what works best, and we follow that theory in making our decisions. Rodgers (1991) labels these kinds of informal theories as theories-in-use (p. 206). He goes on to say, in part, "that usually we do not make informal theories-in-use explicit. Hence neither student affairs staff members nor students are clearly aware of the assumptions or bases for existing programs and actions. Usually one tends to accept what supports his/her views and ignores what does not. Theories-in-use may be good theories; however, they need to be made explicit in order to make judgements about goodness"

(p. 206). Formal theories are explicit and relate concepts to each other and to the subject being studied. They provide specific guidance to our professional practice. Although formal theories may be criticized, argued about, dissected, and debated, they have value.

This chapter will discuss the basic issues involved in understanding and using formal theory in professional practice. A review of six major theory groups that influence practice in student affairs then will be presented, including psychosocial theories, cognitive development theories, typology theories, person-environment interaction theories, college impact theories of student change, and marketing theories. This view of theories is by no means exhaustive, but illustrates the rich variety of theoretical constructs that can be used to inform professional practice in student affairs. Finally, practical suggestions regarding the use of theory will be presented.

Issues Involved

Student affairs professional practice was not guided by any theoretical or conceptual foundation for many years (Hurst and Jacobson, 1985). Early practitioners did the best they could relying on personal experiences, intuition, skills, and knowledge. Even fads sometime influenced practice in student affairs. To illustrate, in the sixties, encounter groups could be found on many campuses (Hurst and Jacobson, 1985). Programs and interventions were sometimes built on a foundation of what was popular rather than on a sound theoretical foundation. The practical issues of campus politics, history, tradition of the institution and funding also influenced what was done and what was not done in student affairs just as they do today.

McEwen, however, believes that "theory, some formal and some informal, has no doubt existed in student affairs from the beginning. Some of the early textbooks on student affairs provide evidence of the use of traditional psychological theories and to some degree, theories on management, organizations, and administration" (1996, p. 153). Sanford's seminal work, *The American College* (1962), started the use of theory to guide practice. Much work has been done in the intervening decades regarding the development of theoretical constructs to explain, predict, and guide student affairs professionals in their work with students. McEwen (1996) and others (Rodgers, 1991; Upcraft, 1993) indicate that there is not just one theory to guide practice in student affairs. In fact Upcraft (1993) cites over seventy-five references that contribute to the "theoretical basis for the student affairs profession" (p. 264). How does a practitioner chose between and among theories to guide their work? And how does a practitioner translate theory to practice?

Useful Models

There are at least two useful models to guide the translation of theory to practice. The first was designed by Wells and Knefelkamp (1982) and the second by Rodgers (1991). Both models acknowledge the complexity of using theory to guide practice, and both require practitioners to have more than a passing knowledge of theory.

Wells and Knefelkamp Model

This model (1982) focuses on the translation of developmental theory into practice. As a precondition, the model requires examination of the goals for the program from a theoretical perspective. Then and only then should the practitioner design and implement programs or interventions.

Prior to Program Design. The model instructs practitioners to identify pragmatic concerns as a first step. What is happening or not happening, and why is that condition an issue of concern? The second step of the model requires identification of the ideal educational goals and outcomes. What would or should be different as a result of the program or intervention? In step three, the practitioner examines the goals and objectives for the program in light of theory clusters and determines the concepts that provide best insight into the "developmental content and process" (Upcraft, 1993, p. 265). Steps four and five require the practitioner to use the most relevant theories to analyze both student characteristics and environmental characteristics from the perspective of each relevant theory cluster. The pre-planning analysis is completed in the sixth step when the practitioner identifies sources of specific developmental challenges and support within the students and the environment. Step six can only be accomplished through the application of theory.

Program Design. If the pre-program work and analysis is successfully completed, the actual program design is much easier to accomplish. In step seven, Wells and Knefelkamp (1982) ask practitioners to reanalyze the educational goals and objectives and determine if they should change as a result of the pre-program work. Questions should be asked at this stage regarding the readiness of students and the institution for the new program. Program goals should be modified or changed if necessary as a result of this analysis. During step eight, the practitioner designs the intervention by using methods that will assist the student mastering the educational goals of the program. Both structure and process are important components of this step. Also the question should now be asked as to how the success or failure of the proposed program or intervention will be measured.

Program Implementation and Evaluation. Step nine is the actual implementation of the proposed program. Step ten requires evaluation of the achievement of goals and both staff and student satisfaction. Was the program worthwhile, and did it contribute to the growth and development of students?

Post-Program. The final step in this theory to practice model is to use the data gained in evaluation and to redesign or modify the program as necessary prior to implementation in the future. (Upcraft, 1993)

Rodgers

The concepts proposed by Rodgers (1991) combine both application of theories and process models in order to effectively translate theory to practice. He reminds us that "using developmental and related social and behavior science theories in the practice of student affairs assumes that well rounded development of the whole personality is a primary goal of higher education" (1991, p. 242). He believes that formal theory linked to procedural or process models result in informed professional practice (p. 216). However, Rodgers cautions practitioners that translation of theory to practice is not an easy task and "requires complex methods using multiple specific theories" (p. 211).

Rodgers observes that practitioners must fully understand a range of theories and be able to apply a variety of theoretical constructs depending on the issue at hand. Further, Rodgers believes that it is equally important for practitioners to understand process models and intervention strategies that are grounded in theory. He highlights a number of procedural and process models (p. 244) and urges professionals to become familiar with several of these models. He cautions that "both process models and formal theories are needed in order to use theory in practice. Neither can do the job without the other. Process models provide the order and nature of the considerations used in linking theory and practice. Formal theory and its related measurement technologies provide substance to the steps recommended in process models" (p. 243).

Useful Theories

Six major theory groups have been chosen to be highlighted in this chapter. Not everyone will agree with the selection of these theory groups, but such disagreement only focuses attention on the complexity of the task of understanding and using theory in professional practice.

Psychosocial and Identity Development Theories

Psychosocial and identity development theories provide explanation for how individuals define self and their relationships to others with regard to the world around them. Theories in this cluster outline a sequence of tasks, both personal and interpersonal, that are addressed throughout the lifetime of the individual. Such development occurs due to a combination of biological, societal, and environmental changes.

Erickson's (1959, 1980) model of eight developmental crises was among the first comprehensive psychosocial theories. At each stage of the eight age-linked crises, a task is addressed and resolved. For example, the issue facing traditional-age college students is identity versus role confusion. In this stage, an individual experiments with the definition of self. Trial and error attempts are usually made to find an identity that best fits the individual. If an individual is able to successfully identify a comfortable lifestyle and role, they are equipped to move on to the next stage: intimacy versus isolation. If role confusion still persists when issues of intimacy occur, the individual is unable to accomplish mature intimacy.

Building on the work of Erickson, Chickering (1969) became intrigued by the developmental tasks of traditional-age college students. He examined student development in a systematic way, noting identity development as a task while also recognizing other developmental issues that support the development of identity. Chickering (1969) identified seven sets of issues that surround the task of identity development in traditional-age college students. He labeled the identified issues as vectors because they occurred in an overlapping yet orderly fashion. Each vector functions as a continuum ranging from confusion to clarity.

Chickering's original model was developed from research on traditional-age college men. In 1993, Chickering and Reisser revisited his original theory and indicated that it also is applicable to returning adult students, students of color, and women. The revised vectors in the 1993 model include developing competence, managing emotions, moving through autonomy toward interdependence, developing mature interpersonal relationships, establishing identity, developing purpose, and developing integrity. Chickering and Reisser indicate that the theory provides a general framework for understanding the development of college students. Both theorists admit that "those who . . . want more specificity and complexity, may be frustrated by our level of generality" (Chickering and Ressier, 1993, p. 44).

Indeed some practitioners were frustrated by the general nature of Chickering's vectors noting that the constructs did not account for the different developmental intricacies of personal identity. Although student affairs professionals understood that identity was an issue for all students, it appeared that very few students developed their identity in the same way. Some theorists have found commonalties within groups of students. Theories subsequently developed with regard to the psychosocial development of men (Levinson, 1978) and women (Levinson, 1996, Josselson, 1987). Theories also addressed the unique tasks associated with racial and ethnic identity development, including the specific experiences of whites (Helms, 1993), African Americans (Cross, 1995; Sue and Sue, 1990), Hispanics (Martinez, 1988; Grossman, 1984), Asian Americans (Chew and Ogi, 1987), Native Americans (LaCounte, 1987), and general ethnic identity development (Phinney, 1990; Bennett, 1993). There are also theories that address sexual orientation identity development (Cass, 1979; D'Augelli, 1994; Weinberg, Williams and Pryor, 1994), the unique developmental issues faced by returning adult students (Schlossberg, Lynch and Chickering, 1989), and spirituality as identity development (Fowler, 1987).

Understanding of the differences between and among our students is essential for practitioner success. While Erickson and Chickering helped us understand that identity development is an important task, the specialized identity theorists help us understand what exactly is at issue for each student group.

Cognitive Development Theories

Cognitive-structural development theories account for the ways an individual develops critical thinking and reasoning processes. This cluster of theories does not explain what people think, but rather focuses on how they think. Development occurs due to challenges to the current thought processes, or cognitive dissonance.

Perry (1968) began his research by focusing on understanding the process by which students came to learn in a classroom. He identified several positions of development that are not age-linked, but occur in an orderly fashion. Perry posited that actual development occurred between positions, whereas the positions themselves represent resting points. Although he identified nine positions, they were conceptualized into four major categories: duality, multiplicity, relativism, and commitment. Dualistic thinking is characterized by either/or thinking (e.g., good/bad, right or wrong). Multiplistic thinkers no longer conceptualize answers as right or wrong and believe that all opinions are valid. Relativistic thinkers understand the importance of asserting and supporting opinions. They understand that some opinions hold less value for them, and therefore learn to disagree. Commitment in relativism implies that the thinker has developed a full belief system or identity based on their relativist thinking (Evans, Forney, and Guido-DiBrito, 1998).

To illustrate, dualistic students may only be interested in what it takes to get a good grade in a class versus what will be learned. A multiplistic student might have a difficult time choosing a major because each choice seems equally valid and intriguing to such a person. Finally, a relativistic thinker would probably be a student who is highly involved in social activism and has chosen a career with that orientation in mind.

Many saw problems with Perry's (1968) theory because it was based primarily on white, male subjects. Belensky, Clinchy, Goldberger, and Tarule (1986) stated that the major limitation in Perry's model was the exclusion of women subjects. They noted markedly different development for women related to intellectual processes. Baxter-Magolda (1992) also responded with her examination of the reflection processes of both men and women. King and Kitchener's (1994) theory of reflective judgement was also a direct reaction to Perry's model (Evans, Forney, and Guido-DiBrito, 1998).

Moral development is a form of cognitive-structural development. These theories explain the cognitive processes people use when faced with a moral dilemma. Kohlberg (1976) developed a theory of moral development with six stages categorized into three levels: preconventional, conventional, and postconventional or principled. Preconventional reasoners do not understand the concept of societal rules. They may be looking for loopholes in a policy rather than the spirit of the policy. Preconventional thinking is self-focused and justice is defined only from the perspective of that individual. Conventional thinkers have developed a sense of societal norms and are concerned with rules and consistency of enforcement. Justice is defined as equal treatment for all members of the community, not just for self. Postconventional reasoners believe in universal values and rights. Justice is defined as concern for broad human rights.

Gilligan (1982) examined the moral development of women and girls in her work because Kohlberg's work was based on boys and men. Through her observations of both male and female subjects, Gilligan attempted to understand the development of women. Her model accounted for three levels and the transition between each level. The first level focuses on orientation to individual survival, with a first transition from selfishness to responsibility. The second level is characterized by goodness as self-sacrifice and leads to the second transition from goodness to truth. The focus in the third level is on the morality of nonviolence. Gilligan notes that at the early stages, female subjects experience the same selfishness as males. Females, however, then begin to focus on relationships rather than on concern for consistent rules. This focus on relationships takes attention away from self to a point of self-sacrificing.

The application of the work of Kohlberg and Gilligan can clearly be seen in judicial cases. Observation of a student judicial board with both male and female members highlights the differences between men and women. The task before the board is to be just. Men at the conventional level serving on the board might frame the question as compliance with the letter of the regulation. Women at the second level serving on the board might focus their concern on why the incident happened. Such differing perspectives can lead to interesting conversations and outcomes in judicial board proceedings.

Maturity models also address a more specific facet of cognitive development. Heath's (1968) stages of maturation suggests a matrix that represents the domain of maturing. The matrix includes five growth dimensions (becoming able to symbolize experience, becoming allocentric or other-centered, becoming progressively integrated, becoming stable, and becoming autonomous) in each of four areas of self (intellect, values, self-concepts and interpersonal relationships). This combination of growth dimensions and areas of the self create the domain of maturity with twenty categories.

Typology Theories

The cluster of typology theories explain individual differences in how people perceive and relate to their world. Unlike psychosocial and cognitive development theories, typology theories do not focus on the nature and process of change or development. "Typology theorists identify factors that create consistent ways of coping with the demands of life. When faced with similar developmental challenges or environmental situations, individuals will respond differently depending on their type" (Evans, 1996, p. 179). The most widely used typology theories include the Myers-Briggs Type Indicator (Myers, 1987), Holland (1966), Heath (1968, 1977), and Kolb (1976).

Myers-Briggs. This theory of personality type (1980) is based on the work of Jung (1923, 1971). Myers-Briggs (Myers, 1987) translated this theoretical perspective into four scales that are bipolar: extraversion/introversion; sensing/intuition, thinking/feeling, and judging/perception. Preferences are organized into one of sixteen different types and are useful in helping individuals understand how they approach choices and options as they encounter others and organizations in their collegiate experience.

Holland. This theory of vocational choice examines both the characteristics of the work environment and the interests of people. Holland (1966, 1973) states that individuals engaged in studying for or working in specific careers have similar personalities. He further theorizes that people look for work environments that permit them to use their abilities, reinforce their values, and allow them to pursue their interests. Six personality types and six corresponding work environments are identified by Holland. These include the following types: realistic, investigative, social, conventional, enterprising, and artistic. When people match their personality type to a corresponding work environment, satisfaction and success are the usual result.

Holland's theory aids student affairs professionals in understanding the dynamics of how students pursue major choice and have social interaction. It is no accident, for example, that certain residence units attract students interested in the arts or social service. Such clustering often occurs even if there is no formal designation of a hall as one for artistic students or volunteers. Students simply join communities that display interests similar to their own. Satisfaction in the collegiate experience is increased for students who experience congruence between their chosen environment and their personality type.

Person-Environment Interaction Theories

This cluster of theories addresses the interplay between environment and students. Not only does the collegiate environment account for the experience of the student, but the student also brings a set of experiences and expectations that they use to interpret their environment. The student also becomes part of the environment, thus influencing the experiences of other students. The burden of "fit" does not rest squarely with the student, but the environment also has a responsibility to connect with students. In 1936, Lewin created a formula explaining the relationship between environment and student behavior. In the formula, behavior (B) is a function (f) of the interaction (x) of person (P) and the environment. (Lewin, 1936, p.12)

$$(E) \text{ or } (B) = f(P x E)$$

Moos (1979) outlined two major components of environmental influence: the physical environment and the social environment. Strange (1996) highlighted four aspects of environmental influence that function in the greater college or university community: the physical structure, human aggregate, organizational structure, and the constructed environment. These categories provide a framework through which to view environmental theories.

Physical Structure. Moss viewed the physical environment as made up of multiple variables. He accounted for issues such as weather, architectural design, population density, and noise and air pollution. Questions that might arise regarding a college campus include "What buildings are centrally located? Is accessibility an issue? What does the campus artwork communicate? How does the institution communicate its values non-verbally?"

Human Aggregate. The collective personality (the human aggregate) effects the person-environment interaction. As people, we tend to seek congruent environment where we will be happier and more satisfied. Several typology models, used to explain individual personality differences, have broadened their scope to identify the personality of the human aggregate (Holland, 1973, Myers, 1987). Although the views of Myers-Briggs and Holland are different, Myers does note, however, that when used as a measure of the human aggregate of the environment, the theory is similar to Holland; congruency equals greater satisfaction.

Organizational Structure. Organizational structure theories describe how people, organizations, and governance processes influence one another and how they directly influence the experience of students. "Organizational theory is a window through which to view the behavior of individuals or groups (students, faculty members, student affairs professionals) in the context of a complex organization interacting with and being shaped by external exigencies and special interest groups" (Kuh, 1996, p. 270). Webers's sources of authority (1947), McGregor's Theory X and Theory Y (1960), Blake and Mouton's Managerial Grid (1964), Hersey and Blanchard's situational leadership (1977), Keller's strategic planning model (1983), Hage and Aiken's social change in complex organizations (1970), and Deming's (1982) total quality management contribute to this cluster.

Constructed Environments. Regardless of an institution's physical environment, human aggregate, or organizational structure, students have life experiences through which all non-verbal communication is filtered (Strange, 1996). Students' perceptions about their environment are real to them and each student will have different perceptions, depending on the life experiences they bring with them. To illustrate, an institution in a small town might be perceived as having a rich array of activities through the eyes of a student from a very rural area. The same small town might be perceived as a place where there is nothing to do by a student with an urban background. To each of these students, their perceptions are reality. Lawrence Pervin's transactional theory (1967) explains this phenomena with regard to student satisfaction.

College Impact Theories

Developmental models and theories draw heavily from the psychological tradition. College impact theories, in contrast, draw primarily from the sociological perspective. Pascarella and Terenzini observe that "whereas 'developmental' models concentrate attention on outcomes or the nature of student change (including identity formation, moral or cognitive development), 'college impact' models focus more on the sources of change (for example, institutional characteristics, programs and services, students' experiences, faculty members) (1991, p.18)."

Astin's (1985) theory of involvement focuses on the impact of students' experiences on their development during college. Astin theorizes that students' learning and development is enhanced by involvement, and he offers five important specific observations regarding involvement (1985, pp. 135–136). First, involvement requires physical and psychological energy. Second, involvement occurs on a continuum. Third, there is both a qualitative and quantitative aspect to involvement. Fourth, outcomes are proportional to the quality and quantity of involvement. Finally, the efficacy of a program hinges on its ability to involve students.

Paces's (1984, 1987) "quality of effort" theory is an instructive and useful companion to Astin's theory of involvement. Pace states that the quality of outcomes is proportional to the quality of effort an individual invests in pursuing those outcomes. In essence, Pace's "quality of effort" theory parallels the idiomatic informal theory "You get out of it what you put into it."

Pascarella and Terenzini report, "one of the most inescapable and unequivocal conclusions we can make is that the impact of college is largely determined by the individual's quality of effort and level of involvement in both academic and nonacademic activities (1991, p. 610)." How can student affairs practitioners encourage effort and involvement by students? Offering opportunities for students to design and implement programs of interest is one way. For example, peer educators and peer resource health education programs often have governing boards of directors with student majorities. In those instances, students are guiding the range of programs being offered to their peers. It is also important to help identify and sponsor opportunities for students to engage in collaborative learning that bridges classroom and co-curricular interests such as residential colleges or service-learning. By engaging in such collaboration, student affairs practitioners can help students become more fully engaged in their college experience.

Tinto's (1975, 1987) work takes a different perspective on the impact of college by focusing on the reasons students drop out of college. Tinto hypothesizes that students come to college with experiences and expectations that are subject to change during their enrollment. Students are increasingly likely to persist when their experiences and expectations are aligned with the normative culture on campus and when their interactions with others are positive. Students for whom this is not the case are more likely to drop out, according to Tinto.

Other theorists more explicitly identify elements of students' backgrounds as being important in understanding the impact of college. Pascarella (1985) offers a model that includes the background and pre-collegiate characteristics of the students, the structural and organizational features of the institution, the frequency and quality of interaction between the student and campus socializing agents, and the quality of effort of the student. Pascarella suggests these various elements impact on student change in both direct and indirect ways.

Weidman (1989), like Pascarella and Tinto, offers a college impact model that includes elements beyond the scope of the institution. Weidman's emphasis is somewhat different, however, in that the role of significant others (e.g. parents, peers, community) is more heavily weighted.

How can a student affairs professional use the work of Tinto, Pascarella, and Weidman to inform their practice? Professionals working in admissions might focus on better understanding the expectations of potential students and to clearly communicate how an institution might, and might not, meet those expectations. Mentoring and advising programs designed to help match returning students and faculty members with incoming students of similar backgrounds and interests might be helpful in minimizing the stresses of transition and adaptation to new norms. In addition, health educators and others concerned with the impact of abusive use of alcohol can enlist parents, peers, and the community in shaping and directing the expectations and behaviors of incoming students with respect to alcohol use and abuse.

Schlossberg, Lynch, and Chickering's (1989) mattering theory emphasizes the quality of student interaction with staff and faculty as a means of enhancing the influence of the collegiate experience. They describe five dimensions of mattering: attention, importance, dependence, ego-extension, and appreciation. Schlossberg, Lynch, and Chickering suggest that students who have a sense that they matter at an institution will be more likely to persist and develop. Student affairs professionals can readily use mattering theory. Listening to a story of a student conveys the message of attention. Asking a student how a test or performance went offers a sense of importance to the student. Seeking out a student or group of students for input on a program or policy matter acknowledges the dependence on the part of the department or institution. A simple note of congratulations on an achievement lets a student know that someone noticed their work.

Marketing Theories

Few graduate preparation programs include marketing theories and concepts in the list of theories relevant to student affairs practice. But many of the theories and concepts in marketing are useful, particularly to professionals with enrollment management responsibilities. In addition, such theoretical perspectives can be helpful to residence hall and student activities programmers and student organizations. Familiarity with marketing theory and practice can be an extremely useful tool for the student affairs practitioner.

To some, the term marketing means little more than advertising. Kotler and Fox (1985) indicate, however, that marketing is more "than analysis, planning and implementation and control of carefully formulated programs designed to bring about voluntary exchanges of values with target markets to achieve institutional objectives. Marketing involves designing the institution's offerings to meet the target markets' needs and desires, and using effective pricing, communication, and distribution to inform, motivate, and service the markets" (p. 7). Marketing theories and concepts are useful when seeking to attract more and better students. Such approaches can assist potential students in understanding the college-decision process as well as further the understanding of the level of satisfaction of current students with their collegiate experience. Further, marketing theories can help focus efforts to design programs that carry out the mission of the institution while meeting student needs and encouraging financial support for the college or university.

Many of the theories important to the field of marketing are known to student affairs professionals. For example, the concepts of hierarchy of needs (Maslow, 1970) and Festinger's (1957) theory of cognitive dissonance have been basic concepts in both marketing and student development literature for a number of years. It is instructive to view these theories through the lens of a marketing perspective.

Maslow. According to Maslow (1970) human beings are motivated by unsatisfied needs, and people act to satisfy lower needs (physical, safety, social, and esteem) first before satisfying higher need (self-actualization). Lower-level needs must be adequately satisfied and are essential for the normal growth and development of the individual. As each lower need is satisfied, it ceases to be a motivator. Maslow posits that higher-level needs ("being needs") can never be fully satisfied, but the process of becoming self-actualized is in itself satisfying. Self-actualization focuses on an individual's actions, sense of identity, self-acceptance, and realization of one's talents and capacities.

As students are making the decision to attend college and to attend a specific institution, each individual has a different set of concerns and needs. Some high school seniors may wonder about the quality of food and housing. Others may worry about personal safety in an unsafe world. Still others may be concerned about whether they will fit in and find people like themselves. Understanding this range of basic needs assists practitioners in designing admissions materials, campus tours, and campus visits and orientation programs. If students believe that the institution is concerned with their basic needs, they will view the institution in more favorable terms.

Understanding needs is also an important component in assessing student satisfaction. If the food service, residence hall facilities, and classroom spaces are poorly run and maintained, such actions provide a strong message to students regarding their value to the institution. Student affairs professionals can talk a great deal about their care for students, but if such care is not reflected in the daily lives of the students it is mere rhetoric. Students are also more likely to leave if they believe the institution does not care for them.

Wise practitioners pay attention to basic needs and continue to do so throughout the period of enrollment of the student.

Festinger. A theory of cognitive consistency was developed by Festinger (1957) and has great implications for practice in student affairs. Festinger posits that behavior which is at odds with an established attitude demands change. Change is usually seen through alteration of the original attitude so that it is in greater conformity with the actual behavior. Festinger asserts that when a person behaves differently, he/she will also change his/her attitude about self. Dissonance results if new information is introduced or if there is inconsistency or disagreement between two pieces of information. When dissonance occurs tension is present, and it is that tension that motivates individuals to reduce the dissonance they are experiencing.

In the larger society, the need for consistency has been a driving force in changing behavior and attitudes about smoking. Conflicting messages have been sent to members of the public. The tobacco companies broadcast messages that smoking was sophisticated and fun. Public health officials, on the other hand, sent a strong message that smoking was bad for your health. As more and more evidence mounted that smoking was detrimental to health, the number of smokers dropped, and the social norms surrounding smoking were modified. The same theoretical application can be made to the issue of alcohol abuse. Alcoholic beverage companies have sent messages to young people that alcohol use is fun and exciting. Health professionals have been less successful in providing messages regarding the dangers of alcohol abuse. Careful analysis of the alcohol education effort shows that the message of harm associated with alcohol is more diffuse than is the message regarding the harm associated with smoking.

Suggestions for Practice

Understanding a variety of theoretical perspectives provides a strong foundation for effective practice in student affairs. Such understanding permits professionals to be intentional in the design and implementation of programs, activities, and services. Most professionals in student affairs have been exposed to many types of theory in our graduate education programs. Application of theory to practice, however, is often not explicit. For example, on move-in day in the residence halls, keys must be given out to new students. It can be done in an efficient manner with directions to the new student and their family on how to get to their room and what the fines are for losing keys. Or distribution of keys can be accomplished using the mattering theory where each student is acknowledged by name, his hometown is mentioned in greeting, and the resident assistant is identified by name to the new student and their family. The key is still given out, but the student hears from institutional representatives that they uniquely matter at the institution. Although simplistic, this example of giving out keys illustrates how theory may be used to inform and guide our professional practice.

The suggestions that follow provide practical advice on how to use theory as a basis for professional activities.

1. Learn about theory and decide the specific theories that have the most meaning for you and make sense to you on a fundamental level.
2. When facing a new issue or problem, take a few minutes to think about the problem from a theoretical perspective. For example, how could the work of Kohlberg or Gilligan inform your approach to the impasse between the Interfraternity Council and the Panhellenic Council if they cannot agree on a united risk management policy?
3. When new initiatives are being proposed, inquire about the theoretical underpinnings of the new idea. This may cause staff members to look at the proposal from a different perspective and in the long run enhance the probable success of the program.
4. Assure that some time in staff development activities is devoted to discussions and presentations regarding theory and the use of theory in practice. Examination of case studies based on actual campus events can bring theory into focus in a practical and effective way.
5. Use theory as one of the instructional tools in leadership training. Theory is as valuable to students as it is to professionals in aiding them in explaining and predicting behavior. Understanding why something is happening is very useful to the student leader.
6. Use your own experiences to guide you, and question theory if necessary. Theory is a roadmap, but it does not provide all the needed information for decision-making. If you find issues in applying theory, raise those questions in professional correspondences or meetings with those who develop theoretical constructs. Your perspective usually informs theory and makes it more relevant to other practitioners.
7. Remember that theory provides a perspective, but it is the informed professional that makes the decision.

Theory is not something to be avoided and can be a valuable tool for professional practice in student affairs. Your active awareness of, use of, and reactions to theory can be major contributions to the understanding of why students and institutions do what they do.

References

Argyris, C., and Schon, D. *Organizational Learning: A Theory of Action Perspective*. Reading, MA: Addison Wesley, 1978.

Astin, A. *Achieving Educational Excellence: A Critical Assessment of Priorities and Practices in Higher Education*. San Francisco: Jossey-Bass, 1985.

Baxter-Magolda, M. *Knowing and Reasoning in College: Gender-Related Patterns in Students' Intellectual Development*. San Francisco: Jossey-Bass, 1992.

Belenky, M., Clinchy, B., Goldberger, N., and Tarule, J. *Women's Ways of Knowing: The Development of Self, Voice, and Mind*. New York: Basic Books, 1986.

Bennett, M. "Toward Ethnorelativisim: A Developmental Model of Intercultural Sensitivity." In R. M. Paige (ed.), *Education for Intercultural Experience*. Yarmouth, ME: Intercultural Press, 1993.

Blake, R., and Mouton, J. *The Managerial Grid*. Houston, TX. Gulf, 1964.

Cass, V. "Homosexual Identity Formation: A Theoretical Model." *Journal of Homosexuality*. 1979, 4, 219–235.

Chew, C., and Ogi, A. "Asian American College Student Perspectives." In D. Wright (ed.), *Responding to the Needs of Today's Minority Students*. New Directions for Student Services, no. 38. San Francisco: Jossey-Bass, 1987.

Chickering, A. *Education and Identity*. San Francisco: Jossey-Bass, 1969.

Chickering, A., and Reisser, L. *Education and Identity* (2nd ed.) San Francisco: Jossey-Bass, 1993.

Cross, W. E., Jr. "The Psychology of Nigresence: Revising the Cross Model." In J. G. Panterotto, J. Casas, L. Suziki, and C. Alexander (eds.), *Handbook of Multicultural Counseling*. Thousand Oaks, CA: Sage Publications, 1995.

D'Augelli, A. "Identity Development and Sexual Orientation: Toward a Model of Lesbian, Gay, and Bi-sexual Development." In E. Trickett, R. Watts, and D. Birman (eds.), *Human Diversity: Perspectives on People in Context*. San Francisco: Jossey-Bass, 1994.

Deming, W. *Out of Crises*. Cambridge, MA: Productivity Press, 1982.

Erickson, E. *Identity and the Life Cycle*. New York: Norton, 1959.

Erickson, E. *Identity and the Life Cycle*. (2nd ed.) New York: Norton, 1980.

Evans, N. "Theories of Student Development." In S. Komives and D. Woodard (eds.), *Student Services: A Handbook for the Profession* (3rd ed.) San Francisco: Jossey-Bass, 1996.

Evans, N., Forney, D., and Guido-DiBrito, F. *Student Development in College: Theory, Research, and Practice*. San Francisco: Jossey-Bass, 1998.

Festinger, L. *A Theory of Cognitive Dissonance*. Stanford, CA: Stanford University Press, 1957.

Fowler, J. *Stages of Faith: The Psychology of Human Development and the Quest for Meaning*. San Francisco: Harper and Row, 1987.

Gilligan, C. *In a Different Voice: Psychological Theory and Women's Development*. Cambridge, MA: Harvard University Press, 1982.

Grossman, H. *Educating Hispanic Students*. Springfield, IL: Thomas, 1984.

Hage, J., and Aiken, M. *Social Change in Complex Organizations*. New York: Random House, 1970.

Heath, D. *Growing Up in College: Liberal Education and Maturity*. San Francisco: Jossey-Bass, 1968.

Heath, D. *Maturity and Competence: A Transcultural View*. New York: Gardner Press, 1977.

Helms, J. "Toward a Model of White Racial Identity Development." In J. Helms (ed.), *Black and White Racial Identity: Theory, Research, and Practice*. Westport, CT: Praeger, 1993.

Hersey, P., and Blanchard, K. *Management of Organizational Behavior: Utilizing Human Resources*. Englewood Cliffs, NJ: Prentice Hall, 1977.

Holland, J. *The Psychology of Vocational Choice: A Theory of Personality Types and Model Environments*. Waltham, MA: Blaisdell, 1966.

Holland, J. *Making Vocational Choices: A Theory of Careers*. Englewood Cliffs, NJ: Prentice Hall, 1973.

Hoy, W., and Miskal, C. *Educational Administration: Theory, Research and Practice*. New York: Random House, 1978.

Hurst, J., and Jacobson, J. "Theories Underline Students' Needs for Programs." In M. Barr and L. Keating (eds.), *Developing Effective Student Services Programs*. San Francisco: Jossey-Bass, 1985.

Josselson, R. *Finding Herself: Pathways to Identity Development in Women*. San Francisco: Jossey-Bass, 1987.

Jung, C. *Psychological Types*. (F. Hall [ed.]; G. Baynes, Trans.) Princeton, NJ: Princeton University Press, 1971. (Original work published in 1923.)

Keller, G. *Academic Strategy: The Management Revolution in American Higher Education*. Baltimore, MD: Johns Hopkins University Press, 1983.

Kerlinger, F. *Foundations of Behavorial Research*. New York: Holt, Rinehart and Winston, 1964.

King, P., and Kitchener, K. *Developing Reflective Judgment: Understanding and Promoting Intellectual Growth and Critical Thinking in Adolescents and Adults*. San Francisco: Jossey-Bass, 1994.

Kohlberg, L. "Moral Stages and Moralization: The Cognitive Development Approach." In T. Lickona (ed.), *Moral Development and Behavior: Theory, Research, and Social Issues*. New York: Holt, Rinehart, and Winston, 1976.

Kolb, D. *Learning Styles Inventory: Technical Manual*. Boston: McBer, 1976.

Kotler, P., and Fox, K. *Strategic Marketing for Educational Institutions*. Englewood Cliffs, NJ: 1985.

Kuh, G. "Organizational Theory." In S. Komives and D. Woodard (eds.), *Student Services: A Handbook for the Profession*. (3rd ed.) San Francisco: Jossey-Bass, 1996.

LaCounte, D. "American Indian Students in College." In D. Wright (ed.), *Responding to the Needs of Today's Minority Students*. New Directions for Student Services, no., 38. San Francisco: Jossey-Bass, 1987.

Levinson, D. *The Season's of a Man's Life*. New York: Alfred A. Knopf, 1978.

Levinson, D. *The Season's of a Woman's Life*. New York: Alfred A. Knopf, 1996.

Lewin, K. *Principles of Topological Psychology*. New York: McGraw-Hill, 1936.

Martinez, C. "Mexican-Americans." In L. Comas-Diaz and E. Griffith (eds.), *Cross Cultural Mental Health*. New York: Wiley, 1988.

Maslow, A. *Motivation and Personality*, (2nd ed.) New York: Harper and Row, 1970.

McEwen, M. "The Nature and Uses of Theory." In S. Komives and D. Woodard (eds.), *Student Services: A Handbook for the Profession*. San Francisco: Jossey Bass, 1996.

McGregor, D. *The Human Side of Enterprise*. New York: McGraw-Hill, 1960.

Moos, R. *Evaluating Educational Environments: Procedures, Measures, Findings, and Policy Implications.* San Francisco: Jossey-Bass, 1979.

Myers, I. *Introduction to Type: A Description of the Theory and Application of the Myers-Briggs Type Indicator* (4th ed.) Palo Alto, CA: Consulting Psychologists Press, 1987.

Pace, C. *Measuring the Quality of College Student Experiences.* Los Angeles: University of California, Higher Education Research Institute, 1984.

Pace, C. *Good Things Go Together.* Los Angeles: University of California, Higher Education Research Institute, 1987.

Pascarella, E. "College Environmental Influences on Learning and Cognitive Development: A Critical Review and Synthesis." In J. Smart (ed.), *Higher Education: Handbook of Theory and Research*, vol. I. New York: Agathon, 1985.

Pascarella, E., and Terenzini, P. *How College Affects Students.* San Francisco: Jossey-Bass, 1991.

Perry, W. Jr. *Forms of Intellectual and Ethical Development During the College Years: A Scheme.* New York: Holt, Rinehart and Winston, 1968.

Pervin, L. "Satisfaction and Perceived Self-Environment Similarity: A Semantic Differential Study of Student-College Interaction." *Journal of Personality.* 1967, 35, 623–634.

Phinney, J. "Ethnic Identity in Adolescents and Adults: Review of Research." *Psychological Bulletin.* 1990, 108, 449–514.

Rodgers, R. "Using Theory and Practice in Student Affairs." In T. Miller and R. Winston Jr. (eds.), *Administration and Leadership in Student Affairs: Actualizing Student Development in Higher Education.* (2nd ed.) Muncie, IN: Accelerated Development Press, 1991.

Sanford, N. (ed.) *The American College.* New York: Wiley, 1962.

Schlossberg, N., Lynch, A., and Chickering, A. *Improving Higher Education for Adults: Responsive Programs and Services from Entry to Departure.* San Francisco: Jossey-Bass, 1989.

Strange, C. "Dynamics of Campus Environments." In S. Komives and D. Woodard, (eds.), *Student Services: A Handbook for the Profession* (3rd ed.) San Francisco: Jossey-Bass, 1996.

Sue, D., and Sue D. W. *Counseling for the Culturally Different: Theory and Practice.* (2nd ed.) New York: Wiley, 1990.

Tinto, V. "Dropout from Higher Education: A Theoretical Synthesis of Recent Research." *Review of Educational Research*, 1975, 45, 89–125.

Tinto, V. *Leaving College: Rethinking the Causes and Cures for Student Attrition.* Chicago: University of Chicago Press, 1987.

Upcraft, M.L. "Translating Theory to Practice." In M.J. Barr (ed.) *The Handbook of Student Affairs Administration* San Francisco: Jossey-Bass, 1993.

Weber, M. *The Theory of Social and Economic Organization.* London: Oxford University Press, 1947.

Weidman, J. "Undergraduate Specialization: A Conceptual Approach." In J. Smart (ed.), *Higher Education: Handbook of Theory and Research.* vol. 5, New York: Agathon, 1989.

Weinberg, M., Williams, C. and Pryor, D. *Dual Attraction: Understanding Bisexuality.* New York: Oxford University Press, 1994.

Wells, E., and Knefelkamp, L. "A Process Model of Practice to Theory to Practice." Unpublished manuscript, 1982.

CHAPTER FOURTEEN

ASSESSMENT IN STUDENT AFFAIRS

M. Lee Upcraft and John H. Schuh

Assessment seems to be on everyone's mind in higher education. We may not know what we mean by assessment, or why we should assess, or what to assess, or how to assess, or how to use assessment, but we all feel the pressure to *assess*. This pressure is often more strongly felt in student affairs, which, in an era of increased competition for resources, may be questioned more critically about its rationale, importance, and results. The purpose of this chapter is to introduce readers to some of the basic definitions surrounding the issue of assessment, discuss the reasons to engage in assessment, and offer a comprehensive assessment model for student affairs. The steps in the assessment process will be outlined followed by a discussion on assessment ethics. Finally, advice on how to overcome resistance to assessment will be provided.

Some Basic Definitions

One of the first problems we encounter is confusion over what is meant by assessment. Too often, assessment is thought of as simply doing a survey or running a focus group. Some terms are used interchangeably ("assessment" and "evaluation"), some phrases are used incorrectly ("statistics show . . ."), and some terms are so vague as to strip them of any commonly accepted meaning ("quality" or "excellence"). Let's start with the term *assessment*. There are many definitions in the assessment and evaluation literature, with no conclusive consensus among the so-called "experts." We can only make an admittedly arbitrary, but, we hope, reasoned judgment. Therefore, for the purposes of this chapter, ***assessment*** *is any effort to gather, analyze, and interpret evidence that describes institutional, divisional, or agency effectiveness.* Effectiveness includes not only assessing student learning outcomes, but assessing other important results such as cost-effectiveness, clientele satisfaction, meeting clientele needs, complying with professional standards, and comparisons with other institutions. Assessment in student affairs is not restricted to students, but may include other constituents within the institution such as the faculty, administration, and governing boards, and outside the institution, such as alumni, legislators, funding sources, and accreditation agencies.

One further clarification: when we use the term assessment, we are not referring to assessing individual student or other individual clientele outcomes, *except in the aggregate.* For example, although we may not want any information about why an individual student may persist to graduation, we will want to know why, in the aggregate, students graduate.

Assessment, however, must be contrasted with but also linked to *evaluation.* Here there is less agreement among the experts. Most would agree that ***evaluation*** *is any effort to use assessment evidence to improve institutional, departmental, divisional, or institutional effectiveness.* Whereas assessment describes effectiveness, evaluation uses these descriptions in order to improve effectiveness, in whatever way that might be defined by an institution. For example, determining whether our admissions criteria predict subsequent persistence and degree completion is assessment. Using that assessment to change admissions requirements is evaluation.

Another term also must be defined: ***measurement.*** Measurement refers to *the methods we use to gather information for the purposes of assessment.* Typically, measurement methods are divided into two not very discrete categories: ***quantitative*** and ***qualitative.*** Quantitative methodologies assign numbers to objects, events, or observations according to some rule (Rossman and El-Khawas, 1987). Instruments with established psychometric properties are used to collect data; statistical methods are used to analyze data and draw conclusions. For example, the ability to predict college success might involve gathering all the quantifiable data about those variables that are thought to predict persistence and degree completion, such as high school grades, scores on standardized tests, involvement in high school activities, parents' education and income, etc. These data might then be correlated with subsequent student behavior (dropping out or persisting) to determine which factors and in which combinations best predict college success. For a more complete discussion of how to do quantitative assessment studies, see Upcraft and Schuh (1996).

Qualitative methodologies, on the other hand, are the detailed description of situations, events, people, interactions, and observed behaviors; the use of direct quotations, from people about their experiences, attitudes, beliefs, and thoughts; and the analysis of excerpts or entire passages from documents, correspondence, records, and case histories (Patton, 1990). Using the admissions example again, admissions personnel might want to interview students who persisted and those who dropped out to determine the extent to which their backgrounds and experiences might have contributed to their success or lack thereof. Variables that seem to predict college success but are difficult to measure (e.g. motivation) might be better understood through a qualitative approach. (For a more complete discussion of qualitative methods, see Upcraft and Schuh, 1996.) We should point out that the selection of an assessment methodology may not be an either/or decision; in fact, in many instances the use of both methodologies is not only appropriate but more powerful.

Another definition worth mentioning, although it will not be the focus of this chapter, is *research*. In the 1960s and 1970s, it was fashionable to use the term "student affairs research" to refer to assessment and evaluation efforts. This term proved to be confusing, particularly to faculty, who had a much narrower definition of research. When comparing research and assessment, Erwin (1991) argues that although they share many processes in common, they differ in at least two respects. First, assessment guides good practice, whereas research guides theory and conceptual foundations. Second, assessment typically has implications for a single institution, whereas research typically has broader implications for student affairs and higher education.

Another term that is often confusing is *outcomes assessment*. Often, this term is used to refer to all assessment, but in fact it refers to a very specific type of assessment. Outcomes assessment is an attempt to show a relationship between an intentional intervention (student use of career services) and some desired outcome (finding a job), taking into account pre-college background characteristics (gender, age, race/ethnicity and others) and during-college experiences (major, place of residence, GPA, and others). As we will discuss later in this chapter, there are many other forms of assessment, including tracking clientele use of services and programs, assessing student needs and satisfaction, assessing campus environments and student cultures, using national standards, assessing cost effectiveness, and benchmarking.

Why Assessment in Student Affairs?

National pressures on higher education institutions to demonstrate their effectiveness are continuing to mount. State legislatures and governors, the federal government, the general public, and students and their families are asking tough questions. What's your college's contribution to learning? Do your graduates know what you think they know and can they do what your degrees imply? How do you assure that? What do you intend for your students to learn? At what level are students learning what you are teaching? Is that the level you intend? What combination of institutional and student effort would it take to get to a higher level of student learning? (Marchese, 1990). Is your college accessible to *all* qualified students, regardless of gender, race, age, and demographic and background variables? And perhaps most importantly, as tuition increases at twice the rate of inflation, are students being shut out of education because they can't afford it, and if they can, are they getting a reasonable return on their considerable financial investment in higher education? In short, we can no longer ignore these questions. Assessment helps us answer them in more systematic and valid ways.

Survival

Student affairs is also under considerable pressure to demonstrate its importance and worth. In an era of declining resources and increased competition for what precious few resources we do have, student affairs has come under the institutional fiscal microscope. Issues range from quality and efficiency to the ultimate question: Do we really need this service or program? So the first answer to the question "Why assessment in student affairs?" is ***survival***. There is some evidence that student services have borne the brunt of budget cuts. In order to shield academic programs from severe cuts, budgets of all other categories have suffered a disproportionate share of reductions (Cage, 1992).

One might easily respond, "Isn't there a substantial body of research that demonstrates that students' out-of-class experiences contribute to their learning, personal development, academic achievement, and retention?" The answer is yes (Pascarella and Terenzini, 1991; Kuh, Branch, Lund, Ramen-Gyurnek, 1994), but this doesn't help for two reasons. First, this research is not well known among administrators and faculty. Second, even if it is, the question of local applicability always arises. "Okay, so the research evidence shows that students living in residence halls earn higher grades and are more likely to persist to graduation than students living elsewhere, but is that true at our institution?" National studies may be more elegant in design, sophisticated in research techniques, and more lucid in the presentation and results, but locally produced studies, if well done, will have more impact on a particular campus. In this sense, *all assessment is local.*

In general, we believe assessment efforts can and will demonstrate the effectiveness and worth of student services and programs, and show positive relationships between students' out-of-class experiences and use of student services and programs and student learning, including academic achievement and retention. However, one should be prepared to deal with local results that may not be consistent with the findings of national studies because students make their own environments based on interactions with their institutions (Baird, 1996). Further, even if there are local studies that are consistent with national findings, policy decision-makers may choose this evidence for other reasons. Thus, *all assessment is a risk*: we can never be certain that local assessment studies will have the desired impact of demonstrating the worth of student services and programs or ensuring their survival.

Quality

Although survival may be the primary motivation for assessment in student affairs, there are other reasons. Even if it is demonstrated that student services and programs are essential and needed, a second question is, are they of high *quality*? Assessment can be a very powerful tool in linking goals to outcomes, helping to define quality, and determining if quality exists in student affairs. We strongly believe that a fundamental responsibility of student affairs is to provide services, programs, and facilities that are of the highest quality. Assessment can help us determine if we have been successful in fulfilling that responsibility.

Affordability

A third reason for assessment is to gauge *affordability* and cost-effectiveness. The question to be answered goes something like this: "Sure, this program or that service is needed, and there is evidence of their quality, but in an era of declining resources, can we afford them? Can we continue to fund them at current levels? Can we afford them at all?" Decisions to eliminate services and programs based on their affordability may have to be made, but other affordability questions abound. Might it be less expensive to outsource this service or program? Can this service or program generate income from fees? Can this service do more with less, or less with less? And how do we know? Unfortunately, these decisions are often made without adequate assessment, in part because there are few, if any, cost-effectiveness models used in student affairs.

Strategic Planning

Strategic planning, according to Baldridge (1983), examines the big issues of an organization: its mission, purpose, long range goals, relationship to its environment, share of the market, and interactions with other organizations. Because many higher education institutions are seriously involved with strategic planning, it is important for student affairs to be an active and effective participant in this process. Assessment contributes to strategic planning by helping define goals and objectives and pointing to critical issues or problems that must be resolved successfully if the organization is to achieve its goals. Assessment is especially important in the early phases of strategic planning, to identify strengths, weaknesses, and opportunities for the future. It is also critical in the later stages of planning, when evaluation of policies and programs occurs.

Policy Development and Decision-Making

What evidence do we have to help us make a decision or develop and revise a policy? Assessment can provide systematic information, which can be critical in helping policy and decision-makers make valid judgments about policy, decide on important issues, and make decisions about resource allocations. Making these kind of judgments based on systematic information is not only important within students affairs, it is also important to help student affairs influence policies and decisions within the institution, and with those with something at stake outside the institution, such as boards of control, legislatures, alumni, and the general public.

Politics

Assessment may also be necessary for *political* reasons. Sometimes we must do assessment because someone or some institution of importance wants some information, which makes it politically important to produce. It may be the president of the institution, a faculty governing group, an influential board of control member, an outspoken legislator, or a concerned alumni. We must also be concerned about the political impact of our assessment findings. *All assessment is political*; thus assessment investigators must be attuned to the impact of their studies from the moment an assessment idea emerges. If one of the purposes of assessment is to influence policy and practice, the political context within which decisions are made must be accounted for in the assessment process. This issue will be discussed in greater detail in Chapter 10 of this volume, "The Political Dimensions of Decision Making."

Accreditation

According to the Commission on Higher Education's *Standards for Accreditation* (1992), one of the criteria for accreditation is institutional effectiveness. "The deciding factor in assessing the effectiveness of any institution is evidence of the extent to which it achieves its goals and objectives. The necessity of seeking such evidence continually is inescapable; one of the primary hallmarks of faculty, administration, and governing boards is the skill with which they raise questions about institutional effectiveness, seek answers and significantly improve procedures in the light of their findings" (pp. 17–18). This moves assessment from the "nice to have if you can afford it" category to the "you better have it if you want to stay accredited" category. Because student affairs is an active participant in the accreditation process, it will be required to contribute assessment evidence to this process.

These are among the many reasons for assessment in student affairs. They are important because we believe that the first step in the assessment process is to determine why you are doing a particular study. What you do will in a large part be determined by why you are doing it. We also believe these questions are best answered within the context of a comprehensive assessment program.

A Comprehensive Assessment Model

Too often, assessment is done piecemeal without any real planning or consistency in response to a crisis, or not done at all. Often we don't do anything because we don't know how to start or what to do. This comprehensive assessment model describes various types of assessment and offers choices about which assessments are appropriate.

Keeping Track of Who Uses Student Services, Programs, and Facilities

How many clients use services, programs, and facilities, and how are they described by gender, race, ethnicity, age, class standing, residence, and other demographic variables? This component is very important because if our intended clientele do not use our services, programs, or facilities, our intended purposes cannot be achieved. However, sheer numbers do not tell us the whole story, especially if users or participants are not representative of our clientele. The quantity and distribution of users have important implications for policy and practice, and must be assessed.

Assessing Student and Other Clientele Needs

The basic principle that we should meet the needs of our clientele is a good one, and well supported in the literature, but often is not easy. There are many questions to be answered. What kinds of services, programs, and facilities do students and other clientele need, based on student and staff perceptions, institutional expectations, and research on student needs? How do we distinguish between "wants" and "needs?" How do we know if what we offer "fits" our clientele? Assessing student and other clientele needs can provide answers to these questions.

Assessing Student and Other Clientele Satisfaction

Of those persons who use our services, programs, and facilities, what is their level of satisfaction? What strengths and suggestions for improvement do they identify? Client satisfaction is important because if they are not satisfied, they won't use what we offer again, and they will not recommend them to friends and colleagues. We are also interested in clientele satisfaction because it gives us valuable information about how to improve our services, programs, and facilities.

Assessing Campus Environments and Student Cultures

Although assessing individual use, needs, and satisfaction is important, it is also critical to take a look at their collective perceptions of campus environments and student cultures within which they conduct their day-to-day lives. This component of the assessment model can help answer such questions as "What is the climate for women on this campus? What is the academic environment, both inside and outside the classroom? What is the overall quality of life in residence halls?"

Assessing Outcomes

Of those persons who use our services, programs, and facilities, is there any effect on their learning, development, academic success, or other intended outcomes, particularly when compared with nonusers? Can programmatic interventions be isolated from other variables that may influence outcomes, such as background, characteristics, and other experiences? These kinds of studies are very difficult to design, implement, and interpret, but in some ways they attempt to answer the most fundamental question of all: Is what we are doing having any effect, and is that effect the intended one? These studies are both the most important we do and the most difficult to conduct.

Providing Comparable Institutions Assessment

How does the quality of services, programs, and facilities compare with "best in class" comparable institutions? An important way of assessing quality is to compare oneself to other institutions that appear to be doing a better job with a particular service, program, or facility, often described as "benchmarking." One purpose would be to discover how others achieve their results, and then to translate their processes to one's own environment. The key to this assessment component is to select comparable institutions that have good assessment programs, rather than relying on anecdotes or reputation.

Use of Nationally Accepted Standards to Assess

How do our services, programs, and facilities compare to accepted national standards, such as those developed by the Council for the Advancement of Standards for Student Services/Development Programs, various national and regional accrediting agencies, and professional organizations?

Assessing Cost Effectiveness

Are the benefits students derive from what we offer worth the cost, and how do we know? There is very little guidance offered from existing student affairs literature, except at the crudest level of analysis: divide the cost of a service by the number of students using the service. Such an "analysis" is often fraught with so many methodological problems that its conclusions may be meaningless. Cost/benefit analysis is difficult and somewhat imprecise in a nonprofit, service-oriented organization, but should be attempted nevertheless.

Steps in the Assessment Process

We believe assessment is best implemented in a systematic way if all of the following steps are followed:

STEP ONE: Define the Problem. We assert that all assessment flows from an attempt to solve a problem, so establishing a clear and concise definition of the problem facing the student affairs practitioner is the first step in the assessment process. Another way of framing this step is asking the question, "Why are we doing this assessment?" Everything else flows from this question, for the "why" determines what we do, how we do it, and how we use the results. Other questions that might help define the problem include:

- What specific circumstances or situations are driving assessment efforts? Examples might include low enrollments, consideration of a policy to protect students from being discriminated against on the basis of their sexual orientation, pressures to reduce budgets, commitment to improving services and programs, impending accreditation review, or whatever.
- What external pressures are driving assessment efforts? Pressures external to student affairs might include the general public (costs are rising more quickly than inflation), institutional boards of control (we need to increase minority enrollments), institutional leadership (too many problems arise from students abusing alcohol), alums (the sinking feeling that student life just isn't what it used to be!), and in state supported institutions, legislatures and governors (we need

to cut state allocations by a certain percentage), and from accrediting agencies (assessment is required for reaccreditation).

- What internal circumstances are driving assessment? Student services and programs could always be bettered regardless of their quality, so improvement is a primary internal circumstance that drives assessment efforts. Other internally driven variables may include a concern that services and programs might not be meeting student needs or might not be equally accessible and used by all types of students. We may need to know more about whether our services and programs are achieving their intended outcomes, and if so, whether they are being administered in cost-effective ways.

STEP TWO: Determine the Purpose of the Study. As discussed previously, assessment is the process of gathering, analyzing, and interpreting evidence (information). Given the particular problem identified in Step one, what information do we need to help solve it? What information will be critical to responding to external and internal pressure to perform assessment? The answers to these questions then become the basis for determining the purpose of the study. For example, if we need more information about student satisfaction with our health service, we should conduct a study that's purpose is to measure that satisfaction.

STEP THREE: Determine Where to Get the Information Needed. Information can be retrieved from a wide variety of sources. The most obvious source is students or other clientele, but there are many other sources. Institutional or functional unit records may well contain valuable information needed to solve a problem. For example, if our concern is the differential use of services by underrepresented groups, an analysis of student usage by gender, race/ethnicity, age, disability, and other categories may provide all the information needed to verify the problem. Other sources of information might include institutional documents, student newspaper articles, and field observations.

Most student affairs assessment focuses on gathering information directly from students; however, they may not be the only sources of information. There may be others who might have insight into the problem, including staff, faculty, administrators, community leaders, or even the general public. It may seem obvious, but defining the population precisely is important because the conclusions drawn from a particular inquiry apply only to those studied in the first place.

STEP FOUR: Determine the Best Assessment Method(s). Another way of framing this step is to answer the question, "What's the best way to get the information I need?" Of course, the best assessment method depends on the purpose of the study. Basically we have three choices: quantitative methods, qualitative methods, or a combination of both. According to Patton (1990), qualitative methods focus on gathering information from interviews, observations, and documents, and they require much smaller samples than quantitative measures. Quantitative measures, on the other hand, include gathering data from a survey or other instrument and require much larger samples than qualitative methods. So the question becomes, "Given the information we need, what is the best way to retrieve it?" Generally speaking, if we need information about "what" is going on, quantitative methods are more appropriate. If we need information about "why" something is going on, qualitative measures are more appropriate. Our experience has also taught us that a *combination of methods* may best provide the information to solve the problem that precipitated the study. For example, if one is studying the development of critical thinking in first year students, a pre- and post-test measure of critical thinking would tell us if such development did occur. Focus groups might best tell us why or why not development of critical thinking occurred.

STEP FIVE: Determine *Whom to Study.*

Having decided on the population to be studied, it is rarely possible to include the whole population in a study regardless of the type of study chosen. Sometimes, however, if the population is narrowly defined, it is possible. But most often, a *sample* of the whole population must be selected in ways that ensure that those selected are *representative* of that population according to some criteria. For quantitative studies, the most typical criteria are the demographics of the population, such as gender, age, race/ethnicity, disability, and others. In the collegiate setting, factors such as class standing, grades, place of residence, full-time or part-time enrollment, major field, and others may also be important. If the sample is, in fact, representative, one can *generalize* with much more confidence to the whole population. In qualitative studies, however, although strict adherence to the representativeness is not required, it is still nonetheless important within general parameters.

STEP SIX: Determine *How Information Will Be Collected.*

Data can be collected in a wide variety of ways, including mailed questionnaires, telephone surveys, individual interviews, focus groups, Web-based surveys, and other data collection procedures. Each procedure has its strengths and limitations, but all are intended to get the desired number of participants in the study. For example, mailed questionnaires will most often yield the fewest number of participants, but more thorough information will be collected. On the other hand, telephone surveys will yield a higher percentage of return, but will be limited in the amount of information collected. Individual interviews and focus groups require a more personal touch and incentives such as food or token monetary compensation may be helpful. Whatever data collection procedures are chosen, they should be consistent with the purpose of the study and yield the optimum number of participants needed.

STEP SEVEN: Determine What Instrument(s) Will Be Used. The instrument(s) used to collect data depends on several factors, including which methodologies are chosen. For quantitative methodologies, an instrument must be chosen that yields results that can be statistically analyzed. Beyond that, we need to decide whether we will use an already constructed instrument with appropriate psychometric properties and standardized norms, or a locally constructed instrument that may be more appropriate to the study, but lacks validity, reliability, and other psychometric properties. Generally speaking, instruments available from any one of several national test publishing houses are preferable, if there is an opportunity to add locally developed items. But if the problem under study is unique to a particular campus, test construction experts should be consulted when developing local instruments.

For qualitative methodologies, an interview protocol must be developed, consisting of standardized, open-ended questions that retrieve the information needed for the study. According to Patton (1990), an item is standardized when it is written out in advance *exactly* the way it is to be asked during the interview. Clarification or elaboration should be included, as should any probing questions. Variations among interviewers can be minimized and comparisons across interviews can be made if the interview protocol is standardized. Open-ended means there are no prescribed answers (such as yes/no); respondents are free to provide any answer they choose. Although this may seem obvious, there should be a direct connection between the questions asked and the information needed to help solve the problem.

STEP EIGHT: Determine Who Should Collect the Information. At first glance, this question may not seem to matter much. Obviously, data should be collected by people who are competent to do so. But often the most qualified people are also those who have a vested interest in the outcome. This is less of a problem with quantitative methodologies, where bias is more likely to have occurred in the selection or development of the instrument. In qualitative methodologies, however, where the data is collected and filtered by those who conduct the study and record the data, bias becomes a much larger issue.

There is also the lingering problem of the "face credibility" of the study. Can we really trust a study that was done entirely by those with a vested interest in the outcome? On the other hand, can we really trust a study that was done entirely by outside experts who know little or nothing about the context and nuances of the study? In general, if the study and the people who are doing it have integrity, we have no problem with those who have a vested interest in the outcome being a part of the data collection process.

STEP NINE: Determine How the Information Will Be Analyzed. Analysis of quantitative data depends on the purpose of the study. Probably the most important first step is to determine if the respondents are, in fact, representative of the population to be studied. Then appropriate descriptive and inferential statistical analyses can be applied. Because most student affairs professionals lack the necessary knowledge of which statistical analyses are most appropriate and how to interpret statistically generated results, we recommend using statistical consultants familiar with social science research methodologies for both data analysis and interpretation.

Analysis of qualitative data is somewhat more consistent with the skills and abilities of student affairs professionals, but still must be done in systematic ways, including listening to and searching for meaning in interview/focus groups audio tapes or transcripts, looking for themes, trends, variations, and generalizations. This process should be an inclusive one, with data gatherers collaborating with colleagues, students, and even subjects in the interpretation of the data.

STEP TEN: Determine the Implications of the Study for Policy and Practice. Too often, investigators are content with reporting the findings and conclusions of a study, leaving its implications for policy and practice to various audiences. We believe that in reporting assessment results, the implications of the study should be spelled out. Here we are clearly crossing over from assessment to evaluation. Remember that whereas assessment is the gathering and analyzing of information, evaluation is using assessment information to solve the problem that precipitated the study in the first place. What approaches to solving the problem should be considered in light of the findings? What policies or practices need to be revised, eliminated, or created because of the findings? In assessment reports, there should be clear "calls for action" that motivate the reader to do something about the problem that precipitated the study.

STEP ELEVEN: Report the Results Effectively. After the findings have been reported and analyzed, and the implications for policy and practice identified, how do we report the results? In what form do we report the results? To whom should the study be reported? Should everyone with something at stake get the whole report? Many studies end up filed under "I" for "Interesting" or gathering dust on someone's shelf because we fail to "package" results in ways that move decision-makers to make changes based on the study. In fact, how a study is formatted and distributed may be more important than the results of the study. Probably the biggest mistake we make is to send the full report to all audiences and hope for the best.

There are several ways to overcome this problem. Multiple reports for multiple audiences is one way. Highlight the results most applicable to a particular audience. Executive summaries that summarize the study, its findings, and recommendations for policy and practice are also effective. Getting results to the "right" people (those who can do something about the problem studied) is also very important. Offering to discuss the results in greater detail in person may also be appropriate. Even going so far as to suggest how decision-makers may make best use of the study is not out of the question. Clearly, if the purpose of the study is to solve a problem, the report must not only report the results, but how the results can be used to solve the problem.

We would again assert that these steps should be addressed for each study *before* the study is conducted. To be sure, as the study progresses, changes may have to be made, but a major impediment to good assessment is lack of planning. Following these steps helps ensure that the study will be a good one.

The Ethics of Assessment

Maintaining high standards of ethics and integrity is as important as doing a good study. Whenever we study human behavior, we have an obligation to protect the rights of subjects participating. This includes respecting their autonomy, preventing them from harm, treating them fairly and honestly, ensuring their confidentiality, obtaining their fully informed consent, guarding them from deception, and telling them how the results will be used (Upcraft and Schuh, 1996). To do less means we have not met our ethical responsibilities as professionals. Careful attention must be given to the ethical considerations of assessment if we are to conduct studies that honor the dignity of participants.

Overcoming Resistance to Assessment

Unfortunately, understanding the importance of assessment and how to do it does not necessarily result in getting it done. There are many reasons why assessment doesn't get done. They include the following problems.

Lack of commitment from institutional leadership. Sometimes the leadership of an institution doesn't have a commitment to it. It may be because the leadership doesn't understand the value of assessment, doesn't believe the institution has the expertise, is afraid of possible findings, or other reasons. Whatever the reasons, leaders must be shown that the benefits of assessment outweigh the risks, and that, on the whole, assessment can become an important problem-solving, policy-development, and decision-making tool.

Lack of time. Assessment requires a lot of staff time, if we subscribe to the principle that those affected by the assessment should be involved in it. Often those staff members most resistant to assessment are those who are unwilling to take time away from their jobs or students to get involved. Although this is an admirable point of view, it may also be somewhat shortsighted. For example, if the very existence of a service or program is being questioned, there may have to be some temporary reduction of direct service to ensure its continuance. The reality may be that staff members do what they have to do in order to keep doing the things they want to do.

Lack of money. Assessment costs money. Sometimes funding for assessment comes from external sources, but most often the cost of assessment is expected to be covered within existing fiscal and human resources. Again, if the very existence of a program or service is being questioned, spending money to demonstrate its importance and impact is money well spent. The cost of assessment may well be, in the long run, of benefit to students.

Lack of expertise. Too often we are intimidated by the lack of assessment technical expertise particularly on statistical analysis and design. Although this may be true, we may be more qualified than we think when is comes to qualitative approaches, especially individual interviews and focus groups. Most student affairs professionals claim some interpersonal and group skills that can readily apply to these data collection procedures. This barrier may be overcome through retraining of existing staff and students, hiring consultants as needed to help with specific projects, and reconfiguring existing professional and staff positions to include assessment.

Fear of Results. As we have discussed, all assessment is a risk. There is no guarantee that assessment will necessarily make us look good or yield positive results. For example, we know that generally speaking, living in residence halls is associated with persistence to graduation, even when other variables that contribute to that outcome are taken into account. What if an institution does a study which shows that there is no relationship, or worse yet, a negative relationship between living in residence halls and retention? In this instance, isn't the fear legitimate? It all depends on the reason the study was done in the first place. If it was to improve residence halls, there is less risk than if it was done to determine whether or not the institution should continue to have residence halls. The risk must be considered in the light of the potential consequences. Put another way, can we live with all the possible results?

Overcoming barriers to assessment is an important part of assessment in student affairs, and should be considered in the light of specific institutional conditions.

Summary

Assessment is not just another educational fad that will disappear when newer fads emerge. The very existence of the student affairs profession may be at stake if we are unable to justify what we do and, most importantly, demonstrate that student affairs services, programs, and facilities contribute to student learning, especially student academic and psychosocial development. We must be certain that our services, programs, and facilities serve all our students, meet their needs, result in their satisfaction, create positive campus climates, are cost-effective, meet nationally accepted standards, and most importantly, contribute to student learning.

But even if there were no pressures to justify our existence, student affairs should be committed to the very highest quality student services, programs, and facilities. A comprehensive assessment effort that is well thought-out, systematic, and produces credible results is the only way to know for sure that we have, to the best of our ability, served well our students, our institution, and other stakeholders.

References

Baird, L.L. "Learning from Research on Student Outcomes." In S.R. Komives and D.B. Woodard, Jr. (eds.), *Student Services: A Handbook for the Profession* (3rd 3d). San Francisco: Jossey-Bass, 1996.

Baldridge, V. J. "Strategic Planning in Higher Education: Does the Emperor Have Any Clothes?" In V. J. Baldridge (ed.), *Dynamics of Organizational Change in Education*. Berkeley, CA: McCutchan, 1983.

Cage, M. C. "To Shield Academic Programs from Cuts, Many Colleges Pare Student Services." *Chronicle of Higher Education*, Nov. 18, 1992, A25–A26.

Commission on Higher Education. *Standards for Accreditation*, 1992.

Erwin, T. D. *Assessing Student Learning and Development: A Guide to Principles, Goals, and Methods of Determining College Outcomes*. San Francisco: Jossey-Bass, 1991.

Kuh, G. D., Branch, Douglas, K., Lund, J. P., Ramin-Gyurnek, J. *Student Learning Outside the Classroom: Transcending Artificial Boundaries*, ASHE-ERIC Higher Education Report, vol. 23, no. 8. Washington, D.C.: George Washington University Press, 1994.

Marchese, T. J. "Assessment's Next Five Years." *Association of Institutional Research Newsletter*, 1990, Fall-Winter, 1–4, (Special Supplement).

Pascarella, E. T., and Terenzini, P. T. *How College Affects Students: Findings and Insights from Twenty Years of Research*. San Francisco: Jossey-Bass, 1991.

Patton, M. Q. *Qualitative Evaluation and Research Methods* (2nd ed.) Newbury Park, CA: Sage Publications, 1990.

Rossman, J. E., and El-Khawas, E. *Thinking About Assessment: Perspectives for Presidents and Chief Academic Officers*. Washington, D.C.: American Council on Education and American Association for Higher Education, 1987.

Upcraft, M. L., and Schuh, J. H. *Assessment in Student Affairs: A Guide for Practitioners*. San Francisco: Jossey-Bass, 1996.

CHAPTER FIFTEEN

MEASURING STUDENT SATISFACTION AND NEEDS

John H. Schuh and M. Lee Upcraft

Without question, there is a strong emphasis on quality in contemporary higher education. Haworth and Conrad (1997, p. xi) evaluate the situation this way: "Program quality—how to enhance it and how to evaluate it—has been placed squarely on the contemporary agenda in higher education. Among the reasons for the current interest in program quality, none is more important that a widely-shared belief that the quality of our nation's colleges and universities is declining." Quality is defined in a variety of ways: by retention and graduation rates, by the quality experiences for students, and by a variety of other measures (for examples, see Taylor and Massy, 1996).

One of the ways of determining quality in higher education is to conduct periodic assessment studies to measure the level at which an institution or program functions. Stark and Thomas (1994, p. 3) describe assessment this way: ". . . the term assessment as currently used has a broader meaning that generally applies to the gathering of information to indicate the extent to which an institution or unit within the institution is achieving what it purports to do, that for which it is accountable . . ." Banta, Lund, Black, and Oblander (1996, p. xvii) add, " . . . questions about how to think about assessment and what methods to use are being asked by more people and with more intensity than ever before."

Two essential elements in developing an assessment program are determining the specific needs of students and other clients, and then determining whether those needs have been met. Practically speaking, this means that institutions need to conduct needs assessments and satisfaction assessments because these two forms of assessment are linked.

This chapter is concerned with two aspects as assessment: needs assessment and satisfaction assessment. These are forms of action inquiry, meaning that they occur in the field with students. Often they are tied to specific issues that challenge student affairs practitioners. Consider the following scenario confronting a newly-hired director of a student affairs department.

You have just been appointed the director of services for students with disabilities on your campus. This position did not exist before your appointment. Your campus, which is a public university of 10,000 students, has an unknown number of students with disabilities. Before your appointment, academic services for persons with disabilities were coordinated by the dean of students, but this task simply became too complex and the responsibilities were turned over to you.

The dean's office has some records of individuals for whom accommodations were made. In the Admissions Office is a file of students who have identified themselves as having a disability, but this was never cross-checked with the dean's file. The campus police department has a list of students and others for whom special accommodations have been made regarding campus parking, and student housing has information about accommodations that were provided for students who wanted to live in the residence halls. The Testing Office has information about tests administered related to learning disabilities for diagnostic purposes, but the office has no idea about any degree of follow-up that was done for these students after they received the results of the test.

Your job is to coordinate services, develop a plan to make the campus more accessible to students, and serve as the person who can provide information to students who need specific accommodations. How might you proceed?

The problem inherited by the newly appointed director of services for students with disabilities on the campus identified previously is challenging. An early task this person must accomplish is to identify the potential clients by working closely with the other agencies and departments that heretofore have provided services to persons with disabilities. Assuming that can be accomplished successfully, the next step is to develop a program of services and learning experiences for the students. This leads to the primary discussion of this chapter: How are needs and satisfaction assessment accomplished in support of the practice of student affairs administration? More specifically, this chapter is designed to provide a rudimentary introduction to these two forms of assessment. The problem identified previously will be used to illustrate the assessment methods recommended in the chapter. In dealing with these two forms of assessment, it is important to remember that in the view of some (for example, Holmes, 1996), such concepts as needs, wants, quality, and satisfaction are linked. Another linkage, assessment methodology, is just as important. Although approaches to quantitative and qualitative assessment will be discussed separately, it is increasingly common for these two approaches to be linked in the literature on research methods (for example, Gall, Borg, and Gall, 1996) and in reports of assessment projects (for example, Kelley, 1994).

The Role of Institutional Mission in Needs and Satisfaction Assessment

Before defining needs and satisfaction assessment, it is important to discuss the role an institution's mission plays in shaping assessment projects. The institution's mission has a tremendous influence on the array of programs and services that are found on a particular campus. For example, at a residential college that offers no graduate programs, the need for a complex system of day-care centers to serve the children of students probably is unnecessary because of the nature and mission of the college. Very few, if any, students may have children for whom they have custody. To propose this kind of intervention would reflect a lack of understanding of who attends the college and for what reasons. On the other hand, at a commuter institution with no residence halls where the average age of the student body is over 30 years old, a proposal to reshape the student health service into a complete hospital with infirmary care likely would be received as foolish. Both adoption of the day-care proposal at the commuter school and development of a more complex array of services at the student health service of the residential college may make perfect sense for the same reason: the proposal would provide a higher quality of student experience consistent with the purposes of the institution.

As Barr asserts, an institution's mission has an influence on all student affairs activities, programs and operations, including assessment (see Chapter 2 in this volume). Supporting this assertion are Gall, Borg, and Gall (1996, p. 701), who conclude that one of the underlying problems with needs assessment is that ". . . the values underlying needs often are not clearly articulated." Again, the institutional mission statement will help in identifying what institution values will help frame a needs assessment. From a practical point of view, the director of the office of services for students with disabilities should make sure that the department's mission is consistent with the mission of the division of student affairs and the mission of the institution. After this is in place, the assessment process can begin.

Definitions

Arriving at definitions for needs assessment and satisfaction assessment is an important step in developing the assessment process. Following are brief definitions of needs and satisfaction assessment.

Needs Assessment. A number of definitions of needs assessment are available in the literature including those provided by Rossett (1990); Stufflebeam, McCormick, Brinkerhoff, and Nelson (1985); and Lenning and MacAleenan (1979). All these authors offer excellent contributions about needs assessment, but their work is somewhat broader than what might be most appropriate for needs assessment within the context of student affairs. When we think about needs assessment in the context of student affairs, we see that students are the primary object of our services and programs. Their needs are somewhat narrower than the general population because their relationship with the institution is limited to just a few years, and especially at a traditional, residential campus, the range in age of students is limited. Contrast measuring the needs of college students with the citizens of a medium-size institution and city and the differences are obvious. Consequently, a fairly narrow definition of needs assessment is warranted.

Five different kinds of needs have been identified by Roth, 1977 (cited by Gall, Borg, and Gall, 1996). These include ideals, norms, minimums, desires (meaning wants), and expectations. Clearly there are dramatic differences in this per se, because the range is the very best to the absolute minimum. In developing a needs assessment, the framers will have to decide what they mean by need with some degree of precision.

Kuh (1982) cautions that determining student needs must be separated from student wants. Students might want a campus food service that provides gourmet food for the price of fast food, available any time day or night, with refunds provided for all meals missed. Although that would be a highly desirable food service operation from a student perspective, it is highly unlikely that it could be provided for competitive prices, which is usually one of the objectives of the campus food service.

We urge student affairs officers to define needs assessment within the context of an institution's mission as was asserted previously. Institutions use their mission to map out what they aspire to be, and within the context of their mission they place an emphasis on certain kinds of programs, services, and resources, as was explained previously. In this context, we define needs assessment as " . . . determining the presence or absence of the factors and conditions, resources, services, and learning opportunities that students need in order to meet their educational goals and objectives within the context of an institution's mission" (Upcraft and Schuh, 1996, p. 128).

Satisfaction Assessment. In the simple terms, satisfaction assessment is about determining how students and other clients evaluate the quality of their experiences. All institutions have the potential to provide quality experiences within the context of their educational mission. Satisfaction, however, can be a bit deceiving. For example, many students might find the concept that they would not have to pay for items at the campus bookstore attractive. As appealing as this might be, the fact is that such an approach is unrealistic in a fiscal sense and would result in income having to be derived from other sources to keep the bookstore solvent.

Hartman and Schmidt (1995) indicate that two variables, performance and outcomes, have a relationship with satisfaction. They conclude that " . . . students' satisfaction with an educational program is dependent on that program's success in meeting students' needs" (1995, p. 214). Performance and outcomes are crucial because satisfaction results when the level of performance is high within the definition of outcomes expected by clients. That leads to a definition of satisfaction assessment.

Levine and Cureton (1998) conclude that contemporary traditional age college students have a consumer mentality. "They prefer a relationship like those they already enjoy with their bank, the telephone company, and the supermarket" (p. 50). Whether this is appropriate is a subject for debate, but the fact is that satisfaction assessment is an important element in serving people with this point of view on their relationship with their college.

Satisfaction assessment has a direct link to the movement to improve the overall quality of institutions of higher education. Improving the quality of our institutions is a concern that has received intense national interest according to Bogue and Saunders (1992, p xi), who assert that such questions as "What are we trying to achieve?" and "How good a job are we doing and how do we know?" are central in higher education. The total quality management movement has emerged, in part, as an attempt to improve how our institutions function. Lembcke (1994, pp. 53- 55), in describing the purpose of customer research as part of Total Quality Management (TQM), indicates the following:

> "The purpose of customer research is to understand the degree of and reasons for customer satisfaction (or dissatisfaction) with the services and products received so improvements can be made. Customer satisfaction research, which is performed after the fact, reveals the gap between customer needs or expectations and customer perceptions. Data explaining customer dissatisfaction are used to add, eliminate, or redesign services and products and to improve processes in ways that decrease nonconformance to standards (errors, omissions, and delays) in the services and products provided. Customer satisfaction data help department managers to determine future quality improvement

needs as well as to monitor the improvements in customer satisfaction expected to result from past investments in TQM."

For the purposes of assessment in student affairs, satisfaction assessment is defined as that form of assessment that is concerned with the extent to which students and other clients evaluate their experiences as of high quality. For students, these experiences should contribute to growth and development within the context of the institution's mission.

Building the Case for Needs and Satisfaction Assessment

Needs and satisfaction assessment are essential elements of student affairs practice. The logic for this assertion is obvious. In the case of needs assessment, it would be imprudent and perhaps foolish to develop programs, services or learning experiences for students without considering the institution's mission and the needs of the student body. The influence of the mission has been discussed previously in this chapter. Satisfaction assessment helps determine if the needs of students have been met. One of the assertions of this chapter is that these two forms of assessments are linked. That is, to conduct one form of assessment without the other is to have an incomplete assessment program. To simply measure student needs without knowing if they have been met is as much a mistake as determining if students are satisfied with campus programs, services, and learning experiences without knowing if they are the right ones; that is, that they have been developed in response to a careful study of student needs.

Needs Assessment

Student affairs practitioners have numerous opportunities for personal growth and development (see Nuss, 1993). They attend conferences, read the literature, cruise the World Wide Web, and use other means to identify ways of advancing their practice. In short, student affairs practitioners are very good at sharing information with their colleagues and they are equally adept at starting new programs. But, if there is no student need for the particular intervention, the activity is a waste of time, energy, and resources.

In the example, the Office of Services for Students with Disabilities (OSD), students may be quite independent and able to negotiate their way through the college. In this scenario they may not require much, if any, institutional support except for monitoring the physical environment to make sure that facilities are accessible. If this is the case, the approach of the director will be to oversee physical accessibility but not do much else. Suppose that the physical facilities are in very good repair and accessible, but faculty members are unwilling or unable to make accommodations for students to complete their courses successfully, such as allowing extra time for certain students to complete their exams because of a documented learning disability. In this case, an advocacy role for the office would be indicated. Yet another approach might be that the college has good facilities and a cooperative faculty, but that the diagnosis of students with apparent learning disabilities was inadequate. In this circumstance, a third form of intervention would be required. The point becomes obvious: without knowing students' needs, it is very difficult for a director to frame the program.

Satisfaction Assessment

Satisfaction assessment is an equally important building block in providing a solid foundation for student affairs practice. After needs have been identified and an intervention developed to meet these needs, the reaction of clients (students and others served by the office) to the intervention needs to be measured. In effect, the use of satisfaction assessments provides a formative assessment of the activity. It provides planners and others responsible for the activity with information about what changes, if any, need to be made in the intervention. It is highly possible that the intervention is very successful and needs only minor changes to meet the needs of clients more effectively. But it is also possible, though perhaps less likely, that the intervention has been completely off-target. This could be due to a variety of reasons, including a faulty needs assessment, exorbitant costs to be borne by the clientele or others, or other reasons. Regardless of the reasons, the implementation of a satisfaction assessment can provide information that can be used to improve the service.

More specifically, assessment has a direct relationship with student affairs in trying to improve the quality of programs, services, and learning opportunities. Scott (1996, p. 73) asserts that "student affairs professionals want to satisfy customers (student, parents, and the institutions) with the level and variety of services offered while promoting student development concepts and student learning in the framework of those services and programs." Scott (1996, p. 78) adds that "using assessment is another way of responding to questions of improvement and accountability."

An Assessment Model

The multistage assessment model described by Upcraft and Schuh in this volume has a direct application to the office of disability services. This circumstance is quite complex in that nothing in the way of coordinated services is in place, and no one has measured the extent to which the minimum services provided have met client needs. Determining the problem, identifying the purpose of the study, carefully describing the information needed, choosing the best method of assessment, deciding whom to study, determining the way to collect the data and the instruments to be used, deciding how to record and analyze the data and how to use the results, and then reporting the results, are important steps to be followed. As Upcraft and Schuh point out, these steps should be addressed *before* the study is conducted.

A Quantitative Approach to Needs Assessment

Refer back to the case description that was introduced at the beginning of this chapter to refresh your memory about the situation. A director of services for students with disabilities has been recently appointed, and very healthy debate about the services of the office has been ongoing. A quantitative approach to determining student needs would be to administer a questionnaire to the potential clients served by the office established to meet the needs of individuals with disabilities. After the director was able to identify the population of individuals served, students and perhaps some selected faculty or staff, a quantitative needs assessment could be conducted. A few basic steps would guide this study.

Sampling. Depending on the number of individuals potentially to be served by the office, a random sample of students and others could be drawn from the larger population. In all probability, the number of individuals would not be particularly large, so a census sample could be conducted, meaning that all the people potentially served by the office could be studied.

Instrumentation. In determining what instrument to use, the director has the choice of using a commercially developed instrument or preparing an instrument specifically tailored to address the exigencies of the campus. Advantages and disadvantages are associated with each method. For example, the College Student Needs Assessment Survey (ACT, Inc., 1996) or the Adult Learner Needs Assessment Survey (American College Testing Program, 1994), are commercial instruments that will help determine general needs. Their validity and reliability (sometimes referred to as psychometrics) have been calculated.

The other option is to develop an instrument specifically for the study. This is a complex process. If a campus-based instrument is developed, validity and reliability will have to be established. Blaxter, Hughes, and Tight (1996, pp. 157–158) observe, " . . . as anyone who has tried to put a questionnaire together

—and then tried to interpret the responses—will tell you, it is not as simple as it might seem." They provide a number of good suggestions in terms of how to develop an instrument. Gall, Borg, and Gall (1996) provide a step-by-step process for developing questionnaires. They strongly recommend that a questionnaire be pilot-tested before it is used in the field. Using this strategy, problems with the instrument can be addressed and corrected in advance of data collection, which will assist in making sure that the instrument appropriately addresses the information you are trying to collect. Other advantages and disadvantages are associated with using a commercial instrument or developing your own and are discussed by Ory (1994).

Data Collection. Typically, quantitative data are collected by the use of questionnaires mailed to respondents. This approach can be time-consuming and disappointing. An alternative is to collect information by administering questionnaires over the telephone. Rea and Parker (1997) have identified the strengths and weaknesses of collecting data by using the telephone compared with mailed surveys. Mailed surveys are relatively inexpensive, provide ample time for the respondent to complete the survey, can assure anonymity, and create an authoritative impression. On the other hand, they generally have a poor response yield, take a long time to conduct, and have no assurance that the person to whom the questionnaire was mailed actually completed it.

Telephone surveys are more expensive, but quicker, to complete. They provide for a widespread accessibility of respondents, but can be conducted, quite obviously, only with people who have telephones and for whom correct telephone numbers have been secured. Mechanisms are available to improve the rate of mailed questionnaires, but our advice is to use the telephone if that is an option.

An emerging form of data collection is the use of the World Wide Web. A survey can be put on the Web for students to respond at their leisure. A cautionary note is that one needs to be sure that those people who complete the questionnaire are the people the investigator wishes to respond. Software for this purpose is evolving rapidly, and this issue will be less of a problem as time passes.

Data Analysis. Typically, data are analyzed through the use of various statistics. Frequency distributions, measures of central tendency (means, modes medians), and other forms of comparison and correlation can be used, depending on the level of analysis and what is sought. In the case of this problem, the data needed may be nothing more than measures of central tendency and then some analysis of subgroups within the population, such as students of color, women, international students, or other groups of students about whom additional information is needed.

In other studies, measures of association and tests of association might be necessary, depending on the purposes of the study. Rea and Parker (1997) provide excellent advice on data analysis, as do Briley and Moreland (1998). These sources can be referred to for more information about analyzing data.

Using the Results

After the assessment process has been completed, the next step is to determine what changes, if any, need to be made with the program or service, based on what the data reveal. This would be true for a needs assessment or a satisfaction assessment, and should be considered regardless of one's methodological approach. However, it is quite appropriate to use a qualitative approach as a means to elicit information that will provide direction for organizational change. For example, if a large percentage of individuals report that parking services for students with disabilities is a problem in the scenario identified previously, a series of follow-up questions could be used to determine the nature of the problem. Is parking a problem throughout the campus, or near certain buildings? Is parking a problem for all vehicles, or just for those who drive vans? These kinds of issues lend themselves very well to qualitative inquiry. By learning more specifically what the problems are, and how they might be corrected, meaningful change can be developed, which is one of the purposes of conducting assessments in the first place. Additional information about using assessment results is provided in Chapter 16, "Translating Theory and Assessment Results to Practice."

A Qualitative Approach to Needs Assessment

Another way of measuring student needs would be to conduct a qualitative study. The format for this type of assessment is different than what one might use in a quantitative assessment, but we will follow the general outline listed previously for the quantitative assessment. It is important to remember that qualitative research includes more than just interviewing people. It also involves observing people in a natural setting and reviewing documents.

Sampling. Generally, sampling in a qualitative study is purposeful, meaning that sampling " . . . is based on the assumption that the investigator wants to discover, understand, and gain insight and therefore must select a sample from which the most can be learned" (Merriam, 1998, p. 61). Merriam (1998) adds that criteria must be identified for selecting participants and an explanation must be provided as to why the criteria are important. Michael Patton (cited by Upcraft and Schuh, 1996) identifies fifteen different approaches to sampling in qualitative methods. In the case of this project, people who are to be served by the office would be likely candidates to be included in the study. We might want to look at individuals with various kinds of disabilities as opposed to one specific challenge, such as interviewing only those who use wheelchairs.

Instrumentation. In this case, rather than identifying an instrument to administer to our respondents, we would need to decide the kind of interview protocol we would use. These range from being highly structured to being completely unstructured (Merriam, 1998). In a structured situation, " . . . all respondents receive the same set of questions, asked in the same order or sequence, by an interviewer who has been trained to treat every interview situation in a like manner" (Fontana and Frey, 1994, p. 363). Unstructured, informal interviews " . . . are particularly useful when the researcher does not know enough about a phenomenon to ask relevant questions. Thus there is no predetermined set of questions and the interview is essentially exploratory" (Merriam, 1998, pp. 74–75).

Data Collection. Data are collected in the field through the use of interviews, observations and document review. The number of interviews to be conducted cannot be predicted with great accuracy before the interviewing begins. Morgan (1998) indicates that the number will run from three to five, but the important point to remember is that interviewing should continue until the point of redundancy has been reached. That is, interviewing can cease when no new information is gleaned from the interviewing process. Morgan adds, "When the groups become repetitive, you have reached a point of 'theoretical saturation,' and there is little to be gained by doing more groups." The number of individuals in each group can range from seven to ten according to Carnaghi (1992) or six to ten, based on the advice of Morgan (1998).

Document Analysis. Document analysis is another form of data collection used in qualitative methods. "Documents tend to be ignored in favor of more active or interactive forms of qualitative (or verbal) data collection, such as interviews and observations" (Whitt, 1992, p. 79). In our needs assessment, a number of documents would be useful. Among them would be all the records that the various offices that heretofore had assembled in providing services to students: documents that address such issues as what kinds of disabilities have been identified, what budgets have been developed by the various units to provide services, what plans have been developed to address problems in the future and so on.

It is important to place a document in the historical context of when it was written, as Hodder (1994, p. 398) asserts, "Past and present meanings are continually being contested and reinterpreted as part of social and political strategies." Whitt (1992) points out a number of advantages and disadvantages of documents. Among their advantages are that they are readily available, they are a stable source of data, they are grounded in the setting and the language in which they occur, and they may be the only way to study some aspects of a phenomenon. Conversely, she points out some disadvantages of documents. Documents may be incomplete, they may be inaccurate or of questionable authenticity, and they may raise questions they cannot answer.

It should be noted that some researchers divide documents into two categories: documents and records. Records fall under an umbrella of official materials whereas documents exist more for personal reasons, such as memos, letters, and fields notes (Hodder, 1994). To this set, Merriam (1998, p. 117) adds physical materials that are ". . . physical objects found within the study setting. Anthropologists typically refer to these objects as *artifacts* . . . ."

Observation. The other primary data collection technique is observation. Observation is one of several unobtrusive measures identified by Terenzini (1994). He explains, "Unobtrusive measures . . . offer an important methodological counterweight to the unknown and unbalanced reactive bias in interview- and questionnaire-generated data sets, such as those upon which we now rely to assess outcomes of college. Merriam (1998) identifies two advantages of observations: they take place in the natural setting instead of in a location designed of the purpose of interviewing, and they represent a firsthand encounter with the phenomenon of interest.

Participant observation ranges from being a complete participant to being a complete observer (Whitt, 1991, citing Marshall and Rossman, 1989). "Researchers may choose to focus on a group where they intentionally place themselves in a particular location to observe subjects' behavior, or they may observe the behavior of those falling naturally around them" (Adler and Adler, 1994, p. 379). The nature of the problem to be studied and the exigencies of the circumstance will help define the extent to which the researcher will be participant, an observer, or both.

Merriam suggests six general categories of observations for the person involved in this form of data collection: the physical setting, the participants, activities and interactions, conversation, subtle factors, and the observers' own behavior. Clearly, trying to keep track of all of this in the field is a daunting task. One option is to use a video recorder, although that presents certain ethical challenges that will be addressed later in this chapter.

In the case of the needs assessment of the Office of Disability Services, wandering around the campus might be a good place to start the observational process. Watching how students negotiate their way through parking lots, the library stacks, and through heavy doors will begin to help paint a picture of the accessibility of the physical facilities of the campus. Attending classes where students with various disabilities are enrolled as an observer also will be helpful. Another possibility would be to use a wheelchair for a day and determine how easy it is to get around the campus, negotiating bumps, curbs, stray dogs, and so on. Admittedly, not all situations involving students with disabilities will be observed or experienced, but unfiltered data can be collected so that the next time the person who directs a specific program or operates a facility claims that people with disabilities have problems with access, you can agree or disagree based on the data you have collected in the field.

Data Analysis. Data collection and data analysis are simultaneous in qualitative assessment (Whitt, 1991). One of the more common methods of analysis is the constant comparative method. "The basic strategy of the method is to do just what its name implies—constantly compare" (Merriam, 1998, p. 159). The data are organized into units—representing chunks of meaning (Carnaghi, 1992). Themes begin to emerge and "smaller categories can be collapsed into broader, more overarching, defined themes" (Carnaghi, 1992, p. 119).

Data analysis is a complicated process in qualitative assessment. The data are reduced to information bits, sometimes referred to as chunks, and from these bits come the themes, patterns, and trends upon which the larger report is based. Preparing the final report is a particularly challenging task. Among the factors to contribute to this challenge are the following, according to Merriam (1998): because data collection and analysis are continuous and simultaneous, there is no clean cutoff when everything stops; a great amount of data needs to be sorted through, selected, and woven into a coherent narrative, and there is no standard format for reporting such data (citing Wolcott, 1990). Krueger (1998) provides an outline for the various elements of a report. Although he concedes that although reports usually run from 10 to 30 pages in length, at times a report could be closer to 100 pages. His format includes a cover page, summary, table of contents, purpose and procedures, results or findings, summary or conclusions, recommendations, and an appendix. Other approaches to report writing can be a more abbreviated version or executive summary that might contain nothing more than a statement of the problem, the findings of the inquiry, and recommendations for practice. This format is especially effective in working with senior administrators, board members, or others who have volumes of reports to read and who are looking for recommendations on how to deal with existing problems.

In the case of the needs assessment project, a description of the problem and recommendations for practice might suffice as an executive summary. In the executive summary, it is useful to indicate where additional information can be obtained should the reader want to learn more about the study.

Quantitative and Qualitative Approaches to Satisfaction Assessment

After completing the needs assessment for our Office of Services for Students with Disabilities (OSD), submitting a report, making certain changes in the services available for clients of the office, the next logical step, after a period of time, is to determine if the changes that were instituted made a difference. In short, are the clients of the OSD satisfied with the changes that were made? To answer this question, a satisfaction assessment project could be undertaken. The general approach to satisfaction assessment would be the same as the approach taken to needs assessment. This process is as follows.

Quantitative Assessment

A quantitative approach to satisfaction assessment will follow many of the same steps employed in a needs assessment. A brief discussion of these steps follows.

Sampling. Our sampling approach would be much the same. Because the total number of people who use the services of the office is not great, we would use a census sample, meaning that all clients would be included in the sample. If, for some reason, the number grew dramatically, we would want to use random sampling.

Instrumentation. We would need to decide to use a different instrument than was used in the needs assessment project, quite obviously. Our decision would rest on the same factors: is a commercially published instrument available that would measure the constructs important to us or would we need to develop our own?

Data Collection. Data would be collected either by mail or perhaps through the use of a telephone poll. Our general preference is for telephone polling because response rates tend to be quite good and the data can be collected quickly, as was discussed in the previous section on needs assessment.

Data Analysis. Data are analyzed through various statistical procedures, including measures of central tendency, frequency distributions, and perhaps some comparisons of groups. We might want to compare the responses of students with disabilities with those of faculty and staff who have disabilities, and so on.

Qualitative Assessment

As was the case with the quantitative satisfaction assessment, our approach to measuring satisfaction through qualitative means would mirror the needs assessment.

Sampling. We would engage in purposive sampling; that is, we would choose members of certain groups to be interviewed. We certainly would want to interview individuals who represented the various kinds of disabilities of OSD clients. We might also want to interview politically sensitive cases as the situation would demand (such as those who had been highly critical of the services provided before the changes were made on campus) as well as any other information-rich sources. We would use the snowball sampling approach to make sure that we were able to reach an appropriate number of students and other clients who have information and perspectives to offer on our subject.

Instrumentation. We would develop an interview protocol that is semi-structured. Clearly, there is some information we would need to have, but we would want to be sure to give the clients a chance to express their views, no matter how wide-ranging, about the services on campus.

Data Collection We would want to use focus groups, document review, and observation. Documents might include complaint forms filed with the office, letters to the president's office, requests for service, and so on. Observation would have to be done in the field and could take virtually the same form as the needs assessment.

Data Analysis. As was the case with the needs assessment, the data are collected and analyzed simultaneously. We would continue to collect data until we reached the point of saturation, meaning that the data are redundant and no new information is presented.

Static Assessment Measures

Besides the quantitative and qualitative measures described previously, other approaches are available to provide additional information to those interested in assessing student needs and satisfaction. They are described briefly in this section of this chapter with examples from various units typically located in a division of student affairs.

Persistence and Participation Rates

Persistence and participation rates may help identify how students evaluate their experiences on campus. This can be as simple as which residence hall floors, year after year, have a waiting list, which health care provider is the most popular with students, or which classes fill immediately after registration. All of these are measures of how well students evaluate services and service providers. Now, there certainly may be other reasons for high participation rates. More students may eat in one dining hall rather than another because of its location, not because they perceive that the food is any better. But, by paying attention to persistence and participation, one can begin to measure satisfaction, and by working backwards, develop hypotheses about student needs. These data can be followed up with assessment studies, and asking questions as uncomplicated as why students would like to live in one residence hall rather than another can provide an excellent start.

Spending Patterns

Students can buy their books and supplies from a variety of sources. They can order food at the campus food court or go off campus to the local pizza parlor. In short, students have lots of places where they can spend their money. Is anyone paying attention to where students spend their money and why? Do students buy their books off campus because of the initial cost, buy back programs, special promotions, or other reasons? The days of students as a captive market are over. Studying spending patterns can generate the same kinds of data as persistence and participation rates. They can provide a point of departure for needs and satisfaction assessment projects.

Membership Recruitment and Retention

Why is it that some organizations have to work very hard to recruit students while others have a waiting list? One answer might be that student needs are met by joining the latter rather than the former. Or, students are more satisfied with the latter than the former. Maybe it is both; perhaps neither. The point is, studying recruitment and retention data for student organizations is a good way to get a basic understanding of student interests and how to meet them. Again, these data will not by themselves provide definitive answers to these questions, but they will provide a point of departure for addition analysis.

Student Newspapers

Simply reading the student newspaper will not provide a complete picture of campus life, what students are interested in, what they complain about, and so on, but it will provide an interesting periodic snapshot of campus life. Students send letters to the editor presumably about topics that concern them deeply. If a series of letters is printed about a campus problem, that may reflect an emerging student need. Or, after a new service is implemented, letters that reflect satisfaction (or frustration) may reflect areas for additional inquiry. Additionally, checking with the editor of the student newspaper is a good assessment strategy. Periodic meetings with this person to discuss campus life may generate interesting perspectives for a student affairs practitioner.

Institutional Databases

One other form of static measures of assessment can be found in institutional databases. Institutions collect all kinds of data but too infrequently, in our opinion, are these databases used for assessment and evaluation purposes. Among the data that are collected routinely are residence hall transfers, police reports, student health center statistics, drop and adds in the Registrar's office, and so on. These data by themselves may not indicate anything significant, but on the other hand, they may point staff in the direction of further inquiry.

An Active Assessment Measure

One other form of assessment is worth discussing: the secret shopper program. Secret shoppers are individuals who make routine contacts with various offices on campus and report on their interaction. They answer such questions as, "How long did you have to wait to be helped in an office? Were you treated well? Was your problem taken seriously? If you were referred, were you referred to an office where you could be helped?" and so on. Private businesses use secret shoppers to get a sense of customer satisfaction and employee effectiveness. For these same reasons, secret shoppers can be used by colleges and universities to determine the effectiveness of staff.

Institutional Sources of Assessment Data

An overlooked source of assessment data about students lies in institutional databases, or data that are collected for other purposes. For example, students provide information on applications for admission, applications for financial aid, applications for student housing, and so on. These databases can provide very useful information about students and can then be used in the assessment process. Through the sources of information identified previously, the following pieces of information can be obtained regarding students: hometown; whether they are first-generation college students; the extent to which they will need to work; their standardized test scores; high school grade point averages; race; gender; and a host of other important pieces of information. From this information, strategies can be developed to generate plans to collect information and develop programs. The institution's database played an integral role in the development of outcomes indicators and model of the freshman experience in a study of student satisfaction conducted by Sanders and Burton (1996).

The other important source of information are the results of various studies such as the Cooperative Institutional Research Program (CIRP) annual study, various studies of alumni and alumnae, and so on. These studies also can be used to provide various useful information about students and former students. An important principle to follow is this: if information is available from another source on campus, there is no point in collecting it a second time.

Summary

This chapter has introduced basic concepts about two important assessment issues: needs assessment and satisfaction assessment. These two approaches to assessment are linked because needs assessment can be used to identify and shape programmatic initiatives, and satisfaction assessment can be used as a measure to determine the level of success of the initiatives.

An institution's mission plays an important role in shaping assessment projects. Mission statements help determine the role and nature of student affairs on a given campus, and within the framework of the institution's mission, various initiatives can be developed.

This chapter identified an eleven-step model that can be used in the assessment process. The most important steps in this model are to identify the problem the assessment will address and then determine the purpose of the activity. We believe very strongly that the use of multiple methods makes for the best assessments. Both quantitative and qualitative methods have a place in needs and satisfaction assessment, depending on the nature of the problem and the kind of data needed. The best studies make use of both research traditions.

Reporting the information learned from the study requires careful thought. Not every person who should be informed about the results of the study needs to receive a complete, unabridged version. Rather, short reports with charts and graphs can be very effective in communicating the message of the study. We urge investigators to recommend potential action steps in addition to reporting the results of the inquiry. That can help move the conversation into a phase where improvements in student experiences and learning can be realized.

This chapter ends where it started—with the assertion that quality is an overarching concern in higher education. Being able to demonstrate that programs, services, and learning opportunities are of high quality is essential for a division of student affairs. Careful applications of needs and satisfaction assessment are crucial in this process and must be incorporated into the annual routines of student affairs practitioners. To do less is a disservice to our most important constituents, our students.

References

Adler, P. A., and Adler, P. "Observational Techniques." In N. K. Denzin and Y. S. Lincoln (eds.), *Handbook of Qualitative Research*. Thousand Oaks, CA: Sage Publications, 1994.

ACT, Inc.. *College Student Needs Assessment Survey*. Iowa City, IA: ACT, Inc., 1996

ACT, Inc.. *Adult Learner Needs Assessment Survey*. Iowa City, IA: ACT, Inc., 1994.

Banta, T. W., Lund, J. P., Black, K. E., and Oblander, F. W. "Preface." In T. W. Banta, J. P. Lund, K. E. Black, and F. W. Oblander, (eds.), *Assessment in Practice*. San Francisco: Jossey-Bass, 1996.

Blaxter, L., Hughes, C., and Tight, M. *How to Research*. Bristol, PA: Open University Press, 1996.

Bogue, E. G., and Saunders, R. L. *The Evidence for Quality*. San Francisco: Jossey-Bass, 1992.

Briley, G., and Moreland, N. *A Practical Guide to Academic Research*. London: Kogan Page, 1998.

Carnaghi, J. E. "Focus Groups: Teachable and Educational Moments for All Involved." In F. K. Stage and Associates, *Diverse Methods for Research and Assessment of College Students*. Alexandria, VA: American College Personnel Association, 1992.

Fontana, A., and Frey, J. H. "Interviewing: The Art of Science." In N. K. Denzin and Y. S. Lincoln (eds.), *Handbook of Qualitative Research*. Thousand Oaks, CA: Sage Publications, 1994.

Gall, M. D., Borg, W. R., and Gall, J. P. *Educational Research* (6th ed.) White Plains, NY: Longman, 1996.

Hartman, D. E., and Schmidt, S. L. "Understanding Student/Alumni Satisfaction from a Consumer's Perspective: The Effect of Institutional Performance and Program Outcomes." *Research in Higher Education*, 1995, 36, 197–217.

Haworth, J. G., and Conrad, C. F. *Emblems of Quality in Higher Education*. Boston: Allyn and Bacon, 1997.

Hodder, I. "The Interpretation of Documents and Material Culture." In N. K. Denzin and Y. S. Lincoln (eds.), *Handbook of Qualitative Research*. Thousand Oaks, CA: Sage Publications, 1994.

Holmes, T. A. "TQM: Finding a Place in Student Affairs." In W. A. Bryan (ed.), *Total Quality Management: Applying Its Principles to Student Affairs*. New Directions for Student Services, no. 76. San Francisco: Jossey-Bass, 1996.

Kelley, L. H. "Utilizing Multiple Measures to Assess Student Satisfaction." Paper presented at the meeting of the Association for Institutional Research Annual Forum, New Orleans, LA, May, 1994.

Krueger, R. A. *Analyzing and Reporting Focus Group Results*. Focus Group Kit 6. Thousand Oaks, CA: Sage Publications, 1998.

Kuh, G. D. "Purposes and Principles of Needs Assessment in Student Affairs." *Journal of College Student Personnel*, 1982, 23 (3), 202–209.

Lembcke, B. A. "Organizational Performance Measures: The Vital Signs of TQM Investments." In D. Seymour (ed.), *Total Quality Management on Campus: Is it Worth Doing?* New Directions for Higher Education Sourcebook, no. 86. San Francisco: Jossey-Bass, 1994.

Lenning, O. T., and MacAleenan, A. C. "Needs Assessment in Student Affairs." In G. D. Kuh (ed.), *Evaluation in Student Affairs*. Alexandria, VA: American College Personnel Association, 1979.

Levine, A., and Cureton, J. S. *When Hope and Fear Collide*. San Francisco: Jossey-Bass, 1998.

Marshall, C., and Rossman, G.B. *Designing Qualitative Research*. Newbury Park, CA: Sage Publications, 1989.

Merriam, S. B. *Qualitative Research and Case Study Applications in Education*. San Francisco: Jossey-Bass, 1998.

Morgan, D. L. *Planning Focus Groups*. Focus Group Kit 2. Thousand Oaks, CA: Sage Publications, 1998.

Nuss, E. M. "The Role of Professional Associations." In M. J. Barr and Associates, *The Handbook of Student Affairs Administration*. San Francisco: Jossey-Bass, 1993.

Ory, J. C. "Suggestions for Deciding between Commercially Available and Locally Developed Assessment Instruments." In J. S. Stark and A. Thomas (eds.), *Assessment and Program Evaluation*. Needham Heights, MA: Simon and Schuster, 1994.

Rea, L. M., and Parker, R. A. *Designing and Conducting Survey Research*. San Francisco: Jossey-Bass, 1997.

Roth, J. "Needs and the Needs Assessment Process." *Evaluation Needs*, 1977, 5, 15–17.

Rossett, A. "Needs Assessment: Forerunner to Successful HRD Programs." In J. W. Pfeiffer (ed.), *The 1990 Annual: Developing Human Resources*. San Diego, CA: University Associates, 1990.

Sanders, L., and Burton, J. D. "From Retention to Satisfaction: New Outcomes for Assessing the Freshman Experience." *Research in Higher Education*, 1996, 37, 555–567.

Scott, R. M. "Using Assessment to Achieve Quality in Student Affairs." In W. A. Bryan (ed.), *Total Quality Management: Applying Its Principles to Student Affairs*. New Directions for Student Services, no. 76. San Francisco: Jossey-Bass, 1996.

Stark, J. S., and Thomas, A. "Introduction." In J. S. Stark and A. Thomas (eds.), *Assessment and Program Evaluation* . Needham Heights, MA: Simon and Schuster, 1994.

Stufflebeam, D. L., McCormick, C. H., Brinkerhoff, R. O., and Nelson, C. O. *Conducting Educational Needs Assessment*. Norwell, MA: Wolters Kluwer, 1985.

Taylor, B. E., and Massy, W. F. *Strategic Indicators for Higher Education*. Princeton, NJ: Peterson's, 1996.

Terenzini, P. T. "The Case for Unobtrusive Measures." In J. S. Stark and A. Thomas (eds.), *Assessment and Program Evaluation*. Needham Heights, MA: Simon and Schuster, 1994.

Upcraft, M. L., and Schuh, J. H. *Assessment in Student Affairs*. San Francisco: Jossey-Bass, 1996.

Whitt, E. J. "Artful Science: A Primer on Qualitative Research Methods." *Journal of College Student Development*, 1991, 32, 406–415.

Whitt, E. J. "Document Analysis." In F. K. Stage and Associates, *Diverse Methods for Research and Assessment of College Students*. Alexandria, VA: American College Personnel Association, 1992.

Wolcott, H.F. *Writing Up Qualitative Research*. Thousand Oaks, CA: Sage Publications, 1990.

CHAPTER SIXTEEN

TRANSLATING THEORY AND ASSESSMENT RESULTS TO PRACTICE

Mary K. Desler

Over the last thirty years, three events have occurred that influence how student affairs administrators approach their work. First, an impressive number of theories have been identified that now serve to guide our everyday practice. Second, researchers have begun to test these theories. Their findings provide valuable insights into how college affects students. Third, in the last decade, the topic of assessment and the issues related to it have emerged as one of the top priorities in higher education. This is due, in part, to the increased competition for resources and declining public trust in education. More and more student affairs administrators are being asked to account for how efficiently and effectively they use the resources allocated to them from inside and outside the institution. The confluence of these three events puts emphasis on a competency required of student affairs administrators: the knowledge and the skill to translate theory, research, and assessment results to practice.

The importance of using research and assessment results in practice is noted in the document, *Principles of Good Practice for Student Affairs* (1997), sponsored by the American College Personnel Association (ACPA) and the National Association of Student Personnel Administrators (NASPA).

Good practice in student affairs uses systematic inquiry to improve student and institutional performance. Good practice in student affairs occurs when student affairs educators ask, 'What are students learning from our programs and services, and how can their learning be enhanced?' Knowledge of and ability to analyze research about students and their learning are critical components of good student affairs practice. Student affairs educators who are skilled in using assessment methods acquire high-quality information. Effective application of this information to practice will result in programs and strategies for change that improve institutional and student achievement (American College Personnel Association and the National Association of Student Personnel Administrators, 1997, p. 4).

Although theory is not mentioned in the previous principle, King and Baxter-Magolda (1996) argue convincingly for an integrated view of learning and personal development. From this perspective, the cognitive and affective dimensions are seen as parts of one process. "Knowledge construction, meaning making, and awareness of self are presumed to be integrated within the developing human being" (King and Baxter-Magolda, 1996, p. 163). Good practice in student affairs then includes knowledge of theory, at least development theory, and the effective application of this information to practice.

This chapter begins with a definition of terms. Next, a number of valuable sources of research about students and their learning are identified. The topic of assessment, including several principles of good practice, is then summarized. This discussion is followed by a focus on the ways in which theory, research, and assessment results can be translated to practice. A case study illustrates how a vice president for enrollment management and student affairs uses theory and assessment results to develop a strategic plan addressing student retention. The chapter concludes with a discussion of several cautions to be aware of when using theory, research, and assessment results in practice.

Many books have been written about each of these subjects—theory related to student affairs, research about students and their learning, and assessment practices. All that can be accomplished in a chapter is to provide an overview. Readers are encouraged to utilize the references provided to further explore each topic.

Definition of Terms

Before we begin, it is important to define three terms: theory, research, and assessment. All three are used throughout the chapter.

What is theory? McEwen (1996) writes, "Theory can be thought of as a description of the interrelationships between concepts and constructs. These interrelationships are often represented by a particular set of hypotheses—about human development, about organizations, about how persons and environments interact —developed by an individual or a group of individuals. Some hypotheses are empirical in nature, evolving from the collection and examination of quantitative or qualitative data. Others are rational in nature, based not on formal data but rather on ideas and relationships that attempt to explain a particular phenomenon" (McEwen, 1996a, p. 150).

Sometimes the terms "research" and "assessment" are used interchangeably. However, as Erwin (1996) suggests, there are differences between them, particularly in terms of scope and purpose. Research has implications for student affairs or higher education in general. Assessment is focused on a particular institution. "Research is concerned both with forming new theories and conceptual approaches and with confirming or refuting existing theories and educational practices. Assessment, on the other hand, is primarily concerned with the confirmation or refutation of approaches" (Erwin, 1996, p. 417).

Theory Related to Student Affairs

Numerous authors have reviewed the theoretical bases relevant to student affairs (Widick, Knefelkamp, and Parker, 1980; Moore, 1990; Miller and Winston, 1991; Pascarella and Terenzini, 1991; Evans, 1996; Evans, Forney, and Guido-DiBrito, 1998). Most consolidate the theories related to student development into several clusters that "share certain basic assumptions and uses similar constructs to describe development or point out influential factors in development" (Widick, Knefelkamp, and Parker, 1980, p. 78). Pascarella and Terenzini (1991) identify another cluster of theories relevant to student affairs: college impact models of student change. Other theories focus on the organization, or how people, organizational structures, and governance processes influence one another. More recently, student affairs administrators with enrollment management responsibilities have begun to use marketing theories to guide their strategic planning efforts.

Many of the early development theories, although useful in understanding traditional-age students and their experiences in college, are somewhat problematic. They do not fully explain the development of student groups that are coming to college in larger and larger numbers—women; minority racial and ethnic groups; older students; international students; gay, lesbian, and bisexual students; student-athletes; commuters; and others. Consequently, new theories are emerging and existing theories are being modified to take into consideration the different experiences of these "new" students.

An overview of relevant theories and models for student affairs practice can be found in Chapter Thirteen in this volume, "An Overview of Relevant Theories and Models for Student Affairs Practice." The list of theories relevant to student affairs is long and the field of student affairs is ever-changing. New theories from a variety of disciplines, but applicable to student affairs, will no doubt continue to emerge.

Research About Students and How They Learn

Good practice in student affairs includes understanding research about students and how they learn. It is well beyond the scope of this chapter to review all the research about students and their learning. However, others have done so. In 1991, Pascarella and Terenzini synthesized twenty years of empirical research and over 2,600 studies about students and how they change in college. Two years later, Astin (1993) described the influence of college on students based on the results of the longitudinal study—the Cooperative Institutional Research Program (CIRP). Their findings have numerous implications for policy and practice. *Involving Colleges* (Kuh, Schuh, Whitt, and Associates, 1991) is based on a year-long qualitative study of fourteen four-year colleges and universities. The results described in the book provide "a framework that can be used by administrators, faculty members, and others to examine their own campuses and identify ways in which their practices can be modified to enhance student learning" (Kuh, Schuh, Whitt, and Associates, 1991, p. xiii).

Listed below are a few of the findings from these research studies that should be considered when shaping policies, programs, and practices.

- "A large part of the impact of college is determined by the extent and content of one's interactions with major agents of socialization on campus; namely, faculty members and student peers" (Pascarella and Terenzini, 1991, p. 620).
- "The strongest single source of influence on cognitive and affective development is the student's peer group" (Astin, 1996, p. 126).
- "The most critical issue regarding campus environments and student involvement is . . . creating a sense of belonging, a feeling on the part of the students that the institution acknowledges the human needs of social and psychological comfort, and that they are full and valued members of the campus community" (Kuh, Schuh, Whitt, and Associates, 1991, p. 321).
- What counts most in terms of college outcomes is what students do, not who they are or where they go to college. The most important factor in student learning is the quality of effort students themselves invest in their institution's resources and facilities, such as the amount of time they spend studying and using the library (Astin, 1993; Pascarella and Terenzini, 1991).
- Students who live or spend time with someone from a different racial and ethnic background gain an understanding of human differences and appreciation for the aesthetic qualities of life (Astin, 1993).
- "Residential institutions, compared with commuter schools, are more likely to provide their students with the kinds of interpersonal academic and social ex-

periences associated with change . . . . Ways must be found and resources provided to bring the educational experience of commuter college students closer to that of their residential peers" (Pascarella and Terenzini, 1991, p. 639–640).

- "The effects of a single experience in college appear to be smaller than the overall net effect of college . . . the enhancement of the educational impact of a college is most likely if policy and programmatic efforts are broadly conceived and diverse" (Pascarella and Terenzini, 1991, p. 655).

In addition to these findings, other national studies have been conducted that provide valuable insights about students. In 1998, Levine and Cureton described the results of a national study involving senior student affairs administrators and a diverse group of undergraduate students across the country in their book, *When Hope and Fear Collide*. Their findings are helpful in understanding today's college students and how they are different from ten years ago. For example, Levine and Cureton (1998) report today's students appear more optimistic about the future than the students of 10 years ago and they believe their generation has the capacity to make a difference. On the other hand, today's college students are frightened. Levine and Cureton (1998) found through surveys and focus groups that students are frightened of getting hurt, frightened about their economic prospects, and concerned about relationships. "The effect of the accumulated fears and hurts that students have experienced is to divide and isolate them" (p. 96).

The Cooperative Institutional Research Program (CIRP) has been conducting a national freshman survey since 1966. Their annual reports provide valuable data about the students who are coming to college each fall and describe how these students are the same or different (background characteristics, behaviors, values, attitudes and goals) from their peers 5, 10, even 30 years ago.

Since 1989 the Core Institute, located at Southern Illinois University at Carbondale, has annually published valuable data on alcohol and drug use by American college students. The Harvard School of Public Health also periodically publishes the results of the College Alcohol Study, which explores the problem of binge drinking on American college campuses.

Some professional associations conduct national surveys with college students. Their conclusions are disseminated in various publications, including local newspapers and professional journals. For example, the American College Health Association has begun to survey youth and young adults about their health risk behaviors. Their information, coupled with the results from local assessment efforts, can give direction to health educators in the program planning process.

Finally, the *Chronicle of Higher Education* frequently reports the results of research conducted across the country as well as findings from their own collection efforts.

Often the data are sorted by institution, allowing readers to compare results from their campus to those from like institutions across the country.

Assessment Methods

When we hear the word "assessment," we often think of a survey or questionnaire of some kind. Although one-time assessment studies are "assessment," they are only part of what most agree must be an ongoing and comprehensive program (Banta, Lund, Black, and Oblander, 1996).

Upcraft and Schuh (1996) define assessment broadly as "any effort to gather, analyze, and interpret evidence which describes institutional, departmental, divisional, or agency effectiveness. Effectiveness includes not only assessing student learning outcomes, but assessing other important outcomes as well (cost effectiveness, clientele satisfaction, meeting clientele needs) for other constituents within the institution (the faculty, administration, governing boards) and outside the institution (alumni, legislators, funding agencies, accreditation agencies)" (Upcraft and Schuh, 1996, p. 18). Ernest Pascarella and Elizabeth Whitt (1999) underscore the importance of linking measures of effectiveness to the educational mission of the college/university.

Taking a broad view of assessment, the American Association for Higher Education (1992) outlined several principles of good practice for assessing student learning. These principles, although focused on student learning, provide valuable guidelines for any assessment effort.

1. The assessment of student learning begins with educational values.
2. Assessment is most effective when it reflects an understanding of learning as multidimensional, integrated, and revealed in performance over time.
3. Assessment works best when the programs it seeks to improve have clear, explicitly stated purposes.
4. Assessment requires attention to outcomes and to the experiences that lead to those outcomes.
5. Assessment works best when it is ongoing, not episodic.
6. Assessment fosters wider improvement when representatives from across the educational community are involved.
7. Assessment makes a difference when it begins with issues of use and illuminates questions that people really care about.
8. Assessment is most likely to lead to improvement when it is part of a larger set of conditions that promote change.
9. Through assessment, educators meet responsibilities to students and to the public (American Association for Higher Education, 1992, p. 2–3).

In his chapter in this volume, "Understanding Campus Environments," Kuh makes another suggestion that could be added to the previous list of principles: "Data collected by multiple methods of data collection almost always are mutually reinforcing and add legitimacy to the findings as those who prefer either the qualitative or quantitative paradigm will be able to locate information that they can believe."

Comprehensive assessment programs, as well as individual assessment studies —if they are to provide useful results—must be carefully planned from the beginning. They must be connected to issues or questions that people really care about. "It means thinking in advance about how the information will be used, and by whom" (AAHE, 1992, p. 3).

In planning an assessment program or an individual assessment study, the following questions are usually asked: What is the purpose of the study? What will be assessed? Who will be assessed? How will the assessment be conducted? When and how often will the assessment be conducted? How will the results be analyzed? How will the results be reported? (Upcraft and Schuh, 1996; Erwin, 1991).

The Purpose of the Study

Upcraft and Schuh (1996) identify a number of ways that assessment results can be used. Each identifies a different purpose for which a study might be conducted. Assessment results can help answer questions of accountability and quality; help gauge affordability and cost-effectiveness; provide valuable data in a strategic planning process; and aid in the policy and decision-making process. In addition, Hanson (1990) notes that assessment results allow us to describe students in meaningful ways—what they are like when they enter, what they learn by the time they leave, how they learn, and whether what they learn is a result of what we do.

After the purpose of the study has been clarified, it is often useful to generate a list of specific questions the study should attempt to answer.

Selecting What or Whom to Study

According to Upcraft and Schuh (1996), there are six components to a comprehensive assessment model: keeping track of who uses services, programs, and facilities; assessing student needs; assessing clientele satisfaction with services, programs and facilities; assessing campus environments and student cultures; measuring outcomes; and comparable institutions assessment. These six components help identify "what" can be studied. More information on these components can be found in the Chapter Fourteen in this volume, "Assessment in Student Affairs."

Who is selected to participate in an assessment study depends, again, on the purpose of the study. It may be appropriate to study an entire population, or to draw a sample. Sampling has a technical side and must be done with some level of sophistication if the data are to be useful. The best sample is representative of the population being studied. Samples may be drawn randomly or they can be stratified or clustered on the basis of one or more characteristics. Some studies follow a cohort of students over a period of time. Certain cohorts of students may have something in common that other students do not. The size of the sample is also important. Size is usually based on the expected rate of return, the amount of sampling error that can be tolerated, and cost. Sampling techniques are described simply in a number of publications (Fink, 1995; Upcraft and Schuh, 1996).

Data Gathering Techniques

When conducting an assessment study, data can be collected in two ways: using a qualitative technique or a quantitative technique. Qualitative techniques include observation, document review, individual interviews, and focus groups (Whitt, 1991). Quantitative methods generally utilize existing student records or data gathered by questionnaires. Deciding which assessment method is most appropriate and then choosing or creating the assessment instrument are important steps in the process. Multiple data collection methods are desirable whenever feasible.

Qualitative Techniques. Qualitative methods are particularly useful when rather little is known about a phenomenon of interest. As a result, they are often used early in an assessment project and are often followed by other types of data collection that provide more quantifiable data from a larger group of respondents. But qualitative methods are also useful when interpreting the results following the analysis of a large-scale, quantitative survey. Used at this juncture, qualitative assessment mechanisms help explain the "why" behind the numerical results. Structured interviews and focus groups allow individuals to respond in their own words, using their own categorizations and perceived associations (Stewart and Shamdasani, 1990).

There are several drawbacks to qualitative studies. First, gathering the data is labor-intensive. Second, data analysis can be a protracted process. And third, it is questionable whether the results can be generalized.

Quantitative Techniques. Quantitative methods are more structured and are designed before the study is carried out to test a particular hypothesis or theory. In quantitative studies, how data is collected, when data is collected, what is collected, and how it is analyzed depends on the purpose of the study.

Data can be gathered from existing records or, if new data must be collected, by an assessment instrument. Existing records (or secondary sources) include admission files, transcripts, registration data, health records, and so on. Assessment instruments are available from commercial vendors or may be developed on a local level. The choice of which to use depends on the goals of the assessment project and the availability of time, money, and expertise.

There are several advantages in using assessment instruments available commercially. First, these instruments generally have established reliability and validity. However, this is not always the case (Komives, 1992). Just because a commercial vendor sells an instrument does not mean its psychometric properties have been established. A second advantage in using standardized assessment instruments is that comparative and normative data based on national samples of students are often available and can be useful in the interpretation of assessment results. Finally, such instruments are usually more efficient to administer and score, given the established procedures and support services provided by the vendors. They can be costly, however.

Researchers have developed instruments to measure a number of the theories relevant to student affairs described previously that can be used on local campuses to measure needs and outcomes. For example, the Student Developmental Task and Lifestyle Inventory (SDTLI) (Winston, Miller, and Prince, 1987) and the Iowa Student Development Inventories (Hood, 1986) attempt to assess psychosocial development as outlined in Chickering's theory (1969). The Intercultural Development Inventory (IDI) (Hammer and Bennett, 1994) was designed to measure five of the six major stages of the Developmental Model of Intercultural Sensitivity (Bennett, 1993). Two major instruments exist for measuring moral reasoning: Kohlberg's Moral Judgment Interview (MJI) (Colby and others, 1987) and Rest's Defining Issues Test (DIT) (Rest, 1986). Upcraft and Schuh (1996) and Evans, Forney, and Guido-DiBrito (1998) identify numerous instruments available to test the theories relevant to student affairs.

Still other assessment instruments are available that provide institutions with local data while at the same time providing comparison data from other institutions. For example, the Association of College and University Housing Officers-International (ACUHO-I), in conjunction with Educational Benchmarking, Incorporated (EBI), developed the Resident Satisfaction Survey, which measures students' perceptions of the quality of residence life. Peer comparisons are available.

Despite the advantages, student affairs administrators often find established instruments unsuited to their needs. Locally developed instruments can take into consideration specific local conditions. Comparative national data is lost, but the direct applicability of the results may make this option preferable. Theory and research should be considered when developing local assessment instruments. For example, marketing theory can be helpful when constructing needs assessments and satisfaction questionnaires. Tinto's (1987) theory of college student departure can be helpful in designing exit interviews. Chickering's (1969) vectors of development can be helpful in creating the questions for a series of senior focus groups. Guidance on how to develop quantitative and qualitative assessment instruments on a local level is provided in Chapters Four, "Understanding Campus Environments," Fourteen "Assessment in Student Affairs" and Fifteen, "Measuring Student Satisfaction and Needs."

Sometimes the challenge for the student affairs administrator is not creating an instrument, but in connecting data from other sources. As Banta, Lund, Black, and Oblander (1996) observe, "a great number of institutions find themselves awash in data. The data collected include everything from pre-entry test scores to surveys of student satisfaction with the general college environment" (p. 43). Offices of institutional research and the Registrar usually maintain a number of databases that are useful in a comprehensive assessment effort. In addition, other campus units may conduct surveys that could provide valuable insight about students, their needs, the campus environment, the impact of a program or service, and a learning outcome.

Assessment results from other institutions—although difficult at times to generalize to other populations—can be helpful in understanding students, issues, or problems faced by student affairs administrators on their campuses. These assessment efforts and the results are reported in professional journals and at professional conferences. Many institutions, in fact, are willing to share locally developed assessment instruments. The American College Personnel Association Commission IX sponsors a Clearinghouse for Assessment in Student Affairs that can be accessed through the ACPA homepage. The contents of the Clearinghouse vary from brief descriptions of assessment instruments and the addresses used to obtain the instruments to full descriptions of the instruments and brief reviews.

When and How Often Is Data Collected?

When and how often data is collected depends on the purpose of the study. Data collected at a single point in time can provide valuable information when exploring a specific problem or issue. For example, assessment information is sometimes collected at the beginning of a program and used immediately for diagnostic purposes. Data can be collected during orientation, before students have been influenced by attendance at the institution. Often data is collected at the end of the first year or enrollment or during the senior year. Data can even be collected after students graduate.

On a local level, understanding how a specific group of students or cohorts change over a specified period of time on various dimensions—hopefully as a result of some institutional intervention—is useful outcome data. In this case, assessment information is collected more than once, often at orientation, in the middle of the undergraduate experience, and in the senior year. This type of study is generally coupled with theory and is longitudinal in scope.

Analyzing Data

"Analysis is the process of aggregating students' responses to various assessment stimuli, and of describing the overall characteristics, patterns, and parts of these student data to obtain answers to questions" (Erwin, 1991, p.111).

In qualitative assessment studies, particularly focus groups and individual interviews, the analysis of the data begins with a transcript of the interview. There are occasions, however, when transcripts are unnecessary. Instead a brief summary may be all that is needed. The interviewer identifies categories or themes through a cut-and-paste technique or through content analysis, analytical induction, or comparative analysis (Stewart and Shamdasani, 1990; Erwin, 1996). Additional information about analyzing data from qualitative assessment studies is provided by Upcraft and Schuh in Chapter Fourteen, "Assessment in Student Affairs."

In quantitative studies, the data may be analyzed in many ways ranging from simple descriptive statistics (frequency counts and percentages or mean scores), measures of relationships (correlation), inferential statistics (chi-square, t-tests, analysis of variance, discriminant analysis), multivariate analysis, and multiple regression (step-wise regression, hierarchical regression, logit analysis, and probit analysis). Again, the method depends on the purpose of the study.

Many assessment studies done on a local level rely on the use of simple descriptive statistics: frequencies, percentages, means, standard deviations, and cross tabulations. As Lenning (1980) observes, "Much useful information can be obtained from such simple statistics, especially if they are profiled graphically and patterns of similarities and discrepancies across information items and across groups are examined. Means, by themselves, can be quite misleading if the frequency distributions are not also examined. Also, response bias should be analyzed in questionnaire and interview studies" (Lenning, 1980, p. 241).

Often it is useful to make comparisons across groups using t-tests, chi-square, analysis of variance, correlational analysis, and discriminant analysis. El-Khawas (1996) provides two dimensions of student characteristics that may be helpful in identifying groups by which to compare data. The first dimension, diversity of background, includes key background factors like race, ethnicity, class, gender, sexual orientation, disability, country of origin, and age. The second dimension, situational, includes differences of enrollment status (full- or part-time), degree objective, intermittent versus continuous enrollment, transfer status, commuter versus residential, and institution. Groups may also be identified on the basis of levels of campus involvement, type of intervention, or campus environment (Erwin, 1996).

Sometimes it is helpful to compare assessment data from one institution to another or to compare local results to that of the rest of the country or like institutions. These comparisons can help identify institutional or program strengths and weaknesses, understand institutional image, and understand students and their needs. In recent years, the practice of "benchmarking" has become commonplace. "Through this process, 'best practices' from comparable organizations are studies to improve products, services, or processes, in order to become 'best in class' among competitors" (Upcraft and Schuh, 1996, p. 240].

More sophisticated statistical procedures are needed if the purpose of the study is to measure students' change over time. For a discussion of the important methodological and analytical issues in measuring change, readers should consult Pascarella and Terenzini (1991). Detailed descriptions on the use of quantitative methods can be found in Fred Kerlinger's book, *Foundations of Behavioral Research* (1986).

Interpreting Data

"Analyzing assessment information can be a complex task, just as interpreting the findings is a particular responsible task" (Erwin, 1991, p. 131). Interpreting the results takes time and higher-order thinking skills, including critical-thinking skills (Bloom, 1956; Miller, Williams, and Haladyna, 1978). Moreover, regardless of who analyzes the data, someone familiar with the subject of the assessment study must be involved in interpreting the results.

Interpretation involves making meaning of the themes (qualitative) or numbers (quantitative). Interpretation involves making connections—connections between theory and data, or connections between data from one source with another source. Interpretation involves seeing the interrelationships between one question and another question, or between one group and another group. Interpretation involves identifying patterns in responses or the data. It involves explaining, confirming, or not confirming information and formulating alternative explanations and interpretations where appropriate. Interpretation involves making judgments about the value of the data. It involves "the process of working with pieces, parts, elements, etc., and arranging and combining them in such a way as to constitute a pattern or structure not clearly there before" (Bloom, 1956, p. 192). The ability to interpret data requires knowledge of relevant theory, research, and results from other studies, as well as skill, common sense, and experience.

Reporting the Results

"Once assessment data is collected, analyzed and interpreted, it must be disseminated in compelling ways" (Banta, Lund, Black, and Oblander, 1996, p. 44). This process can be considered the first step in translating the results to practice. What is reported and how it is reported sets the stage for the recommendations that will follow.

Assessment reports come in many forms. In qualitative assessment studies, the end product is usually a written report that "will put the reader in the setting being studied, allowing the reader to experience the setting as the participants do and to view their world from their perspectives" (Whitt, 1991, p. 413). The themes identified through the analysis are described and verbatim quotations are used to illustrate feelings, perceptions, and insights. The form of the study—case study, historical analysis, life history, single- or multiple-site research, and culture audit —and the audience will ultimately dictate the format of the report (Whitt, 1991).

Similarly, in quantitative assessment studies, how the results are presented depends on the two things: the purpose of the study and the audience for whom the report is intended. Written reports, newsletter articles, press releases, computer-accessible reports, and stand up presentations are all options. Statistical packages make it easy to illustrate data in many ways (bar charts, line charts, pie charts, area charts, scattergrams, histograms, and more).

Most assessment reports—qualitative and quantitative—include a set of recommendations for action that are consistent with the major findings of the study. These recommendations suggest how the results can be translated to practice. Occasionally, the recommendations can be implemented easily, especially if the suggestions are ones over which the student affairs administrator has responsibility. Far more often, the recommendations enter into the resource allocation process; that is, funds must be requested.

Translating Theory, Research, and Assessment Results to Practice

Jacobi, Astin, and Ayala (1987) suggest a "continuum of utilization" that is helpful in understanding how theory, research, and assessment results, used separately or together, can be translated to practice. On one end of the continuum is everyday practice. Theory, research on students and their learning, and assessment results can inform our everyday decisions, our interactions with individual students and groups of students, and the way in which we approach our tasks. On the other end of the continuum is immediate and direct action. A program is initiated, a policy is adopted or changed, or a practice is reconsidered and altered on the basis of a theory (or combination of theories), research findings, or assessment results. Between these two ends are multiple opportunities for student affairs administrators to use theory, research on students and their learning, and assessment results to shape institutional—and student affairs—policies, programs, and practices.

Everyday Practice

Using theory, research, and assessment results in everyday practice assumes knowledge of each. For some student affairs administrators, theory, research on students and their learning, and assessment results are so internalized they may not recognize when they are putting them to use. "Over time we all develop a repertoire of techniques that we know will work in a given situation and it is the utilization of these day-to-day skills that is guided by our theories" (Widick, Knefelkamp, and Parker, 1980, p. 112). For others, it takes conscious effort to identify a theory, a research study, or an assessment study that sheds light on a problem to be solved or supports a decision to be made.

Shaping Policies, Programs, and Practices

Using theory, research, and assessment results to shape institutional and student affairs policies, programs, and practices can be as much a political as a practical dilemma. Student affairs administrators have an obligation to make appropriate use of what they know, but it must be done in a time, place, and manner in which it will be heard. Student affairs administrators can use theory, research, and assessment results to stimulate a campus-wide discussion about a particular issue that may later result in action. The discussion may encourage the "buy in" that will be necessary when the action plan is made public. Student affairs administrators can use theory, research, and assessment results to formulate questions that can be posed when institutional decision-makers are reviewing several possible courses of action. Student affairs administrators can use theory, research, and assessment results to defend budget requests and grant proposals. Student affairs administrators can use theory, research, and assessment results to help explain an issue to the board of trustees and craft a response to a myriad of student issues.

Program Initiatives

Of course, the ideal is that theory, research on students and their learning, and assessment results will be used in immediate and direct action involving policies, programs, or practices. Translating theory, research, and assessment results directly to practice is easiest when the focus of the "action" is in an area for which the student affairs administrator has direct responsibility.

Over the years, there have been numerous attempts aimed at providing guidance on translating theory to practice that may be useful in designing *program* interventions (Rodgers, 1991; Evans, 1987; Knefelkamp, Golec, and Wells, 1985; Rodgers and Widick, 1980; Morrill, Oetting, and Hurst, 1974). One of them, the Grounded Formal Theory Model, includes the use of theory and assessment results (Rodgers and Widick, 1980). The six phases in the Grounded Formal Theory Model are as follows.

Phase I—Focus on practice: a problem, a context, and a population;

Phase II—Select useful and usable formal theories to enlighten or define the problem in principle;

Phase III—Assess the population, context, and interaction using the formal theories;

Phase IV—Formulate goals and objectives from the assessment data and formal theories;

Phase V—Design interventions (programs) using the theories and assessment data; and

Phase VI—Evaluate the intervention/program (Rodgers, 1991, p. 227).

The Developmental Intervention Model proposed by Evans (1987) recognizes that interventions may be targeted at either the individual or the institution. Institutional interventions focus primarily on creating campus environments that encourage development.

Both of these models focus on the practical applications of translating theory, research, and assessment results to practice. Neither addresses the political aspects. Politics is often involved when theory, research, and assessment results suggest the need for change on an institutional level or in an area over which the student affairs administrator has no direct responsibility.

A number of authors (Jacobi, Astin, and Ayala, 1987; Banta, Lund, Black, and Oblander, 1996) do account for some of the political aspects when it comes to applying the assessment results to policy, program, or practice. They identify a number of factors that will reduce the chances that the recommendations will go unheeded that should be considered when planning an assessment study.

1. The assessment study should be a collaborative effort. Involving stakeholders in the gathering and interpretation of data generates feelings of ownership and increases the chances that the recommendations will be enacted.

2. Stakeholders accept the underlying theory, agree on the purpose of the study, the variables selected, the instruments used, and the sample selected.
3. The assessment study was done well.
4. The final report and recommendations contained no surprises. Unexpected findings, particularly those that may not be popular, should be communicated to target audiences at an early stage. Seeking assistance in understanding and explaining these findings builds trust.
5. Recommendations for changes in policy, program, or practice were developed collaboratively with the stakeholders. Full consideration was given to all of the possible alternatives for action suggested by the data.
6. The recommendations were written to benefit the stakeholders, not pass judgment on them.

In the end, however, the results from assessment studies, theory, and research may not be all that are considered when deciding whether to implement the recommendations. "Decisions are not based exclusively on information available in the organization. Decisions are based partly on political considerations regardless of what the data show. Administrators may act on friendship, immediate tensions, current moods, subjects' conversations, costs, or deference to preserve an image or reputation" (Erwin, 1991, p. 147).

Other Ways

There are three other ways in which theory, research on students and their learning, and assessment results can be translated to practice. They can be used to inform one another. For example, student affairs administrators are often asked to explain assessment results. Theory, or combinations of theories, and research about students can help with this task. Looking at data from a variety of perspectives (including theory, research, common sense and experience) can help administrators understand the dynamics involved in a situation and generate a list of possible explanations and recommendations based on the findings.

Theory and research should be considered when developing local assessment instruments. For example, marketing theory can be helpful when constructing needs assessments and satisfaction questionnaires. Tinto's (1987) theory of college student departure can be helpful in designing exit interviews. Chickering's (1969) vectors of development can be helpful in creating the questions for a series of senior focus groups.

Sometimes assessment results, research, common sense, or experience suggest a missing concept, variable, or link in a theory that, if accounted for, might increase the explanatory power of an existing theory or suggest a new theory. A single theory will seldom completely explain the complexity of the real world. It is difficult to construct theories that do not oversimplify complicated issues. Moreover, it is sometimes difficult to take apart phenomena and put the pieces back together in a meaningful way (Blalock, 1969).

A Case Study

In the following case study, Joe, the new vice president for enrollment management and student affairs at Normal College, is faced with a challenge that is familiar to many student affairs administrators. He has been asked to develop a plan to increase the retention rate among undergraduates. Joe's approach to the task illustrate the number of ways theory, research, and assessment results can be translated to practice.

Normal College is a small, private liberal arts institution in the Midwest. When Joe arrived, the retention rate at the college was below that of comparable institutions of its size and selectivity, a situation that was of great concern to the board of trustees. Every five years, the college engaged in a strategic planning process. The new five-year plan was to be presented to the board of trustees at their annual fall meeting. The board asked that the strategic plan specifically address the retention rate. It was February. The board of trustees meeting was in October.

Joe began by asking his colleagues to share copies of any assessment studies that had been conducted at Normal College within the last five years. Among the documents were the final report from the accreditation team that visited the campus three years before, hard copies of the results from the freshman survey conducted by CIRP for five years, the results of a survey of admitted students completed by the Admissions Office for the last three years, a report written by the director of career planning and placement detailing the results of a telephone survey of graduating seniors conducted the last two years, and the results from a satisfaction survey conducted five years before.

Joe also read the undergraduate catalog, paying specific attention to the mission statement. The statement contained the usual lofty rhetoric, but it emphasized the college's commitment to educating future leaders. Joe also collected and reviewed the college's admission materials. He was most interested in learning how the institution was being marketed.

After review of existing assessment studies Joe noted that

1. The CIRP data revealed that Normal was the first college choice for only one half of the entering class. In addition, CIRP data revealed that sixty percent of the entering students were first generation college students.

2. Both the admitted student survey and CIRP indicated that financial aid was extremely important to new students. A very high percentage of new students planned to work while in school.

3. A high percentage of graduates reported being employed in their major field of study after graduation.

4. Students reported being fairly satisfied with their academic experience, but were concerned about academic advising.

5. The accreditation team expressed concern about a lack of an assessment plan.

While reading the reports, Joe began to think about the theory and research that was relevant to this problem. He was familiar with Tinto's (1987) theory of student departure and John Bean's (1990) longitudinal model of the type of factors that affect retention decisions. Joe knew from the theory and research about students (Pascarella and Terenzini, 1991) that when it came to retention, what happened after a student arrived on campus was probably more important than the student's background characteristics. Furthermore, Tinto's (1987) concept of academic and social integration reminded Joe of Astin's (1985) theory of student involvement. "Uninvolved" students were more likely to withdraw from college than those who devoted considerable energy and time to the academic and out-of-class experience (Astin, 1993). Joe knew from research on college students that orientation programs were important in the socialization process. Good orientation programs, especially those that extend throughout the first semester, lead to earlier and more enduring involvement in the academic and social systems of the institution (Pascarella and Terenzini, 1991).

Joe also understood the concept of "mattering" and how important it was that if students were to be successful, they needed to feel like they belonged (Schlossberg, Lynch, and Chickering, 1989). Joe knew from the work done by Noel, Levitz, Saluri, and Associates (1985) that students often decide to leave an institution within the first two weeks of the freshman year even though they might not physically leave until much later. He knew that certain learning environments can have a greater impact on some students than others and that matching people with environments is important.

These theories, models, and research findings suggested a number of questions for which Joe didn't have answers. Are we admitting the "right" kind of student? Is it a question of fit? Who leaves? When do they decide to leave? When do they leave? Why do they leave? Who stays? Why do they stay? What could be done to prevent students from leaving? And what is a realistic retention goal for an institution like this?

To begin to answer some of these questions, Joe asked the registrar to download some information about the students who matriculated at Normal College for the last ten years. Knowing what variables to include in the analysis came from his knowledge of theory and the retention literature (studies done at other institutions). He was particularly interested in making some comparisons between and among groups of students, so he carefully selected the demographic characteristics he thought were most important.

Using a computer-based statistical package, he discovered

1. The majority of the students who left the college, did so at the end of the first year, often in good academic standing.
2. A higher percentage of commuters than resident students did not graduate.
3. A higher percentage of African American students than other racial/ethnic backgrounds did not graduate.
4. Students who were admitted late in the year were far more likely to leave than students who were admitted early.
5. High school rank was the best predictor of first semester academic success (measured by grade point average) and first semester academic success was a strong predictor of graduation.

This review of records helped Joe answer some questions and also helped to narrow the scope of the problem. He decided to concentrate on improving the first-to-second year retention rate. In order to better understand the issues, Joe decided to use a combination of qualitative and quantitative assessment projects to explore why students were leaving after the first year.

First, he randomly selected a number of freshmen that left the college the year before and telephoned them to ascertain their primary reasons for leaving. He also conducted a series of focus groups with a number of commuter students and students of color. His questions were designed to measure their level of involvement at the institution, their primary concerns, and their overall satisfaction with their educational experience. He also asked them how the institution might better meet their needs. At the same time, he instituted an exit interview process for students who went to or called the registrar's office to formally withdraw. What did he find out?

1. A number of students mentioned they expected the college to be different than it was. Academically it was harder than some thought it would be; others mentioned it was easier than they anticipated. Some thought their academic advisor would be more interested in them. Some thought it would be more "fun" than it was.
2. The students of color talked about feeling isolated within the institution. The transition from high school to a predominantly white institution was harder than they anticipated.

3. Some of the students who had already withdrawn said they transferred to state schools because it cost less. Finances came up repeatedly in the exit interviews.
4. The commuter students had a lot of concerns. They didn't know anyone. They felt they were out of the information flow. They complained about parking.
5. Many of the students complained about the orientation program. They said the activities and the first semester course didn't provide them with the information they needed.

Joe asked the dean of students to develop a satisfaction survey to be mailed to a random sample of students during spring semester. He told the dean of students he was particularly interested in knowing how satisfied students were with the following: student-faculty interaction, student-student interaction, the sense of community on campus, institutional emphasis on diversity, the amount and kind of extracurricular activities available, academic advising, the residence hall experience, and commitment to the institution. Joe knew these variables were consistently found in research and on other assessment studies as being associated with persistence and educational attainment. Also, based on the results of the telephone interviews, focus groups, and exit interviews, he asked her to include some questions about parking and orientation. The dean of students and Joe agreed that they should include the following demographic variables on the survey so they could sort the data by groups: gender, academic status (part- or full-time), racial/ethnic background, commuter/resident status, home state, major, age, grade point average, and hours worked per week. The dean of students suggested they also include an open-ended question at the end of the survey asking students to identify what they were most satisfied and least satisfied with at the college.

Over lunch one day, the associate dean for academic affairs shared an informal theory she had about why students did poorly their first semester. Her theory was based on her years of advising freshmen. She thought that if freshmen took a particular combination of courses (calculus and chemistry) their first semester, they were far more likely to be put on academic probation than were students who registered for these courses in separate terms. Joe asked the associate dean to conduct a transcript review of the students who met the admission criteria of the college, but were put on academic probation at the end of the first semester to see if her theory was correct. At the same time, he asked the associate dean to look for any other "gate-keeping courses," courses that a high percentage of freshmen failed.

A few weeks later the associate dean reported her conclusions. Her theory about calculus and chemistry appeared to be correct. She was anxious to share her results with the freshman faculty advisors. And, much to her surprise, the introductory psychology course also emerged as a gatekeeper course. Joe was pleased to hear she had already set up a meeting with the faculty who teach that course to examine the syllabus, tests, and teaching methods.

In the meantime, the dean of students had completed the satisfaction survey. It took a little longer to complete than she had anticipated because she sought the help of a professor in the sociology department.

Her major findings included the following:

1. Students were dissatisfied with the residence hall experience, particularly the perceived subjectivity of the disciplinary system.
2. Students were satisfied with the opportunity to meet informally with faculty, but dissatisfied with academic advising.
3. Students who worked off campus were far less involved in the academic and social dimensions of the college than those who worked on campus.
4. Students were extremely dissatisfied with the one-credit course required of all freshmen. They indicated it was not relevant and involved far too much reading for the amount of credit given.

One day while meeting with a group of faculty members, Joe mentioned how surprised he was about students' negative reaction to the one-credit course for freshmen. The faculty members weren't surprised. They weren't particularly happy with the course either. Joe was pleased when they offered to ask the vice president for academic affairs to create a committee to explore the issue and include Joe. He was hoping the course could be refocused to address some of the developmental issues identified by Chickering (1969). It might make the course more "relevant" to the freshmen and, at the same time, provide a vehicle for them to make a connection with some of the major agents of socialization on campus—faculty and peer groups (Pascarella and Terenzini, 1991). Joe also hoped the format of the course could be designed to be more interactive.

Joe decided he would explore on Tinto's (1997) recommendation regarding "learning communities" in the first year. He had heard this approach was yielding some important benefits at other schools, not the least of which was increased retention rates.

Almost simultaneously, Joe was also invited to join a group of faculty members and the vice president for academic affairs who were developing an outcome assessment plan that needed to be in place before the next accreditation visit.

Joe found a recent article that listed the retention rates of the majority of colleges and universities in the country. Joe identified the first-to-second year and the six-year graduation rates at similar institutions and institutions his institution wanted to emulate. He noted their retention rates and established a tentative goal.

Joe used the assessment results gleaned from the record review, document analysis, the satisfaction survey (quantitative), the focus group, telephone and exit interviews (qualitative), and the theories and research related to the problem as he drafted his report to the board of trustees describing a institution-wide strategic plan for increasing the first-to-second-year retention rate. He carefully described the problem, using a little theory, research, and his assessment results to bolster his conclusions. Then he outlined his plan of action. His plan included some policy changes, a number of new program initiatives, and some suggestions for changes in practice. Listed are some of the key initiatives.

Policy Implications

1. Create a comprehensive assessment program that regularly collects data from students and would allow Normal College to track students, identify needs, monitor satisfaction, assess environments, and measure outcomes.
2. Require freshmen that go on probation after the first semester to attend an academic assistance seminar the second semester.
3. Communicate financial aid options to students and their families and do not reduce aid after the first year.

Program Initiatives

1. Create a Commuter Assistant (CA) program that replicates the role that Resident Assistants (RA) play with resident students. Identify a space that can be used as a commuter student lounge.
2. Reconfigure the orientation course already required of all freshmen to include more than just an introduction to the intellectual life of the campus.
   - Teach the course in teams of three: the students' faculty advisor, a student affairs staff member, and a continuing student who acts as a peer advisor.
   - Limit enrollment in each class to fifteen students.
   - The content of the class should deal with the major developmental tasks and transitional issues facing freshmen, introduce students to services, and encourage students to become "involved" in the academic and social dimensions of the college.
   - The format of the class should be highly interactive.
3. Implement a parent program that includes a parent orientation program, a newsletter for parents, and a parent association.
4. Institute a six-week summer transition program for underrepresented minority students.
5. Work with students to revive traditions that haven't been celebrated at Normal College for some time.

Changes in Practice

1. Provide on-campus jobs for students when reasonable and appropriate.
2. When possible, allow students more control over their residence hall environments.
3. Conduct an in-service program for faculty advisors identifying combinations of courses that cause students difficulty.
4. In future marketing efforts, emphasize the extremely high employment rate of the graduates from Normal College.

Was he ready for the board of trustees meeting? Not yet. Joe invited a number of key staff at the college, including the president, to review his proposal draft. They made a few suggestions and asked some questions. He also presented his ideas to the faculty committees with whom he had been meeting. They seemed supportive of Joe's recommendations for changes in policy, programs, and practices. A few were skeptical whether these changes would really affect the retention rate at Normal, but were willing to try.

In summary, theory, research, and assessment results helped Joe identify the problem, develop an assessment plan, make sense of the results, and together they suggested the goal, a plan of action and a series of interventions.

Issues in Translating Theory and Assessments Results to Practice

There are several issues to be considered when translating theory, research, and assessment results to practice. First, it is essential that student affairs administrators remain current when it comes to theory relevant to student affairs and the results of research and assessment studies conducted on a national and local level. Theory and research can help focus assessment efforts and vice versa.

Second, students change and campuses change. We need to continually seek to understand students and campuses through theory and assessment and to base our policies, program initiatives, decisions, and plans on up-to-date information in both areas. Basing a policy change or a program proposal on outdated theory or data can be the first step toward failure.

Third, use of theory, research, and assessment results is strongest when it is linked to common sense and experience.

Fourth, knowing when, where, and how to share theory, research about students, and assessment results is as much a political as a practical dilemma. We have an obligation to make appropriate use of what we know, but it must be done in a time, place, and manner in which it will be heard.

Fifth, for some student affairs administrators, particularly those who haven't had a statistics course since graduate school, analyzing data in meaningful ways may be a rusty skill. We should not be shy about asking for help or clarification. Faculty can be particularly helpful in this regard.

Sixth, the faculty can be valuable resources when it comes to understanding students, measuring program effectiveness, planning programs, solving problems, or measuring outcomes. Faculty can help identify relevant theory and appropriate assessment mechanisms, critique assessment methodology, and assist with the analysis of data. Their perspective from inside the classroom complements the student affairs' view from outside the classroom.

Seventh, theory is just that, theory. Assessment results are usually drawn from samples and generalized to populations. It is important to keep in mind that the individual students who come to our offices may not fit the theory, the research, or the data.

References

American Association for Higher Education (AAHE). *Principles of Good Practice for Assessing Student Learning.* Washington, D.C.: American Association for Higher Education, 1992.

American College Personnel Association (ACPA*). The Student Learning Imperative: Implication for Student Affairs.* Washington, D.C.: American College Personnel Association, 1994.

American College Personnel Association (ACPA) and National Association of Student Personnel Administrators (NASPA). *Principles of Good Practice for Student Affairs.* Washington, D.C.: American College Personnel Association (ACPA) and National Association of Student Personnel Administrators (NASPA), 1997.

Astin, A. W. *Achieving Educational Excellence: A Critical Assessment of Priorities and Practices in Higher Education.* San Francisco: Jossey-Bass, 1985.

Astin, A. W. *What Matters in College.* San Francisco: Jossey-Bass, 1993.

Astin, A. W. "Involvement in Learning Revisited: Lessons We Have Learned." *Journal of College Student Development,* 1996, 37(2), 123–133.

Banta, T. W., Lund, J. P., Black K. E., and Oblander, F. W. *Assessment in Practice.* San Francisco: Jossey-Bass, 1996.

Bean, J. P. *The Strategic Management of College Enrollments.* San Francisco: Jossey-Bass, 1990.

Bennett, M. J. "Toward Ethnorelativism: A Developmental Model of Intercultural Sensitivity." In R.M. Paige (ed.*), Education for the Intercultural Experience* (2nd ed.). Yarmouth, ME: Intercultural Press, 1993, p. 1–51.

Blalock, H. M. *Theory Construction.* Englewood Cliffs, NJ: Prentice-Hall, 1969.

Bloom, B. S. (ed.) *Taxonomy of Educational Objectives,* vol. 1. New York: McKay, 1956.

Chickering, A. *Education and Identity.* San Francisco: Jossey-Bass, 1969.

Colby, A., and others. *The Measurement of Moral Judgment: Vol. 2. Standard Issue Scoring Manual.* New York: Cambridge University Press, 1987.

El-Khawas, E. "Student Diversity on Today's Campuses." In S. R. Komives, and D. B. Woodard, Jr. (eds.), *Student Services: A Handbook for the Profession.* (3rd ed.) San Francisco: Jossey-Bass, 1996.

Erwin, T. D. *Assessing Student Learning and Development.* San Francisco: Jossey-Bass, 1991.

Erwin, T. D. "Assessment, Evaluation, and Research." In S. R. Komives and D. B. Woodard, Jr. (eds.), *Student Services: A Handbook for the Profession.* (3rd ed.) San Francisco: Jossey-Bass, 1996.

Evans, N. J. "A Framework for Assisting Student Affairs Staff in Fostering Moral Development." *Journal of Counseling and Development,* 1987, 66, 191–194.

Evans, N. J. "Theories of Student Development." In S. R. Komives and D. B. Woodard, Jr. (eds.), *Student Services: A Handbook for the Profession.* (3rd ed.) San Francisco: Jossey-Bass, 1996.

Evans, N. J., Forney, D. S., and Guido-DiBrito, F. *Student Development in College.* San Francisco: Jossey-Bass, 1998.

Fink, A. *How to Sample in Surveys.* Thousand Oaks, CA: Sage Publications, 1995.

Hammer, M.R., and Bennett, J. J. *Intercultural Development Inventory.* Portland, OR: Intercultural Communication Institute, 1994.

Hanson, G. R. "Improving Practice Through Research, Evaluation, and Outcome Assessment." In M. J. Barr, M. L. Upcraft, and Associates, *New Futures for Student Affairs.* San Francisco: Jossey-Bass, 1990.

Hood, A. B. (ed.) *The Iowa Student Development Inventories.* Iowa City, IA: Hitech Press, 1986.

Jacobi, M., Astin, A., and Ayala, F. Jr. *College Student Outcomes Assessment: A Talent Development Perspective.* ASHE-ERIC Higher Education Report No. 7. Washington, D.C.: Association for the Study of Higher Education, 1987.

Kerlinger, F. N. *Foundations of Behavioral Research.* Fort Worth, Texas: Holt, Rinehart and Winston, 1986.

King, P. M., and Baxter-Magolda, M. B. "A Developmental Perspective on Learning." *Journal of College Student Development,* 1996, 37(2), 163–173.

Knefelkamp, L. L., Golec, R. R., and Wells, E. A. *The Practice-To-Theory-To-Practice Model.* Unpublished manuscript, University of Maryland, College Park, 1985.

Komives, S. R. "Editor's Introduction." In N. Snyder-Nepo, *Leadership Assessments: A Critique of Common Instruments.* College Park, MD: National Clearinghouse for Leadership Programs, 1992.

Kuh, G. D., Schuh, J. H., Whitt, E. J., and Associates. *Involving Colleges: Successful Approaches to Fostering Student Learning and Development Outside the Classroom.* San Francisco: Jossey-Bass, 1991.

Lenning, O. T. "Assessment and Evaluation." In U. Delworth, G. R. Hanson, and Associates, *Student Services: A Handbook for the Profession.* San Francisco: Jossey-Bass, 1980.

Levine, A., and J. S. Cureton. *When Hope and Fear Collide: A Portrait of Today's College Students.* San Francisco: Jossey-Bass, 1998.

McEwen, M. K. "The Nature and Uses of Theory." In S. R. Komives and D. B. Woodard Jr. (eds.), *Student Services: A Handbook for the Profession.* (3rd ed.) San Francisco: Jossey-Bass, 1996.

Miller, H. G., Williams, R. G., and Haladyna, T. M. *Beyond Facts: Objective Ways to Measure Thinking.* Englewood Cliffs, NJ: Educational Technology Publications, 1978.

Miller, T. K., and Winston, R. B. (eds.), *Administration and Leadership in Student Affairs.* Muncie, IN: Accelerated Development Inc., 1991.

Moore, L. V. (ed.) *Evolving Theoretical Perspectives on Students.* San Francisco: Jossey-Bass, 1990.

Morrill, W. H., Oetting, E. R., and Hurst, J. C. "Dimensions of Counselor Functioning." *Personnel and Guidance Journal,* 1974, 52, 354–359.

Noel, L., Levitz, R., Saluri, D., and Associates. *Increasing Student Retention: Effective Programs and Practices for Reducing the Dropout Rate.* San Francisco: Jossey-Bass, 1985.

Pascarella, E. T., and Terenzini, P. T. *How College Affects Students.* San Francisco: Jossey-Bass, 1991.

Pascarella, E.T. and Whitt, E. J., "Using Systematic Inquiry to Improve Performance." In G. S. Blimling, E. J. Whitt, and Associates. *Good Practice in Student Affairs: Principles to Foster Student Learning.* San Francisco: Jossey-Bass, 1999.

Rest, J. R. *The Defining Issues Test* (3rd ed.) Minneapolis, MN: University of Minnesota Center for the Study of Ethical Development, 1986.

Rodgers, R. F. "Using Theory in Practice in Student Affairs." In T. K. Miller, R. B. Winston Jr., and Associates, *Administration and Leadership in Student Affairs: Actualizing Student Development in Higher Education.* (2nd ed.) Muncie, IN: Accelerated Development Inc., 1991.

Rodgers, R. F., and Widick, C. "Theory to Practice: Using Concepts, Logic and Creativity." In R. B. Newton and K. L. Ender (eds.), *Student Development Practice: Strategies for Making a Difference.* Springfield, IL: Thomas, 1980.

Schlossberg, N. K., Lynch, A. Q., and Chickering, A. W. *Improving Higher Education Environments for Adults: Response Programs and Services from Entry to Departure.* San Francisco: Jossey-Bass, 1989.

Stewart, D. W., and Shamdasani, P. N. *Focus Groups: Theory and Practice.* Newbury Park, CA: Sage Publications, 1990.

Tinto, V. *Leaving College: Rethinking the Causes and Cures of Student Attrition.* Chicago: University of Chicago Press, 1987.

Tinto, V. "Reconstructing the First Year of College." In G. Keller (ed.), *The Best of Planning for Higher Education.* Ann Arbor, MI: Society for College and University Planning, 1997.

Upcraft, M. L., and Schuh, J. H. *Assessment in Student Affairs.* San Francisco: Jossey-Bass, 1996.

Whitt, E. J. "Artful Science: A Primer on Qualitative Research Methods." *Journal of College Student Development,* 1991, 32(5), 406–415.

Widick, C., Knefelkamp, L., and Parker, C. A. "Student Development." In U. Delworth, G. R. Hanson, and Associates, *Student Services: A Handbook for the Profession.* San Francisco: Jossey-Bass, 1980.

Winston, R. B. Jr., Miller, T. K., and Prince, J. S. *Student Development Task and Lifestyle Inventory* (Rev. 2nd ed.) Athens, GA: Student Development Associates, 1987.

CHAPTER SEVENTEEN

PROGRAM PLANNING AND IMPLEMENTATION

Joan Claar and Michael Cuyjet

The development and implementation of programs is a central activity for student affairs professionals. Whether the program is a major administrative unit, a major new initiative, a one-time event, or a series of events, the ability to plan and implement effective programs is essential. Barr and Keating identified three essential elements in planning and implementing any program: the context, the goal, and the plan (1985, p.3). Program success, whether the program is large or small, depends on a full understanding of each of these program elements.

The chapter begins with an explanation of the Barr and Keating program planning model. Next, the model is applied to the development and implementation of major campus initiatives such as the creation of a new program unit or the complete refocusing of an existing service or agency. Examples of application of the model with regard to both types of initiatives are then provided along with an analysis of the examples.

The chapter then focuses on the one-time activities or series of activities and programs that take much time and effort on the part of student affairs professionals. Examples of application of the model and specific steps for success in program planning and implementation involving students are provided. Finally, suggestions for practice that should assist student affairs professionals in improving their skills and competencies in the art of program planning and implementation are provided.

THE MODEL

There are three assumptions that underlie this model of program development and implementation. First, the student affairs professional must understand and be able to apply a variety of theories to the task of program development. Second, there are three equal elements involved in program development: the context, the goal, and the plan or method. A third assumption is that all three program elements must be congruent in order for the program to succeed (Barr and Keating, 1985, p.3).

Each element is also essential interdependent and such interdependence is critical to program success. As the following discussion illustrates, successful program planning is both a skill and an art.

Planning and Implementing Major Initiatives

A major initiative involving program planning is an activity that is more than one event and may include the addition or deletion of an office or function, or significant enhancement of an existing program, such as orientation. The components of context, goal, and plan apply to the planning process whether a new program is being created, an existing program is being enhanced, or a program is being eliminated.

Context

A major initiative must be planned with consideration for the culture of the college or university, the need for and possible benefits of the program within the institution, external issues or concerns, interested constituencies, the resources required, availability of human and fiscal resources, and timing. Failure to address these issues of context can result in the failure of an otherwise well-planned program.

The culture of a campus "is the collective pattern shaped by the combination of institutional history, mission, physical setting, norms, traditions, values, practices, beliefs, and assumptions that guide the behavior of individuals and groups in a college or university" (Kuh and Whitt, 1988, p. 37). Developing a program that is contrary to the prevailing institutional culture may be a desirable change, but is likely to generate a considerable amount of resistance. For example, changing a traditionally all-male "animal house" residence hall to a coed hall for students committed to service may be highly beneficial for the improvement of students' experiences in residence halls and for the institution. However, the potential for opposition by students and for women hesitating to move into the building must also be considered and planned for if the change is to be successful.

The need for and timing of a proposed program within the institution also must be considered. No matter how good the plan for an office or program may be, if it is not needed or if the identified need is being successfully met in another way or through another program, the new program initiative should not go forward. Sometimes the realization that the needs are being met in other ways does not occur until after the plan has been implemented and is not successful. For example, starting a "buddy" program in which upper-class students volunteer to mentor a new student may have limited value if, at the same time, improvements are made in the orientation leader program and more of the interpersonal connection needs of new students are met through their relationship with the orientation group leader.

Program planning sometimes requires consideration of factors external to the institution before a new program is initiated. If the institution purchases a large home for the purpose of creating a new multicultural living unit for students and then discovers that the city requires a specific number of parking spaces for multiple dwelling residences, implementation of the new program in that location may not be possible unless the parking space problem can be solved.

Any institution of higher education also has a variety of constituencies with an interest or investment in change. Some of these individuals and groups could include students, faculty, staff, parents, alumni, members of the board of trustees, donors, business, and industry. Depending on the proposed initiative, it may be desirable to consult representatives from any or all of them.

The availability of institutional fiscal resources is a reality that has a direct influence on program planning and implementation. Resource needs for the program include the budget for any new staff required, facilities, and direct programming money. The addition of an office of alcohol education may be needed, but if the budget is frozen and vacant positions are not being filled, development of the office may have to be delayed for some time. It may be possible, however, to reorganize existing programs and resources to begin the program immediately, or there may be ways of achieving the outcomes desired without the creation of a new office. All options should be explored.

Goal

Providing a clearly articulated goal that can be understood and embraced by interested constituencies is critical for building understanding and support for a new program. The program goal must be consistent with the mission of the institution, and there should be widespread agreement within the campus community that the goal is desirable. When eliminating a program, it is important to inform others, especially those who are directly involved with the program, whether the goals of that program will be met when the entity no longer exists.

When developing a goal statement, language that is understandable to all should be used, and terms that confuse and frustrate those who are not in student affairs should be avoided. Frustration can result in creating the suspicion or belief that the language is being used to artificially elevate the importance of the program and that the need for the program is questionable. A goal statement also helps determine if there are other programs on campus with similar or related activities. Faculty and staff involved in those established efforts may see the proposed program as "taking over their territory." If there is a possibility of that response, the proposed program should be discussed with appropriate staff from the other area before planning begins.

When developing a major initiative and establishing the goal, consideration should be given to how success in achieving the goal will be determined. The act of establishing a program, function, or office does not guarantee success. How will you and others know if the program has fulfilled the goal?

Plan

When creating or eliminating an office or function, having a plan is essential. The plan should include the goal, consultation and involvement with others, a preliminary schedule, a proposed budget, facility needs, an outline of the program, and an evaluation mechanism. If the proposal is the elimination of a function, obviously the plan must be different than if it is for the modification or addition of a program.

When ending a program, consultation and involvement is essential, and a thoughtful and articulate goal or reason for the program's demise is essential. Frequently, when a program is eliminated, it is done in order to make resources available to add a function or office in an area with higher priority. The plan, goal, and rationale must be well conceived and well communicated to concerned constituents. An example of such a change would be to eliminate an office of alcohol education in order to establish a volunteer service office. Both are important, but the decision might be that with limited resources the volunteer service office might do more toward changing the campus culture in a positive direction.

The following case examples help illustrate the complexity of developing and implementing major program initiatives.

Case Example: Creation of a Multicultural Living-Learning Center

A residential liberal arts college in the Midwest is located in a rural community. The college has enrolled mostly traditional students; i.e., eighteen to twenty-two years old, Caucasian, and middle class. The campus has twenty-three national fraternities and sororities with their own houses, and approximately well over one-half of the student body is affiliated with one of the groups. Although all first-year students are required to live in residence halls, most students move to fraternity or sorority housing at the beginning of their second year. Most campus social activity takes place through the sororities and fraternities. Student life and academic life are very separate and there is little overlap between the two domains.

A new president has identified a major initiative of dramatically increasing the number of students of color at the college. The response of the faculty, staff, and students has been generally supportive, but uncertain about what this change will mean for the campus. Some assume that these new populations of students will fit into the campus culture that has been relatively unchanged for over 150 years. Others recognize that the change is likely to require significant adjustment in the campus culture if these new populations are going to find a place to belong on the campus.

Staff in both student affairs and academic affairs recognize that the change in the student population requires a change in the culture of the campus and believe that students of color will not feel comfortable in the traditional residence hall environment. The director of residence life and the academic dean proposed applying for a grant to support the establishment of a multicultural living-learning unit. This would consist of a small residence hall for students who are committed to an intensive multicultural living experience and agree to take one class together that would integrate their living experience with theory.

A committee of interested faculty, students, and staff was created and worked for several months to develop the concept. The grant proposal was written and the project was funded for two years, as a model for small residential colleges. A diverse group of students was recruited and a faculty member and the director of residence life agreed to co-teach the course. The first year began with participants full of enthusiasm and highly committed to making the experiment work and to changing the culture of the campus. The project was highly visible and was the recipient of a significant amount of attention and curiosity throughout the campus.

Late in the first semester, problems began to occur. Initially it was thought that the problems were part of the process of creating something new. Students in the program were highly dissatisfied with the faculty member teaching the course, whom they did not think was doing enough to integrate their experiences into the course. Throughout the remainder of the semester, the chasm grew, and the faculty member withdrew from the project at the end of the first semester. At the end of the initial year, some of the participants were disillusioned with the project and moved back into traditional housing, whereas others stayed for the second year and were still committed to the original goals.

During the second year, the project emphasized conflict resolution and the course, with a different faculty member and the director of residence life co-teaching it, improved. The project was evaluated by outside evaluators throughout the year, with participants from both years being interviewed. The director of residence life left the college after the second year. The college was expecting a large class of first-year students and needed the space for traditional housing; the funding period of the grant ended; and the program ended.

Discussion. The context of the program was given careful consideration during the development stage of the new initiative. The goal of the program from the time of its conception was to cause some changes in the traditional culture of the campus: both in student life and in the classroom. Although there was significant verbal support for the program, when it was actually established the extent of change required by individuals became much clearer. The timing appeared to be appropriate, but some of the participants were not ready. The program was successful in some aspects, but did not achieve the original goal. It did provide some institutional experience with change and with the issues that the campus would be required to confront as the student population changed. It clearly demonstrated to both students and faculty that life at the college would not be the same as it had been and that change needed to be planned. The plan for the program was well conceived and there was involvement by the key constituents, but the goal could not be met at that time and on that campus.

Case Example: Changing the Culture in a Residence Hall

The Context. A small, traditional, residential liberal arts college in the Midwest is located in a small rural community. Almost all students live in college housing, which remains predominately single-gender residence halls. Although approximately one-third of the students are affiliated with the local fraternities and sororities, no Greek housing exists and affiliated students live in the residence halls. One of the men's halls has long been the building of choice for athletes because of its extra large rooms and its location across the street from the athletic facilities. This hall has, for more than twenty years, had the well-earned designation as an "animal house." Women did not feel welcome there, vandalism and damage was a regular and accepted occurrence, and many male first-year students were intimidated by activity in the hall and moved out as quickly as possible. Students were generally accepting of behaviors of the men living in the hall because they saw the administration taking no action and felt that "this is just the way it is here."

The Goal. The new dean of students had been at the college for a year and observed that much of what was negative in the out-of-class environment of the college could not be changed until the residence life experience was significantly modified. The goal was to alter the residence life experience and make it more positive by making more halls coed. The men's hall in question was one of those targeted to become coed. A key to the successful fulfillment of the goal was modifying the unacceptable behavior in the men's hall.

The Plan. The final decision about the changes in residence halls had to be made prior to room selection in the spring. The plan included the following steps:

1. Notifying all students about the proposal and setting up opportunities for them to discuss it with residence life staff.
2. Meeting with the coaches of men's sports to obtain their support and discussing the proposal, reasons for needing change, and potential advantages for men's athletics.
3. Presenting the proposal to the student life committee of the faculty.
4. Notifying the chair of the student affairs committee of the board of trustees.
5. Keeping the president's cabinet informed about the status of the proposed changes.
6. Making the decision using the information gathered and making appropriate modifications in the proposal.

The dean of students sent a letter to all students, announcing the proposed changes, enclosing a copy of the proposal, and reporting that the residence life staff would hold a hearing in each of the eight residence halls on campus. As students discussed the issues in the open meetings, many became highly supportive of the plan. They were favorable about the increase in coeducational living opportunities and became increasingly outspoken about the physical and behavioral conditions in the men's hall in question. Some of the men in the hall to be changed were irate and started a campaign to defeat the proposal. Other men who lived in the hall, but did not like the environment, gave quiet, behind-the-scenes support to the plan.

The dean and director of residence life met with the coaches of men's sports and the athletic director, who were supportive and enthusiastic, believing that the changes would improve the image of student athletes and athletics on campus. Faculty, trustees, and the president's cabinet were all supportive of the long-needed changes.

The change of the men's hall to a coed hall was made. Some of the men who were opposed started rumors suggesting that women who moved in would not have a pleasant experience, and women students were concerned about moving into that environment. The residence life staff designated that hall as a leadership and service hall and required all who were interested in living there complete an application committing themselves to involvement in leadership and service activities. Those who had serious disciplinary problems were not permitted to live in the newly-constituted coed residence hall.

The change in the environment in the residence hall was dramatic, and it continues to be one of the preferred living options on campus. Vandalism and damage in the building has significantly diminished.

Discussion. This is an example of a major initiative that seemed to defy tradition in the undergraduate culture. Looking at the issue beyond the surface, however, it becomes apparent that the existing culture was not supported by most of the campus constituencies, but they felt helpless to do anything about it and were silent about their dissatisfaction. The new program initiative gave them a "voice" and a chance to participate in a positive change in their undergraduate experience.

The implementation of major initiatives take a great deal of time and effort and should not be lightly undertaken. Most student affairs professionals, however, spend much of their time and effort on developing and implementing activities and programs such as concerts, plays, lectures, and leadership programs. Success of these programs is also dependent on understanding the context, goal, and plan.

Planning and Implementing Specific Activities

In practice, many event programmers may not think of applying a general programming model to the development of events. They just "do" the program—scheduling the facility, contacting the participants, using the local campus media to inform the audience, and cleaning up afterwards. Although this method may work for some, developing and consistently employing a model has several advantages including training of new staff; reduction of "trial and error" mistakes; establishing greater consistency in the entire programming process across different events; and providing a mechanism for evaluating and improving the program development process. The primary benefit of using a program model is to provide an opportunity to lay an adequate contextual and theoretical foundation for each program before just jumping in and "doing" it.

Context

The Barr/Keating model (1985) calls for consideration of context on three levels—the higher education context as it relates to the greater society, the contextual elements of one's particular college or university, and finally, the assessment of the environment within the student services unit of the campus. Contextual assessment for event programming focuses on the latter and mandates narrowing that focus from student affairs as a single entity to the unique characteristics of a student affairs agency or possibly a sub-unit of such an agency. For example, a resident assistant considering the context for a program she is contemplating for the residents on her floor must be aware of any general programming parameters of the residence life department as well as the influences her individual residence hall may have on program implementation. Moreover, the context of the floor—that is, the needs of the residents, their tastes, their schedules, the ways in which they tend to interact—are also a prime considerations in the planning of any successful activities for this specific population.

Goal Setting

The Barr/Keating (1985) model recommends three general goals for programming on the campus: to provide essential institutional services, to teach life management skills, and to provide links for the integration of knowledge between the curriculum and the co-curriculum (p. 6). This perspective provides an important starting point for the activities programmer, but there are more detailed elements of the goal-setting process that must be considered. A first step might be to select one of these three major goals as a starting point (because only the more complex events and activities might address more than one goal), and then determine exactly which institutional service, life skill, or element of knowledge is to be the specific focus of the program or activity.

Population. Further refinement might include an assessment of the targeted population to determine their specific goals. For example, a career counselor might set out to design a program with the general institutional service goal of providing career planning skills to a group of students. Without further refinement of this goal, the program is likely to be inappropriate for a portion of the potential audience or to miss the mark altogether. In this case, class rank of potential participants might influence whether the goal was long-range career planning activities for freshmen or short-term strategies for seniors. The major field of study of participants might cause a shift in planning strategies. Other characteristics such as gender or ethnicity could also alter the goals for the program, as would the longevity of the program itself—a one-time program would have different expected outcomes than a series of sessions over an extended period of time.

Outcomes. It is important to carefully articulate the desired outcomes of the program. Be clear with what you expect to accomplish and what you expect participants to achieve. For example, outcomes for a career development workshop for freshmen might include familiarizing them with the location of the career development center and the resources available there; establishing early contact between first-year students and career center staff who can help them throughout their enrollment; familiarizing students with lesser-known career options; and explaining the correlation between minimum skills for particular careers and academic courses to acquire them.

Objectives. Because broad-based goals are difficult to assess, specific, measurable objectives should be used to facilitate evaluation and to help determine the success of a program. Objectives for the career program might include attracting a minimum number of participants, having those participants scheduling a certain number of follow-up visits; or reaching a satisfaction level as measured by a summary written evaluation provided by students. Each of these objectives can be measured in a tangible way.

Plan

Barr and Keating (1985) advise that, "Whatever planning techniques are employed, whatever the size or complexity of the ultimate program endeavor, a systematic, time-delineated program plan must be developed if the student services program is to succeed" (p. 9). The program planner in search of a model to follow will have no lack of choices from which to select. A series of models developed in the 1970s that are reviewed by Styles (1985) and include Lewis and Lewis's (1974) Schematic for Change, the Aulepp and Delworth (1976) Ecomapping Model, Drum and Figler's (1973) Outreach Model, Morrill, Oetting, and Hurst's (1974) Cube, and Moore and Delworth's (1976) Training Model can also be useful tools for programmers. There are also several useful models developed more recently that might be helpful for the programmer seeking a blueprint to follow. Included in this group would be the Barr and Cuyjet's (1991) program planning model and Cuyjet's (1996) later adaptation of it. Regardless of which model one chooses to follow, there are a number of essential elements that should be incorporated into the planning stage of the process.

Revisit Objectives. As the actual planning for the program begins, reconsider the goals and objectives and carefully identify the initial intent of the program. Is this a one-time event, a pilot program, a possible precursor to one or more subsequent programs, or a part of a clearly defined series? Are all of the objectives clear at the onset, or is it possible that components may be added to the program in the process of program development? The planning process will need to be much more flexible if links to other programs need to be established or if consideration needs to be made for program components to be added as the event begins to unfold.

Personnel. A second consideration is the staff who will be involved in the program. The event actual requires two teams—a planning team and an implementation team —although these groups often consist of the same people. However, it is sometimes convenient to think of them as two discrete operations in order to better track progress and accomplishments. Thus, the completion of the planning stage of the event should signal a point at which some formative assessment of the event's elements is made and any additional planning elements are added as the actual program is undertaken. Most program planning/implementation teams work best if comprised of a small but effective group that is able to function together as a unit and whose members, collectively, possess all the skills necessary to perform the tasks required. Examples of particular skills that may be important for at least one member of the group to have might include the following:

- the ability to coordinate administrative functions in order to manage the team itself,
- clerical ability in order to maintain good records and process correspondence and other written communications, artistic or design skills for creating publicity materials,
- knowledge of facilities management for selecting and preparing the site of the program, budgeting and financial management skills, a knowledge of local resources, and
- the appropriate contacts for soliciting and securing necessary items. The team should also include members of the target population or others affected by the program, particularly if the target is not a "mainstream" group.

Training. Another consideration related to the staffing is the training provided to the team members. Some general orientation to the goals of the program and the target population usually is needed. Remember that training requires both information and resources, so be sure to allow for both in the planning of the event.

Theoretical Approach. An often overlooked step in the planning of events or programs is to identify a theoretical approach for the program. Initiatives such as *A Perspective on Student Affairs* (National Association of Student Personnel Administrators, 1989) and the "Student Learning Imperative" (SLI, American College Personnel Association, 1996) have focused attention on the need of all forms of student affairs programming to support the academic mission of the institution by contributing to the comprehensive development of students within the academic community. Whether attempting to foster growth by teaching personal behaviors (such as acceptable social interactions in a residence hall), or to impart self-developmental knowledge (such as information to assist with career decision-making), or simply to encourage greater involvement in the life of the campus community, which has been found to enhance retention (Astin, 1984), program planning in the college environment should include a consideration of the development benefits.

Time Line. Planners need to consider two aspects related to the timing of the event. First, because programs do not occur in a vacuum, planners need to be aware of other events scheduled on the campus. This includes other similar programs that may be redundant or provide some of the same service or information and, therefore, split the target audience. However, timing also means avoiding other significant events and programs in the campus community. Certainly, the academic significance of midterm or final examinations precludes many other events from occurring during those periods. Timing also dictates that events celebrating significant campus traditions (for example, Founder's Day, Homecoming, or Commencement) should be respected. Significant community holidays—not just Christian holidays such as Christmas or Easter, but those celebrated in Judaism, Islam, Hinduism, as well as other sects—should be noted and avoided, if possible.

The second aspect of timing relates to the establishment of a time line for the program. The successful programmer identifies the date of the program, identifies all of the tasks that need to be accomplished in order to bring the event to fruition, and then works backwards from the target date to establish a realistic, week-by-week activity plan.

Budget. Another important part of the planning process is the identification of necessary resources to implement the program. The budgeting process generally has two components. First, the programmer determines the actual amount of money necessary to complete the program, including all costs for personnel, materials, space, marketing, telecommunications, postage, food, transportation, and equipment. Second, after a total budget figure is determined, a realistic source of revenue needed to cover these expenses must be identified. Revenues may come easily from a single source, such as an allocation in the career center budget from general university funds to provide resume writing workshops for seniors. On the other hand, the budget for a major music concert may rely on an elaborate web of support from a variety of sources including ticket sales, revenues from related merchandise, student activities fees, grants and gifts, and profits from other student-sponsored entertainment events.

Shared Resources. In addition to the scheduling issues mentioned in the section on timing, event planning should include consideration of how an event fits into the "bigger picture" on the campus. Seeing a program as part of the comprehensive offerings of the campus community not only gives a common purpose to the event, but it can provide opportunities for collaboration and the sharing of personnel, funds, and materials. With the ever-present concern for the efficient use of resources, complementary programming with other agencies should be considered. To illustrate, different floors in a residence hall could cosponsor a lecture by a guest speaker or agree to support each other's programs by their mutual attendance. As a last example, agencies that seem to share target audiences (for instance, the adult student center and the women's center on a computer campus with a large number of older, returning women students) could agree to advertise each other's programs.

Implementation

The last step in the planning phase of the model refers to the actual end product, the program or event itself. To get to that "end product," there are two more steps to the process—implementation and evaluation. The following are several important considerations for the implementation phase.

Delegation. Getting any of the implementation steps accomplished begins with delegating tasks and responsibilities to the members of the program planning team and identifying clear lines of accountability, reporting relationships, and deadlines. Backup responsibilities to cover all tasks in case someone fails to carry out an assignment will provide an additional margin of safety for program completion.

Marketing. Those charged with doing so should develop and initiate a marketing plan well in advance of the program itself, using a variety of media to catch the attention of both the target group and any peripheral audience that can help pass information to that target group. For example, a workshop on developing good study habits targeted at freshman students could also be publicized to faculty who may then encourage their students to attend. The key is to identify those who might be interested in the topic and to discover the optimal ways to reach them.

Venue. Prepare the location you have selected for the program. The site should be barrier-free, highly visible, and easy to find. Parking, accessibility for the physically disabled, aesthetics, and proximity to related programs are additional considerations to be taken into account. If the program consists of a series of events, using a consistent place, day and time is usually recommended.

Equipment. Be certain adequate amounts of all needed materials and devices are on hand and in good working order. If trained personnel, such as lighting, sound, or computer technicians are required, make sure they are available and that you provide all the materials they will need.

Assessment and Evaluation

Collect evaluative responses from as many program participants as is feasible. Use a variety of media, including written forms, face-to-face interviews, suggestion cards, or telephone calls. Because you will want to gather evaluative data on the process (how the planning and implementation went) as well the content (the elements contained in the program itself), be sure to solicit evaluative data from members of the planning and implementation team too.

Upcraft and Schuh (1996) describe assessment as "any effort to gather, analyze, and interpret evidence" (p. 18) and evaluation as "any effort to use assessment evidence to improve . . . effectiveness" (p. 19). Thus, assessment is the process of collecting feedback from program participants (and planners), and evaluation is the use of those data for making decisions about subsequent programming. Please see other chapters in this volume for suggestions for practice.

Administrative Decision. After examining all the information compiled in the evaluation phase, decide on one of three actions for the future of the program: continuation, modification, or abandonment. Continuation decisions should specify a definite period of time and include provisions for ongoing review. Modification decisions should delineate very carefully the changes recommended and the reasons for them. Abandonment decisions should offer compelling reasons and offer suggestions of possible alternate approaches to meet the goals that will be unmet when the program is abandoned. Even if the program was a one-time event, do not omit this step. Instead, make a determination as to which of the three actions you would recommend in case the program is considered for presentation again in the future.

Program planning and implementation is a process, but it is also an art. The following recommendations for practice may provide assistance to program planners.

Recommendations for Practice

1. Do not underestimate the importance of timing and of process. In a controversial program proposal, inadequate attention to either process or timing can result in it, instead of the actual program content, becoming the central issue.
2. Involve students in planning programs and listen to them. Student involvement can result in a program that is more relevant to students, and students can do a great deal to encourage attendance.
3. Communicate with other concerned constituents while in the planning process.
4. Identify the individual with responsibility for leading the initiative and provide support for that person.
5. Do everything possible to succeed, but be willing to fail.
6. Be prepared to make adjustments in the plan as needed.
7. Try to engage as many people as possible in the planning and implementation of programs—there is a great deal of expertise on any campus.
8. Enjoy the process of planning and implementing programs and use the process as an opportunity to teach students and staff.
9. Remember that the context, goal, and plan are important, but that the most important element is a committed and interested staff member. People do make the difference.

References

American College Personnel Association. "The Student Learning Imperative: Implications for Student Affairs." *Journal of College Student Development*, 1996, 37(2), 118–122.

Astin, A. W. "Student Involvement: A Developmental Theory for Higher Education." *Journal of College Student Personnel*, 1984, 25,(5), 297–308.

Aulepp, L., and Delworth, U. "Training Manual for an Ecosystem Model." Boulder, CO: Western Interstate Commission for Higher Education, 1976.

Barr, M. J., and Cuyjet, M. J. "Program Development and Implementation." In T. K. Miller and R. B. Winston, Jr. (eds.), *Administration and Leadership in Student Affairs: Actualizing Student Development in Higher Education*, (2nd ed.) Muncie, IN: Accelerated Development, 1991.

Barr, M. J., and Keating, L. A. "Introduction: Elements of Program Development." In M. J. Barr and L. A. Keating (eds.), *Developing Effective Student Service Programs*. San Francisco: Jossey-Bass, 1985.

Cuyjet, M. J. "Program Development and Group Advising." In S. R. Komives and D. B. Woodard, Jr. (eds.), *Student Services: A Handbook for the Profession,* (3rd ed.) San Francisco: Jossey-Bass, 1996.

Drum, D. J., and Figler, H. E. *"Outreach in Counseling."* New York: Intext Educational Publishers, 1973.

Kuh, G. D., and Whitt, E. J. *The Invisible Tapestry: Culture in American Colleges and Universities.* ASHE-ERIC Higher Education Report, no. 1. Washington, D.C.: Association for the Study of Higher Education, 1988.

Lewis, M. D., and Lewis, J. A. "A Schematic for Change." *Personnel and Guidance Journal,* 1974, 52(5), 320–323.

Moore, M., and Delworth, U. *Training Manual for Student Service Program Development.* Boulder, CO: Western Interstate Commission for Higher Education, 1976.

Morrill, W. H., Oetting, E. R., and Hurst, J. C. "Dimensions of Counselor Functioning." *Personnel and Guidance Journal,* 1974, 52(6), 354–359.

National Association of Student Personnel Administrators. *Points of View.* Washington, D.C.: National Association of Student Personnel Administrators, 1989.

Styles, M. H. "Effective Models of Systematic Program Planning." In M. J. Barr and L. A. Keating (eds.), *Developing Effective Student Service Programs.* San Francisco: Jossey-Bass, 1985.

Upcraft, M. L., and Schuh, J. H. *Assessment in Student Affairs: A Guide for Practitioners.* San Francisco: Jossey-Bass, 1996.

CHAPTER EIGHTEEN

BUDGETING AND FISCAL MANAGEMENT

Dudley B. Woodard, Jr. and Mark von Destinon

The current debate on funding social security is not unlike the debate on funding higher education into the twenty-first century. Many of us had hoped that the financial turbulence of the past two decades was not a precursor of future conditions but rather a temporary condition generated by state and federal fiscal problems. We hoped that legislators and the public would rally around the long-standing notions of "the public good" of higher education and that there would be a reinvestment in higher education. Responding to issues of fiscal and academic accountability, institutions looked to the corporate experience and began the process of downsizing, restructuring, cutting nonessential programs, and measuring outcomes to demonstrate accountability and gain the public's trust. These efforts were helpful to institutions navigating through turbulent times, but the objective of increasing public financial support for higher education simply did not happen. There is a new economic reality for the twenty-first century that will be very different from the unprecedented economic and enrollment growth of the past fifty years. Franklyn Jenifer, president of Howard University, captured the essence of this new reality when he stated that "higher education has to develop a strategy that will be good in the good times and sustain us in the bad times" (Cage, 1991, p. A1).

The winds of change are not simply driven by economic and enrollment changes, but also by the competition for resources from other public sectors and the debate over the soundness and cost-effectiveness of higher education

(Breneman, 1993). This chapter reviews higher education finance and budgeting trends. It discusses budget definitions and process, including types of budget and revenue sources. Strategies and models for the student affairs practitioner are offered in the context of this new reality and six theoretical approaches to budgeting are presented. The budgeting cycle in student affairs and analytical guidelines are reviewed and some practical tips are offered.

Financial Context for Budgeting

During recent decades, costs have risen faster than inflation—personnel, supplies, library, utilities, and technology. The Higher Education Price Index has risen more than five-fold since 1961 and the Consumer Price Index has risen four-fold. The share of state government budgets to higher education decreased since the mid-1970s from eight percent to six and a half percent by 1994. This represents a twenty percent decrease. The picture for federal funds is similar. Higher education's share of the federal budget has fallen from four percent in 1975 to two percent by 1985 and has remained at this level through 1995 (Carroll and Bryton, 1997, pp. 2–29). A study on institutional costs noted that with two exceptions, "in each decade since 1930 tuition in both public and private sectors has gone up more than general inflation as measured by the Consumer Price Index" (Halstead, 1991, p. 16). Overall, tuition and fees increased at a rate between two and three times the rate of inflation from 1980–1990 (Higher Education Surveys, 1990) and by 1994, tuition and fees increased by more than 100 percent compared to 1976. While institutional costs have outstripped inflation and state and federal support has declined in real dollars, the net effect on the cost of attendance for both public and private institutions has been dramatic. Adjusted for constant dollars, cost of attendance (tuition, fees, and room and board) has risen by forty percent for public universities and sixty percent for private universities. (Benjamin, 1998, p. 16). However, per capita personal income increased only eighteen percent in constant dollars during this same period and during the 1980s, the federal share of financial aid decreased from eighty-three to seventy-three percent. Loans grew faster than grant aid for students, resulting in an increase in debt at graduation, and the maximum Pell grant award decreased by fifty-four constant dollars during this period. Based on these trends, the conclusion was that "neither student aid nor family incomes kept pace with rising college costs in the 1980s" (The College Board, 1990, p. 3).

The context is clear. Enrollments and costs have risen rapidly during the past two decades, but public support has not kept pace. This is the new reality for the foreseeable future. Some may view the events of the past few decades as a function of hard times, competition for resources, and an unenlightened public. But there is another interpretation of these events. States and the federal government have set into motion policies that are moving institutions from an insular position to one wherein institutions are more responsive to market forces. Similar to the public quest for accountability in government, the new policies "allow universities and colleges to become more responsive to a market-driven economy and to public accountability" (Pew Policy Perspectives, 1998, p. 5).

This is the marketization of higher education—"viewing higher education as a commodity provided by competitive suppliers and educational services priced to meet market demands and consumers' ability to pay" (Quping and White, 1994, p. 217). Slaughter and Leslie describe this as institutions adopting market-like behaviors as a consequence of increasing dependency on external private and public resources and a decline in block grants from state and federal government (1998). Dill (1997) explains it as the "introduction into higher education of government reforms encouraging competitive research grants systems, greater reliance on tuition fees, and providing incentives for private fund-raising are therefore examples of the application of market instruments in academic reform" (p. 172).

This new reality means that institutions are moving closer to the marketplace and using their human capital to secure funds to offset losses in state and federal funding. This is often described as the privatization and commercialization of higher education. The question is not whether this is a good idea—the evidence is clear that institutions have adopted these market-like behaviors in recruiting students, targeting academic programs for students supported by their employers, outsourcing services, and entering into entrepreneurial arrangements with the private sector. Rather, the question is how do institutions function in this new fiscal and market reality while maintaining the core principles and values that have served our institutions well for over three centuries? Budget planning and implementation must take into account this reality.

Politics and Policy

Federal and state policy have a powerful role in shaping higher education. Many faculty and administrators do not appreciate how federal policy, in particular, has shaped higher education and moved higher education into playing a competitive role in the marketplace. For example, the shift from financial aid money as a direct allocation to institutions to a direct grant to students forced institutions to see students as consumers in a competitive market (Slaughter, 1997). This led to increasing services and targeting students for niche programs.

Another example is the deliberate change in federal policy that encouraged and permitted institutions to engage in technoscience strategies and partnerships as a way of stimulating the economy and maintaining the United States as the premiere international economic power. This federal legislation "promoted privatization, deregulation and commercialization, bringing universities, or segments of universities, into market and market-like activities" (Slaughter, 1997, p. 9).

These examples simply illustrate the powerful role the government has played in moving institutions closer to the marketplace and adopting market-like behaviors. Budgeting must take into account the historical role of state and federal policy and their probable future roles. Not understanding or underestimating this force likely would lead institutions and departments to make choices that would not serve the institution well into the future.

According to Wildavsky (1988), classical budgeting theory prior to the 1980s was characterized by annularity and a balanced budget. Incrementalism was the instrument for change and allocation. But by the 1980s, consensus was replaced by dissent because the rise in entitlements and increasing deficits made it very difficult to achieve consensus on issues when there was competition for a very small amount of discretionary money. This state of dissension continues today and most decisions are based on partisan politics. This dissension has found its way into both state and college/university budget activities. Most decisions are, in the final analysis, made on a political basis and not necessarily the merits of an argument or program (Wildavsky, 1988, pp. 92–134). This condition is another factor that decision-makers must be aware of: they must understand how to work within a system of dissent and political decision-making.

Budget Definitions

The budget process can be viewed either as a creative process or a routine task. The latter view frequently results in showcasing activity designed to satisfy an institutional or governing board requirement. However, the budgeting process can be a creative process and designed to sort out priorities, make strategic decisions, and agree on a plan for the future.

Budget Process

Meisinger and Dubeck (1984) describe budgeting as a process, a plan of action, a control mechanism, a way of communicating, a contract, and a political tool. As a process, a budget allows for the participation of constituents and consensus building with regard to levels of funding by program, revenue source, and standards of accountability. As a plan, it is a mechanism for setting priorities for activities consistent with the institution's strategic plan and forecasted resources. The budget is a contract based on commitments reflected in the strategic plan and as the recipient of restricted funds from donors, federal agencies, and state appropriations. As a control mechanism, the budget regulates the flow of resources to support each activity in accordance with approved institutional policies and procedures. As a communication network, the budget allows each department/unit to communicate its objectives, needs, and the resources required to fund those needs. Finally, a budget is a political tool because it reflects the outcomes of negotiations with different constituents about funding sources and over which activities will be supported and at what level (Meisinger and Dubeck, 1984, pp. 3–5). The budget process should be viewed as a dynamic, creative, consensus-building process that involves key decision-makers in an effort to set priorities that best serve students and societal needs.

Budget Types

An institution, depending on size, complexity, and type of control, will generally have two major budgets: the operating budget and the capital budget. It is also possible that there will be other separate budgets for local funds, auxiliaries, and special function units such as hospital operations. The operating budget is the main budget and includes "all of the regular unrestricted income available to the institution plus those restricted funds (for example, endowed professorships and sponsored programs) that are earmarked for instructional activities and department support" (Meisinger and Dubeck, 1984, pp. 7–8).

As the core budget, the operating budget includes funds allocated to support instructional activities, instructional support, student services, libraries, administration and finance, public service and development, and the unrestricted portion of endowment income, gifts, and student aid. The capital budget usually includes cost of approved new construction and renovation. Local fund or restricted budgets usually encompass federally sponsored research, grants and contracts, nongovernmental grants, some endowment and gift income, and student aid from federal and other external sources. Auxiliary budgets fund those activities that are self-supporting such as residence halls, intercollegiate activities, the student union, and copy centers (Meisinger and Dubeck, 1984, pp. 7–8).

Sources of Revenue

There are many sources of revenue such as tuition and fees, fees for services, auxiliary income, state appropriations, endowment, federal grants and contracts, federal and state financial aid programs, commercial activity, and fund balances. Based on type of institution and state statutes, the mix of these funds will vary considerably. For example, public colleges rely more on state appropriations than private colleges; however, public institutions, have increasingly relied more on tuition because of gradual decreases in state assistance. The mix of funds has changed considerably during the last two decades, and monitoring and anticipating changes is a prerequisite to sound budget planning.

Budget Models

During the last decade, most institutions of higher learning have developed a strategic plan, based on the outcomes of environmental scanning, designed to capture the future requirements and needs of the institution. The strategic plan serves as the plan around which the academic, support services, facilities, and financial plan are built. The strategic financial plan then represents the required funding to implement the academic, support services, and facility plans. In addition, after the financial plan for a given year is developed, an operating budget is generated that supports the strategic goals and objectives for that fiscal year. Monthly operating statements then allow for comparison to the budget and evaluation of how well the goals and objectives are being met (Morrell, 1989).

There are many different budget models; however, the shifts in public confidence, enrollment declines, and sources of revenue have rendered some approaches less useful than others. The following models represent an array of budget approaches and any one, or a combination, will fulfill the requirement of establishing an annual budget. The budgeting process, however, must take into account the assumptions and decisions on which the financial plan is based by providing the tools and information necessary to successfully implement and evaluate the institution's long-range strategic plan (Morrell, 1989).

Incremental

Incremental budgeting is based on the previous year's allocation—the budget is adjusted based on guidelines provided by the budget office. The underlying assumptions are that financial resources from one budget cycle to another change only modestly; expenditure patterns for the department represent continuing commitments and, therefore, it is difficult to change these commitments; and that institutional needs and priorities remain relatively unchanged from one budget cycle to the next (Meisinger and Dubeck, 1984, pp. 182–183). For example, the next year's budget adjustment factors might represent a salary projection of a five percent increase, a two percent increase in operations, and no increase in travel and capital expenditures. General practice is to adjust all unit budgets by these projected changes rather than making adjustments based on changing needs and priorities of an individual unit. It does not force the institution to examine priorities in a way that encourages annual reallocation, reductions, and elimination of programs.

Its strengths are also its weaknesses. It is flexible and easily implemented, but encourages building on past decisions and choices rather than discussing strategic decisions. Conflict is minimized by focusing on extending existing commitments and avoiding a reexamination of programs and priorities. Managers, therefore, engage in budget behaviors that are self-serving and politically driven rather than behaviors that lead to an open assessment of needs and opportunities.

Zero-Based

Zero-based budgeting is one of the more appealing approaches, but also one of the most cumbersome. It is appealing in that "administrators must justify from base zero all of their departmental or agency budgeted expenditures . . . Nothing is taken for granted or simply continued at some previous level. Everything must be justified or discontinued through the use of cost benefit analysis" (W. L. Boyd in Schuh, 1990, p. 15). Zero-based budgeting builds in an annual review of each department's performance, cost benefit, and relationship to the institution's strategic plan. It is easier to consolidate, reduce, or eliminate programs under a zero-based model, but it also can be very disruptive or anxiety-producing because commitments may be viewed as no longer than one year. Also, it is time-consuming, difficult to reach consensus on priorities, and generates a lot of paper work. Many institutions that use such an approach fix the budget base at some percentage, such as ninety percent, and then use the principles of zero-based budgeting to allocate the remaining ten percent. However, this variation undercuts the basic principle of complete program reviews based on performance, cost, and relationship to the strategic plan (Meisinger and Dubeck, 1984).

Planning, Programming, and Budget Systems (PPBS)

PPBS is a way of linking strategic planning elements to resource allocation. PPBS focuses on a clear and detailed description of program activities and the cost-effectiveness of those activities in terms of attaining desired objectives. The institution's strategic plan is used to establish priorities and a cost/benefit analysis study is done. The cost/benefit analysis is used to determine alternative ways of reaching the goals and objectives through an examination of resources required for each program activity and the estimated benefits to be gained. Agreed upon performance indicators are used to help select the cost-effective approach while maintaining effectiveness (Morgan, 1984). Projecting the costs and outputs of programs over a number of years as a way to provide a long-term view of the fiscal implications of those programs is an important feature of program budgeting (Meisinger and Dubeck, 1984, p. 183).

According to Schuh (1990), some of the difficulties of PPBS are defining outputs of higher education, quantifying program activities, determining cost/benefit ratios, and calculating cost/benefits of alternative programs. Also, the costs of information gathering and analysis of program alternatives can be overwhelming. Because of these time-consuming activities and costs, PPBS has not been successfully implemented in governmental and educational settings.

Formula

Formula budgeting is a way of allocating or appropriating dollars to an activity based on quantifiable workload measures. The most common measure is the conversion of enrollment into a mathematical ratio; for example, every student enrolled for fifteen instructional hours is equivalent to one full-time student and each full-time student is worth X dollars. According to Brinkman (1984), formula budgeting is both a political and technical process. This means that policy is forged out of political agreements and mathematical equations that express the agreements. Brinkman (1984) cites several criteria to ensure the validity of formula budgeting. Formula budgeting should recognize the varying costs of different activities, only use factors which can be quantified, make comparisons only to comparable peer institutions, use a factor or methodology appropriate to the activity to be funded, and take into account differing needs of the institution. "Taken together, then, the evaluative criteria indicate that a good formula is technically correct, representative of certain basic values, and helpful in making the budgeting process work smoothly" (Brinkman, 1984, p. 25).

The advantages of formula budgeting are appearance of objectivity because the activity is quantified; reduced conflict because individuals understand the basis of funding; built-in equity; diminished uncertainty of the budgeting process; and more autonomy for public institutions because state appropriations are formula-driven (Meisinger and Dubeck, 1984, pp. 187–188). Among the weaknesses of formula budgeting are that it is not anticipatory because it is usually based on past behavior, such as the previous year's enrollment; calculations tend to be simplistic (therefore economies of scale, variable costs, and enrollment shifts are not easily accommodated); and it has the tendency to treat all institutions alike, resulting in a "leveling effect." Also, it discourages new program development to meet emerging needs because dollars are tied to existing activity (factors such as, for example, the number of electrical engineering majors); has a reward structure aimed at achieving specific goals, such as enrolling more students, that encourage institutions to behave in ways that favor the reward but disfavor the teaching environment; and reacts slowly to price changes in the marketplace. For instance, faculty and staff salaries may not be adjusted at the same rate of change as service and production employees (Brinkman, 1984, pp. 26–28).

Formula budgeting is widely used, but its utility should be questioned because it does not encourage program assessment, respond in a timely way to emerging needs, or recognize differences among institutions.

Cost-Centered

Cost-centered budgeting is based on the principle that every unit/department pays its own way. Each unit is viewed as self-supporting and the unit is expected to raise sufficient revenues to cover its costs. This type of budgeting works more successfully with "units that are relatively independent in the sense that the instructional and research programs are self-contained" (Meisinger and Dubeck, 1984, p. 188). It has been a useful approach for units like auxiliaries, research, and development, but not as useful for instructional and support services such as academic and student services.

Responsibility-Centered

Responsibility-centered budgeting has evolved, more recently, as a way to extend centralized planning and decision-making and to make each instructional unit financially responsible for its activities. Units are taxed to meet institutional fixed expenses, and the remaining funds are allocated by the unit to meet operating expenses. Deficits must be made up in the following fiscal year and units are allowed to carry forward generated savings for reallocation. The major advantage of this approach is that it provides "incentives to solve problems and meet shifting challenges . . . faculty have a greater sense of responsibility for, and control over, their own destiny and that of their department, thus increasing morale" (Stocum and Rooney, 1997, p. 52). The major disadvantage is that it can lead to the segmentation of units by creating competition "for students and resources, making it difficult for them to work toward a common vision or set of academic goals" (p. 51). The marketization of academic units encourages units to seek out opportunities to generate income while moving these units further away from the core mission of the institution. Adams (1997) summarizes this trend as the "fractionalization of what remains of the university," and states that it will "greatly lessen its [the university's] ability to fulfill its core educational, cultural, and social mission" (Stocum and Rooney, 1997, p. 61).

No one budgeting model is sufficient to meet the changing financial landscape and shifting needs of higher education. Budgeting should be based on the mission and stated priorities (planning process) of the institution; performance indicators (accountability); devolution of decision-making (incentives and responsibility); meeting the challenges and shifting needs of the marketplace; and fulfilling society's educational, cultural, and social mandate. Too often, the budget process is politicized, and vested interests lead to dissension and poor choices. The following section is designed to help the reader avoid these pitfalls while incorporating the previously stated principles in developing a budget.

Student Affairs Budget Cycle

It is not uncommon for a department head to be simultaneously involved in three budget cycles. The first cycle is closing out the previous fiscal year. This is an important activity from the standpoint of determining whether budgetary program and expenditure goals were met. This information is critical to the allocation process for the next fiscal year and preparation of the budget request for the subsequent fiscal year.

The second cycle is the next fiscal year. Many institutions use a fiscal year of July 1st through June 30th. This cycle represents the allocation of resources based on the final budget request and subsequent allocation to student affairs. It is essential to establish an ongoing monitoring process in order to make certain that expenditures are in line with actual resources and, equally important, that progress is being made towards meeting program goals. The most frequent mistake made by department heads is waiting until near the end of the fiscal year to check on progress. A monthly review process should be implemented for each budget unit and adjustments made based on the rate of expenditures and any approved variations from the approved budget; for example, unanticipated expenses or changes in direction based on new information or needs.

The third cycle is the preparation of the budget request for the succeeding year. This request usually begins fourteen to sixteen months in advance of the actual fiscal year, such as March of 2000 for July of 2001. Preparing for the budget cycle for the succeeding year is the main focus of this section.

There are seven distinct steps in preparing a budget request for the next fiscal year. These steps do not include the institutional stages of governing board review and action, legislative submission and action, and the final institutional process of allocation based on actual and projected resources for the coming fiscal year. The practitioner should be well acquainted with the following steps in order to anticipate likely resources, timing of budget decisions, and, most importantly, points of intervention. It is important to know when to take action to clarify a budget issue, when to provide additional information, or to simply argue to protect the integrity of the request or offer an alternative based on current and projected conditions.

Establish Assumptions and Constraints

The first step in developing the succeeding budget request is to gather information about next year's likely fiscal environment (Meisinger and Dubeck, 1984). Will enrollments change? If so, how? Has the stock market negatively or positively affected projected earned interest? What are the prospects for new gifts? Are there changes in program offerings? What is happening with federal financial aid? What is the prospect for grants and contracts? What are the costs of any new mandated changes? What is the outlook for the state economy? These are some of the many questions that must be addressed by senior management in setting the framework for preparing the budget. Assumptions about sources of revenue, enrollment, program offerings, and constraints such as mandated requirements and fixed costs must be understood and shared with all individuals responsible for developing the budget.

Guidelines and Timetable

After the assumptions and constraints have been established, the division head should send out written guidelines to be used in preparing the budget. These guidelines should be reflective of the general guidelines previously outlined, institutional assumptions and constraints, and other limitations agreed to regarding the budget process. Make certain expectations are clear and an opportunity is provided to discuss the instructions. Also include a time line for hearings and final submission of budget request.

Involvement

Divisional or unit instructions should encourage the involvement of departmental staff, students, and, where appropriate, faculty. This is also an opportunity for the division or unit head to review financial conditions, institutional priorities, and likely financial scenarios. This is a time to share information and excite individuals to think creatively about achieving goals with a likely changing mix of resources.

Hold Hearings

Schedule hearings for each unit in student affairs and invite students, staff, and faculty. This is a time for a department to demonstrate whether it has been a good steward of its resources and how well it has met its objectives. It is a time to ask tough questions of the department head—including what alternatives were considered in preparing the budget request. A public hearing will help individuals be more sensitive to the needs of the community, perceptions on how well the needs are being met, and highest priorities. Before you engage in a hearing process, be sure it fits the organizational climate of your institution.

Central Staff Debate

Each department should finalize its budget and submit it to the central staff, management team or budget committee of the division. These are the staff members of the division of student affairs who have the responsibility of finalizing the division's budget request for approval and action by the senior student affairs officer (SSAO). These individuals will need to take into account assumptions, constraints, unit requests, results of public hearings, as well as short- and long-term divisional priorities. The SSAO should be a member of this group and should participate fully.

Develop Alternatives

Each department as well as the senior management team should develop alternatives based on likely financial scenarios. This requires a great deal of goodwill and trust. In some cases, alternatives may include a reorganized division of student affairs, elimination of programs or units, or the transfer of functions to academic departments or other college units. Maintaining adaptability will help the division effectively respond to new opportunities as well as tough financial challenges.

Stay Informed and Keep Others Informed

In today's environment, the budget news is like the daily newspaper. There are always new headlines, and yesterday's news is old news. Keep people informed of changing events and hold occasional briefing sessions. This will help to control rumors and keep people involved in the process and committed to working through the eventual budgetary circumstances.

Budget Guidelines

This section is a guide to help the student affairs practitioner successfully navigate the shifting tides of the budget-setting process. The analytical guidelines will assist the student affairs practitioner in preparing a budget regardless of the fiscal climate. These guidelines should be used to evaluate the contributions of each student affairs unit both to the mission of the student affairs division and mission of the institution. Careful application of the guidelines will determine whether the student affairs unit should remain as is, grow, be reduced, eliminated, or consolidated with another unit(s). These suggestions are targeted at developing a strategy for the "good times and the bad times."

Does the Unit Contribute to Divisional and Institutional Mission? The connections between the unit and institutional mission should be clear and documentable. Lyons indicated that all "programs and activities are important, but not all are equally important" (Lyons, 1991, p. 3). Although this sounds much like Orwell's admonition to society that "all animals are equal, but some animals are more equal than others" (Orwell, 1954), it is true that the mission, purpose and nature of programs do make some "more equal than others." The tighter the connection is to the mission, the stronger the rationale is for keeping the program.

Has Each Unit Developed Credible Workload Factors? The scope and magnitude of a service or program and who is served and benefited by these functions is important to document (Lyons, 1991). Each unit should develop workload measures and document the characteristics of its clientele. These data will help you solicit support, for example, from the mathematics department if you can demonstrate that you serve a fair number of their students, students value the service, and student performance is enhanced.

Are There Measurable Outcomes? Beyond developing workload factors, each unit should attempt to quantify the desired outcomes for their service/program in relation to the institution's stated outcomes for the educational experience. Does the collegiate experience facilitate the ability of the student to think reflectively, analytically, and critically? Does it facilitate personal growth and identity? (Pascarella and Terenzini, 1991). Developing outcome measures and demonstrating the role of the unit/division in facilitating student growth in these areas will greatly enhance the unit's worth and future role.

Do Most Activities Help Students Do Things for Themselves? The authors of *Involving Colleges* observed that "involving colleges encourage student responsibility and freedom of choice . . . . Students are trusted and expected to be responsible for their own learning and development, as well as for handling violations of community norms. For the most part, students are given the freedom to learn from their own decisions, experiences, and, in some cases, mistakes" (Kuh, Schuh, Whitt, and Associates, 1991, p. 137). It is clear that activities that promote individual responsibility and help students to do things for themselves should be valued and protected in the budget-setting process (Lyons, 1991).

Protect Services Designed to Maintain Ethical, Health, and Safety Standards. The difficult decisions made during tight fiscal times must protect essential services. This does not mean that such services are exempt from cuts, but rather that responsible action should be taken to maintain campus standards for those services. Responsible actions may include competitive bidding for the services, using students for safety and health tasks, or seeking volunteers for low-risk functions in order to protect high-risk activities (Lyons, 1991).

Progress Made in Building Community and Diversity Must Be Protected. Frequently, programs that were created to meet Affirmative Action goals and diversity are the first to see the ax-blade of budget cuts. These programs are a necessary condition for today's institution to meet the highly publicized statements of commitment to diversity and community. Actions that undercut these trends will seriously jeopardize the academy's long-stated goal of a community that values and celebrates diversity.

Change Operating Practices to Effect Cost Savings. This is a difficult and essential task and the practitioner should examine alternative ways of providing services. Some examples of possible alternatives are contracting out services in order to generate cost savings or new revenues without reducing quality; developing appropriate, improved workload standards; taking advantage of staff openings to consolidate and reorganize functions; targeting high-cost goods and services such as computing, printing, and reproduction for cost-containment; utilizing creative personnel policies and practices to reduce costs (for example, early retirement, flex-time, ten-month contracts); reducing administrative services inefficiencies, such as duplicate accounting practices; and streamlining reporting and recording activities (University of Arizona, 1991).

New Sources of Revenue. The erosion in federal and state funding and the rapid increases in tuition and fees have forced student affairs divisions to think more creatively about generating new sources of revenue without placing the burden solely on students. Some examples are fundraising and creating endowments, sale of goods and services to the general public, indirect cost recovery from grants, training contracts, fees for services, voluntary fees, and outsourcing (Levy, 1995). In building a budget, managers have an obligation to think about ways to generate new sources of revenue to support new initiatives or enhance existing programs.

Delete Some Programs In Order to Protect Other Programs or Establish New Programs. In times of budget cuts, across the board or vertical cuts simply reduce everything to a lower level of functioning and effectiveness. Instead, it is possible to protect the efficiency and effectiveness of some programs by eliminating weak, low-demand, or inappropriately duplicative programs as well as freeing up dollars for new programs (University of Arizona, 1991).

Savings Should Be Real

A reduction in one unit will not generate a savings or funding for reallocation if another unit will be pressed to compensate (Lyons, 1991). Cuts should not be made in isolation. Each unit has the obligation to discuss the probable impact of certain actions with those affected in order to avoid later finger-pointing and confusion among students. The community should be well advised in advance of the curtailment in services and elimination of programs.

Partnership with Faculty Must Be Genuine

Boyer (1991) and others say we need "to re-engage faculty." This means that there are functions that faculty should be encouraged to assume as a trade-off for downsizing support services or reallocating funds to support emerging needs. If these kinds of negotiations are not articulated and battles rage over turf, students will continue to be the losers. Student services will not be eliminated, but we must look at new arrangements and how some student service functions might be assumed by faculty in exchange for protecting the integrity of the instructional mission through a reallocation of student service dollars to the instructional budget or new programs.

Suggestions for Practice

This section provides practical advice for thinking about and participating in the budget-setting process. These tips cover most sins and should be occasionally reviewed to maintain perspective and a sense of humility.

Be Flexible

The practitioner must be open to new ways of doing things even if the current method is successful. Change occurs either by force or cooperation. Maintaining an open stance will help facilitate a thorough discussion of options and the eventual discarding of dysfunctional ideas and the adoption of new strategies.

Do Not Dawdle

As Lyons so aptly states, "there is more pain and institutional trauma when the decision and implementing processes are stretched out over a long period of time" (Lyons 1991, p. 2). Determine a reasonable timeframe for completing the task, communicate that time frame, and then stay on task. Be decisive and do not fret about consulting with everyone. If you have designed a solid process with respect to input from staff, students, and faculty, you should pay attention to agreed-upon procedures and get the job done.

Play It Straight

Nobody likes to find out after the fact that information had been withheld or even edited to serve a self-interest. Provide useful information such as cost, workload measures, outcome data, and peer comparison data up front. Respond to requests on a timely basis and ask for feedback as to whether the information was understood and useful. "A lie, an attempt to blatantly cover up some misdeed, a tricky move of any kind, can lead to an irreparable loss of confidence" (Wildavsky, 1988, p. 106).

Accept Responsibility

Make certain staff understands the decision-making tree and line/staff functions (Halfond, 1991; Lyons, 1991). Accept responsibility for your actions and do not look for scapegoats. Reallocation and downsizing is not a pleasant business, but remember: you are paid to make decisions.

Involve People

Building a sense of community and shared responsibility is a function of involving people in the information-gathering and decision-making process. In order for decisions to have validity and be accepted by the larger community, campus leaders must be valued for their input and be seen by others as an involved member of the process designed to make budget recommendations. This will reduce friction and help mute dissidents.

Seek Advice

There are many knowledgeable students, staff, and faculty. Create an advisory committee and test out ideas and possible alternatives. "Advisory groups are rarely professional student affairs folks. That's their strength. They can, among other things, ask some brilliant dumb questions—the very kind that often result in some very imaginative thinking" (Lyons, 1991, p. 2).

Avoid Extreme Claims

In an effort to support the worth of a program, we sometimes make claims we believe are right, but cannot support with any evidence. Do not make sweeping claims or lead with your heart when candor would score more points. Faculty have the same problem in terms of documenting the outcomes of the educational experience. Indicate what the research does demonstrate, but don't go beyond a reasonable interpretation of the evidence (Wildavsky, 1988).

Decentralized Decisions

Seek unit heads' involvement and allow for decision-making at that level. "Central leaders are best at setting the parameters and the goals. Leaders (and their followers) in the units are in the best position to bring good judgment to bear and hence, to find the most sensible and creative alternatives to choose from" (Lyons, 1991, p. 2).

Secure Feedback

Everyone claims that their service or program is popular and serves its clientele well. Before making such a claim, make certain you have secured feedback from the individuals you serve and from secondary sources likely to be affected, such as the students' department, residence hall, or place of employment. Direct clientele feedback can be helpful, but be certain, if possible, you are aware of its content in advance of any presentation. This will help you to check on the accuracy of the information and be prepared to answer questions. Do not try to avoid bad news. Objective listeners will sort through the noise and determine what was helpful based on client feedback and your response to questions (Wildavsky, 1988).

Be a Good Politician

Wildavsky (1988) states that being a good politician requires three things: "cultivation of an active clientele, the development of confidence among other governmental officials, and skill in following strategies that exploit one's opportunities to the maximum. Doing good work is viewed as part of being a good politician" (Wildavsky, 1988, p. 101). The student affairs practitioner should lobby for key programs and services as long as the process is open and does not run counter to the priorities established by the division. Spending time explaining the nature of a valued program and resulting student benefit to a faculty colleague, an academic department head, or a dean is a practice that should be ongoing—not prompted solely because of a budgetary crises.

Conclusion

Budgeting, at one time viewed as someone else's job and a tiresome task, has become an important management tool for today's practitioner. Every practitioner should develop an understanding of the financial and budgetary practices of their institution. This understanding is essential for successful participation in budget-setting practices. The budgetary process should be viewed as a creative process. To meet the challenge of a cost-containment, accountability-driven environment, practitioners must develop the sophistication to model the costs of different program options that are linked to the priorities of the institution's strategic plan and find alternative revenue sources. Anything less will be a disadvantage to the division of student affairs in the preparation of the budget and the allocation of resources for the coming year.

References

Adams, E. M. "Rationality in the Academy: Why Responsibility Center Budgeting Is a Wrong Step Down the Wrong Road." *Change*, September/October 1997, 29(5), 59–61.

Benjamin, R. "Looming Deficits: Causes, Consequences, and Cures." *Change*, March/April 1998, 30(2), 13–17.

Boyer, E. L. *Scholarship Reconsidered.* Princeton, NJ: Carnegie Foundation for the Advancement of Teaching, 1991.

Breneman, D. W. "Higher Education: On a Collision Course with New Realities." Association of Governing Boards of Universities and Colleges, Occasional Paper No. 22, Washington, D.C.: Association of Governing Boards of Universities and Colleges, 1993.

Brinkman, P. T. "Formula Budgeting: The Fourth Decade." In L. Leslie (ed.), *Responding to New Realities in Funding.* New Directions for Institutional Research, no. 43. San Francisco: Jossey-Bass, 1984.

Cage, M. C. "Recession Expected to Bring Long-Term Changes in State Colleges' Relations with Governments." *Chronicle of Higher Education,* 1991, 37(44), A1.

Carroll, S., and Bryton, E. "Higher Educations's Fiscal Future." American Council on Education, Washington, D.C., February 1997.

The College Board. *Trends in Student Aid: 1980 to 1990.* New York: College Entrance Examination Board, 1990.

Dill, D. D. "Higher Education Markets and Public Policy." *Higher Education Policy: The Quarterly Journal of the International Association of Universities.* September/November 1997, 10 (3/4), 167–185.

Halfond, J. A. "Too Many Administrators: How It Happened and How to Respond." *AAHE-Bulletin.* March 1991, pp. 7–8.

Halstead, K. *Higher Education Revenues and Expenditures: A Study of Institutional Costs.* Washington, D.C.: Research Associates of Washington, 1991.

Higher Education Surveys. *The Finances of Higher Education Institutions.* Higher Education Survey Report Number Eight, November. Sponsored by the National Science Foundation, the National Endowment for the Humanities, and the United States Department of Education, 1990.

Kuh, G. D., Schuh, J. H., Whitt, E. J., and Associates. *Involving Colleges.* San Francisco: Jossey-Bass, 1991.

Levy, S. R. "Sources of Current and Future Funding." In *Budgeting as a Tool for Policy in Student Affairs.* D. B. Woodard, Jr. (ed.), New Directions for Student Affairs, no. 70, Summer 1995, San Francisco, Jossey-Bass.

Lyons, J. W. "A Perspective on Cutting Student Affairs Budgets or How to Run a Blood Bank When Your Only Volunteers are Turnips." Paper presented at the National Association of Student Personnel Administrators Richard Stevens Institute, July 1991.

Meisinger, R. J., and Dubeck, L. W. *College and University Budgeting: An Introduction for Faculty and Academic Administrators.* Washington, D.C.: National Association of College and University Business Officers, 1984.

Morgan, A. W. "The New Strategies: Roots, Context, and Overview." In L. L. Leslie (ed.), *Responding to New Realities Funding.* San Francisco: Jossey-Bass, 1984.

Morrell, L. R. "Financial Strategy in Higher Education." *Business Officer,* 22(10), April, 1989, pp. 34–38.

Orwell, G. *Animal Farm.* New York: Harcourt Brace Jovanovich, 1954.

Pascarella, E. T., and Terenzini, P. T. *How College Affects Students.* San Francisco: Jossey-Bass, 1991.

Pew Policy Perspectives. "A Very Public Agenda." Pew Charitable Trust: Philadelphia, PA, September, 1998, pp. 1–12

Quping, P., and White, G. "The Marketization of Chinese Higher Education: A Critical Assessment." *Comparative Education,* 1994, 30(3), 217–237.

Schuh, J. (ed.). *Financial Management for Student Affairs Administrators.* Alexandria, VA: American College Personnel Association, 1990.

Slaughter, S. *Who Gets What and Why in Higher Education? Federal Policy and Supply-Side Institutional Resource Allocation.* Presidential speech presented at the annual meeting of the Association for the Study of Higher Education, Memphis, TN, 1997.

Slaughter, S., and Leslie, L. *Academic Capitalism.* Baltimore, MD: John Hopkins University Press, 1998.

Stocum, D. L., and Rooney, P. M. "Responding to Resource Constraints: A Departmentally Based System of Responsibility Center Management." *Change,* 29(5). September/October, 1997, pp. 51–57.

University of Arizona *Advisory Budget Priorities Planning Task Force.* Unpublished report. Tucson, AZ: University of Arizona, 1991.

Wildavsky, A. *The Politics of the Budgetary Process.* (3rd ed.) Boston: Little, Brown, 1988.

CHAPTER NINETEEN

UNDERSTANDING THE LEGAL IMPLICATIONS OF STUDENT AFFAIRS PRACTICE

Donald D. Gehring

Justice Cardoza once said "The law never is, but is always about to be," recognizing that the law is always changing. Indeed, since the original publication of this chapter in 1993, the law has changed. Kaplin's (1985) statement that the law "has spoken forcefully and meaningfully to the higher education community and will continue to do so" (p. ix) is, however, still true today.

This chapter will familiarize the reader with the legal relationships that students have with their institutions by including the most up-to-date laws, regulations, and interpretations that exist at this writing. The chapter begins with a brief discussion of the institutional relationship with students and an overview of the judicial system. Discussion then focuses on torts, contracts, statutes, and constitutional issues. A brief summary is then provided.

Student/Institutional Relationship

Administrators have an obligation to stay abreast of the law and to understand the legal parameters defining the institution's relationship with students. The policies, programs, and practices of the institution must be in accord with current laws, rules, regulations, and judicial interpretations. The best way to understand these parameters is to become familiar with the different types of legal relationships students have with their institutions.

Students, as residents of the United States, have certain guarantees set forth in the amendments to the federal constitution. They are also residents of a particular state and thereby enjoy certain rights provided for in state constitutions. It is necessary to understand the rights that students have under both the federal and state constitutions and to apply those to student affairs programs, policies, and practices. Careful analysis must be made because constitutional protections are not necessarily guaranteed in private institutions.

Another legal relationship stems from the rights and responsibilities pertaining to students as defined in specific state and federal laws. These laws are often very general in nature and, therefore, rules and regulations are written to enforce the law. Such rules and regulations carry the full force of the law.

Students also contract for goods and services with their college or university. These contracts are both explicit and implicit and define yet another relationship with the college or university. Finally, students and all others have a right to be free from intrusion upon their person, their property, and their reputation. In almost all states, certain minimum rights and duties are defined by judicial precedent developed from English common law and, thereby, define our relationships with others. A violation of these minimum standards constitutes a tort. Thus, the four primary relationships between students and their institutions can be classified as torts, contracts, statutes, and constitution.

The Judicial System

The function of our judicial system is to settle controversies, decide the constitutionality of laws, and to interpret laws. State courts generally decide disputes between state residents, decide on the constitutionality of state laws, or interpret them. They are limited in their jurisdiction to the laws of that state and its geographic area. Federal courts, in terms of this discussion, decide questions pertaining to federal laws and settle disputes between citizens of different states. These courts also have jurisdiction over a specific geographic area. The decision of a court of geographic jurisdiction is only binding on that particular geographic area. A decision by a California court, therefore, does not bind administrators in New Jersey. However, the reasoning of the California court may be persuasive and adopted by New Jersey courts (see, for example, *Tarasoff v. Regents of the University of California*, 1976 and *McIntosh v. Milano*, 1979). Similarly, a decision by the United States Fifth Circuit Court of Appeals is not binding on and may even be the opposite of a similar case decided by the Fourth Circuit Court of Appeals (see *Rowinsky v. Bryan Independent School District*, 1996 and *Brozonkala v. Virginia Polytechnic Institute*, 1997). Only cases decided by the United States Supreme Court are binding on all United States citizens.

Finally, administrators must understand that the laws of the various states as well as the interpretations of their courts may differ. To illustrate, in a tort situation in Pennsylvania, a student organization may be held liable in the case of someone injured by an intoxicated guest who was served alcoholic beverages at one of the organization's parties. The same situation in Virginia might not attach any liability to the organization.

Torts

The word *tort* comes from the Latin word *torquere,* meaning to twist. Thus, a tort would constitute a "twisted relationship." Specifically, a tort is a civil wrong other than the breach of a contract for which the courts will provide a remedy. The remedy is generally in the form of monetary damages, of which there are two types: compensatory and punitive. Compensatory damages seek to make injured persons "whole" again, or as much as possible, put them back into the position they were in before the injury was suffered. It is, therefore, easy to understand why damages are sometimes assessed at such high levels. Punitive damages, by contrast, are assessed where the injury is caused by willful acts without regard for another's person, property, or reputation and serve as punishment.

Negligence

The tort of negligence involves the breach of a duty owed. To be found liable for negligence, four elements must exist. First, a duty must be present. Second, the duty must have been breached. Third, an injury must occur, and fourth, the breach of duty must be the proximate cause of the injury.

If there is no duty, there can be no breach and thus no negligence. It is imperative to understand what duties exist. Prosser (1971) cautions " . . . 'duty' is not sacrosanct in itself, but only an expression of the sum total of those considerations of policy which lead the law to say that the particular plaintiff is entitled to protection" (p. 326).

The courts have recognized three general duties of institutions of higher education: to provide proper supervision; to furnish proper instruction; and to maintain equipment in a reasonable state of repair. College students are generally legal adults and therefore require less supervision (*Mintz v. State*, 1975); however, as those under 18 years of age are considered "children of tender years" by the courts, the concept of *in loco parentis* may still be applicable. In one case, a high school student enrolled in a special summer program at Montana State University (MSU) was injured after attending a party where alcoholic beverages were served. The Montana Supreme Court noted that, "when MSU undertook to have

Kimberly live on its campus and supervise her during the MAP program, it assumed a custodial role similar to that imposed on a high school because Kimberly is a juvenile. Once MSU assumed that role, it was charged with exercising reasonable care in supervising the MAP participants" (*Graham v. Montana State University*, 1988 at 304). After a university permits the enrollment of a student, reasonable care in supervision must occur. With minors, an entirely separate and more restrictive set of regulations may be imposed in order to meet the obligation of closer supervision (*Stone v. Cornell University*, 1987).

Several jurisdictions have held that unless a "special relationship" exists, there is no custodial duty or duty to control the conduct of students (*Bradshaw v. Rawlings*, 1979; *University of Denver v. Whitlock*, 1987; *Smith v. Day*, 1987). However, in Delaware the Supreme Court recognized a unique relationship between students and their institutions in which the university does exercise some control over the lives of students and may be held liable for failing to exercise supervision over fraternity hazing activities (*Furek v. University of Delaware*, 1991).

Student affairs practitioners engage in a variety of instructional activities and in doing so are held to a standard of providing proper instruction. They must provide careful information on the operation of equipment such as the use of stage equipment in productions (*Potter v. North Carolina School of Arts*, 1978) or how to adjust ski bindings on a spring break outing (*Meese v. Brigham Young University*, 1981).

The institution is also required to inspect its premises for defects and then make the necessary repairs. When a student was injured attempting to open a window, an Ohio court of appeals held that a university had not met a standard of reasonable care, regardless of the fact that it had made periodic inspections of every window in the residence halls (*Shetina v. Ohio University*, 1983). Intramural directors should also regularly inspect playing surfaces (*Drew v. State*, 1989; *Henig v. Hofstra University*, 1990).

Violence. Violence is a significant problem on campuses (Palmer, 1993). Although colleges and universities are generally under no duty to protect students from the violent acts of third persons (Prosser, §314, 1971), there are certain special relationships that involve a duty to protect. The landlord-tenant relationship is a well defined special relationship; although "[t]he landlord is no insurer of his tenants' safety, . . . he certainly is no bystander" (*Kline v. Massachusetts Avenue Apartment Corp.*, 1970 at 481). Not being a bystander includes taking preventative action to minimize predictable risks (*Miller v. State*, 1984). A university is also a common carrier when it operates elevators and as such has a special relationship exists with those who ride, requiring that the institution protect them from unreasonable risk of harm (*Houck v. University of Washington*, 1991). In addition, a landowner (university) has a duty to protect invitees (students and others who come on the property to do business with the institution) from unreasonable risks (*Bearman v. University of Notre Dame*, 1983; *Schultz v. Gould Academy*, 1975). Where the risk is not foreseeable, liability will not attach (*Relyea v. State*, 1980; *Hall v. Board of Supervisors, Southern University*, 1981). As a general guide, what must be remembered is that "[t]he risk reasonably to be perceived defines the duty to be obeyed" (*Palsgraf v. Long Island R.R. Co.*, 1928 at 100).

Universities do not normally take custody of students, and the courts generally agree that colleges and universities do not exercise control over adult students. Nevertheless, in at least one jurisdiction, it has been held that when students elect to live in campus housing they yield control of their own protection. (In other words, they cannot protect themselves with weapons or dogs and are not allowed to change or modify door hardware.) Thus, they surrender control to the institution (*Duarte v. State*, 1978). In this case, the university has a special relationship to resident students and, thus, a duty to protect them from foreseeable violence.

The courts have also defined the relationship between a therapist and a client to be a special one. If, in the exercise of professional judgment, the therapist determines that the client's conduct needs to be controlled, and there is a foreseeable victim, the therapist has a legal duty to warn or protect the intended victim (*Tarasoff, supra*; *McIntosh, supra*). The circumstances will determine whether the therapists need only warn the intended victim or whether they have a duty to protect. This duty is applicable to *professional* therapists, and an attempt to apply the standard to a paraprofessional who failed to report a suicidal youth was rejected in the same jurisdiction that decided *Tarasoff* (*Nally v. Grace Community Church of the Valley*, 1987). In at least one case, it has been held that the intended victim need not be a person, but could be property (*Peck v. Counseling Service of Addison County, Inc.*, 1985). Many states now have specific legislation defining the duties of mental health professionals who deal with violent clients. Because significant differences exist between the states in this area of law, administrators should consult with counsel concerning the applicable law in their state. It is also helpful to develop a policy of consulting with other mental health professionals when dealing with dangerous clients because the law will hold therapists to a standard of care exercised by members of the profession (Gehring, 1991).

Providing security or police services on campus creates yet another duty related to care. The law recognizes that if an institution voluntarily renders a service for the protection of another and the other person relies on that service, reasonable care must be exercised in providing it (Prosser, §323, 1971). This duty was the basis for finding Pine Manor College liable for the rape of one of its students (*Mullins v. Pine Manor College*, 1983). The Supreme Judicial Court of Massachusetts stated, in part: "Colleges generally undertake voluntarily to provide their students with protection from criminal acts of third parties. . . . Adequate security is an indispensable part of the bundle of services which colleges, and Pine Manor, afford their students" (at 336).

Alcoholic Beverages. Violent acts and alcoholic beverages often seem to be connected (Gadaleto and Anderson, 1986; Wechsler, Moeykens, and DeJong, ND). Administrators should know the laws of their state pertaining to liability associated with the violation of alcoholic beverage statutes. In some states, violating alcoholic beverage laws constitutes negligence *per se*. Two of the more significant areas of alcohol-related liability are dramshop and social host liability. The two are similar except that dramshop liability applies to licensed vendors, whereas social host liability applies to those who are not licensed but gratuitously provide alcohol to others. The potential for liability arises when one sells or provides alcoholic beverages to a minor or an intoxicated person and that individual causes injury to another as a result of their intoxication. In addition to suing the person who caused the injury, the dramshop and social host liability theories hold that the injured person may also sue the provider of the alcoholic beverages for negligence. Not all states recognize dramshop liability and even fewer recognize social host liability. The trend, however, seems to favor the imposition of liability on the provider (Gehring and Geraci, 1989). Most recently the state of Arizona has recognized social host liability (*Estate of Hernandez v. Board of Regents*, 1994).

At least two states, Louisiana and Wisconsin, hold the provider of alcoholic beverages liable for injuries suffered by individuals who have been forced to consume or who have been falsely told a beverage contains no alcohol. In Illinois, the courts have held that fraternities have a duty to refrain from requiring pledges to consume excessive amounts of alcohol; in South Carolina, the court held that fraternities have a duty not to harm pledges (*Quinn v. Sigma Rho Chapter Beta Theta Pi Fraternity*, 1987; *Ballou v. Sigma Nu General Fraternity*, 1986).

Because of the differences in state laws and judicial interpretations, student affairs administrators must stay current regarding statutes involving alcoholic beverages. Added incentives are the Drug Free Schools and Communities Act Amendments of 1989, which require that institutions annually notify *each* student of the local, state, and federal laws for the unlawful possession, use, or distribution of alcohol.

Defamation

False statements about students, or others, that hold them up to ridicule or disgrace may constitute the tort of defamation. Both libel (written) and slander (spoken) are included in defamation. In order to be defamatory, a statement must be a false statement made by one person to another about a third person that ridicules or disgraces the third person. Generally the false statement must injure the third person's reputation; however, it is often not necessary for that person to show injury if he or she is falsely accused of having a loathsome social disease, being unchaste (*Wardlaw v. Peck*, 1984), or having committed a crime (*Melton v. Bow*, 1978). The best advice is to speak and write the truth. If the statements being made are professional opinions, the recipient of that communication should be so informed and the basis of the opinion should be stated (*Olsson v. Indiana University Board of Trustees*, 1991).

Student editors are accountable for what they publish and, therefore, risk liability when they print false information (*Ithaca College v. Yale Daily News Publishing Co., Inc.*, 1980). When a student editor responded to a critical letter with a rebuttal that contained sexual innuendoes, the court held that the statement presented a libel question for a jury (*Brooks v. Stone*, 1984). In New York, student editors were held liable for defamation when they published a letter purportedly sent by two students who said they were gay. The two complained that they had never written the letter and were not gay, and the newspaper printed a retraction and an apology. The court held that the failure of the editors to check the authorship of the letter was irresponsible, negating any qualified privilege they might have had (*Mazart v. State*, 1981). It will become even more important for student newspaper editors to understand the legal parameters of defamation as they seek and obtain information on campus judicial hearings under the newly enacted Higher Education Amendments of 1998 (Sec. 951).

Finally, as students log onto the Internet and chat rooms, where their messages have the potential to be read by people all over the world, it is imperative that they be familiar with the parameters of defamation. It's all too easy to write something that is not true about another person that causes them injury while sitting in front of one's own computer in one's own room—it feels very private, but it is very public (Washington Post, 1996). Damages in defamation cases are predicated on how much harm was done. When a false statement is communicated to thousands, even millions of others, the damage to someone's reputation can be astronomical. Institutions should provide students and faculty with training in the law of defamation before ever issuing an account to use the university server. As long as the university is simply a conduit and not the publisher of the defamatory material, it would probably not be liable for defamatory statements made by students or others using the university server as long as the university was not aware it was circulating defamatory material (*Zeran v. America Online, Inc.*, 1997).

Tort Liability Defenses

The best defense is to fulfill all duties. The courts will not generally attach liability when students engage in activity known to be dangerous. When a twenty-five-year-old student with documented health problems died after completing a two-and-a-half-mile race in the tropics, the college sponsoring the race was not held to be liable. The student assumed the risk of injury by participating in the activity with the knowledge of his condition and the environment (*Gehling v. St. George University School of Medicine*, 1989). In addition, students who contribute to their own negligence may be barred from recovering damages. Some states, however, have comparative liability where damages are assessed on the basis of the degree of fault (*Zavala v. Regents of University of California*, 1981). Sovereign immunity, which insulates public officials from suit when carrying out their duties, should generally not be relied upon as a defense. Sovereign or governmental immunity only applies to public institutions, and many states have now abrogated the concept. The best defense against tort liability is to know the legal duties and fulfill them. If the act is reasonable and treatment to others is proper, liability will probably not attach.

Contracts

Contract law is a civil matter that can lead to damages, and differs from state to state. Although there is no way to cover all the differences and nuances of contract law in this chapter, several general principles will be provided. Understanding some of these will aid in avoiding liability.

A *contract* is defined generally as "[a] promise or set of promises for the breach of which the law gives a remedy or the performance of which the law in some way recognizes as a duty" (*American Law Institute*, 1981, p. 5). The elements that must be present in a contract are a promise or a set of promises; an offer and an acceptance; an agreement of what is to be gained and what is to be given up to gain it; and an agreement between the parties so that both have the same understanding.

Contracts may either be explicit or implicit, written or oral. An implicit understanding exists that if students pay tuition and meet the established academic and social requirements, they will receive a degree.

> The elements of a traditional contract are present in the implied contract between a college and a student attending that college, and are readily discernible. The student's tender of an application constitutes an offer to apply to the college. By 'accepting' an applicant to be a student at the college, the college accepts the applicant's offer. Thereafter, the student pays tuition (which obviously constitutes sufficient consideration), attends classes, completes course work and takes tests. The school provides the student with facilities and instruction and upon satisfactory completion of the school's academic requirements (which constitutes performance), the school becomes obligated to issue the student a diploma [*Johnson v. Lincoln Christian College*, 1986 at 1348].

One court has even held that this implied contract contemplates that the degree awarded will be an accredited one if that is required for the licensure examination (*Behrend v. State*, 1977). Where students are not required to be graduates of accredited programs to take such licensure examinations, failing to inform them that the degree was not accredited does not constitute a breach of contract (*Lidecker v. Kendall College*, 1990).

Explicit contracts are created with students for housing and other services and for admission to the institution. When a medical college stated in a brochure that applicants would be judged on the basis of the criteria listed in the brochure and then assessed them on an additional financial criterion, the action was held to be a breach of contract with the applicant (*Steinberg v. Chicago Medical School*, 1977). The terms and conditions of the contract found in brochures, handbooks, and other documents published by the institution that set forth promises are usually interpreted by the courts by applying the normal meaning of the words (*Warren v. Drake University*, 1989; *Delta School of Business, Etc. v. Shropshire*, 1981).

Not all contracts are written, and even oral statements can constitute promises offered. United States Merchant Marine Academy officials promised several midshipmen immunity if they spoke freely about marijuana use at the Academy. After admitting their own use, the midshipmen were dismissed from the Academy. The court reversed the suspensions, saying, "as agents, the questioners were authorized to make promises . . . Plaintiffs, by speaking freely, accepted this offer, and a contract was made. The Academy is bound by this agreement" (*Krawez v. Stans*, 1969 at 1235).

In some cases, the terms and conditions of the contract may be changed by the institution without breaching the contract. When Vassar changed its rules to allow male visitation in the residence halls, the mother of one of the students unsuccessfully sued for breach of contract (*Jones v. Vassar*, 1969). When a graduate student was obliged to take a comprehensive exam that was not part of the requirements for a degree listed in the catalog, the change was not held to breach the contract (*Mahavongsana v. Hall*, 1976).

The courts have also recognized disclaimers published in institutional catalogs. These disclaimers disavow the catalog as a contract and allow the institution more flexibility. A nursing student who was unsuccessful in appealing his failing grade claimed the university breached its contract with him by failing to follow the terms outlined in the catalog. The court, however, noted that the catalog contained a disclaimer statement and thus there was no enforceable contract (*Tobias v. University of Texas*, 1991). The Supreme Court of Montana found that a catalog statement allowing the university to change its curriculum and apply the new requirements to current as well as new students was not an abuse of discretion (*Bindrim v. University of Montana*, 1988).

It may be tempting to entice students with promises of extraordinary programs and services. Yet that practice is also risky. The best advice is to provide everything that is promised and do not promise anything that can not be provided. Catalogs, brochures, and handbooks should be reviewed with input from legal counsel. As a final word of caution, administrators should always sign both their names and their official titles to protect themselves against individual liability for goods and services they may contract for as agents of the institution. This practice will indicate that the officials were acting for the institution and were not contracting in an individual capacity. Finally, administrators should be careful not to use legal terminology in their codes of conduct. Public institutions that define sexual assault as "rape" as an offense or private colleges that use "due process" may be held to proving the criminal elements of rape or providing all the elements of due process respectively. Stoner and Creminara (1990) also suggest avoiding legal terminology for additional reasons.

Statutes

Many state and federal laws provide students with specific rights in their relationship with institutions. Violating these rights can lead to criminal action as well as civil liability. Administrators must be aware of these laws and their proscriptions. Although it is not possible to cover the laws of each state in this chapter, the campus library will usually maintain a set of state statutes. These volumes are indexed and can be retrieved by looking under headings for "Colleges and Universities" or "Schools and Colleges."

This section will focus only on the federal laws that affect student affairs programs, policies, and practices. Such statutes are authorized by the power of the Congress to regulate interstate commerce and to provide for the general welfare. After it is enacted, the law must be implemented by the appropriate agency of the executive branch. Statutes are sometimes interpreted by the judicial branch. It is not enough to know the law; those in student affairs must also understand what the regulations say and the judicial interpretations of those laws and regulations.

Title VI

Although the federal government has been making laws affecting higher education since before the 1862 Morrill Act, the most recent and direct impact has been the Civil Rights Act of 1964. Title VI of that Act provides: "No person in the United States shall, on the ground of race, color or national origin, be excluded from participation in, be denied the benefits of, or be subjected to discrimination under any program or activity receiving federal financial assistance" (42 USC 2000(d)).

Title IX of the Education Amendments of 1972 (prohibition against sex discrimination) and Section 504 of the Rehabilitation Act of 1973 (prohibition against discrimination on the basis of handicap) were modeled after Title VI. Therefore, cases interpreting the general application of Title VI would be the same for Title IX and Section 504. Although Title VI has been interpreted to mean that a recipient of federal financial assistance was any institution where even one student attended under any type of federal aid (*Bob Jones University v. Johnson*, 1974; *Grove City College v. Bell*, 1984), the question of how to define a program or activity remained. The Civil Rights Restoration Act of 1987 defined a program or activity under all three statutes to constitute all the operations of the college or university. Thus, whether a specific program receives any federal funding is immaterial. If there is one student attending the institution who receives federal financial aid, everything that school does must conform to Title VI, Title IX, and Section 504, including noncredit and nondegree courses (*Radcliff v. Landau*, 1989; *United States v. Board of Trustees for University of Alabama*, 1990).

The most famous Title VI case involved the denial of admission to medical school of a white applicant because the institution had specifically reserved a number of spaces for minority candidates (*Regents v. Bakke*, 1978). The Supreme Court held that an admissions quota violated Title VI, but institutions could *consider* race as one of several factors in their admissions decisions. Two subsequent cases in which race was considered, but was not the sole factor in the admission decision, were *McDonald v. Hogness* (1979) and *DeRonde v. Regents of University of California*, (1981). The state supreme court in both cases upheld the process. Thus, when race is the sole factor in making an admission or other decision, it probably violates Title VI (*Uzzell v. Friday*, 1979).

Two more recent decisions, one by the Fourth Circuit Court of Appeals (*Podberesky v. Kirwan*, 1994) and the other by the Fifth Circuit Court of Appeals (*Hopwood v. University of Texas*, 1996), however, have rejected using race as a factor in the distribution of financial aid and admissions, respectively. In striking down the use of race as a factor, the courts applied the traditional equal protection test of the 14th Amendment rather than the Title VI analysis that was used in *Regents of University of California v. Bakke* (1978) and subsequent cases. The courts sought to determine two questions: does the racial classification serve a compelling governmental interest; and is the racial classification narrowly tailored to achieve the goal? Using race as a factor failed on both counts. The Fifth Circuit specifically rejected the rationale of Justice Powell that using race as a factor would be justified as a means of diversifying the student body. Citing more recent Supreme Court opinions, the Fifth Circuit specifically held that using race as a factor to overcome past discrimination could be justified only if the entity trying to correct the present effects was the one that had discriminated in the past. The Supreme Court denied a review, but that does not mean the Court agrees or disagrees with the Fifth Circuit (*Texas v. Hopwood*, 1996). This is an area of the law that bears careful watching in the future.

Regulations implementing Title VI (34 C.F.R. 100), Title IX (34 C.F.R. 106), and Section 504 (34 C.F.R. 104) each provide a mechanism for administrative procedures against those who violate the law. If those attempts are not successful, the Department of Education must seek the approval of Congress to revoke the institution's federal financial assistance, the penalty for violations. Students, however, may initiate their own legal action and need not wait for the government to act (*Cannon v. University of Chicago*, 1979).

Title IX

While Title IX was originally enacted to provide an equal opportunity for women in programs and activities, it has also been held to prohibit sexual harassment by faculty and staff (*Alexander v. Yale University*, 1980; *Bougher v. University of Pittsburg*, 1989). This includes both *quid pro quo* (something for something) and hostile environment sexual harassment (*Patricia H. v. Berkeley Unified School District*, 1993). The Supreme Court has also held that under Title IX a student may recover damages for sexual harassment (*Franklin v. Gwinnett County. Public Schools*, 1992). The court has also defined the standard to be used to determine the liability of the institution when faculty or staff sexually harass a student (*Gebser v. Lago Vista Independent School District*, 1998). Although this case arose in a secondary school, it would be equally applicable to a college or university. The court held that for the institution to be liable for the sexually harassing actions of employees, someone with power over the offending employee must be notified of the harassment. In addition, the person in power who was notified must act with "deliberate indifference" in failing to take action. The issue of student-to-student sexual harassment is not as clear. Several circuit courts of appeals are in disagreement over whether an institution may be liable under Title IX for the sexual harassment of one student by another (compare *Rowinsky v. Bryan Independent School District*, 1996 and *Davis v. Monroe Board of Education*, 1996 to *Doe v. University of Illinois*, 1998 and *Brozonkala v. Virginia Polytechnic Institute*, 1997). As of this writing, the Supreme Court has decided to hear the *Davis* (1996) case, which will help to clarify this significant and increasing area of litigation.

Regulations implementing Title IX (34 C.F.R. 106) also have specific sections dealing with campus rules, athletics, student organizations, and the provision of housing, counseling, and placement services.

Section 504

Section 504 prohibits discrimination against "otherwise qualified handicapped" persons. A handicapped person is one who is physically or mentally impaired to the point that one or more major life activities is substantially limited, has a record of having such an impairment, or is considered to have the impairment. An otherwise qualified handicapped individual is one who can perform the essential functions in spite of the handicap (*Southeastern Community College v. Davis*, 1979); *Doe v. New York University*, 1981). Although institutions are required to make reasonable accommodations for disabled students, they are not required to eliminate courses essential to the nature of the degree (*Guckenberg v. Boston University*, 1997, 1998). This is particularly significant in medical and other health-related degrees (*Doherty v. Southern College of Optometry*, 1988; *Ohio Civil Rights Commission v. Case Western Reserve*, 1996), but blanket decisions that there would be absolutely no substitutions for foreign language or mathematics are a violation (*Guckenberg v. Boston University*, 1997). However, reasonable accommodations such as providing a guide dog, taped lectures, or a sign language interpreter may be required to permit the handicapped individual to perform essential functions. Several judicial decisions have indicated that auxiliary aids are to be paid for by the state rehabilitation agencies and not colleges and universities (*Jones v. Illinois Department of Rehabilitation Services*, 1981; *Schornstein v. New Jersey Division of Vocational Rehabilitational Services*, 1981). The requirement to provide auxiliary aids to disabled students applies whether the student is enrolled in credit or noncredit courses and must be provided unless doing so creates an "undue financial or administrative burden." The courts construe this latter term strictly (*United States v. Board of Trustees for University of Alabama*, 1990). The Washington Supreme Court, however, has upheld the denial of state rehabilitation funds to a blind student who wanted to pursue a ministerial degree because the state constitution prohibited providing public moneys for religious instruction (*Witters v. Washington Department of Services for the Blind*, 1989). Although drug addicts and alcoholics are considered handicapped, they, like all handicapped students, must conform to the institution's reasonable rules and regulations (*Anderson v. University of Wisconsin*, 1988).

In *School Board of Nassau County, Florida v. Arline* (1987), the United States Supreme Court ruled that a contagious disease constituted a handicap under Section 504. The disease in *Arline* was tuberculosis, and the Court held that fear of contagion alone was not sufficient for dismissal of a handicapped person. In determining whether the handicapped person is otherwise qualified, administrators should seek medical advice including how the disease is transmitted, how long the carrier will be capable of transmitting the disease; what the potential risk is to third parties; and what the probability is that the disease will be transmitted and cause harm. Obviously symptomatic AIDS is a contagious disease, but even more difficult to transmit than tuberculosis. Two federal courts have applied the above test to a third-year dental student (*Doe v. Washington University*, 1991) and in both cases found the individuals posed a significant risk to the health and safety of others.

For purposes of Section 504 as it relates to employment, the Civil Rights Restoration Act of 1987 indicates that a handicapped person "does not include an individual who has a currently contagious disease or infection and who, by reason of such disease or infection, would constitute a direct threat to the health or safety of other individuals, or who by reason of currently contagious disease or infection, is unable to perform the duties of the job" (42 USC 2000d – 4a).

FERPA

Other federal laws directly affecting colleges and universities include the Family Educational Rights and Privacy Act (FERPA or the Buckley Amendment). FERPA provides that "No funds shall be made available . . . to . . . any institution of higher education . . . which has a policy of denying, or which effectively prevents the parents of students attending . . . the right to inspect and review any and all official records . . . " [PL 93–380 Sec. 438(a)(1)]. The rights of the parent revert to the student when the student attains eighteen years of age or enters a postsecondary institution unless the student remains financially dependent on the parent for tax purposes.

Administrators should read the law (20 USC 1232g) and the implementing regulations (34 CFR 99) in their entirety to understand both requirements and exceptions. The Higher Education Amendments of 1998 amended FERPA to allow institutions to notify parents or legal guardians of any student who is under twenty-one years of age and has committed a disciplinary violation governing the use or possession of alcohol or a controlled substance (Higher Education Amendments of 1998, Sec. 952). However, the law is permissive and also allows institutions to withhold such information from the parents under institutional policy. Any policy, however, must be written and available to everyone in the college community. Students may not sue to enforce their FERPA rights (*Smith v. Duquesne University*, 1985), but must rely on the government to effectuate compliance. However, students whose FERPA rights have been violated may bring suit under 42 USC 1983 for a deprivation of federal rights (*Tarka v. Cunningham*, 1989; *Lewin v. Medical College of Hampton Roads*, 1996). Such suits only result in nominal damages ($1.00) unless the student can prove actual damages.

Under the revised rules, police incident reports are not protected by FERPA (34 CFR 99.8). There is some question whether FERPA prohibits disclosure of disciplinary records. Although the regulations define disciplinary records as "educational records" (60 Fed. Reg. 3465), which may not be disclosed without the consent of the students involved, the Ohio Supreme Court has held that individual student disciplinary records are not "educational records" (*State ex rel The Miami Student v. Miami University*, 1997). The Georgia Supreme Court has held that campus disciplinary records related to student organizations are not protected from disclosure (*Red and Black Publishing Co., Inc. v. Board of Regents*, 1993), whereas courts in Louisiana (*Shreveport Professional Chapter of the Society of Professional Journalists and Michelle Millohollon v. Louisiana State University in Shreveport*, 1994) and North Carolina (*D.T.H. Public Corporation v. University of North Carolina at Chapel Hill*, 1998) have held that individual disciplinary records are protected from disclosure by FERPA. A suit by the Department of Education to enjoin enforcement of the courts' order in the Ohio case and to declare disciplinary records as "educational records" has, however, been brought in federal district court. The outcome should clarify the issue (*United States v. Miami University*, 1998).

The Higher Education Amendments of 1998 provide that FERPA does not preclude institutions from disclosing the nature of the violation, sanction, and name of a perpetrator who has been found responsible for an act of violence (as defined in 18 U.S.C. 16) or a nonforcible sexual offense (Higher Education Amendments 1998, Sec. 951). For public institutions, this means that because the record is not protected by law, access to this information may probably be gained through state freedom of information acts (FOIA). Caution must be exercised in disclosing information, however, because college disciplinary hearings do not involve proving the elements of a crime of violence and falsely accusing someone of a crime could be defamation. Administrators should read the law and consult with counsel before complying with this section of the law.

Other Statutes

Two newer federal laws influencing student affairs programs, policies, and practices are the Drug Free Schools and Communities Act of 1989 (20 USC 1145) and the Student Right-to-Know and Campus Security Act (20 USC 1092(f)). The Drug Free Schools and Communities Act Amendments of 1989 mandate that institutions annually distribute to each student and employee specific written information regarding standards of conduct that prohibit unlawful possession, use, and distribution of drugs and alcohol; a description of applicable local, state, and federal laws concerning the unlawful possession, use, or distribution of illicit drugs and alcohol; a description of health risks associated with the use of illicit drugs and alcohol; a description of rehabilitation and treatment programs available; and a statement that the institution will impose sanctions for violations of its standards.

It is not enough to simply make the information available; it must be provided in writing to every student and employee (see Comments 55 FR 33595). Institutions must also conduct a biennial review of drug and alcohol programs to determine if they are effective, what changes need to be made, and whether disciplinary sanctions are consistently enforced.

The Student Right-to-Know and Campus Security Act as amended by the Higher Education Amendments of 1998 requires institutions to report graduation rates for athletes and others, revenues and expenses for men's and women's teams, and crime statistics. The Campus Security Act section of the law requires the publication of campus crime statistics and a variety of other information in a security report that must be provided to each current student and employee. Prospective students must be given a summary of the contents of the report and an opportunity to request a copy. The Act also mandates that victims of sexual offenses "must" be informed of the outcome of disciplinary hearings against the perpetrator and institutions "will" change a victim's academic and living conditions after an alleged sex offense if, after notice of this option, the victim requests it and the change is reasonably available. The regulations appear at 34 CFR 668.46–.49. There are aspects of this law that are somewhat troubling (Gehring, 1991) and administrators must stay abreast of the developments.

The Civil Rights Act of 1871 (42 U.S.C. 1983) creates civil liability for public officials who violate the constitutional or statutory rights of others. The law has been interpreted to apply to public officials carrying out their duties when doing so violates the "basic unquestionable" rights of students (*Wood v. Strickland*, 1975). Damages assessed under 42 U.S.C. 1983 are limited to $1.00 unless specific injury, beyond the violation of one's rights, can be shown (*Carey v. Piphus*, 1978). The Supreme Court has also held that 42 U.S.C. 1983 can be used as the basis for liability "where the failure to train amounts to deliberate indifference to the rights of persons with whom the police come into contact" (*City of Canton, Ohio v. Harris*, 1989 at 426). The same reasoning was applied in a case where police received no training about AIDS and told a woman that she needed to wash after touching her neighbor's truck because he had AIDS (*Doe v. Borough of Barrington*, 1990). Thus, resident assistants, campus police, or any other state employee who works directly with students must be properly trained, as actual damages are likely where there is a "deliberate indifference" judgment; and actual damages will be considerably higher than the $1.00 nominal charge that can be assessed under 42 USC 1983.

Many other federal laws have a more indirect influence on student affairs programs and policies. These include the Copyright Revision Act (Title 17 United

States Code with regulations at 37 CFR 201–204), Human Subjects Research Act (45 CFR 46), and Americans with Disabilities Act (42 USC 12101 et seq.). In addition, personnel laws affect hiring and employment. Some examples are Title VII of the Civil Rights Act (42 USC 2000(e)2 with regulations at 29 CFR 1601 and sexual harassment guidelines at 24 CFR 1604), the Equal Pay Act of 1963 (29 USC 206(d) with regulations at 29 CFR 806), the Age Discrimination in Employment Act of 1967 (29 USC 621 with interpretations at 29 CFR 860), the Fair Labor Standards Act of 1938 (29 USC 201), Executive Order 11246 as amended (32 FR 14303 with regulations at 41 CFR 60, 41 CFR 60–2, and Employee Selection Guidelines at 41 FR 29016), and the Age Discrimination Act of 1975 (42 USC 6101). Institutional personnel offices can assist in understanding both rights and obligations under these laws.

Constitutional Issues

The United States Constitution is the highest law in the land and describes the relationship between the three branches of government. The Bill of Rights sets forth the minimum rights of persons residing in the country. No state constitution or federal or state law may conflict with the federal constitution. Although no state constitution may grant fewer rights than the federal constitution, many states grant more rights than are found in the federal constitution (e.g., *State v. Schmid*, 1980; *Witters, supra*; *Washington v. Chrisman*, 1982). The guarantees set forth in the federal Constitution, however, protect persons against actions by the government or its agencies only. The Constitution "erects no shield against purely private conduct" (*Shelley v. Kraemer*, 1947 at 1180). Only if private colleges are shown to be engaged in "state action" are they required to conform to the guarantees found in the Constitution.

The courts determine state action by "sifting facts and weighing circumstances" (*Burton v. Wilmington Parking Authority*, 1961). The mere receipt of federal or state funding is certainly not enough to show state action (*Grossner v. Trustees of Columbia University*, 1968; *Torres v. Puerto Rico Junior College*, 1969), nor is the fact that the state approves the curriculum, accredits the institution, or grants it a tax exemption or powers of eminent domain (*Rowe v. Chandler*, 1971; *Berrios v. Inter American University*, 1976; *Browns v. Mitchell*, 1969; *Blackburn v. Fisk University*, 1971 respectively). The courts are generally reluctant to find state action. However, racial discrimination weighs heavily—where it has been present, a private college has been held to have engaged in state action and thus required to comply with constitutional mandates (*Hammond v. Tampa*, 1965).

The First Amendment

The First Amendment, which permeates almost every aspect of student affairs administration, provides that "Congress shall make no laws respecting the establishment of religion or prohibiting the free exercise thereof: or abridging the freedom of speech or of the press; or the right of the people peaceably to assemble; and to petition the Government for a redress of grievances."

Establishment and Free Exercise of Religion. This prohibition is primarily involved in situations in which federal or state assistance of some type is provided to religiously affiliated institutions. The assistance need not be financial; it can be any type of assistance that puts the government's "stamp of approval" on a sectarian activity. Determination if there is a violation of the establishment clause rests on a three-pronged test established by the Supreme Court. The test asks whether the aid reflects a clearly secular purpose, has a primary effect which neither advances nor inhibits religion, and avoids excessive entanglement between the church and government (*Lemon v. Kurtzman*, 1971). Balancing the establishment clause against the rights of free speech was the essence of a case involving the allocation of student activity fees to a student organization "whose purpose was [t]o publish a magazine of philosophical and religious expression" (*Rosenberger v. Rector and Visitors of the University of Virginia* at 2510, 1995). The Supreme Court, noting that "Vital First Amendment speech principles are at stake here" (at 2535) held that withholding funds from the organization constituted viewpoint discrimination. Further, denial of free speech could foster an attitude of hostility to religion, thereby undermining the "neutrality" the establishment clause requires. When a public university placed a student teacher at a parochial school, a federal court found that although the placement served a valid secular purpose, it advanced religion by creating a perception that the state endorsed the school's religious mission (*Stark v. St. Cloud State University*, 1986).

State and federal financial aid may be provided to students at church-related institutions or to the institution itself without offending the establishment clause so long as the aid meets the *Lemon* test (*Tilton v. Richardson*, 1970; *Roemer v. Board of Public Works*, 1976; and *Americans United v. Rogers*, 1976). If public institutions permit student religious groups to use facilities for religious services, there is no violation of the establishment clause, but prohibiting such use could violate the group's right to free speech (*University of Delaware v. Keegan*, 1975; *Widmar v. Vincent*, 1981).

Freedom of Speech and Press. The freedom of speech and press guaranteed in the First Amendment is not absolute. One can not yell "fire" in a crowded theater (*Schenck v. United States*, 1919) and "utterances in a context of violence, involving a definite and present danger, can lose significance as an appeal to reason and become part of an instrument of force unprotected by the Constitution" (*Siegel v. Regents of the University of California*, 1970 at 838). In *Tinker v. Des Moines Indep. Community School District* (1969), the Supreme Court held that institutions may regulate speech and expression that would "materially and substantially disrupt the work and discipline of the school" (at 742). The institution, however, must bear the burden of showing clear and convincing evidence that the speech or expression would be disruptive (*Molpus v. Fortune*, 1970). The mere belief that speech will become disruptive is not enough (*Brooks v. Auburn University*, 1969). Colleges and universities may impose reasonable time, place, and manner restrictions on the exercise of free speech and expression (*Bayless v. Martine*, 1970; *Sword v. Fox*, 1971), but those restrictions are valid only when there is no reference to content; regulations are narrowly tailored to serve a compelling governmental interest; and ample alternatives for communication are available (*Students Against Apartheid Coalition v. O'Neil I*, 1987).

Whenever decisions are made on the basis of the content of oral, symbolic, or printed expression, a violation of the First Amendment will probably be found. Thus, institutional officials have been found to be in violation when they have eliminated editorials critical of the state governor (*Dickey v. Alabama Board of Education*, 1967), removed editorial advertisements (*Lee v. Board of Regents of State Colleges*, 1969; *Lueth v. St. Clair County Community College*, 1990), restricted speakers (*Pickings v. Bruce*, 1970), prohibited the wearing of black arm bands to protest a war (*Tinker, supra*), or prohibited students from erecting shanties to protest South Africa's policy of apartheid (*University of Utah Students Against Apartheid v. Peterson*, 1986; *Students Against Apartheid Coalition, supra*).

The landmark decision of the Supreme Court in *Papish v. Board of Curators of University of Missouri* (1973) involved a student distributing newspapers that showed a police officer raping the Goddess of Justice and another raping the Statute of Liberty with a headline of "M____ F____ Acquitted." The university suspended the student for violating regulations prohibiting indecent conduct or speech. The Court reaffirmed that colleges and universities " . . . are not enclaves immune from the sweep of the First Amendment." (*Healy v. James*, 1972 at 279) said, ". . . the mere dissemination of ideas—no matter how offensive to good taste—on a state university campus may not be shut off in the name alone of 'conventions of decency'" (*Papish, supra*).

Incidents of racially motivated behavior have caused colleges and universities to promulgate speech and behavior regulations. This is not a new phenomenon. A student editor at a historically black public institution published an editorial espousing segregationist views. The president of the university withheld funds that supported the newspaper on the grounds that funding the editorial violated the Civil Rights Act and the equal protection clause of the Fourteenth Amendment

(*Joyner v. Whiting*, 1973). The court ordered the funding reinstated because the Civil Rights Act and the Fourteenth Amendment only prohibited the state from actually discriminating, but not from advocating segregation.

The policy of the University of Michigan prohibiting "[a]ny behavior, verbal or physical, that stigmatizes or victimizes an individual on the basis of race, ethnicity, religion, sex, sexual orientation, creed, national origin, ancestry, age, marital status, handicap or Vietnam-era veteran status . . . " was struck down as overly broad and vague as its prohibitions could include speech protected by the First Amendment (*Doe v. University of Michigan*, 1989 at 853). Any rule designed to regulate speech will bear a heavy burden of showing that it is narrowly tailored to serve a compelling governmental interest (Neiger, Palmer, Penney, and Gehring, 1998 model hate speech code). The Supreme Court has also struck down portions of the Communications Decency Act (CDA) found to be an unconstitutional infringement on free speech. In doing so, the Court clearly stated that it would apply traditional First Amendment principles to communication on the Internet (*Reno v. American Civil Liberties Union*, 1997).

Right to Peaceably Assemble. Institutions are not required to provide any sort of official recognition or endorsement of student organizations; however, after they open the door to recognition they must treat all who request it equally and may not determine recognition on the basis of the goals or philosophy as long as they are lawful. In *Healy v. James* (1972), the Supreme Court said that merely disagreeing with the philosophy of the organization was not sufficient to deny recognition. However, the Court also stated that recognition could be denied if the organization should advocate views directed to inciting or producing imminent lawless action, failed to show a willingness to comply with reasonable institutional rules, or engaged in unlawful or disruptive action.

Organizations recognized by an institution gain no new rights, nor is the institution required to assist them to exercise any rights (*National Strike Information v. Brandeis*, 1970; *Maryland Public Interest Research Group v. Elkins*, 1977). When recognized, organizations must have the rights and privileges generally accorded to other recognized groups. The law does not require equal support for each group, but it does not permit the denial of privileges based on a disagreement with the group's lawful goals (*Gay and Lesbian Student Association v. Gohn*, 1988).

The right of association also guarantees the reciprocal right not to associate. Institutions sometimes impose a student activity fee that is used in part to support the student government association and other campus activities. In some instances, students who pay this fee automatically become members of the student government association. The Washington Supreme Court was asked if this practice was constitutionally permissible and had " . . . no hesitancy in holding that the state, through the university, may not compel membership in an association, such as ASUW, which purports to represent all the students at the university" (*Good v. Associated Students*, 1975 at 768). Courts have, however, permitted institutions to collect and distribute activity fees from all students to provide a forum for the expression of ideas (*Veed v. Schwartzkoph*, 1973).

More recent cases have refined how activity fees may be used. Several courts have held that using mandatory activity fees to support political and ideological organizations violates the free speech and association rights of students who disagree with those groups (*Smith v. Regents of University of California*, 1993 and *Southworth v. Grebe*, 1998).

The clear language of the First Amendment guarantees students the right to assemble on campus and to demonstrate for particular causes as long as those demonstrations are not disruptive (*Esteban v. Central Missouri State College*, 1969). Prior registration may be required to ensure that the demonstration does not interfere with other scheduled activities and to prepare for the demonstration. The right to assemble cannot be denied on the basis of the content of the message (*Shamloo v. Mississippi State Board of Trustees, Etc.*, 1980).

The Fourth Amendment

The Fourth Amendment provides that "[t]he right of the people to be secure in their persons, houses, papers, and effects, against unreasonable searches and seizures, shall not be violated, and no warrants shall issue, but upon probable cause, supported by oath or affirmation, and particularly describing the place to be searched, and the persons or things to be seized."

The Supreme Court in *New Jersey v. T.L.O* (1985) allowed a warrantless search of a fourteen-year-old school girl's purse stating that " . . . when there are reasonable grounds for suspecting that the search will turn up evidence that the student has violated or is violating either the law or the rules of the school" (at 735). The Court said that "reasonableness" would be determined by the age of the student, that which is sought, past history, and the degree of individualized suspicion. The Supreme Court has yet to address the issue as warrantless searches relate to college students who are adults. Prior to *New Jersey, supra*, many state and federal jurisdictions had upheld warrantless searches of student rooms where administrators had reasonable cause to believe that the student had contraband in the room (*Moore v. Student Affairs Committee of Troy State University*, 1968). Warrantless searches of students' suitcases (*United States v. Coles*, 1969), automobiles (*Keene v. Rodgers*, 1970), and rooms (*Ekelund v. Secretary of Commerce*, 1976) have all been conducted to maintain discipline and not to obtain criminal evidence.

Although it appears that the greater weight of precedent supports warrantless searches under the conditions previously outlined, college officials may not delegate the lower standard of "reasonable cause" to police who seek criminal evidence. Where criminal evidence is sought, police must meet the higher standard of "probable cause" and obtain a warrant as called for in the First Amendment (*Piazzola v. Watkins*, 1971).

There are, in addition to the reasonable-cause standard, other reasonable searches and seizures that do not require a warrant. Contraband observed in "plain view" may be seized and used for disciplinary purposes (*State v. Kappes*, 1976).

An emergency situation also provides an exception to the necessity for a warrant. The California Supreme Court upheld the conviction of a student for possession of marijuana where the drug had been treated with a chemical substance and caused a foul odor to emanate from his library carrel where it was stored. The discovery of the student's briefcase with small bags of greenish-colored weeds by a custodian prompted the librarian to call police. The police recognized it to be marijuana and seized it. The Court held that it was reasonable to assume control of the briefcase under the emergency doctrine (*People v. Lanthier*, 1971). The Court also held that it was also reasonable for officials to call police for an identification and that the police had obtained the evidence under the "plain view" doctrine. Good faith inventories of lost and found items are also reasonable and contraband observed in the inventory may be seized (*State v. Johnson*, 1975).

Fourteenth Amendment

The Fourteenth Amendment was passed shortly after the Civil War to protect former slaves. The Amendment provides in part: " . . . nor shall any State deprive any person of life, liberty, or property, without due process of law; nor deny to any person within its jurisdiction the equal protection of the laws." The Amendment refers to any *person* rather than any *citizen*. Thus, the protections of due process and equal protection are guaranteed to everyone in the United States including international students.

The *Dixon* case was the landmark decision applying the due process guarantees of the Fourteenth Amendment to student discipline (*Dixon v. Alabama State Board of Education*, 1961). Chambers (1972), however, uncovered a decision by a county court in Pennsylvania seventy-four years before *Dixon* that also required due process rights be afforded to students facing disciplinary charges (*Commonwealth ex rel Hill v. McCauley*, 1887).

The process that is due depends upon the nature of the right that is deprived. Thus, a minor noise violation in a residence hall would not demand the same amount of process as if the student faced expulsion. Due process is not a fixed standard; rather, it is defined "by the gradual process of judicial inclusion and exclusion" (*Davidson v. New Orleans*, 1877 at 104).

Many institutions use the same process for minor offenses as they do for serious breaches of the code of conduct. This is not necessary (Gehring, 1999). The Supreme Court has held that even in the case of a ten-day suspension, due process only requires that the student be given "some kind of notice and afforded some kind of hearing" (*Goss v. Lopez*, 1975, at 579). The Court characterized this as an " . . . informal give-and-take between student and disciplinarian . . ." (p.584).

The Fifth Circuit Court of Appeals in *Dixon, supra* set standards for due process when students face serious consequences. First, the court indicated that students should receive a specific notice of charges and grounds that, if proven, would justify expulsion. Second, the notice should include the nature of the evidence; furnish the time, date, and place of the hearing; and provide reasonable time for the student to prepare a defense. Third, the court indicated the circumstances of a specific case would influence the specific type of hearing to be held. Serious cases required the institution to have a more formal hearing with an opportunity to hear both sides of the case in considerable detail. Fourth, students should be given the names of witnesses and an oral or written report of their testimony. Fifth, students should be provided an opportunity to present a defense, including written or oral testimony of witnesses. Sixth, the hearing must be held before an impartial individual or board. Finally, the findings of the hearing should be furnished in written form for the student's inspection. "If these rudimentary elements of fair play are followed in a case of misconduct of this particular type, we feel that the requirements of due process of law will have been fulfilled" (*Dixon v. Alabama State Board of Education*, 1961 at 159).

When considering due process, administrators should read the *General Order on Judicial Standards of Procedure and Substance in Review of Student Discipline in Tax-Supported Institutions of Higher Education* (1968) issued by a federal district court in Missouri. The *General Order* differentiates between college discipline and criminal jurisprudence and concludes that the analogy between them is not sound. It also points out the lawful missions of higher education and provides an excellent set of procedural standards for campus discipline.

The procedural requirements outlined in *Dixon, supra* and the *General Order* have been refined over the years. Students should be given a written notice of the charges in enough detail to allow them to prepare a defense (*Esteban, supra*). Violated regulations must be specific enough to provide a reasonable person with notice of what is prohibited (*Soglin v. Kauffman*, 1969). Students may not frustrate the notice process by moving or failing to keep the university apprised of their current address (*Wright v. Texas Southern University*, 1968). There is no general requirement that witnesses be confronted or cross-examined (*General Order*, 1968), but where questions exist about the credibility of witnesses, cross-examination may be essential (*Blanton v. Statue University of New York*, 1973). A hearing may also be conducted when, after proper notice, the student charged decides not to attend the hearing (*Swanson v. Wesley College*, 1979). Special circumstances, such as when the university uses an attorney to present its case (*French v. Bashful*, 1969), require that the student be allowed to be represented by counsel. Where the student faces criminal charges, the advice of counsel at the hearing may also be required (*Gabrilowitz, supra*). Students have no absolute right to record hearings (*Gorman v. University of Rhode Island*, 1988). It is not necessary for the university to make a full transcript of the hearing (*Sohmer v. Kinnard*, 1982; *Due v. Florida Agricultural and Mechanical University*, 1963). Hearings on campus need not wait until criminal charges are settled (*Nzuve v. Castleton State College*, 1975). Hearings must be closed unless those students defending against the charges agree in writing to have them open and then the choice is the institution's (*Marston v. Gainesville Sun Publishing Co., Inc.*, 1976). Decisions should be based on substantial evidence (*Dixon, supra*; *Mc-Donald v. Board of Trustees of University of Illinois*, 1974; *Jackson v. Hayakawa*, 1985) and although it is prudent to have someone review the decision, there is no right to an appeal (*District of Columbia v. Clawans*, 1936; *Reetz v. Michigan*, 1903). Finally, administrators need not wait for the time-consuming due process procedures of criminal law to run their course before protecting the community from those who present a real and serious threat to the health, safety, or welfare of persons or property. A student who poses such a threat may be suspended immediately, on an interim basis, pending a subsequent hearing (*Gardenhire v. Chalmers*, 1971; *Swanson v. Wesley College*, 1979). This is a very serious step and should be carefully considered before being taken.

The Supreme Court has held that where students are being suspended or expelled for academic reasons, the decision rests on the academic judgment of college officials and they refused to require a hearing (*Board of Curators v. Horowitz*, 1978; *Regents of the University of Michigan v. Ewing*, 1985). Questions of acts of academic dishonesty, however, are disciplinary in nature and would require some form of due process (Gehring, Nuss, and Pavela, 1986).

The Fourteenth Amendment also guarantees that the government not deny to anyone the equal protection of the law. The equal protection clause means that if an institution is engaged in state action, *similarly situated* individuals must be treated equally. Unless a fundamental right (such as voting or interstate travel) is denied to a class of people or a "suspect class" (based on race, alienage, or national origin) is created, only a rational relationship between the class of people created by the different treatment and the legitimate interests of the state must be demonstrated. For example, requiring all students under twenty-three years of age to live on campus for educational reasons has been upheld (*Pratz v. Louisiana Polytechnic Institute*, 1971), whereas, requiring all women, but only freshmen men, to live on campus has been held to violate the equal protection clause (*Mollere v. Southeastern Louisiana College*, 1969).

Although admission to an institution of higher education is not a fundamental right, classifying students on the basis of their alienage creates a suspect class and thus the state must be able to show a "compelling interest" in creating the classification. During the hostage crisis in Iran, the state of New Mexico passed legislation denying enrollment to any student whose home country held American citizens hostage. The law was held to be a violation of the equal protection clause because a suspect class was created and the rationale for doing so did not serve a compelling state interest (*Tayyari v. New Mexico State University*, 1980).

Classifications based on gender are not suspect and, therefore, do not require a compelling interest, but they have been held to require more than a simple rational relationship to be justified. In a case involving the admission policy of Mississippi University for Women (which excluded men), the Supreme Court held that gender classifications must serve "important governmental objectives" and the classification must be "substantially related" to accomplishing those objectives. Furthermore, the classification must be free of stereotypes concerning the roles and abilities of men and women (*Mississippi University for Women v. Hogan*, 1982). Applying those same tests to the male only admission policy of Virginia Military Institute and the Citadel also resulted in striking down the male only admission policies of those institutions (*United States v. Virginia*, 1996; *Faulkner v. Jones*, 1995).

Summary

The law has definitely arrived on campus. It permeates every program, policy, and practice of the institution. Because student affairs programs and practices are often where the student and the institution come together, administrators must understand the legal guidelines that define the basic relationships between students and their institutions. The law is not static, but ever-evolving. Thus, administrators must not only understand these basic guidelines, but must also stay current. The specific facts, the current state of the law, and the private or public nature of the institution of higher education all influence the legal aspects of the work of student affairs. Competent legal advice is necessary and should be sought. This chapter has attempted to provide the basic information for understanding student and institutional relationships. It becomes the responsibility of the astute student affairs administrator to stay current.

References

American Law Institute. *Restatement of Contracts. 2d.* St. Paul, MN: American Law Institute, 1981.

Chambers, M. M. *The Colleges and the Courts: The Developing Law of the Student and the College.* Danville, IL: Interstate, 1972.

Gadaleto, A., and Anderson, D. "Continued Progress: The 1979, 1982, and 1985 College Alcohol Surveys." *Journal of College Student Personnel,* 1986, 27, 499–509.

Gehring, D. "Abreast of the Law." In *National Association of Student Personnel Administrators Forum.* Washington, D.C.: National Association of Student Personnel Administrators, Nov. 1991.

Gehring, D. "Do We Really Need All This Process?" *Proceedings of the Twentieth Annual National Conference on Law and Higher Education,* Stetson College of Law, 1999.

Gehring, D., and Geraci, C. *Alcohol on Campus: A Compendium of the Law and a Guide to Campus Policy.* Asheville, NC: College Administration Publications, 1989.

Gehring, D., Nuss, E., and Pavela, G. *Issues and Perspectives on Academic Integrity.* Washington, D.C. National Association of Student Personnel Administrators, 1986.

General Order on Judicial Standards of Procedure and Substance in Review of Student Discipline in Tax-Supported Institutions of Higher Education. 45 FRD 133 (W.D. MO 1968).

"Internet Message Alleges Mother Mistreated Girls." *Washington Post,* Feb. 14, 1996, p. 32.

Kaplin, W. A. *The Law of Higher Education: A Comprehensive Guide to Legal Implications of Administrative Decision Making.* (2nd ed.) San Francisco: Jossey-Bass, 1985.

Neiger, J., Palmer, C., Penney, S., and Gehring, D. "Addressing Hate Speech and Hate Behaviors in Codes of Conduct: A Model for Public Institutions." *National Association of Student Personnel Administrators Journal,* 1998, 35(3), 193–206.

Palmer, C. *Violent Crimes and Other Forms of Victimization in Residence Halls.* Asheville, NC: College Administration Pubs., Inc. 1993.

Prosser, W. *Law of Torts* (4th ed.) St. Paul, MN: West, 1971.

Stoner, E., and Creminara, K. "Harnessing the Spirit of Insubordination: A Model Student Disciplinary Code." *Journal of College and University Law,* 1990, 17(2), 89–121.

Wechlser, H., Moeykens, B. and DeJong, W. "Enforcing the Minimum Age Drinking Law: A Survey of College Administrators and Security Chiefs." The Higher Education Center for Alcohol and Other Drug Prevention, N.D.

CASES CITED

Alexander v. Yale University, 631 F. 2d 178 (2nd Cir. 1980).

Americans United v. Rogers, 45 L.W. 3429 (1976).

Anderson v. University of Wisconsin, 841 F. 2d 737 (7th Cir. 1988).

Ballou v. Sigma Nu General Fraternity, 352 S.E. 2d 488 (SC App. 1986).

Bayless v. Martine, 430 F. 2d 873 (5th Cir. 1970).

Bearman v. University of Notre Dame, 453 N.E. 2d 1196 (App. IN, 3rd Dist. 1983).

Behrend v. State, 379 N. E. 2d 617 (Ct. App. OH, Franklin Cty. 1977).

Berrios v. Inter American University, 535 F. 2d 1330 (1st Cir. 1976).

Bindrim v. University of Montana, 766 P. 2d 861 (MT 1988).

Blackburn v. Fisk University, 443 F. 2d 121 (6th Cir. 1971).

Blanton v. State University of New York, 489 F. 2d 377 (2nd Cir. 1973).

Board of Curators v. Horowitz, 46 L.W. 4179 (1978).

Bob Jones University v. Johnson, 396 F. Supp. 597 (D. SC Greenville Div. 1974).

Bougher v. University of Pittsburgh, 882 F. 2d 74 (3rd Cir. 1989).

Bradshaw v. Rawlings, 612 F. 2d 135 (3rd Cir. 1979).

Brooks v. Auburn University, 296 F. Supp. 188 (M.D. AL E.D. 1969).

Brooks v. Stone, 317 S.E. 2d 277 (GA App. 1984).

Browns v. Mitchell, 409 F. 2d 593 (10th Cir. 1969).

Brozonkala v. Virginia Polytechnic Institute, 132 F. 3d 949 (4th Cir. 1997).

Burton v. Wilmington Parking Authority, 365 U.S. 715 (1961).

Cannon v. University of Chicago, 99 S. Ct. 1946 (1979).

Carey v. Piphus, 98 S. Ct. 1024 (1978).

City of Canton, Ohio v. Harris, 103 L. Ed. 2d 412 (1989).

Commonwealth ex rel Hill v. McCauley, 3 PA Co. Ct. 77 (1887).

Davidson v. New Orleans, 96 U.S. 97 (1877).

Davis v. Monroe Board of Education, 74 F. 3d 1186 (11th Cir. 1996).

Delta School of Business, Etc. v. Shropshire, 399 So. 2d 1212 (LA App. 1st Cir. 1981).

DeRonde v. Regents of University of California, 172 CA Rptr. 677 (1981).

Dickey v. Alabama Board of Education, 273 F. Supp. 613 (M.D. AL E.D. 1967).

District of Columbia v. Clawans, 300 U.S. 617 (1936).

Dixon v. Alabama State Board of Education, 294 F. 2d 150 (5th Cir. 1961); cert. den. 386 U.S. 930 (1961).

Doe v. Borough of Barrington, 729 F. Supp. 376 (D. NJ 1990).

Doe v. New York University, 666 F. 2d 761 (2nd Cir. 1981).

Doe v. University of Illinois, 138 F. 3d 653 (7th Cir. 1998).

Doe v. University of Michigan, 721 F. Supp. 852 (E.D. MI So. Div. 1989).

Doe v. Washington University, 780 F. Supp. 628 (E.D. MO 1991).

Doherty v. Southern College of Optometry, 862 F. 2d 570 (6th Cir. 1988).

Drew v. State, 536 NY S. 2d 252 (A.D. 3rd Dept. 1989).

D.T.H. Public Corporation v. University of North Carolina at Chapel Hill, 496 SE 2d 8 (NC App. 1998).

Duarte v. State, 148 CA Rptr. 804 (CA App. 4th Dist. 1978).

Due v. Florida Agricultural and Mechanical University, 233 F. Supp. 396 (N.D. FL 1963).

Ekelund v. Secretary of Commerce, 418 F. Supp. 102 (E.D. NY 1976).

Estate of Hernandez v. Board of Regents, 866 P. 2d 1330 (AZ 1994).

Esteban v. Central Missouri State College, 415 F. 2d 1077 (8th Cir. 1969).

Faulkner v. Jones, 51 F. 3d 440 (4th Cir. 1995).

Franklin v. Gwinnett County. Public Schools, 503 U.S. 60 (1992).

French v. Bashful, 303 F. Supp. 1333 (E.D. LA N.O. Div. 1969).

Furek v. University of Delaware, 594 A. 2d 506 (DE 1991).

Gabrilowitz v. Newman, 582 F. 2d 100 (1st Cir. 1978).

Gardenhire v. Chalmers, 326 F. Supp. 1200 (D. KS 1971).

Gay and Lesbian Student Association v. Gohn, 850 F. 2d 361 (8th Cir. 1988).

Gebser v. Lago Vista Independent School District, 118 S. Ct. 1989 (1998).

Gehling v. St. George University School of Medicine, 705 F. Supp. 761 (D.E.D. NY 1989).

Good v. Associated Students, 542 P. 2d 762 (WA 1975).

Gorman v. University of Rhode Island, 837 F. 2d 7 (1st Cir. 1988).

Goss v. Lopez, 419 U.S. 565 (1975).

Graham v. Montana State University, 767 P. 2d 301 (MT 1988).

Grossner v. Trustees of Columbia University, 287 F. Supp. 535 (S.D. NY 1968).

Grove City College v. Bell, 104 S. Ct. 1211 (1984).

Guckenberg v. Boston University, 957 F. Supp. 306 (D. MA 1997).

Guckenberg v. Boston University, 8 F. Supp. 2d 82 (D. MA 1998).

Hall v. Board of Supervisors, Southern University, 405 So. 2d 1125 (App. LA 1st Cir. 1981).

Hammond v. Tampa, 344 F. 2d 951 (5th Cir. 1965).

Healy v. James, 33 L. Ed. 2d 266 (1972).

Henig v. Hofstra University, 533 NY S. 2d 479 (A.D. 2nd Dept. 1990).

Hopwood v. University of Texas, 78 F. 3d 932 (5th Cir. 1996).

Houck v. University of Washington, 803 P. 2d 47 (App. Wash. 1991).

Ithaca College v. Yale Daily News Publishing Company, Inc., 433 NY S. 2d 530 (S. Ct. 1980).

Jackson v. Hayakawa, 761 F. 2d 525 (9th Cir. 1985).

Johnson v. Lincoln Christian College, 501 N.E. 2d 1380 (IL App. 4th District 1986).

Jones v. Illinois Department of Rehabilitation Services, 504 F. Supp. 1244 (N.D. IL E.D. 1981).

Jones v. Vassar, 299 NY S. 2d 283 (S. Ct. Duchess City 1969).

Joyner v. Whiting, 477 F. 2d 456 (4th Cir. 1973).

Keene v. Rodgers, 316 F. Supp. 217 (D. ME N.D. 1970).

Kline v. Massachusetts Avenue Apartment Corp., 439 F. 2d 477 (D.C. Cir. 1970).

Krawez v. Stans, 306 F. Supp. 1230 (E.D. NY 1969).

Lee v. Board of Regents of State Colleges, 306 F. Supp. 1097 (W.D. WI 1969).

Lemon v. Kurtzman, 403 U.S. 602 (1971).

Lewin v. Medical College of Hampton Roads, 931 F. Supp. 443 (E.D. VA 1996).

Lidecker v. Kendall College, 550 N.E. 2d 1211 (IL App. 1st Dist. 1990).

Lueth v. St. Clair County Community College, 732 F. Supp. 1410 (E.D. MI S.D. 1990).

McDonald v. Board of Trustees of University of Illinois, 375 F. Supp 95 (N.D. IL E.D. 1974).

McDonald v. Hogness, 598 P. 2d 707 (WA 1979).

McIntosh v. Milano, 403 A. 2d 500 (NJ Sup., Law 1979).

Mahavongsana v. Hall, 529 F. 2d 488 (5th Cir. 1976).

Marston v. Gainesville Sun Publishing, 341 So. 2d 783 (Dist. Ct. App. FL 1st Dist. 1976).

Maryland Public Interest Research Group v. Elkins, 565 F. 2d 864 (4th Cir. 1977).

Mazart v. State, 441 NY S. 2d 600 (Ct. Clms. 1981).

Meese v. Brigham Young University, 639 P. 2d 720 (UT 1981).

Melton v. Bow, 247 S.E. 2d 100 (GA 1978).

Miller v. State, 478 NY S. 2d 829 (1984).

Mintz v. State, 362 NY S. 2d 619 (App. 3rd 1975).

Mississippi University for Women v. Hogan, 73 L. Ed. 1090 (1982).

Mollere v. Southeastern Louisiana College, 304 F. Supp. 826 (W.D. AR Fayetteville Div. 1969).

Molpus v. Fortune, 311 F. Supp. 240 (N.D. MS 1970).

Moore v. Student Affairs Committee of Troy State University, 284 F. Supp. 725 (M.D. AL N. Div. 1968).

Mullins v. Pine Manor College, 449 N.E. 2d 331 (MA 1983).

Nally v. Grace Community Church of the Valley, 240 CA Rptr. 215 (App. CA 2d Dist 1987).

National Strike Information Center v. Brandeis, 315 F. Supp. 928 (D. MA 1970).

New Jersey v. T.L.O., 83 L. Ed. 2d 720 (1985).

Nzuve v. Castleton State College, 335 A. 2d 321 (VT 1975).

Ohio Civil Rights Commission v. Case Western Reserve, 666 N.E. 2d 1376 (OH 1996).

Olsson v. Indiana University Board of Trustees, 571 N.E. 2d 58 (Ct. App. IN 4th Dist. 1991).

Palsgraf v. Long Island Railroad Co., 162 N.E. 99 (NY 1928).

Papish v. Board of Curators of University of Missouri, 35 L. Ed. 2d 618 (1973).

Patricia H. v. Berkeley Unified School District 830 F. Supp. 1 288 (N.D. CA 1993).

Peck v. Counseling Service of Addison County. Inc., 499 A. 2d 423 (VT 1985).

People v. Lanthier, 97 CA Rptr. 297 (1971).

Piazzola v. Watkins, 442 F. 2d 284 (5th Cir. 1971).

Pickings v. Bruce, 430 F. 2d 595 (8th Cir. 1970).

Podberesky v. Kirwan, 38 F. 3d 147 (4th Cir. 1994).

Potter v. North Carolina School of the Arts, 245 S.E. 2d 188 (NC App. 1978).

Pratz v. Louisiana Polytechnic Institute, 316 F. Supp. 872 (W.D. LA. 1970); cert. den. 401 U.S. 1004 (1971).

Quinn v. Sigma Rho Chapter Beta Theta Pi Fraternity, 507 N.E. 2d 1193 (IL App. 4th Dist 1987).

Radcliff v. Landau, 883 F. 2d 1481 (9th Cir. 1989).

Red and Black Publishing Company, Inc. v. Board of Regents, 427 S.E. 2d 257 (GA 1993).

Reetz v. Michigan, 188 U.S. 505 (1903).

Regents of the University of Michigan v. Ewing, 106 S. Ct. 507 (1985).

Regents of University of California v. Bakke, 98 S. Ct. 2733 (1978).

Reno v. The American Civil Liberties Union, 521 U.S. 844 (1997).

Roemer v. Board of Public Works, 96 S. Ct. 2337 (1976).

Rosenberger v. Rector and Visitors of the University of Virginia, 115 S. Ct. 2510 (1995).

Rowe v. Chandler, 332 F. Supp. 336 (D. KS 1971).

Rowinsky v. Bryan Independent School District, 80 F. 3d 1006 (5th Cir. 1996).

Schenck v. United States, 249 U.S. 47 (1919).

School Board of Nassau County, Florida v. Arline, 55 L.W. 4245 (1987).

Schornstein v. New Jersey Division of Vocational Rehabilitational Services, 519 F. Supp. 773 (D. NJ 1981).

Schultz v. Gould Academy, 332 A. 2d 368 (ME 1975).

Shamloo v. Mississippi State Board of Trustees, Etc., 620 F. 2d 5168 (5th Cir. 1980).

Shelley v. Kraemer, 92 L. Ed. 1161 (1947).

Shetina v. Ohio University, 459 N.E. 2d 587 (OH App. 1983).

Shreveport Professional Chapter of the Society of Professional Journalists and Michelle Millohollon v. Louisiana State University in Shreveport, no. 393, 332 (First Judicial Dist. Ct., Caddo Parish, LA 1994).

Siegel v. Regents of the University of California, 308 F. Supp. 832 (N.D. CA 1970).

Smith v. Day, 538 A. 2d 157 (VT 1987).

Smith v. Duquesne University, 612 F. Supp. 72 (W.D. PA Civ. Div. 1985).

Smith v. Regents of University of California, 844 P. 2d 500 (CA 1993).

Soglin v. Kauffman, 418 F. 2d 163 (7th Cir. 1969).

Sohmer v. Kinnard, 535 F. Supp. 50 (D. MD 1982).

Southeastern Community College v. Davis, 442 U.S. 397 (1979).

Southworth v. Grebe, 151 F. 3d 717 (7th Cir. 1998).

State ex rel The Miami Student v. Miami University, 680 N.E. 2nd 956 (OH 1997).

Stark v. St. Cloud State University, 802 F. 2d 1046 (8th Cir. 1986).

State v. Johnson, 530 P. 2d 910 (AZ App. Div. 2 1975).

State v. Kappes, 550 P. 2d 121 (Ct. App. AZ Div. 1 Dept. A 1976).

State v. Schmid, 423 A. 2d 615 (NJ 1980).

Steinberg v. Chicago Medical School, 371 N.E. 2d 634 (IL 1977).

Stone v. Cornell University, 510 NY S. 2d 313 (A.D. 1987).

Students Against Apartheid Coalition v. O'Neil I, 660 F. Supp. 333 (W.D. VA 1987).

Swanson v. Wesley College, 402 A. 2d 401 (DE Sup. Ct., Kent Co. 1979).

Sword v. Fox, 446 F. 2d 1091 (4th Cir. 1971).

Tarasoff v. Regents of University of California, 551 P. 2d 334 (CA 1976).

Tarka v. Cunningham, 891 F. 2d 102 (5th Cir. 1989).

Tayyari v. New Mexico State University, 495 F. Supp. 1365 (D. NM 1980).

Texas v. Hopwood, 518 U.S. 1033 (1996).

Tilton v. Richardson, 403 U.S. 627 (1970).

Tinker v. Des Moines Indep. Community t School District, 21 L. Ed. 2d 731 (1969).

Tobias v. University of Texas, 824 S.W. 2d 201 (TX App. Ft. Worth 1991).

Torres v. Puerto Rico Junior College, 298 F. Supp. 458 (D. PR 1969).

United States v. Board of Trustees for University of Alabama, 908 F. 2d 740 (11th Cir. 1990).

United States v. Coles, 302 F. Supp. 99 (D. ME N.D. 1969).

United States v. Miami University, Case #C298–0097 (S.D. OH 1998).

United States v. Virginia, 518 U.S. 515 (1996).

University of Delaware v. Keegan, 349 A. 2d 14 (DE 1975); cert. den. 424 U.S. 934 (1975).

University of Denver v. Whitlock, 744 P. 2d 54 (CO 1987).

University of Utah Students Against Apartheid v. Peterson, 649 F. Supp. 1200 (D. UT C.D. 1986).

Uzzell v. Friday, 591 F. 2d 997 (4th Cir. 1979).

Veed v. Schwartzkoph, 353 F. Supp. 149 (D. Nebr. 1973); affd. 478 F. 2d 1407 (8th Cir. 1973); cert. den. 414 U.S. 1135 (1973).

Wardlaw v. Peck, 318 S.E. 2d 270 (SC App. 1984).

Warren v. Drake University, 886 F. 2d 200 (8th Cir. 1989).

Washington v. Chrisman, 102 S. Ct. 812 (1982).

Widmar v. Vincent, 102 S. Ct. 269 (1981).

Widmar v. Vincent, 454 U.S. 263 (1981).

Witters v. Washington Department of Services for the Blind, 771 P. 2d 1119 (WA 1989).

Wood v. Strickland, 95 S. Ct. 992 (1975).

Wright v. Texas Southern University, 392 F. 2d 728 (5th Cir. 1968).

Zavala v. Regents of the University of California, 178 CA Rptr. 185 (App. 2nd Dist. Div. 4 1981).

Zeran v. America Online, Inc., 129 F. 3d 327 (4th Cir. 1997).

CHAPTER TWENTY

DEVELOPING EFFECTIVE CAMPUS AND COMMUNITY RELATIONSHIPS

C. Arthur Sandeen

Why is it important to student affairs leaders to establish good campus and community relationships? Don't we know what our professional obligations are? Why spend all this time involving others in what we do? My job description doesn't include anything about these relationships. Why am I evaluated to such a degree on the success of these relationships? With so many diverse constituencies for student affairs leaders, how can anyone be expected to work effectively with all of them?

These are questions student affairs leaders often ask themselves when thinking about their responsibilities and as they work to establish good campus and community relationships. In this chapter, these questions will be addressed and suggestions will be made about developing effective campus and community relationships. The discussion will cover the essential elements of good campus relations, developing key campus and community relationships, expected outcomes from such relationships, and questions every professional should consider about their role in campus relations.

The following assumptions are made in discussing this issue:

- Student affairs leaders are most effective when they are highly visible and active with the campus and community.
- Involving others in policies, programs, staffing, and evaluation is likely to result in more support and understanding for what student affairs leaders do.

- The overall evaluation of student affairs professionals depends heavily upon the effectiveness of their campus and community relationships.
- The best way to fail is for student affairs leaders to isolate themselves, thinking that they can do their jobs without involving others.

Essential Elements of Good Campus Relations

It takes hard work and time to establish good campus relationships; they don't happen by accident! Establishing good relationships requires attention to detail and to the constituent groups involved in the situation. It is founded on certain essential elements: the student affairs leader's personal and ethical characteristics; staff competence; willingness to listen and involve others; commitment to confidentiality; and effective planning and follow-up.

Be Trustworthy and Honest

Without trust and honesty, policies and programs simply cannot succeed. These are the most important qualities in establishing good relationships with the campus and the community. Issues must be represented in an open manner and when problems are encountered, they should be acknowledged and confronted. Trust is not granted automatically in an academic community; it has to be earned, and student affairs leaders must be worthy of it every day in their actions and words. It can be lost as the result of a single incident, and when a student affairs leader is viewed as distrustful or dishonest, it is very difficult to recover. Most student affairs staff should be quite visible in the academic community and thus are subjected to frequent scrutiny. Misrepresenting or exaggerating a program, problem, or issue will be quickly noticed and will result in a lack of credibility; moreover, there can be a "spillover" effect on the entire student affairs division due to the actions of just one staff member. This situation is especially true of relationships with students, who may be testing their "elders" to see if they are honest and consistent in their actions. Senior student affairs officers should be sensitive to the integrity of their staff and their dealings with the campus community and set an example with their own actions. Programs and policies, no matter how brilliantly they might be conceived or written, do not succeed on their own simply because they are good ideas; they succeed because student affairs leaders make honest and persuasive proposals regarding them and implement them with skill and sensitivity. The most important factor in achieving such success is the trust that student affairs leaders have established in the campus community.

Be Competent

Senior student affairs officers are always pleased to get reports from students, faculty, and others outside their divisions about the good work their staff is doing. It is essential to demonstrate a high level of competence in every project, policy, consultation, or program that student affairs staff encounter. The best way to "sell" a program or policy is to do a very good job with it. If a student, faculty, or community group benefits, it is likely to continue to support the program. A poor performance by an individual can damage the reputation of the entire student affairs division; thus, a strong emphasis on high quality work should characterize all the staff members' efforts. This is not to suggest that high-risk or controversial initiatives should not be undertaken for fear of failure. However, the staff should understand their limitations and not assume the lead role in areas for which they are not prepared. Some student affairs staff are so anxious to serve others and to be helpful that they may become involved in areas beyond their training. This practice can be damaging to students and will certainly erode the confidence of others. When student affairs staff demonstrate that they can handle difficult problems with competence and sensitivity, their campus relationships will be enhanced. It is important that the staff use its skills and training effectively in areas where they can make a positive contribution.

Listen and Involve

Earning the support, respect, and confidence of students, faculty, other administrators, and community groups is greatly enhanced by careful listening to their concerns and involving them in programs and policies. Student affairs leaders rarely establish good relationships as a result of speech making or authoritative announcements. In their eagerness to establish themselves as "powerful" administrators, some in student affairs have erred by equating strength with the title of their position or with bold-sounding statements. Such actions inevitably antagonize others and damage, rather than develop, campus relationships. Moreover, they are often cited as major reasons why student affairs staff are removed from their positions. The most successful staff take the time to learn about the special talents of faculty, students, and community members and then find useful ways to involve them in program and policies. This approach requires sensitivity to the various campus and community cultures and a recognition that the campus is not one community, but several. Staff should have an open mind and be able to understand these several communities and their needs. The ability to help the campus recognize and respond effectively to these many communities is an important leadership role for student affairs staff. To accomplish this task, it is essential to listen to the many voices on the campus and in the community.

A common error that student affairs staff who are new to a campus may make is to put programs and policies in place before listening to and understanding the special nature of the group being targeted. There are many similarities from one campus to another, but staff should not assume that what they have done before will automatically work again on their new campus.

Maintain Confidentiality

Student affairs staff often learn about personal problems and sensitive issues that involve students, faculty, other administrators, and community members. To establish and maintain good relations with these various groups, student affairs leaders must demonstrate that they can be trusted with confidential information. Engaging in campus gossip will surely diminish respect for student affairs staff, and, more important, sharing confidential information without adequate justification is a violation of professional ethics and the law. If students, faculty, other administrators, and community members perceive that student affairs staff do not protect confidential information, it will be impossible to create positive relationships with them.

Ensure Effective Planning

The worst time to try to establish good relationships with various campus and community groups is during a crisis. Thus, it is important to build trust and get to know student, faculty, administrative, and community groups before there are difficult problems to face. Student affairs leaders should know key elected officials, the local and campus police, community mental health staff, hospital personnel, and the city manager. They should also know the informal leadership structures in the community and know the key people to work with on specific issues. Student affairs leaders will benefit from knowing the most influential faculty on campus, as well as the elected leaders in the academic senate. They should be active and visible participants and contributing members of campus and community organizations. This activity is supportive of building effective relationships and is essential to the successful resolution of problems when they occur. All of this requires student affairs staff to get out of their offices and into the campus's many communities! Planning ahead by creating strong support with these groups is often the basis of solving difficult problems.

Continue to Build Relationships

Good campus and community relations need continuous attention and support. Student affairs leaders ought not to be seen only when there is a crisis, or when the assistance of faculty, student leaders, other administrators, or community officials is needed. Relationships must be genuine and strengthened over time and should reflect a sincere effort to understand and involve other groups. Showing support by attending a meeting of a group or organization or participating in one of its activities can help student affairs leaders build strong campus and community relations. There is no substitute for being there.

Key Campus and Community Relationships

The President

Student affairs officers serve at the pleasure of the institution's president. It is their responsibility to carry out the president's goals and objectives and to represent the president to a wide range of people concerning the institution. If student affairs is to be successful, it must have the confidence and trust of the president. Establishing an effective relationship with the president is the most important responsibility of the senior student affairs officer; everything else that happens in student affairs depends upon this relationship.

Developing an effective relationship with the president does not happen overnight, and student affairs officers should work hard to understand the educational priorities, personal values, and administrative styles of their presidents. Perhaps most important, they should decide if the working relationship can be a good fit; the president and the senior student affairs officer are likely to have strong beliefs and neither may be willing to compromise if the differences are too great. This important two-way assessment should be done before accepting a position or when a new president comes to the campus; it is much wiser to confront incompatibility early on and to sever the relationship rather than avoiding it and facing the inevitable conflicts later on.

Presidents have different styles and strengths just as senior student affairs officers do. Some presidents enjoy frequent personal involvement with students and campus programs, and student affairs staff can benefit from encouraging this activity. Other presidents prefer to spend their time on external affairs or are not very comfortable being directly involved with student life. Some enjoy and are very good at informal debate with students on campus issues; others prefer to avoid any public confrontation with students where the results are unpredictable and the publicity may be unfavorable. Senior student affairs officers must take the lead in understanding their president's interests and strengths and build relationships based upon this understanding. Presidents want to be successful with their students, and one of the responsibilities of the senior student affairs officer is to find ways to assure the president's success with students.

Although the job of establishing an effective relationship with the president rests primarily with the senior student affairs officer, all members of the student affairs division have a role in this ongoing effort. When presidents see student affairs staff engaged in successful programs, effective problem-solving, and creative responses to difficult issues, they will develop confidence in the staff. When presidents find student affairs staff with little imagination, scant insight into student problems, and low campus visibility, they will wonder if student affairs staff are needed. The most effective way for the student affairs division to earn the respect and support of the president is to demonstrate a high level of performance in carrying out the institution's mission.

Almost all presidents can benefit from the knowledge and insight student affairs staff have about students and the various issues that affect them. Presidents get information and advice from almost everyone; the senior student affairs officer should make sure the president also gets consistent and accurate messages from the student affairs division. It is likely that there are many different views within the student affairs staff about policies concerning financial aid, admissions, student activities, housing, student health, and student fees; however, these issues should be settled within the student affairs division. The senior student affairs officer should represent the division to the president with one voice. Presidents, of course, do not need to be shielded from controversy; in fact, they need to be aware of the most difficult and unpleasant problems on their campuses; but they need to hear clear, consistent, and credible messages from student affairs.

Establishing an effective relationship with the president is an ongoing process and because of the volatile nature of many issues in student affairs, this relationship can be fragile. All campuses are vulnerable to incidents that can damage the institution's public image almost overnight, and the best way to assure the continued support of presidents is to earn their trust through hard work, effective policies and programs, and personal integrity.

Other Key Administrators

Effective student affairs leaders know their successes rarely come from acting alone. Successes usually occur as the result of close collaboration and planning with key colleagues on the campus, most of whom are not in student affairs. Most often, these are business, academic, medical, and development officers and their staffs. The senior student affairs officer should provide the leadership in increasing the knowledge and awareness of student-related issues and programs among key campus administrators. At the same time, the student affairs staff should work hard to become well aware of issues, problems, and practices in other administrative areas outside of their own division.

Successful collaboration with key administrators outside of student affairs does not occur because of power, position, or placement on an organizational chart. It takes place as the result of good ideas, effective follow-up, cooperation, and especially, proven competence. Student affairs staff and others are rarely invited into policy-making groups simply because of a position or title they hold; they are included because they have something substantive to contribute and are viewed as useful.

When a new residence hall is being planned, a child care program is being considered, an admissions strategy is being developed, or a career program is being rethought, student affairs leaders ought to involve other key administrators on the campus. But when the general education program is being revised, the campus bus system is being revamped, a new capital campaign plan is being developed, or a new basketball arena is being planned, the student affairs staff should be involved as well. Relationships with key campus administrators are developed when the talents and knowledge of several people are needed; it helps, of course, to be cordial and visible, but it is most important to be able to contribute something useful to the project.

Many campus administrators outside of student affairs can be effective participants in student programs, and the awareness gained from such participation can result in better understanding and support. Moreover, many campus administrators greatly enjoy the opportunity to interact with student groups and help them with projects related to their professional expertise.

Student affairs leaders often deal with volatile problems and student traumas; the support and understanding of key campus administrators is essential in such situations. The effectiveness of relationships with key campus administrators, of course, depends on credibility and trust developed over time. Student affairs staff will benefit from the time and effort they expend in developing these relationships.

Faculty

The faculty represents the most important campus resource available to student affairs staff. Without the support, understanding, and participation of the faculty, no student affairs division can succeed for long. On every campus, there are faculty whose talents can be tapped for the benefit of students and their out-of-class education. All student affairs staff—in admissions and orientation, residence life and student counseling, financial aid, career development, and student health —should be actively engaged in efforts to involve the faculty in their programs and policies. Establishing positive relationships with faculty entails getting to know individual faculty members and their specific interests, and then finding ways to invite their participation in programs. Some staff, feeling that they have sufficient knowledge and independence to implement programs on their own, may be reluctant to approach the faculty. Yet failure to make this connection often results in the isolation of the student affairs staff from the faculty, a situation that eventually harms the division and does not serve students very well either. Younger staff may not be as confident as those more experienced in initiating these contacts for program and policy development and may benefit from some encouragement in this regard.

The most successful student affairs staff understand that the faculty, even on small campuses, is comprised of many smaller groups, often related to academic disciplines, but sometimes to other interests as well. Student affairs staff must know faculty members well enough to be able to match their talents with particular student needs. A student affairs staff should know, for example, what faculty member can be asked to help a Chinese student facing a family tragedy; which one should (and should not!) be invited to moderate a debate on gay and lesbian issues; which one should mediate a dispute between African American and Hispanic students; which should be recommended to the president for membership on the trustee committee on student life; and which faculty members should be the most helpful in reviewing the fraternity and sorority system. These are only a few examples of how the student affairs staff can work with faculty. In each of them, the success of the effort depends on a strong student affairs-faculty liaison. Student affairs needs faculty support in order to thrive and its staff should initiate these contacts, which can improve the education and growth of students.

Governing Board Members

The senior student affairs officer, on behalf of the president, should keep the staff informed about the activities, objectives, and priorities of the governing board. Some board members may not be very visible in campus programs and student life, whereas others may enjoy being frequent participants. At times, this situation can be awkward for the student affairs staff; for example, a board member may express a view contradicting what the president has stated. Those on the staff should understand that it is the president who speaks for the institution to the board. They should not attempt to do so or to initiate contacts with board members on their own. In the course of their work, however, it is very likely that they will get to know various members of the board, and in many cases, such interactions can be good for the institution. The staff should keep the senior student affairs officer informed of these contacts.

Many governing boards include a standing committee on student affairs, and such committees demand the time and attention of senior student affairs officers. This board committee can become a very positive asset for student affairs, resulting in better understanding and support for policies, new facilities, or new programs; it can also become an obstacle, resulting in the imposition of policies and programs that do not fit current student needs. Careful planning and trusting relationships must be developed between committee members and the senior student affairs officer. This can become a delicate issue, as the senior student affairs officer must follow the lead of the president on all matters, and at times, committee priorities may conflict with the president's. With the president's knowledge and permission, the senior student affairs officer should develop a plan to educate and inform committee members about student life. This may include visits to the campus to meet with staff and student groups, learning the realities of financial aid, admissions, student activities, or counseling. Most board members who serve on student affairs committees are eager to learn about student life, and with good planning over a period of time, the senior student affairs officer can have a positive influence on what the committee does.

If a president feels the people in student affairs are misrepresenting the institution to the board, a very serious situation has developed. Board members may be quite interested in issues such as student demonstrations, the disciplinary status of a student, the registration of a controversial student group, the status of an applicant for admissions, or the invitation of a speaker to the campus. If the student affairs staff has done its homework and has taken the time to get to know individuals on the board, their conversations on issues such as this can be more candid and helpful. In all of its dealings with board members, the staff should remember that it must defer to the president and keep the senior student affairs officer well informed.

Parents

On campuses with significant numbers of traditional age students, establishing strong ties to parents can be very helpful to student affairs. Many institutions have well developed parent programs, with staff members assigned to this function. Everyone in student affairs should have contacts with parents and be sensitive to their concerns and interests. Parents can be excellent partners with the institution in the education of students, and student affairs staff should be the initiators of programs to increase their involvement. The senior student affairs officer should make sure that the institution's contacts with parents produce a coordinated and coherent message—especially in large universities, where many departments and colleges may want to conduct their own separate parent programs. Special weekends, seminars, advisory groups, fund-raising efforts, publications, and other programs may be developed by the student affairs staff, but the success of all these efforts depends on relationships with parents. These can begin, of course, with the introduction of the institution to prospective students and their parents and should continue with a variety of academic, student life, financial, and other activities through graduation. In establishing connections with parents, student affairs staff should listen carefully to their concerns before initiating programs and policies. When parents feel a real sense of involvement in the activities of their children's university, they are more likely to be helpful participants.

Alumni

The student affairs staff can often improve the quality of student life by establishing good relationships with alumni. Staff can speak about the kinds of experiences and opportunities and programs that are of interest to alumni. These contacts can often result in enhanced support and understanding of student affairs programs and policies. With the assistance of the development staff, student affairs can establish good relationships with key alumni on specific issues. These relationships can be enhanced by inviting alumni to campus events and by involving them in discussions of important policy and program issues. With the increasing complexity of student affairs divisions, it is very important that the efforts of the staff not contradict or duplicate each other. It is likely that housing, admissions, financial aid, placement, recreation, and student health all have compelling programs and proposals to present to alumni, so it is essential that the senior student affairs officer coordinate these efforts. The development staff is the key to success for student affairs in this area, and with the knowledge they have about former students, the student affairs staff can often make very helpful suggestions to their colleagues in development.

Community Members

Student affairs staff should know the history and culture of their communities and understand how they operate. Whether the institution is located in a large city or small town, senior student affairs officers should be visible and active participants in the community. They should know the elected officials, the city manager, the mayor, the police, the business leaders, the clergy, and personnel from the various health-related agencies. Such relationships are essential if problems are to be solved or if campus and community services and support are to be coordinated. When a troublesome issue arises in an off-campus apartment complex, a student death occurs, or the student government petitions a city commission on a controversial issue, it is crucial for students affairs staff to have forged strong links with community officials in advance. The leadership for this should come from the senior student affairs officer, but those working in functional areas also have much at stake. At many institutions, the campus-community relationship is very close, and regular meetings throughout the year may be called to ensure good coordination and communication. Student affairs staff should be very active in initiating such contacts and should find ways to involve students in the process. With the rapid turnover of students from year to year, this is an effort that requires constant attention. The staff may have a tendency to get involved with community leaders only at times of crises; this is not the time to establish good relationships. Moreover, it may give the impression that the only reason student affairs staff care about the community is to protect their own interests. By establishing regular and positive relationships with community leaders, student affairs staff can enhance the quality of life for students.

Students and Student Organizations

Students, of course, are the most important constituency for student affairs. Building strong and trusting relationships with students is essential for success in any program or policy initiative. Student affairs staff should work to establish good relationships with all students, not just those who are the most visible, accessible, or compliant. Among the various offices, many different insights about students exist and can be shared with others. Among financial aid, recreational sports, housing, admissions, counseling, student activities, registration, and career development, there should be valuable and diverse insights about the various student cultures that exist on every campus and good ideas about how to connect with them. Faculty advisers to student organizations discover student interests and talents that can improve the quality of student life. Staff working in student religious centers can also provide very valuable information. Staff members will usually get a distorted and limited notion of student life if they restrict their contacts to those who visit their offices during the day. Every college or university comprises many smaller student communities; understanding student life on any campus requires that the staff learn about their needs, concerns, and customs. Student affairs staff should be the campus experts on student culture and should be able to gauge its effect on programs and policies. All campuses, large and small, are complex, and no one staff member can know or be effective with every student group. However, the staff as a whole should be able to develop good working relations with most groups. Being sensitive to the special traditions and thinking of smaller student communities will enable student affairs staff to earn their respect and support. Without this, little can be accomplished.

Students and student groups, of course, sometimes engage in inappropriate activities that violate institutional rules or standards. Relationships between student affairs staff and students in such situations are often negative, especially when the staff must intervene in efforts to change behavior or to impose sanctions. Even in these situations, very little can be achieved if the student affairs staff has not earned the respect of the group beforehand. Student groups involved in negative behavior need to be approached with consideration and candor. If constructive change is to occur, the staff will need to work with individuals in the group over a period of time. Very little education takes place as a result of authoritative decisions imposed by the staff on student groups; after harsh disciplinary action is taken, the real education should begin by working with the group in efforts to rebuild its strengths. The same principle obviously pertains to individual students. Student affairs staff build well known reputations among students and student groups over a period of time. Most frequently, student perceptions of the staff are accurate, as they are based on actual experience. Good relationships with students are earned as a result of taking the time to reach out to them in all corners of the campus community, of listening to their concerns, and of demonstrating through consistent actions a commitment to them.

Expected Outcomes

Effective campus and community relations should result in positive outcomes for the institution and its students. Some of these expected outcomes are discussed:

Improved Understanding and Support

Involving others in student affairs programs and policies is likely to result in greater support and understanding by students, faculty, staff, parents, and community members. Much of what student affairs leaders do is the result of cooperation and collaboration with such groups. When there is a trusting relationship among these groups, the chances are much greater that difficult decisions, policy changes, and new program initiatives will be accepted. The best student affairs leaders understand that their success depends upon the good relations they develop with various constituent groups.

Improved Sense of Community

Student affairs leaders work to create strong campus communities, but understand that they cannot do this alone. They must work with others on and off campus to encourage values supportive of a caring and open institution. They can bring people from diverse groups together to improve the sense of community, but they must realize that such efforts depend on the relationships they have built over a period of time.

Improved Problem-Solving

Student affairs staff are engaged in helping individual students and student groups in solving problems. These may involve personal matters, financial difficulties, political and ethnic disputes, or conduct problems. Indeed, some student affairs leaders are evaluated in terms of their effectiveness as problem-solvers, so it is very important for them to be successful in these tasks. But most problems faced by student affairs leaders are not ones easily solved by themselves; they require involvement with others on and off the campus, and thus, establishing good relations with faculty, parents, other campus staff, and community groups is essential to solving problems.

Improved Quality of Programs

By establishing positive relations with academic departments, student groups, parents, alumni, and community organizations, student affairs leaders can increase the quality of cocurricular programs for students. Few student affairs organizations have sufficient financial or creative resources to conduct all programs on their own; the quality of what can be done in health education, orientation, career development, or leadership programs can be greatly enhanced with the involvement and participation of others outside of student affairs. The best leaders know and understand this, and work to develop positive relationships that can make this happen.

Improved Education for Students

The reason student affairs staff exists is for the education of students. The staff recognizes that students learn better when they are involved in an activity and when they have opportunities to interact with others while engaged in real projects. Most of what student affairs staff do in their work with students is based upon these assumptions. Thus, it is important for staff to link students with many others on the campus and in the community for a variety of learning opportunities. If student affairs staff has established good relations with its constituent groups, it can make these learning opportunities much more likely for students.

Questions to Consider

As student affairs staff work to establish good relations on their campuses and in their communities, the following questions are offered for consideration.

Who Should Decide Division Priorities?

The staff in each of the division's offices may be eager to create close ties with various groups on and off the campus. There is more than enough work for everyone! However, it is important to convey a coordinated and consistent message from the student affairs division; of course, the senior student affairs officer must ensure that this happens. There are persons on every staff whose talents and interests are particularly suited to certain groups and issues. Efforts should be made to ensure that relationships between staff members and community members are not left entirely to chance. Not every staff member needs to have a close working relationship with the city police, the community health providers, the faculty in the pharmacy school, or the alumni association staff. However, the senior student affairs officer should make sure that someone on the staff works very closely with each of these groups and that what they hear is consistent. The information gathered by staff in their dealings with such groups must be shared with others in student affairs in regular conversations about the campus community and its many components. Only through this sharing can the best education programs and policies continue to improve. The senior student affairs officer should create an atmosphere within the staff that encourages such contacts and stimulates such creativity.

How Can Staff Learn the Importance of Campus Relations?

Most student affairs staff probably do not need much encouragement to move out and meet new campus and community groups. They understand that developing such relationships is essential to the success of what they do. There may be a tendency among some staff, however, to think that they simply offer a "service" and that their only job consists of providing it to students who happen to visit their office. Such staff may be reluctant to reach out to groups simply because they have not done it before or because they lack the confidence to try. More experienced staff can be of real assistance, not by lecturing to them, but by asking them to join in some activity. When staff learn how new relationships with campus and community groups can enhance their work with students, they usually do not need any more prodding. In many ways, student affairs administration is the art of the possible, and the most valuable assets staff can possess are their imagination and initiative.

Which Approach Works Best?

Is there a single most effective way to establish good relations with the campus and the community? The same approach may not work for each staff member, as some are more comfortable with informal contacts and others may prefer more structured and planned meetings. There does not seem to be any substitute for personal, face-to-face contacts with campus and community groups. The staff will learn that the same method will probably not work equally well with the Filipino Student Union, the Rugby Club, the Gay and Lesbian Association, the Coalition for Conservative Action, and a social fraternity. Some groups may be offended by direct contacts initiated by student affairs staff; thus, the preferred approach may be to arrange an invitation from within the organization. Others may have felt unwanted or unappreciated for some time and may welcome the attention and concern expressed by the student affairs staff. Sometimes the best way is to work through others who already have established contacts within the group. It is not uncommon for some staff to fail in their efforts to establish good relations with campus and community groups because they have not taken the time to learn how to contact them appropriately. The process requires that those in student affairs be careful listeners and observers and that they adapt their approach to fit the special nature of the group.

What If Others Resist Cooperation?

Student affairs staff members must recognize that not all of their efforts to establish good relations will be successful. Some student groups may actively resist almost any attempt at involvement, and some faculty members may be openly skeptical about what student affairs may have to contribute. Indeed, such resistance certainly contributes to the decisions of student affairs staff to conduct their programs in isolation, for there are fewer obstacles and difficulties. However, very little of consequence can be achieved in this manner, and eventually, isolation can result in obscurity. The best student affairs leaders are always seeking better ways to approach campus and community groups, especially those that present the biggest challenges. They may at times have to resort to authoritarian methods (such as disciplining a fraternity) in order to get the attention of some groups. However, staff members must realize that if they want to have any positive influence over time, they must establish good relations. Persistence and consistent performance are excellent strategies to use in student affairs. Eventually, at least one member of the staff is usually able to build a trusting relationship with a group.

Who Is Accountable?

It is obvious that when student affairs staff members enter into cooperative arrangements with campus and community groups, things become more complicated. With more people from different backgrounds sharing the workload, some campus administrators may become nervous about who is in charge and even about who may be responsible. This situation presents a dilemma at times for senior student affairs officers, who, on the one hand, encourage coalitions with student, faculty, and community groups and, on the other, are worried about how predictable the results might be and who might be held accountable for them. Establishing good relationships with various groups should lead to more creative and worthwhile programs and policies, but it also increases the risk of failure, as a good deal of the control may be lost. But there really is no workable alternative in student affairs because the very nature of the profession is cooperation and collaboration. Of course, the senior student affairs officer is ultimately accountable for what happens in the division. However, each staff member should be actively involved in establishing good relations with campus and community groups and should understand the responsibility the institution and the division assume in any cooperative project or program.

Summary

Student affairs administration is not an end unto itself. Success of the enterprise depends on the quality and diversity of the relationships that staff can develop with campus and community groups.

Trustworthiness and honesty, proven competence, good listening skills, a commitment to involve others effectively, respect for confidentiality, and skill in planning are all essential in developing strong relations with campus constituency groups and individuals. The time and effort spent is important, for the result is inevitably improvement in the quality of programs, policies, and the educational experience of students. The senior student affairs officer must demonstrate commitment to building relationships, set priorities, purposely involve staff, and take responsibility to assure that attention is paid to this important aspect of student affairs work. Staff who understand the special nature of diverse constituent groups will prove valuable to their institution.

CHAPTER TWENTY-ONE

MANAGING CONFLICT CONSTRUCTIVELY

Leila V. Moore

Colleges and universities mirror the greater society in their experiences with differences and the conflict that often results. In fact, many faculty, staff, and students would agree that managing conflict is one of the most frequently called-for skills in their daily interactions on college campuses. Yet, when faced with conflict, many of us feel uncomfortable and unskilled in responding to these situations. Perhaps we anticipate a negative outcome or hold the misconception that if we ignore it the conflict will go away.

Christopher Moore makes this observation:

> All societies, communities, organizations and interpersonal relationships experience conflict at one time or another in the process of day-to-day interaction. Conflict is not necessarily bad, abnormal, or dysfunctional; it is a fact of life. Conflict in disputes happen when people are engaged in competition to meet goals that are perceived as, or actually are, incompatible. However, conflict may go beyond competitive behavior and acquire the additional goals of inflicting physical or psychological damage on or destroying an opponent. It is then that the negative and harmful dynamics of conflict take their full costs [1987, p. ix].

Thus, when faced with conflict, many of us are like the people in conflict noted by Moore, anticipating or often experiencing the negative result of conflict.

In these circumstances, we tend to avoid conflict, preferring to remain unresponsive rather than risk the very likely chance of a negative result. If we do not avoid the conflict, we may rely on a limited range of responses based on our prior experiences. The result of approaching conflict in these ways on college campuses is a hostile or distrustful campus climate marked by recurring interpersonal problems with those involved in conflict, polarization of issues, and avoidance of the attitudes, opinions, and individuals who are parties to conflict.

All of us know of situations in which a conflict was handled poorly or not at all. We cite the professor who refuses to teach any of her classes until her schedule is rearranged to eliminate early morning and late afternoon sections. The department chairperson accommodates her demands even though it means overloading another professor with the unwanted sections. In residence halls, we learn of roommate situations that have been festering for an entire semester when they explode. When asked why they didn't come forward sooner, the students often reply, "We didn't want to cause trouble." We see student government officers and members of the student senate engaged in a debate in the student newspaper over student fees, but the same debate never takes place in face-to-face meetings between the officers and the senators. We know of senior student affairs officers or college presidents who, when confronted by angry students, their lawyers, and their parents objecting to a judicial board sanction, overturn the judicial board's decision to pacify the complainers. Growth and productive change are lost as outcomes in these examples. As administrators, we find ourselves caught in a "do-loop," fully aware of the negative consequences of avoiding or otherwise ineffectively responding to conflict yet stuck in our own apprehensions about conflict.

This chapter begins by analyzing the origins of assumptions about conflict, in particular noting cultural influences over these assumptions. The next section includes definitions of conflict, negotiation, and mediation, along with a review of Moore's (1987) discussion of a continuum of types of conflict based on approaches to conflict and desired outcomes. The third section introduces the ideas that different approaches to conflict will shape outcome, and that being able to use a range of approaches is more effective than relying on some variation of one approach for all conflicts. Skills of responding to and managing conflict are reviewed next. Three case studies are then presented and discussed. The chapter closes with a summary and recommendations for practitioners.

Challenging the Negative Assumptions

One's view of conflict is influenced in part by cultural values about conflict and interpersonal relationships (Myers and Filner, 1997; Pedersen, 1994). According to Pedersen (1994), those of us whose values most closely resemble mainstream America have learned the values of Western culture. These values, delineated by Ho (1987), include placing more importance on the individual and his or her achievements than on the group's interests, giving permission to challenge authority, supporting direct communication (saying what you mean), and stressing the importance of recognition for one's personal achievements. Ho also points out that these Western cultural values are significantly different from the values of other major world cultures. Pedersen (1994) observes that the values of the Western culture lead to culturally-biased assumptions, including the assumptions that everyone has the same definitions of "good" and "bad," of "right" and "wrong," and that there is a common view of human behavior that is "more or less universal across social, cultural, economic, and political backgrounds" (Pedersen, 1994, p. 46). With such a focus on the individual and the assumption that there is a common view of the world, it is difficult for those of us influenced by these values to see other values or to see them arranged on continuums that represent individuals from all cultures. Thus, when we view conflict, we see the conflict from our worldview that may or may not include positive experiences with conflict. Whatever that view may be, we do not recognize the existence of other worldviews of the same conflict.

Moving from aspects of culture that serve to differentiate Western culture from all others, Myers and Filner (1994) discuss the cultural values that most relate to conflict. They identify these values and place each of them on a continuum:

Competition	Collaboration
Egalitarian	Hierarchical
Admission of Error	Saving Face
Individualistic	Collectivistic
Youth-Oriented	Respect for Age
Emotional Responses	Controlled Responses
Deadline Intensive	Time Not an Issue
Casual Behavior	Formal Behavior
Authoritative Decisions	Consensus
Contractual	Implied Agreement
Openness to Change	Reluctance to Change (p. 32)

They make no statement that the item to the left of each value continuum represents Western culture. Instead, they acknowledge that culture influences these values, observe that each person involved in a conflict can fall anywhere on a continuum for each value, and state that it is important for each of us to know where we fall on each continuum. Such a view tends to eliminate the need to characterize conflict as either positive or negative.

Knowledge about Conflict

Conflict may be defined as "a situation between two or more parties who see their perspectives as incompatible" (Cohen, Davis, and Aboelata, 1998, p. 4). The term parties may apply to individuals as well as groups. Therefore the constructs discussed in this chapter may be applied to disputes between two people as well as those between and among groups. Power imbalances between parties to a conflict may significantly affect the range of approaches that might be used to address conflict.

Our knowledge about conflict can be organized according to approaches taken to address it. According to Moore (1987), the range of approaches moves from conflict avoidance to direct action in the form of violence. Moore observes that approaches including avoidance, informal discussion and problem-solving, negotiation, and mediation are characterized as involving private decision-making by the parties involved in the conflict, with low potential for coercion or win-lose tactics. This range of approaches is based on mutual willingness to participate in addressing the conflict, depends on identifying mutually acceptable solutions and, in the case of mediation, results in a mutually agreed-upon approach to resolving or reducing the conflict.

The National Institute for Dispute Resolution (1999) defines negotiation as "communication for the purpose of persuasion; a way of solving problems; or a process for reaching decisions." Parties to the conflict discuss possible outcomes, each presents and advocates for their ideas or solutions, and the discussion continues until the parties agree on a solution or agree that there is an impasse.

Mediation is defined as "the intervention into a dispute or negotiation by an acceptable, impartial, and neutral third party who has no authoritative decision-making power to assist disputing parties in voluntarily reaching their own mutually acceptable settlement of issues in dispute" (Moore, 1987, p. 14).

Mediators or third-party negotiators present in these approaches to conflict remain nonjudgmental in their efforts to assist the parties to the conflict. Their role includes helping the parties communicate more clearly with one another, identifying misunderstandings or misconceptions that seem to be impeding communication, helping to sort out multiple issues related to the conflict and assisting the parties to agree on which issues need attention first, offering ways to improve the parties' skills in discussing solutions, and helping to sort out perceived incompatibilities from actual differences (Moore, 1987; Pedersen, 1994; Myers and Filner, 1997). Most of our daily conflicts on college campuses fall within this range of approaches to conflict.

Moore's continuum of approaches to conflict moves next to third-party decision making such as arbitration, judicial decisions, and legislative decisions. The final aspect of his continuum includes "extralegal nonviolent and violent action" (p. 5). As the range of approaches takes more control away from the parties to the conflict and from legal third-party decision-makers, there is an increased chance that coercion and win-lose outcomes will be the result. The knowledge and skills needed in using these more formal approaches include awareness of case law, familiarity with due process, and clarity about the roles of judicial boards and judges, and how these roles interact with the role of the student affairs administrator. Because of the specific and far more complex discussions needed to characterize these approaches to conflict, this chapter will not include these more formal approaches. The reader is directed to Chapter Nineteen, "Understanding the Legal Implications of Student Affairs Practice," by Donald D. Gehring for further information.

A final perspective for this section on knowledge about conflict is a discussion of the relationship between violence prevention and conflict. Recall that, on Moore's continuum of conflict discussed previously, violence is considered to be an extralegal approach, not at all associated with the earlier approaches to conflict. Cohen, Davis, and Aboelata (1998) have made a compelling case for the need to consider violence prevention as a necessary component in approaches to conflict. They cite recent developments in violence prevention programs across the country as evidence of the need to change norms about conflict and its perceived inevitable outcome as violence. The widespread efforts to move social and cultural norms toward nonviolence speaks volumes about the urgency in student affairs administrators to respond more effectively to conflict. Workshops designed to teach anger management skills, for example, have taken on an increased visibility as part of educational programs. Because violence prevention is clearly the work of many constituencies in a community, student affairs administrators may take some reassurance from the fact that they are part of a much larger coalition of concerned individuals for whom nonviolence is their common value.

Attitudes Toward Conflict

Much of the discussion in this chapter reflects attitudes toward conflict as they are shaped by cultural values and prior experience. Added to these influences is an attitude about approaches to conflict. Some models of managing conflict seem to be built on an assumption that doing something is better than doing nothing at all, or that collaboration is always better than compromise when it comes to managing conflict. These characterizations of approaches add an unrealistic and limiting attitude toward conflict management, namely that certain approaches are never as good as others. Such a linear approach to conflict is challenged by the work of Thomas and Kilmann (1974), who begin with the assumptions that the situation shapes approaches to conflict, and that based on the situation all approaches have value.

Thomas and Kilmann developed the Conflict Mode Instrument (1974), a self-report instrument used in workshops on conflict to help participants understand their typical approaches to interpersonal conflict. The resulting scores are then displayed as a combination of two dimensions: the extent to which the approach satisfies the individual's needs or concerns related to the conflict; and the extent to which the approach satisfies the other person's needs or concerns. Five conflict modes are presented: competing, collaborating, compromising, avoiding, and accommodating. Competing is described as "power-oriented" (p.10) and focused on winning. Collaborating is described as full acknowledgment of both the individual's and the other's needs or concerns and a focus on finding common ground within a conflict on which to base some mutually agreeable approach to the conflict. Compromising is characterized as a more expedient approach to conflict that partially responds to both parties. It usually involves giving up something in order to solve the problem, seeking a middle ground. Avoiding is characterized as responding to neither the individual nor the other person. Thomas and Kilmann say that avoiding: " . . . might take the form of diplomatically sidestepping an issue, postponing an issue until a better time, or simply withdrawing from a threatening situation." (p. 10). Finally, Thomas and Kilmann characterize accommodating as responding entirely to the other's needs or concerns while neglecting or ignoring one's own. Thomas and Kilmann provide examples of accommodating behavior, including obeying another's order when one might prefer not to, or yielding to another's opinion.

The Conflict Mode Instrument (1974) is then used to assess an individual's tendency to rely too much on certain approaches or to avoid using other approaches. The message of the instrument and its interpretation is that all approaches have value, depending on the situation surrounding the conflict. The authors cite several situations for which each approach might be appropriate. A competing style, for example, might be used when an unpopular decision such as cutting the budget needs to be implemented. The needs of others are acknowledged but not responded to. A collaborating style might be used when the needs of both parties are too important to be compromised. A common or integrated solution must be found that supports both parties. A compromising style might be used when other approaches have failed, or when time pressures require a solution. An avoiding style might be used when tempers are too hot for a reasonable discussion to occur, or when the issue seems to be unimportant in the face of other issues. Accommodating might be used in developing the skills of a supervisee by allowing the other to "call the shots" in order to learn.

Thomas and Kilmann's situation-based approach to conflict rests on the concept that a clear idea of the outcomes sought will help those involved in a conflict to select approaches that match these outcomes. Thus, the work of finding outcomes that the parties can agree on is often the most important action in managing conflict.

Skills in Managing Conflict

Many of the skills related to managing conflict are those related to counseling. Active listening, clarifying statements made by others, expressing empathy, and building trust are four examples. As well, the basic skills of problem solving apply here. Examples include defining a problem, developing options to solving the problem, evaluating each option for effectiveness, selecting and implementing an option, and following up to determine whether the problem has abated. Skills developed in leadership education programs also apply, including summarizing; reframing comments to reduce negative perceptions of the ideas of others; helping group members respond to issues and ideas and not to personality; assuring that all have the opportunity to state their opinions and thoughts; identifying power imbalances among group members that seem to be a potential detriment to clear communication; and being aware of nonverbal communication. Intercultural communication skills include the skills mentioned previously. Other examples of these skills include being aware of one's own frame of reference as well as that of others; identifying and checking out with the other person assumptions and inferences made about the other's perspective; and paying attention to the variety of meanings assigned by different cultures to nonverbal behaviors. McFarland (1992) offers a clear discussion of interpersonal conflict resolution and the behaviors or skills associated with constructive management of conflict. Although he focuses on the role of counselor in teaching others, his discussion has equal value in its application to many other situations involving interpersonal conflict.

It is the experience of many of us that, under stress, some if not all of our newly-learned skills are not available to us. We rely instead on old, familiar ways, even when we know that those ways have not been as effective as we would like them to be. It is certainly the case that being in the presence of conflict or being part of a conflict is one of the most stressful experiences for student affairs professionals. In the face of what seems to be ever-increasing time spent by staff on conflict management, it is clear that skill practice should be a central component in graduate program practica and a mandatory part of staff development programs.

Pedersen's (1994) comments about developing multicultural skills apply as well to the development of other skills. His comments relate to preparation programs, but their application can be extended to professional staff development activities. According to Pedersen, the development of skills is accomplished effectively through modeling and demonstration, the use of videotaping to provide students with feedback about their skill level, supervising students in the application and use of skills, and practicing the skills and behaviors in as many settings and different situations as possible. On the job, skill practice and feedback should be part of the supervisor relationship, including performance appraisal and evaluation, and might also occur regularly through such means as special training programs in mediation or case study discussions. The following section is a presentation of three case studies used to illustrate the application of skills, knowledge, and attitudes about conflict.

Case Examples

Case Example One: Roommate Conflict

Case One is a roommate conflict. Alice Adams and Brenda Brown are freshmen. They were assigned to their residence hall room randomly, except that both requested a nonsmoker as a roommate. When they moved into their room in the fall, they were both pleased to know that the other was a nonsmoker, and they quickly identified several other interests that they had in common. They were both optimistic about their relationship as roommates and settled into the year enthusiastically.

About a month after school began, Brenda told Alice she and her old boyfriend had gotten back together again and she was sure "this is it." Shortly after that, Brenda invited her boyfriend to spend time in their residence hall room, and it wasn't long before Brenda's boyfriend was spending several nights a week in the room. Alice agreed to sleep in another room when Brenda's boyfriend stayed over, but soon became tired of this arrangement. She complained to another friend, who reminded her that she needed to see her hall director to discuss the matter. The policy in the residence department was quite clear: guests are permitted in student rooms only when the roommate(s) are in full agreement with the arrangement. Guests are not permitted to be in the rooms on weeknights. When a student is found in violation of these arrangements, the guest is asked to leave immediately and the host of the guest is officially warned that another violation could result in the host's eviction or a sanction of disciplinary probation.

Alice refused to speak to her director about this matter. She was upset with herself for not being able to handle this situation and did not want to rely on rules or an adult to help her out. She did not complain to Brenda either because she felt that Brenda and her boyfriend had rights too.

As the semester continued, Alice's grades began to drop. She seemed distracted and unable to concentrate on her work. Her relationship with Brenda had deteriorated, and Alice found herself arguing with Brenda about everything from music in the room to Brenda's choice of friends. When mid-semester grades came out, Alice received a failing grade in one class, one B, and all the rest Cs. She called home to talk about the grades, and soon she had told her mother everything about her roommate situation. Alice's mother was surprised and upset she was just learning about this problem. She called Alice's hall director and described the call she had received from Alice. She also asked the director to tell Alice that she had called.

The director called Alice to her office and told her about her mother's call. Alice became very angry that her mother had called. She told the director that the roommate arrangement was no big deal, and that she and Brenda were having some differences of opinion that she was sure could be worked out. When the director asked Alice whether she wanted to change rooms, Alice said no.

The director then met with her supervisor to discuss this situation. There seemed to be some truth to Alice's mother's concerns, as the floor counselor for Alice and Brenda had observed a general deterioration in the friendship of the two women. She reported hearing arguments when she passed their door, and observed that Brenda's boyfriend was spending a lot of time in the room. The director and her supervisor agreed that the director would keep an eye on the situation, and would use any opening to start conversations with either Brenda or Alice about their roommate relationship. The floor counselor would increase her observation of the boyfriend's time in the room. If she found evidence of violation of the guest policy, she would refer Brenda for disciplinary action.

Two weeks later, Alice's mother called the director to ask what the director had done to separate the two roommates. She reported that Alice had been calling regularly, first angry at her mother for calling the director and then in tears about her living situation. Alice still refused to complain to the director. She asked her mother if she could see a counselor because she couldn't seem to handle this situation in a mature manner. After hearing what Alice's mother said, the director decided to make an appointment to see Brenda. She told Brenda that the floor counselor had noticed Brenda's boyfriend spending quite a bit of time in Brenda's room and reminded Brenda of the guest policy. She said that Brenda would be referred for disciplinary action if she learned that Brenda had violated the guest policy. She then asked Brenda how she and Alice were doing. Brenda said that they were "okay." She volunteered the observation that Alice seemed stressed and tense lately, and mentioned that she thought she'd see a counselor. Brenda did not know what was on Alice's mind. The director asked Brenda if she thought there was anything about their living situation that seemed to stress Alice, and Brenda thought perhaps her boyfriend's staying over was hard on Alice. At the director's suggestion, Brenda agreed to talk with Alice about her boyfriend being in the room so much.

The next day, Brenda saw the director. She had talked with Alice, who finally admitted that she was disturbed by Brenda's boyfriend being in the room so much. Brenda offered to reduce the time her boyfriend spent there, Alice seemed relieved, and Brenda reported that both she and Alice seemed to have a very good conversation after that. Alice told Brenda about her stress, and they both agreed that Alice should be more truthful with Brenda about her concerns.

At first glance, this conflict situation seemed to resolve itself. The hall director's conversation with her supervisor seemed to lead to an avoidance approach, as Alice was reluctant to acknowledge a conflict with Brenda. Alice seemed to acknowledge the conflict as one within herself, a conflict between the value of standing up for her rights in the situation and her assumption that the mature response to Brenda and her boyfriend was to accommodate Brenda. Alice's mother's first telephone call changed the dynamic somewhat by adding power or influence to the belief that there was a conflict between Brenda and Alice even though Alice denied it to campus officials. In fact, the mother's call triggered increased observations of Brenda and Alice by the resident counselor. The hall director could have waited until the resident counselor had accumulated sufficient evidence for hall staff to intervene by declaring a rules violation on Brenda's part. Subsequent judicial board action could have resolved at least the guest policy abuse contributing to the stress that Alice was feeling. This might have been a perfectly adequate approach to the conflict. The "system" would have handled the conflict.

The second telephone call from Alice's mother added an increased urgency to the issue, as Alice's stress had escalated to the point where she was willing to seek counseling. The hall director decided to contact Brenda about a potential guest violation even though she had insufficient information to make a judicial board referral. She then ran a risk in opening a conversation with Brenda about how she and Alice were getting along, hoping that she would be able to turn the conversation toward the quality of the roommate relationship. The risk paid off, as Brenda was open to the idea that her behavior with her boyfriend might have something to do with Alice's increased stress level. Thus, the director succeeded in returning the responsibility for managing the conflict to the parties to the conflict. When Brenda was willing to modify her behavior in having her boyfriend stay over, the relief that Alice demonstrated was sufficient evidence that Brenda's behavior did have something to do with Alice's stress. The added beneficial outcome was that Alice and Brenda reestablished some of the rapport that they had had before.

It should be noted here that Alice's lack of assertiveness in dealing with her roommate's behavior did not become part of the director's approach in this situation. Although it may be the case that Alice needs to learn assertiveness, it may also be the case that Alice's cultural values rule out standing up for her rights, either assertively or aggressively, as a valid approach to this conflict.

Case Example Two: Staff Issues

Case Two involves a long-standing lack of trust between two employees working on the same staff. Carl Samson and Derek Williams are both employed as career counselors. Carl was hired five years ago, and Derek was hired three years later. Their current supervisor hired them both. His rationale for hiring Derek was that he is sufficiently different from Carl in perspective and working style; the resulting diversity of style and opinion could only benefit the career development staff. However, as soon as Derek was hired there was friction with Carl. Carl, a task-oriented person, was put off by Derek's insistence on a more inclusive approach to matters related to the office. Carl complained that Derek wasted valuable time in "nothing but chatter," and Derek defended his approach by referring to greater commitment and buy-in as positive results. Their supervisor chose to ignore the clash, believing that the two would eventually sort out their differences.

As time passed, however, each man became more extreme in his defense of his own style. Carl, who at one time had seen the value of longer discussions and a more inclusive approach in certain situations, became virtually intolerant of this approach. Derek took every opportunity to slow down staff discussions in the name of inclusivity even when no one on the staff saw the need for further discussion. The supervisor met with each person separately to discuss this growing rift. He appealed to their professional ethics and asked them to seek common ground in the name of the future of the staff. He brought the two men together in joint sessions to discuss the effect of their differences on the health of the staff. Each time he intervened, the two agreed to try again to get along and to find ways of becoming more tolerant of one another's styles. After a while, however, the resolve of Carl and Derek dissolved into the same friction as before.

As time passed, the supervisor noticed that both Carl and Derek were carefully avoiding serving on the same committees and managed to avoid speaking with one another during staff meetings. Each was beginning to complain to him about the behavior or attitude of the other, and each found ways to diminish the work of the other. Other members of the career development staff complained to the supervisor that the clash between the two men was affecting their work too. Some began to take the side of one or the other staff member, until most of the career development staff members either blamed Carl or Derek for the low morale of the staff.

The supervisor consulted with the vice president for student affairs. They agreed that although the clash between Carl and Derek had been a significant influence in eroding the trust and sense of "team" that once characterized the career development staff, the negative effect on the staff could be reduced or removed. The supervisor planned a staff retreat in order to reestablish a common vision for the staff and to build a sense of team spirit and the beginning of trust among staff members. The retreat was a success in terms of establishing a common vision and building a sense of team spirit among all staff members, including Carl and Derek. The supervisor also noticed the reemergence of a sense of trust among all staff members. Only Carl and Derek continued to demonstrate a low level of trust between them.

Soon it was time for performance evaluation. The supervisor decided to make an official statement on each person's performance evaluation about the their mutual inability to reconcile what seemed to be reconcilable differences. He gave low ratings to each staff member for their ability to get along and placed each on warning to resolve their differences before the next evaluation period.

Several months after the performance evaluations, the student chairperson of the career development board asked to meet privately with the supervisor. She wanted to tell the supervisor that students had noticed the clash between Carl and Derek and that several of the students were going to file written complaints about the unprofessional behavior of both people. The written complaints appeared on the supervisor's desk the next day. The supervisor met separately with Carl and Derek to discuss the complaints, and for the first time each man saw his role in contributing to the clash between the two. Through continued conversations, the supervisor came to see that neither man had the skill to begin the process of managing the conflict. He established that each man wanted to resolve the conflict and would be willing to discuss the problem with a disinterested third party. They agreed to participate in a mediation session with a trained mediator. After long hours of discussion (a process that frustrated Carl immensely), Carl and Derek found an approach to their conflict that each was willing to try. In the course of the mediation, the mediator discovered, however, neither Carl nor Derek knew how to begin to make the changes that they agreed were required. They asked the mediator for coaching and regular appointments to help them through the process.

With their permission, the mediator met with the supervisor to discuss the results of the mediation and to let the supervisor know of Carl and Derek's need for coaching and follow-up. The supervisor offered to participate with the mediator in the coaching and follow-up appointments, and Carl and Derek agreed. In about eight months, both Carl and Derek had developed sufficient comfort with their new behaviors that they requested a period of time without the extra meetings. Their differences in style and perspective remained through this time, but there was a gradual diminishment of the acrimony and alienation that marked the reaction of each man to the differences.

This conflict was marked with several well intended efforts to manage the differences between two staff members. Each time an effort was made, the parties to the conflict agreed that there was a problem that needed to be attended to, and each agreed to make an effort to resolve the problem. The process stalled at this point, as follow-up by the supervisor was absent or at a very low level, and there was no specificity involved in the resolve to change. Even the presence of a poor performance rating did little to produce the changes needed for the conflict to be managed constructively. The supervisor relied almost exclusively on an approach that stopped with a definition of the problem, assuming that after the problem was agreed upon, the solution would follow. Both Carl and Derek knew which behaviors exhibited by the other were inappropriate, but had little or no idea of which of their own behaviors would need to change in order to address the problem.

The supervisor missed the fact that Carl and Derek were both without the necessary tools to change. The block to progress was the refusal of each person to see his behavior as in need of change, and none of the interventions addressed this attitude. The use of a third party to address the conflict could have been brought in much earlier had Carl and Derek each seen that they needed to change as much as the other person did. In the end it was the letters of complaint from students that forced each man to see his own shortcomings.

Case Example Three: A Sit-In

The final case involves a sit-in in the offices of the provost and the vice president for student affairs. The Black Student Alliance had been in the forefront regarding complaints about the climate for minorities on campus. Three years ago, they had identified problems with campus climate, inadequacies in campus response to racist incidents, poor recruiting efforts, and lack of effort to improve the low retention rate for minorities when compared with the retention rate of other students on campus. The president of the university at the time promised change in response to the BSA's complaints but produced no plan to make the changes. Because their complaints were first communicated to the campus, a new president, provost, and vice president for student affairs were appointed. The new administrators were aware of the students' concerns and developed a report to the BSA and other members of the campus community about plans to address the complaints. Approximately six months after this report was delivered, members of the BSA occupied both the provost's and the vice president's offices. They stated that they had read the report, found it to be "full of double talk," and demanded a face-to-face meeting with all involved in writing the report. They wanted the provost, vice president, and others to set specific recruitment goals, make concrete policy changes, and pledge to improve minority retention rate until it equaled the retention rate of the rest of the campus. The students resolved to stay in the vice president's and provost's offices until their demands were met.

The vice president and provost agreed to meet with representatives of the BSA and arranged for other staff to join the meeting. They made no effort to have the students removed from their offices while the meetings were taking place, reasoning that the students' complaints were legitimate and that to attempt to remove the students would further erode the already low level of trust the students had for the administration. The students were not convinced that the report was a real plan or that the university intended to make good on its pledge to change. With the support of the president, the provost, vice president, and other administrators then met with the student representatives. They reviewed each of the complaints of the students and discussed the action they had taken to address the complaint. At first, their discussions were marked by a high amount of confusion and misunderstood messages. The discussions were adjourned frequently in order for the students to consult with one another about what they were hearing. The administrators also met separately, attempting to understand what the students still did not trust about their messages and looking for alternative ways to talk about the complaints. As time passed, both sides began to understand how the breakdown in communication around the progress report had happened. The report had been written in a formal way and its writers had attempted to provide great detail about the plans for addressing the complaints of the BSA. The net result in the eyes of the students was a report that "talked the talk" but failed to "walk the walk." It had omitted an explanation of the outcomes sought in addressing the complaints. When both sides saw how the report had failed to communicate its message, they began to add outcomes to the original report. A reference to "monitoring campus climate," for example, was amended to include a specific method for collecting baseline data about hate crimes and reports of racist behavior, and establishing reasonable goals for reducing the numbers of hate crimes and reports of racist behavior over a three-year period of time. "Improvements in faculty and staff awareness of cultural differences" was amended to specify the proportion of faculty and staff members who participated in six hours or more of workshops in improving knowledge and skills in cross-cultural communication. The students' expectations for change were realistic, and there was general agreement on the length of time that was needed to change campus climate and policy to respond more effectively to the complaints of students.

The university was criticized strongly by some for "giving in" to student demands, for not having the students arrested, and for not holding students accountable through the judicial system for their conduct. Allegations of double standards and reverse discrimination came from many sources, including parents, the general public, alumni, and donors. At the same time, the university received praise and support from others in the same constituencies for listening and for having the courage to do the right thing.

The turning point in managing this conflict seemed to be the decision on the part of the provost and vice president not to have the protesting students removed from their offices. By accommodating their resolve to stay in the administrative offices during the discussions, the provost and vice president demonstrated an act of faith in the students and the value of their concerns. To have them removed would have been a manifestation of the imbalance of power that exists between students and administrators and would have established a win-lose tone that precludes the use of collaborative approaches to conflict. There would have been little or no chance for students to explain their complaints or to feel that they had finally been heard. The discussions that followed were focused on the outcome of understanding how to communicate in such a way that both sides felt heard and their expectations for action specified. The discussions succeeded in revealing the fact that there were common expectations for action.

Summary

The purpose of this chapter has been to establish the notion that conflict is inevitable, and that its lack of constructive management is both common and problematic. Seeking the goal of eliminating conflict in our work setting is both unrealistic and unhealthy. Conflict can as easily produce positive outcomes as negative ones, depending on our perspective on conflict and the goals or outcomes we establish for addressing conflict. Learning to deal with conflict is one of the most important and difficult skills student affairs administrators can develop. As conflict becomes a more common part of the work of student affairs staff at all levels, and as conflict becomes more contentious, our ability to manage it constructively is critical. Graduate preparation programs and staff development programs need to provide frequent opportunities for practicing the skills of conflict management, add opportunities for discussing case studies involving conflict, and include more systematic study of knowledge about conflict as part of professional development.

Although preparation programs may be helpful in creating a greater awareness among graduate students of the importance of managing conflict constructively, the real work lies on the campus. The practitioner should address management of conflict as part of a campus culture change. Students need skills workshops on managing conflict. Peer educators can be a very effective means of delivering these workshops. Student leadership development programs should contain workshops and case studies about conflict. Student conduct staff should offer skills-building among parties involved in conflicts. The senior student affairs officer must endorse and exemplify flexibility in approaches to conflict and serve as a spokesperson with other campus constituencies about the importance of developing conflict management skills. Employee grievance procedures should include skills-building in managing conflict, and staff evaluations should speak directly to an employee's conflict-management capabilities. The value of nonviolent responses to conflict must be underscored by public statements regarding violence. Academic deans should recognize and address classroom incidents involving faculty-student conflicts. Members of the campus community should know where to go on campus to find information, support, and education on matters related to conflict.

In conclusion, becoming skilled and knowledgeable about constructive conflict management should be a professional development goal of every student affairs professional. A similar focus in elementary and secondary schools underscores the urgency of developing constructive managers of conflict. It also provides sufficient impetus for practitioners to advocate institutional change that supports and rewards constructive conflict management among all members of the campus community.

References

Cohen, L., Davis, R., and Aboelata, M. "Conflict Resolution and Violence Prevention: From Misunderstanding to Understanding." *The Fourth R*, 1998, 84, 1, 3–7, 13–15.

Ho, M. K. *Family Therapy with Ethnic Minorities*. Newbury Park, CA: Sage Publications, 1987.

McFarland, W. P. "Counselors Teaching Peaceful Conflict Resolution." *Journal of Counseling and Development*, 1992, 71, 18–21.

Moore, C. W. *The Mediation Process: Practical Strategies for Resolving Conflict*. San Francisco: Jossey-Bass, 1987.

Myers, S., and Filner, B. *Mediation Across Cultures: A Handbook About Conflict and Culture*. Amherst, MA: Amherst Educational Publishing, 1994.

Myers, S., and Filner, B. *Conflict Resolution Across Cultures: From Talking It Out to Third-Party Mediation*. Amherst, MA: Amherst Educational Publishing, 1997.

National Institute for Dispute Resolution *Glossary of Dispute Resolution Terms.* [http://www.crenet.org/info/glossary.html], Jan. 31, 1999.

Pedersen, P. *A Handbook for Developing Multicultural Awareness* (2nd ed.) Alexandria, VA: American Counseling Association, 1994.

Thomas, K. W., and Kilmann, R. H. *Thomas-Kilmann Conflict Mode Instrument.* Tuxedo, NY: XICOM, Inc, 1974.

CHAPTER TWENTY-TWO

MAINTAINING HIGH ETHICAL STANDARDS

Jane M. Fried

Maintaining high standards for ethical behavior is an ambiguous and demanding task. Institutional complexity, competing demands from multiple constituencies, and the increasing permeability of institutional boundaries all contribute to the problem. Recognizing the existence of an ethical dilemma is often the most daunting task of all (Canon, 1993). In this chapter we will discuss some of the reasons why ethical thought and behavior have become so complex in higher education and offer a template for analyzing ethical dilemmas. The three-dimensional template includes 1) the principles used in ethical decision making, 2) the character of the decision makers and 3) the context in which ethical dilemmas evolve. This roadmap for ethical discussion can be helpful in unwrapping some of the complexities of the ethical dilemmas we face on today's campuses.

Why has ethical decision making become so complex? This trend reflects national and international developments. Since the end of the Vietnam War, our campuses have welcomed students, staff, and faculty from every segment of the American population and almost every other part of the world. American campuses are connected to universities and other kinds of organizations all over the world. Collectively, they are making decisions about issues that simply did not exist 50 years ago, in areas ranging from biotechnology to cyberspace.

Ethics and Cultural Values

All ethical systems reflect the values of the cultures that produce them. The ethical beliefs of the student affairs profession are grounded in Anglo-American culture. This culture believes in scientific materialism, individual autonomy, achievement and responsibility, a belief in the necessity of progress, and a strong emphasis on the future, rather than the present or past (Fried et al. 1995). Our individualist culture is quite different from collectivist cultures throughout Africa, Latin America, the Middle East, and Asia. The major points of contrast include emphasis on the individual over the group, which might be a family group, a tribal group, or a work group, and the dominance of materialism over spirituality and awareness of the future over awareness of the past or present. Of course, most human communities share certain values as well. These include emphasis on the reliability of one's promises within one's own group and helping or not hurting members of one's own group or other groups except under hostile intergroup conditions like war (Okun, Fried, and Okun, 1999). The relationship between human values, which are shared among many groups, and cultural values, which differ among groups, shifts constantly in a dynamic process. Few cultures in the world are untouched by others. Studying at universities abroad or working with colleagues in different countries are two of the activities that contribute to the constant and dynamic interchange among cultures. This interchange leads to a transformative process in which interacting systems shape each other in unpredictable and irreversible ways.

Five Ethical Principles That Guide Student Affairs

Ethical principles are expected to provide relatively stable guidelines for decision-making across all types of situations and contexts. Kitchener (1985) synthesizes five important principles that have been widely used in student affairs:

Respect Autonomy. Individuals have the right to decide how they live their lives as long as their actions do not interfere with the welfare of others. One has freedom of thought and choice.

Do No Harm. The obligation to avoid inflicting either physical or psychological harm on others and to avoid actions that put others at risk is a primary ethical principle in the helping professions.

Help Others. There is an obligation to enhance the welfare of others. Those in the helping professions assume that the welfare of the consumer or client comes first when other considerations are equal.

Be Just. To be just in dealing with others means to offer equal treatment to all and to afford each individual her or his due. It presumes reciprocity and impartiality.

Be Trustworthy. One should keep one's promises, tell the truth, be loyal, and maintain respect and civility in human discourse. Only insofar as we deserve it can we expect to be seen as trustworthy (cited in Canon, 1993, p.30).

With the exception of the first principle, respect autonomy, all the others are shared by a wide range of cultures. Differences occur in context and emphasis. In collectivist cultures, one is trustworthy, loyal, and helpful to those who are members of one's group and the rules tend to be different for those who are considered outsiders (Kotkin, 1992). In Anglo-American culture, commitments and obligations are made by contract between individuals and generally are not based on family or group membership. The Anglo-American definition of fairness implies that rules are applied impartially, regardless of family or group membership.

Ethical Systems in Conflict

Fairness is an extremely important value in Anglo-American culture. People who believe that they have been unfairly treated are often outraged. Fairness is a guiding principle that implies impartiality and enforces rules equally without regard to social status. When the student activities staff holds a scheduling meeting on a campus in the U.S., all groups are expected to follow the same process to apply for the use of building space. The rules are usually spelled out in detail before the meeting. As long as the explicit rules are followed, some groups may be dissatisfied with the results of the process, but they do not generally challenge the process or consider it unfair. The reaction would be quite different if all groups were treated the same way, except for groups that have special relationships to campus authority figures. If the President's fraternity, as an example, always received first choice for space and all other groups had to follow the rules, there would be a general perception of unfairness among other groups.

In collectivist cultures, rules are implicit and typically based on relationships among families. Individual relationships are governed by family relationships. Preferential treatment is often given to individuals or groups because their families hold high status in the society or have historical privilege for some other reason. This approach is taken for granted in collectivist cultures. Fairness or impartiality, as understood in the U.S., is not a value. Rules in these cultures are always embedded in a relational context. Rules for decision making in the U.S. are typically separate from personal relationships and granting special privileges to relatives or friends is typically considered unfair. In some cases, it is illegal. Most Native American tribes are collectivist in social organization. In many tribes, the chief's son always wins athletic competitions. Other players defer to him because he is the chief's son. The game is not totally based on athletic prowess and individual competition as it would be in Anglo-American society. It is also based on social rank.

When people from both individualist and collectivist cultures work together on a campus in the U.S., ethical decision making requires thoughtfulness and care. If a student activities staff on a U.S. campus gave preferential treatment to the president's sorority or fraternity, American students would be outraged, although students from collectivist cultures might shrug and accept the situation. If the student activities staff were composed of people who were born in the U.S., their judgment would be questionable. If some of the staff belonged to cultures with more collectivist values, they would be in conflict or confused by the reactions of the other groups. The process would also be shaped by the reality that the campus existed within the U.S. and that Anglo-American values shaped the policies and procedures of the larger organization. At first glance, most Americans and most student affairs professionals in the U.S. would follow the prescribed process exactly and object to any attempt to interfere. Ethical decision making in this circumstance would require a lot of respectful dialogue.

Attempts to interfere with fair practices on campus are not unusual. Public officials may call with requests for special preferences in housing for constituents' children. Alumni may attempt to intrude in a disciplinary procedure against star athletes who have committed assault. Major donors may request special favors or attempt to influence policy or purchasing decisions in ways that benefit their business interests but do not necessarily benefit the institution. According to the dominant belief system in the U.S., all such attempts constitute interference and suggest unfair practices that are also considered unethical. Persons from cultures outside the U.S. may engage in similar attempts to influence decisions. They may or may not realize that their efforts are unacceptable within the American system.

Virtue Ethics in the Helping Professions

"Virtue ethics shifts the focus from principles to characteristics of particular people in particular contexts. Virtues are traits considered to be personal qualities that are deemed meritorious in a particular context" (Fried, 1995, pp. 13–14). Virtue ethics have provided us with a little more flexibility than we had using principles alone. Meara, Schmidt, and Day (1996) identified four virtues that psychologists consider essential for ethical behavior in the helping professions: prudence, integrity, respectfulness, and benevolence. These traits are character attributes, not abstract principles. The current practice that many teenagers have adopted of wearing bracelets with WWJD? (What Would Jesus Do?) on them is an example of an attempt to practice virtue ethics. In a Christian culture, that would be a powerful question for a young person to ask before deciding how to act in a difficult situation. What virtues did Jesus manifest? If I could behave as he might have, what would I do?

The definition of these virtues depends on the cultural context. A person who demonstrates these traits in a specific culture could be considered prudent, respectful, and benevolent or as one who demonstrates integrity. In a highly demonstrative culture, prudence might consist of shouting only under specific types of distressing circumstances, rather than shouting as part of everyday conversation. In a nondemonstrative culture, prudence might consist of never showing emotions or never taking action in controversial circumstances until all parties have been consulted. In one set of circumstances, respectfulness is demonstrated by not challenging authority figures and in another it is demonstrated by preparing to debate authority figures in a way that indicates that the challenger has prepared extensively for the discussion and respects the superior knowledge of the authority figure.

The four virtues identified by Meara and others (1996) were gleaned from a survey of counseling psychologists. The four traits represent a consensus among the community of counseling psychologists in the U.S. In other countries, the traits might differ from these. Although there has not been a similar set of desirable traits generated for members of the student affairs profession, our work is sufficiently similar, as far as values go, with that of counseling to make comparisons convincing. In daily practice, using the notion of virtue ethics requires that at least two sets of questions are raised in a problem situation: 1) What principles are involved in making a decision about how to handle this problem and 2) What would a virtuous practitioner do under these circumstances?

Case Example

Because student affairs professionals work very closely with subordinates, supervisors, and students, there are numerous opportunities for dual role relationships to develop at work. This problem is particularly difficult in residential life where professional staff, student staff, and students live and work in the same buildings and often see each other at all hours of the day and night.

Joe, the RA, falls in love with one of his students. What does the hall director do? Tell Joe he can't love Shameka? Ask Shameka to move? Tell Joe to break up with her? Fire Joe? Move Joe? What principles are involved? Shameka has the right, under the principle of autonomy, to date Joe. Under the principle of being just and treating all students and staff fairly, has he the right to date her? Do rights have anything to do with love? If Joe remains romantically involved with Shameka, his ability to behave ethically may be compromised. Perceptions, in such circumstances, often become reality and others may question his capacity to be fair to other students and help them if their welfare comes into conflict with Shameka's. Questions may arise about his capacity to maintain other student confidences and to help the other students in his jurisdiction.

Because the ethical codes of the student affairs profession prohibit dual role relationships, Magdalena, the hall director, would be obligated to intervene in the situation and alter it in some way. The virtues would support her perspective as a supervisor who cares about her students and staff and prefers to resolve the problem in a manner that is both fair and respectful of the emerging relationship as well as of the other students under Joe's supervision. Her obligation to be benevolent would require that she speak with both people. She would take an educational/counseling approach in which she reminds them that their relationship could not be sustained under the present circumstances, but that they all needed to work together to create new circumstances that they could all accept. Benevolence in this situation requires consensus decision making, not the imposition of fairly rigid principles. Both Magdalena's integrity as a supervisor and the integrity of her relationship with staff and students require a resolution that conforms both to the ethical principles and to the virtues that maintain respectful relationships. All three parties must be involved in the final resolution.

This case often occurs in slight variations outside residence hall work settings. People who work together on campus may become romantically involved with one another. This involvement may or may not have ethical implications for their work. The prohibition of dual role relationships derives from several of the ethical principles. Respecting autonomy forbids letting personal relationships and feelings interfere with a staff member's freedom of choice in doing her or his job. Doing no harm mandates avoiding behavior that has a high probability of leading to adverse consequences. Work-related romances often incur harmful consequences if the partners separate. Being just mandates fairness. In romantic relationships, a staff member might be treated unfairly during the relationship, when she might receive more lenient treatment than colleagues, and after the relationship, when she might receive more punitive treatment. Both principles and virtues clearly prohibit these kinds of relationships between supervisors and subordinates. How does one decide what to do when such relationships occur between peers/colleagues, between people who work in different offices but one outranks the other, or between people who work in different offices but often collaborate on projects? An examination of the principles highlights key concerns in any of these situations. An examination of the virtues of all participants can guide the participants toward an ethical solution in a manner that respects all persons and leaves as few ill feelings as possible.

Contextual Issues in Ethical Decision Making

In addition to ethical principles and virtues, a number of contextual issues should be taken into account in ethical decision making. Four such issues are the cultural values of the participants, the participants' phenomenology, the time frame in which the situation emerges, and the dynamics of the evolving situation (Fried and Malley, 1998).

Definition of Terms

Cultural values of the participants are those aspects of the participants' belief systems that can be traced to their cultural origins, and that tend to be held in common by the majority of people who are members of that culture. Cultural values exert a powerful influence on the beliefs of most people. For example, American culture tends to value fairness, equal treatment, attention to individual needs, recognition of individual accomplishments, and financial rewards for hard work. Southeast Asian cultures tend to value social harmony, recognition of group accomplishment, differential treatment according to age and gender, and maintaining family honor. A significant part of African American culture involves honoring the role of faith in one's life and public discussion of gratitude to God for one's blessings.

Phenomenology refers to the individual value systems and perspectives of the people who are involved in an ethical dilemma. Phenomenology is shaped by the interaction between the cultural values one inherits and the individual belief systems one creates in reflection on personal experience. For example, a student may receive a hostile or obscene message via e-mail. In current student culture or in the individualistic, self-defensive culture of the U.S., that student might be expected to return the message with something equally hostile. However, if the student has given the subject serious thought, he might have decided that hostility only leads to more hostility and that he does not want to respond. A second ethical issue he would have to consider is whether or not to report the incident to the system administrator or the student affairs judicial officer. The student might decide on an individual level that he does not want to participate and on an institutional level that he still doesn't want to get involved in prosecuting the first offender. His configuration of the ethical issues on a personal level is his phenomenology.

Time frame refers to the temporal elements that affect a situation and the various ways in which it could be resolved. The situation might have developed in the past day or so or it may have been going on for years. Participants might know each other well and for a long time or have just met when they began work on a particular project. The dilemmas might challenge a process that a university has been using for a long time or might involve creating new process for a problem that has never happened before. If the resolution of the problem must occur immediately, it will be handled differently than if there are weeks, months, or years to consider possible resolutions and consequences. The time of the academic year in which the incident occurs is also significant. Time frame may also refer to the particular time of history, the *zeitgeist*, in which the situation occurs. Some eras are liberal and others conservative, some ethnocentric and others expansionist, and so forth.

Dynamical is a new and unusual term. Dynamical systems are "open to the environment, exchanging matter, energy, and information" (Caine and Caine, 1997, p. 58). People, money, events, and organizational concerns flow through the system at unpredictable times and rates. The ethical dilemma also evolves over time in the context of the dynamical system that is the university. Dynamical systems exist along a continuum from more to less stable. The more stable a system is, the more drastic an event must be to provoke change. When a system is disturbed, disequilibrium increases. Interactions between the system, in this case, a college or university, and its environment tend to become more unpredictable the farther the system gets from stability. Ethical considerations tend to become cloudier. Some factors that may destabilize universities include changes in federal funding programs, specific incidents on campus that generate a lot of public interest, unexpected increases or decreases in enrollment, huge financial donations for specific purposes, an untimely death, and so forth.

The dynamical nature of ethical dilemmas on our campuses suggests that a series of questions to consider before making ethical decisions might serve us well. Questions identified in advance of considering a particular problem can guide decision makers through a thoughtful process that is in line with the values of the institution. Some suggested questions are as follows:

1. What are the current circumstances in which the ethical dilemma is embedded, including competing values, interests, and priorities?
2. How long has this situation been in place? Are conditions close to or far from stability?
3. How motivated are the people involved to change their interpretations of events or behavior? What phenomenological perspectives are operating? Are

any identifiable factors or interests in this situation that dominate possible outcomes? Is there any specific constituency that has the power to demand certain outcomes?

4. Can the persons or interests involved achieve consensus about ethical outcomes or ethical guidelines by which outcomes can be evaluated?

Case Example

A fraternity composed primarily of Latin American students had been given permission to use a display case in the student union to inform the rest of the student body about its values and activities. The symbol of this fraternity was *El Conquistador*. Their statue in the display was about three feet high, brightly colored, and very attractive. No one would be likely to walk past the case without noticing the statue. The Conquistador is a highly controversial figure in the history of Central and South America. It represents the Spanish conquerors who brought European diseases with them and committed rape and murder among the native people. They built gold mines, forced the native people to work in the mines, and returned the gold to Spain, leaving the native people with no benefit and much pain. The association between the arrival of the *conquistadores* and the exploitation, pain, and suffering of the peoples of Central and South America is strong.

The display created a great deal of controversy. How could a Latin American fraternity use the symbol of a conqueror to represent itself? The fraternity brothers interpreted the meaning of the symbol as representing survival and overcoming adversity. The other students thought that the symbol represented oppression and actively objected to the display. They equated display of the Conquistador as comparable to displaying a swastika by a Jewish fraternity because it represented survival in the face of holocaust. No compromises in interpretation seemed to be available and hostility escalated over a period of several days.

What were the ethical issues that the advisors of this group had to consider before an effective response could be made?

1. **Current circumstances and competing priorities.** There were two competing sets of priorities in this situation. The first was the priority of the fraternity to display its symbol and make the general student body aware of its values and activities. This group was particularly proud of its work with poor Latino children in the surrounding community. They valued the notion of strength in the face of adversity very highly. The larger community, which included both Latino-Americans and other groups on campus and in town, held contradictory views about the meaning of the symbol. They associated

the conquistador with oppression, exploitation, and violence. They were not open to the students' interpretation. Both sides held their beliefs strongly and were unwilling to reconsider.

2. **Duration of the problem and stability of the situation.** The specific problem existed only briefly, but the controversy created a very volatile and unstable situation.

3. **Motivation for change and powerful constituencies.** People on both sides of the argument were entrenched and not motivated to change. Powerful constituencies included: a) the administration of the college, which had a strong interest in not being seen as racist or discriminatory by the student body or the general public, b) the local civic groups that contained many Latin American and Mexican-American members, and c) the national fraternity that had an interest in supporting its student chapter but did not want to alienate its alumni and other supporters.

4. **Possibility of achieving consensus.** The fraternity and its advisor were committed to discussion but not to the achievement of consensus. They considered discussion an opportunity to convince other students that their viewpoint should dominate. The opposing group was not interested in conversation.

All the ethical principles were involved in the resolution of this situation: autonomy, justice, doing good, not doing harm, and being trustworthy. The students, their advisors, and representatives of the administration and of local civic groups had to be treated respectfully and with benevolence. Since the administration of the college is both legally and morally responsible for what happens on campus, administrators had the ultimate responsibility to decide how to handle the problem. Their behavior, in order to be ethical, had to demonstrate both prudence and integrity. Ultimately, the weight of broader public opinion about the interpretation of the meaning of *El Conquistador* prevailed. The administrators came to agree with the public that display of the symbol did more harm than good. In order to take prudence and integrity seriously, it was also necessary for the administration to help the fraternity find other, less controversial ways to get its message out and continue its good work.

Clinical Skills for Use in Addressing Ethical Issues

A serious discussion of ethical dilemmas generally involves processes that are similar to those involved in conflict resolution. Concerned individuals need to be able to raise issues in a serious but non-judgmental manner. They must be able to remain calm and impartial in the midst of a somewhat volatile conversation. They should be able to express viewpoints clearly and remain open to the perspective the other people. They must be able to weight pros and cons and consider the context of the situaion (Guthrie, 1997). Finally, they must be able to translate the discussion about beliefs, values, and ethical perspectives into some practical plan so that action can be taken.

Creating Environments for Ethical Discussion

Professional Associations

Professional associations such as the National Association of Student Personnel Administrators (NASPA) and the American College Personnel Association (ACPA) provide the context in which ethical environments can be discussed among members of specific professions on a campus. Two types of ethical codes are used by these associations. NASPA's code is considered aspirational (NASPA, 1998). It identifies the optimal level of ethical functioning it expects its members to use or aspire. The code suggests appropriate standards for members to use in guiding their work with students, their relationship with their institution, the means they use in conducting research, and their own self-representation when they discuss their personal qualifications for the work they do. ACPA has a more detailed ethical code that identifies baseline ethical standards for all. ACPA's code is divided into four segments dealing with 1) professional responsibility and competence, 2) student learning and development; 3) responsibility to the institution and 4) responsibility to society. ACPA also has a detailed enforcement procedure and gives members guidelines about the process to be used when anyone is concerned about the ethics of another person's professional behavior. Both codes focus on the behavior of individual members and do not address the ethics of institutional decision making in any specific fashion.

Institution-wide Environment

Decision making is most complex at the institutional level. Establishing an organizational culture in which the discussion of ethics is included in all decision making takes time, patience, and a high level of cognitive and political skill. When the issue of ethics is raised in the course of a discussion about policy or procedure, it is not unusual for at least one person to assume that the ethical course of action inevitably conflicts with the practical or expedient course. One or two people cannot shift the course of an entire institution, but they can initiate conversation that provokes a wider awareness of the ethical implications of decisions. Ultimately, institutional awareness of ethics in decision making rises to become a regular part of these conversations. A review of the ethical implications of any decision can also help decision makers think carefully about both the intended and the unintended consequences of their choices.

Brown has suggested that, "Appropriate ethical behavior is often determined by relating it to what is thought to be the common good, which is usually influenced by community norms" (Brown, 1985, p. 70). This approach is likely to be the most fruitful. It begins with a campus-wide discussion of institutional norms and the ideas of the campus community about its common good. This discussion can be conducted in faculty meetings, in staff meetings, within the administration, within student groups, and between and among all groups. Creation of consensus about the "common good" of the community makes the development of a process of ethical decision-making possible. This type of conversation will never be finished. Beginning it and carrying it on over time is its major virtue. This conversation keeps ethics in institutional awareness.

Staff Development

Discussions about ethics tend to make staff members nervous. People begin to look for things they have done "wrong" recently and wonder if they are going to get caught. We tend to think of ethics questions as helping us figure out what not to do or what we should not have done. A discussion on ethics, as part of professional development and unrelated to any specifics, can be a very useful tool in informing staff members about recent trends in ethical thought and emerging national ethical issues in higher education. These discussions are also useful in helping people realize that skill in ethical thinking can help them decide what to do in complicated situations and how to recognize ethical issues that are not obvious.

Dozens of fascinating ethical dilemmas in higher education right now can serve as case examples for a staff development discussion. A few examples are 1) the ethics of serving part-time adult students adequately when the resources of the institution are configured to serve younger, full-time day students, 2) financial aid and other support services for international students, particularly those who come from economically unstable areas of the world and may lose their financial support from home, 3) housing arrangements for married undergraduates and other nontraditional students, and 4) the role of diversity as an admissions or hiring criterion in areas where states have eliminated affirmative action. The important thing to remember in conducting ethics discussions as part of staff development is that the purpose is to help staff learn how to think about ethics, to translate theory to practice. These are not problem-solving discussions. The responsibility of the discussion leader is to help people realize the value of the thought process.

Graduate Education

Graduate preparation programs are perhaps the easiest venue in which to discuss ethics. There are two key challenges in integrating ethics education into graduate programs: 1) to present ethics information in a manner that integrates theory and practice and 2) to manage the program and establish norms of faculty and student behavior within the program that are ethical and congruent with the subject matter in ethics coursework. Studying ethics is not only a matter of learning content; it is about understanding principles, virtues, and context and applying one's understanding to practical situations. Students must learn an effective thought process so that they can use what they know in applied situations. This process requires a high degree of cognitive complexity and the ability to tolerate ambiguity and confusion (Guthrie, 1997). In the midst of a difficult discussion of ethics, one of this author's students recently burst out, "You have to be really smart to understand this stuff." Her insight provided a moment of delight for me as a teacher. She realized that ethical thinking could not be obtained from a cookbook.

Ethical issues in program management and faculty behavior are the same in any student affairs academic department. Admissions and evaluation processes should be fair; students should be informed about requirements before they agree to attend, particularly in the areas of required counseling and group courses where self-disclosure is an expectation; dual role relationships should be avoided; and colleagues should follow the ethical codes of the professional associations in their relationships with peers, students, and all other areas of their academic work that are covered in these codes. All of these expectations are covered under the virtue of integrity.

Advising and Training with Individuals and Groups

Everything that a staff member knows about ethical thought and action should be used in their work with students.

Training. Discussions of ethics should be integrated into leadership training and the orientation of student groups. This approach also serves to establish the norm that ethics is part of the environment in which these groups are working. Ethics training for undergraduates should focus on practical applications and case studies. When possible, the students should generate their own cases. If not, presenters should use cases that typically fall within the domain of these groups. For example, many student employees use time cards to punch in and out of work. They may assume that everybody cheats a little and spend some of their on-clock time doing personal business or visiting with friends. This unexamined behavior provides a good opportunity for a discussion of the ethics involved. Dual role relationships are also an ongoing problem in many student affairs work environments. Before the year begins, this issue can be discussed in the context of an ethics workshop. This discussion informs staff in advance that these relationships are considered a problem so the staff can make informed choices about their behavior.

Advising Groups. If a student group has been well trained, the advisor's role is to raise issues that the students may not notice in the course of doing their organizational work. Ethically ambiguous situations often arise because students do not realize the conflicts inherent in them. For example, students may take the rule of the majority for granted without realizing that this decision-making process always subordinates groups that cannot achieve a majority in the voting. A residence hall student government may be dominated by people who like a certain type of music and may not realize that their idea of what everybody wants is not really what some groups would prefer. Student groups also make purchasing decisions and may not realize that potential suppliers do not use fair employment practices in hiring or are offering them questionable purchasing arrangements.

Advising Individuals. Much of the work done in career counseling and academic advising offices involves advising individual students. Some of the most important decisions students make occur in these venues. In both situations, students can and should learn to consider the ethical consequences of their choices and actions. Constructing a resume can become an exercise in ethics. How students present themselves to potential employers and represent their work, life experience, and skills involves interpretation and accuracy. A responsible career counselor not only helps a student choose which experiences and skills to identify, but he or she also helps the student understand the process by which these choices are made and the consequences of accurate or inaccurate representation.

Academic advising, if practiced from a developmental perspective, presents another opportunity for ethics education. Discussions about majors, choice of courses, study abroad, leaves of absence, and so forth are often connected to family expectations about a student's future and the student's value system. The advisor is in a position to identify ethical issues within the decision-making process, ask the student relevant questions, and point out potential consequences of the choices available to the student.

Conclusion

The processes of managing institutions ethically, educating students for ethical decision making, and dealing with all of our colleagues in an ethical fashion remains one of the most important issues facing the profession of student affairs. Sound ethical decisions must take at least three analytic dimensions into account: the application of ethical principles, understanding the virtues that the community values, and an examination of the multilayered context in which the dilemma has arisen. Higher education leads by both precept and example. Colloquially, we need to talk the talk and walk the walk. Since humans are social creatures, we will probably be more successful in attempting to live ethical lives if we do so within the context of communities that are committed to the examination of ethical issues and values. The question we must now ask ourselves is how we create ethical communities and how we set norms within our communities in higher education. How much energy and time are we willing to put into the effort? The ways in which we answer these questions will shape the future of our democracy. President Clinton was an honors student at Georgetown University. Most of the members of Congress, the business leaders of our nation, and the leaders in all of our professions are college graduates. What are we, in student affairs, teaching our students about how to live in the human community? What are we showing them about how we live in our own communities?

References

Brown, R. "Creating an Ethical Community." In H. Canon and R.D. Brown (eds.) *Applied Ethics in Student Services*. San Francisco: Jossey Bass, 1985.

Caine, R. and Caine, G. *Education on the Edge of Possibility*. Alexandria, VA: Association for Supervision and Curriculum Development, 1997.

Canon, H. "Maintaining High Ethical Standards." In M.J. Barr and Associates. *The Handbook of Student Affairs Administration*. San Francisco: Jossey-Bass, 1993.

Fried, J. and Malley, J. "Ethical issues on Multicultural Campuses." Paper presented at the annual conference of the American College Personnel Association, St. Louis, MO, March, 1998.

Fried, J. and Associates. *Shifting Paradigms in Student Affairs*. Lanham, MD: University Press of America/American College Personnel Association, 1995.

Guthrie, V. "Cognitive Foundations of Ethical Development." In J. Fried (ed.) *Ethics for Today's Campus: Education, Student Development, and Institutional Management*. San Francisco: Jossey Bass, 1997.

Kitchner, K.S., "Ethical Principles and Ethical Decisions in Student Affairs." In H. J. Canon and R.O. Brown (eds), *Applied Ethics in Student Services*. New Directions for Student Services. No. 30, San Francisco: Jossey-Bass, 1985.

Kotkin, J. *Tribes*. New York: Random House, 1992.

Meara, N., Schmidt, L., and Day, J. "Principles and Virtues: A Foundation for Ethical Decisions, Policies and Character. "*The Counseling Psychologists*, 1996, 24(1), 1–77.

National Association of Student Personnel Administrators, *Member Handbook*, Washington, D.C.: NASPA, 1998, pp. 19–20.

Okun, B., Fried, J., and Okun, M. *Understanding Diversity*. Pacific Grove, CA: Brooks/Cole, 1999.

CHAPTER TWENTY-THREE

DEVELOPING PARTNERSHIPS WITH ACADEMIC AFFAIRS TO ENHANCE STUDENT LEARNING

Cathy McHugh Engstrom and Vincent Tinto

Many student affairs professionals and faculty across the country are working together in exciting endeavors such as residential living-learning centers or colleges, supplemental instruction programs, new student seminars, service-learning activities, and learning communities to create enriched educational experiences for students. They have done so because they recognize the importance of shared learning (Tinto, 1997) and shared authority (Olyer, 1996). In addition, there has been recognition of the need to design activities that integrate the social, intellectual, and emotional components of learning, and link the in- and out-of-class activities of students (Love and Love, 1995). To build such "seamless learning" environments (Kuh, 1996), faculty and student affairs professionals have been willing to take risks and be vulnerable, seek connections and relationships, display empathy, and challenge their own assumptions, perceptions, and myths. They have been open to examining and renegotiating their own attitudes and assumptions about each other and are comfortable with the conflict that emerges from welcoming diverse perspectives and voices into their classrooms, educational programs, meetings, and informal conversations. In doing so, faculty and student affairs professionals have willingly constructed a truly collaborative learning environment in which all members take part.

Though still uncommon, these efforts mirror a growing body of literature that emphasizes the interrelatedness of the intellectual, social, and emotional processes in learning (Belenky, Clinchy, Goldberger, and Tarule, 1986; Gabelnick,

1997; Love and Love, 1995) and a shift that is leading us to rethink what we know, and the way we teach and learn (Baxter-Magolda, 1992; Liu, 1995). At the same time, greater emphasis on access, affordability, accountability, and efficiency; concerns about increasing costs and return on investment; and other issues have combined to put pressure on higher education to refocus efforts on student learning (Guskin, 1997; Schroeder, 1998; Wingspread Report, 1993). This focus on student learning and the need to construct learning environments that bridge the academic and social lives of students could be the unifying bridge to bring more faculty and student affairs together in ways that benefit us all (American Association Higher Education/American College Personnel Association/National Association for Student Personnel Administrators, 1998; American College Personnel Association, 1994; American College Personnel Association/National Association for Student Personnel Administrators, 1997).

This chapter describes ways to construct bridges between student affairs and faculty so that opportunities for promoting integrated learning experiences for students are maximized. We first describe the barriers that typically have hindered partnerships between faculty and student affairs. A continuum of the types of partnerships between faculty and student affairs is also discussed. We then identify the characteristics of authentic, enduring, collaborative relationships, and the potential that partnerships have for fundamentally transforming how student affairs and faculty understand their work and how student learning is constructed in the academy. Finally, we describe several organizational models that provide fertile ground for these relationships and offer a series of recommendations for promoting collaborative partnerships between faculty and student affairs professionals.

Barriers to Partnerships

Achieving collaborative partnerships between faculty and student affairs professionals is far from simple. Strong forces in higher education have acted as barriers to developing meaningful, lasting partnerships between student affairs and faculty. Separatism, specialization, and competition have existed in higher education for over 100 years and have led to the development of cultural differences between student and academic affairs that hinder efforts at collaboration. The value of highlighting these barriers is to bring to a conscious level the powerful forces that have made the task of developing relationships between faculty and student affairs so difficult. At the same time, it provides a critical context for understanding how the strategies recommended later may be successful in dismantling obstacles.

Separatism, Specialization, and Competition

American higher education was founded on the notion of development of the whole person, particularly the development of student character and civic and religious leadership (Schroeder and Mable, 1994). With the emergence of the German research university model in the mid-nineteenth century, the purpose of higher education shifted from developing the whole person to the developing of the intellect. The tasks that faculty no longer deemed directly relevant to student academics were assumed by student affairs professionals (Kuh, Shedd, and Whitt, 1987). While faculty were busy nurturing students' intellect, student affairs professionals assumed responsibility for discipline and regulated student behaviors outside the classroom. The result was an increased specialization of functions, a growing tension between student affairs professionals and faculty reinforced by the presence of separate structures for in-class and out-of-class experiences (Blake, 1979). In the 1970s, there was a concerted effort to embrace practices that moved student affairs professionals from "regulators of student behavior" to educators dedicated to promoting student development. The proliferation of student development theories during this period provided a knowledge base for student affairs practices. Brown (1990) shared a list of activities in which faculty and student affairs interacted, activities that reflected different levels of intensity and commitment (such as faculty attendance at a residence hall dessert versus faculty member and student affairs professionals co-instructing credit-bearing new student experience course). However, despite these efforts, the literature in the 1980s was dominated by the theme that little progress had been made in faculty-student affairs relationships. Smith (1982) argued that part of the problem stemmed from faculty's lack of understanding or acceptance of the "whole person" mission of the institution.

Scarce financial resources in the late 1980s and early 1990s also intensified the disdain and distrust between faculty and administrators. Concerns about reporting structures, territorialism, and ownership were part of the daily activities of faculty and administrators. Recently, scholars such as Boyer (1987, 1990), Palmer (1987), and Astin (1988) challenged the competitive values and structures embedded in higher education institutions and stressed the need to foster community and a more expansive view of scholarships.

Cultural Differences

A consistent theme is that faculty and student affairs represent fundamentally different cultures. Culture can be defined as "the social or normative glue—based on shared values and beliefs—that holds an organization together" (Kuh and Whitt, 1988). Faculty and student affairs groups each have developed value systems, ways of knowing, norms of behavior, roles and responsibilities, customs, language, and styles. These cultural assumptions and norms have resulted in differences in organizational structures, backgrounds and training, goals and priorities, and reward systems. The strength of these cultures has "contributed to an inability on the part of institutions to change quickly in response to changing needs of students" (Love and Love, 1995, p. 21). Granted, within each of these two cultures, many subcultures exist. For example, the values, norms, and assumptions of a humanities faculty tend to be strikingly different than those of an engineering faculty. The culture of a career development office varies dramatically from that of a housing/residential life office in terms of their respective histories, day-to-day activities, professional association affiliations, and even the typical graduate training experiences obtained by the professional staff (Kuh and Whitt, 1988; Love, Kuh, MacKay and Hardy, 1993; Tierney, 1990; Kuh, 1993; and Schroeder, Nicholls, and Kuh, 1983).

An examination of the attributes of these two cultures highlights why the two groups have been described as "opposites" and the barriers between them have been perceived to be insurmountable. Consequently, relationships between faculty and student affairs are often characterized by misunderstanding, mistrust, disrespect, conflict, disdain, and antagonism (Blake, 1979; Knefelkamp, 1991; Schroeder, 1998). Table 23.1 summarizes perceived differences that traditionally have been described in the literature on student affairs and faculty. Note that these descriptions reflect cultural perspectives and are not intended to describe the attitudes and behaviors of all faculty or all student affairs professionals.

Blake (1979) believed that faculty and student affairs administrators engage in symmetrically opposite, complementary educational functions. Brown (1990) wrote:

> Traditionally, faculty have considered the primary functions of the university to be creating, preserving, and transmitting knowledge while promoting and safeguarding the so-called life of the mind. Their professional rewards have followed from these values. Moreover, recognition, promotion, and tenure at most institutions are based more on scholarly contributions to an academic discipline than on professional contributions to the education of students or to the welfare of the institution. The orientation of student affairs professionals is quite different. For them, the institutional emphasis is on the student and the process of growth and development that students, regardless of age, undergo during their time in college [p. 246—47].

Faculty have been described to be more isolated, reflective, theoretical, cautious, and likely to move at their own pace. Student affairs administrators are often

TABLE 23.1 FACULTY AND STUDENT AFFAIRS TRADITIONAL CULTURAL CHARACTERISTICS, NORMS, ATTITUDES

Student Affairs	Faculty
Emphasis on student personal growth dimensions (social and affective); value experiential education	Emphasis on student critical thinking, acquisiton of knowledge. Pedagogy relies heavily on lecture.
Value subjective, relational, dimensions of knowing and learning	Privilege objective, rational, independent ways of knowing
Believe student affairs and faculty have shared purposes-education of the whole student. Student affairs is central to promoting student learning	Believe intellectual/academic activities in the classroom are superior to other nonrational or nonintellectual activities occurring outside the classroom
Characterized by hierarchical structures, centralized decision-making, defined responsibilities and lines of authority; maintenance of status quo. Loyalty is to one's department and institution.	Characterized by structures that emphasize collegiality through shared governance, peer leadership, Loyalty is to academic discipline.
Values defined goals, task completion and productivity, accountability, systems to control	Values ambiguity, autonomy, flexibility, nonconformity, creativity and innovation, and critical analysis
Individuals tend to be interpersonally adept, extraverted, problem-solvers. Interested in moving up the administrative ladder	Individuals tend to be introverted. No interest in moving up administrative ladder. Desire to increase scholarly prominence in academic community
Doing, action-oriented, little time for reflection. Work characterized by practicality, brevity, variety, and unpredictability	Thinking and reflecting, future-focused. Value order and predictability in their work
Work collaboratively, in groups, to solve immediate problems with real deadlines	Engage in solitary, autonomous, independent work
Encourage cooperative efforts and contributions within a defined set of community expectations of behavior. Perspectives or conflicts that impede the group from meeting goals are not valued. Expected to uphold institutional policy in public	Encourage nonconformity. Dissent perceived as normal, healthy, and expected in a community that values freedom of inquiry. It is a right and responsibility to challenge structures that are threats to academic freedom.
Seek student involvement in decision-making; serve as student advocates, particularly for voices that are often marginalized and not heard	Sees faculty as the expert and authority. Students are the receptacles of their wisdom and knowledge. Believe they know what is best for the students

(continued)

TABLE 23.1 FACULTY AND STUDENT AFFAIRS
TRADITIONAL CULTURAL CHARACTERISTICS, NORMS, ATTITUDES

Student Affairs	Faculty
Areas of expertise: Experts at understanding and appreciating diverse cultures, student subcultrues, popular culture. Experts in student characteristics and developmental needs. Knowledge of interpersonal dynamics, team building, managing group conflicts. Skilled at diverse pedagogical strategies to promote student learning. Understand how institutional processes and politics work	Area of expertise: Their academic discipline, teaching the content related to their academic discipline, research, writing, and publishing skills
Training: human development theories, counseling theories, organizational development, and administration	Training: Scholarship in their academic discipline and writing
Reward system often based on loyal behavior to supervisors and adherence independent work (often of current administrative norms	Reward system based on scholarly productivity and and acceptance narrowly defined as research productivity as evaluated by a group of scholars outside the university who are experts in that discipline).

Sources for this infomration include: Blake, 1978; Brown, 1990; Fried, 1995; Kuh, Douglas, Lind, & Ramin-Gyurnek, 1994; Kuh, Shedd, & Whitt, 1987; Love & Goodsell, 1995; Love, Kuh, MacKay, & Hardy, 1993; Schroeder, Nicholls, & Kuh, 1983.

depicted as action-oriented, focused on products or results, and skilled at securing resources, managing crises, and problem solving. Blake observed that based on these cultural norms, it is "hardly surprising that different human personalities tend to end up as professors or administrators of student affairs. In caricature the professorial extreme is almost the mirror image of the student personnel administrators extreme" (1979, p. 284).

Currently, the organizational structures in higher education seem to promote individual, isolated, passive learning and forms of discourse limited to the narrow boundaries of separate disciplines (Tinto, 1997) and administrative functional areas. Faculty and student affairs professionals often speak different languages literally and metaphorically (Knefelkamp, 1991) and operate from different theoretical bases. Members of each group also tend to be suspicious of those who cross borders (Brown, 1997).

A Window of Opportunity for Innovative Types of Partnerships

Although the obstacles just described are real and formidable, recent societal trends and forces affecting institutions of higher education create significant promise for a reconceptualization of faculty and student affairs partnerships so we might create "seamless curriculums" (Knefelkamp, 1991) or "seamless learning environments" (Kuh, 1996). These environments are characterized by the recognition that "cognitive and affective development are inextricably intertwined and the curricular and out-of-class activities are not discrete, independent events" (Banta and Kuh, 1998).

Paradigm shifts about knowledge and the teaching-learning process are occurring in education, the humanities, and the social sciences. Educators are challenging the objective and cognitive assumptions about knowledge and are advocating that the individualist, independent, and competitive climate of our institutions be complemented with inclusive, caring elements of community (Belenky, Clinchy, Goldberger, and Tarule, 1986; Palmer, 1987). These scholars emphasize the importance of recognizing and valuing the relational, instrumental components of how we learn, come to know, and come to live (Baxter-Magolda, 1992; Liu, 1995; Palmer, 1987). Increasing numbers of scholars in the social sciences, humanities, and education disciplines *and* professionals in student affairs are advancing perspectives that are more inclusive, collaborative, egalitarian, and less hierarchical (Rhoads and Black, 1995). In addition, the academy is beginning to embrace a broader notion of scholarship that recognizes innovative *applications* of research and the *integration* of research, teaching, and service are important scholarly activities (Boyer, 1990; Angelo and Cross, 1992). Boyer argues that faculty reward systems must value scholarship that arises through teaching and service activities, where the faculty member makes connections across disciplines leading to new insights and interpretations, and innovatively applies knowledge (Whitt and Nuss, 1994). A faculty reward structure that supports this more expansive view of scholarship opens up new, exciting possibilities for how faculty construct their work and the type of relationships that might be meaningful in this design.

In response to these trends and forces, leaders in student affairs have called for professionals to work with faculty to develop partnerships on behalf of student *learning* (AAHE/ACPA/NASPA, 1998; ACPA, 1994; ACPA/NASPA, 1997). A student-learning paradigm requires a new way of thinking and acting at both individual and institutional levels (Barr, 1998). The focus moves from providing instruction to promoting learning. The interrelationships among the social, emotional, and academic domains of learning are recognized and respected, thereby leading to deeper, more meaningful student experiences. A student-learning paradigm also suggests different roles and responsibilities for faculty, student affairs, and college and university structures (Love and Love, 1995; Kuh, 1996).

Brown (1997) emphasizes that the most effective way of actualizing the student-learning paradigm is to extend the learning environment into the workplace of faculty and administrators. Embedded in promoting a student-learning paradigm is the need to transform institutions of higher education into "learning organizations" (Senge, 1990). Members of learning organizations are committed to discourse where shared learning among faculty, student affairs, and students is commonplace; the perspectives and experiences of all are equally valued as important sources of knowledge; participants are open to examining their own assumptions and attitudes; and conflict is assumed essential to developing community. These characteristics are indicative of cross-disciplinary, cross-functional, collaborative learning approaches. Minimally, boundaries become permeable; optimally, they become obsolete. Organizational structures, as we know them today, are open to reconceptualization and design.

Evolution of the Partnerships Between Student Affairs and Faculty

Student affairs and faculty have managed to come together to develop meaningful educational experiences for students with frequency and success despite barriers. Methods range from serving as information clearinghouses for faculty, being cooperative partners, and recently establishing collaborative relationships with faculty.

Working together is something we learn to do and requires the individuals involved to experience change. Working with faculty in any of these functions illustrates a continuum integrating the dimensions outlined in Table 23.2. The table illustrates how these dimensions vary, depending upon the type of relationship. Roles are not clear-cut or absolute; the dimensions are intended to focus on critical elements to consider when examining how faculty and student affairs work together.

This role is assumed by student affairs when departments pull together resource information that faculty members (and other constituent groups such as students, families, and alumni) find useful in their teaching and other educational interests of their students. For example, an office may have information about tutors or information about ADA compliance and institutional expectations and procedures for faculty to follow. At the University of Maryland, the National Clearinghouse on Student Leadership can be an important scholarly reference for faculty members whose interests lie in leadership. This role assumes more of a one-way service function to faculty and is more directly tied to an office than a

TABLE 23.2 CHARACTERISTICS OF PARTNERSHIPS BETWEEN STUDENT AFFAIRS AND FACULTY

Serving as Information Clearinghouses	Working Cooperatively with Faculty	Working Collaboratively with Faculty
LOW LEVELES REQUIRED	*HIGH LEVELS REQUIRED*	
Commitment to Relationship	<————————————————>	
Commitment to shared learning and challenging one's "mental maps"	<————————————————>	
Construct shared purposes regarding desired learning outcomes	<————————————————>	
Degree of interdependence	<————————————————>	
Degree of reciprocity	<————————————————>	
Commitment to create integrated student learning experiences	<————————————————>	
Ease of and time required for implementation	<————————————————>	
Institutional leadership support needed	<————————————————>	
Funding required	<————————————————>	
Ambiguity in the roles and responsibilities assumed by faculty and student affairs	<————————————————>	
Change required in how we do our work	<————————————————>	
Need to be "multi" cultural Information Clearinghouse Role	<————————————————>	

specific individual. The student affairs member (or unit) and the faculty work very autonomously from one another. Student affairs professionals can dictate their own priorities about what and how information will be collected and disseminated. However, hopefully, the importance of obtaining feedback from its "clients" will be incorporated into the unit's ongoing activities so the resources will be relevant and valued by the targeted audiences.

Cooperative Ventures

Such ventures have increased dramatically over the past two decades. In cooperative ventures, faculty and student affairs staff typically come together with identified outcomes in mind. For example, a committee to design a residential living-learning floor for women engineering students is announced. In this process, the goal of establishing a residential living-learning floor (the product) cannot be accomplished without each partner(s) doing his/her part. The roles and responsibilities of the faculty members and student affairs staff are often defined by their respective expertise and functional area or discipline. In other words, they are still operating from their "functional silos." Faculty and student affairs assume the roles and responsibilities traditionally relegated to their group (for example, faculty oversee the academic components, while student affairs coordinate the administrative functions and attend to the social/psychological needs of students).

The student affairs staff may worry that curriculum of the engineering faculty may not address important transitional and social issues or educate students about university rules and regulations. Therefore, the residence life staff may develop some initial community-building activities and orientation sessions that educate the engineering students about important campus resources and university expectations for behavior. The planning group may have to address areas that overlap such as staffing structures, roles and responsibilities, publication materials, and assessment strategies. Often, the final authority for these decisions may rest with the part of the group with the needed financial resources to fund proposed ideas.

In this example, engineering faculty and student affairs conduct their work in a rather independent fashion, but share progress on their assigned responsibilities. They come to appreciate one another and the contributions each group makes to promote students' educational experience. Both groups are committed to the defined goals of the project, but it is not necessary they come to a shared understanding of desired *learning* goals for this program. However, this type of experience has not typically made individuals aware of the underlying assumptions and values that guide actions, nor led faculty and student affairs to work collectively to develop a shared vision (and language) about what factors contribute to student learning (Kuh, 1996). Faculty and student affairs professionals are not challenged to reflect upon ways in which institutional boundaries inhibit the development of educational experiences for students that integrate the social, emotional, and intellectual dimensions of the learning process (Love and Love, 1995). Faculty and student affairs may act respectfully toward each other, but the development of mutually strong, trusting relationships has not been essential to completing a project. Boundaries and territories have remained unchallenged and intact.

There are countless examples of the first two roles and the important educational contributions that have resulted, but, as Terenzini and Pascarella (1994) observed, cooperative partnerships are limited in their potential to develop integrated, institutionalized, learning experiences for students. "Organizationally and operationally, we have lost sight of the forest. If undergraduate education is to be enhanced, faculty members, joined by academic and student affairs administrators, must devise ways to deliver undergraduate education that are as comprehensive and integrated as the ways students actually learn. A whole new mindset is needed to capitalize on the interrelatedness of the in- and out-of-class influences on student learning and the functional interconnectedness of academic and student affairs divisions" (Terenzini and Pascarella, 1994, p. 32). We contend that, in order to make any substantial progress to meet the challenges of the *Student Learning Imperative* (ACPA, 1994) and move toward "learning organizations" where learning is shared and *jointly* constructed across disciplines and functional areas, student affairs and faculty must develop *collaborative relationships*. It is these types of relationships that have the greatest potential to create structural reform and a conceptual rethinking of higher education in ways that value emerging epistemologies or ways of knowing and their related pedagogies (such as experiential, active learning). The importance of inclusivity, community, and conflict are embraced in learning-centered institutions. The presence of collaborative partnerships is just beginning to find expression and value in institutional structures and processes.

Moving Toward Collaborative Partnerships

A discussion about a vision of collaborative relationships requires imagination. A commitment to work toward collaboration will require us to head down unknown, uncharted paths in which the roles and responsibilities of those involved will be open to constant negotiation, organizational boundaries will be more permeable and fluid, and participants will be pushed to become skilled at "comparing learnings, sharing learnings, and acting on new learnings" (Brown, 1997, p. 7). We will first describe characteristics of collaborative partnerships, and second, we will provide examples of emerging collaborative relationships. Finally, we end with recommendations to consider for promoting collaborative partnerships between student affairs and faculty.

Characteristics of Collaborative Partnerships

The focus of collaborative partnerships is not on producing a final "product." Rather, the purpose of these partnerships is to mutually construct the vision, goals, and processes for developing student-learning experiences that integrate the emotional, social, and cognitive dimensions of learning (Love and Love, 1995). Participants seek to develop a democracy that includes many voices, many ideas, many perspectives, and multiple commitments (Gabelnick, 1997) focused on student learning and community responsibility. In this non-hierarchical structure, all group members are perceived and recognized as holding important knowledge and experiences that can contribute to the group's learning process. The responsibilities and roles of participants are in constant negotiation; authority is shared and shifts continually based on the knowledge and experiences of group members. As a result, this process often feels ambiguous. Conflicts and difficult dialogues are deemed essential to establishing trusting, respectful, forgiving relationships (Bruffee, 1995; Matthews, Cooper, Davidson and Hawkes, 1995), community, and different ways of knowing and pedagogies (Palmer, 1987).

In this process, participants recognize and confront their biases and presuppositions of one another. This reflection initiates the "re-acculturation" process (Bruffee, 1987, p. 7) in which both faculty and student affairs renegotiate membership in groups or cultures that they have affiliated with as they now learn to become members of another group or culture. Since faculty and student affairs members often represent numerous subcultures, in this re-acculturation process, participants are challenged to be "multicultural." Bruffee (1987) notes that the educational process of re-acculturation is extremely difficult, painful, and typically incomplete. In this re-acculturation process, boundaries become permeable and even reconstructed. Consequently, group members must be flexible and embrace cultural change. They are called to exercise new levels of ingenuity and innovativeness (Bruffee, 1987). As a result of this shared process of inquiry, participants develop the knowledge and skills to solve complex, sophisticated problems and issues.

Organizational Models that Promote Collaborative Partnerships

Two recent initiatives, learning communities and service learning, embrace the principles of collaborative learning and have the potential to transform our institutions into true learning-centered organizations. Focus on these initiatives is not intended to dismiss other promising collaborative partnerships in such areas as freshmen experience programs, retention efforts, career development initiatives, leadership development, or multiculturalism. These specific models are used as a vehicle for highlighting the characteristics of collaborative, learning-centered relationships between student affairs and faculty. In addition, they demonstrate a rich potential for engaging students in more integrated learning experiences as current, limiting organizational structures and barriers are challenged.

Learning Communities. Partly in response to a series of reports by the National Institute of Education (1984) and the Association of American Colleges (1985) as well as studies in the late 1980s and early 1990s by scholars such as Astin (1987), Boyer (1987), and Tinto (1987), a growing number of institutions have begun to reform educational practice and restructure classrooms to more actively involve students in learning. One such effort is encompassed by learning communities and the collaborative pedagogy that underlies them. Unlike many programs that exist at the periphery of the academic experiences of students, learning communities seek to restructure the classrooms in which students find themselves and alter the way students experience both the curriculum and learning within those classrooms. It should be noted that learning communities are not new. In the United States, they date back to the early work of Meiklejohn and to the Experimental College at the University of Wisconsin (Meiklejohn, 1932). However, like Tussman's experiment at the University of California at Berkeley (1969), early learning communities were limited in scope and in the students they served. The current movement, led over the past twelve years by the Washington Center at The Evergreen State College, is different not only because it involves a greater range of institutions public and private, two- and four-year, but also because it is being adapted to the learning needs of a broad range of students.

Learning communities begin with registration scheduling that enables students to take courses together rather than apart. In some cases, learning communities link students by tying two courses together. In other cases, it may mean sharing the entire first-semester curriculum. In some large universities such as the University of Oregon and the University of Washington, the twenty-five to thirty students in a learning community may attend lectures with two to three hundred other students, but stay together for a smaller discussion section led by a graduate student or upperclassman. In still other cases, students will take all their classes together either as separate but linked classes (cluster learning communities) or as one large class that meets four to six hours at a time several times a week (coordinated studies).

The courses in which students register are not coincidental or random. They are typically connected by an organizing theme that gives meaning to their linkage. The point of doing so is to engender a coherent, interdisciplinary or cross-subject learning that is not easily attainable through enrollment in unrelated, stand-alone courses. For example, the Coordinated Studies Program at Seattle Central Community College entitled "Body and Mind," which links courses in human biology, psychology, and sociology, asks students to consider how the connected fields of study pursue a singular piece of knowledge, namely how and why humans behave as they do.

As described by Gabelnick and her colleagues (1990), many learning communities do more than register students around a topic. They change the manner in which students experience the curriculum and the way they are taught. Faculty have reorganized their syllabi and their classrooms to promote shared, collaborative learning experiences among students across the linked classrooms. This form of classroom organization requires students to work together in some form of collaborative group and to become active, and responsible, for the learning of both group and classroom peers.

Though the content may vary, nearly all learning communities have three things in common. First is shared knowledge. By requiring students to take courses together and organizing those courses around a theme, learning communities seek to construct a shared, coherent curricular experience. In doing so, they seek to promote higher levels of cognitive complexity that cannot easily be obtained through participation in unrelated courses. Second is shared knowing. Learning communities enroll the same students in several classes so they get to know each other quickly, fairly intimately, and in a way that is an essential component of their academic experience. By asking students to construct knowledge together, learning communities seek to involve students both socially and intellectually in ways that promote cognitive development as well as an appreciation for the many ways in which one's own knowing is enhanced when other voices are part of that learning experience. Third is shared responsibility. Learning communities ask students to become responsible to each other in the process of learning. They participate in collaborative groups that require students to be mutually dependent on one another so that the learning of the group does not advance without each member doing her or his part.

As a curricular structure, learning communities can be applied to any content and any group of students. Most often, they are designed for the needs of beginning students. In those instances, one of the linked courses may become a freshman seminar. Increasingly, they are also being adapted to the needs of undecided students and students who require developmental academic assistance. In these cases, one of the linked courses may be a career exploration and/or developmental advising course or, in the latter case, a "learning to learn" or study skills course. In residential campuses, some learning communities have moved into the residence halls, creating "living-learning communities" with shared courses and shared living.

When applied to particular groups of students, as previously described, the faculty of the learning community almost always combines the work of academic and student affairs professionals. Such learning communities require the collaborative efforts of both parties. Take the case of learning communities for students requiring developmental assistance. In cluster learning communities, for example, the "faculty" of the learning community may consist of a faculty person who teaches a regular introductory course in political science and two members of a learning support center who teach developmental writing and mathematics.

Regardless of their focus, evidence mounts that such learning communities are powerful tools to enhance both the education and retention of college students (Tinto, Goodsell, and Russo, 1993). Students report not only greater involvement and enhanced learning—as one student puts it, "we learn better together"—they also persist at rates that are substantially higher than those for similar students in stand-alone courses (Tinto, Goodsell, and Russo, 1994).

To be effective, however, learning communities require their "faculty," the academic and student affairs professionals who staff the learning community, to collaborate on both the content and pedagogy of the linked courses. They have to work together, as equal partners, to ensure that the linked courses provide a coherent, shared learning experience. One of the many benefits of such collaboration is that the academic staff "discovers" the wealth of knowledge that student affairs professionals bring to the discourse about teaching and learning. One of the ironies of this situation is that the typical student affairs professional knows more about student learning than the typical faculty member. Least we forget, faculty members are the only members of the teaching profession, from kindergarten through college, who are not trained to teach their own students.

When faculty and student affairs leave their respective silos, both discover the benefits of looking at one's work as an educator from fresh eyes. The result is that a new appreciation for conversations about how we teach our students can enrich our own teaching. As one faculty member in a learning community says, "We are all realizing the strengths we bring to our teaching, but we are also introduced to new ways to deal with the same content" (Gablenick, MacGregor, Matthews, and Leigh-Smith, 1990, p.81).

Learning communities offer not only an organizational vehicle for increased cooperation between faculty and student affairs, but also a setting for the development of truly collaborative relationships that lead both parties to rethink their work. Little wonder then that the recent movement to reintroduce a university college into the organization of the university, such as the University College at Indiana University-Purdue University, Indianapolis (IUPUI), has looked to learning communities as a structure around which to build such colleges.

Service Learning. Jacoby defines service learning as "a form of experiential education in which students engage in activities that address human and community needs together with structured opportunities intentionally designed to promote student learning and development. Reflection and reciprocity are key concepts of service-learning" (Jacoby, 1996, p. 5). As a pedagogical model, service learning recognizes the power of interdisciplinary approaches to solve the complex core problems facing society and is proving to be capable of transforming traditional teaching and learning practices (Engstrom and Tinto, 1997; Howard, 1998; Liu, 1995; Rhoads and Howard, 1998). Research indicates that students involved in service learning increase their levels of social responsibility, develop critical thinking skills, and examine the values, beliefs, and understanding of self and others (Checkoway, 1997).

Many factors are responsible for the increasing adoption of service learning in institutions of higher education. A few key forces include the creation of Campus Compact in 1985 by a group of college presidents invested in promoting the importance of civic responsibility in students' learning, the development of the "Principles of Good Practice for Combining Service and Learning (Honnet and Poulsen, 1989) (see Table 23.3), and federal support for such initiatives as Learn and Serve: Higher Education and Americorps. After examining the Principles of Good Practice for Combining Service and Learning, it is evident that the potential to actualize these conditions can be maximized by having faculty and student affairs work together on behalf of service learning. The manner in which these groups work together varies tremendously. Many student affairs-faculty partnerships exist where student affairs staff assumes a clearinghouse role. A cooperative relationship between student affairs and faculty is also common on campuses.

For example, an English faculty member contacts a student affairs service learning/community service office and asks the student affairs staff to make arrangements to place his/her students in community agencies. The faculty member shares his/her syllabus with student affairs staff members to orient them about how this activity relates to the course goals. The teaching assistant for the course facilitates reflection sessions and picks up a booklet from the student affairs office that offers some tips for facilitating these sessions. The faculty member meets regularly with the teaching assistant to clarify what connections he/she hopes students will make between the course material and community service experiences. Students evaluate this experience very highly and indicate how useful it was to connect their agency experience with the course material. However, they also share that they felt somewhat isolated and didn't have anyone to speak to about the experience. They explain they were uneasy about bringing non-course-related ideas or issues in the TA-run sessions.

In this cooperative endeavor, the faculty member and student affairs staff worked rather independently and autonomously. They did not construct a shared vision about the purposes of this learning experience or work together to construct processes that reflect an integrated notion of learning. The roles of the faculty member, teaching assistant, and student affairs staff were well-defined, understood, and respected. Opportunities did not materialize for the faculty and student affairs members to learn from each other. Their respective territories remained intact and unchallenged. Clearly, in this cooperative partnership, an important learning experience was provided to a group of students. In addition, the experience was designed with relative ease, speed, and minimal new financial resources.

Increasingly, institutions are demonstrating more collaborative partnerships in which faculty and student affairs are working together to conceptualize shared meanings of service learning as it relates to the institutional mission. In these ex-

TABLE 23.3   WIDESPREAD PRINCIPLES OF GOOD PRACTICE FOR COMBINING SERVICE AND LEARNING

Learning
An effective and sustained program that combines service and learning:

Engages people in responsible and challenging actions for the common good

Provides structured opportunities for people to reflect critically on their service experience

Allows for those with needs to define those needs

Clarifies the responsibilities of each person and organization involved

Matches service providers and service needs through a process that recognizes changing circumstances

Expects genuine, active, and sustained organizational commitment

Includes training, supervision, monitoring, support, recognition, and evaluation to meet service and learning goals

Ensures that the time commitment for service and learning is flexible, appropriate, and in the best interests of all involved

Is committed to promote participation by and with diverse populations

Source: Porter Honnet and Poulsen, 1989

amples, service learning is beginning to transform faculty and student affairs work, particularly related to the assumptions and practices of teaching and learning. These outcomes have also resulted in institutional changes that value a more expansive view of scholarship, teaching, and learning.

For example, at the University of Utah, thanks to the leadership of the Bennion Center staff (student affairs staff), the Bennion Center Faculty Advisory Committee, and individual faculty members, the campus offers over 80 service-learning courses in forty-five different departments (Engstrom and Tinto, 1997). Faculty and student affairs staff work together to advocate the benefits of service learning at the highest levels of the university. As partners, they have developed a statement articulating an institutional rationale for integrating service learning within departmental, college, and administrative structures. In addition, they work together to educate departments interested in service learning and provide consultation to faculty about how to write service-learning proposals. Over $70,000 of institutional support has been awarded to support service-learning grant initiatives. The Bennion Center and faculty also oversee several prestigious awards that have been created to recognize the innovative efforts of faculty. The faculty contributes their expertise by approving service-learning courses and providing leadership with Center staff for developing guidelines for tenure and promotion for departments to evaluate faculty involved in service-learning activities (Engstrom and Tinto, 1997). The faculty are critical in shaping policies that result in service learning becoming a valued and important scholarly endeavor (Ward, 1998, p. 76), efforts that are positively recognized in the university rewards structure.

The student affairs staff works with individual faculty members to help them develop service-learning proposals that meet the standards used by departments to evaluate faculty involved in service learning. They also serve as the central liaison with community agencies. Staff members fund and supervise teaching assistants who work with faculty who are integrating service learning into their classes for the first time. The teaching assistants are trained in group facilitation, designing meaningful reflection activities, and pedagogy. In addition, the teaching assistants arrange the site placements and facilitate the reflection component of the course. Clearly, in these partnerships, the expertise of faculty and student affairs staff have been tapped. However, those involved do not work independently. They develop a shared vision of the purpose of service learning at their institution and to work, as partners, to educate the institution about its benefits and to secure a high level of institutional support.

The University of Michigan's Center for Learning through Community Service (a unit in student affairs) is another example of collaborative efforts between student affairs and faculty. This center is dedicated to "strengthen student learning, assist faculty members, and develop university-community partnerships that address unmet community needs and enhance the educational process" (http://www.state.outreach.umich.edu/cgi-bin/urel/viewitem?77 +). Since 1973, the Division of Student Affairs, Sociology, and Education has involved over 600 students per year to combine academically accredited learning with meaningful service to the community (Engstrom and Tinto, 1997). The requirements for this experience include community service work, a weekly reflection seminar, readings, and writing. The Center's staff work with faculty and graduate student instructors to develop this comprehensive learning experience for students. They work together to develop a common understanding of the underlying course tenets and a seminar manual for the graduate student instructors (see http://www.umich.edu/~crltmich/pubs.html). In partnership, both are involved in training graduate students. Specifically, faculty discuss how to make connections between sociology and the course content with the field experience. Student affairs staff also consult with the graduate assistants about seminar design issues and offer ideas for facilitating student involvement and critical reflection. The staff serves as a liaison with community agencies and makes the site placements.

The Center also plays a significant role in supporting the scholarly activities of faculty and student affairs staff. For example, it publishes the first nationally distributed, refereed service-learning journal, the *Michigan Journal of Community Service Learning*. The Center also sponsors a Brown Bag Lunch Series where scholars can present papers on pedagogy and research in service learning. One of the principles that was developed by the University Task Force on Community Service Learning was to "generate resources and share power between and among students, faculty, the university and the community, and develop relationships that are reciprocal, collaborative, and focus on building community" (www.umich.edu/~ocsl/). Clearly, these elements are characteristic of collaborative as opposed to cooperative partnerships, as they seek to challenge current organizational structures and processes.

Finally, Michigan State University has developed meaningful incentives for faculty or units who consider service as a critical viable scholarly activity. Funding is offered for faculty and staff on a peer-reviewed, competitive basis and for units proposing projects that strengthen service as scholarship. These actions have resulted in the integration of service initiatives into the annual planning and budgetary process of the university and generated new ways of thinking about service.

Service learning represents the principles of learning that recognize the neo-Deweyan approach of "learning by doing" (Dewey, 1916) and the shared construction of knowledge among faculty, student affairs staff, and students. It is a pedagogical model that emphasizes new roles for each of these groups. This pedagogy encourages faculty and student affairs staff to come together and establish common ground about purposes and pedagogical strategies to use to promote learning. As a result, "teaching roles are shared with others, instruction is more public, knowledge sources are decentralized, and learning experiences are less predicable" (Bringle, Games, and Malloy, 1999, p. 11). Faculty and student affairs learn from and with each other as they work together to institutionalize service learning into the infrastructure of the campus. These colleges and universities recognize that institutional change cannot occur from scattered service-learning courses. Institutional transformation has been accompanied by changes in the rewards system, allocation of resources, leadership at senior levels, and assessment of initiatives.

Together faculty and student affairs are conceptualizing, as partners, the purpose and shared values of service learning. They are working interdependently, rather than autonomously, in ways that result in mutual benefits for both parties and for student-learning outcomes. At these institutions, service learning is crossing many boundaries and diffusing many barriers to collaboration. Service-learning initiatives have created exciting opportunities for faculty and student affairs to reflect more intentionally and creatively about their relationships, roles, and responsibilities, as they reconsider and reimagine the values and priorities of higher education (Weigert, 1998).

Recommendations for Promoting Collaborative Relationships

As we seek to create partnerships with faculty colleagues across campuses that endure and succeed in offering students integrated learning experiences, what can be learned from the examples just described? In order to move from periodic, cooperative efforts that surface to meet individual/unit goals, the fundamental structures and processes in our institutions must be altered. Knefelkamp (1991) argued that "It is the season in which we must give up the notion of privilege, mastery, and control, and venture into the uncharted territory of creating a new educational culture" (p. 6).

The recommendations that follow address interrelated strategies that foster collaborative relationships between faculty and student affairs. We believe these relationships can promote the transformation of our institutions into "learning organizations" (Senge, 1990) where an ethos of learning begins to permeate (Kuh, 1996) and colleges and universities recognize the interrelatedness of in- and out-of-class influences in student learning.

Senior Leadership

The president and other senior leaders must call for faculty and student affairs to work together to link the academic and out-of-class dimensions of students' lives. In addition, senior administrators and faculty must model what it means to be a member of a "community of learners." Leaders are needed who will take risks and be vulnerable in the spirit of collaboration as they emphasize learning (including their own) and community (Palmer, 1987).

The leadership of divisions and departments should be evaluated based on their level of collaboration with other groups on behalf of student-learning initiatives and for creating organizational climates where its members see themselves as "teachers, learners, and collaborators in service to learning" (AAHE/ACPA/NASPA, 1998). In these environments, ideas are invited and can be shared, discussed, and debated without risk (Brown, 1997). Administrators and faculty should be challenged (and rewarded) for how they have contributed to the ethos of learning at that institution, rather than the number of students they have taught or programs or services they have implemented. Leaders whose egos are "in check" and a low tolerance for territoriality are needed at all levels and all segments of the campus. We need to develop and reward leaders who demonstrate flexibility and comfort with ambiguity; value multiple perspectives; develop relationships built on mutual trust, forgiveness, and learning (Gabelnick, 1997); and appreciate the importance of conflict and promoting win-win solutions. In addition, leaders are necessary who recognize and confront institutional practices that are espoused to be collaborative, but really are only cooperative (that do not require faculty members or administrators to leave their functional silos or reconsider the way in which they work).

Interdisciplinary, Cross-Functional, University-Wide Task Forces and Design Teams

It is critical that institutional leadership promotes activities that bring people across campus together to envision an integrated notion of learning (Love and Love, 1995) and develop processes for enacting this vision. Committees that include respected leaders from academic and student affairs should be formed continually to address issues and problems that hinder student-learning experiences (that is, "triggering opportunities") (Schroeder, 1998, p. 1) and work together to identify common ground and shared learning agendas. For example, assessment, retention, student leadership, citizenship, community, and multiculturalism represent complex areas affecting student learning. Institutions would benefit from representatives across campus working together as they create a shared vision of what matters and as they address these issues.

Overall, group members must work to uncover their "mental models" or ideas in their "head about how things work" (Brown, 1997, p. 7). They should be encouraged to be open to learn from one another and recognize and value the knowledge and experiences that each member brings to the group. They must reflect upon the organizational structures that are hindering the development of both principles and practices that infuse an integrated ethos of learning into their institution. Through involvement on committees, student affairs and faculty must identify ways to tap and blend their strengths, particular expertise, and interests. Members must also be ready to acknowledge the tensions that will come from cultural differences represented in the group and be willing to facilitate difficult conversations in order to understand, anticipate, and positively channel these differences. Group members must be willing to exercise courage and vulnerability as they begin to challenge decision-making norms and the territories and boundaries that inhibit collaborative endeavors and integrated student-learning experiences.

Reward Systems. Administrative and faculty reward systems necessarily mirror institutional priorities. Faculty tenure and promotion policies must recognize and legitimize a broader, more inclusive view of scholarship that values interdisciplinary and cross-functional approaches to research, teaching, and service. Embedded in interdisciplinary approaches and diverse forms of scholarship are acts of collaboration that are too often discounted in promotion and tenure committee evaluations of faculty work. The unfortunate question is still asked, "How can we judge the person if we do not know whose work it is?" Without these paradigm shifts in how scholarship is viewed, it is doubtful that partnerships between student affairs and faculty will reflect anything more than fragmented efforts at the periphery of campus life.

Institutions also must engage in "serious cultural campaigns" (Checkoway, 1997, p. 313) to inform the community about collaborative initiatives and their benefits for enhancing student learning. All accomplishments should be well publicized so that the language and processes of these initiatives begin to be well understood across campus and there is a growing appreciation of a changing paradigm of learning and collaboration being infused into the fabric of the institution. However, when sharing our joint successes, we must be cognizant and respectful of appropriate ways to give praise and credit in the other disciplinary and administrative cultures. For example, it is not enough that a student affairs colleague shares in a divisional or institutional publication that he/she wrote an article for or made a presentation at a national conference with a faculty member. It is critical that this information be presented in a way that represents the rules of the scholarly community for primary and secondary authorship.

In addition, professional associations and disciplinary societies (including scholarly publications) must advocate the benefits of interdisciplinary interaction. Collegial collaboration should be encouraged through fiscal support; an openness to publish works exemplifying the paradigm shifts in teaching, learning, and a broader notion of scholarship; the support of faculty colleagues facing external reviews; and an acceptance of scholarly papers and presentations for regional and national conferences and meetings. These conditions are critical to how faculty and administrators prioritize their work activities.

Faculty and Staff Development Programs

In order to engage in a re-acculturation process, as described by Bruffee (1995), faculty and student affairs staff initially must be able to work across the many cultures found in the academy. This process involves unmasking and understanding our own assumptions, values, and norms of work. In addition, efforts must be made to understand the ways in which our partners view the world, their priorities, challenges, responsibilities, and work habits. We must move away from "partial knowledge" (Knefelkamp, 1991) and misinformed attitudes that we have of one another that often develop from jargon-filled language and cultural ignorance

(Creeden, 1988). For example, we would never criticize a third-grade teacher for being unavailable for consultation or work in the summer, yet student affairs staff often perceive faculty who are inaccessible during the summer or breaks as inflexible, indifferent, uncaring of students, or unsupportive of student affairs. This attitude often surfaces from a misunderstanding of faculty work responsibilities. Many student affairs staff members are surprised to learn faculty members are not on twelve-month appointments and do not accrue vacation days. Faculty vacations do coincide with students, although most faculty are reading papers, preparing classes, and conducting research far into semester and unpaid summer breaks.

Although student affairs staff would probably react more favorably to staff development sessions that educated participants about perceived cultural differences between faculty and student affairs, faculty development sessions would probably be perceived by faculty as intrusive administrative gestures. Probably one of the most powerful ways in which student affairs staff can understand the faculty culture and its many subcultures is through nurturing one-on-one relationships with individual faculty members. Student affairs staff should begin by tapping like-minded faculty and students are fabulous resources for identifying these faculty members.

Infrastructure

Institutions must dedicate resources—staff, time, space, financial, technological—to support collaborative efforts. Note that the initiatives described in this chapter frequently are accompanied with additional staff, released time for faculty, funding support through new initiative grants, and substantial financial commitment to renovate spaces for seminar rooms, informal social gathering, eating spaces, computer laboratories, and faculty offices. Collaborative learning endeavors are not cheap, but Barr (1998) challenges higher education to take the lead of Silicon Valley companies that dedicate one-third of their budgets to the examination of new methods and processes. For example, in spring 1998, the Provost Office at Iowa State University awarded $28,000 to a cross-disciplinary Learning Communities Working Group (LCWG). These financial resources were used to conduct site visits to exemplary learning community institutions, coordinate a learning communities workshop for faculty and staff, fund assessment efforts, provide financial support for writing across the curriculum efforts, and pay for learning community publications and the costs of hosting a two-day LCWG retreat (http:///www.public.iastate.edu/~learncommunity/LCREPORT98.html). In fall 1998, this working group received a presidential grant of $1,500,000 ($500,000 annually for three years) to fund new learning communities and develop the peer mentors program, assessment initiatives, and communication vehicles (http://public.iastate.edu/~learncommunity/itsworking..html).

Institutions should consider as well the benefits of establishing a senior-level administrative unit dedicated to lead the effort to change the university culture to value collaboration, community, and learning. This office could provide focus to campus-wide learning initiatives, resource support, external funding assistance, and coordinate and recognize campus-wide partnerships. The creation of this unit could represent a powerful symbolic gesture of the transformative changes that are occurring and being supported by senior leaders in the institution.

Graduate Education

Love and Love (1995) and Knefelkamp (1991) emphasize that higher education must rethink how it prepares (and socializes) both the future professoriate and student affairs professionals. Graduate education is a critical opportunity where we can begin to nurture the qualities, skills, and knowledge required for both parties to enter and develop a commitment to collaborative partnerships. Kuh (1996) has outlined several components to include in student affairs preparation programs to aid student affairs contributions in faculty partnerships. It is equally important that graduate students preparing for the professoriate have opportunities to learn about pedagogy, cooperative and collaborative learning, and student-learning assessment. In addition, future faculty members and student affairs professionals should be encouraged to examine issues from the interdisciplinary lens. They also need to be exposed to collaborative partnerships and learn how they are valued at their institutions, disciplinary societies, and professional associations.

Summary

These recommendations intend to nurture relationships between student affairs and faculty that are based on mutual respect, equality, trust, and shared learning. These strategies will stimulate the creation of institutional structures and processes that are more flexible, versatile, creative, fluid, and responsive to the complex challenges and issues that lie ahead. The recommendations also imply that collaborative relationships are not a panacea. They are very difficult to establish and are quite time-consuming. Senior-level support, financial assistance, and institutional rewards are critical factors in promoting sustaining relationships. In addition, one's institutional mission, culture, and history of relationships between student affairs and faculty may result in conditions that are not conducive to establishing collaborative relationships. Clearinghouse and/or cooperative relationships may be more appropriate places to start to plant the seeds required for future collaborative ventures.

However, as suggested by the literature (Brown, 1997; Kuh, 1996; Love and Love, 1995), many institutions of higher education are now fertile ground for establishing collaborative partnerships; student affairs professionals and faculty must waste no time in asserting leadership to promote these efforts. It is time to move to interdependent relationships between faculty and student affairs where the respective values, goals, interests, and paradigms for teaching and learning are jointly constructed and the knowledge and contributions of academic and student affairs professionals are valued equally. Win-win, integrated, learning-centered processes must prevail not just for faculty and student affairs, but most importantly for the students we serve.

References

American Association for Higher Education (AAHA), American College Personnel Association (ACPA), National Association of Student Personnel Administrators (NASPA). *Powerful partnerships: A shared responsibility for learning.* Washington, D.C.: American Association for Higher Education, American College Personnel Association, National Association of Student Personnel Administrators, 1998.

American College Personnel Association (ACPA). *The student learning imperative: Implications for student affairs.* Washington, D.C.: American College Personnel Association, 1994.

American College Personnel Association (ACPA)/National Association of Student Personnel Administrators (NASPA). *Defining principles of good practices for student affairs.* Washington, D.C.: Author, 1997.

Angelo, T.A., and Cross, K.P. *Classroom Assessment Techniques: A Handbook for College Teachers* (2nd Ed.). San Francisco: Jossey-Bass, 1992.

Association of American Colleges. *Integrity in the curriculum: Report to the academic community.* Washington, D.C.: Association of American Colleges, 1985.

Astin, A.W. *Achieving Academic Excellence.* San Francisco: Jossey-Bass, 1987.

Astin, A.W. "Implicit Curriculum: What are We Really Teaching Our Undergraduates?" *Liberal Education*, 1988, 74 (1), 6–10.

Banta, T., and Kuh, G.D. "A Missing Link in Assessment: Collaboration Between Academic and Student Affair." *CHANGE*, 1997, 30 (2), 40–46.

Barr, R. "Obstacles to implementing the learning paradigm: What it takes to overcome them." *About Campus*, 1998, 2(3), 18–25.

Baxter-Magolda, M. *Knowing and reasoning in college: Gender-related patterns in student intellectual development.* San Francisco: Jossey-Bass, 1992.

Belenky, M., Clinchy, B. M., Goldberger, N., and Tarule, J. *Women's Ways of Knowing: The development of self, mind, and voice.* New York: Basic Books, 1986.

Blake, E. S. "Classroom and context: An educational dialectic." *Academe*, 1979, pp. 280–292.

Boyer, E. L. *College: The undergraduate experience in America.* New York: Harper and Row, 1987.

Boyer, E. L. *Scholarship reconsidered: Priorities of the professoriate.* Princeton, NJ: Carnegie Foundation for the Advancement of Teaching, 1990.

Bringle, R. G., Games, R., and Malloy, E. A. "Colleges and universities as citizens: Issues and perspectives." In R. G. Bringle, E. A. Malloy, and R. Games (Eds.), *Colleges and universities as citizens.* Boston: Allyn-Bacon, 1999, pp. 1–16.

Brown, J. "On becoming a learning organization." *About Campus*, 1997, 1 (6), 5–13.

Brown, S. S. "Strengthening ties to academic affairs." In M. J. Barr and M. L. Upcraft, (Eds.). *New futures for Student Affairs: Building a vision for professional leadership and practice.* San Francisco: Jossey-Bass, 1990, pp. 239–269.

Bruffee, K. A. "The art of collaborative learning." *Change*, 1987, (3), 42–47.

Bruffee, K. A. "Sharing our toys: Cooperative learning versus collaborative learning." *Change*, 1995, (1), 12–18.

Checkoway, B. "Reinventing the research university for public service: Comments and observations." *Journal of Planning Literature*, 1997, 11, 308–19.

Creeden, J. "Student affairs biases as a barrier to collaboration: A point of view." *NASPA Journal*, 1988, 26, 60–63.

Dewey, J. *Democracy and education: An introduction to the philosophy of education.* New York: Macmillan, 1916.

Engstrom, C. M. and Tinto, V. "Working together for service learning." *About Campus*, 1997, 2(3), 10–15.

Fried, J. "Border crossing in higher education: Faculty/student affairs collaboration." In J. Fried and Associates (Eds.), *Shifting paradigms in student affairs: Culture, context, teaching, and learning.* Landam, MD: American College Personnel Association, 1995, pp. 171–188.

Gabelnick, F. "Educating a committed citizenry." *Change*, 1997, 29 (1), 30–35.

Gabelnick, F., MacGregor, J., Matthews, R., and Leigh-Smith, B. "Learning communities: Building connections among disciplines, students, and faculty." *New Directions for Student Services*, 1990, no. 41.

Guskin, A. "Learning More, Spending Less." *About Campus*, 1997, 2(3), 4–10.

Honnet, P. E., and Poulsen, S. J. *Principles of Good Practice for Combining Service and Learning.* Racine, WI: Johnson Foundation, 1989.

Howard, J. P. "Academic service learning: A counternormative pedagogy." In R.A. Rhoads and J.P. Howard (Eds.), *Academic service learning: A pedagogy of action and reflection.* New Directions for Teaching and Learning, no. 73. San Francisco: Jossey-Bass, 1998, pp. 21–30.

Jacoby, B., and Associates. *Service-learning in higher education: Concepts and practices*, 1996.

Knefelkamp, L. L., and others. *Is this good for our students?* (1992) Two papers from the 1991 CIC Dean's Institute. Keynote address from the Council of Independent College Dean's Institute (November 2, 1991). Washington, D.C. ED 356 720.

Kuh, G. D. "Guiding principles for creating seamless learning environment for undergraduates." *Journal of College Student Development*, 1996, 37, 135–148.

Kuh, G. D. *Cultural perspectives in student affairs work.* Lanham, MD: University Press of America, 1993.

Kuh, G. D., Douglas, K. B., Lind, J. P., and Ramin-Gyurnek, J. *Student learning outside the classroom: Transcending artificial boundaries.* ASHE-ERIC Higher Education Report No. 8. Washington, D.C.: The George Washington University, 1994.

Kuh, G. D., Shedd, J. D., and Whitt, E. J. "Student affairs and liberal education: Unrecognized (and unappreciated) common law partners." *Journal of College Student Personnel*, 1987, 28, 252–60.

Kuh, G. D., and Whitt, E. J. *The invisible tapestry: Culture in American colleges and universities.* ASHE-ERIC Report, No. 1. Washington, D.C.: ASHE, 1988.

Liu, G. "Knowledge, foundations, and discourse: Philosophical support for service learning." *Michigan Journal of Community Service Learning*, 1995, 2, 5–18.

Love, P. G., and Goodsell Love, A. *Enhancing student learning: Intellectual, social, and emotional integration.* ASHE-ERIC Higher Education Reports, No. 4. Washington, D.C.: George Washington University, 1995.

Love, P. G., Kuh, G. D., MacKay, K. A., and Hardy, D. M. "Side by side: Faculty and student affairs culture." In G. D. Kuh (Ed.). *Cultural perspectives in student affairs work.* Landham, MA: ACPA, 1993, pp. 37–58.

Matthews, R. S., Cooper, J. L., Davidson, N., and Hawkes, P. "Building bridges between cooperative and collaborative learning." *Change*, 1995, 27, (4), 34–40.

Meiklejohn, A. *Experimental college.* New York: Harper and Row, 1932.

National Institute of Education. *Involvement in Learning: Realizing the Potential of American Higher Education.* Washington, D.C: U.S. Department of Education, 1984.

Olyer, C. "Making room for students: Sharing teacher authority in room 104." New York: Teacher's College, Columbia University, 1996.

Palmer, P. J. "Community, conflict, and ways of knowing." *Change*, September-October 1987, 19 (5), 20–25.

Rhoads, R. A. and Black, M. "Student affairs practitioners as transformative educators: Advancing a critical cultural perspective." *Journal of College Student Development*, 1995, 36, 413–421.

Rhoads, R. A. and Howard, J .P. *Academic service learning: A pedagogy of action and reflection. New Directions for Teaching and Learning*, no. 73. San Francisco: Jossey-Bass, 1998.

Schroeder, C. C. "Developing collaborative partnerships that enhance student learning and educational attainment." ACPA Senior Scholars Trend Analysis Draft Essays, 1998 (http://www.acpa.nche.edu/srsch/charles_schroeder.html).

Schroeder, C. C. and Mable, P. *Realizing the educational potential of residence halls.* San Francisco: Jossey-Bass, 1994.

Schroeder, C. C., Nicholls, G. E., Kuh, G. D. "Exploring the rain forest: Testing assumptions and taking risks." In G. D. Kuh (Ed.), *Understanding student affairs organizations. New Directions for Student Services*, No. 23, pp. 51–64. San Francisco: Jossey-Bass, 1983.

Senge, P. M. *The fifth discipline: The art and practice of the learning organization.* New York: Doubleday, 1990.

Smith, D. "The next step beyond student development: Becoming partners within our institutions." *NASPA Journal*, 1982, 19 (4), 53–62.

Terenzini, P. T. and Pascarella, E. T. "Living with myths." *Change*, 1994, 26 (6), 28–32.

Tierney, W. *Assessing academic climates and cultures. New Directions for Institutional Research*, No. 68. San Francisco: Jossey-Bass, 1990.

Tinto, V. "Universities as learning communities." *About Campus*, 1997, 1(6), 2–4.

Tinto, V., Goodsell, and Russo, P. "Building community among new college students." *Liberal Education*, 1993, 79 (4), 16–21.

Tinto, V., Goodsell, and Russo, P. *Building learning communities for new college students.* A publication of the National Center on Postsecondary Teaching, Learning, and Assessment. Pennsylvania: Pennsylvania State University, 1994.

Tussman, J. *Experiment at Berkeley.* London: Oxford Press, 1969.

Ward, K. "Addressing academic culture: Service learning, organizations, and faculty work." In R. A. Rhoads and J. P. Howard (Eds.), *Academic service learning: A pedagogy of action and re-*

flection. New Directions for Teaching and Learning, no. 73, pp. 73–80. San Francisco: Jossey-Bass, 1998.

Weigert, K. M. "Academic service learning: Its meaning and relevance. In R. A. Rhoads and J. P. Howard (Eds.) *Academic service learning: A pedagogy of action and reflection. New Directions for Teaching and Learning*, no. 73, pp. 1–14. San Francisco: Jossey-Bass, 1998.

Whitt, E. and Nuss, E., "Connecting residence halls to the curriculum." In C. Schroeder, and P. Mable (Eds.), *Realizing the educational potential of residence halls*, pp. 133–164. San Francisco: Jossey-Bass, 1994.

Wingspread Group on Higher Education. *An American imperative: Higher expectations for higher education*. Racine, WI: Johnson Foundation, 1993.

CHAPTER TWENTY-FOUR

DEALING WITH CAMPUS CRISIS

Marsha A. Duncan and Keith M. Miser

It is almost impossible to work for any period of time in student affairs without facing a campus crisis, whether it be a student death (from murder, suicide, or an accident), a student demonstration, a violent act (assault or rape), or a natural disaster (hurricanes, tornadoes, or earthquakes). Volumes have been written on the subject of crisis management, many of which provide clear information on the elements and development of formal organizational crisis management plans.

This chapter is not intended to provide guidance on the development of a formal institutional crisis management plan. The intent is, instead, to focus on those issues and circumstances that every student affairs administrator will face in the midst of a campus crisis. Lagadec (1993) writes that the Chinese ideogram for crisis consists of the combined symbols representing danger and opportunity. Student affairs professionals can use the Chinese wisdom and see an opportunity in each crisis and the subsequent recovery process to create a better program, a stronger institution, more accurate and inclusive communication systems, and a more organized, close-knit staff. Planning for and moving through a crisis from response to recovery is a natural part of the process of organizational development in any history of a high-performing organization.

This chapter will concentrate on two kinds of crisis situations facing student affairs administrators. First, the chapter will focus on situations involving the death or injury of a student(s). Four broad issues will be addressed, including the hands-on management of the crisis, media management, attorney management, and personal issues. The second section of the chapter shifts to a discussion regarding management of a natural disaster such as a flood, tornado, hurricane, major fire, or earthquake. Practical suggestions for preparing for a crisis, defining the leadership role for student affairs, coordinating an administrative responses, and responding to members of the community will be given.

Confronting a Crisis Involving a Student

When that dreaded call comes, what do you do? How do you do it? How do you establish priorities? The answers to those questions will vary, depending upon the nature of the crisis and the specific circumstances at the institution. However, a number of actions are predictable and necessary if a crisis is to be managed well.

Inform the President

The president should be informed immediately and must be given *all* the facts as well as an understanding of the current circumstances (for example, have parents been informed?). In a crisis, the entire institution needs to work together and the president is key to that effort.

Encourage Coordination

The president should be encouraged to identify a "point person" and communicate that decision to the campus. The key campus players in any crisis usually include the chief of campus police, the chief student affairs officer, and the director of public information. It is, however, unlikely that those holding these positions report to the same person. Thus, someone must be assigned the responsibility for coordinating a response across administrative units and ensuring that efforts are not duplicated or counterproductive.

Coordination should not stop at the boundaries of the campus during a crisis. Open communication needs to also occur with local law enforcement agencies and other representatives of the criminal justice system. Remember that communication during a crisis will be enhanced if relationships are developed with these individuals prior to an actual crisis.

Contact the Top Public Relations Official

The top person in the public relations-information office on campus should be contacted and fully involved at the scene and in all subsequent communications.

This person's knowledge and understanding of the circumstances must be complete if he or she is to be effective.

Call the Institution's Attorney, If Necessary

If the crisis involves a death or serious injury, contact the attorney for the institution immediately. There is, of course, no way to know whether or not a crisis will result in a lawsuit. However, the likelihood is often great, and the institution will be well served if you operate as if that will be an outcome.

Identify Concerned Parties

Early identification of the individuals and categories of people who have been or will be affected by the crisis is important if you are to make certain that the information and support is provided quickly and appropriately. The list of individuals and groups that require a response includes not only the parents and friends of the victim, but the student body, the faculty and staff, the parents of other students, alumni, members of the board of trustees, the media, various law enforcement agencies, and the specific staff members who will be directly involved in the crisis and its aftermath.

Although the priorities will differ depending on the circumstances, it is important to provide timely and accurate information, respond to rumors (which will be rampant), and provide direct support for whatever specific requirements may arise. Written communications, if timely and specific to the audience, can be particularly useful. Every individual and group will need the facts that can be shared. In addition, a letter to the faculty and staff might ask for their assistance in identifying and supporting students who require special attention. Another letter to the governing board might include how the campus is responding to the various aspects of the crisis. A third letter to the student body might supply information about temporary changes in policies and practices or encourage students to seek assistance if needed. It is unlikely that a single written communication to each group will be sufficient. Circumstances change rapidly, and periodic updates will be expected and necessary.

Use Existing Support Systems

Existing support services should be mobilized to respond to the particular requirements of students and the close friends and family of the victim. The period immediately following the crisis will bring both predictable and unanticipated challenges. Residence hall, counseling center, and chaplaincy staff members are often the most significant and obvious resources; it is important to determine how these individuals can be used most effectively.

Although individual circumstances will differ, consider whether or not a professional counselor should be available "on site." To what extent do more seasoned staff members need to be directly involved in supporting both students and the less experienced staff? What are the wishes, needs, and demands of those most directly affected? Are you being responsive to these concerns?

All student affairs divisions have support services in place that are theoretically prepared to respond to emergency situations. This is one area of our services that should be taken most seriously. The successful delivery of support in times of crisis will depend, however, upon your care and flexibility in developing a response.

Establish Communication Links

Depending upon the nature of the crisis, a temporary telephone hotline may be appropriate. Such a hotline can be a valuable tool in disseminating accurate information, responding to rumors, and providing direct assistance to callers. However, the individuals who staff the hotline must be carefully selected. They should be experienced individuals who have the capability to deal with both rational and irrational calls and who have the confidence and judgement to know when a situation must be handled immediately or can be referred to ongoing support systems. It is, of course, essential to keep those staff members answering inquiries fully informed and constantly updated about the facts and the response of the institution to the crisis.

Define the Role of Staff

The role that the staff plays in furnishing support for various police agencies, the district attorney's office, and the coroner's office (if appropriate) is critical. The role may take many forms, depending on the specific requests or demands of those agencies, as well as the nature of the relationship that the university has with them. Regardless of what expectations those agencies have, the police, the coroner, and the district attorney office are central players over which the university has no formal authority or control. Putting the staff at the disposal of agency representatives and responding efficiently and positively to their needs will increase the likelihood that the university will be better informed and involved in all aspects of an investigation. A voice of authority (usually the Chief Student Affairs Officer (CSAO) or the institutional attorney) should be identified. This person can help staff members sort out how to respond to a request from law enforcement when compliance would violate institutional policy.

The list of responses that are required at the time of a crisis is almost endless, and the circumstances will dictate priorities. However, the complex responses that are necessary must often be accomplished almost simultaneously at a time of enormous emotional stress. As a result, staff involvement in thinking about responses to a crisis before they happen will be time well spent.

Two critical issues must be addressed when confronting an individual student crisis or a national disaster. The first is the relationship of the student affairs professional with legal representatives. The second involves managing the media.

Attorney Management

Though there will be many major incidents and crises on campus that will not require the involvement of the legal world, it is clear that a general understanding of the law and litigation is increasingly necessary for those in student affairs administration. Yet attorney management involves an entirely different skill that is also important: how can student affairs staff members use institutional attorneys most effectively? What are the realities of relationships with legal counsel?

Understand the Nature of the Relationship

It is important to understand the nature of the representation. Does the university employ the attorney? Are they retained by the university for general purposes? Are they appointed by your insurance company? Are they representing you or the university? What are his or her specialties? Does that person have experience in or understand higher education and college campuses? For public institutions, the issues may even be more complicated. Depending on state statutes, the university may be represented by the office of the attorney general or the state's attorney in litigation matters. Knowledge of these factors is essential if the crisis is going to be managed effectively and the institution represented competently.

Be Realistic

Unless your attorney works "in house," you should be aware that you and your campus crisis are not likely to be as high a priority for your attorney as it is for you; this situation also means that your attorney may not always be fully prepared. In addition, the process of preparing that person may be extensive one if he or she has no previous experience with your institution and its values.

Understand the Protections Available to You

Before a suit is filed, you should understand the extent to which the university and you, as an individual and an employee, are protected. Institutions take many precautions to provide adequate protection, but does your carrier for standard liability exclude coverage when personal damages are sought or when punitive damages are part of the suit? Do your policies cover legal fees for your institution and for you?

You should know what is excluded and included in your coverage and, equally important, what circumstances can alter the coverage. As an example, your failure to immediately inform your insurance company of a suit could result in its failure to cover you. It is a complex world that can be best understood before a suit is filed.

Make No Assumptions

Never assume that any attorney that is retained or employed by you knows anything at all about colleges and universities in general, your institution in particular, or student life on a college campus. Educating your attorney about the world of higher education may be the most important thing that you do.

Take Notes

Careful notes are necessary; write down everything that you say and do when you say and do it. You should also document what you have been told to do by attorneys; they do not always give good advice and that advice can sometimes be contradictory.

Get Approval

Obtain attorney approval on everything you write that is in any way related to the circumstances of the lawsuit. Annual reports, correspondence, and policy statements may be documents that you find yourself explaining in a deposition.

Train for a Deposition

If you are going to be deposed, make certain that your attorney takes the time to train you for that experience in advance. A number of standard guidelines may seem obvious and are little more than common sense, but understanding and thinking through the guidelines before a deposition will significantly improve the likelihood that you will do a good job.

Review and Proof

Do not fail to review and proof everything that your attorneys write. Your role is not to approve the legal language; it is, however, your responsibility to see that the tone is consistent with the university's position and that the facts are correct. You should not hesitate to ask questions or disagree. Take your role as a client-consumer seriously.

Consider Settlement Carefully

The decision of whether to settle a lawsuit or to allow it to go to court is difficult, both institutionally and personally. The likelihood of winning or losing the suit will be only one of many factors. The decision will also depend on whether settlement is an option that all parties agree to pursue and whether you and the institution are willing to prolong the process and the expense (both human and financial) for months and often years.

Attorneys are not only a critical part of our lives in student affairs administration, but they can be magnificent resources as well. However, monitoring and managing those relationships are responsibilities that are increasingly critical to our effectiveness.

Media Management

Interaction with the media takes many forms, from formal press conferences and interviews for the print or broadcast media to responses to individual inquiries and the preparation of a press release. At the time of a crisis, such interactions are often complicated by the fact that the institution is communicating bad news.

Most campuses have public relations-information offices with responsibilities for managing the institution's relationships with the media. The public relations-information staff and the relationship you have with them will become critical assets during a crisis. Interaction with the media is complex and risky. As a result, the student affairs staff should establish and develop a close working relationship with the public relations-information office and seek assistance in understanding the complexities of the media world before a crisis happens. Then, when a crisis does occur, the institution will be poised to maximize the opportunities and minimize the difficulties.

Depending on the magnitude of the crisis, the institution will be besieged with requests for information and interviews. Those requests may come from national and regional media, as well as the local press. Although the pressure on the staff is often intense, a number of actions can reduce that pressure as well as increase the likelihood that the relationships with the media will be positive.

Explain the Context to Your Media Representative

Having the top public relations-information person on site and fully informed is not enough. That person also must understand the context of the crisis and response of the campus. For example, if the crisis involves a student death and if both the victim and the perpetrator are students, the friends of both will be dealing with the reality of what has happened. However, the friends of the perpetrator will also be confronting a different kind of loss and betrayal. Some students will be numbed by the crisis, others will take an activist role, and some may even seek revenge. If the crisis involves a natural disaster, also be prepared for a wide range of emotional responses from the community. It is those complex interactive dynamics that provide the context for effective support from the public relations-information office.

Listen to Advice

It is important to remember that the public relations-information officer is a professional in the media world and knows and understands this arena better than you do. Once the facts and context are discussed fully, it is time to listen to that person's advice and trust in his or her instincts. That certainly does not mean blind acceptance, but it does mean that the public relations-information officer is better trained and positioned than you are to make difficult decisions.

Use the Resources

The public relations-information office should be responsible for calls and inquiries from the media. If that office is fully informed, many of the requests for information will be handled immediately. An additional tool that may prove helpful is a question-and-answer list that is jointly prepared by the student affairs staff and public relations-information personnel. Such a list will not only enable an immediate response to many more inquiries, but its development will also provide an occasion to think through the appropriate responses to complicated or sensitive questions.

Decide Who Will Speak for the Institution

The institution must decide who will be available for interviews and press conferences. Although the public relations staff can provide basic facts, the media will want an opportunity to hear from individuals who are directly engaged in managing the crisis. The president may or may not be the right person for this task, but he or she should be involved in deciding who is best able to handle that delicate role for the college or university.

Balance Student Privacy and Press Interests

Protecting students while simultaneously meeting the demands of the press will be a constant problem. Members of the media will not be pleased if you remove them and their cameras from a residence hall or prevent them from entering a building. Yet the primary responsibility of student affairs staff is to provide support and care for the students. The approach that is taken may depend upon whether or not the institution is public or private. It is therefore crucial to determine the press contact that will be allowed by the institution and then communicate this decision to the students, the staff, the police, and the press.

Engage the Student Press

It will also be important to fully engage your student press. They are important players and will be covering the story long after the local, regional, and national media have left the campus. Give the editor of the student newspaper the facts, keep him or her current on developments, and ensure direct access to the significant individuals managing the crisis.

Exercise Candor

You can never control what the media prints or broadcasts, but you can manage how your institution is perceived by being cooperative, responsible, and truthful. There is no alternative to candor.

Handle Privileged Information with Care

There may be circumstances or facts that cannot be communicated to the press. However, hiding behind the "no comment" response is not a good alternative. When handling a question from the press, it should either be answered directly, or you should indicate that you simply cannot respond at that time, but will follow up as soon as possible.

Confront Errors and Misinformation Prudently

No matter how clearly, openly, or thoroughly you communicate with the media, you should be prepared for the fact that there will be many times when you will be misquoted or quoted out of context. In addition, many of the "facts" that are reported will simply be wrong. Although it is a natural inclination to attempt to clarify or correct, that is often impossible and imprudent. Seeking or even achieving a public correction, apology, or retraction may seem the right thing to do, but it can often result in unwanted extended coverage, with little to be gained.

Regardless of your skill or competence in dealing with the media, the student affairs staff will most certainly be expected to interact with the press. The time to develop those skills and to establish positive working relationships with the public relations-information office is before a crisis occurs. Working with the media is an excellent opportunity for a high-quality staff development program. The development of written protocols and procedures on events, such as responding to a student death, is also useful preparation for crisis management.

To manage the media during any crisis, as well as the response and subsequent recovery period, requires extensive expertise and experience. In today's environment of instant information, a major campus crisis can bring hundreds of reporters representing print, television, and radio media outlets to the campus. Lagadec (1993) says that any event is defined by how it is perceived. In many ways, the media portrait of a campus crisis defines its magnitude and the attitudes of both internal and external constituents regarding how the crisis is being handled. Reporters demand information and decisions on the course of action being taken, even though the complexity of a crisis does not lend itself to instant decision making. Nevertheless, media reports will determine the perception of whether campus leaders are handling the crisis appropriately. This image in turn can build or lose confidence both inside the organization and among external constituents. If confidence is gained, most likely the institution will be successful in dealing with the crisis. If confidence is lost, the campus may struggle effectively to respond and recover from the crisis.

Maguire (1993) suggests that by responding through the media outlets, administrators and campus leaders will be able to communicate with parents, students, and external constituents. This particular arena is where student affairs staff often play a central role by working with the institution's public relations department.

Personal Management

Personal management could be the most important element of the crisis with which you must contend. If you cannot keep yourself under control and function at the top of your form, chances are not very good that any other aspect of a crisis will be well managed.

It is always difficult to perform efficiently when you are tired and under stress. In the midst of a crisis, you are not likely to be sleeping much, eating regularly, or finding any time for yourself. Those circumstances will make your body, your emotions, and your judgements vulnerable. Obviously and unfortunately, there is no one plan for personal management that works for everyone; however, several suggestions can be kept in mind.

Stay Calm

Remember that your colleagues will need you and your support more than ever. No matter what the circumstances, it will be important to stay visibly calm and exude confidence (even if you have to fake it).

Identify a Confidant

Find that single person in whom you can confide for support. That individual should be someone with whom you can safely share confidential information, a person who understands you well enough to help you manage your emotions, and someone with whom you can be emotional. It may be a colleague on your campus or a friend from far away that you can talk with openly and freely. An escape valve is essential, and finding and using it will enhance your ability to think clearly and respond with care.

Attend to Your Health

Take care of yourself. Eating and sleeping may seem like distractions, but they are critical to your effectiveness.

Clear the Decks

Get everything that you can that is unrelated to a major crisis off your desk and off your mind. You will find that colleagues are more than willing to help with ongoing functions and responsibilities that cannot be postponed. If you try to do everything, you will most surely realize after the fact that deadlines have been missed and opportunities lost. Focusing your efforts on the management of the crisis while delegating other current issues to your staff will not only result in a better managed crisis and operation, but will also give the staff a wonderful opportunity to expand its understanding, to test new skills, and to contribute in new and significant ways.

Maintain a Sense of Humor

There will be nothing funny about the crisis that you are facing, but amusing things may happen. Let yourself enjoy those moments. Only you can know what will serve you well, but maintaining strength and confidence in the midst of a crisis will be essential survival and management skill.

Other crisis situations also occur that have both emotional and practical components. Dealing with and effectively managing catastrophic situations also presents very specific challenges for student affairs administrators.

Managing a Natural Disaster

Prepare

Although major campus crises rarely occur, it is important to develop an institutional plan as well as a plan within the division of student affairs to effectively deal with a catastrophe. Although it seems logical to develop detailed plans outlining options and choices on decisions to be made during such a crisis, this is not practical or even effective. Each major campus crisis is unique and likely occurs only once during an institution's history. Detailed and rigid planning does not place institutional and student affairs leaders in positions flexible enough to deal with the crisis and the following events as they unfold.

Developing a Plan

A good crisis plan includes a framework for decision making during the actual period of a crisis. The plan should outline both philosophical and pragmatic issues and should identify individuals in positions who should participate on the decision making team. Finally, the crisis plan should articulate the lines of organizational authority and responsibility within the institution. Such clarity will facilitate both the decision-making process and implementation of decisions.

A comprehensive communication and media plan should be in place before a natural disaster occurs. The plan's components should include a means to contact key personnel, so leaders and other staff can be notified quickly as the crisis unfolds. Second, communications methods must be designed to allow communication with internal constituents including students, staff, and faculty from the beginning of the incident until the crisis has been resolved. Third, a framework needs to be in place to communicate effectively with external constituents such as government officials, local citizens, parents, alumni, and other interested individuals and groups. Internal and external constituents and the media will demand information about the campus's response to the crisis. Without a comprehensive communication plan in place, chaos will result because decision makers will be drawn into designing a communications plan, rather than addressing the responses to and the recovery from the crisis itself.

Policy Review

To prepare for a possible crisis, each campus must review policies and procedures that may be needed during such an event. These documents could include financial policies; expenditure and authorization procedures; purchasing, bidding, and approval policies; insurance documents; construction approval policies; environmental, health, and safety policies; and student records policies and procedures. Many of the standard processes, including any approval procedures a campus uses, may have to be altered significantly to allow the campus to respond quickly to the crisis.

The procedure for responding to a crisis can and should be planned in advance, allowing for maximum flexibility and knowing that even during an actual event these planned procedures may need to be altered. In many ways, the response to a crisis is an art more than a science in a continually unfolding and unstable post-crisis environment.

The Leadership Role of Student Affairs

When a campus crisis occurs, there usually is a short period of chaos before the actual process of response and rebuilding begins. The regular routine and institutional responsibilities are disbanded and the response to the crisis becomes the norm. During a crisis, the best in an institution appears when politics are set aside and the usual visions are gone, as the institution strives to mitigate the effects of the crisis (Siegel, 1991).

When a physical crisis occurs, people's safety is the first concern, followed by immediate efforts designed to implement temporary solutions for facilities. Such efforts aid a return, as quickly as possible, to normality. Frequently, the initial response is directed toward the physical plant, particularly when the media focus on the intense and dramatic visual images showing the campus destruction. However, the trauma to and impact on people may exceed the damage to the buildings. It is critical for campus leaders, especially in student affairs, to focus a significant amount of effort on assisting and supporting people effectively. In the end, this response will determine whether the campus response was of high quality.

Student affairs professionals are trained to work with people, and from these foundations, they become key leaders in responding to campus crises. Needs include counseling, loss therapy, the rescheduling of academic programs, communicating with families, supporting faculty colleagues, and working with individuals who may have lost their life's work and research. Facilities, such as student unions,

Greek houses, residence halls, and student health centers, under student affairs management responsibilities may be demolished or damaged during a natural disaster. Student affairs leaders must be actively involved throughout the entire process of rebuilding the physical plant. If there is loss of life or severe injuries, a significant time must be spent with family, friends, and colleagues of those individuals affected by the crisis. The campus will depend on student affairs staff to use their experience and skills to make significant contributions to the human community through the response period and the rebuilding process.

Each campus is a unique organization with a special culture, shaped by history, mission, and leadership. The important role of student affairs in a crisis will be defined both by the campus culture and the nature of the crisis. The senior student affairs leader often serves as a key figure and as a central campus leader during this period. This individual should define the specific responsibilities of student affairs programs and staff during the crisis. In any crisis, the contributions of student affairs professionals are significant in determining the outcome of the response and rebuilding process, especially with regard to the well-being of the campus community.

Crisis Coordination and Administration

In the administration of a crisis, the key organizational structure that contributes to successful outcomes in the recovery effort is a campus-wide coordinating committee. Depending on the nature of the campus, the extent and nature of the crisis, and the resources needed to analyze the issues and to make decisions, the institution's president should appoint a special crisis coordinating committee to accomplish this task of response and recovery.

During a crisis, there usually is a breakdown of the normal systems of communication and analysis on campus. Consequently, the core crisis coordinating team should be relatively small, and members need to be professionals with specific expertise. The team must analyze and make decisions with regard to the structures and processes to deal with the crisis. When issues are brought before the committee, decisions must be made quickly. After each meeting, committee members must implement the decisions made at the meeting within their own department or organization as well as gather more information from their units to bring back to the next meeting. This structured process guarantees smooth decision making and eliminates confusion and miscommunication. Student affairs representatives typically are key members of such a committee and indeed may chair the group. Following the 1997 flood that caused a significant crisis at Colorado State University, a crisis coordinating committee was appointed with members including the vice president for administrative services, vice president for student affairs, director of housing, director of the student union, director of purchasing, director of facilities services, university general counsel, director of public relations, provost, director of telecommunications and information services, chief financial officer, and the student body president.

Financial Management

During crises involving damage to buildings and personal property, excellent financial management is essential. Decisions must be made about immediate expenditures to bring the campus into a position where normal functions and activities can be resumed. A long-term financial strategy also must be implemented to return the campus back to its pre-crisis state and do so in a financially stable way.

Insurance plays a large role in the financial recovery from a campus crisis. Student affairs professionals must be involved in the damage assessment process as well as the implementation of the recovery using insurance funds. In particular, students may suffer from great personal and financial losses, including the contents of residence hall rooms, cars, and other personal materials. These losses must be assessed immediately and verified to allow students to make insurance claims and receive funds as soon as possible for housing, food, and daily necessities. At times, state and federal insurance agencies may be involved in the recovery, creating an environment of conflicting rules, procedures, and outcomes. Student affairs professionals are key in assisting colleagues and students with these issues and their successful resolution.

Legal Issues

As with any issue today, many complex legal concerns have to be addressed during a campus response to a natural disaster. Institutional lawyers must be involved with every decision from the beginning of the crisis through the entire recovery process. Primary issues include student information privacy laws, financial aid, regulations, and insurance claims. Legal counsel must be consulted to review insurance claims and policies, state and federal regulations affecting the crisis recovery, open record laws, and possible lawsuits.

Technology

With the growth of the use of computer technology, particularly e-mail, campus leaders can use this tool in managing a campus crisis. However, this medium also can cause great disruption. In a recent crisis at a large state university, administrative offices received over 5,000 e-mails. Through this ripple of e-mails and rumors they generated nation-wide, the communication about the crisis not only became misleading, but also inaccurate, thus creating false perceptions to readers, many of whom were family members and supporters. The campus nearly became paralyzed in an effort to respond to and manage the e-mail communications. The institution used its Internet Web site to release press statements about the crisis, but this did not significantly reduce the e-mail challenge. Thus, the readily available and heavily used medium of e-mail can create problems yet also can provide solutions for student affairs professionals in their effort to communicate information accurately and in a timely manner to students and other internal constituents, as well as to external groups.

Student Affairs Response to the People on Campus

Student affairs professionals are critical in establishing and maintaining a climate of support during a campus crisis, the immediate response, and recovery period. Of course, campuses that have developed a supportive environment before such a crisis occurs are able to continue and advance this ethic during a time of high stress.

Students and Their Families

Students are the key target constituency for a student affairs response. Teams should be created within the division of student affairs to assist students in any way possible by using their resources, skills, and training. Helping students process the personal meaning of the disaster and, through this process, helping them deal with all their losses are important responsibilities of student affairs staff. Many students feel disoriented and frightened. All students, particularly seniors, will struggle to learn how the crisis impacts their academic progress or their graduation. A number of students will have lost personal possessions of great value to them. Some may have lost friends or relatives to death. In all these cases, student affairs staff can be the student's vital link to the campus by providing counseling, academic advising, financial advising, grief counseling, personal support, and information about the institution's decisions and actions through the recovery process.

Student affairs staff are also often the connection to students' families. Often, 800-number telephone lines are installed immediately to allow parents, family members, and friends access to a single information source after a crisis. These lines can be staffed by student affairs professionals who give accurate and up-to-date information about the response and recovery process. Newsletters sent to parents and other external constituencies after the crisis are another vehicle to provide an update on the recovery process. Student affairs professionals may ask for the assistance of parent organizations and others to assist with newsletters and other forms of communication during a crisis period. For families who have not received information, the unknown usually is much worse than the known, especially if a family lives a great distance from campus. If communication with students' families and friends is handled well, their support likely will expand and continue to grow long after the campus has returned to its normal routines.

Student Leaders

In a crisis situation, student affairs professionals play another critical role by immediately and actively involving student leaders in the response and recovery process. Student leaders have excellent ideas in how to effectively communicate with their fellow students. Student leaders, along with student affairs professionals or institutional officials, should sign letters, memoranda, e-mails, and press releases. Student government leaders usually are more than willing to become involved, and they are an invaluable communication link in reaching the general student population. They have good ideas on how to solve problems that will better meet student needs.

In addition to engaging student leaders in problem solving and facilitating good communication, many other campus and external constituents and governance systems should be directly involved. Faculty councils, staff councils, the alumni board, governing board, city council, and chamber of commerce may be helpful and will appreciate being asked to share their expertise and leadership. Specific student affairs staff also are central to helping with internal and external communication, including residence hall staff, Greek advisors, student union advisors, and student government advisors. These staff members will help disseminate information to student constituencies and bring ideas and concerns to the central coordinating committee.

Responding to Staff

During a crisis, student affairs staff will also have personal and professional needs. Student affairs staff will work extraordinarily hard for very long hours to help students with their emotional, financial, and personal needs. At the same time, these staff members likely will have some of the same needs, fears, and concerns as students. Senior student affairs professionals and counselors are instrumental in this effort throughout the recovery process. The strategies of taking scheduled breaks, changing venues, seeking personal support, getting appropriate rest, and eating nutritious meals are critical to maintaining a staff who continues to be effective, even after the first several days. It is critical for student affairs leaders to communicate to staff members the importance of taking care of themselves during a crisis and subsequent recovery so they can be effective in supporting others around them, particularly students, during this difficult period.

After the immediate shock and disarray of the disaster and the beginning of the orderly and often mechanical response and recovery process, student affairs leaders and staff must develop strategies for healing that will return the total campus community to a normal routine. A mandatory step in a return to normalcy is for the campus community individually and collectively to find ways to grieve for their losses. There must be a period of mourning, transition, and regeneration for everyone, whether they are concerned about buildings, organizational design, administrative structure, or relationships, or any combination of these. Regardless of the nature of the crisis, it also is important to recognize that the campus likely will never be the same as it was before the incident happened, and student affairs staff play an integral role in ensuring a positive outcome in this process of rapid change. One essential word of caution: leaders and staff at colleges and universities often make the serious mistake of believing that when buildings are repaired and furniture, books, and other supplies are replaced, everything is back to normal. Only later do they find that personal scars from the crisis have so negatively impacted the community that the new post-crisis organization is dysfunctional. So, equal concern about the attention to these hidden wounds will promote healing and an optimistic attitude toward the future, in spite of the losses.

After the response and recovery period, it is entirely possible that the restored institution will be better than it was before the event occurred. Replacement of and repair to buildings may improve and update them to better meet campus needs. Relationships among staff are strengthened through their participation in the process of crisis management and working together. New relationships and linkages developed during the crisis can improve communication and coordination throughout the institution. Through innovative and steady leadership, the institution's culture can be strengthened because it now believes it is strong and able to accomplish anything by working together. Student affairs staff and leaders are essential in helping to ensure these positive outcomes at the end of the crisis period.

Debriefing and Evaluation

Debriefing and evaluating all components of the crisis and the subsequent campus response are critical. This may be almost as important as the actual recovery process, because it helps bring closure for those who were intimately and directly involved with the crisis from beginning to end. It provides useful insights and information into the processes and policies that might be changed for a future crisis response. This period of debriefing and evaluation also allows the campus leaders to personally and publicly thank everyone who helped with the response and contributed to the recovery.

The review process is especially significant for the student affairs staff who are the campus human resource specialists. Occasionally, student affairs staff feel they could have done a much better job during a crisis. This comment is common during a situation when there is such organizational and physical disarray that staff members, who are usually perfectionists, are not able to maintain their normal expectations in responding to needs and demands. In truth, no one can meet every immediate human and institutional need during a major crisis. It is important for student affairs leaders to continually assure staff and to believe themselves that they have done an excellent job, especially in view of the complexity and the comprehensive nature of any crisis.

The final step is to transition the student affairs staff into a more routine and normal work environment, and to address the myriad of projects that were postponed or delayed during the crisis. If this closure process is handled successfully, not only will much be learned in order to handle a future campus crisis, but also the campus community will feel empowered and capable of overcoming any challenge.

Summary

Bejin and Morin (1976) discuss the origins of the word crisis. In the religious language of ancient Greece, "Krisis" signified the interpretation of the flights of birds and of dreams and choices of sacrificial victims. Krisis required judgement and interpretation, rather than the mechanical response to a plan. In Greek tragedies, Krisis meant a critical event that required a decision. This interpretation of the word crisis suggests a flexible process for colleges and universities to assume when responding to a crisis. Consequently, when leaders plan how to approach a crisis, they will leave the maximum number of options open to consider, reflect upon, and discuss, so the decision making process occurs in the most efficient way.

The effective management of a crisis is an essential skill for a student affairs administrator. In fact, a successfully managed crisis can result in positive visibility, increased confidence, and deepened appreciation for an understanding of the role of student affairs on campus. By that same token, a poorly managed crisis can result in a very different outcome. Loss of respect, influence, and trust, individual reassignment, or even dismissal is also possible if the crisis is major and if it is poorly handled.

More importantly, how student affairs professionals deal with crisis will have a lasting influence on the lives of the students who are touched. No greater opportunity exists for our profession to provide support and understanding than to individuals who are affected personally by a crisis. Many will come through that experience either strengthened or diminished. The role that student affairs plays in the management and response both to the crisis and its aftermath can make the crucial difference.

In many respects, the student affairs profession is uniquely positioned to manage these most difficult moments. We have support services in place, we work in communities with shared values, and our ongoing communication and relationships with students, faculty, and staff provide a positive context for dealing with crisis effectively.

In other respects, we are not so well positioned or prepared. We may have a general understanding of the federal and state laws, as well as case laws, that apply to higher education. However, our legal knowledge rarely extends to the world of litigation and the complexities of that process. The same gap often applies to the world of media relations. We all have a basic appreciation of the importance of public relations, and we often have regular interaction with the student press, but how many in our profession have the training to be successful in a press conference or to appreciate the subtle differences in dealing with the print versus the broadcast media or with the national "entertainment" journalists versus the national or regular news?

The process of becoming more familiar with such areas as litigation and media relations increases the likelihood that we will be better equipped to handle a crisis when it comes. Moreover, those issues provide wonderful opportunities for staff development and interaction within the student affairs division and across campus.

The successful practitioner will recognize that crisis management can be as critical a task as any that we engage in and will take whatever steps are necessary to prepare for a sound performance in that role.

References

Bejin, A., and Morin, E. "Introduction." *Communications*, 1976, No. 25, 1–3.

Lagadec, P. *Preventing Chaos in a Crisis: Strategies for Prevention, Control, and Damage Limitation.* London: McGraw Hill, 1993.

Maguire, M. *Here Comes Trouble: During an Emergency, A Run-of-the-Mill Crisis Plan Isn't Enough.* Currents, March 1993, 19(3), 26–30.

Siegel, D. *Campuses Respond to Violent Tragedy.* Phoenix, AZ: Oryx Press, 1994.

Other Resources

Allen, R.D. *Handbook of Post-Disaster Interventions.* Corte Madera, CA: Select Press, 1993.

Derrington, M. "Calming Controversy." *Executive Educator,* February 1993, 15(l), 32–34.

Hoverland, H., C.S. McIntruff, T. Rohm *Crisis Management in Higher Education.* San Francisco: Jossey-Bass Publishers, 1986.

Mitchell, J.T. *Critical Incident Stress Debriefing: An Operations Manual for the Prevention of Traumatic Stress Among Emergency Services and Disaster Workers.* Ellicot City, Maryland: Chevron, 1993.

Mitroff, I. and Pearson, C. *Crisis Management. A Diagnostic Guide for Improving Your Organization's Crisis-Preparedness.* San Francisco: Jossey-Bass Publishers, 1993.

Pruett, H.L., and Brown, V.B. *Crisis Intervention and Prevention.* San Francisco: Jossey-Bass Inc., Publishers, 1990.

Smart, C.F., and Stanbury, W.T. *Studies on Crisis Management.* Toronto: Institute for Research on Public Policy, 1978.

Snyder, T. "When Tragedy Strikes." *Executive Educator,* July 1993, 15(7), 30–31.

Stevenson, R. (Ed.) *What Will We Do: Preparing a School Community to Cope with Crises.* Amityville, New York: Baywood, 1994.

PART FOUR

COMMITMENT TO PROFESSIONAL EDUCATION

When it comes to professional development, student affairs administrators have responsibilities to self as well as their staff. Professional development activities can help keep student affairs staff up-to-date on new theory, research and good practices and they can provide training in areas of deficiency. Academic training and preparation, regardless of how thorough, may not provide us with all of the skills and knowledge that is required to function effectively as a student affairs practitioner. The question becomes one of identifying what skills and competencies we must further develop, what knowledge we need to gain, and what experiences would be helpful in meeting these goals. We can then design a plan to meet those requirements. Part Four discusses the means and methods to improve, update, or acquire the com-

petencies necessary to be an effective administrator within student affairs and identifies the ingredients of an effective continuing education program for staff.

Staff salaries are by far the largest item in our budgets and staff members are our most important investment. Well-crafted staff development programs provide one method to maximize this investment, and in Chapter Twenty-Five, James Scott, discusses practical methods to assess staff needs for development and methods to institute a high-quality, creative development program.

Professional associations create many opportunities for student affairs professionals to gain indispensable skills, competencies, and support. Elizabeth Nuss, in Chapter Twenty-Six, considers the role of professional association in the ongoing development of staff. In addition, she provides suggestions for student affairs staff members to match their individual requirements with opportunities within such associations.

Many middle managers wrestle with the question of whether to get a doctoral degree. In Chapter Twenty-Seven, Susan Komives and Deborah Taub explore the issues involved in choosing a graduate program, the possibilities associated with such a decision, and the alternatives available if a professional does not choose to pursue doctoral study.

In Chapter Twenty-Eight, Kevin Kruger reviews a number of new alternatives for professional development. These include writing for publication, attending executive training programs, participating in executive intern programs, and studying abroad.

Each of these approaches can create opportunities for student affairs professionals to acquire the needed skills and competencies to be a successful administrator and manager and to provide opportunities for staff to gain new knowledge and skills. The commitment to improve professional skills and competencies rests, however, with each of us.

CHAPTER TWENTY-FIVE

CREATING EFFECTIVE STAFF DEVELOPMENT PROGRAMS

James E. Scott

Creating effective staff development programs for student affairs staff can contribute to the positive development of staff and enhance the overall health and effectiveness of a student affairs division. Kaufman (1994) offers additional support and asserts that (1) investing in human capital is important in order to have a high-quality labor force and an effective organization and (2) when supervisors invest in their employees, including helping them gain greater skills, increase their knowledge, and maintain good health, the investment will result in a better skilled, happier, more motivated, and more effective workforce. Clearly, staff at all levels including new professionals, middle managers, and senior student affairs officers can benefit from staff development activities that facilitate and support professional, career, skill, and personal growth. Moreover, in order to successfully respond to the challenges, demands, and expectations associated with student affairs work, it is essential that institutions and student affairs leaders establish well-planned and comprehensive staff development programs. Such programs are critical in helping staff achieve continuous professional growth, including the acquisition of skills and knowledge and the tools for professional, career, and personal success. Advocacy for staff development in literature has been significant (Stamatakos and Oliaro, 1972; Komives, 1986, 1992; Barr, 1990; Preston, 1993). Careful attention must be paid to the development and implementation of high-quality staff development programs. Staff members are our most important resource and investment in the training and education of staff will pay dividends in the future.

This chapter will address a model for creating effective staff development including (1) a rationale for staff development, (2) organizational factors associated with the development and implementation of programs, (3) the need for a multi-level approach to staff development, and (4) practical suggestions and recommendations to be considered in program development.

A Rationale for Staff Development

The dynamic nature of student affairs work supports the need for staff to be engaged in continuous professional growth opportunities in order to effectively serve students and their institutions. Further, increasing expectations from students, parents, faculty, presidents, alumni, trustees, legislators, and others require student affairs staff to be experts on students, knowledgeable about public policy issues, and equipped with the skills to deal with contemporary problems and issues confronting students and institutions.

Rapidly expanding technology, changing demographics of students on campus, legal issues, crisis management, diversity and multiculturalism, assessment and evaluation, and personnel and financial management are examples of matters that require an increasingly wide knowledge base for practitioners at all levels. This point is affirmed by Cox and Ivy (1984), who assert that staff development programs are needed that enhance the abilities of student affairs professionals to implement change strategies, milieu management, consultation, and instruction in their work with students. Accordingly, organized staff development activities offer an excellent opportunity for staff to develop a broad repertoire of skills and knowledge to address the day-to-day challenges and complexity of student affairs in a pro-active and structured approach.

Competence and Professionalism

Another factor supporting the need for effective staff development is related to practitioner competence and professionalism in student affairs. Some authors assert that student affairs is not and probably never will be considered a classic profession (Stamatakos, 1987; Bloland, 1987). Others argue that the challenge is to increase knowledge and skill foundations within functional areas of student affairs (Rickard, 1988). Regardless of the debate on this issue, student affairs staff are best served by developing professional competence as practitioners. Effective student affairs programs provide campus-wide leadership for issues related to students and set standards for excellence and provide effective and efficient delivery of services. Staff development programs contribute to the field by (1) participation in and service to state, regional, and national professional associations and activities, and (2) by conducting scholarly writing and research. Young (1994) supports the need for professionalism and asserts that as practitioners develop they improve their individual practice and the profession as a whole. If student affairs professionals limit their personal development then practitioners, their students, and the field of student affairs will suffer. Supporting professionalism (Nuss, 1994) calls for a greater emphasis on professional training and staff development to ensure that student affairs professionals maximize their contributions to their organization.

Ownership

Several authors have discussed the important relationship between organizational effectiveness, staff development, and ownership. Ashton (1985) and Peters (1988) call for the professional development for practitioners in areas likely to increase organizational effectiveness. Porter (1989) supports this proposition saying in part that

1. A sense of ownership is directly related to a sense of competence in an ongoing cycle. Each one in turn is supported by the other.
2. Owning a task helps ensure at least eventual competence with that task. At the same time, developing skill in a particular activity helps ensure deepening ownership of that activity.
3. Student affairs organizations must create opportunities for staff to develop progressively greater skills in role-related activities. Staff need to feel competent.
4. Successful professional development experiences not only lead to increased knowledge and skills, they also lead to increased ownership.

Young (1994) offers additional support, suggesting that students are better served by practitioners who are themselves working to strengthen their skills. Clearly, those responsible for creating staff development programs need to understand this important relationship between staff development, organizational effectiveness, and ownership in the development of staff competence.

Staff Retention

Retaining a high-quality, culturally and ethnically diverse professional student affairs staff is an ongoing concern for most institutions. At the middle manager level, Blum (1989) reports that 26 to 27 percent of student affairs professionals leave the field each year. Studies on preparation program graduates (Burns, 1982;

Saddlemire, 1988; Blum, 1989) suggest that 24 to 40 percent of those graduates leave the student affairs profession within five years. Further, according to Saddlemire (1988), the likelihood of those remaining in the field is influenced by their personal and professional development.

Clearly, these findings suggest the critical need for student affairs leaders to structure staff development activities that assist staff in matters related to personal and professional development. Lawing, Moore, and Groseth (1982) assert that a key to the retention of staff is the creation of professional development programs, and they argue that professional development, career enhancement, and career development go hand in hand.

Effective professional development can have a significant positive impact on staff retention. Through activities that focus on personal and professional renewal and career development and enhancement, institutions can increase their ability to retain committed and connected staff.

Career Satisfaction and Personal Development

An effective staff development program must also consider matters related to individual career satisfaction and personal development. Borelli (1984) recommends that managers provide ongoing development programs with opportunities for professional and personal growth and self-renewal available for all staff.

Providing opportunities for staff to work toward their career goals is essential. Staff development activities should be structured in a manner that enables staff to identify their career aspirations and at the same time assist in the development of strategies that can help them progress toward these professional goals. Senior student affairs leaders can play an important role in this process by helping staff realistically examine their personal and career goals and collaborating in the development of opportunities that support career and personal plans. Opportunities stemming from this context may include involvement in professional associations, moving up the student affairs career ladder, conducting research, teaching opportunities, and seeking opportunities for leadership development. Personal development is also very important. Staff development activities that facilitate growth toward professional maturity, good judgement in making decisions, the development of personal ethics, and effective interpersonal skills can serve student affairs staff at all levels.

Organizational Factors in Staff Development Programs

Colleges and universities use a variety of different organizational approaches in creating and implementing staff development for student affairs staff. The methods and models used are influenced by different factors, including but not limited to the size of the staff, resources available, staff needs and interests, program goals and expectations, and the level of institutional commitment. One common approach to staff development used by many institutions is the creation of a staff development committee. Often such a committee is made up of staff from various student affairs departments and is charged with the responsibility of designing and implementing staff development program activities.

Another approach often used is to assign the responsibility of staff development to a staff member along with other job duties. Scott (1998), in a survey of senior student affairs officers, reports that staff at different levels may be responsible for staff development. On some campuses, the senior student affairs officer is responsible for this area, while on other campuses those with assistant and/or associate titles had the responsibility for staff development.

Regardless of which model or approach is used in the administration of staff development, the following factors are most important:

1. The responsibilities for staff development within a student affairs division should be clearly identified.
2. The goals and objectives for staff development programs should be established and communicated to all staff.
3. Staff needs and interests should be formally assessed and priorities established.
4. Staff should have input into the program design of the staff development efforts.
5. The implementation and delivery plan for staff development should be communicated to all staff.
6. Those in management and supervisory positions should be charged with the responsibility of reducing or eliminating obstacles for staff participation and involvement in staff development activities.
7. Senior student affairs leaders should communicate their commitment to the staff development program. This includes their expectations for staff participation and support of the effort.
8. Resources for staff development should be identified and earmarked in appropriate budgets.
9. Staff development programs and related activities should be regularly evaluated for improvement.
10. Annual performance evaluations for staff at all levels should include professional development goals.

Attention to these ten issues will go a long way toward reducing individual and institutional barriers for effective staff development.

Funding Staff Development Programs

Another major factor associated with the organization of staff development programs is funding support and available resources. Preston (1993) asserts that staff development generally falls into one of two extreme positions on the financial continuum: either as a wise and long-term investment or as a token effort and sometimes burdensome expense. In examining financial support for staff development, Miller (1975) reports the following funding approaches: (1) 33 percent of the staff development funding at postsecondary institutions was spent for off-campus staff attendance at annual conventions and professional association meetings; (2) 19 percent of funds went to off-campus professional workshops; and (3) 9 percent of funds were allocated for specific on-campus, in-service education programs. The remaining 39 percent supported acquisition of materials for use on the campus. In another study, Scott (1998) reports that 40 percent of the respondents indicated that their annual expenditures for on-campus staff development activities were $2,000 or less, 50 percent reported annual expenditures between $3,000 and $10,000, and 10 percent reported expenditures of $20,000 or more.

Funding strategies for staff development may take a variety of approaches. Each has strengths and weaknesses, as the following descriptions indicate.

Staff Development Grants. Staff development grants are provided for individual staff. These may be used to support travel and attendance at conventions and conferences or special workshops and seminars. Unless a method is employed to bring what is learned back to the campus, the impact of such approaches is minimal on the staff at large.

Tuition Remission. A number of colleges and universities provide opportunities for staff to take courses and waive the payment of tuition and fees. This approach may aid an individual staff member but has less influence on the total organization than some other approach.

Job Training. Support is often provided to help staff acquire needed skills to improve job performance. Examples include paying for staff to attend workshops to improve computer skills, customer service training, or enrollment management strategies. This approach can immediately increase production and staff efficiency.

Cost Sharing. Opportunities to share expenses with other units, departments, or institutions helps to maximize staff development resources. For example, local institutions may share the costs of video teleconferences or jointly sponsor speakers and other programs. Likewise, opportunities to share costs may be possible with other institutional areas including athletics, academic advising, and institutional research. This approach has an added advantage of providing opportunities for staff interaction.

Divisional and Institutional Funding Support. Senior student affairs managers may earmark funds specifically to support staff development programs. These may include allocations for travel to professional meetings and conferences, bringing in off-campus speakers to address specific topics, or funding teleconferences and other initiatives related to staff training and in-service programs.

Program Delivery

The third factor associated with the organization of staff development is the packaging and delivery of programs and activities. Fey and Carpenter (1996) have reported on the preferred methods for professional development: conferences (74.4 percent); workshops (58 percent); reading (47.2 percent); discussions with colleagues (44.9 percent); mentors (23.9 percent); staff meetings (14.8 percent); sabbaticals (9.1 percent); and other (4 percent).

Scott (1998) identified the following several methods for staff development from his survey of senior student affairs officers:

Topic-specific workshops. Such workshops provide opportunities for staff to attend workshops on specific topics of interest. Examples might include dealing with cults on campus or improving customer service.

Teleconferences. As technology improves, institutions are taking advantage of teleconferences for staff development. The opportunity to hear from experts and reach small or large groups of staff on important and timely topics has great appeal to those responsible for staff development.

Discussion groups. Interaction among staff provides opportunities for interested staff to discuss special problems, issues, trends, and concerns.

Training videos. Such videos on various topics are available and can be helpful additions to staff training. Examples include improving customer service or conflict resolution. When supplemented by meaningful discussion, these are powerful training tools.

Administrative sabbaticals. While unusual, such sabbaticals are available at some institutions. The institutions offer administrators the equivalent of a faculty sabbatical that provides a paid leave for a specific period of time to work on a research project or participate in professional development activities.

Self-directed programs. A more complex approach is to provide individual staff members with opportunities to develop personalized professional development plans tailored specifically to their needs and interests. These may include attending selected conferences, readings, or committee opportunities.

Administrative internships. An internal program of internships can provide staff with the opportunity to gain administrative experience by serving in a specific office or department. The internship is usually for a specific period of time and the intern is given opportunities to gain experience and enhance his or her administrative skills.

Administrative shadowing. This is an approach that provides an opportunity for staff to spend time with administrators and senior managers and gain insight into the daily routines of selected administrators.

Administrative exchange programs. This is a more complex approach and provides an opportunity for staff to work in different departments and in some instances at different institutions to gain experience in different settings. It takes a great deal of coordination and agreement on the value of the program.

Site visits to other institutions. Such visits provide an excellent opportunity for staff to visit other campuses and interact with and learn from their colleagues and/or counterparts.

Orientation for new staff. Many institutions and student affairs divisions offer a formal orientation program for new staff. The duration of the program may range from a few hours or a day to an entire term or year. Goals of the program may include helping to acquaint new staff with policies and procedures and learning about institutional culture. Mentoring is often a part of ongoing orientation for new staff.

A review of these activities and programs indicates that institutions utilize a wide range of approaches in providing staff development. Moreover, staff development programs and activities are significantly influenced by such factors as available resources, staff needs and interests, program goals and objectives, and the institution's level of commitment. Clearly, those responsible for creating and implementing staff development must tailor programs to match institutional expectations with available resources and support.

Staff Development: A Multi-Level Approach

Any effort in creating staff development must take into account the different levels of staff and their corresponding professional, personal, and career development needs. The staff development needs of new professionals, middle managers, and senior student affair leaders tend to be quite different and each must be addressed accordingly. Miller and Carpenter (1980) in applying human development principles to professional development offer five propositions that provide an applicable framework:

1. Professional development is continuous and cumulative in nature, moves from simpler to more complex behavior, and can be described via levels or stages held in common.
2. Optional professional development is a direct result of interaction between the total person striving for professional growth and the environment.
3. Optional professional preparation combines mastery of a body of knowledge and a cluster of skills and competence within the context of personal development.
4. Professional credibility and excellence of practice are directly dependent upon the quality of professional preparation.
5. Professional preparation is a lifelong learning process.

From a general and practical perspective, what are the staff development needs of new professionals, middle managers, and senior student affairs leaders? What resources are available to those who are responsible for creating effective staff development programs? The following section identifies the general development needs of staff at different levels along with examples of applicable staff development opportunities.

New Professionals

For the purposes of this chapter, a new professional is defined as a practitioner beginning a career in student affairs with up to five years of full-time experience.

Personal, Professional, and Career Needs. The following needs are important to new professionals:

- Understanding student development theory
- Learning to apply theory to practice
- Career development
- Learning how to network
- Developing a sense of professionalism
- Learning how to effectively work with students including student leaders and student groups

- Skill development (writing memos, serving on committees)
- Using technology
- Developing professional ethics
- Professional association involvement
- Relating to peers, colleagues, and supervisors
- Balancing work and personal life (time management, stress management)

Staff Development Opportunities. The following opportunities may address these needs:

- The National Association of Student Personnel Administrator's (NASPA) new professionals institutes and other special programs for new professionals
- Mentoring programs for new professionals
- Enrolling in graduate courses on counseling, psychology, sociology, higher education administration, and personnel management
- Attending state, regional, and national conferences, attending sessions for new professionals and first-time participants, serving as a volunteer, attending social functions, and networking to meet other professionals
- Taking advantage of teleconferences on current issues
- Reading professional journals (such as the *NASPA Journal* and the *Journal of College Student Personnel*) and other relevant books and articles
- Participating in workshops on computers and technology
- Joining a discussion group on campus with other new professionals to discuss issues of mutual concern and interest
- Identifying role models and observing them in action
- Developing a personalized staff development plan with specific goals and expectations on an annual basis
- Developing short-term and long-term career goals and assessing and evaluating them regularly

Middle Managers

For purposes of the chapter, the middle manager is defined as a student affairs practitioner with five to eight years of experience in student affairs and budget/personnel responsibilities.

Personal, Professional and Career Needs. Middle managers may have the following skill deficits:

- Fiscal responsibilities, such as budgeting and financial planning
- Personnel management, such as supervision and performance evaluation

- Conflict resolution and mediation skills
- Mentoring
- Consultation
- Advising student leaders and student groups
- Professionalism
- Competency, broad-based
- Career issues including mobility and assessment of goals
- Family—balancing work, family, and career goals
- Contributions to the profession
- Technology management
- Understanding the big picture— developing broader perspectives
- Networking
- Skill development in chairing committees, writing reports, and problem solving

Staff Development Opportunities. These opportunities may meet the needs outlined above:

- Access to NASPA's middle manager institutes and other professional association programs directed toward middle managers and, when appropriate, NASPA's symposium for women aspiring to be chief student affairs officers
- Courses on personnel management, higher education administration, and psychology
- Assessments of short-term and long-term career goals
- A personalized staff development plan with specific goals and expectations
- Identifying of role models and observing them in action
- Participating in specific topic workshops to enhance skills and knowledge, such as computers and technology, supervision, conflict resolution, and mentoring. Certification should be sought where possible, such as diversity training or Alternate Dispute Resolution (ADR)
- Contributing to professional associations by attending conferences and volunteering for committees and task forces, as well as writing for professional journals such as the *NASPA Journal* and *Journal of College Student Personnel* or seeking co-authorship opportunities
- A reading list of journals, articles, and books to increase knowledge

Senior Student Affairs Leaders

For purposes of this section, the senior student affairs leader is defined as a practitioner with 10 or more years of experience in student affairs. Further, it is assumed that the senior staff member has division-wide responsibilities and can include individuals at the assistant and associate vice president level.

Personal, Professional, and Career Needs. The needs of student affairs vice presidents, directors, and deans include:

- Leadership development
- Personnel management
- Fiscal accountability and financial planning
- Crisis management
- Public relations
- Marketing
- Conflict resolution
- Legal issues
- Team building
- Strategic planning
- Managing technology
- Fund raising
- Campus politics—understanding power and influence
- Assessment strategies
- External affairs—working with alumni, trustees, and legislators
- Working with the president
- Media management

Staff development opportunities. Some options to meet the needs of senior staff include

- NASPA's Academy for Senior Student Affairs Leaders and the Stevens Institute, Harvard University's Management Development Program (MDP), and the Institute for Educational Management (IEM)
- Attending national meetings and conferences of professional associations such as NASPA, ACPA, AAHE, and NASCLGU
- Participating in executive development programs
- Enrolling in continuing education short courses on personnel management, marketing, fund raising, public relations, and other management or executive leadership opportunities
- A personalized staff development plan with specific goals and expectations
- Contributing to professional associations by providing leadership and service
- Contributing to the field of student affairs and higher education through scholarly writings and research
- A reading list of books, journals, and periodicals. In addition to student affairs and higher education literature, materials are needed from business, management, and corporate development.
- An informal network of professional colleagues for consultation and support

Practical Suggestions and Recommendations for Staff Development

The following suggestions and recommendations are offered to senior managers and others with responsibilities for staff development:

1. Create a staff development planning committee. This group should be charged with assessing staff needs, developing staff development goals and objectives, and program implementation.
2. Utilize divisional staff meetings on a periodic basis for staff development activities.
3. Utilize faculty expertise for on-campus staff development programs where appropriate.
4. Provide a continuing orientation program for new professionals.
5. Establish mentoring programs as a staff development program component.
6. Set up a staff development library, resource room, or Web site with a collection of appropriate books, journals, periodicals, and other relevant materials
7. Senior managers should take the initiative to reduce or eliminate institutional and individual barriers to staff participation in staff development.
8. Staff development programs and activities should be evaluated for improvement on a regular basis.
9. Funding support for staff development should be earmarked and annually budgeted in divisional accounts.

Summary

Effective staff development represents an important investment in people. Such an investment facilitates personal, professional, and career growth and contributes to the development of knowledgeable, well-trained, and competent student affairs practitioners. Further, effective staff development provides staff with the tools and skills needed for success in student affairs work. This is particularly important given the demands and expectations facing staff today and the complexity of contemporary issues and concerns requiring a broad knowledge base for practitioners at all levels.

Effective staff development positively influences the retention of staff and enhances career satisfaction and personal development. Competency, professionalism, and a sense of ownership are among the outcomes associated with the continuous professional growth of individual student affairs staff members. Persons responsible for staff development should focus increased attention to these outcomes in order to maintain dedicated and committed personnel.

In planning for staff development, care should be taken to consider the needs of staff at all levels. The general needs of new professionals, middle managers, and senior student affairs officers are different and varied. Considerable attention should be directed towards assessing the needs of staff and designing programs and activities accordingly.

Finally, senior student affairs leaders and others responsible for staff development play a critical role in influencing the success of staff development initiatives. On one hand, they are responsible for allocating resources including funding support needed for these efforts. Equally important, senior student affairs leaders can give credibility to staff development by setting expectations for program excellence, communicating to staff the importance of the programs and activities, and encouraging staff involvement and participation. In essence, staff development must be a priority for student affairs leaders committed to fostering the professional growth of staff as well as for staff who benefit from such efforts.

References

Ashton, P. "Motivation and the Teacher's Sense of Efficacy." In C. Ames and R. Ames (eds.), *Research on Motivation in Education*. Vol. 2. Orlando, FL: Academic Press, 1985, 141–171.

Barr, M. J. "Growing Staff Diversity and Changing Career Paths" In M. J. Barr, M. L. Upcraft and Associates, *New Futures for Student Affairs: Building a Vision for Professional Leadership and Practice*. San Francisco: Jossey-Bass, 1990.

Bloland, P. A. "Are We a Profession?" Paper presented at the joint national conference of the American College Personnel Association and the National Association of Student Personnel Administrators. Chicago, IL, March, 1987.

Blum, D. E. "24-pct Turnover Rate Found for Administrators. Some Officials are Surprised By Survey Results." *Chronicle of Higher Education*, A – 13, March 29, 1989.

Borelli, F. "The Art of Administration." *NASPA Journal*, 1984, 22(1), 14–16.

Burns, M. "Who Leaves the Student Affairs Field?" *NASPA Journal*, 1982, 20(2), 9–12.

Cox, D. W. and Ivy, W. A. "Staff Development Needs of Student Affairs Professionals." *NASPA Journal*, 1984, 22, 26–33.

Fey, C. J. and Carpenter, D. S. "Mid-level Student Affairs Administrators: Management Skills and Professional Development Needs." *NASPA Journal*, 1996, 33(3), 218–231.

Kaufman, B. E. *The Economics of Labor Markets*. Fort Worth, TX: The Dryden Press, 1994.

Komives, S. R. "Facing Crises: Counselors' Personal and Professional Responses." In M. Rose and S. Alexander (eds.), *Power Keys in America: Counseling Interventions*. Alexandria, VA.: American Association of Counseling and Development, 1986.

Lawing, M. A., Moore, L. V. and Groseth, R. "Enhancement and Advancement: Professional Development in Student Affairs." *NASPA Journal*, 1982, 20(2), 22–26.

Miller, T. K. "Staff Development of College Student Personnel." *Journal of College Student Personnel*, 1975, 16(4), 258–264.

Miller, T. K. and Carpenter, D. S. "Professional Preparation for Today and Tomorrow." In D. G. Creamer (ed.), *Student Development in Higher Education: Theories, Practices, and Future Directions.* Washington, D.C.: American College Personnel Association, 1980.

Nuss, E. "Leadership in Higher Education: Confronting the Realities of the 1990's." *NASPA Journal*, 1994, 31(3) 209–216.

Peters, T. *Thriving on Chaos: Handbook for a Management Resolution.* New York: Knopf, 1988.

Porter, J. "Leadership and Ownership within Student Affairs." *NASPA Journal*, 1989, 27(1), 11–15.

Preston, F. "Creating Effective Staff Development Programs." In M. J. Barr and Associates, *The Handbook of Student Affairs Administration.* San Francisco: Jossey-Bass, 1993.

Rickard, S. T. "Toward a professional paradigm." *Journal of College Student Personnel*, 1988, 29(5), 388–394.

Saddlemire, G. L. "Young Professionals' Mobility." Paper presented at a meeting of the American College Personnel Association, Miami, FL, March, 1988.

Scott, J. "Student Affairs Staff Development Survey." Office of Student Services, Georgia State University, 1998.

Stamatakos, L. C. and Oliaro, P. M. "In-Service Development: A Function of Student Personnel" *NASPA Journal*, 1972, 9, 169–273.

Stamatakos, L. C. "Unsolicited Advice for New Professionals." *Journal of College Student Personnel*, 1978, 19, 325–29.

Stamatakos, L. C. "Are We a Profession?" Paper presented at the joint national conference of the American College Personnel Association and the National Association of Student Personnel Administrators. Chicago, IL, March, 1987.

Young, R. "Student Affairs Professionals' Perceptions of Barriers to Participation in Development Activities." *NASPA Journal*, 1994, 31(4), 243–251.

CHAPTER TWENTY-SIX

THE ROLE OF PROFESSIONAL ASSOCIATIONS

Elizabeth M. Nuss

Seven out of ten Americans belong to at least one professional association and one in four belong to four or more (Maurer and Sheets, 1998). Professional associations have an important function in American higher education. The purpose of this chapter is to demonstrate to student affairs professionals how these organizations can help them enhance or develop their administrative and professional skills. The chapter provides a brief history of professional associations and describes what they are and do. It reviews the wide variety of forms of participation and the ways that involvement in a professional association may vary over the span of a career. Suggestions about how to become involved, tips for managing time commitments and personal resources, and issues related to affiliation in multiple associations are also discussed.

The chapter gives examples of many professional associations but is *not* intended to be a definitive summary of the universe of professional associations. The sample listing is included for illustrative purposes only. Moreover, the chapter does not advocate membership in any particular organization. As should be evident from the following discussion, decisions about which professional associations to join and when to join them are based on the reader's current professional goals, talents, and institutional needs. Nevertheless, participation in these organizations is the hallmark of a professional, and involvement is often considered to be one of the more rewarding aspects of a professional career. At a minimum, anyone intending a serious career in student affairs should be a member of at least one professional association.

A Brief History of Professional Associations

Professional associations have many objectives, but above all, they do for the membership what the members cannot do for themselves as effectively (Maurer and Sheets, 1998). They seek to advance understanding, recognition, and knowledge in the field; to develop and promulgate standards for professional practice; to inform the public on key issues; to stimulate and organize volunteerism; and to provide professionals with a peer group that promotes a sense of identity. The oldest American professional society still in existence is the American Philosophical Society, founded by Benjamin Franklin in 1743. As societies grow and become technically and socially more complex and specialized, associations are created to represent those specialized interests (Bloland, 1985).

The founding of the major student affairs professional associations follows the history and development of higher education and the profession itself. Student affairs as a distinct entity emerged in the early 1900s as a result of changes in the American professoriate. Deans of men and women were appointed to resolve student problems and to administer campus discipline systems (Nuss, 1996). In 1914, the first formal program of study in vocational guidance was offered at the Teachers College of Columbia University (C. Johnson, personal communication, August 12, 1993). The increased size and specialization of higher education fostered the establishment of appropriate professional associations to articulate the shared concerns of each institutional group (Bloland, 1985). The development of the professional associations was influenced by the fact that many student services in the early 1900s were organized by gender and that racial discrimination prevented the full participation of minorities.

The National Association of Deans of Women (NADW) was organized in 1916. Since its founding, the organization has focused its mission on serving the needs of women in education. In 1956, NADW became the National Association of Women Deans and Counselors (NAWDC). In 1972, a decision was made to change the group's name and purpose; the organization became the National Association of Women Deans, Administrators, and Counselors (NAWDAC) (Sheeley, 1983). In 1991, the organization's name was changed to the National Association for Women in Education (NAWE) to reflect more accurately its contemporary scope and focus. NAWE no longer views itself as one of the three major student affairs organizations, but rather as an association for those who have interests in women's issues and concerns in higher education (L. Gangone, personal communication, October 27, 1998).

In January 1919, a meeting referred to as the Conference of Deans and Advisers of Men was held at the University of Wisconsin. That meeting is now recognized as the founding of the National Association of Deans and Advisers of Men (NADAM). After two earlier attempts in 1948 and 1949 failed, the organization officially adopted the National Association of Student Personnel Administrators (NASPA) as its name in 1951. This broadened the base of the association, and for the first time NASPA began to recruit members (Rhatigan, 1998).

The American College Personnel Association (ACPA) traces its founding to 1924, when it began as the National Association of Appointment Secretaries (NAAS) (Sheeley, 1983; Bloland, 1972). The title of appointment secretary referred to persons who assisted in placing teachers and other college graduates. NAAS's first meeting in 1924 was held jointly with NADW. In 1929, NAAS's name was changed to the National Association of Placement and Personnel Officers to reflect its broader professional role. In 1931, the name was again changed to ACPA (Bloland, 1972). In 1991, ACPA members voted to disaffiliate from the American Association for Counseling and Development (AACD). The separation became effective in September, 1992 (ACPA, 1998). Bloland (1972) describes the historical cooperative relationships among these three major associations.

In 1954, two minority professional organizations, the Association of Deans of Women and Advisers of Girls in Colored Schools and the National Association of the Deans of Men in Negro Education Institutions, met to plan, organize, and develop the National Association of Personnel Workers (NAPW) (Barrett, 1991). Membership was open to deans, counselors, and other personnel workers. In 1994, the NAPW changed its name to the National Association of Student Affairs Professionals (NASAP) (S. Whitaker, personal communication, May 19, 1995).

As professional roles expanded and became more specialized, associations for housing, student activities, financial aid, and other officers developed in the 1950s and 1960s. In 1987, the Association for Student Judicial Affairs (ASJA) was organized.

A sample listing (not by any means a complete one) of some other national higher education and student affairs associations and their founding dates is included in Table 26.1. The list provides a historical context for the development of the different associations and provides the frequently used acronyms. For complete information, consult the *Encyclopedia of Associations* (Maurer and Sheets, 1998).

It should also be noted that over time many regional or state associations developed independently of the national organizations. Examples include the Western Deans and the Pennsylvania Association of Student Personnel Administrators.

TABLE 26.1 A SAMPLE LISTING OF PROFESSIONAL ASSOCIATIONS BY YEAR OF FOUNDING

Year	Founding
Association of American Universities (AAU)	1990
American Association of collegiate Registers and Admissions Offiers (AACRAO)	1910
Association of College Unions International (ACU-1)	1914
National Association for Women in Education (NAWE)	1916
American Council on Education (ACE)	1918
National Association of Student Personnel Administrators	1919
American Association of Community Colleges (AACJC)	1920
American College Health Association (ACHA)	1920
Association of Governing Boards of Universities and Colleges (AGB)	1921
American College Personnel Association (ACPA)	1924
National Association of College Admissions Counselors (NACAC)	1937
National Orientation Directors Association (NODA)	1947
Association of International Educators (NAFSA)	1948
National Association of College and University Business Officers (NACUBO)	1950
American Counseling Association (ACA)	1952
Association of College and University Housing Officers, International (ACUHO-I)	1952
National Association of Student Affairs Professionals (NASAP)	1954
American Association of State Colleges and Universities (AASCU)	1961
National Association of State Universities and Land Grant Colleges (NASULGC)	1962
National Association of Independent Colleges and Universities (NAICU)	1967
National Association for Campus Activities (NACA)	1968
National Association for Student Financial Aid Administrators (NASFAA)	1968
American Association for Higher Education (AAHE)	1969
Council for the Advancement and Support of Education (CASE)	1974
Association for Student Judicial Affairs (ASJA)	1987

Source: Adapted from Maurer & Sheets, 1998.

Role of Professional Associations

The mission of each organization describes the fundamental reasons for its existence, establishes the scope of its activities, and provides its overall direction. Like many other social institutions, these purposes evolve and change over time. It is also true that, like a college or university, an association's mission may or may not be explicit or readily understood by its members or a wider professional audience. One of the marks of excellence in a voluntary association is the degree to which its mission is clearly articulated and serves as a guidepost for determining the appropriateness of the association's activities (Independent Sector, 1989). The financial and human resources of most associations are limited. As board members consider alternative programs and services, choices must be made among several desirable options. Determinations should be based on how centrally related the particular program or service is to the organization's mission.

Generally, associations are described by both their mission and scope. They may be local, regional, statewide, national, or international. They may be an organization composed of individual members, institutional members, or both. The specific types of services and programs offered may vary. As a general rule, most professional associations perform the following functions: to conduct research; publish and disseminate research, information, and opinion; provide educational training and professional development programs; advocate on behalf of public policy or broad professional issues affecting members; assist members with career development issues; promulgate standards for professional preparation and practice; and create opportunities for professional peers to interact (American Society of Association Executives, 1988).

Professional associations are governed by their members and exist to serve their interests and needs. Most associations are legally incorporated nonprofit entities. Various formal rules and structures for governance exist and are described in documents such as the articles of incorporation, constitution, or bylaws. A governing board composed of elected and/or appointed individuals has the fiduciary responsibility to govern the association in compliance with the published bylaws.

A key characteristic of most student affairs professional associations is the degree to which their operations are managed by volunteers. Organizations such as NASPA, NAWE, ACPA, the Association of College and University Housing Officers-International (ACUHO-I), and others have relatively small office staffs that provide administrative services and assistance to the hundreds of volunteers responsible for program development and execution. During the past ten years, there has been some increase in the size of the professional staff as the multiple demands on volunteer members' time and energy has increased and as the associations have been successful in receiving foundation grants to support special initiatives.

Professional associations are funded primarily by member dues; fees for programs, services, and publications; and corporate or foundation grants. Like other organizations, associations are distinctive for many reasons, including those attributable to organizational culture. That culture is constantly evolving, incorporating changes in the beliefs, values, and attitudes of society as well as those of the members (Kuh, Schuh, Whitt, and Associates, 1991). The culture of the association determines in large measure how the governing board, staff, and volunteers behave, regardless of written policies (Independent Sector, 1989). Examples of organizational culture might include the dominant values espoused by the association (such as the degree to which volunteers have responsibility for program development); the emphasis placed on service to members, technology, or public policy matters; and the priority assigned to multicultural participation and involvement.

As mentioned earlier, the roles and purposes of associations evolve and change over time. Several examples of recent changes include computer technology, international involvement, and the development of research foundations.

Computer technology and the Internet have had considerable impact on professional associations. For most associations, the Internet provides an unprecedented opportunity to reach both members and the world at large in ways that were unthinkable just a few years ago (Valauskas, 1997). Enhanced communication and information are fundamental benefits of the on-line presence of associations.

As higher education worldwide has placed new emphasis on student development and support programs, there has been a growing participation of student affairs colleagues from Europe, Asia, and Africa in American associations as well as the founding of organizations in their own countries. NASPA has organized several exchange programs and has hosted a growing number of international participants at the annual conference.

Demonstrating the growing role of professional fund raising for student affairs on campus, the role of the association foundation has shown increased activity in the 1990s. Celebrating its 75th anniversary in 1996, the NASPA Foundation launched its Diamond Club campaign to raise additional funds from members to support and expand the research role of the NASPA Foundation. ACPA followed suit in 1999. Both organizations solicited funds in honor of the contributions and accomplishments of the leaders in the profession.

Many associations collaborate on issues of common concern. For example, the American Council of Education (ACE) coordinates the Washington Higher Education Secretariat, composed of over 30 higher education associations based in Washington, D.C. The National Association of College and University Business Officers (NACUBO) coordinates the Council of Higher Education Management Associations. Many of the organizations listed in Table 26.1 are members of one or both of these coordinating councils.

Reasons for Belonging to a Professional Association

Why do institutions and individuals belong to professional associations? There are a host of answers, but the majority of reasons fall into one of the following categories: opportunities for professional growth, a means to benefit from the services and programs provided, a chance to test professional competencies, a desire to join with others of similar interest to influence the future direction of the association or profession, and a professional sense of obligation to help advance the status of the profession and fund programs that assist it. Bloland (1985) argues that colleges and universities join the higher education associations based in Washington, D.C., because they need to have their case presented to Congress and the administration.

Fisher (1997) notes that with "the plethora of associations one wonders about the value of each" (p. 321). Two key values of an association are the extent to which it encourages and supports research that contributes to the theoretical knowledge base of the profession and the professional development opportunities it brings to its members (Fisher, 1997). Some of the common barriers to involvement include time, whether or not the college supports attendance with released time or reimbursed costs, and whether staff are encouraged or supported in their leadership roles (Gallemore and Ming, 1997).

There are many different forms of participation and involvement, ranging from consumer to board member. These forms of involvement and the typical skills and time commitments required are

Consumer. A consumer is an individual who is not a member but may, for example, periodically read the publications in the library; purchase a publication or audiotape; subscribe to a teleconference as a staff development tool; or attend a state, regional, or national conference.

Member. A member is a professional who has joined the association and receives copies of newsletters, journals, and other publications. The member follows the news of the association and responds to surveys on professional issues. These individuals have an opportunity to influence the direction and priorities of the association and are able to attend conferences or purchase resource materials and services at reduced costs. They may also volunteer and serve a variety of leadership roles.

Contributor. A contributor may or may not be a member of the association. Working alone or in conjunction with colleagues, the contributor submits program proposals for workshops or conferences, makes presentations, prepares newsletter articles, or submits research results for publication. These tasks require good oral presentation and written communication skills and a solid conceptual understanding of research and the professional issues being addressed. The time commitment will depend on the scope and nature of the project.

Volunteer. A volunteer is a member who agrees to assist with an activity, project, or program. The assignment may be for as little time as an hour or an ongoing assignment that requires a considerable investment of time and expertise (such as service on a committee). A volunteer must have an ability to handle independent tasks as well as work as a team member. Examples of possible jobs include posting signs; planning programs; helping with registration, newsletter preparation, or surveys; conducting research; and recruiting members.

Coordinator. The coordinator is a member responsible for planning, coordinating, and directing the efforts of other volunteers and colleagues to deliver a program, event, or service. The assignment may be on a project, local, state, regional, national, or international level and usually requires involvement for six to eighteen months. The work typically involves coordination, administration, supervisory, interpersonal, and communication skills. Financial management skills may also be necessary. Because committee members may be located across the country, being a coordinator requires an ability to interact with and motivate others in person, on the telephone, or through e-mail and other written materials. Possible assignments may include editing publications, chairing committees, planning educational programs, and coordinating commissions or networks.

Governance. A member can be elected or appointed to an advisory board or a governing board. This person is responsible for establishing major policies and long-range planning. It is work that requires an understanding of budget and finance, a significant time commitment, and an appreciation of the important and emerging issues in the profession.

In summary, the major reasons why professionals join and become involved with associations are (1) to enhance their own professional development, (2) to make a contribution to the association, and (3) to help the profession. Individuals can assist their own professional development through all the forms of participation described previously. However, making a contribution to the association and profession requires membership at a minimum and usually participation as either a contributor, a volunteer, or in a governance capacity. The value one derives from professional association depends on the time and effort one invests in it (Fisher, 1997).

Involvement over the Career Life Cycle

It may be helpful to think about a career in student affairs as a life cycle. During the course of the cycle, we may be at various points or playing many different roles. Consider the student affairs professionals in a typical student affairs division. There are graduate assistants with varying amounts of previous professional experience, new professionals, persons who have made a career transfer from another field or discipline, mid-level professionals, senior student affairs officers, faculty members, and perhaps several retired staff members. In addition to their professional assignments, each of the individuals may have family responsibilities, may be involved in community or church activities, or may be working on an advanced degree. All of these factors influence the degree to which they are able to participate or interested in participating in professional associations and the types of involvement that they seek.

The following examples describe categories of participation and involvement for student affairs professionals.

Consumer and Member. Sally is a graduate assistant with limited time and financial resources. She is a resident director and a member of ACUHO-I. She subscribes to the NAWE journal, *Initiatives*, and reads other publications as required for her course work. Next year she plans to join ACPA so she can attend the annual conference and participate in career services.

Consumer, Member, and Contributor. Jim is a doctoral student who has three years previous professional experience as a Greek advisor. Prior to returning to graduate school, he was a member of ACPA's Commission IV (student activities) and edited the Commission newsletter. As a result, his writing and publication skills improved considerably. This year he joined NASPA and plans to attend the regional conference. He and his faculty adviser have submitted a program proposal and hope to present it at the regional NASPA conference.

Consumer, Member, Contributor, and Volunteer. George is the director of the counseling center. He is a member of the American Counseling Association (ACA), ACPA, and American Psychological Association (APA). In the past fifteen years, he has served in numerous volunteer roles, has made frequent presentations at conferences, and has published his research regularly. Because of the demands of his current position and budget restrictions, he will not be able to attend any professional conferences this year. He has, however, agreed to serve as a reviewer of program proposals for the conference.

Member. Alice has recently been named director of the outdoor recreation program in the student center. Her previous professional experience was as a high school coach. She plans to maintain her membership in the National Intramural/Recreational Sports Association and has recently joined the Association of College Unions-International (ACUI) to learn more about the union field. Alice hopes to attend the summer institute sponsored by the association this year.

Member, Contributor, Volunteer, and Governance Participation. Sue has been a faculty member and a student affairs professional for twenty-five years. She has served as editor of the *NASPA Journal* for three years, was director of the research division, was director of the NASPA summer institute, and served as a member of the board of directors for both NASPA and NAWE. In 1995, she was elected president of ACPA, and she has recently agreed to be the program chair for the upcoming annual conference.

Consumer, Member, and Coordinator. Bill is the dean of students and has been a student affairs professional for ten years. He has been a member of ACUHO-I, ACPA, and NASPA. He now has administrative responsibility for financial aid and the student health service. He has recently joined the National Association for Student Financial Aid Administrators (NASFAA) and plans to accompany the health center director to the American College Health Association (ACHA) conference next year. Occasionally, he also attends the annual ACE meeting with the president of the college.

These are just a few examples of how participation and involvement in professional associations may vary over the course of a career. These examples are based on the patterns of contemporary professionals. Think about your own pattern of involvement and participation. How does it compare to these examples or to the experiences of your colleagues and other processionals whom you respect?

The Role of Associations in Professional Development

Professional associations provide programs and services designed to enhance their members' understanding of contemporary issues and to develop their professional skills. Though the benefits derived from participation often depend on the type of individual involvement, the potential positive outcomes are significant, as described by B.V. Laden.

> The education and training provided by professional associations complement university study in a number of ways. First, they often provide insights into the day-to-day operational problems of administrative life, augmenting the theoretical knowledge offered by university courses. Second, they help recent graduates adjust to new roles by helping them negotiate unfamiliar institutional cultures. Third, they provide new administrators with sponsors and mentors who can build confidence, offer guidance, make introductions, and use their expertise to assist in the socialization of new professionals. In short, they help future leaders make the most of what they have learned in graduate school (Laden, 1996, p. 47).

The most often cited benefits are summarized next.

Colleagues. The reason that is given most frequently for joining an association is the opportunity it offers for professional networks. Individuals encounter colleagues and make friends with whom they exchange ideas, perspectives, and concerns beyond the scope of their current work. The professional can interact with individuals in similar types of institutions and can compare ideas on programs and services, as well as gain a broader perspective on issues from professionals in other types of institutions and parts of the country. Someone who moves from a small liberal arts college in New England to a public four-year college in the Southwest may have an automatic network of colleagues as a result of involvement in professional associations. For many members of underrepresented minority groups and women, participation in professional associations creates valuable contacts. In cases where few women or ethnic minorities are employed on a campus, the organization provides connections to valuable role models and colleagues with similar interests and concerns. Many of the associations have created special caucuses or networks to address the needs of previously underrepresented groups.

The social nature of professional associations is also a legitimate advantage of involvement. Friendships and personal relationships develop during graduate school, in employment settings, and as a result of professional work. As people move to different institutions and regions of the country, professional associations furnish opportunities for continued interactions and get-togethers. Individuals often develop strong friendships with those whom they have served on committees with or in other volunteer roles.

Opportunities for Understanding. The simple act of getting away from a single campus environment is important in gaining new perspectives. The chance to consider issues from the perspective of others working in related campus units is also valuable. For example, health educators can learn more about students use of alcohol by attending a professional association related to residence life. Staff members can also broaden their understanding of different types of institutions and the issues they confront.

Ongoing Professional Development. Participation in professional associations provides access to the latest professional developments through publications and conferences. As a contributor or volunteer, an individual can expand and test a repertoire of skills and experiences beyond those required in a current assignment. It may be possible to perform duties and tasks not included in a full-time position. Many professionals gain the necessary experience and training for broader or more responsible career roles as a result of association involvement. Further, they also have a chance to establish a professional reputation beyond an individual campus as a result of their contributions.

Orientation to the Profession. New professionals and persons who transfer into student affairs from another career receive an important orientation to the relevant issues and literature through participation in association-sponsored programs. Many chief student affairs officers are appointed to their leadership roles from faculty positions. The professional associations provide important opportunities to gain conceptual grounding as well as advice from more experienced colleagues.

Influence on the Direction of the Profession. Individuals do make a difference. The organizational culture, professional priorities, and the association's direction are all shaped by the concerns and perspectives of the members and those responsible for governance. By responding to research questionnaires, voting on membership issues, serving as a volunteer, and contributing to the professional literature, professionals help to document the current issues and influence the emerging ones.

Shaping Professional Practice and Accreditation Standards. Professional associations establish professional standards that describe the characteristics of good individual and institutional practices. The general public's expectations and benchmarks for sound professional and ethical practices are guided by the association's standards and directives. In many cases, accreditation and licensing standards are established, or at least influenced, by professional associations. The Council for the Advancement of Standards in Higher Education (CAS), a consortium of twenty-three professional associations, has published the *CAS Standards and Guidelines,* which enable institutions to assess, study, evaluate, and improve their student services (Council for the Advancement of Standards in Higher Education, 1992).

This chapter has described the functioning of professional associations, the forms of participation and involvement, and the specific benefits to members' professional development and skills, yet several other questions must be considered. These include ways to get involved, decisions about time and resource management, and factors associated with joining more than one professional association.

Ways to Get Involved

If ten student affairs professionals were interviewed, the results might reveal fifteen different views on how to get involved, and they would all work for some people. No one correct way exists, and professionals should talk with respected colleagues and seek their advice. Listed here are some basic suggestions for getting started.

Assess Your Own Situation. What do you wish to accomplish? What contributions can a professional make? What talents do you have? In what areas do you wish to develop? Keeping your own personal and professional needs in focus is an important first step.

Investigate Associations. Once individual goals have been clarified and identified, investigate a variety of associations. The list contained in Table 26.1 is one place to start. Browsing an association's Web site is also an excellent way to learn more about the organization. Consult with faculty members and colleagues. Be wary of persons who may try to persuade you that there is one best professional association. Review the association's publications, conference programs, and membership recruitment materials. Determine as much as you can about the association and its culture, and assess their compatibility with your goals.

Join and Participate. As the examples illustrated, you are free to change your mind and belong to different associations at various points in your career. When possible, attend a state or regional conference so that you can get acquainted with people in an appropriate setting. Here is some straightforward advice for newcomers: attend with a colleague who may already be involved and ask that person to introduce you to the volunteers and leaders; attend sessions, especially those designed for newcomers, and ask questions; participate in group meals and sit with people you do not already know; take part in social events or small-group discussions; and wear your name tag.

Volunteer. Depending on individual needs and interests, a person may decide to become more involved by volunteering or submitting a program proposal, newsletter article, or journal article.

Explore Other Alternatives. Always keep an open mind about other possibilities. As you mature professionally, shift your interests or change positions or institutions, your professional goals and aspirations will invariably change. It may be a good time to seek out new challenges in your professional association or to find another one. Ideally, there should be no limits to your ability to participate and become involved in professional associations. What are some of the realistic constraints?

Your first priority is to your institutional assignment. Most institutions are supportive of staff involvement, but you should not take things for granted. Consult with your supervisor before accepting a volunteer assignment. Be sure you have a clear understanding about the use of university time for association activities; release time to attend meetings; use of institutional resources for copying, mailing, and telephone calls; and so forth. Finally, clarify which types of support the association will provide for the volunteer experience.

Your ability to participate may also be limited by the needs and plans of other staff members. For a variety of sound administrative and financial reasons, not everyone on the staff can attend the same workshop or conference. Someone has to be on duty to handle campus responsibilities. If the majority of the staff in a unit is active in one association, it may be a wise choice to pursue other opportunities. This approach also provides the unit with access to the resources of more than one association and may allow greater possibilities for participation and involvement.

Cost of Membership

In most cases, the individual and the institution combine to pay the cost of membership in professional associations. For example, you may be eligible for reduced membership dues because your college or university is an institutional member of NASPA or ACPA. In other cases, the individual may pay the membership dues and registration fees, but the institution allows release time for attendance and a van for transportation. As a professional, you are ultimately responsible for your own development. Institutional support is an important investment, but lack of campus funding is not a valid excuse for not joining a professional association. Obviously, finite time and financial resources will influence your decisions about whether or not to join more than one professional association.

Multiple Association Affiliations

It is not unusual for professionals to change their association memberships from year to year as their personal and professional circumstances change. It is also common for individuals to belong to more than one organization. The examples discussed previously supplied several reasons, including a desire to learn more about issues in a new field, to collaborate with other colleagues, and to provide financial and moral support for the goals and purposes of several worthwhile organizations.

Good judgment is the determining factor in deciding whether or not to volunteer in more than one association simultaneously, because your time and energy will be limited. Avoid commitments that may cause you to give less than a very best effort to your assignments. The student affairs professional associations depend heavily on volunteers to plan and execute their programs, and your colleagues will rely on you to complete your work. Failure to manage your time effectively can result in disappointments and frustrations for both you and your colleagues.

Much of your professional reputation depends on how well you handle your volunteer assignments. Reliability is an essential characteristic for volunteers.

Equally valued will be the ability to delegate and share responsibilities, to assist or mentor newcomers, to share recognition and credit appropriately with all involved, and to manage your commitments realistically. Of utmost importance are your professional standards and personal integrity.

As the examples illustrate, the degree of participation will vary at different points in your career. Your ability to make mature and responsible decisions about your professional involvement will influence the esteem in which your colleagues hold you.

Summary

Professional associations play an important role in continuing career development and represent a major strategy for professionals to consider when they think about the ways in which they can acquire or improve their professional and administrative skills. Individuals and their institutions both derive advantages from participation in professional associations. The benefits include access to current information for ongoing professional development, a broader perspective of understanding on contemporary issues, a network of colleagues and friends, an orientation to the profession for persons who transfer into student affairs from other disciplines, the standards of professional practice and accreditation, and an opportunity to influence the future direction of the profession and the association. You should also not overlook the intangibles, such as a sense of pride and accomplishment, camaraderie, and the joy derived from participation.

Decisions to join and become involved should be based on your goals and talents, the flexibility and support of your institution, and the needs of the association. There is no one best association, and you should feel comfortable exploring alternatives at various points in your career.

Whether you are a new professional, someone who has made a recent career change, or a senior student affairs officer, associations should play a meaningful and significant part in your professional development. It is never too early or late to consider and reconsider the variety of associations and the forms of participation and involvement available. It is my hope that you are inspired to take charge of your development and carefully analyze the possibilities that the professional associations may create.

References

American College Personnel Association (ACPA). *Brief History of ACPA.* 1998–1999 Member Resource Directory. Washington, D.C.: author, 1998.

American Society of Association Executives. *Principles of Association Management: A Professional's Handbook.* Washington, D.C.: author, 1988.

Barrett, B. N. "The Presidential Issue." *NAPW Journal III,* 1991, 1, 1–35.

Bloland, H. G. *Associations in Action: The Washington, D.C. Higher Education Community.* ASHE-ERIC Higher Education Report, No.2. Washington, D.C.: Association for the Study of Higher Education, 1985.

Bloland, P. A. "Ecumenicalism in College Student Personnel." *Journal of College Student Personnel,* 1972, 13, 102–111.

Council for the Advancement of Standards in Higher Education. *CAS Standards and Guidelines.* Washington, D.C.: author, 1992.

Fisher, W. "The Value of Professional Associations." *Library Trends,* 1997, 46(2), 320–330.

Gallemore, S. L., and Ming, L. "Perceived Barriers to Involvement in Professional Associations: Views of Physical Educators in Georgia." *Physical Educator,* 1997, 54(1), 20–30.

Gangore, L. National Association for Women in Education. Personal Communication, October 27, 1998.

Independent Sector. "Executive Summary." In *Profiles of Excellence: Studies of the Effectiveness of Nonprofit Organizations.* Washington, D.C.: author, 1989.

Johnson, C. Personal Communication, August 12, 1993.

Kuh, G. D., Schuh, J. H., Whitt, E. J., and Associates. *Involving Colleges: Successful Approaches to Fostering Student Learning and Development Outside the Classroom.* San Francisco: Jossey-Bass, 1991.

Laden, B. V. "The Role of Professional Associations in Developing Academic and Administrative Leaders." In J. C. Palmer and S. G. Katsinas (eds.) *Graduate and Continuing Education for Community College Leaders.* New Directions for Community Colleges, No. 95, XXIX, (3). San Francisco: Jossey-Bass,1996, 47–59.

Maurer, C., and Sheets, T. E. *Encyclopedia of Associations.* Detroit: Gale Research, 1998.

Nuss, E. M. "The Development of Student Affairs." In S. R. Komives and D. B Woodard (eds.), *Student Services: A Handbook for the Profession.* San Francisco: Jossey-Bass,1996, pp. 22–42.

Rhatigan, J. J. "NASPA History." In *NASPA Member Handbook.* Washington, D.C.: author, 1998.

Sheeley, V. L. "NADW and NAAS: 60 Years of Organizational Relationships (NAWDAC—ACPA: 1923–1983)." In B. A. Belson and L. E. Fitzgerald (eds.), *Thus We Spoke: ACPA-NAWDAC 1958—1975.* Washington, D.C.: author, 1983.

Valauskas, E. J. "The Virtual Association." *Library Trends,* 1997, 46, (2), 411–421.

Whitaker, S. National Association of Student Affairs Professionals (NASAP). Personal Communication, May 19, 1995.

CHAPTER TWENTY-SEVEN

ADVANCING PROFESSIONALLY THROUGH DOCTORAL EDUCATION

Susan R. Komives and Deborah J. Taub

Y ou may be reading this chapter because you are approaching your thirtieth birthday and are well into the career development stage of committing to student affairs work as a life career, or you are well past thirty and are finally deciding to think about a doctoral program. You may be preoccupied with questions like, do you need a doctorate or not? Is a doctorate necessary to move into new professional roles, engage in meaningful research, or make a career shift into a faculty role? Are you considering graduate work because of a sense of "up or out" (Burns, 1982), a recognition of needing more competencies to handle your role more effectively, or an acknowledgment that you are burned out and need to make a job change? Is the reason that you love to learn and want the stimulation of the classroom to push you to read books again, not just collect them on your shelves? One issue in professional development is the serious consideration of what additional education is needed to achieve your professional goals (Miller and Carpenter, 1980). Now may be time to decide.

Assuming that the reader has earned a master's degree or is engaging in master's-level study, this chapter focuses on the nature of doctoral preparation for student affairs administrative, teaching, and research positions. The chapter, an examination of specialization and growth within the study of student affairs and higher education, will emphasize perspectives on doctoral programs, both in higher education and student affairs administration. Particular attention will be devoted to (1) curricular focus, (2) degree requirements, (3) faculty, (4) Ph.D. or

Ed.D. degrees, (5) criteria and processes for admission, (6) financing doctoral study, and (7) alternative preparation routes. The chapter concludes with observations on evaluating the appropriateness of a doctoral program, including self-assessment and program review, and on how to make a successful early transition into doctoral study. Future issues in doctoral preparation are also briefly explored.

Doctorates for Career Success

Success in student affairs work should not be judged by upward mobility or degrees earned. A professional can stay renewed and effective with the help of good supervision, meaningful work, and the self-learning that can take place beyond a professional master's preparation. Few would argue, however, that there is a growing expectation of doctoral study for both advancement and credibility in student affairs. A current job could be retained without the doctoral degree, and promotions from within are one way that someone without a doctorate can advance, yet most opportunities for advancement or even lateral shifts are likely to be reduced when master's degree applicants are compared to similarly experienced peers who have doctorates. Many mid-management and upper-management positions in most institutions simply are not available without the doctoral credential. Conversely, prospective doctoral students without any prior experience in higher education may find the degree alone insufficient for obtaining an administrative position in higher education.

The doctorate, however, is much more than a "union card," a mere academic hurdle, or a rite of passage to advance further in the academy. A good doctoral program should be a valuable experience establishing the developing professional as an expert on the student experience and student affairs administration. The doctorate should add a strong scholarly focus to an already established practitioner base, empower educational leadership, provide perspectives that enable the role of change agent, and stimulate research inquiry.

The doctorate offers concentrated, formal opportunities for building additional competencies and skills whether one's career path is to be an expert in a functional area (such as career development, residence life, or learning disabilities), assume a faculty position teaching student development or student affairs administration, take an institutional research role, or move into central leadership positions (such as becoming a vice president or dean). Indeed, seeking a doctorate for career advancement often requires shifting from functional-area specialty skills to advanced educational administration skills. Bloland (1979) states that the attitudes, competencies, and roles of vice presidents for student affairs must focus on being administrators and leaders and that new vice presidents actually have "changed career fields from student personnel to professional administration" (p. 58).

Doctorates are increasingly common among senior student affairs officers in all types of institutions. A recent salary survey of National Association of Student Personnel Administrators (NASPA) members (Kruger, 1998) shows that fifty-six percent of the 1,045 Senior Student Affairs Officers (SSAOs) reported holding an earned doctorate. This profile differs by type of institution. Using the Carnegie classification system, Exhibit 27.1 demonstrates that doctorates were the highest degree earned in all categories except community and two-year colleges. Among NASPA members in this survey, doctorates were held by 52.4 percent at small colleges (enrollment is less than 5,000); 78.8 percent at medium-size colleges (enrollment is between 5,000 and14,999) and 89 percent at large colleges (enrollment is over 15,000). Although this report does not include the length of tenure in a particular role, doctorates are clearly common at public universities and that expectation increases with institutional size. The doctorate appears less essential, however, for department head positions. The NASPA salary survey (Kruger, 1998) reports master's as the terminal degree for 64.1 percent of the 1,148 directors, and doctorates are held by only 22.5 percent, including such positions as directors of student life, student services, and student development.

The NASPA data (Kruger, 1998) also does not indicate what the doctoral degree is in, although we are tempted to conclude that the vast majority are professionally prepared in student affairs, higher education, or a closely related field. At the end of the last decade, however, Paterson (1987) found that 25 percent of senior student affairs officers held doctorates in higher education or student personnel administration; of note is that only 63 percent of these senior student affairs officers had any type of doctorate at all. Studies nearly two decades ago found that 13 percent of all administrators with doctorates in four-year colleges and universities have their degrees in higher education (Moore, 1981). The student affairs field clearly needs more definitive information on the discipline of the degrees held by department heads and SSAOs at four-year institutions.

Doctorates in higher education are common in two-year colleges. One study of two-year colleges reports that 39.1 percent of senior student affairs officers and 41.2 percent of presidents have a higher education doctorate (Moore, Martorana, and Twombly, 1985). In another study of 716 presidents, vice presidents for academic affairs, and vice presidents for student affairs in all types of institutions, Townsend and Wiese (1992) find uniformly positive impressions of a higher education degree in the community college sector. Approximately one-third of the presidents and vice presidents for student affairs in this study have doctorates in higher education. Whereas presidents and vice presidents of acad-

EXHIBIT 27.1 HIGHEST ACADEMIC DEGREE EARNED
SENIOR STUDENT AFFAIRS OFFICERS

Degree	Total	Research I & II Public/Private		Doctoral Granting Public/Private		Comprehensive I & II Public/Private		Liberal Arts I & II Public/Private		Community & Two Year
Unknown	77 (7%)	6 (9%)	8 (30.7%)	2 (3%)	4 13%)	15 (6%)	8 (5%)	2 (8%)	14 (6%)	18 (4%)
Bachelors	1	0	0	0	0	0	0	0	0	1 (1%)
Masters	350 (34%)	7 (11%)	5 (19%)	6 (10%)	8 (25%)	42 (18%)	60 (38%)	5 (20%)	100 (43%)	117 (55%)
Post Masters Certificate	34 (3%)	1 (2%)	2 (8%)	1 (2%)	1 (3%)	6 (3%)	7 (5%)	1 (4%)	11 (5%)	4 (2%)
Doctorate	583 (56%)	52 (79%)	11 (42%)	50 (85%)	19 (59%)	172 (73%)	82 (52%)	17 (68%)	105 (45%)	75 (35%)
TOTAL	1045	66	26	59	32	235	157	25	230	215

Source: NASPA Membership Database (Kruger, 1998)

emic affairs at other types of institutions are unlikely to prefer the higher education doctorate for their role, vice presidents for student affairs are more likely to value the degree. Nearly half (47 percent) of the respondents believe that the degree is more beneficial than one in an academic discipline for a vice president of student affairs; 23 percent think it less desirable. Presidents are neutral in this opinion, and student affairs vice presidents are highly supportive. Sandeen (1982) reports that 83 percent of 219 senior student affairs officers in a national study view a professional degree in student personnel services as somewhat or very important for assuming entry-level staff and department-head positions, and 75 percent feel that it is very or somewhat important for the senior student affairs officer role.

The doctorate is clearly valued for student affairs and institutional management positions in all types of institutions. "It is possible that the [higher education] degree is more useful for those seeking career advancement in lower-tier institutions than in those designated as Level I institutions, particularly for positions in academic administration . . . Obtaining the doctorate . . . may now be the means for many prospective students to simply hold their current positions, rather than to advance" (Townsend and Mason, 1990, p. 79).

Specialization in Studying Higher Education and Student Affairs

The ever-growing list of new books in higher education signals the growth and specialization of scholarship in the fields of higher education and student affairs. These publications are an indication of the growing complexity of the American postsecondary system and the increased interest in studying higher education.

Just as College Student Personnel (CSP) is a field that begins professional study at the graduate level, entry-level preparation receives a great deal of attention in the student affairs literature. Many studies and opinions have been published on such topics as career options in student affairs (Komives and Gast, 1996; Rentz and Knock, 1990; Saddlemire, 1988), competencies for new professionals (Hyman, 1988; Ostroth, 1981), comprehensive developmental models (Beeler, 1991; Brown, 1985; Miller and Carpenter, 1980), and the curriculum and related experiences needed for effective practice (Delworth and Hanson, 1989; Knock, 1977; McEwen and Talbot, 1998; Saddlemire, 1988; Spooner, 1979; Task Force on Professional Preparation and Practice, 1989; Woodard and Komives, 1990). Until recently, however, far less attention has been paid to doctoral preparation (Beatty and Stamatakos, 1990; Coomes, Belch, and Saddlemire, 1991).

The latest *Directory of Graduate Preparation Programs in College Student Personnel* (Keim and Graham, 1994), sponsored by ACPA Commission XII, lists over 80 institutions that offer master's or doctoral study in student affairs. No accreditation agencies for higher education or student affairs doctoral programs are offered. The *Directory* indicates which programs meet minimal criteria set by Commission XII of ACPA: one full-time faculty member, one practicum, and two student affairs content courses. The Council for the Accreditation of Counseling and Related Educational Programs (CACREP), an independent accreditation agency affiliated with the American Counseling Association (ACA), has historically been the only accreditation route for graduate programs in student affairs. A small number of CSP master's programs (36), most based within counseling departments, are accredited by CACREP. McEwen and Talbot (1998) chronicle the impact of ACPA's withdrawal from the ACA and from the CACREP board, resulting in CACREP moving toward counseling-type expectations for practice. Most programs choose not to seek this accreditation. It should be noted that standards for professional preparation serve the function of quality assurance and "establish the norms for a profession" (Miller, 1991, p. 60).

Voluntary master's preparation standards, created by the collaborative efforts of the Council for the Advancement of Standards (CAS), were first published in 1986 (Council for the Advancement of Standards for Student Services/Development Programs, 1986); however, no standards for doctoral preparation in student affairs or higher education exist. Recent study groups that considered the role of student affairs doctoral standards within CAS did not recommend any move toward a set of standards. Few, if any, references are made to accreditation in the broader field of study in higher education, although the Association for the Study of Higher Education (ASHE) has just listed graduate preparation programs on its Web page (http://www.ashe.missouri.edu/introduc2.htm).

Prospective doctoral students might explore either a generalist degree of higher education (perhaps with an emphasis on student development or student affairs administration) or a specialized degree in student affairs administration (likely with an emphasis on higher education administration or another developmental focus). More research exists on the higher education doctorate than the student affairs doctorate, but information on both degrees is presented in this chapter. Other doctoral majors may be appropriate and are noted at the end of the chapter.

Perspectives on Doctoral Programs in Higher Education or Student Affairs Administration

The taxonomy of three groups of higher education programs identified by Dressel and Mayhew (1974) remains useful in assessing today's higher education programs (Crosson and Nelson, 1984) and also appears to apply to student affairs graduate programs. The first group contains programs with a *national* perspective and reputation based on the research and professional activity of the faculty, their graduate placements, and their student applicants. Programs in the second group have a *local* or *regional* perspective with an emphasis on practitioner preparation and are frequently composed of part-time students or administrators from area institutions. The third group of programs is small, with little to no formal structure, and consists of several courses designed to serve a *local* need (often geared to community college personnel). Townsend (1990) suggests that very few programs admit to the latter orientation; most blend the national and local perspectives, with many aspiring to a national focus.

Many problems exist with ranking or listing exemplary national programs, and such reviews of a dozen nationally regarded higher education programs reveal few differences between them on such measures as faculty-to-student ratios, size, number of faculty, and courses offered. Indeed, Crosson and Nelson (1984) concluded that such programs are probably "distinguished by qualitative rather than quantitative factors, and that they have more visible, active and 'cosmopolitan' faculty and students" (p. 21). Studies of program quality have generally asked professors of higher education to rank programs or have looked at such objective measures as faculty publications; few studies have looked at student-related outcome measures like the career paths of graduates, persistence in the field, satisfaction, or graduates' subsequent publications and research productivity. *U.S. News and World Report's* new rankings of graduate schools have generated great interest but are often regarded as less informed about specialty programs like college student personnel or higher education administration.

Curricular Focus

Doctoral programs in higher education frequently provide specialization options. Two specialties exist in nearly 75 percent of the programs: student affairs administration or general administration and management. Two-thirds offer a specialization in academic administration or community college administration. Half make available an emphasis on curriculum and instruction, teaching, or adult education; fewer than half empasize the foundations, history, or philosophy of higher education and institutional research, policy analysis, or financial administration or finance; and fewer than 25 percent provide information on planning and comparative or international higher education (Crosson and Nelson, 1984).

The department in which a program is based exerts a strong influence on program design. The *Directory of Graduate Preparation Programs in College Student Personnel* (Keim and Graham, 1994) notes 43 student affairs doctoral programs; slightly more than half are located in higher education or educational leadership programs, and the others are in counselor education, counseling psychology, educational psychology, or other departments. Although 75 percent of all higher education administration doctoral programs claim a student affairs specialization (47 programs), their resources should be examined carefully; the *Directory of Graduate Preparation Programs* lists only 22 doctoral programs in higher education with a student affairs specialization, and not all of those meet the minimal ACPA Commission XII criteria. Even allowing for some differences in the programs that were used in these two data sources, this is a troublesome discrepancy.

Another troubling fact is that, of the doctoral programs in the 1994 *Directory*, 18 reported that they offered no student affairs courses exclusively for doctoral students (McEwen and Talbot, 1998). McEwen and Talbot report that "fewer than five programs appeared to offer substantial specialized, post-masters courses in student affairs" (p. 145).

Both student affairs and higher education are "derivative field[s] of study" (Crosson and Nelson, 1984, p. 7). Course work ranges from applied management theory to sociology. Higher education administration programs and student affairs administrative doctoral programs may have only one thing in common:

neither has paid serious attention to identifying a core of necessary knowledge. "The question that remains unanswered is how doctoral programs continue to prepare professionals for more advanced levels of student affairs administration or prepare faculty for teaching and research in student affairs, without having mutually agreed upon guidelines and standards that relate to the field's needs and expectations" (Beatty and Stamatakos, 1990, p. 222). Miller, Creamer, Gehring, and McEwen (1996) call for a comprehensive description of student affairs doctoral programs.

Delworth and Hanson (1989) indicate that the core of doctoral programs in student affairs should be "competence in research" (p. 613) and mastery of at least one of what they term "role orientations" in student affairs. These role orientations include administrator, counselor, student development educator, and campus ecology manager. They further indicate that leadership in the profession should be the focus of doctoral education.

McEwen and Talbot (1998) agree that research and leadership are the dimensions that should distinguish doctoral study in student affairs from master-level education. They suggest that "the goal of doctoral programs in student affairs should be to develop expert practitioners or scholar-practitioners and also, for some doctoral programs, to develop persons to assume faculty positions" (p. 142). They indicate that this is consistent with Delworth and Hanson's (1989) focus on leadership for the profession.

Beatty and Stamatakos (1990) find agreement among student affairs practitioners and preparation faculty on the competencies needed for effective practice; the exception is that the faculty rank research and evaluation competencies as number one, whereas that skill was rated ninth for student affairs administrators. Based on the general agreement of the practitioners and faculty members in their study, Beatty and Stamatakos (1990) identify six general competence areas that students should seek in a developmental framework for their doctoral preparation:

- Theoretical competence: an in-depth understanding of the historical, philosophical, and theoretical foundations on which student affairs administration is based.
- Scholarly competence: the development and perpetuation of scholarship through inquiry, critical interpretation, investigation, research, and writing.
- Functional competence: the development, maintenance, or enhancement of those skills needed to perform both simple and complex functions in an effective manner.
- Transferal competence: the ability to transfer theoretical and philosophical foundations of student affairs administration to practical situations.

- Environmental competence: an understanding of and the ability to work with and to help shape the environment in which student affairs administration exists.
- Human relations competence: the ability to understand, direct, communicate with, and interact with primary constituents, colleagues, and peers who are a part of the higher education environment.

Those considering doctoral study might use this list as a self-assessment guide. If prospective students can demonstrate high-level competence in each area, then their academic study might extend beyond higher education or student affairs for further enrichment. If self-assessment reveals deficits in master's preparation or in experience, then a doctorate that would best round out those competencies is indicated.

Administrators believe the most useful experience in a higher education doctorate to be an internship, along with courses on finance and budgeting and organization and governance (Townsend and Wiese, 1992). The importance of field experience, including practice and internships, is a consistent theme in master's degree programs related to student affairs (Council for the Advancement of Standards in Higher Education, 1997; Richmond and Sherman, 1991).

Doctoral Degree Requirements

Doctoral degree requirements typically include a residency requirement, dissertation, and a course work core in higher education, as well as statistics or research requirements (Crosson and Nelson, 1984). Student affairs doctoral programs require 3.7 research courses on average and an average of 18.1 courses beyond the master's degree (Keim, 1991).

Comprehensive Examinations. Most programs require comprehensive examinations to measure a necessary minimum subject competence, usually including (1) the history of the field; (2) major professional issues therein; (3) the field's various dimensions, such as governance,organization, finance, and student development theory; (4) research skills sufficient to begin a dissertation; and (5) some applied, integrating, synthesizing experience like a case study, comprehensive question, or practical problem (Peters and Peterson, 1987). Programs may also require preliminary or qualifying examinations for a wide variety of purposes.

Dissertation. The dissertation process is guided by a committee usually chaired by the student's adviser. The committee generally includes a methodologist, someone from outside the host department and often outside the college, and a faculty member from the program. The two major components of the process include the proposal and the oral defense. Students agree that acceptance of the proposal seems more crucial than the oral defense, which virtually everyone should pass (Peters and Peterson, 1987). Doctoral students nearing the end of their program are sorely tempted to accept a professional position before starting their dissertation, but they should be careful. Successfully completing a dissertation from long distance is understandably difficult, and students are advised to stay through the defense of their research if possible and at least conduct the proposal meeting before assuming a new professional role. The bottom line is that All But Dissertation (A.B.D.) is *not* a degree; indeed, it may become an insurmountable hurdle if one cannot establish support systems in the new environment (such as time off or understanding supervisors and employees) to move the dissertation along.

Faculty

Crosson and Nelson (1984) estimate that the number of full-time faculty in higher education doctoral programs increased 50 percent in the 1970s, with approximately 330 faculty members teaching higher education full time. Concurrently, part-time faculty members continue to play a strong role in all higher education programs; 58 percent of the part-time faculty hold appointments as administrators on their host campus. Although the size of the faculty varies greatly, most higher education programs are small, with a mean of 3.7 full-time faculty members along with 5.5 part-time affiliates (p.12). Student enrollment has outpaced increases in full-time and part-time faculty. Over half of all higher education programs report more than 20 students per full-time faculty member (Crosson and Nelson, 1984).

Faculty numbers in student affairs doctoral programs are even smaller and are, in many cases, a subset of a larger group of faculty in the host department. Evans and Williams (1998) report that, according to information in the 1994 *Directory*, there are 95 full-time faculty members in the 83 listed programs; this averages out to only 1.1 full-time faculty per program. Evans and Williams further report that 26 programs (31 percent) list no full-time student affairs faculty. In a national study of CAS and CACREP standards in master's programs, Evans (1988) concludes, "Clearly the lack of staff is a major issue for programs trying to meet standards in terms of courses, supervision, and advising" (p.9). With the number of full-time faculty decreasing in existing student affairs programs, the field faces the problem of improving its professionalization, which requires greater demand on faculty resources.

There are few full-time faculty of color in either higher education or student affairs graduate programs. A survey of full-time faculty members in student affairs graduate programs (Evans and Williams, 1998) reports that 87 percent of the respondents were Caucasian. Moreover, women now compose over half of all higher education and student affairs doctoral student enrollments; yet women make up only 15 percent of all higher education faculty at all ranks, and many programs have no women faculty members. Faculty profiles of full-time and part-time student affairs faculty reflect slightly higher proportions of women (approximately 36 percent) to men (approximately 64 percent) with women predominately at the lower academic ranks (Evans and Williams, 1998).

Ph.D. Versus Ed.D.

Half of all higher education doctoral programs make available both the doctor of philosophy (Ph.D.) and doctor of education (Ed.D.) options; another 24 percent offer only the Ph.D. and 26 percent only the Ed.D. Where both options exist, it is frequently possible to switch programs if one degree becomes more relevant to the student's goals than the other. The Ph.D. is thought to reflect a greater research orientation, and the Ed.D. is often perceived having a practitioner focus. In reality, reviews show little difference between Ph.D. and Ed.D. degree requirements even when a program offers both options (Crosson and Nelson, 1984). One difference is that research requirements in the Ed.D. program range from five to eleven hours, whereas the Ph.D. requires twelve to sixteen credits (Dill and Morrison, 1985). Prospective students often ask, "Which degree is better?" One could reply, "Which degree do you think I have? How about the degree of Professor Smith or well-known researcher Dr. Jones or outstanding Vice President Wilson or the president of one of our professional associations, Dr. Washington? It's probably not the degree, but how good you are that counts!" Little difference exists in reality, leading some (Carpenter, 1990) to encourage academic departments to eliminate the valid but more confusing Ed.D. and offer only the Ph.D., which may be more readily understood.

Criteria and Processes for Admission

More than half of the higher education doctoral programs require similar credentials: letters of recommendation, a master's degree, English proficiency for international students, a satisfactory Graduate Record Exam (GRE) score, and a stated minimum grade point average (GPA) for both baccalaureate and master's work (ranging between a 3.0 to 3.5). A few programs ask for such materials as a career goals statement, two to five years of professional experience, or an autobiographical statement (Crosson and Nelson, 1984). Student affairs programs use similar screening methods. Over 40 percent admit students on a rolling admissions deadline; 83 percent demand a GPA from 3.00 to 4.00 (Coomes, Belch, and Saddlemire, 1991). Approximately two-thirds of the student affairs doctoral programs require a personal interview and 77 percent use prior years of experience in their admissions requirements for doctoral students (Phelps Tobin, 1998).

As many doctoral programs are offered by major research universities, the host graduate school also will have minimum academic standards for admission in good standing. Programs can recommend students who do not meet those requirements for provisional or probationary admission, so prospective students should not be deterred merely by published criteria. There is a movement to seek diverse indicators of academic promise that could influence graduate admissions beyond published cognitive indicators like GPA and test scores. Sedlacek's noncognitive factors to predict academic achievement (Tracey and Sedlacek, 1985) become very useful for effective consideration of racial and ethnic minorities. They are also useful for other students whose undergraduate leadership experiences and motivation signal a better prognosis of success than their test scores or undergraduate grades. Students who do not meet minimal academic standards should assertively build their case around these indicators and request an exception to stated minimums. Even if not requested, applicants should consider recalculating their undergraduate GPA to demonstrate their highest GPA achievement (such as their last sixty credits earned or their major). Applicants should use a persuasive cover letter, write a thorough personal statement, if one is required, and include a resume to build a strong set of credentials that exceed the stated requirements.

Financing Doctoral Study

Assistantships are valuable work experiences for master's students and offer an out-of-class setting to integrate the knowledge, attitudes, and skills needed in the student affairs field. By contrast, for doctoral students, assistantships generally serve as a source of financial support and usually provide less credibility and responsibility than full-time work experience prior to matriculation.

A recent survey of nine nationally-based CSP preparation programs (McLoughlin, 1998) shows all programs offering assistantships that include in- and out-of-state tuition remission covering a range from six credits per semester to full-time course loads. There is a wide variation in salaries and other benefits. Among these nine programs, the ten-month stipends range from $6,600 to $13,500, only one campus noted offering medical benefits, and in most cases, the live-in stipend was half that of the live-out but also covered room and board. An earlier survey of eleven major CSP preparation programs (Olivetti, 1991) showed that only 36 percent of the doctoral students had assistantships, compared to 78 percent of the master's students. Doctoral assistantship stipends varied as much as $7,000 (from $2,500 to $9,700) with a variety of fringe benefits, including tuition remission, office space, computer access, parking, professional travel, health benefits, and housing and meals for live-in positions.

Most assistantships are meaningful professional involvements with developmental supervision. Doctoral students should consider accepting assistantships that offer research experience, particularly in offices that can make subjects or a database available for dissertation research. Students seeking graduate assistantships should carefully assess the campus and office work climate. All professionals know that a supposedly twenty-hour-a-week assistantship as a head resident, student activities adviser, or student union programmer usually involves much more time. Because the relationships and reputation gained from assistantship employment will persist after graduate study, students should carefully assess the true workload, expectations, and office culture as students cannot afford not to do well in this related work experience.

Alternative Approaches

The approach to doctoral study in this chapter has valued an administrative degree in either higher education or student affairs earned in a traditional campus-based program. Other disciplines and modes of learning also should be explored to answer the diverse needs of professionals seeking doctorates.

A Doctorate in Counseling, Counselor Education, or Counseling Psychology

Counseling degrees have become a specialty degree at the doctoral level for those preparing for professional roles in counseling centers, teaching, and human development in community colleges. They are also a legitimate route to becoming a director of agencies such as career development and counseling centers, services for students with disabilities, or learning assistance programs. Three-fourths of counseling doctoral graduates find positions in counseling, and 15 to 19 percent are employed in student personnel work, higher education administration, or higher education teaching (Zimpfer and DeTrude, 1990). For the administratively oriented counselor, this degree may be a means of furthering one's administrative career advancement or teaching and may even be desirable in small college or community college settings. However, noticeably fewer doctoral counseling graduates are entering higher education work environments: 64.4 percent in 1970 compared to only 21.5 percent in 1985. More than 1000 doctoral counseling degrees are conferred annually (Zimpfer and DeTrude, 1990), not including degrees in counseling psychology or clinical psychology.

A Doctorate in Another Discipline

In this era of specialization, some argue for the competencies of a compatible behavioral science field (such as organizational behavior, social psychology, law, psychology, or sociology) as acceptable, if not desirable, for student affairs administrative roles (Canon, 1982). Using the base of a student affairs master's degree, this approach clearly would be a strong option and provide such additional benefits as adjunct teaching in almost any institution of employment and the unspoken credibility of a more clearly understood discipline. These authors believe it essential that professional practitioners earn at least one graduate degree in student affairs or higher education. If another discipline is pursued as the only course of study for both the master's and doctorate, one would be advised to take student development or higher education administrative course work as a cognate area; conduct dissertation research on a related issue in higher education; use students, faculty, or administrators as the population of interest; and in essence develop a specialty in the higher education environment within the selected discipline. Some formal graduate preparation and exposure to student affairs and higher education may be preferable to none, but they will be insufficient for professional practice. This course of action is not recommended.

External Degree Programs

Perhaps graduate education needs a paradigm shift. The known paradigm of a campus-based degree program is comfortable, has rigor, and is effective. If we truly believe in continuous lifelong learning, self-motivated learners, and new technologies that make teleconferencing and video and electronic communication a reality, then we might be more open to external degree programs.

One possibility would be a shift away from a "campus" perspective of traditional learning to explore the merit of external degree programs such as the Union Institute. Accredited by the same regional agencies that evaluate established colleges and universities, many of these programs help the advanced learner establish a doctoral committee of graduate faculty across the country that will guide learning, read papers, and direct research. Often combined with intensive weekend seminars, learning contracts, and regular progress checks, these programs claim that the quality of their doctoral dissertations compares positively with that of traditional programs. This approach may be successful for the most motivated self-directed learner and may be the only opportunity for advanced study for someone without ready access to a campus-based program. The external degree program does have significant disadvantages, including the lack of interaction with peer students and graduate faculty, but learning does occur. Additional competencies can be built through such a program, and the desired outcome—the doctoral degree—is obtained.

If clusters of colleges in a region of a state are not served by a graduate preparation program, special offerings might be developed as a satellite program. This might create a source of new students for a nearby established program, support state outreach for public institutions, and bring degree advancement possibilities to professionals who might not otherwise be able to seek them.

Institutes, Workshops, Extended Study, and Professional Development

Continuous learning is essential for professional practice, whether or not an individual seeks a doctoral degree. Creamer and Shelton (1988) identify two perspectives on in-service education: institutional effectiveness and staff effectiveness. Assuredly, specific staff training in areas of institutional goals can and will advance the accomplishment of objectives. Likewise, staff training designed around staff needs and professional interests can advance individual skills (see the chapter by Scott in this volume).

Adaptation of the model of requiring continuing education units (CEUs) for recertification in such fields as counseling and psychology should be on the national student affairs agenda. Such a credentialing system ensures professional renewal supported by professional associations (Paterson and Carpenter, 1989; Task Force on Professional Preparation and Practice, 1989). A professional could demonstrate a competence in such topics as conflict resolution, multicultural awareness, women's development, facilities development, or the like by earning a designated number of CEUs. Carpenter (1998) calls for the collaboration of professional associations, student affairs practitioners, and preparation program faculty to provide continuing professional education in student affairs and for faculty to provide leadership in identifying content, delivery, and assessment. Even without a formal registry, CEUs need to be embraced as evidence of important experiences beyond a formal degree program. Associations should establish the appropriate mechanisms, and professionals should request, perhaps demand, CEUs to encourage that process.

Assessing a Doctoral Program—Is It Right for You?

Deciding to engage in doctoral study is a complex search for compatibility between the needs and characteristics of the student and the focus and environment of the graduate program. Finding an optimal match between personal needs and program characteristics is worth extensive study and research, for it may be the most important decision in the process.

Self-Assessment

The single most important variable in selecting a graduate program is *you!* Practitioners considering doctoral study should engage in probing self-assessment, including intermediate and long-term career goals, skill and competency strengths and needs, and ways to build on the focus of their master's degree. Perhaps more important is to evaluate family responsibilities and support, necessary financial adjustments, stress and energy levels, and life events that might occur during the duration of graduate study (Belch and Ottinger, 1989). This assessment inevitably leads to the questions of whether you will be a full-time or part-time student, work on or off campus, and how long it will take you to complete the degree.

Part-time or Full-time. A serious preliminary question is whether you will pursue a program part-time while employed (at least part-time) or whether you will enter poverty again as a graduate student and enjoy full-time study. If you plan to be a part-time student, explore your work culture. You should determine the support of members of your organization, particularly those who may feel that they might have to assume some of your responsibilities when you have to leave for class on a regular basis. They may support your effort or may resent the increased workload. You may wish to consult two extensive lists of self-assessment questions: those posed by Moore and Young (1987) and by Belch and Ottinger (1989).

Working on or off Campus. If you are a part-time student, will you work on or off the host campus? Working on campus usually brings tuition-remission benefits, ease in getting to classes, and access to resources. And you do not have to find another parking place. However, on-campus work also brings the possibilities of complex relationships in which your supervisor may now also be a faculty member and an employee in your unit may be a doctoral student ahead of you in the program. These can be healthy experiences or they can be stressful and uncomfortable. Working at a nearby campus provides less role confusion. In fact, colleagues may not even know of your graduate study obligations, but it may not provide needed benefits and support.

Time to Degree. Townsend and Mason (1990) report that the time taken to earn a higher education doctorate has steadily grown, from 5.4 years in 1967 to 6.9 years in 1987. The average age at the time of awarding of the degree has similarly increased, from 36 to 43. Students in student affairs doctoral programs tend to be slightly younger (one-third are 31 to 35 years of age) (Coomes, Belch, and Saddlemire, 1991).

Program Assessment

If you have identified what you want to study, have career and research goals, know if you can enroll in a national program or are adapting your life to accommodate a regional program, and have decided whether you will be part-time or full-time, you are ready to begin reviewing programs.

Locating Programs. Several Web sites have useful sources of information on graduate programs. You should explore the classic *Directory of Graduate Preparation Programs in College Student Personnel* (Keim & Graham, 1994), now updated and available on the ACPA Web page (http://www.acpa.nche.edu). NASPA has also created a graduate programs site with a balance of student affairs and higher education programs (http://www.naspa.org). ASHE has the newest site with their first 1998 listings of higher education programs. E-mail, write, or call these programs for more specific literature from the department; do not rely only on graduate catalog or web site information. You should consider many aspects of the programs of interest to you. The following list is not exhaustive but is representative of basic questions.

Policies. What policies will influence your life: required internships, residency requirements, procedures for interrupted study, language requirements, and policies about class absences due to work or travel?

Faculty. Who are the current faculty members, and what are the faculty staffing projections for the four to six years required for you to get your degree? Are retirements or sabbaticals being planned? What is the nature of student-faculty interaction? To what degree does the faculty act as mentor and sponsor and advise students (Merriam, Thomas, and Zeph, 1987; Rentz and Saddlemire, 1988)? Among full-time and affiliate faculty or campus practitioners, are there professionals that you could consider models for your gender, race, and interests if these are important to you?

Connections with Practice. Is there a healthy connection with the host campus student affairs program and nearby institutions (Komives, 1998)? Are the practitioners and faculty tightly or loosely joined? Is the program well networked with local, regional, and national associations?

Areas of Specialty. What are the areas of specialty in the program? Is there flexibility with department cognate areas, or is the one you want even available? Can you register in other departments' courses, or are they closed to non-majors? Do not just assume you can take a wonderful psychology course or a doctoral-level course in managerial leadership in the business school; check it out. How does the focus of the host department influence core requirements like course work and comprehensive exam questions?

The Academic Experience. What is the sequence of courses and how often are they offered? Can you schedule required courses when needed? What is the mix of master's and doctoral students in the same classes and how does this fit your expectations? How do your interests and experiences fit what you know about other students in the program who will now be your colleagues? What is the student culture?

Teaching Modes. What are the predominant teaching modes in the department: seminar discussions, case studies, lecture classes? What is the nature of the learning activity: readings, research papers, group projects? Are the fieldwork experiences in settings that will stretch and challenge you? Do the modes used build on your preferred learning styles (Forney, 1994)? Is course content on the cutting edge or at least current?

Ethics. What are the climate, culture, tone, and core values of the program? Are departmental relationships ethical and principled (Brown and Krager, 1985)? Is it a collaborative community with norms of supportive relationship, an impersonal atmosphere stressing individual accomplishment, or even a competitive environment providing a richer experience for the scholarly committed student? In which environment would you flourish? How realistic are your expectations?

Research and Dissertations. What are the faculty research interests? What research methods are valued by faculty members Is their work predominantly qualitative, quantitative, or both? How do dissertation titles signal program interests? What supports exist for moving through the dissertation in a timely way (McEwen and Talbot, 1998)?

Financial Support. Are there appropriate assistantships, fellowships, or other financial support if needed? Is there a tuition-remission limit on the number of credits per semester or number of semesters that are covered? What other benefits are included, such as health insurance?

Student Completion. What are graduation rates from the program? What is the average time to earn the degree for full-time and part-time students? What supports exist for job placement, and what positions do recent graduates hold?

Succeeding in Doctoral Study

Having decided that you need the doctorate, assessed yourself and the programs, and made a decision about the right program for your goals, you have already begun the transition to doctoral study. Make no mistake about it—engaging in doctoral study adds major complexity to your already busy life. Whether moving cross-country or adding it to your already complex life, be prepared for major adjustments. Understanding the stages of socialization and transition can help you manage the transition intentionally. This section concludes with tips for success in pursuing the doctorate.

Socialization/Transition

Graduate study has been described as a process of socialization to a profession (Baird, 1995). Entering a doctoral program also means socialization to a new setting, possibly a different institution or department, and to a new role.

Feldman (1976) describes a three-stage model of socialization to an organization, which provides a helpful framework for considering the transition to a doctoral program. The first stage is *anticipatory socialization,* which "encompasses all the learning that occurs before the recruit enters the organization" (p. 434). The tasks of this stage are forming expectations and making decisions. For the prospective doctoral student, anticipatory socialization would include gathering information about programs, assessing programs and one's self, and making decisions about program alternatives.

In the second stage, *accommodation,* the individual finds out what the organization is really like and tries to become a part of the organization. Seashore (1975) observes, "There seems to be a significant discrepancy between what was expected in the program and what is found, including: finding a few things that you did expect, finding a lot of things you didn't expect but really like, finding some things you didn't expect and are sure you don't need, not finding quite a few things you did expect and can't believe are not there" (p. 2). Coming to terms with all of these discoveries is integral to the accommodation stage. The tasks of the accommodation stage include learning new tasks, forming new relationships, clarifying one's roles, and evaluating one's progress. For the new doctoral student, accommodation might include making friends with other doctoral students, getting to know faculty, learning what expectations are in classes and in assistantship assignments, and getting feedback on course work.

In the third stage, *role management,* the individual attempts to resolve conflicts between work life and home life and between various groups in the organization. For the doctoral student, these tasks might include negotiating study time and home responsibilities.

Feldman (1976) identifies the outcomes of socialization as satisfaction, mutual influence (degree of control or power), internal motivation, and involvement; the further along in socialization a person is, the greater the outcomes. According to Feldman, the success of socialization may be assessed at any point in the process; socialization is considered complete when an individual has moved through all three stages and mastered the tasks associated with each stage. Just as a new (or prospective) employee needs to form expectations, make decisions, learn new tasks, form new relationships, manage conflicts, and so on, so does the new (or prospective) doctoral student.

Although some graduate programs offer extensive orientation programs (Taub and Komives, 1998), in general, "there is little formal or systematic effort to socialize doctoral students" (Hawley, 1993, p. 6). Therefore, it is likely that much of the effort and direction to move successively through the stages of socialization and manage the transition successfully will come from you. Likewise, you probably will have to construct your own support system from supportive faculty, new doctoral student colleagues, supervisors, family, and friends.

Tips for Success

A number of authors (Baird, 1995; Hawley, 1993; Peters, 1997) provide suggestions for managing the transitions and achieving success. Here are some tips.

Get Organized. Juggling your multiple roles and responsibilities as a doctoral student will be easier if you get organized. Peters (1997) provides detailed information about a number of organizational topics including setting up a calendar system, organizing a work area, and setting up a filing system for the masses of articles, research ideas, class notes, handouts, and conference materials that you will accumulate.

Negotiate Home Responsibilities. It is almost inevitable that the demands of doctoral study will require you divert time away from responsibilities you have maintained at home and toward studying, reading, and writing. Successfully resolving potential home/graduate school conflicts is critical to completing successfully the final stage of socialization (Feldman, 1976).

Establish Good Working Relationships. It will be important for you to establish good working relationships with a number of people: your fellow students, the faculty in and out of your department, and assistantship supervisors. Seashore (1975) draws the comparison of establishing relationships with other students and "the rather unsettling experience of being assigned eight or ten siblings with whom you are supposed to have some unspecified form of interdependence for a year or two" (p. 3). However, Baird (1995) points out that other students can be critical in helping one feel at home in a program and can be valuable sources of socialization information. Peters (1997) recommends remembering to treat support staff kindly, as they can be extremely helpful to graduate students.

Stay Positive. A number of researchers (Goplerud, 1980; Hodgson and Simoni, 1995; Mallinckrodt, Leong, and Kraij, 1989; Valdez, 1982) have come to the not at all surprising conclusion that graduate students are under stress. It is important, however, to stay positive. Try to avoid falling into the pattern of griping about the program, the requirements, the faculty, or your fellow students. Although letting off a little steam can be helpful, continual complaining breeds a negative attitude that will not help you progress through your doctoral studies and could foster a negative personal reputation. Try to keep a positive attitude and seek out other positive people. It will make things at least seem easier.

Keep a Research Log. Remember that the doctorate is a research degree. Research ideas can come from anywhere—class readings, a situation at your work site, casual discussions with classmates, brown bag presentations in your department, or journals and periodicals that you scan. Get in the habit of keeping a notebook in which you jot down these thoughts and ideas. Particularly valuable is learning the habit of phrasing these ideas as research questions. This is not as difficult as it might sound. We both often ask our students the simple question: "What is it you'd like to know about that?"

Future Content in Doctoral Preparation

Society has become a permanent "white water," with rapid change, ambiguity, and chaos becoming the norm instead of the exception (Vaill, 1989). These complexities are more than simply problems that must be solved (Barr and Golseth, 1990). We seek a community built on the talent and creativity that arises from our differences in an environment that values our shared visions and common dreams. Successful professionals, both those engaging in doctoral study as well as those in practice, will need to learn many new ways to function well in these rapidly changing times. Graduate programs should enrich their course work, experiential learning, research focus, and program culture to honor these changes and shift emphasis from the present, probably most comfortable for practitioners, to the ambiguities and unknowns of the future.

Graduate programs should strive to develop leadership perspectives, attitudes, values, and skills in doctoral students as an intentional outcome. Vaill (1989) admonishes leaders of the future not merely to work harder or longer, but to work collectively, reflectively, and spiritually smarter. New-age leaders must see connections, value collaboration, and empower all stakeholders to make a difference in campus change. It is encouraging that Rogers (1991) finds a commitment to this new collaborative paradigm of leadership among graduate preparation faculty and students.

Other chapters in this book have considered the benefit and challenge of diversity in college environments. Student affairs professionals have always shared a professional commitment to bring all students to the table, to value individual differences, and to ensure that all students' interests are taken seriously by the institution. Though not always implemented with consistency or insight, professionals for the future must possess cultural competence (Ebbers and Henry, 1990; Talbot, 1996) and demonstrate an appreciation of multiculturalism in their attitudes and behaviors. This appreciation embraces all kinds of individuals, regardless of their gender, sexual orientation, race, ethnicity, disability, religion, or other characteristics. These individuals have talents and perspectives to bring to the larger purpose of being an inclusive learning community not because it is "politically correct," but because it is "educationally correct." Indeed, it is an educational mandate. Further, graduate programs must search affirmatively for faculty members who can create more effective links to and models for diverse graduate students (Woodard and Komives, 1990).

The concept of campus community, which in the 1980s was so vigorously endorsed in the pages of the *Chronicle of Higher Education* and many national reform reports, needs nurturing champions: student affairs professionals. Yet few graduate programs teach an understanding of campus culture, elements of building a diverse community, or ways to become "involving colleges" (Kuh, Schuh, Whitt, and Associates, 1991) or developmentally powerful environments. The environmental assessment and redesign skills required to build real learning communities should be a foundation of all student affairs graduate programs.

It would be folly to try to list the many additional competencies and skills necessary for effective student affairs administration in the future. Perhaps instead we should encourage prospective students, program faculty members, and practitioners to find regular mechanisms to bring important issues as well as a discussion of essential generalist skills, attitudes, and values to the seminar table. This "liberal arts" approach to graduate study will serve us as well as it has served the liberal arts undergraduates, who traditionally know how to think, how to learn, and how to communicate within the higher education community.

Summary

Student affairs professionals desiring strong careers as administrators, researchers, graduate faculty members, and informed change agents must consider graduate study beyond their master's degree. Doctoral degrees are necessities in many positions and types of institutions. The reasons for pursuing a degree and decisions about when to start, what and where to study, and with whom are issues requiring personal reflection and self-assessment. Professional practice will advance when those who engage in it are prepared with advanced competencies, knowledge, skills, attitudes, and values and when institutions commit themselves to that kind of practice by hiring such professionals. "Chief student affairs officers who have their own graduate training in student personnel services in higher education attach considerably more importance to such graduate training in their hiring decisions than do their counterparts who have earned their graduate degrees in unrelated fields" (Sandeen, 1982, p. 53). Perhaps the decade's most profound challenge to employing institutions is to advance effective, professional practice by requiring professional graduate credentials of those seeking student affairs leadership roles, and stand for no less!

References

Baird, L. L. "Helping Graduate Students: A Graduate Adviser's View." In A. S. Pruitt and P. D. Isaac (Eds.), *Student Services for the Changing Graduate Student Population*, New Directions for Student Services No. 72. San Francisco: Jossey-Bass, 1995.

Barr, M. J., and Golseth, A. E. "Managing Change in a Paradoxical Environment." In M. J. Barr and M. L. Upcraft, and Associates, *New Futures for Student Affairs: Building a Vision for Professional Leadership and Practice*. San Francisco: Jossey-Bass, 1990.

Beatty, D. L., and Stamatakos, L. C. "Faculty and Administrator Perceptions of Knowledge, Skills, and Competencies as Standards for Doctoral Preparation Programs in Student Affairs Administration." *Journal of College Student Development*, 1990, *31*, 221–229.

Beeler, K. D. "Graduate Student Adjustment to Academic Life: A Four-Stage Framework." *NASPA Journal*, 1991, *28* (2), 163–171.

Belch, H. A. and Ottinger, D. C. "To a Degree: Making a Decision about Doctoral Studies." *Connections*, 1989, *1* (1), 13–18.

Bloland, P. "Student Personnel Training for the Chief Student Affairs Officer: Essential or Unnecessary?" *NASPA Journal*, 1979, *17* (2), 57–62.

Brown, R. D. "Graduate Education for the Student Development Profession: A Content and Process Model." *NASPA Journal*, 1985, *22* (3), 38–43.

Brown, R. D., and Krager, L. "Ethical Issues in Graduate Education." *Journal of Higher Education*, 1985, *56* (4), 403–418.

Burns, M. A. "Who Leaves the Student Affairs Field." *NASPA Journal*, 1982, *20* (2), 9–12.

Canon, H. J. "Toward Professionalism in Student Affairs: Another Point of View." *Journal of College Student Personnel*, 1982, *23* (6), 468–473.

Carpenter, D. S. "Continuing Professional Education in Student Affairs." In N. J. Evans and C. E. Phelps Tobin (eds.). *The State of the Art of Preparation and Practice in Student Affairs: Another Look*. Washington D.C.: American College Personnel Association, 1998.

Carpenter, S. "Professional Development and Career Issues for Mid-Managers." In R. B. Young (Ed.), *The Invisible Leaders: Student Affairs Mid-Managers*. Washington, D.C.: National Association of Student Personnel Administrators, 1990.

Coomes, M. D., Belch, H. A., and Saddlemire, G. L. "Doctoral Programs for Student Affairs Professionals: A Status Report." *Journal of College Student Development*, 1991, *32* (1), 62–68.

Council for the Advancement of Standards for Student Services/Development Programs. *Council for Advancement of Standards: Standards and Guidelines for Student Services/Development Programs.* Washington, D.C.: Council for the Advancement of Standards for Student Services/Development Programs, 1986.

Council for the Advancement of Standards in Higher Education. *The CAS Book of Professional Standards for Higher Education.* Washington, D.C.: Council for the Advancement of Standards in Higher Education, 1997.

Creamer, D. G., and Shelton, M. "Staff Development: A Literature Review of Graduate Preparation and In-Service Education of Students." *Journal of College Student Development*, 1988, *29*, 407–414.

Crosson, P. M., and Nelson, G. M. "A Profile of Higher Education Doctoral Programs." Paper presented at the annual meeting of the Association for the Study of Higher Education, March 1984 (ERIC Document Reproduction Service No. ED 245 604).

Delworth, U., and Hanson, G. R. "Future Directions: A Vision of Student Services in the 1990s." In U. Delworth, G. Hanson, and Associates, *Student Services: A Handbook for the Profession.* (2nd ed.). San Francisco: Jossey-Bass, 1989.

Dill, D., and Morrison, J. L. "Ed.D. and Ph.D. Research Training in the Field of Higher Education: A Survey and Proposal." *Review of Higher Education*, 1985, *8*, 169–186.

Dressel, P. L., and Mayhew, L. B. *Higher Education as a Field of Study: The Emergence of a Profession.* San Francisco: Jossey-Bass, 1974.

Ebbers, L. H., and Henry, S. L. "Cultural Competence: A New Challenge to Student Affairs Professionals." *NASPA Journal*, 1990, *27* (4), 319–323.

Evans, N. J. "College Student Personnel Program Responses to Preparation Standards." Unpublished Report to the American College Personnel Association, 1988.

Evans, N. J., and Williams, T. E. "Student Affairs Faculty: Characteristics, Qualifications, and Recommendations for Future Preparation." In N. J. Evans and C. E. Phelps Tobin (eds.). *The State of the Art of Preparation and Practice in Student Affairs: Another Look.* Washington, D.C.: American College Personnel Association, 1998.

Feldman, D. C. "A Contingency Theory of Socialization." *Administrative Science Quarterly*, 1976, *21*, 433–452.

Forney, D. S. "A Profile of Student Affairs Master's Students: Characteristics, Attitudes, and Learning Styles." *Journal of College Student Development*, 1994, *35*, 337–345.

Goplerud, E. N. "Social Support and Stress During the First Year of Graduate School," *Professional Psychology*, 1980, *11*, 283–290.

Hawley, P. *Being Bright is Not Enough: The Unwritten Rules of Doctoral Study.* Springfield, Ill.: Charles C. Thomas, 1993.

Hodgson, C. S., and Simoni, J. M. "Graduate Student Academic and Psychological Functioning." *Journal of College Student Development*, 1995, *36*, 244–253.

Hyman, R. E. "Graduate Preparation for Professional Practice: A Difference of Perceptions." *NASPA Journal*, 1988, *26* (2), 143–150.

Keim, M. C. "Student Personnel Preparation Programs: A Longitudinal Study." *NASPA Journal*, 1991, *28* (3), 231–242.

Keim, M. E., and Graham, J. W. (eds.). *Directory of Graduate Preparation Programs in College Student Personnel.* Washington, D.C.: American College Personnel Association, 1994.

Knock, G. H. (ed.). *Perspectives on the Preparation of Student Affairs Professionals.* Alexandria, VA: American Association of Counseling and Development, 1977.

Komives, S. R., "Linking Student Affairs Preparation with Practice." In N. Evans and C. Phelps (eds.). *The State of The Art of Professional Education And Practice In Student Affairs: Another Look.* Washington, D.C.: ACPA, 1998.

Komives, S. R. and Gast, L. K. "Student Affairs and Related Careers In Higher Education." In B. B. Collison and N. J. Garfield (eds.). *Careers in Counseling and Human Services* (2nd ed.). Washington, D.C.: Taylor and Frances, 1996.

Kruger, K. "Membership Statistics." Unpublished report. National Association of Student Personnel Administrators. November 17, 1998.

Kuh, G. D., Schuh, J. H., Whitt, E. J., and Associates. *Involving Colleges: Successful Approaches to Fostering Student Learning and Development Outside the Classroom.* San Francisco: Jossey-Bass, 1991.

Mallinckrodt, B., Leong, F. T. L., and Kraij, M. M. "Sex Differences in Graduate Student Life-Change Stress and Stress Symptoms." *Journal of College Student Development*, 1989, *30*, 332–338.

McEwen, M. K., and Talbot, D. M. "Designing the Student Affairs Curriculum." In N. J. Evans and C. E. Phelps Tobin (eds.). *The State of the Art of Preparation and Practice in Student Affairs: Another Look.* Washington, D.C.: American College Personnel Association, 1998.

McLoughlin, P. J. II. "A Comparison of Higher Education Administration Programs." Unpublished report, 1998, University of Vermont (Contact Higher Education and Student Affairs Program at 802–656–2030).

Merriam, S. B., Thomas, T. K., and Zeph, C. P. "Mentoring in Higher Education: What We Know Now." *Review of Higher Education*, 1987, *11* (2), 199–210.

Miller, T. K. "Using Standards in Professional Preparation." In W. A. Bryan, R. B. Winston Jr., and T. K. Miller (eds.), *Using Professional Standards in Student Affairs*, New Directions for Student Services No. 53. San Francisco: Jossey-Bass, 1991.

Miller, T. K., and Carpenter, D. S. "Professional Preparation for Today and Tomorrow." In D. G. Creamer (ed.), *Student Development in Higher Education.* Washington, D.C.: American College Personnel Association, 1980.

Miller, T. K., Creamer, D. G., Gehring, D. D., and McEwen, M. K. "Doctoral Program Standards: Is You Is or Is You Ain't?" Paper presented at the annual conference of the American College Personnel Association, Baltimore, 1996.

Moore, K. M. *Leaders in Transition: A National Study of Higher Education Administrators.* University Park: Center for the Study of Higher Education, Pennsylvania State University, 1981.

Moore, K. M., Martorana, S. V., and Twombly, S. *Today's Academic Leaders: A National Study of Administrators in Community and Junior Colleges.* University Park: Center for the Study of Higher Education, Pennsylvania State University, 1985.

Moore, L. V., and Young, R. B. (eds.). *Expanding Opportunities for Professional Education.* New Directions for Student Services, No. 37. San Francisco: Jossey-Bass, 1987.

Olivetti, S. *Graduate Assistant Benefits Survey Summary.* Unpublished manuscript. University of South Carolina, 1991.

Ostroth, D. D. "Competencies for Entry-level Professionals: What Do Employers Look for in Hiring New Staff?" *Journal of College Student Personnel*, 1981, *22*, 5–11.

Paterson, B. G. "An Examination of the Professional Status of Chief Student Affairs Officers." *College Student Affairs Journal*, 1987, *8* (1), 13–20.

Paterson, B. G., and Carpenter, D. S. "The Emerging Student Affairs Profession: What Still Needs to be Done." *NASPA Journal*, 1989, *27* (2), 123–127.

Peters, D. S., and Peterson, M. A. "Monitoring and Evaluating Doctoral Student Progress in Programs for the Study of Higher Education." Paper presented at the annual meeting of the Association for the Study of Higher Education, February 1987 (ERIC Document Reproduction Service No. ED 281 432).

Peters, R. L. *Getting What You Came For: The Smart Student's Guide to Earning a Master's or Ph.D.* (rev. ed.). New York: Noonday, 1997.

Phelps Tobin, C. E. "Recruiting and Retaining Qualified Graduate Students." In N. J. Evans and C. E. Phelps Tobin (eds.), *The State of the Art of Preparation and Practice in Student Affairs: Another Look*. Washington, D.C.: American College Personnel Association, 1998.

Rentz, A. L., and Knock, G. H. *Student Affairs Careers: Enhancing the Collegiate Experience*. Washington, D.C.: American College Personnel Association, 1990.

Rentz, A. L., and Saddlemire, G. L. (eds.). *Student Affairs Functions in Higher Education*. Springfield, Ill.: Thomas, 1988.

Richmond, J., and Sherman, K. J. "Student-Development Preparation and Placement: A Longitudinal Study of Graduate Students' and New Professionals' Experiences." *Journal of College Student Development*, 1991, *32* (1), 8–16.

Rogers, J. L. "Leadership Education in College Student Personnel Preparation Programs: An Analysis of Faculty Perspectives." *NASPA Journal*, 1991, *29* (1), 37–48.

Saddlemire, G. "Designing a Curriculum for Student Services/Development Professionals." In R. B. Young and L. V. Moore (eds.), *The State of the Art of Professional Education and Practice*. Generativity Project #1. Washington, D.C.: American College Personnel Association, 1988.

Sandeen, C. A. "Professional Preparation Programs in Student Personnel Services in Higher Education: A National Assessment by Chief Student Affairs Officers." *NASPA Journal*, 1982, *20* (2), 51–58.

Seashore, C. "In Grave Danger of Growing: Observations on the Process of Professional Development." Paper presented to the candidates and faculty of the Washington School of Psychiatry Training Program, Washington, D.C., June 1975.

Spooner, S. E. "Preparing the Student Development Specialist: The Process Outcome Model Applied." *Journal of College Student Personnel*, 1979, *20* (1), 45–53.

Talbot, D. "Multiculturalism." In S. R. Komives and D. W. Woodard Jr. (eds.), *Student Services: A Handbook for the Profession* (3rd ed.). San Francisco: Jossey-Bass, 1996.

Task Force on Professional Preparation and Practice. *The Recruitment, Preparation, and Nurturing of the Student Affairs Profession*. Washington, D.C.: National Association of Student Personnel Administrators and the American College Personnel Association, 1989.

Taub, D. J., and Komives, S. R. "A Comprehensive Graduate Orientation Program: Practicing What We Preach," *Journal of College Student Development*, 1998, *39*, 394–398.

Townsend, B. K. "Doctoral Study in the Field of Higher Education." In J. C. Smart (ed.), *Higher Education: Handbook of Theory and Research*, Vol. 6. New York: Agathon, 1990.

Townsend, B. K., and Mason, S. O. "Career Paths of Graduates of Higher Education Doctoral Programs." *Review of Higher Education*, 1990, *14* (1), 63–81.

Townsend, B. K., and Wiese, M. "Value of a Doctorate in Higher Education for Student Affairs Administrators." *NASPA Journal*, 1992, 30, 51–58.

Tracey, T. J., and Sedlacek, W. E. "The Relationship of Noncognitive Variables to Academic Success: A Longitudinal Comparison by Race." *Journal of College Student Personnel*, 1985, *26*, 405–410.

Vaill, P. B. *Managing as a Performing Art: New Ideas for a World of Chaotic Change.* San Francisco: Jossey-Bass, 1989.

Valdez, R. "First Year Doctoral Students and Stress." *College Student Journal*, 1982, *16*, 30–37.

Woodard, D. B. Jr., and Komives, S. R. "Ensuring Staff Competence." In M. J. Barr, M. L. Upcraft, and Associates, *New Futures for Student Affairs: Building a Vision for Professional Leadership and Practice.* San Francisco: Jossey-Bass, 1990.

Zimpfer, D. G., and DeTrude, J. C. "Follow-Up of Doctoral Graduates in Counseling." *Journal of Counseling and Development*, 1990, 69, 51–56.

CHAPTER TWENTY-EIGHT

NEW ALTERNATIVES FOR PROFESSIONAL DEVELOPMENT

Kevin Kruger

Expectations for continuous professional development are key elements of a thriving profession. The student affairs profession, like all professions, is best served when the members of the profession are committed to a culture of lifelong learning. Creamer (1997), in a report prepared for the American College Personnel Association (ACPA) and the National Association of Student Personnel Administrators (NASPA) on quality assurance in the student affairs profession, states the case for continuous professional development, "Continuous learning goes to the heart of professional practice. Continuous professional education is an irrefutable ethical responsibility of practicing professionals" (p. 362).

A commitment to professional development becomes even more critical in the complex, changing environment of higher education. The knowledge, skills, and competencies required of successful student affairs professionals have become far greater than those that can be developed during a one- or two-year master's degree program. Consider a representative list of current issues facing the student affairs practice:

1. The need to work in interdisciplinary, cross-functional ways to support students

2. The need to develop diverse delivery systems that address institutional differences, changing technology, and diverse student populations

3. The reality of complex and evolving legal and public policy environments
4. Confronting chronic student issues related to alcohol and other drugs, violence, sexual health, and psychological and physical disabilities

The complexity and evolving nature of these issues requires the student affairs profession to retain a clear focus on continuous professional education.

Most writing about professional development has focused on the extent to which effective staffing practices include a strong staff development process. Winston and Creamer (1997), Dalton (1996), and DeCoster and Brown (1991) provide a detailed rationale and strong recommendations for the importance of staff development as an institutional priority. This chapter will focus on the need for student affairs professionals to take responsibility for their own professional development and to explore professional growth opportunities that enhance the traditional, organizationally based staff development model.

The chapter begins with background on the rationale for continuous professional development and examines the challenges facing implementation. A brief overview of adult learning principles and recommendations for planning individual professional development opportunities is presented. The heart of the chapter focuses on specific categories of professional development including professional and scholarly writing, internships and externships, conference presentations, service learning and community service, workshops, conferences, institutes, and finally a review of the skills necessary for the new millennium.

Professional Development Background

An expectation for lifelong commitment to professional development and growth is one of the cornerstones of most professions. The very definition of "profession" suggests continuous professional development. "Acquisition of a recognized body of expert knowledge and skills is fundamental to the concept of professionalism. Throughout their career, however, professionals must continually expand and transform their knowledge and skills to reflect advances in their fields." (Klevans, Smutz, Shuman and Bershad, 1992, p. 17) In the teaching and medical professions, for example, professional development is a requirement for licensure or certification. Although the student affairs profession lacks entities that certify, license, or register individual practitioners, the critical importance of professional development is clear. The very practice and philosophy of student affairs implies ongoing, lifelong professional development. The Council for the Advancement of Standards (CAS, 1998), supported by virtually every student affairs-related higher education association, strongly recommends continuing professional development. The National Association of Student Personnel Administrators (NASPA), one of the leading umbrella associations serving student affairs administrators, states in its *Standards of Professional Practice*, "Members have an obligation to continue personal professional growth and to contribute to the development of the profession by enhancing personal knowledge and skills, sharing ideas and information, improving professional practices, conducting and reporting research and participating in association activities" (NASPA Standards of Professional Practice, 1998). It is worth noting that Creamer's "Quality Assurance Model" (1997), called for ACPA and NASPA, the two primary student affairs professional associations, to assume a larger role in developing standards that address professional development.

While standards and ethics statements provide an important rationale for professional development, the need for continuous professional development is also found in the voices of those who practice in the student affairs profession. The 1980s and 1990s have been challenging times for student affairs practice and all current signs suggest that this challenging environment will continue into the next century. Shaffer (1993) suggested that student affairs work will change dramatically in the next 50 years and will demand more creativity and flexibility. Unless the practice of student affairs advances and addresses these changes, Shaffer asserted that other fields will fill the gap and student affairs will be reduced to "performing housekeeping functions." Garland and Grace (1994) supported Shaffer's contention that new skills will be needed. They advocated the importance of developing skills that will allow student affairs professionals to serve as, "environmental scanner, milieu manager, market analyst, legal adviser, development officer, researcher, and quality assurance specialist" (p. 4).

Another compelling argument for professional development relates to the multiple ways in which people enter the student affairs profession. In discussing the "Quality Assurance Model," Creamer (1997) cited four primary avenues for entry into the student affairs profession: through professional preparation programs, related degree programs, unrelated degree programs, and no formal academic training. The latter two avenues in particular underscore the need for systemic, ongoing professional development. Student affairs staff with no formal academic training or from unrelated degree programs may bring valuable personal attributes and skills to their work, but often can benefit from professional development opportunities that focus on the fundamental "content" of the profession.

Despite the strong support for professional development, a number of factors have contributed to make this a difficult goal to reach. Sandeen (1988) stated that senior student affairs officers recognize the importance of professional development through staff development programs. However, the institutional competition for the needed fiscal resources may result in diminished opportunities. Winston and

Creamer (1997), in reviewing staff development practices, found that most student affairs divisions do not have adequate resources to support staff development. Only 40 percent of comprehensive universities have line items for staff development, a practice that is almost nonexistent in liberal arts and community colleges. Fey and Carpenter (1996) in their review of professional development for mid-level student affairs administrators found little research and much criticism about the state of professional development in student affairs work. Contributing to the problem is the perception among mid-level administrators that there is little or no need for professional development to address relevant skill areas (Young, 1990).

Komives (1998) argued that a professional orientation should include attention to both the roles of practitioner and scholar. The role of practitioner attends to program implementation, evaluation, and application of the theory and research of student development into practice. The role of scholar, by contrast, is oriented towards advancing knowledge and promoting inquiry. Komives argues that both roles are critical for student affairs professionals and that a focus on one over the other may result in limited effectiveness. "I expect that most people in this field intentionally try to incorporate some aspect of both scholar and practitioner, yet there are hundreds of people in the student affairs field who have not read a recent journal, do not attend convention programs, have no campus-based continuing education program, have never conducted an outcomes or evaluation study, and conduct no research" (Komives, 1998, p. 179).

There are adequate philosophical justifications for attention to professional development. There are also pragmatic reasons as well: namely, the job market. During the mid- to late 1980s, a weak economic climate in America contributed several of the worst employment years we have seen for higher education positions. The combination of downsizing, reductions in state appropriations to higher education, and an increase in the numbers of students in student personnel graduate preparation programs created a highly competitive job market. Even today as we close out the 1990s, in the middle of tremendous economic expansion, the competition for employment opportunities remains high. This trend was identified by Komives (1998) in her study of placement data from ACPA and NASPA. The ratio of positions to candidates shifted from about two or more *positions* per candidate in the late seventies and early eighties to between 1.4 and 1.5 *candidates* per position by the mid-nineties.

The demands of today's job market create an environment where continuous professional development is a critical aspect for enhanced marketability and the ability to excel in the complex arena of student affairs administration. As Komives (1998) suggests, although graduate preparation programs provide a critical foundation for the work of a student affairs professional, significant gaps are left between course work, the apprenticeship of a graduate assistantship, and the demands of full-time professional practice.

Path to Professional Development

"Conventional understanding has it that knowledge comes from somewhere—books, journals, lectures, tapes—that this knowledge can be stored for future consumption . . . A more recent view is that knowledge is actually created by people in interaction with their environment" (Baskett and Marsiak, 1992, p. 11). Baskett and Marsiak also suggest that professional development and learning does not come from courses, conferences, lectures, and reading, but in fact is "long, circuitous, and far more circumscribed and holistic than previously imagined" (p. 12). Their research supports the importance of a lifelong process of involvement in professional development experiences.

A review of the literature provides little to guide student affairs professionals in seeking professional growth opportunities. DeCoster and Brown (1991) in a review of the literature of staff development found six categories that represent a curriculum for student affairs staff development:

1. Facilitating interaction with colleagues and associates.
2. Developing functional skills and specific competencies.
3. Promoting self-understanding and self-actualization.
4. Exposure to innovative programs.
5. Providing opportunities for professional renewal.
6. Conveying theoretical and philosophical knowledge
   (DeCoster and Brown, 1991, p. 568).

DeCoster and Brown extract from these categories a list of common staff development activities such as national, regional, and state conference attendance; off-campus workshops and seminars; special research and program grants; committee and task force participation; and administrative fellowships and internships. Fey and Carpenter (1996) found the major categories of professional development to be interactive and largely involving the major professional associations through conferences, workshops, discussions, and mentoring.

Many authors (DeCoster and Brown, 1991; Garland and Grace, 1994; Klevan, Smutz, Shuman, and Bershad, 1992; Winston and Creamer, 1997) suggest that professional development is best achieved using a planning process. Although specific "career mapping" processes may be too structured for some, starting with a self-assessment does provide professionals insights into the gap between current skills, abilities, and experiences and a desired state for these same attributes. "The purpose of self-assessment is to help professionals better understand their profession-related learning needs so that they can tailor plans for their professional development" (Klevans, Smutz, Shuman, and Bershad, 1992, p. 17). DeCoster and Brown suggest a self-assessment process that matches career objectives with the knowledge, skills, and personal qualities necessary to achieve those career goals. The resulting matrix is an example of how to incorporate planning and self-assessment into the process of professional development. Winston and Creamer (1997) discussed the need for a developmental plan emphasizing "current personal and professional status regarding attributes needed to perform assigned duties, short and long-term goals, and alternative methods for achieving the goals" (p. 238).

Professional, Scholarly, and Informal Writing Opportunities

A balance between the role of scholar and practitioner is important in the evolution of a successful practitioner (Komives, 1998). Both the NASPA Standards of Professional Practice (1998) and the ACPA Ethics Statement (1993) strongly state the need for professionals to serve the profession through conducting and reporting the results of research. One of the most significant ways of reporting research and advances in the practice of the profession is through professional writing.

Higher education professional associations provide a wealth of writing opportunities. Examples range from the scholarly writing found in the *Journal of College Student Development* (ACPA), *NASPA Journal* (NASPA), *Journal of Blacks in Higher Education* (CH II Publishers Inc.), and *Initiatives* (NAWE) to less rigorous writing opportunities such as NASPA's *FORUM*, ACUHO's *Talking Stick*, or ACUI-I's *Union Wire*.

Scholarly writing in a refereed journal is arguably the most professionally respected form of professional writing. It is also the most demanding, rigorous, and competitive of writing opportunities. It is common practice for most scholarly journals to reject as many as 85 percent of the articles submitted for review. Most articles report new research or developmentally-based innovations in practice with a strong evaluative component. Many professionals in student affairs, faced with fifty-hour-a-week jobs and demanding day-to-day schedules, report little time to *read* professional journals, no less conduct research and write for a professional journal. To make the process more manageable, a brief environmental assessment may help guide aspiring writers and researchers. Several questions might help guide this assessment: 1) What student affairs programs, interventions, or activities in which you are involved are particularly innovative or effective, 2) Can the results and outcomes of these programs or activities be assessed, 3) Is there an area of student development theory or student affairs practice that is intriguing about which there has been little writing and research, and 4) What is missing in the professional literature or what questions are unanswered that would help guide your practice?

These questions allow aspiring writers to incorporate professional writing with job-related activities. Many young authors might consider seeking writing and research partnerships with supervisors, faculty colleagues, or peers who share the same common interests. For example, if you have identified a research interest, seek out a small team of peer professionals who share the same interest. Develop a research plan and report the results in one of the scholarly journals in higher education. The joint accountability of a shared research and writing project as well as the shared workload can make scholarly writing a more manageable task. A brief review of the most recent issues of the journals listed reveals that many articles have multiple authors, supporting the value and prevalence of the collaborative writing process.

For those intimidated by the requirements of writing for scholarly publications, other publications with less rigorous standards provide opportunities to contribute to the profession and develop sound professional writing skills. Newsletters and magazines that address issues of applied practice are excellent opportunities to write professionally about contemporary issues, innovative practices, or controversial professional issues without applying the standards of scholarly research, advanced statistics, and sophisticated assessment. Every professional association provides opportunities to write in this manner. Articles are normally shorter in length and are often focused on the practitioner, rather than the scholar. This form of writing, although less rigorous from a research standpoint, also makes significant contributions to the practice and dialogue of the profession. Because the publications do not count heavily in the faculty promotion process, they have the capability to focus on more timely, non-research-based topics. Good examples of these publications are NASPA's *FORUM*, the Web-based magazine, *Net Results*, ACPA and Jossey-Bass Publishers' *About Campus*, or the magazines of the many constituent-based associations such as ACUHO-I's monthly magazine *Talking Stick*, NACA's magazine *Programming*, or ACUI-I's newsletter *Union Wire*.

One final writing task is involvement in editing, contributing to, or writing a professional book or monograph. ACPA and NASPA both publish books and monographs. The Jossey-Bass *New Directions in Student Services* series, published six times a year, also provides opportunities for writing in monographs. Most of the examples previously listed focus on contemporary issues with a strongly applied, practice-oriented focus and explore "cutting-edge issues" or second-generation student development theory and research. Guidelines for submitting book proposals can be found on publisher Web pages.

Writing for a proposed book or monograph carries little or no compensation for the author. At best, an author may receive several complementary copies of the article or monograph. Authors proposing book or monograph titles should expect that their ideas will be evaluated on the basis of the content itself as well as the potential marketability of the potential book or monograph.

Internships

Internships and practicum are a common element of most student affairs graduate preparation programs. The importance of these field-based experiences is based on the importance of linking theory with practice, a concept that is firmly rooted in the history of the student affairs profession. In addition to the developmental value of internships, these experiences have also been shown to increase marketability for entry-level positions (Garland and Grace, 1994).

Although most graduate students participate in internship experiences as part of their graduate program curriculum, many non-curricular opportunities exist for developing new skills in a field-based, experiential setting. These internships can provide access to broader professional networks, and experiential education in a wide array of professional skill areas.

Professional associations are often the best venue for exploring internship opportunities. ACUHO-I has a long tradition of offering internships though their "Housing Internship" program. This internship program places student affairs graduate students and young professionals in a wide range of campus-based housing internships. These internships often are paid and provide housing. Internships are primarily offered in the summer but have been expanded to include spring and fall terms. ACUHO-I also has entered into a partnership with the National Association of College and University Food Services (NACUFS) to encourage more professional interest in food service management. ACPA also offers a campus-based internship program called the Graduate Preparation Internship Program (GPIP). This program matches host institutions with graduate students who have applied to the program. Although the GPIP program focuses on summer internship opportunities, spring and fall internships are also available. Most of the GPIP internships offer some form of remuneration through a stipend and/or housing.

Opportunities also exist for full-time staff to participate in internship programs as part of a staff development program. These opportunities often are based on an intern-mentor model, providing the staff member with a senior staff mentor and release time from his or her current position to participate in the administrative internship. These models can be based on a campus or can function within a larger system. An excellent example of a system-based model is the Management Internship Program in the Maricopa Community College District (Zabezensky, et al, 1986). This program placed full-time employees in a rotational internship within five senior administrative offices. At the same time, these interns are enrolled in a graduate course focusing on managerial activities. This is a living example of professional development that links theory to practice. It is also representative of the types of professional development activities that exist for mid-level professionals.

Professional associations also offer internships that provide opportunities to work on national issues or programs that serve the student affairs profession as a whole. NASPA and ACPA, for example, offer summer, fall, and spring internships that focus on higher education association management and public policy issues, as well as the opportunity to work on professional development programs that serve the needs of the student affairs profession.

The mainstream internships referenced previously are representative of the types of internship and experiential opportunities most prevalent in student affairs. However, countless other experiences exist that can provide an opportunity for a unique professional development opportunity. National civic organizations sponsor programs that, although not directly related to student affairs and student development, provide significant professional development. Rotary International's Group Study Exchange is a good example. The Group Study Exchange program "provides grants . . . for teams of men and women in the early stages of their professional careers to travel abroad and share vocational information with the representatives of their respective professions in another country" (Rotary International, 1998). The Rotary Foundation funds round-trip air transportation and arranges for lodging and meals. Rotary International sponsors over 500 team exchanges a year.

Another unique experience is the opportunity to serve as staff of the Semester at Sea program. Though technically not an internship program, the Institute for Shipboard Education through the Semester at Sea program hires a full array of student affairs staff for each voyage of the *Universal Explorer* (University of Pittsburgh, 1999). These semester-long positions range from senior student affairs officer positions to entry-level housing positions. This opportunity provides solid student affairs experience working with diverse students within a true multicultural setting.

Many student affairs professionals, more senior in their professional careers, have participated in the American Scholar Program administered by the Fulbright Program. The Fulbright Scholar program is designed to "increase mutual understanding between the people of the United States and the people of other countries" (Council for International Exchange of Scholars, 1998). The Fulbright scholar program affords student affairs professional the chance to lecture, conduct research, and study the practice of student affairs in the host country. The Fulbright scholar program, lasting six to twelve weeks, is a significant professional experience and is geared to senior administrators who have the ability to negotiate a sabbatical arrangement on their campus.

NASPA also offers an opportunity to travel overseas and to study with student affairs professionals from other countries. The NASPA International Exchange program selects teams of student affairs professionals to participate in a one-week exchange program focusing on the administration of student services and student development in non-American institutions. The NASPA International Exchange program sponsors exchanges to Germany, France, the United Kingdom, Mexico, and Australia/New Zealand.

One of most prestigious internship programs available in higher education is the American Council on Education (ACE) Fellows program. The ACE fellows program is a highly competitive program, selecting only 35 fellows annually that are assigned to a senior mentor at a host institution. "The Fellow typically attends high-level decision-making meetings . . . to study leadership in action. Fellows are given meaningful tasks and projects that will both engage them in the life of the institutions and enhance their knowledge and skills" (American Council on Education, 1998). Although selected fellows are largely drawn from the academic affairs, the prestige of the ACE Fellows program and senior leadership skills developed make this a professional development experience worth considering for senior student affairs administrators.

Professional Presentations

In a study of mid-level professionals, Fey and Carpenter (1996) identified leadership and communication skills as two of the most important skills for successful student affairs administration. Research conducted in other related professions, such as business management, find similar emphases. In the business sector, presentation and public speaking opportunities can be defining events in a person's career. "Because modern organizations are so dependent on timely and understandable information, effective speaking and presentations skills are essential requirements for today's business person to get the job done and ensure that the effect (on his/her reputation) is positive" (Olney and Bednar, 1989, p. 161). Although effective presentation skills can be a distinguishing factor in a student affairs career, public speaking opportunities are commonly recognized as extreme anxiety-producing experiences. One strategy for overcoming public speaking anxiety and for enhancing public speaking skills is through participating in professional presentations.

Scores of conference workshops, symposia, and institutes are offered by national associations and their regional and state entities. Often called a "call for presentations," a "call for programs," or a "call for papers," these announcements seek proposals from general members. In virtually all cases, general program presenters are not compensated and are expected to register for the conference as well. Graduate students and new professionals would be wise to begin their career conducting professional presentations at regional or state conferences and workshops. The selection processes for programs at these conferences are less competitive and are designed to be laboratories and a training ground for major presentations at national conferences. There certainly are many examples of graduate students presenting at a national conference; however, the audience will expect a high-level presentation, with substantial content and a polished presentation style. Many graduate students and new professionals seek a more experienced staff member on their campus and work collaboratively to develop the presentation.

Regardless of scope, local or national, it is important to remember that these presentation opportunities are professionally defining, both positively and negatively. To maximize the positive impact, consider the following:

1. Proof and edit program proposal submissions and presentation handouts carefully.
2. Avoid "show and tell" presentations. Use examples from campus programs to highlight broader issues or principles.
3. Provide data where appropriate. Outcome assessments, research results, and evaluative data strengthen your presentation.
4. Carefully write your presentation abstract so that participants know the purpose and focus of your presentation.
5. Develop the program to meet specified criteria and format guidelines found in the program proposal materials.
6. Never read from a prepared paper. Reading of "papers," while acceptable and expected in the scholarly science community, is not common practice during student affairs conference presentations.

Service Learning and Community Service

The educational and developmental benefits to undergraduate students who participate in service learning are well documented in the student personnel literature (Delve, Mintz, and Stewart, 1990; Jacoby, 1996). Service learning and community service can be powerful experiences for staff, provide opportunities to work with the community, and develop and enhance targeted skills. Proponents of service learning make a compelling case for incorporating a service ethos into your life, "People live richer, more useful, and more fulfilling lives when they are able to avoid segmented thinking and view career, relationship, location, and lifestyle choices as a coherent whole. Commitment to community service and social justice is a way of life that all individuals can choose, rather than an option in only certain social-work-type careers or as a separate activity to be done around the edges of other commitments" (Fisher, 1996, p. 208).

In addition to the intrinsic value of service, these community, non-campus-based experiences provide student affairs professionals with opportunities to refine or develop targeted skills or experiential areas not available in their present job. For example, many young professionals recognize the importance of developing sound budgeting and fiscal management skills, particularly as they express interest in mid- and senior-level positions. Student affairs professionals interested in developing this skill area could design a volunteer experience that focuses on fiscal responsibilities. Many community agencies, church groups, and fraternal organizations would welcome participation in a functional area, such as budgeting and finance, that is less glamorous and often receives less public appreciation. Consider a second example of a student affairs professional interested in expanding counseling and crisis management skills. Community-based counseling and outreach services provide opportunities to develop and enhance one-to-one advising and counseling skills. Many of these agencies, such as rape crisis centers, have reciprocal or cooperative relationships with local universities (Orzek, 1983). These reciprocal relationships provide articulated volunteer opportunities for university staff. Other community-based agencies, such as AIDS support agencies and crisis hotlines, may offer similar arrangements or will be interested in staff involvement from a local university. Because of the nature of the work, many of these agencies require extensive training before working with actual cases. These community agencies, which require a more substantial time commitment, have the benefit of hands-on experience and comprehensive training, creating a more powerful professional development opportunity.

Workshops and Institutes

Sandeen (1988) identified attendance at seminars, conferences, and institutes as an important component of an institution's staff development program. Fey and Carpenter (1996) found conferences and workshops as the top two preferred methods of professional development for mid-level student affairs professionals. The array of workshops, institutes, and conferences offered by professional associations provides both focused and general professional development for all levels of staff, new professionals through senior student affairs officers. These programs also vary from one-day drive-in conferences to week-long institutes with resident faculty.

It is useful to consider the type of experience that best fits your professional development goals and plans when considering attending a conference, workshop, or institute. The national conferences sponsored by NASPA, ACPA, NAWE, ACUHO-I, ACUI-I, the National Association for Campus Activities (NACA), and the National Orientation Directors Association (NODA) are excellent opportunities to choose from among hundreds of programs, and to focus learning in short, one-hour time blocks. These conferences are also networking experiences, allowing participants to interact with other professionals who work in similar settings or deal with similar issues. On a much smaller level, regional conferences offered in one of the NASPA regions or the ACPA's state divisions provide a smaller experience and the opportunity to interact with others from your geographical area. Many of the associations also offer workshops focusing on either new professionals or mid-level staff. These programs focus on the common issues professional cohorts face in their career and work.

Also, wide ranges of opportunities exist for student affairs staff who choose to focus on a specific content area for their professional development. NASPA, for example, offers a series of focused workshops on topics such as assessment, fund raising, adjudicating sexual assault, cultural assessment, and dealing with psychological disabilities, to name but a few. The University of Vermont, Stetson University, and the National Association of College and University Attorneys (NACUA) all offer annual programs on legal issues facing higher education. ACPA and James Madison University sponsor a Student Learning Institute. The Manicur Women's Symposium, sponsored by NASPA, is a three-day program for mid-level women administrators who aspire to be senior student affairs officers. All of these workshops are two- to three-day programs and offer participants the chance to focus in-depth on a single issue or topic.

Finally, there are more protracted and in-depth experiences. NASPA's Richard Steven's Institute for senior student affairs officers is a week-long institute focusing on key issues affecting the management of student affairs. The Harvard Institute for Educational Management program, an intensive two-week, residential, classroom-based experience, and the Bryn Mawr Summer Institute for Women Administrators in Higher Education are further examples of more intensive professional development experiences for senior administrators.

Skills for the New Millennium

The new century presents us with many challenges that will affect the very nature of student affairs practices. Two trends straddling the change of the century are worth considering; the impact of the technological revolution and, within higher education, the increased focus on student learning and creating academic/student affairs collaboration opportunities. Each suggests important professional development opportunities.

Levine and Cureton (1998) chronicle the technology revolution and a new generation of college students who came of age in a world filled with the promise and problems associated with meteoric advances in technology. Such students have grown up during a technological revolution where methods of communications have been transformed "thanks to computers, fax machines, e-mail, VCRs, cellular telephones, fiber optics, CDs, cable, phone mail, the World Wide Web, and more" (Levine and Cureton, 1998, p.13). The technological heritage of today's college student has placed enormous pressures on colleges and universities to keep pace. These pressures extend to student affairs professionals to develop new technology skills and to evaluate the way student services are delivered to this new generation of students. Today's students expect access to services and information twenty-four-hours-a-day, seven-days-a-week and reject the traditional nine-to-five models of university administrative offices (Moneta, 1997).

Technology skill development is a new arena of professional development, one that needs as much attention as student development-related issues. The competency gap between technology-proficient student affairs staff and their computer-phobic colleagues grows wider with every generation of new computers, software programs, and computer-driven services (Moneta, 1997).

This is one area where graduate preparation programs lag far behind the practice of the profession. Engstrom (1997) makes a strong case for the inclusion of technology in the graduate curriculum and for graduate students to experience, "creative, innovative, and cutting edge applications of technology that respond to the learning needs and preferences of an increasingly diverse group of students" (p. 59). The same case, of course, can be made for the developing information technology proficiency for full-time student affairs professionals. By the early part of the twenty-first century, information technology skills will be a core competency for every student affairs professional. The student affairs practitioner who has not developed this competency will not be able to meet the dynamic, evolving needs of students (Benedict, 1996).

Engstrom (1997) suggests a set of key technology skills for graduate students that would also apply to any group of student affairs professionals:

1. Technology skills to promote student learning in residence life, counseling, academic advising, career development, student activities, unions, and other student affairs functional areas
2. Knowledge about campus information systems and how to access information to make data-based decisions
3. The ability to work and communicate with campus information technology staff to improve student services and promote access, civility, and community

A few additional skills and competencies that can be a part of an individual professional development plan include the ability to use the Web as a tool to access research, data, and examples of student service applications from other institutions; the ability to use and access listserve discussion groups on topics of professional interest; how to maximize student learning opportunities using Web-based applications; and the ability to use HTML and/or Java (Web programming language tools) to develop new methods of service delivery and information dissemination to students.

Finding opportunities for professional development in information technology may be more challenging than the more traditional avenues discussed previously. Taking information technology classes at community colleges and local adult education centers or through distance learning providers are tangible ways to accelerate the acquisition of technology skills. Perhaps the most direct way to increase competence in information technology is simply to read and practice. Books for the novice and expert are commonplace in every bookstore, allowing for anyone with a desktop computer and access to relevant software to experiment with new technologies.

Developing the technical skills required to develop Web-based applications will be beyond the aptitude or interest of many student affairs practitioners. If this is the case, at a minimum, student affairs professionals need to understand the big picture of how and in what ways technology is changing our world and the extent to which advancing technology will have legal, ethical, and societal implications for higher education. Publications such as *Change Magazine, Internet World, Wired, Fast Company, The Chronicle of Higher Education's* "Information Technology" column, and *Syllabus* are effective sources for keeping updated on technology issues.

The second and equally important set of skills for the new millennium is composed of the knowledge, skills, and abilities necessary to work within new organizational paradigms. One such paradigm is the "learning organization" (Senge, 1990), which creates opportunities for an active discourse between faculty and student affairs staff in support of student learning. Becoming a full participant in this new organizational paradigm requires faculty and staff who can work effectively in a cross-disciplinary, cross-functional, collaborative environment.

Developing collaborative relationships between faculty and student affairs staff challenges old biases and traditional delivery systems. It also focuses attention on the process of student learning. The current dialogue of the profession has suggested that academic/student affairs collaborations and student learning initiatives will be the very heart of the future of the student affairs profession (ACPA, 1994; AAHE/ACPA/NASPA, 1998). This will require new skills and relationships for student affairs staff.

Professional development will play a key role in the development of new skills that will enable the student affairs profession to meet this challenge. In relatively uncharted territory, limitless opportunities exist for student affairs practitioners to develop new connections with faculty and to experiment with collaborative programming. Consider the following strategies:

1. Seek out relationships with potential faculty allies. Faculty interested in student learning initiatives can often be found in the social sciences or humanities, or they can be identified through conversations with students. These new relationships will help break down the "cultural" barriers and will open up possibilities for collaboration.
2. Identify faculty interested in incorporating service learning opportunities into the classroom. Student affairs staff are uniquely positioned to help faculty create integrative learning experiences.
3. Explore opportunities to teach. The classroom teaching experience develops important professional skills and contributes to a better understanding of the faculty culture. Many campus policies do not provide the opportunity for student affairs staff to teach. In those cases, consider the success of "don't cancel that class" programs where student affairs staff present topics related to health or diversity when a faculty member is not available to teach.

The development of partnerships between academic and student affairs will only increase in importance. (See the Engstrom and Tinto chapter for other ideas on collaborations with academic affairs.)

Summary

This chapter began with the premise that a commitment to continuous professional development is vital to the definition of student affairs as a profession. Traditionally, professional development occurs within staff development programs that are a part of most student affairs divisions. Although staff development programs play an important role in professional development, they are usually passive in nature, short in duration, and too often lack a coherence that links individual staff development activities to a set of learning objectives. It is not the recommendation of this author that staff development be abandoned, but that lifelong professional development must go beyond staff development programs and be a part of the individual responsibility of every member of the profession. The illustrations of professional development discussed in this chapter assume an active role for student affairs staff in developing the knowledge, skills, and abilities necessary to advance in the profession.

As student affairs staff consider the professional responsibility of professional development, consider the following suggestions:

1. Lifelong professional development requires time, a commitment to personal growth, and the willingness to take risks and try new experiences.
2. Take the long view. Assess current strengths, assets, and deficiencies when developing a professional development curriculum. Consider both long- and short-term goals for addressing areas for further professional growth.
3. Be creative. The examples listed in this chapter are meant to spur creative thinking and are not a prescription.
4. Consider pursuing an advanced degree. Doctoral-level graduate study is a strong alternative to many of the strategies discussed in this chapter. Refer to Komives' chapter in this volume on postgraduate coursework as a form of advanced professional development.
5. Self-directed professional development should be an expectation of supervisors and be incorporated into departmental reward systems.
6. Remember that professional development has two purposes: to advance us as professionals and, most importantly, to develop new knowledge, skills, and abilities that enhance the ways in which we work with students.

References

American Association for Higher Education (AAHE), American College Personnel Association (ACPA), and National Association of Student Personnel Administrators (NASPA). *Powerful Partnerships: A Shared Responsibility for Learning.* Washington, D.C.: American Association for Higher Education, American College Personnel Association, and National Association of Student Personnel Administrators, 1998.

American College Personnel Association (ACPA). "Statement of ethical principles and standards." *Journal of College Student Development,* 1993, 34, 89–92.

American College Personnel Association (ACPA). *The Student Learning Imperative: Implications for Student Affairs.* Washington, D.C.: American College Personnel Association, 1994.

American Council on Education (ACE). *ACE Fellow Program.* http://acenet.edu/CLD/Fellows, 1998.

Baskett, H. K. M., and Marsick, V. J. "Confronting New Understandings About Professional Learning and Change". In H. K. M. Baskett and V. J. Marsick (eds.), *Professional's Ways of Knowing: New Findings on How to Improve Professional Education.* San Francisco: Jossey-Bass, 1992.

Benedict, L. G. "Technology and Information Systems." In S. R. Komives and D. B. Woodard (eds.), *Student Services: A Handbook for the Profession.* San Francisco: Jossey-Bass, 1996.

Council for the Advancement of Standards (CAS). *CAS Standards and Guidelines for Student Services/Development Programs.* Iowa City, IA: American College Testing Service, 1998.

Council for International Exchange of Scholars. *The Fulbright Program.* http://www.iie.org/cies, 1998.

Creamer, D. G., et al. "Quality Assurance in College Student Affairs." In R. B. Winston and D. G. Creamer (eds.), *Improving Staffing Practices in Student Affairs.* San Francisco: Jossey-Bass, 1997.

Dalton, J. C. "Managing Human Resources." In S. R. Komives and D. B. Woodard (eds.), *Student Services: A Handbook for the Profession.* San Francisco: Jossey-Bass, 1996.

DeCoster, D. A., and Brown, S. S. "Staff Development: Personal and Professional Education." In T. K. Miller and R. B. Winston (eds.), *Administrative Leadership in Student Affairs; Actualizing Student Development in Higher Education.* Muncie, IN: Accelerated Development Inc. Publishers. 1991.

Delve, C. I., Mintz, S. D., and Stewart, G. M. (eds.). *Community Service as Values Education.* New Directions for Student Services, No. 50. San Francisco: Jossey-Bass, 1990.

Engstrom, C. M. "Integrating Information Technology into Student Affairs Graduate Programs." In C. M. Engstrom and K. W. Kruger (eds.), *Using Technology to Promote Student Learning: Opportunities for Today and Tomorrow.* San Francisco: Jossey-Bass, 1997.

Fey, C. H. and Carpenter, D. S. "Mid-Level Student Affairs Administrators: Management Skills and Professional Development Needs." *NASPA Journal,* 1996, 33 (3), p. 218–231.

Fisher, I. S. "Integrating Service Learning Experiences into Postcollege Choices." In J. Jacoby (ed.), *Service Learning in Higher Education.* San Francisco: Jossey-Bass, 1996.

Garland, P. H., and Grace, T. W. *New Perspectives for Student Affairs Professional: Evolving Realities, Responsibilities and Roles.* ERIC Digest Document ED370507, June 1994.

Jacoby, J. (ed.) *Service Learning in Higher Education.* San Francisco: Jossey-Bass, 1996.

Klevans, D. R., Smutz, W. D., Shuman, S. B., and Bershad, C. "Self-Assessment: Helping Professionals Discover What They Do Not Know." In H. K. Baskett and V. S. Marsick (eds.), *Professional Ways of Knowing: New Findings to Improve Professional Education.* New Directions for Adult and Continuing Education., No. 55. San Francisco: Jossey-Bass, 1992.

Komives, S. R.. "Linking Student Affairs Preparation with Practice." In N. J. Evans and C. E. Phelps Tobin (eds.) *State of the Art of Preparation and Practice in Student Affairs: Another Look.* Washington D.C.: American College Personnel Association, 1998.

Levine, A., and Cureton, J. *When Hope and Fear Collide.* San Francisco: Jossey-Bass, 1998.

Moneta, L. "The Integration of Technology with the Management of Student Services." In C. M. Engstrom and K. W. Kruger (eds.), *Using Technology to Promote Student Learning: Opportunities for Today and Tomorrow.* San Francisco: Jossey-Bass, 1997.

National Association of Student Personnel Administrators (NASPA). *NASPA Standards of Professional Practice.* Member handbook. Washington D.C.: National Association of Student Personnel Administrators, 1998.

Olney, R. J., and Bednar, A. S. "Identifying Essential Oral Presentation Skills for Today's Business Curriculum." *Journal of Education for Business,* Volume 50 (4), 1989, p. 22–23.

Orzek, A. M. "Use of Rape Crisis Center Services by a University Community." *Journal of College Student Personnel,* Volume 24, September 1983, p. 465–466.

Rotary International. *Group Study Exchange.* http://www.rotary.org, 1998.

Sandeen, A. *Student Affairs: Issues, Problems, and Trends.* ERIC Digest Document ED290964, 1988.

Senge, P. M. *The Fifth Discipline: The Art and Practice of the Learning Organization.* New York: Doubleday, 1990.

Shaffer, R. H. "Whither Student Personnel Work from 1968 to 2018? A 1993 Retrospective." *NASPA Journal*, 1993, 30, 162–168.

University of Pittsburgh. *The Continuing Education Program.* http://www.pitt.edu/~voyage/adult.html, 1999.

Winston, R. B. and Creamer, D. G. *Improving Staffing Practices in Student Affairs.* San Francisco: Jossey-Bass, 1997.

Young, R. B. (ed.), *The Invisible Leaders: Student Affairs Mid-Managers.* Washington, D.C.: NASPA, 1990.

Zabezensky, F., Becker, T., Bydalek, D., Cardenas, R., Carter, C., and Monreal, R. "Management Internship Program: A Model." *Community College Review.* Volume 13, No. 3, 1986, p. 54–59.

PART FIVE

CHALLENGES FOR THE FUTURE

The future for student affairs and higher education is anything but clear, but there are some things that we know that can help prepare us for change in positive and helpful ways. In Chapter Twenty-Nine, Robert Fenske, James Rund and Jann Contento organize information regarding what we know about the student of tomorrow. Such data is helpful as we examine who we will serve in the years ahead. We know, for example, that our students will be more diverse in the decades to come. In Chapter Thirty, Christine Kajikawa Wilkinson and James Rund explore how student affairs can support diversity through people, programs and organizational structures. Attention is paid, in this chapter, to both student and staff issues involving diversity.

It appears likely that student affairs units will become increasingly involved in fund raising and development activities on the campuses of both public and independent institutions. Michael Jackson provides practical guidance regarding fund raising for student affairs in Chapter Thirty-One.

Success can be measured in many ways. Student affairs programs have two ways to examine structures and programs within their units. In Chapter Thirty-Two, Elizabeth Whitt and Gregory Blimling discuss the application of professional standards and principles of good practice in student affairs units.

Finally, in chapter Thirty-Three, Margaret Barr and Mary Desler summarize the issues in this volume and provide a challenge for leadership by student affairs in the future. That challenge is based on our historical mandate and informed by what we know about students and our institutions.

CHAPTER TWENTY-NINE

WHO ARE THE NEW STUDENTS?

Robert H. Fenske, James A. Rund, and Jann M. Contento

Every campus student affairs administrator is aware of recent changes in the student body and the need to anticipate new changes. These constant changes leaven the administrator's responsibilities with continual renewal as well as frustration. Some of the changes are part of long-term trends begun decades ago, like the "graying of the campus," more women, more part-timers, and racial/ethnic diversity. Some changes have begun more recently, like student attitudes as consumers paying for an increasingly expensive product, student expectations for cutting-edge technology, and increased exposure to crime and violence on campus.

Student body changes every year on each campus are part of larger societal and demographic trends. It is helpful for administrators to be familiar with these larger trends as a means of interpreting changes on their own campus. This chapter provides an overview of current data that can help delineate a possible portrait of tomorrow's students. The first part of the chapter presents a student profile highlighting current trends in demographics, academic skills and preparation, student activities and interests, attitudes and experiences, education and career plans, and student financing strategies.

The second section presents an overview of possible strategies student affairs administrators should consider to help prepare their campuses for tomorrow's students. Increasing student involvement and enhancing the learning process remain issues when considering any changes in the learning environment of the new century. Tomorrow's students will continue to offer higher education a multitude of challenges and opportunities. The role of student affairs administrators in meeting these challenges requires a broad perspective in preparing programs, services, and people. The results of such efforts can influence the success of higher education by better preparing campuses to meet the unique and changing needs of students.

Background

During the first years of the next century, higher education can anticipate a significant increase in the traditional age (18–24) of students. A century ago, such students comprised the vast majority of the student body. Nearly all of them were male, except in teachers colleges (mostly called normal schools) and nursing schools, and most were from relatively wealthy families.

Until mid-century only a minority of 18-year-olds were high school graduates, but that changed dramatically after WWII. The Servicemen's Readjustment Act of 1944 (G.I. Bill) also changed the face of higher education, enabling hundreds of thousands of mostly male veterans to become first-generation college students. The veterans also fathered the largest increase of babies in the country's history between 1946 and 1964. This "baby boom" triggered a rapid expansion in elementary and secondary enrollments, and the subsequent "tidal wave" of college students beginning in the 1960s. In 1950, enrollments in the public sector of higher education exceeded those in the private sector for the first time, and twenty years later the ratio of enrollments was 3:1 between the sectors, a disparity that continued through the rest of the century. Community colleges proliferated in the 1960s and by the 1990s enrolled more first-time full-time freshmen than any other higher education sector.

The changes in demographic characteristics were as dramatic as the growing numbers. By 1980, college students were more likely to be older and attend part-time. Perhaps the most radical change was the gender shift. Fenske and Scott predicted that for the first time in the nation's history, the number of women would exceed that of men, and that the shift would occur during the 1970s (Fenske and Scott, 1973). In fall, 1976, more women than men enrolled as freshmen and, by the mid–1990s, women exceeded men in every enrollment level except in doctoral studies. Increases in the average age of students and in part-time enrollment were largely due to changes in employment patterns, especially as more older-than-traditional-age women entered the job market and sought to enhance employability through academic credentials.

Current Student Profile

Although national public and private elementary and secondary enrollment is projected to increase by only seven percent over the twelve-year period from 1995 to 2007, the number of high school graduates is expected to increase by 21 percent over the same period. The estimated effect on higher education enrollment suggests an increase of 16 percent from 13.9 million to 16.1 million (U.S. Department of Education, 1997a). The College Board reported that college-bound students in 1998 were more racially and ethnically diverse, more eligible for college credits before enrollment, and had higher grades than their predecessors. Despite these positive changes, disparities in academic preparation, test scores, and other factors continue to grow across subgroups (U.S. Department of Education, 1998a).

Demographic Background Influences Enrollment of Traditional Age Students

The Cooperative Institutional Research Program (CIRP) survey of freshmen students has annually reported changes in the family backgrounds of students for more than 30 years. The CIRP survey reports that the proportion of fathers with college degrees has gone up by two-thirds over the past 30 years, while the proportion of college-educated mothers has more than doubled (Astin, Parrott, Korn, and Sax, 1997, p. 1). The increases in parental education levels also reflect changes in occupation. One major change over the past twenty years shows a large decline in the proportion of students with mothers who are homemakers. In 1996, fewer than one in eight students came from a family where the mother was a homemaker, compared to one in three in 1976. The median combined parental income was five times higher in 1996 than in 1966 ($52,600 versus $9,600), without taking into account the effects of inflation (Astin, Parrott, Korn, and Sax, 1997, p. 3). A 30 year comparison describes today's freshmen as having more highly educated parents, less likely to have mothers who are homemakers, much more likely to come from families where both parents are working, and more likely to have parents who are divorced or separated (p. 4).

The National Center for Educational Statistics (NCES) reports that "of the three million students entering postsecondary education for the first time during the 1995–96 academic year, nearly eighty-six percent enrolled in either public two-year, public four-year, or private not-for-profit four-year institutions" (U.S. Department of Education, 1998a, p. 3). The breakdown for these three sectors is 46 percent at public two-year, 25 percent at public four-year, and 15 percent at private not-for-profit institutions. The remaining students are in shorter programs or proprietary vocational technical schools. NCES reports that students whose parents were more highly educated are more likely to be enrolled in four-year institutions, among them public doctorate-granting institutions; private, not-for-profit doctorate-granting institutions; and private, not-for-profit nondoctorategranting institutions. Students with less educated parents are more likely to be enrolled in public two-year institutions and private, for-profit institutions (p. 26).

There is considerable diversity among the three higher education sectors in student demographic characteristics, educational plans, and prior academic achievement. In general, students entering public two-year institutions are likely to be older, have lower socioeconomic backgrounds, have lower educational aspirations, and demonstrate lower prior academic achievement than their counterparts at four-year institutions (U.S. Department of Education, 1998a, p.20). The characteristics of those entering public four-year and private, not-for-profit four-year institutions are fairly similar. However, students entering public four-year institutions are more likely to have somewhat lower socioeconomic backgrounds and to demonstrate somewhat lower prior academic achievements than those entering private, not-for-profit four-year institutions.

Gender/Ethnicity Disparities in Admission Test Scores Continue

The make-up of students taking college admission examinations is continually changing. The general profiles of students taking the SAT exam reflect changing trends in demographics, gender, and ethnicity participation. Women who take the SAT continue to achieve higher grades in high school than men. The average overall GPA for women is 3.30, while men average 3.14 (Rigol, 1996). However, grade differences do not uniformly represent all subject areas. Although women are taking more math and science courses than formerly, they still take fewer advanced mathematics courses and more arts/music courses than men. Women also outnumber men in the SAT population and in college participation levels, yet (average) scores on both verbal and math scores show men scoring higher than women. Results from 1997 data reveal slightly higher average verbal scores for men (507) than for women (503). However, quantitative scores show larger differences with men averaging 530 and women 494 (College Board, 1998b). The average composite ACT scores for 1998 show a score of 21.2 for men and 20.9 for women (The Chronicle of Higher Education Almanac, 1998–99, p. 16).

The proportion of students in 1997 whose first language is not English represented approximately eight percent of the SAT population. Latino groups reflected the greatest proportion of this population, with 27 percent Mexican-Americans and 40 percent Hispanic/Latinos. The verbal SAT test scores for Mexican-Americans and Hispanic/Latinos taking the SAT were 86 and 67 points below the national average, respectively. Overall, minority students represented one-third of the SAT population and 2.8 percent of Advanced Placement (AP) graduates in 1998. Although college-bound African American and Latino students are making progress, they remain on average less academically prepared for college than other racial and ethnic groups (College Board, 1998a).

Average SAT scores also vary for students from suburban, urban, and rural areas. Average scores for the suburban students are consistently higher than those in either urban or rural areas. Suburban students verbal test scores are 17 points above the national average, while respective urban and rural area students are 13 and 9 points below average. SAT math scores show similar differences. These discrepancies are disturbing considering that nearly half of African American and Latino students who take the SAT live in urban areas. In addition, SAT scores of students with less educated parents continue to fall farther below the national average, while the scores for students from more educated parents rise farther above the average.

National data reveals that 43 percent of first-time students in the 1995–96 school year entering public two-year institutions had admission test scores in the lowest quartile of all beginning postsecondary students. In contrast, only 17 percent of students entering four-year public institutions had scores in the lowest quartile and only 12 percent of those entering private not-for-profits had similarly low scores. Conversely, the proportion of entrants obtaining admission test scores in the top quartile was highest at private, not-for-profit, four-year institutions (43 percent), followed by public four-year institutions (29 percent), and public two-year institutions at ten percent (U.S. Department of Education, 1996a, p. 12).

High School Graduates Are Better Prepared for College

Four primary trends are influencing better preparation for college: (a) higher grades and better proficiency test scores; (b) increased involvement in college-level courses by students while still enrolled in high school; (c) more core academic courses as well as a "capstone" examination required for high school graduation in many states; and (d) higher standards for admission to postsecondary education.

The CIRP survey shows academic trends that reflect a steady increase in high school grade inflation. The most dramatic increases occurred during the periods 1970–1978 and 1986–1996. In 1996, "A" grades outnumbered "C" grades by better than two to one, suggesting that grade inflation may continue into the years ahead. The "grade gap," which has always favored women, has narrowed somewhat since the 1960s (Astin, Parrott, Korn, and Sax, 1997). One possible effect of higher overall grades is the optimistic attitude reported by freshmen concerning their academic prospects in college. Grade inflation may increase the tendency for freshmen to overrate their academic abilities.

The National Assessment of Educational Progress (NAEP) reports that for all nine-, thirteen-, and seventeen-year-olds, average mathematics proficiency scores were higher in 1996 than in 1978, and average science proficiency was higher in 1996 than in 1982. Average writing scores of seventeen-year-olds were slightly lower in 1996 than in 1984. NAEP also indicated that some of the larger gaps in achievement between whites and minorities have narrowed somewhat over the past two decades (U.S. Department of Education, 1997b).

Overall participation in college preparatory courses during high school has been on the increase. The College Board reported that over 635,000 students in over half the nation's high schools took Advanced Placement (AP) Examinations in 1998, more than double the number of ten years ago. By the year 2000, 58 percent of the nation's high schools will offer AP classes. Women comprised 55 percent and minority students 29 percent of AP participants in 1998, up from 50 and 19 percent respectively since 1988. The most popular AP subject areas include English, history, and calculus followed by biology, Spanish, and chemistry (College Board, 1998a).

Average SAT scores of AP graduates were also above national averages for the SAT population in both large cities and rural areas. The number of students taking college preparatory courses may reflect a desire to gain a competitive advantage in the college admission process. In addition to AP, the College Board also administers the College Level Examination Program (CLEP). The American Testing Program offers the Proficiency Examination Program, which is comparable to the CLEP. A recent report suggests that the scope of these activities is larger than many may realize. "During the last year alone, over one million exams were administered to learners hoping to earn college credit. While pass rates were unavailable for the specific exam batteries, if we assume an average pass rate of seventy percent with a conservative three credit hours per exam, the result would be over 4,355,974 credit hours earned" (Leader, 1999, p. 1).

Powerful initiatives toward K–12 school reform have emerged in recent years at both the federal and state levels. The reforms are generally aimed at increasing the academic competence of high school graduates, especially in readiness for college. A few states, notably Oregon and Washington, have recently moved to integrate increased competency demands on high school graduation with "competency-based admission standards" for their public colleges. One of the major goals of the school reform initiatives is to move toward competency-based evidence of a student's readiness for college and away from the traditional reliance on tacit assumptions of college readiness based on accumulation of high school credits.

Many states have begun to enhance college readiness by requiring more core high school academic courses. For example, Arizona increased the number of such courses from 12 to 16, effective in the fall of 1997. This change was based on a thorough study of the potential impact on college readiness. "Evidence from various studies, including (a recent) one by American College Testing (ACT), indicates a very strong relationship between achievement in academic courses in high school and success in high education. By increasing the number of courses required for admission to universities, it is expected that grades and persistence to graduation from the universities for Arizona's students will improve." (Arizona Board of Regents, 1994). Rodriguez (1995) has found in a national survey of state reforms to increase college readiness that between 1992 and 1995 at least 12 states have increased academic core course requirements specifically to increase college readiness. The state initiatives reflect a steady trend begun in the 1980s toward increasing competence in the core academic areas. "Between the 1987–88 and 1993–94 school years, the percentage of public school districts with graduation requirements that met or exceeded the National Commission on Excellence in Education recommendations in the four core subject areas (four units in English, and three each in science, social studies, and mathematics) increased from 12 to 20 percent. Additionally, 1994 high school graduates took more mathematics courses at the algebra I level or higher and more science classes at the biology level or higher than did 1982 graduates" (U.S. Department of Education, 1998d, Indicator 24).

Reforms in Oregon and Washington are being watched closely because they represent a significant move away from reliance on credits and grades for college admissions to a total competency-based system. In Oregon, the system is called PASS (Proficiency-based Admission Standards System). The goal of PASS is "to create a means for admitting students based on demonstrated proficiency, thereby allowing students to move continuously through the education system based on their performance" (Conley, 1998, p. 1).

The explicit goal of PASS is to have one set of competency-based standards that seamlessly extends from kindergarten through college admission. In the new system, to be implemented fully by 2005, three events mark successful attainment of the goals. The first and second are certificates of subject matter mastery at two successive levels, and the third is college admission (Conley, 1998, pp. 2–4). It is made abundantly clear in the system that course credits and grades will be considered as optional, supplemental information for college admissions.

Academic Disengagement, Stress, and Remediation

Although more students are taking college preparation courses, they are at the same time exhibiting greater signs of academic disengagement. The number of hours per week students engage in studying or doing homework has decreased from 42.3 in 1989 to 35.7 in 1997. The Fall 1998 CIRP survey of freshmen suggests a linkage between disengagement and other factors: "Given students' apparent disengagement from academics, it is perhaps not surprising that more students are going to college 'to be able to get a better job' and 'to be able to make more money' (74.6 percent) than 'to gain a general education and appreciation of ideas' (62.0 percent). Interestingly, more students than ever are going to college 'because my parents wanted me to go' (39.5 percent, compared with 36.2 percent last year, and a low of 22.9 percent in 1971)" (Higher Education Research Institute, 1999, p. 2). In addition, fewer high school students reported having academic interactions with teachers outside of the classroom (Astin, Parrott, Korn, and Sax, 1997).

Recent trends show today's freshmen are experiencing more stress than previous classes. "The percent of freshmen who report 'being overwhelmed by everything I have to do' has increased steadily from 16.4 to 29.4 percent since 1987. Students also reported that they frequently 'feel depressed' and the percent of students rating themselves above average in 'emotional health' has been on the decline" (Astin, Parrott, Korn, and Sax, 1997, p. 27). Since 1989, the number of entering freshmen who "seek personal counseling" after entering college has also been on the rise. Such trends may cause new and increased demands on areas of student services designed to address the physical and emotional needs of students.

In a summary of remedial education in higher education, institutions reported that 29 percent of first-time freshmen had enrolled in at least one remedial reading, writing, or mathematics course in fall 1995 (U.S. Department of Education, 1996b). Sixty-four percent of those students enrolled in remedial courses took mathematics. Additional courses taken included 39 percent reading, 38 percent writing, 27 percent study skills, and 25 percent English language (U.S. Department of Education, 1998a, p. 35). Students in two-year institutions were more likely than students in four-year institutions to report that they were taking or had taken remedial courses (26 percent versus 16 percent, respectively). Students at public institutions were also more likely than those at private, not-for-profit institutions to indicate they had taken remedial courses (23 percent versus 13 percent, respectively) (p. 36).

Remediation continues to be a concern on several counts. First, the need for it suggests a failure on the part of K–12 education. Second, remediation threatens the cost-effectiveness of the educational system; it is seen as "paying twice for the same education." Third, college faculty often resent the lack of adequate academic preparation. However, remediation continues to be widely recognized as giving students a second chance. School reform efforts often point to remediation as a symptom of a system that needs fixing. So long as the "open door" concept is embraced by higher education, remediation will be a part of the process (Russell, 1998).

Early Intervention Programs Increase College Readiness for At-Risk Students

The National Postsecondary Student Aid Survey (NPSAS) characterized undergraduates according to seven risk factors. These risk factors include delayed enrollment, attending part-time, being financially independent of parents, working full-time while enrolled, having dependents other than a spouse, being a single parent, and receiving a GED rather than having earned a high school diploma. The survey also reports that three-fourths of undergraduates had at least one of these factors. Students having any factors generally had more than one, and the highest proportion of at-risk students attended two-year or less-than-two-year institutions (U.S. Department of Education, 1998a, p. 4).

There is an underlying assumption that intervention early in the educational pipeline will help to prevent dropouts and increase the number of students who pursue higher education. Student intervention programs operate with a variety of objectives and organizational approaches. In general, they have the intent of widening access, increasing persistence, and achieving degree completion. A recent study by Fenske, Geranios, Keller, and Moore (1997) outlines the most popular and successful forms of "early intervention" programs. These authors refer to "academic outreach" programs as those that originate in schools, colleges, and universities as a subset of the broader concept of early intervention. The goals of academic outreach programs are to enhance educational opportunity for underserved students as well as increasing the number of at-risk students enrolled in specific academic disciplines. These programs are mutually beneficial to both underserved students and institutions of high education.

Another popular concept, known as "school-college collaboration," is a cooperative effort of K–12 schools and higher education institutions. The concept of the "middle college" melds the last two years of high school with the two years offered in public community colleges. Such alliances enhance the recruitment of minority students and increase the readiness of entering freshmen. Early intervention programs provide colleges and universities with a powerful tool to recruit disadvantaged students who need a broad base of support to enroll in and graduate from college. "Administrators on college and university campuses play a critical role in the creation of effective school-college partnerships. By providing opportunities for K–12 students to get an early glimpse of university life, programs, and resources, the transition to higher education is rendered less daunting" (Fenske, Geranios, Keller, and Moore, 1997, p. 83).

One study concludes "moderate to high-risk students who participated in high school outreach programs had almost double the odds of enrolling in a four-year college than their peers who did not participate. Although relatively few at-risk students reported such participation (about five percent), the effect on college enrollment was significant" (Horn and Chen, 1998, p. 27). This study also found that intervention, whether on the part of parents or the school, played a positive role in helping moderate high-risk students make the transition from high school to college.

Title IV of the Higher Education Act Amendments of 1998 created Gaining Early Awareness and Readiness for Undergraduate Programs (GEAR UP), designed to prepare underprivileged students for college beginning no later than the sixth or seventh grade. GEAR UP provides both partnership grants and state grants. It is modeled after the High Hopes program advocated by the Clinton administration in the fall of 1997 and extends existing state early college awareness programs. Beginning in 1999, the GEAR UP partnership program will award multi-year grants to locally designed partnerships between colleges and high-poverty middle schools, plus at least two other partners. The GEAR UP state grants will be awarded to states to provide early preparation, awareness activities, improved academic support, information on paying for college, and scholarships. The overall purpose of GEAR UP is to provide more low-income students with the skills, encouragement, and preparation needed to pursue postsecondary education. This program is one of the newest federal initiatives supporting the assumption that students who participate in high-quality college awareness programs and strengthen their academic preparation attend college in higher percentages than those who do not (GEAR UP, 1998).

Social Attitudes Change While Volunteer Community Service Increases

The CIRP survey of freshmen attitudes on personal and social issues reports that students support "liberal" positions on students' rights, equality for women, and homosexuality while their views on "law and order" have become more conservative. The CIRP survey found that "student opposition to capital punishment declined by more than one-half between 1970 and 1996 (56.3 to 22.2 percent)." The number of students who believe that "there is too much concern in the courts for the rights of criminals" increased by more than one-third over the same period (from 51.6 to 71.6 percent). Attitudes toward the legalization of marijuana have fluctuated in an erratic pattern over the past thirty years. Beer drinking among college freshmen rose steadily between 1966 and 1981 (from 53.5 to 75.2 percent), but has decreased steadily to 52.6 percent in 1996 (Astin, Parrott, Korn, and Sax, 1997, p. 21).

Community service participation for many high school students has increased over the past few years. The percent of students participating in community service during 1996 reached nearly 50 percent for students in grades six through twelve (U.S. Department of Education, 1998d). Since 1987, engagement in volunteer work at the pre-college level has increased from 42.0 to 59.0 percent. These figures represent students who reported that they were involved in some volunteer work during the year before entering college. This rise in pre-college volunteering has also been accompanied by a parallel increase in students' intentions to volunteer during college (Astin Parrott, Korn, and Sax, 1997, p. 28). The increase in volunteer community service activities may reflect the encouragement by high schools for participation in community service hours or, for some, it may be a graduation requirement. Data indicates that among freshmen in the fall of 1998 about three-fourths (74.2 percent) reported involvement in volunteer work as high school seniors (Higher Education Research Institute, 1999, p. 3). Another motivation for participation may be the students desire to gain an "edge" in the competitive college admission process.

Increase in Incidents of Crime in Schools

Recent incidents of crime and violence on campus may reflect the overall rise in crime exhibited in society. The pre-college enrollment characteristics and experiences of students may also have an effect on the number of crime incidents on campus. A national survey of violence in public schools found that serious violent crimes tended to be more prevalent in about ten percent of the schools. The report also notes that most college-bound high school graduates have been immersed in an educational environment rife with drug and alcohol usage, classroom disruptions, and threats of violence or actual violence toward students and teachers (U.S. Department of Education, 1998b). The effects of such an environment on the attitudes and acceptance of violent behavior by college-bound students, although not measured directly, may harbor experiences that are bound to be detrimental.

A National Education Longitudinal Study (NELS: 88) reported on the school safety concerns of students from the eighth grade to the twelfth grade. An analysis of specific issues reveals that high school senior females placed much more importance on school safety than males. In response to the question "How important is a low-crime environment in school?," only 18.3 percent of the females indicated it was not important, compared to 31.1 percent of the males. Conversely, 38.5 percent of the females indicated a low-crime environment was "very important" compared to 25.7 percent of the males. It is assumed that contacts with violence in previous school settings are likely to affect student attitudes, expectations, and experiences with violence on the college campus. However, data are not available to draw clear cause-and-effect relationships between violent behavior in K–12 settings and similar behavior in collegiate settings (Fenske and Hood, 1998, p. 31).

The Federal Campus Security Act of 1990 is one of many federal initiatives aimed at stemming the rise of crime and violence in our colleges. Congress continues to debate legislation that would increase campus security by identifying and widely publicizing perpetrators of campus crime and violence. However, at the same time, previous legislation such as the Family Educational Rights and Privacy Act (FERPA) requires maintaining rights to privacy of students accused or convicted of crimes. Solving this apparent contradiction can perhaps lead to ways campus administrators can deal effectively with violence on campus (Fenske and Hood, 1998).

Aspirations and Career Choices

The most popular fields of study chosen in college include degrees in business management, followed by degrees in the humanities and social and behavioral sciences. These degree choices have constituted more than half of all degrees conferred since 1971 (U.S. Department of Education, 1998d).

The proportion of students interested in business as a major and career more than doubled between 1966 and 1986 (from 11.6 to 24.1 percent). However, recent CIRP survey results reveal that interest in business is in decline with preference for business careers dropping to a 20-year low of 14 percent for 1996 freshmen. The interest level for a career in medicine and/or dentistry remains low but has increased from 4.0 percent in 1987 to 6.4 percent in 1996. Engineering careers are somewhat more popular but have shown a decline from 9.0 in 1989 to 7.0 in 1997. Law careers in 1997 reached an all-time low of 3.3 percent, down from 5.4 percent in 1988. The attraction of majors and careers in education has shown some improvement, but such attraction remains lower than it was in the late 1960s (Astin, Parrott, Korn, and Sax, 1997, pp. 21–22). Interest in traditional liberal arts major fields has declined by nearly half over the past 30 years from 43.6 to 22.7 percent (p. 23). However, 30-year freshmen trends indicate that the popularity of "being very well-off financially" has been an important goal of about three-fourths of the freshmen over the entire period (p. 30).

Over the past 30 years, the educational aspirations of freshmen students show a greater number aiming toward postgraduate degrees. The type of institution in which students first enroll appears to influence educational aspiration among college freshmen. A recent national survey reveals that students enrolled at four-year institutions (public or private, not-for-profit) are more likely to aspire to obtain a postbaccalaureate (graduate or first-professional) degree than those enrolled at public two-year institutions (U.S. Department of Education, 1998a). Thirty-year trends show an increasing similarity between freshmen men and women in their educational aspirations, career plans, behavior, and values (Astin Parrott, Korn, and Sax, 1997, p. 12). Gender trends show that women are slightly more interested in pursuing graduate degrees than are men, 67.7 percent versus 65.3 percent respectively (Astin, Parrott, Korn, and Sax, 1997).

Technology Continues to Influence Learning and Employment

The influence of technology in learning will continue to have an influence on both higher education and the future work environment. A recent report on the importance of technology in K–12 education contends that technology used in conjunction with the most recent research and development findings on learning can help all students achieve in school (Illinois State board of Education, 1995, pp. 5-10). Today around the globe, schools and classrooms are using networking technologies to readily find information previously available to few learners. The SCANS report published by the National Committee on Labor provides direction for educational reform by designating the skills that are required in the workplace. The necessary skills include the ability to identify and organize resources to complete tasks; collaborate with others to work productively; acquire, evaluate, and use information; understand complex systems; and work with and continue to master a variety of technologies (Mitchell, 1994, p. 12).

Mastery of technology, as a necessary skill, may be more attainable due to rapid increases in the use of computers and the Internet by high school students. According to CIRP data, 82.9 percent of fall 1998 college freshmen used the Internet for homework during high school. However, there is considerable variance among institutional sectors. For example, 80.1 percent of freshmen in private universities use e-mail, but only about half this rate (41.4 percent) was true for those in public black colleges (Higher Education Research Institute, 1999).

Increased Concern over Time-to-Degree

Time-to-degree has also become an increasingly important issue for public policy and institutional decision making. A study of entering freshmen from 365 baccalaureate-granting institutions reveals that only two in five students (40 percent) are able to complete a bachelor's degree within four years of entering college. The lowest percent to earn a degree in four years was 30.6 percent at public colleges and the highest was 69.2 percent at private universities (Astin, Tsui, and Avalos, 1996). The public perceives the trend of students taking longer than four years to graduate as the result of poor institutional performance. State legislators see prolonged time-to-degree completion as a financial burden to states. Students and their parents have an obvious interest, since attending college is expensive and is of little value in career development unless the student is able to complete the degree in a reasonable length of time.

Financial Aid: Self-help Outpacing Gift-Aid

Students are increasingly concerned about financing college. Recent CIRP data shows record-high percentages of students expressing "major concern" about their ability to pay for college. Additionally, a high percentage of students report their college choice decisions are based on either "low tuition" (31.3 percent, compared to 20.9 percent in 1987) or because of "financial aid offers" (33.1 percent, compared to 20.2 percent in 1987). Among all beginning postsecondary students in 1995–96, sixty percent received some form of financial aid, averaging about $4,900. The average amount of total financial aid received by first-time entrants were lowest at public two-year institutions (about $2,000). Public four-year institutions were a bit higher at $4,900, and private, not-for-profit four-year institutions were the highest at $9,800 (U.S. Department of Education, 1998a, p. 13). This pattern, of course, reflects the predominant needs assessment method that measures both the ability to pay and the cost of attendance.

"Gift-aid" (grants, scholarships, and waivers) often serve as the foundation of student financial aid for students, particularly for low-income students. ("Self-help" comprises loans and/or employment.) The proportions of entering students in 1995–96 receiving gift-aid differed among the three main sectors of higher education. Thirty-five percent of students at public two-year, 53 percent at public four-year, and 73 percent at private, not-for-profit four-year institutions received gift-aid. The average total amount received in 1995–96 ranged from approximately $1,500 at public two-year institutions to $6,400 at private, not-for-profit four-year institutions (U.S. Department of Education, 1998a, p. 13).

Loans are presently the dominant form of student financial aid. According to a report by the College Board (1998b), loans comprise 60 percent of all student aid compared to just over 45 percent 10 years ago (p. 4). The percent share of grants versus loans from 1980–81 to 1997–98 show grants representing 38.9 percent and loans 59.4 percent (p. 12). A study by Mortenson (1990) contends that the reliance on loans as the dominant student financial aid vehicle has lowered low-income students' participation in higher education. For those who have entered higher education over the past ten years, loans have decreased college choice, raised debt burdens, and increased the probability of loan default.

Working More Hours Can Jeopardize Academic Performance

More freshmen students say they will have to get a job to help pay for college expenses, with many planning to work full-time while attending college. In 1995-96, 70 percent of first-time students worked while they were enrolled in postsecondary education (U.S. Department of Education, 1998a). This trend appears problematic for both continued college persistence and timely graduation. Recent studies suggest that working off campus, especially full-time work, increases the likelihood that the student will drop out of college (Astin, Tsui, and Avalos, 1996). Pascarella and Terenzini (1991), in their meta-analysis of how college affects students, found differences between on-campus and off-campus employment. Although the latter appears to be deleterious to retention and degree completion (especially if many hours are worked), the opposite seems to be true for working on campus. These analysts found that working on campus improves retention and degree completion because it enhances "involvement and integration in the institution" (p. 407). An increasing inability of federal financial aid to keep pace with the rising cost of college has forced more needy students and parents to carry a greater share of the financial burden.

A number of reports indicate that most undergraduates in U.S. postsecondary education work while enrolled, and many even work full time. Many students decide to work because they are reluctant to borrow for fear of not being able to repay their education debt (U.S. Department of Education, 1998c).

According to a recent report issued by the U.S. Department of Education, four of five undergraduate students (seventy-nine percent) reported working during their 1995–96 enrollment. Nearly 90 percent of these students worked all or most of the weeks while enrolled. Sixty-four percent of exclusively part-time students worked 35 or more hours, while only 19 percent of full-time students reported working the same number of hours while enrolled. The study also points out that the number of hours students worked is related to their academic performance. One in four students reported that work had a negative effect on their academic program (U.S. Department of Education, 1998b, p. 24). Furthermore, working long hours while enrolled often limits the students' ability to integrate themselves into campus life. Astin (1993) states that "the largest negative effect on retention is working full-time as a student" (p. 196).

A report on postsecondary financing strategies indicates that students who worked 15 hours or less per week had the same persistence rate regardless of whether or not they borrowed to finance their education. However, working 34 or more hours per week and attending part-time were negatively associated with persistence, and borrowing was positively associated (U.S. Department of Education, 1998c, p. iv).

Role of Student Services in Meeting Future Trends

What are the implications for student affairs in meeting the needs of tomorrow's college students? How will student affairs respond to these changing needs? What programs or services should be developed? Which should be eliminated? These questions and others like them will confront student affairs administrators as they prepare for students of the twenty-first century.

The foregoing describing recent and current data may be used to develop a possible portrait of tomorrow's students. When compared to students today, the data suggests that those of the future will be

- More racially and ethnically diverse.
- Better academically prepared.
- More likely to enroll as new students with college credits.
- More selective about institutional choice.
- More service-oriented.
- More likely to be influenced by earning potential when making a career choice.
- More likely to pursue advanced degrees.
- Will be working more hours to offset rising college costs.
- Will be assuming a greater level of financial debt.
- Will be facing greater pressure to meet personal and academic challenges.

From their day-to-day experiences in working with students, student affairs administrators also recognize trends in behavior that will shape future programs and services. These trends capture a number of salient features of students and the institution's adeptness in providing services.

Increasing Expectations of Students as Consumers

The number of applications to colleges has increased precipitously. "The proportion of freshmen who apply to three or more colleges has more than doubled since 1967, and the proportion who send out six or more applications has more than quadrupled" (Astin, Parrott, Korn, and Sax, 1997, p. 17). Part of this trend may reflect an increase in the overall competitive nature of the college admission process.

Most campuses report that students expect a return on their investment of time, money, and energy both inside the classroom and beyond. An increasing number of faculty report confrontations with students about course requirements, faculty expectations, and student performance. Auxiliary services are routinely challenged to meet consumer expectations. Food service programs have become more commercially recognizable to students. Housing facilities are being transformed into more legitimate living-learning environments. Student health centers rival the complexity of health maintenance organizations. Student recreation complexes are indistinguishable from their counterparts in the private sector.

Enhanced Interaction Among Individual Students and Between Student Groups

The increased demographic diversity of most campuses, including the growing number of multi-racial and multi-ethnic students, contributes to new communities being formed within the student body. However, the interaction between and among diverse groups may result in increased tensions. Efforts to promote better understanding are needed by encouraging collaboration through effective communication. In some instances, campus programs, staffing, and organizational structures are out of sync with the expanding multicultural campus.

Growing Awareness of and Commitment to a Healthy Lifestyle

Although the personal challenges that students have faced in the past are likely to be the issues for students of tomorrow, there is a growing interest among students to lead healthy and productive lives. Campus recreation facilities are routinely overflowing with students, wellness programs are well attended, and food services are challenged to meet the healthful expectations of students. Although not all students are making lifestyle choices that institutions endorse, there is growing support for healthy living among students inclusive of and extending beyond their physical well-being.

Application of Technology in All Aspects of the Student's Experience

Students interact with one another, communicate with the faculty, and connect with their families and friends using multiple forms of technology. Today, students apply for admission, register for classes, check their grades, conduct research, receive tutoring, and order pizza all through the use of technology. Students often take courses and, in some cases, complete all degree requirements via technology. While campuses work diligently to keep pace with technological infrastructure and service demands, most campuses struggle to understand the cultural implications of technology on the campus.

Swirling Student Enrollment and Joint Registration

Increasing numbers of students are concurrently enrolled in two- and four-year institutions and/or are taking Internet and televised college courses. Keeping track of and communicating with these students presents an increasing challenge, as does managing their expectations of a "seamless" and uninterrupted collegiate experience.

Other Contextual Issues

The overall characterization of college student behavior is often at risk of over-generalizing on the one hand and over-prescribing on the other. *The American Freshman: Thirty Year Trends* (Astin, Parrott, Korn, and Sax, 1997) data show a trend toward moderation in personal and social issues, but important, if not troublesome, issues remain on the horizon. Student trends in binge drinking are a large concern on campuses. The specter of HIV/AIDS remains constant with disturbing data about students' lifestyle choices, suggesting a lack of awareness or understanding. Campus violence, like the reports of violence in the public schools, concerns student affairs administrators. An expanding and increasingly complex array of mental health disorders and personal adjustment issues place demands on campus counselors and care providers. Substance abuse, like the persistent problem of alcohol, warrants increased time and attention from counselors, psychologists and their colleagues in public safety, health services judicial affairs, and residence halls. These and other issues will persist into the next generation of students. Some will manifest more than others, influenced by institutional and community norms, as well as geographical, social, and cultural characteristics. Comprehensive and accurate assessment of these contextual issues will help prepare campuses to meet the unique and changing needs of students.

Implications for Programs and Services

Meeting the needs of tomorrow's students may be informed from past practices (Astin, 1993, 1977). Student involvement in the learning process is an important dimension of college impact research. Pascarella and Terenzini (1991) further analyzed and validated the impact of active participation in learning and the corresponding impact on student success. Kuh (1996) noted the research of Chickering and Reisser (1993), Astin (1985, 1993), Jacoby (1989), and others in calling for the creation of "seamless learning environments" to improve student development and achievement. Conceptually, Kuh advocates replacing the compartmentalized university where curricular and co-curricular components are separate and discrete. He calls instead for an environment that fuses these dimensions, incorporating the life experiences of students into the learning environment. Moreover, the professional perspectives and talents of faculty and administrators should be augmented through collaborative efforts, transforming and enriching the educational experience for students. Drawing upon the Student Learning Imperative (ACPA, 1994) and Principles of Good Practice in Student Affairs (ACPA/NASPA, 1997), Schroeder (1994) encourages student affairs administrators to abandon their historic practice of working only within their organizational boundaries and to establish a "broader institutional perspective." Sandeen (1998) similarly points to the increasing specialization in student affairs that threatens to reinforce a more insular perspective and further discourages efforts to collaborate within and beyond student affairs.

This call to action for student affairs to partner with others within the academy is a more urgent one when considering the learning environment of the next century. When the Study Group on the Conditions of Excellence in American Higher Education (1984) issued their recommendations, student affairs responded broadly and effectively. Resources for new students were "front-loaded" in the freshmen year, living-learning communities were created within the residential campus, and freshmen orientation courses proliferated, as did improved academic advising and support programs. Additional efforts were made to increase involvement in learning, including the incorporation of co-curricular experiences into the acknowledged realm of learning, increased faculty-student interaction, and the effective use of technology to improve cooperative learning.

These strategies and techniques for increasing student involvement and enhancing the learning process are as relevant to tomorrow's students as they are to today's. Building upon these improvements in undergraduate education has encouraged a movement to focus efforts on the senior year. The Senior Year Experience (Gardner, et al., 1998) addresses three central purposes:

1. To bring integration and closure to the undergraduate experience.
2. To provide students with an opportunity to reflect on the meaning of their college experience.
3. To facilitate graduating students' transition to post college life (p.22).

These goals point to the need for greater synthesis in the learning environment. This synthesis includes a stronger connection between (a) teaching and learning, (b) the curricular and co-curricular, (c) the affective and cognitive, and (d) theory and application. Greater synthesis will include not only the senior year learning experience but will help better prepare graduates for their professional life beyond the academy.

Increasing pressures on education at all levels to perform and produce has encouraged a more comprehensive analysis of how and where student achievement can be better supported and enhanced. Mounting internal pressures on enrollment, increased competition, funding dilemmas, cost increases, limited institutional flexibility, and loss of public trust are among the challenges influencing higher education. In response to these challenges, members of the Kellogg Commission of the National Association of State Universities and Land Grant Colleges authored *Returning to Our Roots: The Student Experience* (NASULGC, 1997), a call to action for institutions to put students first. This endeavor and other similar efforts should generate the necessary dialogue and subsequent action to position student affairs to meet students' needs, institutional goals, and public expectations. When these efforts are incorporated into existing support services, the notion of a "seamless" learning environment draws closer to reality. It also encourages institutions, large and small, public and private, two- and four-year, to more carefully consider the students' total educational experience.

Additional Challenges

Tomorrow's students offer higher education a multitude of challenges and opportunities. One dimension, however, urgently transcends the rest: the acknowledgement and understanding of multicultural communities on college campuses. Institutional commitment to include all members of the learning community is critical in advancing students' goals and institutional objectives (Astin, 1996; Pope, Reynolds, and Cheatham, 1997).

Baxter-Magolda and Terenzini (1999) raised important research questions in educating tomorrow's students. How do cultural, ethnic, racial, gender, and class dynamics differentially affect learning? What are the multiple conceptions of learning styles, learning abilities, and levels of development students possess? Do educators understand or have access to knowledge about diverse characteristics of students and their impact on learning? How do educators and students shift from autonomous to collaborative functioning? How are educators and students engaged in considering multiple perspectives, especially those unlike or in conflict with their own?

These critical questions and others like them require thoughtful consideration and planning. In a student-centered university, our tasks must include helping all students develop essential life skills and values; critical thinking; knowing how to learn; effective oral and written communication; a multicultural and global perspective; respect for individuals and the sources of their individuality; civic and individual responsibility; self-esteem, self-confidence, and a sense of one's own competence; leadership; and the ability to work well with others either as a leader of a member or a team (NASULGC, 1997, p. 12).

Student affairs administrators, likewise, must have their agenda set to prepare their campuses for tomorrow's students. The results of that preparation in programs, services, and people can dramatically influence higher education's success and the success of its students.

References

American College Personnel Association (ACPA) and National Association of Student Personnel Administrator (ANASPA). *The Seven Principles of Good Practice for Student Affairs.* Washington, D.C.: Author, 1997.

American College Personnel Association (ACPA). *The Student Learning Imperative: Implications for Student Affairs.* Washington, D.C.: Author, 1994.

Arizona Board of Regents. Central Office, Phoenix, AZ, Sept. 1994.

Astin, A. W. *Four Critical Years,* San Francisco: Jossey-Bass, 1977.

Astin, A. W. *Achieving Educational Excellence.* San Francisco: Jossey-Bass, 1985.

Astin, A. W. *What Matters in College?: Four Critical Years Revisited.* San Francisco: Jossey-Bass, 1993.

Astin, A. W. "Involvement in Learning Revisited: Lessons We Have Learned." *Journal of College Student Development,* 1996, 37 (2), 123–134.

Astin, A. W., Tsui, L., and Avalos, J. *Degree Attainment Rates at American Colleges and Universities: Effects of Race, Gender, and Institutional Type.* Los Angeles: Higher Education Research Institute, Sept. 1996.

Astin, A. W, Parrott, S. A., Korn, W. S., and Sax, L. J. *The American Freshman: Thirty Year Trends.* Los Angeles, CA.: Higher Education Research Institute, UCLA, 1997.

Baxter-Magolda, M.D., and Terenzini, P.T. "Learning and Teaching in the 21st Century: Trends and Implications for Practice." In C. Johnson and H. Cheatham (eds.*), Higher Education Trends for Next Century: A Research Agenda for Student Success.* Washington, D.C.: American College Personnel Association, 1999, 20–29.

Chickering, A. W., and Reisser, L. *Education and Identity* (rev. ed). San Francisco: Jossey-Bass, 1993.

The Chronicle of Higher Education Almanac, 1998–99, p. 16.

College Board. 1998a. http://www.collegeboard.org/press/senior98.

Ibid. *Trends in Student Aid.* Washington, D.C.: The College Entrance Examination Board, 1998b.

Conley, D. *PASS Update.* Oregon State Board of Education, Salem, OR, 1998.

Fenske, R. H. and Scott, C. S. *The Changing Profile of College Students.* Washington, D.C.: The American Association for Higher Education, 1973.

Fenske, R. H., Geranios, C. A., Keller, J. E., and Moore, D. "Early Intervention Programs: Opening the Door to Higher Education." *ASHE-ERIC Higher Education Report,* Volume 25, No. 6. Washington, D.C.: The George Washington University, Graduate School of Education and Human Development, 1997.

Fenske, R. H., and Hood, S. L. "Profile of Students Coming to Campus." In A. M. Hoffman, J. H. Schuh, and R. H. Fenske (eds.), *Violence on Campus: Defining the Problems, Strategies for Action.* Gaithersburg, MD: Aspen Publications, 1998, pp. 29–52.

Gardner, J. N., and others. *The Senior Year Experience: Facilitating Integration, Reflection, Closure and Transition.* San Francisco: Jossey-Bass, 1998.

GEAR UP. U.S. Department of Education. http://www.ed.gov/gearup/gu1019/html, Nov. 30, 1998.

Higher Education Research Institute. *The American Freshman: National Norms for Fall 1998.* Los Angeles, CA: UCLA Graduate School of Education and Information Studies, 1999.

Horn, L. J., and Chen, X. *Toward Resiliency: At-Risk Students Who Make It to College.* Washington, D.C.: MPR Associates Inc., 1998.

Illinois State Board of Education. *Learning through Technology: Study Group Framework and Profile Tool.* Oakbrook, IL: North Central Regional Educational Laboratory, 1995, pp. 5–10.

Jacoby, B. "The Student as Commuter: Developing a Comprehensive Institutional Response." *ASHE-ERIC Higher Education Report No. 7.* Washington, D.C.: School of Education and Human Development, George Washington University, 1989.

Kellog Commission of the National Association of State Universities and Land-Grant Colleges. *Returning to Our Roots: The Student Experience.* Washington, D.C.: NASULGC, 1997.

Kuh, G. D. "Guiding Principles for Creating Seamless Learning Environments for Undergraduates." *Journal of College Student Development*, 1996, 37 (2), 135–148.

Leader, C. A. *Independent Study and Testing for Credit: A New Spin on an Old Subject.* Washington D.C.: American Association of Collegiate Registrars and Admissions, 1999. http://www.aacrao.com/pubs/po-004.html.

Mitchell, K. "Multimedia Development for Building Knowledge Structures." *School Library Media Quarterly*, Winter 1994.

Mortenson, T. G. "The Impact of Increased Loan Utilization Among Low Family Income Students [Low-Income Students]." *ACT Student Financial Aid Research Report Series*, Vol. 90–1. Iowa City, IA: The American College Testing Program, 1990, 63.

Pascarella, E. T. and Terenzini, P. T. *How College Affects Students.* San Francisco: Jossey-Bass, 1991.

Pope, R. L., Reynolds, A. L., and Cheatham, H. E. "American College Personnel Association Strategic Initiative on Multiculturalism: A Report and Proposal." *Journal of College Student Development*, 1997, 38 (1), 62–67.

Rigol, G. W. College Board, collegeboard.org/press/senior98College Board. http://www.collegeboard.org/press/senior98, August 1996.

Rodriguez, E. M. *College Admission Requirements: A New Role for States.* Boulder, CO: State Higher Education Executive Officers, 1995.

Russell, A. B. "Statewide College Admissions, Student Preparation, and Remediation Policies and Programs." Summary of a 1997 SHEEO Survey. January 1998.

Sandeen, C. A. "Creeping Specialization in Student Affairs." *About Campus*, May-June 1998, 2–3.

Schroeder, C. C. "Developing Collaborative Partnerships that Enhance Student Learning and Educational Attainment." http://www.acpa.nche.edu/srsch/charles_schroder.html. January 1994.

Study Group on Conditions of Excellence in Higher Education. *Involvement in Learning: Realizing the Potential of American Higher Education.* Washington, D.C.: National Institute of Education, 1984.

U.S. Department of Education. National Center for Education Statistics. "National Postsecondary Student Aid Study, 1995–96." (NCES 97–937). Washington, D.C.: U.S. Government Printing Office, 1996a.

U.S. Department of Education. National Center for Education Statistics. "Remedial Education at Higher Education Institutions in Fall 1995." (NCES 97–584). Washington, D.C.: U.S. Government Printing Office, 1996b.

U.S. Department of Education. National Center for Education Statistics. "Projections of Education Statistics to 2007." (NCES 97–382). Washington, D.C.: U.S. Government Printing Office, 1997a.

U.S. Department of Education. National Center for Education Statistics. "Report in Brief: NAEP 1996 Trends in Academic Progress." (NCES 97–986). Washington, D.C.: U.S. Government Printing Office, 1997b.

U.S. Department of Education. National Center for Education Statistics. "Descriptive Summary of 1995–96, Beginning Postsecondary Students." (NCES 1999–030). Washington, D.C.: U.S. Government Printing Office, 1998a.

U.S. Department of Education. National Center for Education Statistics. "Profile of Undergraduates in U.S. Postsecondary Education Institutions: 1995–96." (NCES 98–084). Washington, D.C.: U.S. Government Printing Office, 1998b.

U.S. Department of Education. National Center for Education Statistics. "Postsecondary Financing Strategies: How Undergraduates Combine Work, Borrowing, and Attendance." (NCES 98–088). Washington, D.C.: U.S. Government Printing Office, 1998c.

U.S. Department of Education. National Center for Education Statistics. "The Condition of Education." (NCES 98–013). Washington, D.C.: U.S. Government Printing Office, 1998d.

CHAPTER THIRTY

SUPPORTING PEOPLE, PROGRAMS, AND STRUCTURES FOR DIVERSITY

Christine K. Wilkinson and James A. Rund

Each of our more than 3,000 colleges and universities has its own specific and distinct mission. Their collective diversity among institutions is one of the great strengths of America's higher education system and has helped make it the best in the world. Preserving that diversity is essential if we hope to serve the needs of our democratic society.

Similarly, many colleges and universities share a common belief, born of experience, that diversity in their student bodies, faculties, and staff is important for them to fulfill their primary mission: providing a quality education (American Council on Education, 1998, p. A9).

Almost 50 national professional associations endorsed an open letter in the *Washington Post* on February 9, 1998, including the American College Personnel Association (ACPA) and the National Association of Student Personnel Administrators (NASPA). This public statement to our nation concluded that colleges and universities must make a conscious effort to build healthy and diverse learning environments as the success of American higher education and our democracy depends on it. This public declaration underscored the need to acknowledge who America is and who it is becoming. It was also a call to action for higher education to take the lead in this endeavor. In similar fashion, the Kellogg Commission on the Future of State and Land Grant Universities called for institutions to become "genuine learning communities, supporting and inspiring faculty, staff, and learners of all kinds" (1997, p. 9).

This chapter will briefly review the changing demographics of higher education. The corresponding need to support programs and structures for diversity will be explored and strategies for successful interventions will be discussed. The recruitment, retention, and development of staff who respond to the challenges of developing a multicultural campus will be discussed. Finally, the organizational structures that support the values of diversity will be examined.

Indeed, the call for action is justified and well documented. Demographers anticipate that nearly 40 percent of Americans will be members of the following groups—African American, Latino, Pacific Islanders, or American Indians—by the year 2020. As early as the year 2012, students of color will make up 25 percent of the under-eighteen population (Rendón and Hope, 1996). College enrollment data from 1996 indicated that 26 percent of those attending college were students of color. Regionally, some states reflect more dramatic changes. Colleges and universities in New Mexico and California reported minority student enrollment well above 40 percent in 1996. Six other states (Texas, Louisiana, Alabama, Florida, Georgia, and New York) reported minority enrollments above 30 percent ("Almanac," 1998).

Since 1979, women have outnumbered men enrolled on college campuses throughout the country (Garland and Grace, 1993). In 1996, the percentage of women enrolled rose to almost 56 percent. Meanwhile, the number of students entering higher education with special needs has increased dramatically over the same period. Approximately three percent of enrolled students in 1978 reported disabilities. That percentage rose to nearly ten percent five years later (Garland and Grace, 1993). Although student affairs professionals are perhaps most informed about the changing demographics of their respective campuses, they still may not be as cognizant as they should be of whom they represent and must serve.

One contrasts the 1998 NASPA reported membership with the 1998 student profile of College Bound Juniors (College Board Online, 1998). The differences between these two groups illustrate the potential growing diversity of institutions of higher education. See Table 30.1 for complete information.

Although expectations for increasing the participation rate of students in higher education continue to grow, success among these students varies as barriers impede their ability to matriculate, enroll, and persist (Garland and Grace, 1993; Harris and Nettles, 1996). Acknowledging our demographic future, this chapter will explore the many ways minority student achievement and success can be enhanced by supporting programs, people, and structures for diversity.

TABLE 30.1 DEMOGRAPHIC COMPARISON OF NASPA MEMBERSHIP WITH SAT I TEST TAKERS, 1998

NASPA	SAT I Test Takers	
	RACE	
Asian American	2.3%	9%
African American	12.4%	11%
Hispanic/Latino	3.9%	8%
American Indian	.3%	1%
Caucasian	73.3%	67%
Multiracial	.5%	NA
Other	2.0%	3%
Not Reported	5.3%	—
	GENDER	
Female	55.4%	55%
Male	44.3%	45%

Supporting Programs

The 1997 report issued by the Kellogg Commission on the Future of State and Land Grant Universities called upon public universities to rededicate themselves to student learning. The first report, *Returning to Our Roots: The Student Experience,* declared that anything short of a strong commitment jeopardizes an institution's capacity as a learning community:

> "In a student-centered university, our tasks must include helping all students develop essential life skills and values; critical thinking; knowing how to learn; effective oral and written communication; a multicultural and global perspective; respect for individuals and the sources of their individuality; civic and individual responsibility; self-esteem, self-confidence, and a sense of one's own competence; and leadership and the ability to work well with others, either as a leader or a member of a team" (Kellogg Commission of the National Association of Land Grant Colleges, 1997, p. 12).

From the seminal report by the Study Group on the Condition of Excellence in American Higher Education (1984) and *Involving Colleges: Successful Approaches to Fostering Student Learning and Development Outside the Classroom* (Kuh et al., 1991), as well as *What Matters in College: Four Critical Years Revisited* (Astin, 1993), we have understood the power of involvement in learning. Astin (1996) refers to involvement as the amount of time and energy (physical and/or psychological) a student invests in learning. Scores of subsequent studies have validated Astin's assertion that the greater the students' degree of involvement, the greater the learning and personal development (Pascarella and Terenzini, 1991).

What we have become more aware of over time is the degree to which students are able to be involved or have access to involvement opportunities (Cheatham and others, 1991; Maloney and Shively, 1995; Pope, 1995). Socioeconomic background, cultural heritage, college preparedness, academic preparation, and campus environment all influence a student's ability to engage in an institution and be an active participant in the learning process. Institutional commitment to involve all members of the learning community is critical in advancing students' goals and institutional objectives (Astin, 1996; Pope, Reynolds, and Cheatham, 1997).

More specifically, Astin's research (1993) indicates that institutional and faculty diversity emphases have a positive impact on cultural awareness and commitment to providing racial understanding among students. Moreover, the same positive effects are found where students have had diversity experiences (ethnic studies courses/workshops or social interaction and dialogue with another racial/ethnic group). The research is especially compelling in identifying students' personal commitment to promoting racial understanding as well as their overall satisfaction with college and student life when these opportunities occur. Yet Pope (1995) makes clear the need for new and better strategies to involve students in a multicultural campus: "creating a multicultural campus requires more than . . . increasing diversity. Instead, new strategies that alter goals, expectations, perceptions, and practices are needed to transform and create multicultural campuses" (p. 234).

Multicultural, as a term, should be used to define a campus that recognizes the broad array of cultural characteristics of racial and ethnic minorities, women, or others who may feel disempowered by policies or practices of college campuses (Stage and Manning, 1992). Although encouraging participation of all students in the active life of a campus enhances the learning environment, the students who benefit most from increasing their understanding of others are white (Pascarella, Edison, Nora, Serra Hagedorn, and Terenzini, 1996). For students of color, the process of learning about those unlike themselves predates cultural diversity efforts (Stage and Manning, 1992). Additionally, Cheatham and others (1991) encourages caution to avoid the common institutional strategy of socializing rather than educating students about a multicultural campus. All students benefit from structured, positive interactions with peers. A healthy and productive learning community requires an opportunity for autonomous involvement in cultural, racial, ethnic, or special interests within the broader community. Cortes (1998) puts it this way:

> "As the United States grows in size and complexity, individuals of all backgrounds are increasingly seeking to discover and develop smaller group affinities to accompany their larger American identity . . . the challenge and opportunity for student affairs administrators is to meet the special needs of diverse groupings of students, including student organizations, while at the same time building bridges among groups as part of a healthier, multiculturally constructive college community" (p. 29).

How Do We Make Progress?

Stage and Manning offer a critique of long-standing institutional strategies and why they fail. "The reasons that piecemeal strategies may be helpful but not adequate . . . can be described in terms of several central issues: (1) assuming that diverse students must change, (2) making multicultural student, faculty, staff, and administrators . . . responsible for socializing new multicultural students, (3) encouraging multicultural students to adapt to the dominant culture, (4) helping only 'identifiable' multicultural students, (5) failing to provide equitable educational opportunities to all students . . . (6) failing to educate those of the dominant culture about their multicultural colleagues" (1992, p. 11–12). This list of central issues may bring to mind a failed attempt on one's own campus: a well-intended but uninformed or ill-conceived effort to advance a multicultural community.

Moore, Fried, and Costantino (1991) offer a host of strategies to plan effectively for and implement programs to support cultural pluralism. These strategies include preparing the campus for change, garnering administrative support, employing a theory-based rationale in program planning, and pacing efforts to avoid over-challenging a campus. Cheatham and others (1991) encourage the application of identity development theory to assess campus climates effectively and appropriately develop vital programmatic responses. He notes specifically that institutions with demonstrated success in developing multicultural campuses are those with "the will to challenge the normative system and its assumptions" (1991, p. 35). Likewise, Banning and Bartels (1997) note how powerfully the physical artifacts of a campus communicate non-verbal messages to students about the values of a campus. They offer a taxonomy through which campus artifacts may be assessed, and they encourage campuses to utilize this system as a vehicle for multicultural education. The content of non-verbal messages transmitted through physical artifacts may send strong signals about those who belong, about the safety of the campus, about role behavior, or about equality.

Stage and Manning (1992) offer a model that campuses can utilize to transform their environments through organizational and systemic change. The model encourages participation from the entire campus community as a means of removing barriers to involvement. A multicultural campus, they argue, is an inclusive campus, responsive to all persons regardless of race, ethnicity, culture, gender, and background. The model's components of learning to think constructively, spanning boundaries, ensuring optimal performance, and taking action are applicable in multiple settings and apply to all members of the multicultural campus.

These models for change are just a few of the multifaceted and complex strategies that help colleges and universities support and encourage the success of their students. Employing intentional strategies for change is critical and must be accompanied by a fundamental commitment from those in student affairs.

Intentional Strategies for Change

Acknowledge individuals. While developing programs and services to involve and positively impact all students, it is also important to recognize students as individuals. Acknowledging each student as an individual learner can become the student's invitation to become a contributing member of the learning community. Failing to connect in a personal way often leaves a student ambivalent at best and, more often, alienated or detached. Regardless of the reported success of many campus programs, the data on institutional climate, or the number of students involved in campus activities, the powerful impact of acknowledging students as individuals should not be underestimated.

Affirm Groups. It naturally follows that if an institution is effective at attending to the human scale of the campus, the next step is to affirm the commonalties within the multicultural community. Although student bodies and campus cultures have become increasingly diverse, the phenomenon of group affiliation is a familiar one to colleges and universities. As an historical example, fraternities and sororities have long represented the collegiate tradition of students sharing a common set of goals and interests. As the multicultural campus evolves in its diversity and its richness, so should it flourish and multiply in its groups and organizations. Affirming the presence and place for each group within the broader community will distinguish a twenty-first century campus from a twentieth century one.

Invest In Others. Educators are aware of the place higher education holds in American society, as a critical element of a successful democracy is an educated citizenry. If higher learning is, at least in part, preparation for responsible citizenship, it follows that campus communities should model principles consistent with democratic goals: shared governance, full representation, and a commitment to the public good. Inherent in these ideals is the concept of interdependency where individual success is made possible through the guidance and help of others. Acknowledging interdependency supports inclusiveness, involvement, and full participation in the multicultural campus.

Supporting People

As higher education prepares the future leadership of the country, the minimum standard for staffing should reflect both current and future society. The growing ethnic diversity throughout the United States presents a visible and compelling reason for staff and faculty to be role models. In addition, the presence of a more diverse staff clearly symbolizes the value the institution places on diversity.

Higher education, while at the forefront of educating the larger society about diversity, still falls short of employing a staff that reflects the nation's diversity. Female administrators increased by 51 percent and minority administrators increased by 56 percent from 1983 to 1993 (Carter and Wilson, 1996). In 1993, 42 percent of administrators in higher education were women, and 14 percent of administrators were minorities (Snyder, Hoffman, and Geddes, 1997).

Preparing a campus for its multicultural future requires an immediate investment in human capital. This investment constitutes one of the most critical issues practitioners now face on a daily basis. Ensuring that the broadest spectrum of talent is reflected on one's campus remains a significant challenge and one that must be addressed if the institutional work force is to mirror in any appropriate way the students and society of the future. For those in student affairs, the implications are significant. Programs supporting young adults through the educational pipeline and engaging them in experiences that will encourage them to consider student affairs as a profession are vital for future success.

A Case for Diversity

Examining professional association membership provides insight into the diversity of the profession. NASPA reported in April 1998 (Metter K., personal communication, November 16, 1998) that 19 percent of its membership comes from a minority background, an eight percent increase from 1991, and that 55 percent are female, an 11 percent increase from 1991 (NASPA).

Membership in associations for specialized student affairs professions broadens the picture of diversity in higher education. The National Intramural Recreational Sports Association (NIRSA), which began at black colleges as the National

Intramural Association, became interracial in 1954; women, first included and then voted out in 1960, were invited back in 1972 (Amundson, 1997). NIRSA's December 1998 membership reports show a membership that is nearly one-third female; ten percent identify themselves from a minority background (L. West, personal communication, November 19, 1998). In 1998, the American College Health Association (ACHA) had a membership that was primarily female and primarily reported itself white (E. Wilson, personal communication, December 7, 1998).

Although many people choose not to indicate personal information on membership applications, some associations are beginning to expand their demographic descriptions on their applications. NASPA recently added the multiracial category to its request for membership demographics (K. Metter, personal communication, November 16, 1998). Although less than one percent of the members select that category, this change in reporting is an indication of the evolution of diversity in higher education and in the country.

The presence of female professionals and administrators has become more prevalent, but they still remain for the most part at the lower levels of the organization (Blackhurst, Brandt, and Kalinowski, 1998). Like their corporate counterparts, women are often found in support roles, rather than line positions, decreasing the opportunity for advancement.

Addressing quality of life issues becomes important for this segment of professional staff. Retaining quality staff requires that managers address the quality of the staff member's professional life, including available and successful role models. Mentors appear to make a key difference, regardless of whether the mentors are male or female (Blackhurst, et al., 1998).

A critical number of diverse staff must be in place so that individuals who are in the minority are not isolated. This critical mass also underscores an institution's commitment beyond tokenism and the tremendous value added by a diverse staff. As a by-product, the capacity of the campus to become more open is enhanced and encourages participation by those who would normally be on the periphery. Any effort to become more aware of the additional pressures and expectations faced by minority staff is a good foundation from which to start.

"Oneness" as a concept occurs when the person of a specific background, ethnicity, gender, sexual orientation, or other distinguishing characteristic is the only one in a peer group. The tendency is often for these individuals to become torchbearers. Whether the expectations are self-imposed or external, it is a reality among minority staff who often feel as though they must represent all of one race, one gender, or one group. For minority women, there may be a double bind. The clear lack of role models, along with having few or no peers, contributes to a feeling of isolation. In an environment that offers little affirmation, doubts may linger about one's performance and ability (Trimble, 1991).

In an informal survey of minority administrators, the authors identified several themes common to most. In the case of an overperformer, the administrator is often asked to take on multiple assignments that extend beyond primary duties. This often includes service, committee work, and stewardship within the university community. Externally, the administrator is asked to participate in community activities and to represent the institution at large. The better the performance in each of these roles, the greater the burden. A compromising and sometimes destructive cycle may result, as these additional assignments may jeopardize one's success in his or her primary professional role.

Beyond one's individual professional success and well being is the issue of group identification. Are minority staff perceived as credible within their ethnic or gender group? How much time, effort, and commitment is required by the group—demands not made of majority group individuals? How comfortable are the individuals in identifying with the group? The delicate balance between group affiliation and over-commitment to the group poses an additional dilemma, as these commitments may sometimes detract from primary duties. This is often a challenge for young professionals.

What if the person is successful? If the individual succeeds, then others like the person have a much better chance of being considered for a future appointment. However, if the first person fails, then the chances of others of a similar background will be much more difficult. Rather than the hiring authority understanding that the previous person may have not succeeded due to lack of competencies or was just not a match for the particular situation, the decision maker may instead classify all the individuals of the same ethnic group in the same category of weakness (Belch, 1994). Minority individuals often feel that they must prove that they are worthy of the position from day one. So, minorities often start with a deficit in the organization. In reality, there will be only a few stars, regardless of ethnic background. If managers are fortunate to hire a star, why would they believe that hiring stars on a routine basis is a common occurrence? That is just not a reasonable assumption.

Being cognizant of the influences of each person's own cultural upbringing will help others understand that each person brings a wonderful but different set of cultural values, with a unique work ethic and outlook on life. Further, each minority individual does not think alike nor understand other minorities any better than a majority person does (Ebbers and Henry, 1990). Biases develop over a number of years and experiences, and they often impact each of us unconsciously. Having a critical mass of minority staff helps to dispel the myths of stereotyping. Only through the successes and failures of many will others rethink their position about clustering all of one race together and instead consider all persons on their own merit.

Strategies for Hiring a Diverse Staff

When hiring opportunities arise, administrators should take the time to consider the organization and the skills and competencies needed to advance it. To encourage a diverse candidate pool, job qualifications should be reviewed to ensure that requirements are relevant to the current duties and not unduly restrictive or narrow. The hiring process should also be examined, with great consideration given to recruitment strategies for the position.

Promoting from Within. Take an inventory of current employees. Where are the women and minorities in the organization? Who might have the potential and be ready for additional responsibilities? Have individuals been encouraged for interim assignments? Have young professionals been encouraged to consider graduate study? Minority administrators are often in entry or middle management positions. They are also located frequently in specialized functions that target other minorities. Although those are extremely important positions and functions, an opportunity also needs to exist to broaden one's skills and outlook if the individual staff member is so inclined. Often these individuals are also involved with programs that are funded by grants or are in staff (versus line) capacities, which places them more on the periphery, and are less able to learn about opportunities for career advancement (Sagaria and Johnsrud, 1991; Rapp, 1997).

People should be promoted for their competencies and promise, not exclusively on seniority. When forming task forces to meet institutional needs, include individuals from nontraditional units within the management structure. Only by reaching out beyond the formal structure is an administrator able to diversify the work force and provide opportunities for professional growth.

Include new professionals and middle management staff in work beyond their particular department. Select them for search advisory committees so they can become acquainted with different search processes while simultaneously learning from reviewing the credentials of others, including the work experience needed for other positions.

Hiring from Outside. The pressure to fill vacant positions often results in most administrators doing what is most expedient, rather than doing what may produce much better long-term results. The administrator should first take the time to reflect on the changing needs of the organization. Rapp (1997), Patitu and Terrell (1998), Freeman, Nuss, and Barr (1993), and others have identified a series of strategies that do not require a great amount of resources or time, but rather a definite commitment to increasing diversity. Broadening the applicant pool becomes one of the most standard of processes. This can be accomplished by personally contacting known individuals who may be strong candidates, identifying individuals through networks, and advertising in multiple sources including minority-focused newspapers and journals, as well as announcing the opening through rapidly developing Web sites.

Screening committees can also be actively engaged in this regard. Candidates should be screened for potential beyond cumulative years of experience. Resumes should be read for parallel competencies that may translate to other positions.

Retaining and Developing

Intentional strategies are required to further support minority staff, affording additional access and advancement within the profession. For those in current management positions, a series of strategies could include some or all of the following:

- Opportunities to direct or coordinate student affairs initiatives
- Summer institutes and academies
- Summer management internships for currently employed individuals who are underrepresented in the field
- Involvement in professional organizations
- Graduate program preparation

Staff development programs are also critical and can be implemented with few resources when necessary. Consider establishing a middle managers staff development program where a professional is invited by the director of a department to join a representative from each of the student affairs departments. These individuals could participate in a series of seminars that focus on general management, the roles and functions of student affairs departments, and the like. This type of program provides an opportunity to learn about student affairs more extensively, become better acquainted with colleagues across student affairs, and also become more knowledgeable about general management principles.

Graduate Preparation Programs

The concept of "growing your own" is a positive one. It should not be the only way to hire; it should be one of many. Students who have been nurtured and supported as undergraduates and worked alongside student affairs professionals can often be strong candidates (Sagaria and Johnsrud, 1991).

Student affairs administrators should take appropriate measures to encourage undergraduates who show an interest in the profession, and they should inform these individuals about graduate programs that have an emphasis in student affairs administration. The Undergraduate Minority Program sponsored by NASPA provides one such vehicle as well as practical experience.

Graduate programs should address their commitment to diversity and ensure that the information disseminated underscores this commitment. Traditional admissions criteria should be reviewed to determine that candidates with less traditional backgrounds or preparation are not excluded from consideration.

To address the inclusion of the topics into the curriculum, faculty must assess both the knowledge base of their students as well as the mission and goals of the department. McEwen and Roper (1994), through their study of 28 student affairs preparation programs, found that most of the students reported a comfort level with a general knowledge of race such as demographics and cultural differences. However, a majority felt they needed to gain more understanding. In addition, the comfort level between what the respondents considered their knowledge of race issues versus the actual knowledge in content areas was vastly different.

To establish a more comprehensive curriculum that integrates a multicultural focus, the faculty should review the existing program as a whole and then discuss how diversity can be incorporated in each of these areas. McEwen and Roper (1994) provide a substantive approach in developing an entire graduate curriculum that includes aspects of diversity throughout the preparation. They offered specific content and sources for 15 different modules within a graduate program that covered a spectrum from human development theory and the American college student to topics on performance appraisal and supervision.

Graduate students need to be assured that the actual practices of their respective faculty match the rhetoric in the classroom (Talbot, 1996). The composition of the faculty needs to reflect the diversity they espouse. In addition, students want to see that the faculty support events highlighting diversity and that they sponsor students of diverse backgrounds.

Programs should also be reviewed for their sensitivity to gender. For example, from a programmatic dimension, what issues are distinctly different for women than men or are more predominant for one gender than another? What should these graduate students learn that could help them in their future work with collegiate women as well as men? Moreover, for those female students who are entering the profession, what additional challenges will they face as a result of their gender?

In researching the inclusion of courses on theories of women's development and/or topics related to women's issues, there was a wide variation as to the commitment in graduate preparation programs (Blackhurst and Hubbard, 1997). Most students had been educated in this area as a topic within a course or courses within a larger context, rather than a course devoted specifically to the topic of women's development and related topics.

To compound the issue, women in large measure compose the majority of students in master's degree programs, while males still dominate the faculty. Therefore, there continues to be a need for more female role models in faculty positions and administrators in leadership roles (Blackhurst and Hubbard, 1997).

Supporting Organizational Structures

Student affairs organizational structures, like others, reflect the changing profile, the needs of college students in general, and their institutional needs in particular. Organized along program and service needs, student affairs administrators must consider the implications for staff.

Although administrators strive to serve both institutional and student needs in more effective ways, structures should be reviewed periodically to determine their effectiveness. Some student affairs organizations have chosen to combine departments into a few clusters of emphasis (Ballou, 1997), while the majority of campuses continue to follow the more traditional organizational constructs. Each of these approaches has the potential to limit or promote minority individuals. With the former, the elimination of entire departments may mean downsizing staff and often affects those with the least seniority or those from fairly specialized areas. In many cases, this means the loss of minorities or women.

In a decentralized organization, there is the potential for specialization early in one's career. This is even more evident on larger campuses (Sandeen, 1998). The tendency is for supervisors to believe that certain skills or competencies are not as easily transferable when, in reality, the opposite is true. For example, if an individual spends two years as a residence hall administrator, why wouldn't the person be eligible for positions in other areas of student affairs and not just another position in residential life? Without the opportunity to gain a broader set of experiences, individuals lose any chance of gaining additional skill sets. For those who are place-bound, it becomes more difficult, even though they may be quite talented and show great potential.

If one looks to organizational structures outside of academe, one easily recognizes the shifting paradigm from a hierarchical, multi-tiered workplace to one that is much flatter and flexible. This allows for greater mobility of staff and enables the organization to evolve as people develop (Helgeson, 1995a, 1995b; Hesselbein, Goldsmith, and Beckhard, 1996).

Summary and Future Implications

Diversity has traditionally been focused on underrepresented ethnic groups and women. In the future, the application of diversity principles will become broader. As an illustration, both gay/lesbian/bisexual students and students with disabilities will become more prominent in their enrollment and participation on campuses. With the former, there have probably been more enrolled as students and more employed as professionals than the institution has known about. However, for these individuals there is still a great amount of fear that their acceptance as students or their job security as professionals will be in jeopardy if they reveal their orientation more openly.

With the latter, federal disabilities legislation alone has resulted in the establishment of comprehensive departments to respond to the growing population of students with temporary or permanent disabilities (Kellogg, 1997). Like other groups in a minority status, issues should be considered well in advance of potential vacancies. What, for example, do some of these staff have as particular challenges that other staff do not need to worry about? According to Belch (1994), the architectural barriers, while still present on many campuses, are less problematic than those of a psychological nature.

Attitudinal barriers and those that result from prior and/or continuing policies and procedures that inhibit participation are much more defeating and demoralizing. As with other populations in the minority, a number of strategies need to be put in place that are strategic and institutional to encourage more open settings that are supportive of all types of diversity.

Definite progress has been made in diversifying the college environment from students to faculty. However, a sustained effort must continue if higher education is to remain a significant contributor to the workforce of the future. The programs and services will need to evolve from ones of exclusively ethnic focus to ones that help students not only identify with their particular race or culture, but clearly assist them with the multicultural aspects of their environment. Just as student affairs professionals teach and enhance competencies for students' career development, they must be partners with the faculty in preparing students for broader life skills (Kellogg, 1997).

The people who serve as role models will need to reflect the dramatically changing demography of the students. Staff and faculty must remain active in their dialogue and personal commitment. The communication, both formally and informally, should be clear.

Lastly, the organizational structure should not be a static one. Student affairs administrators should review the structure in a comprehensive manner and within each department regularly and strategically. They should take the opportunity to ensure that the structures reflect the vision and direction for the future.

References

"Almanac." *Chronicle of Higher Education*. Aug. 28, 1998, p. 10.

Admundson, A. "NIRSA and You." *Changes, Challenges and Choices: A Collection of Readings Submitted for the 48th NIRSA Annual Conference*. Corvallis, OR: National Intramural-Recreational Sports Association, 1997, pp. 7–15.

American Council on Education. "On the Importance of Diversity in Higher Education." *The Washington Post*, Feb. 9, 1998, p. A9.

Astin, A. W. *What Matters in College?: Four Critical Years Revisited*. San Francisco: Jossey-Bass, 1993.

Astin, A. W. "Involvement in Learning Revisited: Lessons We Have Learned." *Journal of College Student Development*, 1996, *37* (2), 123–133.

Ballou, R. A. "Reorganizing Student Affairs for the Twenty-First Century." *About Campus*, Nov.-Dec. 1997, 24–25.

Banning, J. H. and Bartels, S. "A Taxonomy: Campus Physical Artifacts as Communicators of Campus Multiculturalism." *NASPA Journal*, 1997, *35* (1), 29–37.

Belch, H. A. "Professionals with Disabilities." In D. Ryan and M. McCarthy (eds.), *A Student Affairs Guide to the ADA and Disability Issues*. NASPA Monograph Series No. 17. Washington, D.C.: National Association of Student Personnel Administrators, 1994, 125–146

Blackhurst, A. and Hubbard, J. "The 'New' Scholarship on Women: Progress Toward an Inclusive Curriculum in Student Affairs Preparation Programs." *Journal of College Student Development*. 1997, *38* (5), 453–460.

Blackhurst, A. E., Brandt, J. E., and Kalinowski, J. "Effects of Career Development on the Organizational Commitment and Life Satisfaction of Women Student Affairs Administrators." *NASPA Journal*, 1998, *36* (1), 19–34.

Carter, D. J., and Wilson, R. *Fourteenth Annual Status Report on Minorities in Higher Education*. Washington, D.C.: American Council on Education, 1996.

Cheatham, H. E. and others. *Cultural Pluralism on Campus*. Washington, D.C.: American College Personnel Association, 1991.

College Board Online. "SAT Program Background Information." http://www.college-board.org/index_t . . . t/cbsenior/yr1998/nat/natbk198.html. December 1998.

Cortes, C. E. "Beyond Affirmative Action: Student Affairs Administrators in a Multicultural America." http://www.net-results.org/members/archive/carlos.cfm. November 1998.

Ebbers, L. H. and Henry, S. L. "Cultural Competence: A New Challenge to Student Affairs Professionals." *NASPA Journal*, 1990, *27* (4), 319–323.

Freeman, M. A., Nuss, E. M., and Barr, M. J. "Meeting the Need for Staff Diversity." In M. J. Barr and Associates (eds.), *The Handbook of Student Affairs Administration*. San Francisco: Jossey-Bass, 1993.

Garland, P. H. and Grace, T. W. *New Perspectives for Student Affairs Professionals: Evolving Realities, Responsibilities and Roles*. ASHE-ERIC Higher Education Reports No. 7. Washington, D.C.: The George Washington University, School of Education and Human Development, 1993.

Harris, S. M. and Nettles, M. T. "Ensuring Campus Climates That Embrace Diversity." In Rendón and Hope (eds.), *Educating A New Majority.* San Francisco: Jossey-Bass, 1996.

Helgesen, S. *The Female Advantage: Women's Ways of Leadership.* New York: Doubleday/Currency, 1995a.

Helgesen, S. *The Web of Inclusion.* New York: Currency/Doubleday, 1995b.

Hesselbein, F., Goldsmith, M., and Beckhard, P. *The Leader of the Future: New Visions, Strategies, and Practices for the Next Era.* San Francisco: Jossey-Bass, 1996.

Kellogg Commission of the National Association of Land Grant Colleges. *Returning to Our Roots: The Student Experience.* Washington, D.C.: National Association of State Universities and Land-Grant Colleges, 1997.

Kuh, G. D. and others. *Involving Colleges: Successful Approaches to Fostering Student Learning and Development Outside the Classroom.* San Francisco: Jossey Bass, 1991.

Maloney, G. D. and Shively, M. "Academic and Social Expectations and Experience of First-year Students of Color." *NASPA Journal,* 1995, *33* (1), 3–18.

McEwen, M. K. and Roper, L. D. "Incorporating Multiculturalism into Student Affairs Preparation Programs: Suggestions from the Literature." *Journal of College Student Development,* January 1994, *35* (1), 46–53.

Metter, K. Membership Marketing Director, National Association of Student Personnel Administrators, Personal Communication, Nov. 16, 1998.

Moore, L. V., Fried, J. H. and Constantino, A. A. "Planning Programs for Cultural Pluralism." In H. Cheatham (ed.), *Cultural Pluralism on Campus.* Washington, D.C.: American College Personnel Association, 1991.

National Association of Student Personnel Administrators. *Annual Report.* Washington, D.C.: National Association of Student Personnel Administrators, 1991.

Pascarella, E. T., and Terenzini, P. T. *How College Affects Students.* San Francisco: Jossey-Bass, 1991.

Pascarella, E. T., Edison, M., Nora, A., Serra Hagedorn, L., and Terenzini, P. T. "Influences on Students' Openness to Diversity and Challenge in the First Year of College." *Journal of Higher Education,* 1996, *67* (2), 174–195.

Patitu, C. L. and Terrell, M. C. "Benefits of Affirmative Action in Student Affairs." In D. D. Gehring, *Responding to the New Affirmative Action Climate.* New Directions for Student Services, No. 83. San Francisco: Jossey-Bass, 1998.

Pope, R. L. "Multicultural Organizational Development: Implications and Applications in Student Affairs. In J. Fried (ed.), *Shifting Paradigms in Student Affairs: A Cultural Perspective.* Washington, D.C.: ACPA Media, 1995.

Pope, R. L., Reynolds, A. L., and Cheatham, H. E. "American College Personnel Association Strategic Initiative on Multiculturalism: A Report and Proposal." *Journal of College Student Development,* 1997, *38* (1), 62–67.

Rapp, J. L. "Staff diversity: The need for enhancing minority participation in student affairs." *College Student Affairs Journal,* 1997, *16* (2), 73–84.

Rendón, L. I. and Hope, R. *Educating the New Majority: Transforming America's Educational System for Diversity.* San Francisco, CA: Jossey-Bass, 1996.

Sagaria, M. A. and Johnsrud, L. K. "Recruiting, advancing, and retaining minorities in student affairs: Moving from Rhetoric to results." *NASPA Journal,* 1991, *28* (2), 105–120.

Sandeen, C. A. "Creeping Specialization in Student Affairs." *About Campus,* May-June 1998, 2–3.

Snyder, T. D., Hoffman, C. M., and Geddes, C. M. "Digest of Education Statistics." Report No. NCES 98–015. ERIC Document Reproduction Service No. ED 411 612. Washington, D.C.: U.S. Department of Education, 1997.

Stage, F. K. and Manning, K. *Enhancing the Multicultural Campus Environment: A Cultural Brokering Approach.* New Directions for Student Services, No. 60. San Francisco: Jossey-Bass, 1992.

Study Group on the Conditions of Excellence in Higher Education. *Involvement in Learning: Realizing the Potential of American Higher Education.* Washington, D.C.: National Institute of Education, 1984.

Talbot, D. M. "Multiculturalism." In S. R. Komives and D. B. Woodard Jr. (eds.), *Student Services: A Handbook for the Profession.* (3rd ed.) San Francisco: Jossey-Bass, 1996.

Trimble, R. W., Allen, D. R. and Vidoni, D. O. "Student Personnel Administration: Is It For You?" *NASPA Journal*, 1991, *28* (2), 156–162.

Washington Post, February 9, 1998.

West, L. National Intramural and Recreation Student Association. Personal Communication, Nov. 19, 1998.

Wilson, E. American College Health Association, Personal Communication, Dec. 7, 1998.

CHAPTER THIRTY-ONE

FUND-RAISING AND DEVELOPMENT

Michael L. Jackson

This chapter discusses how many student affairs leaders have become more engaged in fund-raising and development efforts to support and enhance co-curricular programs, build facilities, and reduce the need for additional fees and tuition dollars for such activities. This chapter also considers the strategies student affairs leaders, their staff members, and students can employ to maximize effectiveness in gaining additional financial support for student affairs programs beyond institutional funding. Included is a review of projects and programs likely to garner support from external sources, possible sources for external fund-raising and development, strategies student affairs leaders must use within their home institutions to be successful, and methods to leverage unexpected opportunities to secure external funds. Last, there will be a review of ideas student affairs leaders might consider as they plan for fundraising and development in the future.

For the purposes of this chapter and to simplify language, the words "fund-raising" and "development" will be used interchangeably. Both terms are intended to convey seeking external funds to support programs at colleges and universities. These funds may come from donors, foundations, grants, and contracts from local, state, federal governmental agencies, sponsorships from corporations, and the sale of products. However, it should be noted that the term "development" is a bit broader than the term "fund-raising." It includes work performed to establish the foundation for fund-raising through "friend-raising" activities, the cultivation of prospects, and research that creates the opportunities to ask individuals for gifts and to apply for grants from foundations, corporations, and government agencies. In addition, different names are used by institutions to describe the office charged with the responsibility for fund-raising. Some colleges and universities call them "offices of development." Others call them "offices of (institutional) advancement." For simplicity, the term "office of development" will be employed throughout this chapter.

Student Affairs and Institutions Respond to a Changed Financial Environment

What has changed in the financing of higher education that has either forced or provided student affairs leaders opportunities to become involved in fund-raising? In the first edition of *The Handbook on Student Affairs Administration*, there was no substantial discussion of the fact that fund-raising might become an important part of the strategic thinking and planning of student affairs in the future. For many decades, most student affairs programs were adequately funded by their institutions. This was true for both public and private institutions, with the possible exception of appeals to alumni and other donors to provide student scholarships. Another important exception that might have directly involved the senior student affairs officer in fund-raising depended on whether athletic programs were included in the administrative portfolio of student affairs. On occasion, donors were asked to support the building of student residences and student unions. However, professional fund-raisers, presidents, and trustees did the vast majority of the development work. Senior student affairs officers were generally not involved in direct fund-raising. They provided information on projects and served in a support role. Student affairs officers were not hired with the expectation that they would have to raise funds to support the programs for which they provided leadership.

As Schuh indicated, colleges and universities have been under increasing pressure since the early 1980s to develop financial resources and strategies to fund their programs without raising tuition and fee levels beyond the financial capability of students and their families (Schuh, 1993, p. 49–68). Financial issues have made institutions think differently about the way their programs are funded. Institutions have examined a range of strategies including budget cutting, outsourcing administrative and program activities, developing more corporate and industry partnerships, and broadening their approach to fund-raising and development.

For student affairs, this has meant an encouragement to seek external funds for programs and the ability to appropriately advocate and compete in the institutional prioritization process for the support of fund-raising activities. This requires specific support from their central development offices, president, provost, faculty, deans, and others important to successful fund-raising on campuses.

Student organizations have also been encouraged, within certain restrictions, to solicit donors to support their activities. Student groups can be very helpful in developing programs that may be attractive to donors because they are rooted in programs that promote broader educational and professional development for students in a wide variety of fields. Appropriately directed student involvement in development activities helps them learn how to be supportive alumni when they graduate. Many institutions benefit from the financial support of alumni because they personally experienced involvement with donors who supported them when they were students at their alma mater.

Colleges and universities increasingly recognize that student affairs programs provide attractive opportunities for fund-raising to support programs and facilities for students outside the classroom. New external funding also means that financial resources can be reallocated to support academic programs.

Creating the Foundation for Successful Fund-raising

Any fund-raising activity by student affairs leaders must be accomplished within the academic mission, values, and strategic plans of their colleges and universities. The chief student affairs officer should also

1. Assess how the president, provost, deans, key faculty committees and councils, senior administrators, and trustees think about student affairs' role in the institution and involvement in development activities. Schedule meetings to discuss student affairs projects, ask colleagues to review ideas and plans, and get on the agenda of meetings where institutional development priorities will be discussed.
2. Work to develop allies and appropriate partnerships with institutional leaders within and outside the institution. Try to develop common projects with faculty and staff in academic programs, find out what they are trying to accomplish, and offer support and contacts.
3. Determine, to the extent possible, alumni support for student affairs initiatives, particularly if they were involved in co-curricular programs during their time in school. Meet with the leaders of your alumni association to learn their views and survey alumni who were student leaders to gauge their interest in supporting activities they were involved in as students.

4. Develop an overall approach to fund-raising and the development of student affairs including a clear set of priorities, guidelines, and donor stewardship protocols. Develop a "white paper" that outlines the approach of student affairs to these issues and discuss this with organizational leadership and selected faculty, such as the president, provost, deans, and student leaders. Reach a consensus on direction and then develop fund-raising plans and strategies.

5. Take advantage of central development office information and training programs that increase the ability of student affairs staff to be successful in development activities. Participate in activities that reinforce student affairs' interest in fund-raising. Get key staff invited to programs that will help them learn more about the development process and stimulate relationships with fund-raising staff.

6. Create a process within student affairs to determine which programs will receive clearance and administrative support for seeking external financial support. Be clear about the decision-making process that will be used to consider which projects are eligible for fund-raising. It must be consistent with the overall institutional project and donor-clearance protocols. Have the student affairs process approved by the president, provost, and senior development officer.

Programs Likely to Receive External Financial Support

As student affairs leaders consider the development of a plan for fund-raising to support co-curricular activities, a variety of opportunities should be considered. Student affairs programs often appeal to donors because they have the potential to promote the improvement of the quality of life for students through leadership development, personal development, values clarification, ethical behavior, and caring for others and society. In addition, donors often want to foster the professional development of students, support education about diversity, and contribute to the extension of educational opportunities to those who do not have the financial resources to attend college. The facilities and programs described may also stimulate donor interest because they may have been involved in similar programs and activities when they were students and value that involvement. This list also provides an opportunity for donors to create a legacy that honors and serves as a tangible symbol of their institutional involvement and commitment.

Facilities.
- Health center
- Student residences, including residential colleges
- Student union, including internal facility-naming opportunities

- Public/community service center
- Intramural and recreation center
- Recreation fields

Programs.
- Student leadership programs
- Student scholarships
- Diversity, pluralism, and cross-cultural education programs
- Equal education enrichment programs
- Health promotion programs
- Summer internship and mentor programs
- Student residential, educational, social, and cultural programs
- Career center workshops
- Greek organization philanthropies and community service projects
- Religious and moral education programs
- Student-led summer programs for economically disadvantaged youth
- Community service projects

Principles that Guide Student Affairs Fund-raising Efforts

The development of a student affairs fund-raising program should be based on principles that have been discussed and endorsed by the chief student affairs officer, program directors, and the university officer to whom student affairs reports, usually the president or provost. In some cases, it is appropriate to include faculty leadership in the process of determining the underlying principles in support of the program. The establishment of principles provides the foundation for the development of priorities that will guide choices about those programs for which external support will be sought. Such a process also helps eliminate conflicts about institutional priorities, guides staff energy, and possible interests by donors. Principles will help build a consensus among student affairs program directors regarding what should be done. Also, given the prestige and positive symbolism associated with securing external funds to support programs, student affairs can strengthen its standing within the body politic of the institution by demonstrating the values and priorities that guide its development activities.

Principles. Student affairs will:
- Seek funds consistent with missions of the institution and student affairs
- Whenever possible, seek funds for programs that do not compete with academic priorities

- Seek funds for programs that may attract external support but, if discontinued, will not diminish core programs and services for students
- Not seek funds to support core services and programs unless absolutely necessary
- Seek funds for programs that allow staff to experiment with new ideas and program models that might improve core programs and services for students
- Seek external funds, only after appropriate internal review, clearance, and support from senior student affairs officer
- Maintain a process that guides student organization solicitation of external support for their programs
- Maintain an effective donor stewardship program that appropriately acknowledges gifts, fulfills programmatic commitments, and continues cultivation of their personal and institutional interests
- Fulfill institutional fiduciary responsibilities by complying with all reporting requirements of funding agencies and individuals
- Work closely with institution's development office in discussing prospects and strategies

Constituencies Likely to Support Student Affairs Programs

When developing a fund-raising program, it is important to develop an overview and understanding of those individuals, groups, and entities that are likely to support student affairs' programs. This is particularly important when trying to secure funds that are not competitive with academic programs or other important institution priorities. This provides for the development of "target of opportunity" development activities. These are opportunities to solicit funds from donors who are only interested in supporting a specific activity. Some of those constituencies include

1. Alumni who, as students, participated in co-curricular activities as leaders and members of student organizations, fraternities and sororities, and former student employees,
2. Parents of current and former students who express an interest in supporting activities that enhance student scholarship, leadership, and community service projects (in some cases, they may also be approached about large-scale building projects),
3. Corporate sponsors and businesses that participate in career fairs, job placement, and student internship programs,
4. Trustees, particularly those who serve on student affairs, alumni, or athletic committees.

The Role of Senior Student Affairs Officers in Development

The role of the senior student affairs officer in unit-specific and institution-wide fund-raising activities is very important to the success of these development efforts. Their active involvement in providing overall leadership and participation in fund-raising, making "asks" for financial support, writing grant proposals, and stewardship activities is vitally important. This involvement inspires staff, encourages donors, and demonstrates to institutional leadership the student affairs officer's commitment to development. Active involvement also reinforces to the institution's development staff that a commitment of resources to student affairs' fund-raising efforts is a worthwhile investment, especially when they see tangible results. As Bernard R. Gifford, dean of the school of education at the University of California at Berkeley, says, "Be a true believer. I have a clear vision of the school's mission, and I am absolutely convinced that the school will fulfill [it]. I think I convey my beliefs, and the result is a band-wagon effect. People are always looking for a winning cause to support" (Gifford, 1988, p. 17). This philosophical approach to fund-raising applies very well to the work of senior student affairs officers.

Specific strategies that the senior student affairs officer should employ to be successful in providing leadership for student affairs staff and the institution are as follows:

1. Create the vision and need for fund-raising based on a persuasive case statement for projects.
2. Make the case for student affairs fund-raising for specific projects and programs using results from student surveys, benchmarks from similar institutions and competitors for students, and the need to rectify long-standing problems that cannot be solved exclusively with institutional resources. Expensive building projects, for example, often need a combination of funding sources.
3. Understand and support institutional priorities.
4. Develop support for facilities programs and projects from deans and faculty leaders.
5. Develop the support of other administrative leaders, vice presidents, and associate deans of schools for the priorities of student affairs.
6. Work with staff in central development to develop a fund-raising strategy and prospect list.
7. Become appropriately trained on how to approach donors, do research, and cultivate prospects.
8. Get institutional volunteers to help create excitement about giving and solicit other friends to become involved in fund-raising efforts.

9. Keep appropriate university leaders involved and informed of progress.
10. Host social functions that cultivate prospects and thank volunteers and donors for their efforts.
11. Send personalized thank-you notes and acknowledgments to those who give.
12. Consistently market the institution and student affairs programs.

Employ some of the strategies Donald Meyers of the University of Pennsylvania provides. The article reviews guidelines that the University of Pennsylvania developed to shape the work of development staff in fund-raising efforts. He cites a number of ideas that can be very useful in the development of a student affairs development program (Myers, 1993, pp. 17–19).

1. Provide appropriate guidance for staff based on their experience in fund-raising.
2. Understand the nature of your prospect pool and take into account location, proximity to campus or project (the closer that prospects live to the campus or project, the more connection they feel with it), ability to give, and inclination to give.
3. Encourage faculty involvement with student affairs development efforts.
4. Delegate some work to volunteers who can function as an extension of student affairs staff.
5. Provide appropriate administrative support of clerical work, writing, and research.
6. Manage and mediate staff expectations of fund-raising efforts.
7. Make sure appropriate budget support is available for staff to travel to see prospects and host them for meals and special events.

Partnering with Your President in Fund-raising

It is important that senior student affairs officers and the staff with whom they work understand the important role the president plays in raising funds for student affairs projects, particularly buildings. The president is crucial in setting priorities, clearing access to the largest donors, and putting student affairs funding proposals before donors. The president can mobilize central development staff and deans. He or she can devote institutional resources to projects that help potential donors see their relative priority in comparison with other needs. For example, if student affairs is trying to raise funds for a new student union or residence hall, a presidential decision to use tuition dollars to fund a portion of the facility demonstrates an institutional commitment to the project and makes it more attractive to potential donors.

When working with presidents, make them your partner, as Barden discussed in 1988. His ideas apply very well to developing a relationship with presidents in the fund-raising arena. This activity is similar, but quite distinct, from the other tasks senior student affairs officers generally work on with their presidents. Barden's ideas can also be modified and applied to working with the provost or dean of the college, depending on the type of institution:

1. Develop a relationship of trust: It is your responsibility to ensure that the president understands what he or she wants to accomplish and why. And you are in a position to help the president accomplish it. There must be no question that both of you are acting in good faith.
2. Remember your president is an individual: Different people need different kinds of guidance. I have worked for four presidents and chancellors: a biologist, a geophysicist, a law professor/attorney, and an electrical engineer. Each has a unique way of approaching his job, assimilating information, and fundraising. You have to understand their style and complement it when you are working together, particularly when you are making calls on donors.
3. Establish a style: Show the president how you conduct business and let him or her know what to expect from your day-to-day demeanor. Presidents must know exactly what your style will be when you call on donors.
4. Get the rules straight: Establish at the start what must be done and who will do it. Presidents know that they have a responsibility for fund-raising, but it must be clear that you will use their time judiciously. Be sure you are clear on how much is to be raised, for what, and within what time frame.
5. Be interested in your president as an educator and institutional leader: Show your president that you view your work within the larger context of the entire institution, not just the bottom line of your fund-raising success in student affairs. This will lead to conversations about other important institutional issues that will help you better understand key issues facing the institution.
6. Assimilate the president's style: Your working partnership should encompass style as well as purpose. You will probably do some ghostwriting, so draw from the president's writing and speaking, the key phrases and stylistic idiosyncrasies that will help the president accept what you provide as his or her own (Barden, 1988, pp. 22–25).

Dedicating Student Affairs Resources to Development

If the chief student affairs officer is considering dedicating resources to development activities and hiring staff fund-raisers, it is important to learn about institutional and national standards and ratios that guide investment versus dollars raised. This will help establish fund-raising goals and expectations, allow for the evaluation of efforts, and determine if such an investment is worthwhile. In 1990, a four-year study was conducted by the Council for Advancement of Schools and Education (CASE) and the National Association of College and Business Officers (NACUBO) funded by the Lilly Foundation. Ellen Ryan reviewed this study stating that:

> Rigorous study of 51 American colleges and universities sheds new light on the ubiquitous question: How much does it take to raise a dollar? The latest answer is an average of 16 cents—though the range is great among campuses in the study. Eleven cents is the median cost (half the institutions spend more, half less). And the middle 50 percent spend between 8 and 19 cents. The group of cost-per dollar figures covers all direct fund-raising staff and programs, but no portion of presidents' or deans' salaries or overhead costs such as space and utilities.

> The compiled data helps quantify the relationships among gift income, advancement program expenses, and selected institutional characteristics. On average, for example, the institutions in this study spent just over 2 percent of their educational and general (E and G) budgets raising money, while gifts raised for current operations contributed about 10 percent of that budget. The sample institutions spend an average of 1 percent of the E and G budget on programs for public relations and slightly less for alumni relations.

> Keep in mind, however, that these data are not the last word on costs and cost effectiveness at the participating institutions, let alone others that want to use the numbers. The full report warns against simplistic interpretation of the results. After all, institutions vary as greatly in their fund-raising potential as alumni do in their capacity to give. The numbers in the report are aggregate data only; individual institutions should compare themselves only with others of similar type, size, and circumstances. The report gives details about how to make their comparisons.

> Yet another caveat: The data accumulated by the institution that tested the new guidelines confirm conventional wisdom that aggregate fund-raising costs usually run about 15 cents per gift dollar. But again, this finding doesn't mean that a good fund-raising program will cost that much or less. After all, as the report points out, efficiency should not be confused with effectiveness: "The objective of an institution's program should not be to spend as little as possible each year

to raise money, but to maximize net" [Ryan, 1990, p. 58].

It is clear that some student affairs programs can be more successful than others at fund-raising because they carefully develop plans and make clear choices about what they want to accomplish and the type of resources they are willing to devote to reach their goals. In addition, senior student affairs officers of successful units consider a variety of factors when thinking about allocating space, money, and staff time to development efforts. These positive and negative factors, and others unique to the individual campus, will be crucial factors in determining a thoughtful approach to development activities.

Positive Factors.
1. An organized development program can create a clear focus for fund-raising efforts, commitment, support, and participation by staff, volunteers, and donors.
2. Successful fund-raising promotes friend-raising and helps recruit alumni and others who have never made donations. As a result of this positive experience, they may be attracted to other institutional needs.
3. Success in fund-raising demonstrates student affairs' resolve and skill in helping the campus find external funds to underwrite programs.
4. Successful development activity demonstrates student affairs' interest in broader institutional programs and generates allies and support for initiatives.
5. An organized effort in the new arena of fund-raising can provide professional development opportunities for staff.

Negative Factors.
1. Lack of success or failure with regard to development activities can generate internal and external ill will towards student affairs and cause political problems.
2. Managing volunteers will require an investment of staff time and financial resources.
3. Inappropriate management of donor stewardship can reduce the commitment of donors to the institution.
4. Failure to accomplish fund-raising goals can negatively affect staff and student morale if they are depending on the new funds to support a particular project or set of activities.

Relationships with the Office of Development

It is imperative that the senior student affairs officer has a thoughtful and productive relationship with the institution's development staff in both central and school-based offices. Participation in training programs that help student affairs staff learn how to access institutional research about individuals, foundations, corporations, and federal government programs is essential. Involvement in development prospect clearance committees that review funding proposals and the approval of requests for gifts from prospects provides excellent experience. Volunteer to appropriately support fund-raising efforts of academic programs to enhance their success, develop allies, and learn about their priorities whenever you can. Share information about what student affairs is doing, the progress it is making with its fund-raising efforts, and any problems that you need development office assistance to resolve.

It is also important to get to know the leadership of your campus development office. Attend development events, volunteer to host potential donors, and go the "extra mile" to provide information they may need about projects. If you have potential contacts for development opportunities, even if they do not pertain to student affairs, let your development office know and provide any information you believe will be helpful in approaching the individual or entity for a gift. Remember that the development staff is, in many respects, the institution's sales division and must produce results. The more you help them be successful, the more likely it is they will support your efforts when you need their assistance.

The overall goal is to develop a real partnership with development staff. As Barden asserts, "The development officers job, then, boils down to identifying the five Ws and H: whom to see, where and when to see them, why the visit is important, what the visit should accomplish and how to do it" (Barden, 1988, p.22).

Stewardship Is the Key to Future Success

Commitment to the effective stewardship of gifts and donors is of paramount importance. The following steps will assist student affairs units in demonstrating good stewardship of resources in support of projects:

1. Appropriately acknowledge gifts: Send letters, cards, and gifts. Invite donors, and when appropriate, family members, to institution events. List the donor's name in event programs. Encourage campus media to write stories about donors and the projects they support.
2. Follow through on promises to provide information the donor has requested. Stay in touch with them without being a burden. Try to develop a positive professional relationship.
3. If donors ask for information or privileges that are inappropriate, tell them so in a way that helps them understand the reasons. Most donors are reasonable

people who can accept the truth, or already know they are stretching the possibilities about what they are entitled to, as a result of their gift.

4. Complete program projects and reports within the agreed-upon time frame.
5. Spend gift money only on purposes for which they are intended. If you believe there is a legitimate reason for altering the agreed-upon purposes of the gift, discuss this with the donor. Verify in writing any changes and inform appropriate institution offices of changes.
6. Fulfill institutional fiduciary responsibilities by complying with all reporting requirements of funding agencies and individuals.
7. When working with alumni, provide opportunities for them to be engaged with student affairs programs.

The Role of Volunteers

Volunteers can be very helpful in securing external support for student affairs projects. They can also present problems unless they are well managed, given clear responsibilities, and kept informed of progress in achieving the aims of a particular fund-raising effort. As J. Barry McGannon, chancellor of St. Louis University, noted in his discussion of the role of volunteers, they add enthusiasm, lend their professional and personal reputations, and bring credibility and prestige to solicitation meetings. They can also use their personal contacts to open doors for the senior student affairs officer and development staff. They can also advise the institution on prospects for planned giving programs (McGannon, 1992, pp. 15–17).

The role volunteers play in the direct solicitation of funds for student affairs or any other segment of the institution should always be discussed and determined after consultation with your central development staff and other key institutional officers. As McGannon says, "Would IBM entrust its biggest customers to an amateur? Of course not. IBM wants more quality control than that, and so should we" (McGannon, 1992, p. 15; Von Schlegell, 1992, p. 22). Volunteers require extensive staff time to manage. If you use volunteers, clarify what you want them to do and thoughtfully manage their involvement.

The Role of Students in Development Activities

As student affairs units develop plans to seek external funds, they must incorporate student needs. This is particularly important, because students are generally unaware of the larger institutional mission, development protocols, appropriate stewardship of donors, political ramifications of certain types of requests of university supporters, and the fact that their requests may have an impact on larger student affairs or institutional requests for funds. Given this dynamic, students and student organizations, including fraternities and sororities, must be given guidelines about terms and conditions under which they seek funds from donors, the amounts, and when they can solicit funds during the academic year. This information should be incorporated in information provided to institutionally-recognized student organizations and student leadership training materials. For example, in 1996, Stanford University wanted to increase the number and amount of alumni contributions to the annual fund for undergraduate education. The university realized that both the development office and many student organizations were soliciting alumni for support during fall and winter quarters, which diluted the institution's ability to increase contributions to the annual fund in support of undergraduate education. The associate vice president for development and the dean of students worked with students to reduce this competition for alumni support. Students agreed to dramatically reduce soliciting funds during this time period and work for the university-administered annual fund program in the Student Leadership Program Fund to earn dollars they would have received during the fall and winter quarter solicitations. Student organizations can earn up to $300,000 annually to support their organizations through this program by writing thank you letters to donors and volunteers. Students shift most of their fund-raising, if they need additional income, to the spring quarter. This change, along with a streamlining of the annual fund appeals, helped the university significantly improve the percentage of annual alumni giving from 25 percent in 1992 to over 34 percent in 1996 (Stanford Annual Fund Report, 1998).

Students can also play a role in the solicitation of donors by attending social functions and making presentations about student affairs programs from which they will benefit. Many colleges and universities, like the Stanford example cited previously, have students say thank you to donors by writing letters and calling them on the telephone. Some even incorporate students in telethons, soliciting alumni and their fellow seniors for contributions to the annual fund. Students can be terrific assets in student affairs' fund-raising efforts, particularly when they learn how they fit into the larger institutional mission and plan. Take advantage of their energy, commitment, and enthusiasm. You will be pleasantly surprised.

Summary

Student affairs programs now have the opportunity to help their institutions finance projects that may not have been funded by external sources a decade ago. It is important that senior student affairs officers and their staffs take advantage of opportunities to gain support for programs in a manner similar to deans, faculty, and staff in academic departments. They should get involved in fund-raising for academic initiatives to demonstrate that they can help their institutions accomplish broad-based initiatives and develop allies for their fund-raising efforts. This will help student affairs attract support for programs important to student development and co-curricular activities.

Successful fund-raising also demonstrates that student affairs leaders can accomplish what is considered to be the most complex yet prestigious form of institutional work: obtaining external support for programs. Increased institutional status is accorded to staff and programs that garner external support from donors, foundations, corporations, governmental agencies, businesses, and other entities. As this chapter demonstrates, methods of fund-raising can be learned and incorporated into the mission of student affairs in a wide variety of institutions, including public, private, large, small, rural, urban, or church-affiliated schools. Senior student affairs officers and their staffs must learn more about these methods and employ them on behalf of their institutions and the students they serve.

References

Barden, D. M. "Two for the Money," *Case Currents,* June 1988, 22–25.

Gifford, B. R. "The Deans List," *Case Currents,* June 1988, 16–20.

McGannon, B. J. "Who Should Ask for the Gift? The Staff," *Case Currents,* January 1992, 15–17.

Myers, D. G. "Major Gifts Marching Orders," *Case Currents,* March 1993, 17–19.

Ryan, E. "The Cost of Raising A Dollar," *Case Currents,* September, 1990, 58–62.

Schuh, J. H. "Fiscal Pressures on Higher Education and Student Affairs." In M. J. Barr (ed.) *The Handbook of Student Affairs,* San Francisco, CA: Jossey-Bass, 1993.

Stanford Annual Fund Report, Palo Alto, CA: Stanford University, 1998.

Von Schlegell, A. J. "Who Should Ask for the Gift? Volunteers," *Case Currents,* January 1992, 20–23.

CHAPTER THIRTY-TWO

APPLYING PROFESSIONAL STANDARDS AND PRINCIPLES OF GOOD PRACTICE IN STUDENT AFFAIRS

Elizabeth J. Whitt and Gregory S. Blimling

It should be obvious to anyone engaged in postsecondary education that we face many challenges. The Kellogg Commission on the Future of State and Land-Grant Universities in the report *Returning to Our Roots: The Student Experience* (National Association of State Universities and Land-Grant Colleges [NASULGC], 1997) identified two such challenges as increasing competition for students and funding and the declining public trust in higher education. These and other challenges have combined to create widespread and persistent pressure on colleges and universities, including student affairs organizations, to demonstrate both efficiency and effectiveness in achieving their missions. The university presidents who wrote the NASULGC (1997) report asserted that responding to this pressure requires changing traditional ways of thinking about productivity in higher education and, indeed, "unless we become the architects of change, we will become its victims" (p. 9).

Suggestions for ways to "become architects of change" abound. In the past 15 years, more than 20 reports have called for and suggested ways to achieve reform in higher education. Two of the most recent examples are the aforementioned NASULGC (1997) report and *Reinventing Undergraduate Education: A Blueprint for America's Research Universities* (Boyer Commission on Educating Undergraduates in the Research University, 1998). Despite the varied purposes and audiences for these reports, most share a common recommendation: Colleges and universities must focus attention and resources on students and their learning. Although these reports advocate a renewed emphasis on the teaching mission of higher education, they also recognize that student learning is not solely a classroom activity. For example, "As we understand the term, learning is not something reserved for classrooms or degree programs. It is available to every member of the academic community, whether in the classroom or the administration building, the laboratory or the library, the residence halls or the performing arts center . . . Learning is available to all and all serve learning" (NASULGC, 1997, p. 17).

In response to these reports, several strategies have been proposed to help colleges and universities "put student learning first" (Wingspread Group, 1993, p. 3). This chapter focuses on two: (1) the development of examples of "best practice" or "principles of good practice" for a variety of objectives, including conducting assessments of student outcomes, developing learning communities, and creating shared values for learning, and (2) the use of standards as a means to develop and measure progress toward goals. This chapter describes these strategies' usefulness in student affairs organizations. Both are important in the process of improving student affairs *and* the standards against which the process is measured.

Principles of Good Practice in Student Affairs

The *Student Learning Imperative* (SLI) (American College Personnel Association [ACPA], 1994) was student affairs' response to this emphasis on student learning and the SLI helped focus the conversation about higher education reform in student affairs. This document captured the central issue of the ongoing discussion about learning in higher education, that is, creating conditions "that motivate and inspire students to devote more time and energy to educationally purposeful activities, both inside and outside the classroom" (ACPA, 1994, p. 1). In addition, the document outlined the role of student affairs in fostering student learning. Among other things, the SLI described student learning—broadly defined to include cognitive competence, intrapersonal competence, interpersonal competence, and practical competence— as the primary mission of student affairs. The SLI also called for student affairs professionals to create learning-oriented student affairs divisions. These are places where the achievement of learning outcomes is the goal of student affairs programs and services, collaboration across student affairs and institutional functions is the norm, resources are allocated with learning goals in mind, and what and how much students learn are the criteria by which effectiveness is evaluated (ACPA, 1994).

As significant and valuable as the *Student Learning Imperative* (ACPA, 1994) is, it does not describe the means of creating student-learning-oriented student affairs divisions. The *Principles of Good Practice for Student Affairs* (ACPA/National Association of Student Personnel Administrators [NASPA], 1998; Blimling and Whitt, 1998; Blimling, Whitt, and Associates, 1999) were developed to respond to the need for suggestions about how to implement the SLI. Student-learning-oriented student affairs divisions can be created through good student affairs practice, such as engaging students in active learning, helping students develop coherent values and ethical standards, setting and communicating high expectations for learning, using systematic inquiry to improve student and institutional performance, using resources effectively to achieve institutional missions and goals, forging educational partnerships that advance student learning, and building supportive and inclusive communities.

The *Principles of Good Practice for Student Affairs* demonstrate and reinforce the student affairs profession's commitment to student learning and institutional effectiveness. Grounded in compelling research on college students and a wealth of practical experience in student affairs work, the principles are intended to help create learning-oriented student affairs divisions. Thus, the document should change how we think about our responsibilities, communicate our purpose to others, and engage students. As a guide to planning, resource allocation, and program design, the principles offer unambiguous advice on the most productive investment of the time, energy, and resources of student affairs. At the same time, we do not live in a static environment where the results, and directions, of change are predictable. Time and experience teach that adaptability, flexibility, and collaboration are the best companions on the journey through shifting terrain. Without a strong footing on the basic principles of student affairs practice, change can move us to cling to the status quo or run toward quick fixes, both of which hinder our ability to meet our commitments to students and our institutions.

It should be emphasized here that the *Principles of Good Practice for Student Affairs* are not standards (Blimling, Whitt and Associates, 1999). Rather, they are suggestions for a *process* or for the *means* of responding effectively to student affairs' learning imperatives. A detailed description and explanation of each of these seven principles follows.

Seven Principles for Good Practice

Good Practice in Student Affairs Engages Students in Active Learning. Active engagement in their own learning is necessary to help students move from current ways of thinking and acting toward those consistent with the educational mission of higher education, including complex meaning-making, critical thinking and analy-

sis, and integrated cognitive and affective development (Baxter-Magolda, 1992, 1999). Active learning draws students into the learning process by using and valuing their perspectives, asking them to integrate and apply new ways of thinking into their behavior, and giving them opportunities to reflect on their experiences (Baxter-Magolda, 1992, 1999). Thus, good student affairs practice provides students with opportunities for experimentation, application, involvement, and reflection through a wide range of programs and functions focused on engaging students in learning experiences, both in and out of class. These opportunities include experiential learning, collective decision making, peer instruction, and shared educational experiences that advance knowledge acquisition and more complex ways of thinking. Obvious examples would be creating intentional linkages between students' courses in political science or small group development and involvement in student government (Kuh, Branch Douglas, Lund, and Ramin-Gyurnik, 1994).

What distinguishes the notion of "experiential learning," as implied by this principle, from typical student affairs practice is the requirement that such activities as shared decision-making about community standards or leadership training be designed and implemented to achieve specific goals for student learning (Baxter-Magolda, 1999). The focus of this principle, then, is not simply action or experience, but *learning* through action or experience.

Good Practice in Student Affairs Helps Students Build Coherent Values and Ethical Standards.

Many higher education reformers have voiced concern about character development on campuses and the extent to which colleges and universities are adequately preparing students for good citizenship and leadership in helping solve societal problems such as poverty, racism, sexism, and incivility (Boyer Commission, 1998; NASULGC, 1997; Wingspread Group, 1993). Good student affairs practice challenges students to identify, examine, and develop meaningful values for a life of learning and citizenship, and provides opportunities for students, faculty, staff, and student affairs educators to share and act on the values and commitments that define an academic community. Such opportunities include creating a caring community ethos, developing campus governance structures that give students true responsibility and accountability, helping students clarify values in real-life settings, and orienting students to standards and conduct of academic integrity (Dalton, 1999). Note that this principle takes an explicit, rather than relative, stance toward values and ethics and assumes values such as justice, honesty, equality, civility, freedom, dignity, and responsible citizenship are essential to effective learning communities. This implies, of course, that student affairs professionals' work with students should be grounded in clear statements of organizational and professional values (Dalton, 1999). Examples of this principle in practice include judicial and disciplinary processes that give students meaningful responsibility, such as serving as hearing officers, specific learning goals for those "charged" with violations of community rules, and shared responsibility for identifying and maintaining community values.

Good Practice in Student Affairs Sets and Communicates High Expectations for Student Learning. Another key element of higher education reform efforts involves calls to "expect more" from colleges and universities (Chickering and Gamson, 1987; Education Commission of the States, 1995; Study Group on Conditions of Excellence in Higher Education, 1984; Wingspread Group, 1993). The Wingspread group asserts that "the American imperative for the 21st century is that society must hold higher education to much higher expectations or risk national decline" (p. 1). These reports and others demonstrate strong support for setting high and clear expectations for student and institutional performance (Kuh, 1999). Consistent with this effort, good student affairs practice provides clear information about what students are expected to learn from programs, policies, and practice and provides clear expectations for learning from student affairs practitioners. In effect, student affairs says to students from their first contact with the college: "This is what it means to be a student here. This is what we expect of you. Here are our learning goals for you and for ourselves and the experiences and outcomes that will comprise your life as a student at our institution. And we will give, and receive, regular and specific feedback about progress toward those goals."

Often, we assume students know what is expected of them and that they know how to be students, so they figure things out without our assistance, not always with desirable results (Kuh et al., 1994; Kuh, Schuh, Whitt, and Associates, 1991).

Putting this principle into practice requires (1) identifying what expectations are desired, (2) identifying what expectations are actually communicated, (3) identifying the gaps between what is desired and what is communicated, and (4) implementing strategies to close the gaps (Kuh, 1996, 1999). How do students spend their time? What messages do student affairs staff communicate about how students ought to spend their time? Do staff members imply, for example, that residence halls are places for fun, rather than study, or that the most important college experiences take place outside the classroom (Kuh, 1999)? Are these messages consistent with the outcomes desired and valued by the institution? If not, how should they be changed in order to establish clear, high, and appropriate expectations for students (Kuh et al., 1991)?

Good Practice in Student Affairs Uses Systematic Inquiry to Improve Student and Institutional Performance. Recall that the SLI (ACPA, 1994) describes a learning-oriented student affairs division as a place where, among other things, staff are experts on students, their learning, and the environments in which learning takes place and where "student affairs policies and programs are based on promising practices from the research on student learning and institution-specific assessment data" (p. 3–4). Good practice in the form of systematic inquiry is therefore necessary to create learning-oriented organizations. Systematic inquiry, for the purposes of this principle, is defined as an intentional, organized, and ongoing search for valid, reliable, and believable information (Whitt and Pascarella, 1999). Therefore, systematic inquiry encompasses three processes that are (or should be) familiar to student affairs professionals: research, assessment, and evaluation. Good practice requires, however, that the data obtained from these processes be used to inform and support all decisions and policies, and that systematic inquiry be viewed as an absolutely essential element of student affairs work.

This recommendation includes a commitment to using evidence and information from research in all aspects of practice, including routine decisions, planning processes, problem solving, policy making, and integrating systematic inquiry into the daily operations of the student affairs organization. Implementing this principle effectively requires a commitment to systematic inquiry on the part of organizational leaders, especially the chief student affairs officer (CSAO). Indeed, "CSAO's are in a position to remodel the entire profession's orientation toward research" (Brown, 1991, p. 135). This also means hiring staff members who are skilled at systematic inquiries and making staff development on inquiry-related topics an expectation.

The principle also implies a rigorous assessment and evaluation of students, staff, and institutional learning environments. Not just satisfaction surveys, but an assessment of specific learning outcomes (Banta, Lund, Black, and Oblander, 1996). What do students learn and what do they learn from the work of student affairs? Finally, good student affairs practice requires knowledge of research about students and their learning, skill in using assessment methods to enhance institutional and student achievement, and the ability to critically analyze, understand, and use varied sources of information about students (Whitt and Pascarella, 1999).

Good Practice in Student Affairs Uses Resources Effectively to Help Achieve Institutional Missions and Goals. It almost goes without saying that the current climate of accountability, with its emphasis on increasing both effectiveness and efficiency, and the increased competition for funds demand an effective use of resources. All indications are that the pressure on colleges and universities to prove that higher education does what it claims to do, and does so efficiently and effectively, is here to stay (Banta, Lund, Black, and Oblander, 1996; Guskin, 1994a, 1997; Upcraft and Schuh, 1996). Also, all signs point to the fact that programs, services, and activities that fail to implement effective assessment processes and/or fail to demonstrate specific contributions to the educational mission of the institution are in peril (Guskin, 1994, 1997; Upcraft and Schuh, 1996). What deserves emphasis, and what this principle is intended to communicate, is that good practice in student affairs uses resources effectively to achieve the institution's mission and goals for learning. Although the press for the assessment of and accountability for learning affects all aspects of a college or university, there is some evidence that student affairs is particularly vulnerable. For example, Guskin makes the following assertion:

> "Strategically, enhancing student learning and reducing student costs are, in my judgment, the primary yardstick [for organizational effectiveness]. Since the faculty and academic areas are most directly tied to student learning, alterations in the lower priority support areas must precede [major changes in the role of the faculty] [emphasis added]" (p. 29).

This statement is one perspective on what happens when student learning is the measure of institutional productivity; the aspects of the university that are most clearly associated with student learning take priority for funding and indeed for surviving reductions in funding and personnel (ACPA, 1994; Guskin, 1994a, 1994b). Because "there is no presumption that out-of-class activities result in student learning consistent with educational goals," (Blimling and Alschuler, 1996, p. 214), student affairs work can indeed be viewed as "a lower priority support area." And, so, by implication, Guskin's statement reflects what happens to resources available to student affairs organizations if they cannot demonstrate that their programs, services, and people are, in fact, an integral aspect of student learning.

Similarly, the SLI (ACPA, 1994) noted, "If learning is the primary measure of institutional productivity by which the quality of undergraduate education is determined, what and how much students learn also must be the criteria by which the value of student affairs is judged as contrasted with numbers of programs offered or clients served" (p. 2).

Putting this principle into practice means conducting such activities as program planning, program evaluation, responsible fiscal management, ethical and legal personnel management, and strategic organizational development (Reisser and Roper, 1999). Equally important, however, is assessment; demonstrating through systematic inquiry that student affairs resources are used effectively and in ways that are clearly linked to the educational mission of the institution (Whitt and Pascarella, 1999).

Good Practice in Student Affairs Forges Educational Partnerships that Advance Student Learning. A long-standing critique of higher education is its fragmentation. This criticism has taken on strength as evidence mounts that lack of communication and cooperation within institutions hinders effective undergraduate education (Baxter-Magolda, 1996; Pascarella and Terenzini, 1991; Terenzini, Pascarella, and

Blimling, 1996; Terenzini and Pascarella, 1994). Reflecting on their synthesis of twenty years of research on the impact of college on students, Terenzini and Pascarella (1994) commented, "Organizationally and operationally, we have lost sight of the forest. If undergraduate education is to be enhanced . . . [we] must devise ways to deliver undergraduate education that are as comprehensive and integrated as the ways students actually learn" (p.28). In addition, collaborative decision making and strong work relationships demonstrate a healthy institutional approach to learning by fostering inclusiveness, using multiple perspectives, and affirming shared educational values (Schroeder, 1999). Good student affairs practice initiates partnerships for learning with students, faculty, administrators, and other constituent groups inside and outside the institution, and develops structures that support the development and maintenance of collaboration. Implementing this principle requires some self-examination. To what extent do student affairs staff understand and support the academic mission of the institution and the efforts of faculty to carry out that mission? What assumptions do student affairs staff make about faculty—assumptions that might interfere with effective partnerships? What barriers are implied in our language, such as "the academic side of the house"? The image of a house divided, and therefore, as the adage says, likely to collapse, is vivid.

Examples of this principle in practice include identifying institutional opportunities and problems that require collaboration (such as student attrition and creating residential learning communities), contacting faculty and academic administrators to find out what student affairs can do to assist them in their work, and recognizing faculty contributions to collaborative efforts (Schroeder, 1999). Most important, however, is making the effort and taking the risk to leave the comfort of one's own organizational or functional home to forge partnerships for learning.

Good Practice in Student Affairs Builds Supportive and Inclusive Communities.
Concerns about higher education's willingness or ability to prepare students for life after college include uncertainty about whether colleges and universities are committed to creating diverse learning communities that are both inclusive and supportive. Such communities value diversity in all its forms, promote social responsibility, foster a sense of belonging, encourage debate, and foster interaction and connections among all their members (Reisser and Cross-Brazzell, 1999). Good student affairs practice cultivates communities by creating links among students, faculty, and student affairs practitioners; assisting the development of a shared vision of a learning community; ensuring true diversity of perspectives, experiences, and histories; and encouraging open discussion about controversial issues (Reisser and Cross-Brazzell, 1999). Putting this principle into practice also requires attitudes, language, and behavior that reflect awareness of, respect for, and sensitivity to differences.

Using the Principles of Good Practice

The principles of good practice are designed to be incorporated into our daily work and to shape how we think about our responsibilities, communicate our purposes, and interact with students. They also are intended as a guide for assessing our contributions to student learning and for examining and implementing our missions, policies, programs, and services. Like most aspects of higher education, student affairs has become increasingly specialized. Some student affairs professionals can easily see how the principles advance their contributions to students' educational experiences. Others might not see their immediate usefulness in routine encounters with students, but will discover their value as a foundation for collaboration with faculty, academic administrators, and others in student affairs. An example of how the Principles might be used is offered here.

The Case of Ivy College. Ivy College is a residential liberal arts college located in the heart of a large eastern city. Although Ivy's academic programs have a strong local reputation, it is known to the nation through the success of its theater graduates. Ivy College productions, famous for being at the cutting edge of experimental theater, attract audiences from throughout the region, and, in turn, the cultural and ethnic diversity of the city are mirrored in the plays staged at Ivy. This commitment to artistic diversity translates to the college as a whole; Ivy is considered a "safe place" for students of color as well as majority students. The play selected as Ivy's spring production this year was the story of a group of young men who are white supremacists. According to the playwright, the violent hatred portrayed toward African Americans in the play was intended to provoke examination of the racism inherent in United States society. Although they understood the importance of this message, African American students at Ivy College, including theater students, were offended and felt threatened by the racist language used in the play and asked that it not be produced. The theater program faculty insisted, however, that artistic freedom should not be abrogated under any circumstances, even at the expense of offending members of the community. The issue divided the campus and the surrounding community. The local chapter of the NAACP became involved and nightly demonstrations involving students, faculty, and community members accused theater faculty and Ivy administrators of racism. Others were equally vocal about the need to protect artistic freedom. And the local media documented every angry word and deed.

Ivy's Vice President for Student Affairs, Dean Mary Margaret Smith, was appointed to bring the situation to closure. She used the *Principles of Good Practice for Student Affairs* as a framework to address the myriad issues involved. A very brief description of some of the steps she took follows.

Good Practice in Student Affairs Engages Students in Active Learning. Although the situation had escalated to affect much of the community, it began with students' concerns. Dean Smith decided to bring the focus back to the students and give them substantial responsibilities for constructing and implementing workable solutions. She identified long- and short-term goals for the students' learning: that they would understand the implications of Constitutional protections of speech, that they would understand the feelings of the students who felt offended and threatened, that they would learn and practice a process for dealing effectively with such an emotional and divisive issue, and that they would develop skills at facilitating problem-solving discussions across the campus community. She worked with campus student leaders and students on both sides of the theater controversy to identify key issues and develop strategies to foster discussion and resolution.

Good Practice in Student Affairs Helps Students Build Coherent Values and Ethical Standards. Dean Smith and her student task force began their deliberations by talking about their differences. They agreed, in advance, to "rules of conduct" for their discussion. These rules were developed from the Ivy College mission statement that describes the values on which the college was founded, including commitment to democratic government, intellectual freedom, and preparing students for civic participation. Each student articulated how he or she was affected by the play and the fallout it generated. The discussion came to focus on the precarious balance between the need for safe places, free of hateful speech, and the need for freedom of artistic (and other) expression. From this conversation, students developed a statement of common values that would inform their strategies for addressing the theater controversy. They decided that a similar discussion was needed on a broader scale, so they planned an Ivy College forum on hate, civility, and freedom in the academy.

Good Practice in Student Affairs Sets and Communicates High Expectations for Student Learning. Giving students responsibilities for dealing with the theater controversy said to them, in no uncertain terms, that much was expected of them. Dean Smith made sure, however, that the students had help and support as well as challenges. Faculty and administrators volunteered to serve as "mentors" to assist students through the process of planning and implementing a response process.

Good Practice in Student Affairs Uses Systematic Inquiries to Improve Student and Institutional Performances. As part of her long-range plan for addressing the controversy, Dean Smith used the situation as an opportunity to examine the racial climate of Ivy College. Although the campus community was assumed to be a comfortable place for all kinds of differences, no one had examined that assumption in light of data. Students, faculty, and members of the campus institutional research staff met to devise an assessment plan thatwould take a broad and deep look at student life and learning environments at Ivy.

Good Practice in Student Affairs Uses Resources Effectively to Help Achieve Institutional Missions and Goals. Assessment data would be used to inform decisions about the allocation of resources, including fostering continuing communication among the various groups within the student body. In the short term, however, Dean Smith decided to reallocate program funds to provide space and support for the campus community forum. In addition, interested students received training to facilitate peer discussions about diversity, and a series of dialogues about race, sex, and gender was organized in the Ivy College residence halls.

Good Practice in Student Affairs Forges Educational Partnerships. The short- and long-term efforts undertaken by Dean Smith required communication and effort across the campus community. The relationships necessary to make this work had been formed long before the theater controversy, of course, but she did not forget to keep information, ideas, decisions, and feelings flowing freely through her office and around the campus.

Good Practice in Student Affairs Builds Supportive and Inclusive Communities. The outcome of all of these efforts reaffirmed the commitments of the Ivy College community to democratic processes and respect for differences. The drama of the controversy drew attention from those commitments for a time, but the multi-faceted approach of Dean Smith, emphasizing students' and organizational learning, reminded Ivy members of their common values and goals.

Standards

It is also important to be able to judge programs, services, and activities against a set of nationally recognized standards. Efforts have been in place since 1979 within student affairs to define such standards. "As the expectation for institutional effectiveness and accountability becomes increasingly evident, student affairs will be required to demonstrate that it does in fact make a difference in the learning and performance evidenced by students" (Mable and Miller, 1991, p. 358). For many student affairs practitioners, demonstrating effectiveness requires clearly defined professional standards (Mable and Miller, 1991; Miller, 1997).

During the past two decades, increasing attention has been paid to developing guidelines and standards in a variety of student services, including counseling, admissions, academic advising, international education, recreation, and graduate student personnel preparation programs (Bryan and Mullendore, 1993). Given the limitations of space, the focus here is on one aspect of the standards movement in student affairs, the Council for the Advancement of Standards (CAS) (Miller, 1997).

The CAS was established in 1979 "to develop and promulgate standards of professional practice to guide practitioners and their institutions, especially their work with college students" (Miller, 1997, p. 1). These standards were grounded in assumptions and values of student affairs work, including a holistic view of student development, commitment to multiculturalism and diversity, the need for ethical practice, and a commitment to providing students with healthy environments for learning. For example, the first "fundamental principle" (Miller, 1997, p. 7) on which the standards were based is "(t)he individual student must be considered as a whole person" (Miller, 1997, p. 7).

From the beginning, CAS was intended to embrace all aspects of student affairs and thereby "speak for the profession as a whole" (Miller, 1997, p. 2) on matters of standards, assessment, and evaluation. In addition, CAS standards and guidelines "represent best practices that are reasonably achievable by *any and all* programs of quality within all institutions of higher learning" (Miller, 1997, p. 3).

The list of functional areas addressed by CAS guidelines and standards is lengthy and includes academic advising, admissions, alcohol programs, campus activities, career planning and placement, disability services, Greek programs, housing, student orientation, judicial programs, outcome assessment, religious programs, and graduate preparation programs. Each set of standards includes a statement of context (such as general values and assumptions regarding the function described) and a description of standards and guidelines organized by categories, including mission, program, leadership, organization and management, human resources, financial resources, legal responsibilities, diversity, ethics, and evaluation. Standards regarding programs for fraternities and sororities, for example, state "Fraternity and sorority advising programs must be (a) intentional, (b) coherent, (c) based on theories and knowledge of learning and human development, (d) reflective of developmental and demographic profiles of the student population, and (e) responsive to special needs of individuals" (Miller, 1997, p. 85).

CAS standards have been used to organize self-study efforts for accreditation or other program reviews, to provide a rationale for new programs, and to establish the value of existing programs (Bryan and Mullendore, 1993; Bryan, Winston, and Miller, 1991; Miller, 1997). Above all, CAS standards are designed to promote self-regulation and self-assessment. "CAS believes this approach is preferable to externally motivated regulation, because those within an institution generally have the clearest perceptions of its mission, goals, resources, and capabilities" (Miller, 1997, p. 16). Although CAS offers clear standards and guidelines, they can be shaped, adapted, and implemented as appropriate to particular institutional and organizational contexts. At their most effective, self-assessment and self-regulation promote communication about values, expectations, priorities, and shared decision making (Miller, 1997).

Using Professional Standards

Bryan and Mullendore (1993) identify ten ways in which professional standards can be used "to create, develop, expand, explain, and defend important campus services and student development programs" (p. 513).

1. Program development: standards and guidelines can provide an excellent blueprint for program establishment and enhancement as divisions of student affairs seek to determine ways to respond to the unique needs of students.
2. Staff development: using professional standards sets the stage for self-assessment and evaluation and the comprehensive study of one or more different program areas; this can lead to positive development experiences when staff members are involved in the assessment of their areas of responsibility as well as those beyond their purview.
3. Comparative data across institutions: using professional standards and guidelines provides the opportunity for staff members to compare their programs with those at similar institutions due to consistency of language and format.
4. Development and enhancement of program credibility: professional standards can be helpful in reducing the credibility gap between the student affairs staff and other constituencies when the process of their development involves varied university personnel and when many different occasions and settings are used to deliver information.
5. Institutional acceptance of programs and departments: professional standards assist student affairs divisions to define clear missions and objectives; articulate the value of services and student development programs to many different university constituencies; and involve students, faculty, and staff in identifying the needs for programs and services.
6. Education of the campus community and external constituencies: professional standards and their implementation make it possible for faculty, staff, and students to participate collaboratively in the assessment and evaluation of functional areas; they create an occasion for these constituencies to understand the value of division-initiated proposals and recommendations.
7. Improved political maneuverability: as in the academic, business, and athletic arenas, student affairs professional standards can provide a minimal national statement that is easily understood and accepted as a rationale for needed institutional and political change.

8. Budgetary assistance: professional standards, as a minimum statement of expectations, can be helpful in making a case for additional program financial support that can be developed over a period of time.

9. Accreditation self-study: the development of program statements for functional areas following the outline of CAS standards can be extremely helpful in completing divisional self-studies.

10. Program evaluation and assessment: professional standards provide a comprehensive and consistent framework for program evaluation and assessment activities (p. 512–513).

An example of how the CAS standards might be used is described next.

The Case of State University. State University is a public institution located in a rural community in the Midwest. Its new student orientation program, coordinated by staff in the Division of Student Affairs, has been in existence since the late 1970s. Recently, an associate provost position was created at the university in response to the state legislature's focus on undergraduate education. The provost asked the new associate provost for undergraduate education and the assistant vice president for student affairs to co-chair a committee whose charge was to review the orientation program. In addition to the associate provost and the assistant vice president for student affairs, the committee was composed of two faculty members who served as freshman advisors, two associate deans (one from engineering and one from nursing), the director of residential life, and three students. The associate provost and the assistant vice president agreed that the work of the committee should be divided into four phases. First, the committee should focus their discussion on the following question: If time, money, and space were not factors, how would we structure an "ideal" orientation? The committee should then shift its focus to an evaluation of the current orientation program at State University. Once the evaluation is completed, the committee should compare the two—the ideal and the current—and identify the gaps. The final phase would be to generate a set of recommendations for restructuring the orientation program.

At the first meeting, the assistant vice president for student affairs was surprised at how difficult it was for the committee to identify the elements of an "ideal" orientation program. She shared her observation with the director of residential life when they got back to their offices. During the conversation, she thought about the CAS standards. They would provide the committee with a set of standards and guidelines that would be useful in the evaluation process.

The standards were well received by the committee. They helped identify the "ideal" because they provided an independent, objective set of criteria by which to evaluate the current program. The process, as outlined, could then move forward.

Conclusion

The *Principles of Good Practice for Student Affairs* and professional standards have similar goals: creating effective learning environments for students and ensuring productive, high-quality student affairs organizations. Whereas standards, such as CAS standards, provide "criteria that every program of quality should meet" (Miller, 1997, p. 10), the *Principles of Good Practice* are statements of means to a common end, not ends in themselves. But to the extent that either or both can help us create learning-oriented student affairs divisions, they are equally valuable and viable.

References

American College Personnel Association (ACPA) and the National Association of Student Personnel Administrators (NASPA). *Principles of Good Practice for Student Affairs*. Washington, D.C.: Authors, 1998.

American College Personnel Association (ACPA). *The Student Learning Imperative: Implications for Student Affairs*. Washington, D.C.: Author, 1994.

Banta, T., Lund, J. P., Black, K. E., and Oblander, F. W. *Assessment in Practice: Putting Principles to Work on College Campuses*. San Francisco: Jossey-Bass, 1996.

Baxter-Magolda, M. B. *Knowing and Reasoning in College: Gender-Related Patterns in Students' Intellectual Development*. San Francisco, CA: Jossey-Bass, 1992.

Baxter-Magolda, M. B. "Cognitive Learning and Personal Development: A False Dichotomy." *About Campus*, 1996, *1*(3), 16–21.

Baxter-Magolda, M. B. "Engaging Students in Active Learning." In G. S. Blimling, E. J. Whitt, and Associates, *Good Practice in Student Affairs: Principles to Foster Student Learning*. San Francisco: Jossey-Bass, 1999.

Blimling, G. S. and Alschuler, A. S. "Creating a Home for the Spirit of Learning: Contributions of Student Development Educators. *Journal of College Student Development*, 1996, *37*, 203–316.

Blimling, G. S. and Whitt, E. J. "Creating and Using Principles of Good Practice for Student Affairs." *About Campus*, 1998, *3* (1), 10–15.

Blimling, G. S., Whitt, E. J., and Associates. *Good Practice in Student Affairs: Principles to Foster Student Learning*. San Francisco: Jossey-Bass, 1999.

Boyer Commission on Educating Undergraduates in the Research University. *Reinventing Undergraduate Education: A Blueprint for America's Research Universities*. Stony Brook, NY: State University of New York, 1998.

Brown, R.D. "Student Affairs Research on Trail" In K.J. Beeler and D.E. Hunter (eds.), *Puzzles and Pieces in Wonderland: The Promise and Practice of Student Affairs Research*. Washington, D.C: National Association of Student Affairs Personnel Administrators, 1991, 124–142.

Bryan, W. A. and Mullendore, R. H. "Applying Professional Standards in Student Affairs Programs." In M. J. Barr and Associates, *The Handbook of Student Affairs Administration*. San Francisco: Jossey-Bass, 1993.

Bryan, W. A., Winston, R. B. Jr., and Miller, T. K. (Eds.) *Using Professional Standards in Student Affairs.* New Directions for Student Services, No. 53. San Francisco: Jossey-Bass, 1991.

Chickering, A. and Gamson, Z. "Seven Principles for Good Practice in Undergraduate Education." *AAHE Bulletin*, 1987, *39* (7), 3–7.

Dalton, J. "Developing Coherent Values and Ethical Standards." In G. S. Blimling, E. J. Whitt, and Associates (eds.), *Good Practice in Student Affairs: Principles to Foster Student Learning.* San Francisco: Jossey-Bass, 1999.

Education Commission of the States. "Making Quality Count in Undergraduate Education. Denver, CO: Author, 1995.

Guskin, A. E. "Reducing Student Costs and Enhancing Student Learning, Part I: Restructuring the Administration." *Change*, 1994a, *26* (4), 22–29.

Gustin, A.E. "Reducing Student Costs and Enhancing Student Learning, Part II: Restructuring the Role of Faculty." *Change*, 1994b, September/October, 26, 16–25.

Guskin, A. E. "Learning More, Spending Less." *About Campus*, 1997, *2*(3), 4–9.

Kuh, G. D. "Guiding Principles for Creating Seamless Learning Environments for Undergraduates." *Journal of College Student Development*, 1996, *37*, 135–148.

Kuh, G. D. "Setting the Bar High to Promote Student Learning." In G. S. Blimling, E. J. Whitt, and Associates, *Good Practice in Student Affairs: Principles to Foster Student Learning.* San Francisco: Jossey-Bass, 1999.

Kuh, G. D., Branch Douglas, K., Lund, J. P., and Ramin-Gyurnek, J. *Student Learning Outside the Classroom: Transcending Artificial Boundaries.* ASHE-ERIC Higher Education Report, No. 8. Washington, DC: George Washington University, 1994.

Kuh, G. D., Schuh, J. H., Whitt, E. J., and Associates. *Involving Colleges: Successful Approaches to Fostering Student Learning and Development Outside the Classroom.* San Francisco: Jossey-Bass, 1991.

Mable, P. and Miller, T. K. "Standards of Professional Practice." In T. K. Miller, R. B. Winston Jr., and W. R. Mendenhall (eds.), *Administration and Leadership in Student Affairs: Actualizing Student Development in Higher Education.* Muncie, IN: Accelerated Development, 1991.

Miller, T. K. (Ed.) *The Book of Professional Standards for Higher Education.* Washington, D.C.: Council for the Advancement of Standards, 1997.

National Association of State Universities and Land Grant Colleges (NASULGC). *Returning to Our Roots: The Student Experience.* Washington, D.C.: Author, 1997.

Pascarella, E. T. and Terenzini, P. T. *How College Affects Students.* San Francisco: Jossey-Bass, 1991.

Reisser, L. and Roper, L. "Using Resources Effectively." In G. S. Blimling, E. J. Whitt, and Associates (eds.), *Good Practice in Student Affairs: Principles to Foster Student Learning.* San Francisco: Jossey-Bass, 1999.

Reisser, L. and Cross-Brazzell, J. "Creating Supportive and Inclusive Communities." In G. S. Blimling, E. J. Whitt, and Associates (eds.), *Good Practice in Student Affairs: Principles to Foster Student Learning.* San Francisco: Jossey-Bass, 1999.

Schroeder, C. C. "Forging Partnerships for Learning." In G. S. Blimling, E. J. Whitt, and Associates (eds.), *Good Practice in Student Affairs: Principles to Foster Student Learning.* San Francisco: Jossey-Bass, 1999.

Study Group on Conditions of Excellence in Higher Education. *Involvement in Learning: Realizing the Potential of American Higher Education.* Washington, D.C.: National Institute of Education, 1984.

Terenzini, P. T. and Pascarella, E. T. "Living With Myths: Undergraduate Education in America." *Change*, 1994, *26*, 28–32.

Terenzini, P. T., Pascarella, E. T., and Blimling, G.S. "Students' Out-of-Class Experiences and Their Influence on Cognitive Development: A Literature Review." *Journal of College Student Development*, 1996, *37*, 149–162.

Upcraft, M.L., and Schuh, J.H. *Assessment in Student Affairs*. San Francisco: Jossey-Bass, 1996.

Whitt, E. J. and Pascarella, E. T. "Using Systematic Inquiry to Improve Performance." In G. S. Blimling, E. J. Whitt, and Associates (eds.), *Good Practice in Student Affairs: Principles to Foster Student Learning*. San Francisco: Jossey-Bass, 1999.

Wingspread Group on Higher Education. *An American Imperative: Higher Expectations for Higher Education*. Racine, WI: The Johnson Foundation, 1993.

Author's Note

The twelve members of the study group that developed the seven *Principles of Good Practice for Student Affairs* are Gregory Blimling (Appalachian State University, co-chairperson), Elizabeth J. Whitt (University of Iowa, co-chairperson), Marcia Baxter-Magolda (Miami University), Arthur Chickering (Vermont College, Norwich University), Johnetta Cross-Brazzell (University of Arkansas), Jon Dalton (Florida State University), Zelda Gamson (University of Massachusetts), George Kuh (Indiana University), Ernest Pascarella (University of Iowa), Linda Reisser (Portland Community College), Larry Roper (Oregon State University), and Charles Schroeder (University of Missouri-Columbia).

The case described here was adapted from one presented by Jamie Berman (University of Iowa) and Heather O'Neill (University of Iowa) for the Master's Case Study competition sponsored by Region IV-East, NASPA, February 1, 1999. The case study used for the competition was developed by Peter Magolda (Miami University), Robert Gatti (Otterbein College), and others.

CHAPTER THIRTY-THREE

LEADERSHIP FOR THE FUTURE

Margaret J. Barr and Mary K. Desler

The future of higher education and student affairs is anything but predictable. But no matter what the future brings, student affairs professionals need to take leadership and responsibility for shaping the educational climate in the decades ahead. This volume has identified a number of issues and concerns that will influence professional practice in student affairs in the future. It is clear that we will be dealing with change on many fronts and in many forms. New students will enroll. New problems and issues will emerge. New expectations will be set for the enterprise. New technologies will influence our practice. New fiscal realities will increase pressures for accountability and alternative funding sources. What will be the role of student affairs in this ever changing and evolving landscape of higher education? What is our shared future?

It is clear to us that student affairs professionals must exercise leadership within their institutions in the future. For if we adhere to Milton's view that "they also serve who only stand and wait," we will not contribute our unique knowledge, talents, and skills to the educational enterprise.

This chapter will focus on the leadership issues for the future that are most salient for student affairs professionals. First, the alternate futures of postsecondary education will be reviewed. Next, discussion will focus on the foundation documents for our shared profession and the focus those documents bring to our leadership role within higher education. Third, we will identify the knowledge base, skills, and competencies student affairs professionals can and should bring to the leadership of our educational institutions. Finally, the chapter concludes with some recommendations for practice based on the collective wisdom in this volume and from our own experience.

Alternative Futures for Higher Education

Some looking into the future envision colleges and universities that are far from the traditional models of campuses with buildings and a faculty in residence. This view of the future of higher education is rooted in technology and posits that distance learning will be the chosen mode of higher education in the future. In fact, the investment in the Western Governor's University is a testimony to this view of our shared educational future. What role, if any, should student affairs have in such institutions? Clearly, some of the services traditionally associated with student affairs in a campus setting, such as health care, will be absorbed in the various communities where students live and study. It is less clear how the functions associated with career services, psychological care, academic advising, and out-of-class learning experiences can be integrated into this new model of education.

On the other end of the spectrum, some prognosticators see higher education emphasizing practices relating to the control of student behavior and the out-of-class life of students. "What is evolving is a tamer campus and an updated and subtler version of *in loco parentis*, the concept that educators are stand-in parents. College administrators are struggling with the two questions that are emerging as central: Are undergraduates really adults? And should they be seen as the college's customers or more of its products?" (Bonner, 1999). Even a cursory review of current enrollments demonstrates that this view of the future of college is focused on institutions with undergraduate populations of traditional age. Still, important questions need to be answered in this changing climate. Is a modified view of *in loco parentis* one that we wish to embrace as a profession? What can and should student affairs do to provide leadership in this important debate at hundreds of institutions across the country?

Still others view higher education as a dispersed model of education. In this view, education is equated to training to meet specific needs of the economy. Business and industry provide the basic training for the positions that they need to have filled within their organizations. The General Motors Institute and worldwide training initiatives such as Motorola University are but two examples of this approach to education. Those who believe in this model posit that traditional higher education will continue to have a place within society, but business and industry provide the majority of post-secondary education opportunities. Research and development under this model is transferred from the college campus to the research and development units of the private sector. Liberal education, in the traditional sense, is not as great a part of the educational process. What can and should student affairs professionals contribute if this model of the educational enterprise becomes prevalent in the future?

Still others view higher education as a slowly evolving and changing phenomena. This view of education embraces a central premise that the history and tradition of the educational enterprise has survived from the time of the University of Bologna and will continue to do so in the future. Although degrees and curriculums may change and the composition of the student body may be altered, the central functions of research and teaching will continue to go on in the future just as they have done for hundreds of years. This view has some validity, but all the evidence points to rapid change in at least part of the educational environment and "a head in the sand" approach will not help either students or our institutions. What is the role of student affairs in shaping this view of the future of higher education?

The truth is that all of these views and at least a dozen more will be part of the fabric of higher education in the future. Our unique and diverse American system of higher education does not have a uniform approach to education and that reality is unlikely to change. All of these scenarios are likely to emerge in some form within the educational landscape of postsecondary education. A combination of these scenarios may even occur within a single institution of higher education. Under such conditions, the challenge for student affairs professionals is to identify the leadership that needs to be brought to the process of determining educational priorities and futures. Further, we must determine the ways and means that student affairs can contribute to the leadership of our individual institutions in the future.

Leadership: An Essential Function for Student Affairs

Who carries the responsibility for leadership in student affairs? The vice president or dean? All managers within the division of student affairs? The new professional? May staff members within the division of student affairs exercise leadership on a broader institutional plane? Of course, the answers to each of these questions is yes. Leadership is not a sole responsibility of any one person within the organization; all student affairs professionals have a mandate to lead. The question is really one of defining the purpose of leadership and the methods to exercise leadership from a professional base in student affairs.

Our Shared Foundation. Although the term leadership is not expressly used in *The Student Personnel Point of View, 1937* (NASPA, 1989), it is an implicit theme of that document. A major emphasis in the document is the coordination of efforts within institutions, including a dominant theme focused on working with faculty that is as relevant today as it was in 1937. Further, this document charges student personnel workers with the responsibility to interpret the problems of college students through the publication of "a short volume with some such title as 'The College Student and His Problems.' . . . The purpose of this volume would be to inform administrators, faculty, and the general public of the complex human problems that are involved in education" (NASPA, 1989, p.60). The Student Personnel Point of View, 1949 (NASPA, 1989) built on the foundation of the 1937 statement but also broke new ground. In this period after World War II, emphasis was placed on the individual student and his or her growth and development. Many of the conditions outlined in this statement that judge whether a student has had a successful collegiate experience are still relevant today. The conditions include

- Successful orientation to the collegiate environments
- Satisfactory living facilities
- Growth in self-understanding
- Development of significant interests
- Understanding of and control of personal financial matters
- Progress toward vocational goals
- Development of individuality and responsibility
- Discovering ethical and spiritual meaning
- Effectively living with others
- Progressing toward satisfactory and socially acceptable sexual adjustments
- Preparation for post-college activity (NASPA, 1989, pp. 27–34)

Emphasis remains on the importance of collaboration and cooperation across the institution (an essential function of leadership) for student affairs. Further, the 1949 statement declares "Personnel workers at all levels of specialization and administrative responsibility should be given appropriate opportunity and responsibility for participating in planning and policy making for all phases of the institution's instructional and public relations program" (NASPA, 1989, p. 42). Clearly, the statement was urging our shared profession to participate in institutional governance, policy making, and leadership.

A Perspective on Student Affairs (NASPA, 1989) also reflects the need for student affairs professionals to be leaders on their respective campuses. "Student affairs assumes a major role in encouraging and establishing open and humane methods of campus decision making and the rational resolution of conflict" (NASPA, 1989, p. 15). Although a major emphasis in the document is on the assumptions and beliefs that support our professional practice, a consistent focus is on student affairs professionals being "experts of students and their cultures" (NASPA, 1989, p. 15).

Each of these documents reflects the times in which they were written and identifies the corresponding leadership challenges for student affairs. The same is true of contemporary efforts such as the Council on the Advancement of Standards (CAS, 1986), the *Student Learning Imperative* (ACPA, 1994), and the *Principles of Good Practice for Student Affairs* (ACPA/NASPA, 1997). These documents affirm the values and commitments of the earlier documents and reinforce the need for leadership and partnership by student affairs within colleges and universities. At the same time, they focus on another method to exercise leadership, stewardship, and they provide a framework by which student affairs leaders can continually respond and adapt to change within the many institutional contexts where we work.

Stewardship involves the careful and responsible management of the resources entrusted to our care. The CAS standards (CAS, 1986) serve as guidelines for minimum expectations for practice. The *Student Learning Imperative* (ACPA, 1994) reminds us that the criteria by which the value of our work is judged must be what and how much students learn. This document further suggests that the use of resources must be linked to student learning and the *Principles of Good Practice for Student Affairs* (ACPA/NASPA, 1998) provide guidelines for the productive use of resources for learning. It is clear that student learning must be a central focus for student affairs.

In the next decade, change is inevitable and it will require leadership that is nimble and adaptive. Our traditional or comfortable practices may no longer meet the needs of students and/or support the changing mission of the institution. We must be willing to change agents and innovators. The CAS Standards, the *Student Learning Imperative*, and the *Principles of Good Practice* all provide guidance and standards so that we may continually assess and redesign our work to respond to changing needs and conditions.

Too often, as a profession, we have not engaged in true institutional leadership. Student affairs professionals have been diffident about our roles and have spent too much time and energy focusing on our connections with others within the academy. We have written countless journal articles about the relationship between student affairs professionals and faculty members. We have sought legitimization in a variety of ways within the academy. We have been slow to change. Sometimes we have been our own worst enemy.

If we are going to assert leadership in the new century, such self-defeating behaviors must stop. Student affairs needs to clearly, concisely, and forcefully define the added value that we bring to the decision making, educational, and management structures within higher education.

The Value Added by Student Affairs

What is the value added by student affairs within institutions of higher education? What do student affairs professionals uniquely contribute to the educational enterprise? What would be missed if our institutions did not have a division of student affairs and student affairs professionals?

Assumptions and Beliefs

The history and tradition of student affairs is rooted in a set of assumptions and beliefs that guide our professional practice (NASPA, 1989). General leadership theorists also support the notion that effective leaders understand and act on a set of principles to guide their professional practice. Kouzes and Posner (1996) assert that "clarity of personal values" (p. 103) is essential. Moreover, they stress the importance of talking about these beliefs and values frequently and consistently. They add that "shared values make a difference" (p. 103). No matter which of the many alternatives are adopted by institutions of higher education in the future, our assumptions, beliefs, and values are important to the vitality of our institutions. We cannot be silent. Our voice is important in institutional decision making.

Simultaneously, the skilled student affairs practitioner must be able to apply the assumptions and beliefs that guide our professional practice. For if we believe that "feelings affect thinking and learning" (NASPA, 1989, p. 14), then we need to help students deal with those feelings wherever the locus of their learning occurs.

For example, one alternative future may be to provide carefully constructed referral services to provide help for distance learners in local communities. Another might be to improve 800-number services, Web-based information sources, and "hotline" services as part of a distance learning community. The needs will be the same, although they may manifest themselves in different ways. No matter which alternative futures are adopted, student affairs professionals must be creative in adapting essential institutional services to new milieus.

Knowledge

Effective student affairs professionals have an array of knowledge about students and their cultures. Our knowledge base is a leadership tool that can be used to assist colleges and universities who are struggling with issues of student enrollment, retention, and accountability. Our responsibility is to identify ways to disseminate this knowledge to those to whom it is relevant. Theories can inform the teaching/learning process and help faculty members gain understanding about how students learn. Student affairs professionals can use knowledge about students and their cultures to evaluate the potential consequences of alternative courses of administrative action. But if we do not share our theoretical constructs and expose faculty members to new ways of knowing, then we have not met our obligations to our communities of learning. The question should not be whether or not we share theoretical perspectives, but how we do so. In combination with research and evaluation efforts, student affairs professionals can provide important and useful feedback to colleagues both within and without student affairs.

To be sure, others in the academy study developmental issues involving both traditionally and non-traditionally aged students. However, student affairs professionals must move a step beyond abstract study of student behavior and use theories in daily practice in their daily work. We should act as Combs and Snygg (1949) declare, in a "self as instrument mode" as we apply theory to everyday problems and issues within student affairs organizations. To illustrate, the behavior of male students in a fraternity when caught in a violation of the rules is fairly predictable if you understand Kohlberg's (1976) theory of moral development. With that knowledge base, the practitioner can design a preventative intervention strategy regarding ethical decision making on the part of fraternity men. To use another example, conflict among men and women serving on a judicial board is much more understandable when you view the differences between men and women on the issue of justice (Kohlberg, 1976; Gilligan, 1982). This knowledge base might inform practitioners that they need to include moral development theories and ethical decision-making perspectives in the orientation and training sessions of judicial board members.

Theoretical constructs can also shape institutional policies and practices. Student affairs professionals have an obligation, based on our history and tradition, to raise ethical concerns about policies and practices in the institution.

There are countless ways in which our knowledge about students and their cultures can be helpful in daily practice and can provide opportunities for us to provide leadership at the institutional level. Our knowledge about students and their cultures can be useful as institutions identify outcomes and devise assessment strategies and mechanisms. Our knowledge about students and environmental impact is useful when writing program statements to be used by architects designing new facilities.

At the same time, student affairs practitioners must be in the business of developing new theories and new knowledge. In order to prepare for the multiple futures facing higher education, we need to support practitioners who aspire to be such scholars. They can help the profession identify ways to share new knowledge in helpful ways to support learning on the part of students. As Brown notes, "True scholars of higher education and college students are too few" (Brown, 1999, p.16).

Data

Data about many issues come in many forms and from a variety of sources. Yet on most of our campuses this data is bound in reports and is not easily accessible to those who could use it to inform decision making and improve campus teaching and learning. Student affairs professionals are often the people who sort through this data, interpret it, and then suggest ways to use it to inform practice in and out of the classroom. But as with knowledge, too often we do not share this data about our students and their experiences in helpful ways with our academic colleagues on campus.

To illustrate, we have ample evidence to support the notion that the out-of-class life of students affects learning and academic success. Data illustrating the need for financial aid, the need to reduce work, the need for support, and the need to confront abuse is also available. The implications of these findings need to be considered when formulating policy and evaluating practice.

Further, we know that on some of our campuses, differences exist between and among ethnic groups in the way that they evaluate their educational experience on campus. To illustrate, let's say that faculty members are made aware that Asian-American students believe that faculty members do not know the students' names and that this perception contributes to a disconnection with faculty. If faculty members then learn that the differences between Asian-American students and other ethnic groups on this issue are statistically significant, then and only then can faculty members begin to examine the causes of this perception and work to correct it.

Further, many studies document the powerful influence out-of-class experiences, personal problems, friendships, and family can have on the academic achievement and success of students. Yet on most of our campuses that data is bound in reports and not easily accessible to those who could use it to improve campus teaching and learning.

Student affairs has a unique and important contribution to make to the decision-making processes based on our knowledge base alone. Why do students come? Why do students stay? Why do they leave? We can help answer those questions.

Skills and Competencies

Because the work of student affairs is people-intensive, we use an array of skills and competencies in our work. These include assessment and evaluation, budget and fiscal management, conflict management, crisis management, program planning, and personnel management. On larger campuses, specific individuals may be considered an expert in one or more of these areas. On smaller campuses, staff are more likely to play multiple roles and act as generalists. Regardless of size, within a well-functioning student affairs unit, there is specialized expertise to be brought to bear on some of the most pressing problems facing an institution of higher education.

Skills in conflict resolution, honed by dealing with student-to-student conflicts, student organization-to-student organization conflicts, landlord tenant conflicts, parent/child conflicts, sexual harassment complaints, and sexual assault, can also be useful in solving other difficult points of contention influencing the institution. Student affairs staff skilled in these areas could be helpful in developing solutions to vexing town/gown relationships, alumni issues, and even some staff and faculty issues on a campus. Student affairs staff members often know and have worked with outside agencies in their conflict resolution roles. These prior relationships with the local chief of police, city manager, fire marshal, and others can be used by other campus administrative staff when problems arise.

Crisis situations occur far too often on college campuses and student affairs staff members are often the first responders when a crisis occurs. The death of a student, a serious injury, fire, flood, or tornado all require sensitive responses on behalf of the institution and for those effected by the tragedy. "When a crisis occurs, effective leaders ensure that they are fully informed about the situation . . . they share responsibility with others on the campus, pulling key people together for the purposes of sharing information, seeking input and making decisions" (Clement and Rickard, 1992, p. 164). Such skills can make a valuable contribution to the management of crisis situations directly outside the domain of students and student affairs.

Most student affairs professionals develop and implement programs as a regular part of their professional role. Assessing needs, developing goals, and planning, implementing, and evaluating programs are invaluable skills to an institution. To illustrate, on many campuses the responsibility for large ceremonial occasions is vested in the development or public affairs office. It is in the best interest of the institution to have these ceremonial occasions occur with minimal problems and maximum success. Many of the individuals charged with such responsibilities have no expertise in program planning and at times less than optimal events take place at the institution. Although student affairs staff members do not need to take a lead role in planning such events, they can volunteer their expertise on the practical arrangements needed for program success.

On some campuses, this practical and helpful approach has resulted in student affairs assuming responsibility, in the name of the institution, for events such as commencement. Such opportunities for contribution to the leadership of the institution also occur in day-by-day events, such as helping the graduate school design and implement the first orientation program for graduate students or giving technical advice to a faculty group organizing a symposia. Volunteering our time and energy in these important ways can contribute to the well-being of the institution. In all cases, we do not have to do the work but rather provide consultation and guidance to the academic community on how to get things done.

In some cases, one or more student affairs staff members may have expertise in quantitative and qualitative assessment methods. We can be helpful to others in the academy as they design studies. This may include drafting questions, facilitating focus groups, consulting on sampling techniques or possible return rates, assisting in the dissemination process, helping interpret results, generating recommendations, and providing multiple forums where the findings can be disseminated.

Opportunities and Services

Student affairs programs provide numerous opportunities for students to reflect, practice, and apply what they are learning in the classroom. We do this in career development as we aid students in sorting out their interests and skills and then link those interests and skills to possible careers. We do this when we assist students in locating internships. We do this when we help students deal with issues between and among student organizations. We do this through leadership training. Community service and service learning programs provide potent vehicles for students to apply what they have learned.

The programs and services we provide also support students in their multiple roles in the institutional governance structure. We work with students who attend governing board meetings. We include students in search advisory committees. We advise students who are elected to student governments and we hire students to work as paraprofessionals in our residence halls, student unions, and offices.

Eyes and Ears

Finally, student affairs staff members are often the "eyes and ears" of the campus. We are close to our clients/students. Unlike most of our academic colleagues, we live with our students, eat with them, and see them at their best and at their worst. We are often the first to hear about a problem or to identify a student who may be experiencing difficulties that will influence their academic success. Because we know students, we are often asked to deliver the unpopular messages and/or to intervene when no one else knows how. The fact that we know students is extremely valuable to most educational institutions.

We can hear our colleagues saying that we already are busy, overworked, and underpaid. How can you expect us to take on a broader array of responsibilities within the institution? Our simple answer is that we must get involved in broader institutional roles. For if we fail to do so, we cannot be a player in shaping the agenda for higher education on our individual campuses in the future.

Recommendations for Practice

The following recommendations for practice are gleaned from the collective wisdom in this volume and from our own experiences.

Understand Your Institution. It is critical that each professional in student affairs know the institutional mission, the governance structure, and the key relationships on campus. Institutional context influences how we do our work. Student affairs never stands alone and must be an integral part of the decision making, policy development, and ongoing work of the institution. Each professional must appreciate the unique characteristics of the institution and translate that understanding into appropriate management structures, staffing patterns, programs, and services.

Pay Attention to Issues of Management. It is impossible for student affairs professionals to believe that management is the responsibility of someone else in the institution. Fiscal constraints, facilities, a litigious society, diverse students, and complex, diverse staffs require each of us to hone our management skills. Technological advances must be carefully evaluated and integrated into management tasks to increase efficiency and effectiveness. In an era of more restricted fiscal support, lack of sound management judgement will result in less support for student affairs.

Take Assessment and Evaluation Seriously. Everyday there is more pressure from inside (students, faculty, parents, and trustees) and outside (state agencies, accrediting boards, and foundations) our institutions to account for how efficiently and effectively we use our resources. The call for systematic evidence of what students learn and what they can do as a result of their collegiate experience grows louder each year. Careful evaluation of programs in concert with a commitment to modify or abandon ones that no longer meet student needs or institutional goals is essential. Prerequisites for a total evaluation include a solid needs assessment, good program planning, and the ability to set goals that are measurable and observable. We must be able to answer the key question of what will *not* be accomplished if a particular program or activity in student affairs is unavailable to students.

An assessment requires each student affairs professional to think beyond the immediate and to look at the long-range influence those student affairs programs and services have on the growth and development of our students. Assessing outcomes and measuring the impact of our services and programs on those outcomes is not easy work. New skills and competencies will be necessary; no longer will our many publics be satisfied with vague answers about outcomes.

Make a Personal Commitment to Continuing Education. Continuing education can take many forms. At a minimum, student affairs professionals should read the literature and attend professional conferences whenever possible. The literature not only includes journals and books related to higher education and students, but also books and news magazines on major world and national issues. To be effective, the student affairs professional must remain current about the issues, the facts, and how to address potential issues before they become problems on campus.

Use Technology as a Tool, Not as a Distraction or a Panacea. Advances in the use of technology to enhance service delivery and promote student learning are changing the ways we approach and do our work. Knowing how to use technology will become increasingly important in the coming years and this knowledge is essential for institutional leaders. Technology will not answer all of our questions or solve all of the problems we face in student affairs and in our institutions. Our decisions about the use of technology should be guided by the same assumptions, beliefs, and values that serve as the foundation for student affairs. As Pavela notes, "technology should not determine how our mission is defined; our mission should determine how technology is used" (Pavela, 1996, p. 41).

Develop Specific Expertise. Most student affairs professionals are generalists and claim knowledge and skill in many areas. However, if we are to exercise leadership on an institutional level, developing expertise in one or more areas might be advantageous. Legal issues, assessment and evaluation, conflict resolution, and leadership development are just a few of the areas where advanced knowledge and expertise are valuable in determining solutions to the complex problems facing higher education.

Adopt a Philosophy of Continuous Improvement. We face unparalleled change in the years ahead. In this context, we must continually ask whether the services and programs we offer are meeting the needs of students and enhancing the learning process. Evaluation and assessment are tools that can help us consistently improve what we do in both big and small ways. To adopt a philosophy of continuous improvement, we must truly listen to what stakeholders in the institution say. We must pay attention to feedback and learn from it. From that learning, positive changes can be made.

Stay Close to Students. Peters and Waterman (1982) identified eight basic lessons from America's best-run companies. One of those lessons is instructive to those of us in higher education. It is "Stay close to the customer," or in our case, "the student" (Peters and Waterman, 1982, pp. 157–201). They attribute the following quote to Lew Young, editor in chief of *Business Week*. "Probably the most important management fundamental that is being ignored today is staying close to the customer to satisfy his needs and anticipate his wants. In too many companies, the customer has become a bloody nuisance whose unpredictable behavior damages carefully made strategic plans, whose activities mess up computer operations, and who stubbornly insists that purchased products should work" (p. 157). This lesson is applicable to student affairs as well. We must remain focused on students, their needs, their wants, and their learning. Evaluation and assessment help with this process, but we also need to listen to them in careful and attentive ways.

Embrace Diversity. Diversity in its many and complex forms is now an imbedded factor in higher education. We must, as individuals and as a profession, not only understand diversity, but celebrate how we can grow and learn from it. Our students are and will be different, as will our colleagues across the institution. We need to take advantage of a rich learning opportunity.

Keep a Sense of Perspective. Our profession has been functioning well for decades and is likely to be around for some time to come. We do not do anyone a favor when we are burdened by our work and take no joy in it. We must keep perspective of the problems and issues we face and do the best we can. Above all, we need to celebrate our chosen profession and the opportunities it provides for us to make a difference.

These recommendations are not exhaustive, but they are one way to think about our shared future as a profession. We face the challenge of change and must do so with open hearts and minds. As change agents and innovators, we need to risk and invest our time and energy. In doing so, we must understand the past, hold on to the assumptions, beliefs, and values that support our professional practice, hone our skills and competencies, and move ahead with vigor. Although he was specifically discussing chief student affairs officers, Sandeen's advice is pertinent to all student affairs professionals. "They must be good managers, mediators, and educators, and they must know how to work effectively as a part of the institutions management team. They must have compassion for students and must understand that everything they do depends on their integrity and personal trust they establish with others. Their major responsibility is to do everything they can to make their colleges work for the education of their students" (Sandeen, 1991 p. 222). It is advice well worth remembering as we enter the future.

References

American College Personnel Association (ACPA). *The Student Learning Imperative: Implications for Student Affairs.* Washington D.C.: Author, 1994.

American College Personnel Association/National Association of Student Personnel Administrators (ACPA/NASPA). *The Principles of Good Practice in Student Affairs.* Washington, D.C. Author, 1998.

Bonner, E. "In a Revolution of Rules, Campuses Go Full Circle." *New York Times,* March 3, 1999.

Brown, R. D. "Shaping the Future." *Developments.* Washington D.C.: American College Personnel Association, 1999, p. 1 and 16.

Clement L. and Rickard, S. *Effective Leadership in Student Services: Voices from the Field.* San Francisco: Jossey-Bass, 1992.

Combs, A. and Snygg, D. *Individual Behavior.* New York: Harper, 1949.

Council for the Advancement of Standards for Student Services. (CAS) Development Programs. *Council for the Advancement of Standards: Standards and Guidelines for Student Services/Development Programs,* Washington, D.C.: Author, 1986.

Gilligan, C. *In A Different Voice.* Cambridge, MA: Harvard University Press, 1982.

Kohlberg, L. "Moral Stages and Moralization: The Cognitive-Development Approach." In T. Lickona (ed.) *Moral Development and Behavior: Theory, Research and Social Issues.* New York: Holt Rinehart and Winston, 1976, pp. 31–53.

Kouzes, J. and Posner, B. "Seven Lessons for Leading the Voyage to the Future." In F. Hesselbein, M. Goldsmith and R. Beckhard (eds.) *The Leader of the Future: New Visions, Strategies and Practices for the Next Era.* San Francisco: Jossey-Bass, 1996.

National Association of Student Personnel Administrators (NASPA). "A Perspective on Student Affairs." In *Points of View.* Washington, D.C.: National Association of Student Personnel Administrators, 1989.

Pavela, G. "Thinking About the Electronic Future." *Synfax Weekly Report,* January 29, 1996.

Peters, T. and Waterman H. *In Search of Excellence: Lessons from America's Best-Run Companies.* New York: Warner Books, 1982.

Sandeen, C.A. *The Chief Student Affairs Officer: Leader, Manager, Mediater, Educator.* San Francisco: Jossey-Bass, 1991.

NAME INDEX

SUBJECT INDEX